AMERICAN EXPERIENCE

Education and Learning in America

Catherine Reef

Facts On File
An imprint of Infobase Publishing

Education and Learning in America

Facts On File, Inc.
An imprint of Infobase Publishing
132 West 31st Street
New York NY 10001

Library of Congress Cataloging-in-Publication Data

Reef, Catherine.
Education and learning in America / Catherine Reef.
p. cm. — (American experience)
Includes bibliographical references and index.
ISBN-13: 978-0-8160-7024-4 (alk. paper)
1. Education—United States—History. I. Title.
LA205.R395 2008
370.97309—dc22   2007040658

Facts On File books are available at special discounts when purchased in bulk quantities for businesses, associations, institutions, or sales promotions. Please call our Special Sales Department in New York at (212) 967-8800 or (800) 322-8755.

You can find Facts On File on the World Wide Web at http://www.factsonfile.com

Text design by Joan M. McEvoy
Cover design by Dorothy M. Preston
Maps and graph by Jeremy Eagle

Printed in the United States of America

VB FOF 10 9 8 7 6 5 4 3 2 1

This book is printed on acid-free paper
and contains 30 percent postconsumer recycled content.

In the life of the individual, education is always an unfinished task. And in the life of this Nation, the advancement of education is a continuing challenge.
—*President Lyndon Baines Johnson, 1965*

Contents

Acknowledgments

I wish to thank Kathleen Rice of Turning the Page and Jeanne Hamrick of St. Albans School, both of Washington, D.C., for providing such fine photographs. Kathleen and Jeanne were generous with their time, and their contributions enriched this book.

Introduction

"American education seems destined to become a major testing ground for democracy," declared Sterling M. McMurrin, U.S. commissioner of education, in 1963.[1] McMurrin wrote these words while the American psyche was still reverberating from the shock wave generated by the 1957 launch of the world's first artificial satellite, *Sputnik*, by the Soviet Union. As people asked why such a great nation as the United States had not led the world into space, blaming fingers pointed toward America's schools, which had fallen down on the job of producing a citizenry proficient in science and mathematics—and able to defend democracy at home and abroad.

McMurrin also wrote as the effort to secure equality of opportunity for African Americans was being played out in the nation's schools. In 1957, through the news media, the American people had watched nine black teenagers take their rightful places as students in previously all-white Central High School in Little Rock,

A boy watches a group of people, some carrying American flags, as they march to protest the admission of nine African-American teenagers to Central High School in Little Rock, Arkansas. *(Library of Congress, Prints and Photographs Division, LC-U9-2906-15)*

Arkansas, under the protection of federal forces. In 1962 the public had seen James Meredith become the first African American to register for classes at the University of Mississippi, also with armed federal protection. The integration of schools represented democracy in action, and the military support given to these courageous students made plain the government's commitment to safeguarding the rights of all.

The Earliest Efforts

In 1962, when President John F. Kennedy called education "both the foundation and the unifying force of our democratic way of life," he could have been speaking about education not only in his own time, but also throughout the nation's past, because Americans of every period have expected their schools to do more than convey information.[2] They have looked to their primary and secondary schools, as well as to their colleges and universities, to mold a diverse population into a unified American people bonded by a common culture and shared knowledge.

Opinions on how best to accomplish this goal and what it means to be an American have changed over time. To the Puritans who settled in New England in the 17th century and their colonial descendants, educating the young was a religious and moral obligation. Only the literate could read the Bible and seek salvation, and young minds occupied by study were less inclined to harbor evil thoughts than those left idle. The responsibility for a child's education fell to his or her parents or to the master craftsman, if the child was bound as an apprentice. Laws required masters to provide minimal book learning, but busy artisans, like work-worn parents, often neglected this duty.

The first colonial law to call for the establishment and support of schools was enacted in Massachusetts Bay Colony in 1642. It required towns of 50 or more families to appoint an instructor to teach reading and writing to any child who came to him to learn. Towns of 100 households were additionally required to operate a Latin grammar school, which was a secondary school offering instruction in Latin and classical Greek for the academically inclined. Six years later, in 1648, Dedham, Massachusetts, became the first North American community to tax property to fund the building of a school and the salary of a teacher, thus instituting what would become the standard system for supporting schools in the United States.

In 1700, there were 39 grammar schools in New England as well as a number of private academies, which were secondary schools for the sons of affluent families, and private boarding schools for girls or boys. Private schools were more desirable places to teach than public schools, especially those in rural areas, which consequently faced the continual challenge of finding suitable schoolmasters. "If they could read a chapter in the Testament, teach the Shorter Catechism, and whip the boys, they were sufficiently qualified," recalled one Esquire Stiles of Temple, New Hampshire, in 1782.[3] The pay for teaching in a community school was low, and the job often entailed such unrelated tasks as delivering messages or digging graves.

Calvinist teachings dominated lessons in reading and recitation in New England, but not in the middle colonies, where various immigrant groups had settled and employed approaches to education that were in keeping with their heritage. In Pennsylvania, which was one-third German by the 1750s, schools that taught in German proliferated. To the majority English population, the presence of so many German speakers threatened the colony's unity, language, and way of life. The English colonists tried, with very limited success, to create a unified population by educating German children in English. Most Germans determinedly continued to operate their own schools, but they gradually became English speakers without outside help.

School development came latest to the South, where a wealthy white planter class had set itself above the poor white subsistence farmers who lived among them and the African-American population, which was largely enslaved. The planters hired tutors and governesses to teach their children at home, or they sent their sons and daughters to private schools in England. Most impoverished youngsters, white or black, free or enslaved, learned only the skills needed to live and work, although a few cooperative and charity schools educated poor white children, and a missionary group, the Society for the Propagation of the Gospel in Foreign Parts, made forays into the South to bring literacy—and with it Christianity—to the enslaved. Beginning in 1704, the society also operated a nighttime school for enslaved Africans and American Indians in New York City.

The Native people of North America had a long cultural tradition in which formal schooling was unknown. Learning, for Indian children, was woven into the fabric of everyday life. From their parents and other adults, they learned such skills as hunting, fishing, raising crops, preserving and preparing food, and constructing a home. Under adult guidance they also mastered decorative arts and absorbed the religious teachings and myths of their people.

Indians numbered among the first students admitted to Dartmouth College, one of several colleges established during the colonial period, which was founded in Hanover, New Hampshire, in 1769. The first was Harvard College, founded in Massachusetts in 1636, and the first in the South was the College of William and Mary, in Williamsburg, Virginia, founded in 1693. These colleges limited acceptance to men, because it was thought that only males possessed the intellectual stamina needed to pursue advanced learning, and they offered courses of study that emphasized theology and classical languages.

This view of Harvard University was published in 1790. *(Library of Congress, Prints and Photographs Division, LC-USZ62-45523)*

Education and Independence

Faith-based education began to fall out of favor as relations with Great Britain deteriorated and the colonies moved toward independence. The ideas of the Enlightenment, a European philosophical movement based on individual rights, reason, and observable reality, influenced political leaders such as Thomas Jefferson. In 1779, during the American Revolution, Jefferson submitted to the Virginia Assembly a plan for a statewide school system that excluded religion from the curriculum. Preoccupied with wartime matters, the assembly rejected Jefferson's plan, but Americans continued to consider how best to educate the populace after the Revolution ended and the United States was an independent nation. They debated whether Latin and Greek belonged in the schools of a republic, and whether children should use the Bible as a textbook. The Constitution made no mention of education, thus leaving the establishment of schools in the hands of state governments—that much, at least, was clear.

Gradually the states developed systems of public, or common, schools supported by state and local funds. A common school typically was a one-room schoolhouse where children of all ages learned together from a single teacher. Most resembled the Griggsville, Illinois, school of the 1840s, which one of its pupils recalled as having "no desks but instead there was a plank on each side of the school-house fastened to the walls." The pupils sat together on benches hewn from logs, facing the teacher; "and when the older scholars wrote, they had to turn and face the wall."[4]

By the middle of the 19th century, some cities and large towns, including Boston and Quincy, Massachusetts, built multiroom schools and divided the pupils into grades, according to age and achievement. Going to school remained a voluntary activity, though, and it was not unusual for children to interrupt or terminate their education to work on the family farm or in a factory.

Another question that some people pondered was this: How could education promote a national identity? Noah Webster, a teacher in Goshen, New York, set out to make language the great unifier. Seeking to standardize American English and set it apart from the English of Great Britain, in 1783 he began publishing textbooks based on American pronunciation and usage. His *American Spelling Book* was widely used throughout the 19th century, and in 1825 he published the first edition of his *American Dictionary of the English Language*, containing a record 70,000 entries, including scientific terms, in keeping with Enlightenment thinking.

Other minds, meanwhile, were pondering the nature of education itself. The Swiss educator Johann Heinrich Pestalozzi, whose ideas reached the United States in the early 1800s, theorized that children learn first with all their senses and that their understanding proceeds from concrete objects to abstract concepts. Horace Mann, secretary of the Massachusetts Board of Education in the 1830s and 1840s, brought professionalism to teaching by founding in Lexington, Massachusetts, the first public normal school, or teacher-training academy, in the United States. He also created and edited the *Common School Journal*, which contained articles relevant to teaching.

Advanced Study of Science

Some institutions of higher learning in the young United States took the bold step of emphasizing science and engineering in their courses of study. At the innovative Rensselaer School in Troy, New York (the forerunner of Rensselaer Polytechnic Institute), students worked in a laboratory, applying the latest scientific knowledge to agriculture, mechanics, and other disciplines. Engineering formed the basis of study at the U.S. Military Academy at West Point, New York, which was founded in 1802 to produce a corps of highly trained army officers.

Little by little, women and African Americans gained opportunities for higher education. The first college for women in the United States, the Wesleyan Female Seminary, opened in Macon, Georgia, in 1836, and the first private college for African Americans, Wilberforce University, opened near Xenia, Ohio, in 1856.

Efforts to educate African-American children in the North met with mixed success. A school established in New York City by the Manumission Society, a Quaker organization, in 1787, served as a model for schools in other cities. Yet a private school for African-American girls that was opened in 1832 in Canterbury, Connecticut, by a Quaker woman, Prudence Crandall, became the target of mob violence and was forced to close.

Slavery, after 1804, remained legal only in the southern states, where laws forbade teaching people of African descent to read or write. Some enslaved people learned to read from their owners despite the ban, and many received religious instruction, which the law permitted, although it was often laced with lessons about accepting one's lot in life.

Proscription of education was intended to keep the enslaved population powerless and subservient, but the instruction of American Indians had as its objective amalgamation, or the blending of Indians into the dominant culture. Missionary groups such as the American Board of Commissioners for Foreign Missions opened schools near Indian settlements to instruct children and adults in English, the ways of the non-Indian farming society, and the teachings of Christ.

Religion remained at the core of educational efforts directed toward poor children as well. Beginning in 1790, Protestant and Catholic groups operated Sunday schools for the children of the urban poor, to start them on the path toward salvation and inoculate them against environmental temptations that included drink, dishonesty, and laziness, which would lure them into lives of vice and crime. Gradually, Sunday schools lost their association with the poor and became vehicles for the religious instruction of children at all economic levels.

Educators were also attending to the learning needs of the disabled. Schools for the deaf, blind, and developmentally disabled were residential facilities such as the American School for the Deaf, which opened in Hartford, Connecticut, in 1819, and the New England School for the Blind, in Boston, which welcomed its first students in 1829. The courses of study at these schools emphasized oral and written communication, in manners deemed most suitable by the school administrators, and simple work skills.

War Disrupts Education

An educational system had barely taken form in the United States when schooling—like many aspects of American life—was interrupted by the Civil War. The war that began on April 12, 1861, and divided the nation drew male teachers and students into the armed forces. There were other kinds of interference as well: Southern students departing from Northern schools; an economic depression in the North forcing young people to leave public schools and go to work, and making private school tuition hard for many parents to afford; the danger of conducting classes close to the battle lines. As Baltimore and other cities made teachers swear allegiance to the United States, the army established a base at Annapolis, Maryland, forcing the U.S. Naval Academy to relocate temporarily to Rhode Island.

Throughout the war, many teachers, South and North, focused their energy on the children of the Confederacy. Southern educators, no longer able to rely on Northern suppliers, wrote and published textbooks for the future white citizens of their emerging nation, the Confederate States of America, although around them schools shortened their terms and colleges closed for lack of students, faculty, and funds. The new reading, spelling, and arithmetic books replaced Northern place names with Southern ones in problems and examples and referred positively to slavery. The ongoing war was an honorable fight for independence, according to these texts, and the Confederate military leaders were national heroes. In order to "unite their efforts for the advancement of the cause of education in the Confederacy," Southern teachers and school administrators also formed the Educational Association of the Confederate States of America, which convened twice before the Union victory in the war led to its dissolution.[5]

Northerners, in contrast, attended to the learning needs of black Southerners. The necessity for educating the African-American population was evident by 1862, as thousands of people fleeing slavery placed themselves in the hands of the conquering Union forces. Called contrabands by the army and freedmen by most Northerners, the former slaves lived crowded into camps established by the military. Northern missionary and charitable groups and the army established schools for the freedmen, to teach them to read and to impart skills that children and adults required for life after slavery. These schools functioned in defiance of local whites, some of whom burned and vandalized the schoolhouses and terrorized and killed several teachers.

In March 1865, with the war drawing to an end, a federal agency assumed responsibility for educating many of the former slaves. The Bureau of Refugees, Freedmen and Abandoned Lands—better known as the Freedmen's Bureau—distributed provisions to Southerners who had been uprooted by war. Its schools trained hundreds of thousands of African Americans in reading, writing, arithmetic, hygiene, homemaking, and manual trades. The Freedmen's Bureau also cooper-

The Zion School of Charleston, South Carolina, shown here in 1866, had 13 teachers and 850 pupils. *(Library of Congress, Prints and Photographs Division, LC-USZ62-117666)*

A student from the Hampton Institute, a school for African Americans in Hampton, Virginia, teaches former slaves to read, ca. 1880. *(Courtesy of Hampton University Archives)*

ated with private benefactors to establish institutions of higher learning for African Americans, including Atlanta University, founded in 1865, and Howard University, which opened in Washington, D.C., in 1867.

In the late 19th century, two prominent African-American educators disagreed publicly about how education might best serve their race. Booker T. Washington, director of the Tuskegee Normal and Industrial Institute, a vocational school for African Americans, favored practical, industrial training that would permit blacks to play a useful, if lowly, role in society. After several generations, when they had begun to gain acceptance by whites, black Americans could start filling roles that permitted them to use their full intellectual power, he said. W. E. B. DuBois, the Harvard-educated professor of sociology at Atlanta University, took issue with Washington's philosophy, which he said kept African Americans from improving their situation economically or socially. Washington's plan "startled and won the applause of the South, it interested and won the admiration of the North," DuBois wrote; "and after a confused murmur of protest, it silenced if it did not convert the Negroes themselves."[6] DuBois called for equal opportunity in education for blacks and whites and for African Americans to participate fully in U.S. society.

During this period the federal government and private individuals also were addressing the perceived needs of another group, the Native American population. The U.S. Indian Service was creating day and boarding schools for Indian youth that were places of cultural reeducation, where students were required to dress like the non-Indian American majority, speak English, and abandon their Indian names, beliefs, and traditions. Among the best known was the boarding school that was opened in 1879 in Carlisle, Pennsylvania, by a former army officer, Captain Richard Henry Pratt. More than 10,000 children, most from the far-off West, attended this school before it closed in 1918. Changed by their boarding-school experience, students often felt out of place when they returned to the reservations. Yet prejudice prevented them from gaining full acceptance among non-Indians.

Learning by Doing

In keeping with the progressivism that characterized the late 19th century, social scientists had begun to study how children learn, and teachers were applying their findings in the classroom. Chief among these investigators was John Dewey, who tested new teaching methods in a laboratory school at the University of Chicago. For Dewey, learning resulted from activity and problem solving. Teachers best served pupils, he said, by creating challenges for them to overcome and planning activities that matched their interests.

On March 2, 1867, the U.S. Office of Education came into being, to gather and distribute information on school development and educational progress nationwide. One trend that the office monitored was the proliferation of a relatively new and controversial type of institution: the high school. The public generally accepted responsibility for supporting elementary schools, but using local tax dollars to fund high schools, which only a small number of students attended, led to verbal feuding and lawsuits. A decision by the Michigan Supreme Court in 1874, when high schools served fewer than 25,000 students nationwide, largely settled the matter for communities throughout the United States. The court stated that it was important to maintain public high schools, even if they served a minority of students, because they enabled young people without great financial means to prepare for college. In other words, high schools furthered democratic, rather than elitist, aims.

Over the next two decades, high schools explored their role, with some concentrating on an academic curriculum that readied students for college and others favoring vocational training that equipped students for jobs in skilled trades or for unpaid careers as homemakers. Course offerings became so diversified and objectives so inconsistent that in 1892, the National Education Association, a professional organization, appointed a commission known as the Committee of Ten to develop national guidelines for high schools. The committee's recommendation of a strong academic foundation for all students, whether bound for college or heading to work, standardized high school education and continues to influence curriculum.

As high schools gained acceptance, kindergarten education, a modernism imported from Germany, was spreading as well. Kindergartens moved the schooling of young children out of the home and into the classroom, where pupils learned through guided play. St. Louis had a citywide kindergarten program in 1873, but it was not until three years later, when a model kindergarten at the Philadelphia Centennial Exposition attracted national attention, that the kindergarten movement took off.

The development of public education throughout the United States was anything but uniform. While progressivism, high schools, and kindergartens broadened the educational experiences of youngsters in cities and towns, many young people in rural communities continued to attend one-room schools and learn by rote. Compulsory education had begun in Connecticut in 1813, with a law requiring factory owners to provide child laborers instruction in reading, writing, and arithmetic. Nearly 40 years later, in 1852, Massachusetts became the first state to require all children to attend school, and it was not until 1918 that education was compulsory in every state. The southern states mandated separate public schooling for black and white children in accordance with the 1896 Supreme Court ruling in *Plessy v. Ferguson*, which permitted "separate but equal" public facilities for the races, but schools for African Americans in the South were uniformly inferior to those for whites.

By the early 20th century, immigration was straining the resources of public school systems in New York, Philadelphia, and other cities with large numbers of new residents from Europe. Children sat two to a desk, crammed into classrooms and hallways; many had to be turned away because there simply was no room for them. Immigrant children in school underwent indoctrination in the American way of life,

Washington, D.C., children study the Pilgrims, ca. 1899. *(Library of Congress, Prints and Photographs Division, LC- USZ62-68345)*

often instructed by teachers with no appreciation of foreign cultures. The shortage of space and parents' desire to pass down their Old World heritage contributed to the expansion of parochial education. By 1884, there were nearly 3,000 Catholic schools in the United States and smaller numbers of private schools for children of other faiths.

Higher Education Keeps Abreast of Technology

Science and engineering were changing the way Americans raised crops and livestock and manufactured and moved goods. Machines stitched shoes, pressed bricks, sharpened drills, sawed lumber, and separated copper from its ores. Farmers used machinery to cultivate the soil, harvest crops, and thresh wheat. To prepare young people to work in an increasingly mechanized environment, Congress in 1862 created the land-grant college system. The government granted 30,000 acres of western land to each state to form the basis of an endowment that would support at least one college for the teaching of agriculture and the mechanical arts.

Land-grant institutions accounted for some of the 369 colleges and universities that were active in the United States in 1870. In contrast to most colleges and universities of the colonial and early national periods, these institutions tended to be coeducational and to offer degrees in the sciences, engineering, agriculture, education, and in some cases medicine and law.

Three Great Crises

Three catastrophic events—World War I, the Great Depression, and World War II—affected the lives of most Americans in the first half of the 20th century. Each altered the role of government in social welfare and the course of progress in education.

During 1917 and 1918, the years of U.S. participation in World War I, the federal government influenced what was taught in U.S. public schools in a way that was unprecedented. Curriculum guidelines distributed by the U.S. Bureau of Education outlined lessons that were intended to encourage "patriotism, heroism, and sacrifice," such as studies of historical figures from the United States and Allied countries for elementary school children and surveys of the historical background of the war for high school students.[7] Pupils learned that conserving food and making their clothing last could help win the war, and through the U.S. School Garden Army, an agency formed by the U.S. Department of the Interior, they contributed to the national food supply by raising vegetables. Schools also acted on their own initiative in response to the war by taking such steps as adding physical education to their requirements in order to produce male graduates who were fit for military service.

The government became a presence on college campuses through the Students' Army Training Corps (SATC), a program for preparing military officers. SATC terminated after a few months of operation, because the war ended; nevertheless, it brought more than 52,000 young men to colleges and universities for scientific and technical training. The army also pioneered and popularized intelligence testing by administering I.Q. tests to 1.75 million recruits in 1917 and 1918. Government efforts included as well vocational education on military bases and in veterans' hospitals and training for civilians in shipbuilding skills through the Emergency Fleet Corporation, an agency created to oversee commercial shipping during wartime.

Following the armistice, Americans enjoyed a decade of prosperity during which many rural schools consolidated, the high school population grew, and colleges and universities established departments of education to produce a more qualified teaching force. Much of this progress halted abruptly following the stock-market crash of October 29, 1929, the event that announced the start of the Great Depression. This sustained period of severe economic hardship confronted hundreds of thousands of Americans with job loss, hunger, uncertainty, and encroaching poverty.

For a time the educational system held steady, but then declining revenues began taking a toll. Public school systems cut their staffs, eliminated electives and classes in the arts, shortened terms, and postponed purchases and repairs. Even after taking cost-cutting measures such as these, however, many schools had no choice but to close. By spring 1932, school closings had interrupted the education of 330,000 children. In 1932, college attendance dropped for the first time since World War I, because many students and their families could no longer afford to pay tuition. It rose again as the depression lingered and young people sought higher education as an alternative to unemployment.

His inaction and apparent insensitivity to people's needs cost President Herbert Hoover, a Republican, the 1932 election. Voters instead gave their support to his Democratic opponent, Franklin Delano Roosevelt, who promised a greater government response. Roosevelt implemented a broad, ambitious legislative program known as the New Deal. Its principal aims were to revive the economy and put people to work, but some of its programs addressed learning needs. For example, the Civilian Conservation Corps (CCC), which was established in 1933 to employ young men on public-works projects, offered voluntary classes in vocational skills, basic literacy, and artistic enrichment. "What are we trying to teach these men? Anything they want to be taught," said C. S. Marsh, educational director of the CCC.[8] The classes benefited some 500,000 participants.

Another New Deal agency, the National Youth Administration (NYA), oversaw a work-study program for high school and college students and gave jobs and training to young men and women who were unemployed. Participants received classroom and on-the-job instruction in such varied skills as surveying, sales, masonry, typing, and child care. Out-of-work teachers were among the thousands given jobs by the largest New Deal agency, the Work Projects Administration (WPA). Teachers on the WPA payroll taught classes to NYA enrollees, illiterate adults, and immigrants preparing for citizenship. They conducted nursery schools as well as summer classes for elementary and secondary school students. The federal government also attended to the education of some of the children uprooted by the severe drought that afflicted the Southwest in the 1930s by creating schools at the 10 camps for migrant families operated by the U.S. Farm Security Administration in California and other western states.

The New Deal helped Americans weather the Great Depression, but the economy failed to rebound until the late 1930s, when U.S. factories began producing weapons and vehicles for World War II. As soon as the December 7, 1941, attack on Pearl Harbor drew the United States into the war, educators responded with lessons in preparedness. Students needed to know what to do in the event of another air raid, and they needed to understand the background of the war.

Schools also took on the burden of organizing children's participation in patriotic home-front activities, such as selling war bonds and collecting scrap materials. Many high schools offered accelerated schedules to better serve students headed for military service or war work, and they supplemented course offerings to include

Children relax during recess in Tipler, Wisconsin, May 1937. *(Library of Congress, Prints and Photographs Division, LC-USF34-010981-E)*

Young men receiving vocational training through the National Youth Administration (NYA) in Maine work on telephone poles. *(Library of Congress, Prints and Photographs Division, LC-USZ62-100280)*

classes in aeronautics and other subjects thought to be useful for young people entering the "air age."

The federal government was less directly involved in the schools during this war than it was during the First World War, because public support for the nation's cause was so strong. Still, in 1942 U.S. Commissioner of Education John W. Studebaker created the High School Victory Corps to organize teens' home-front efforts. The government also provided teachers and school supplies for the Japanese-American children who had been transported with their families from the West Coast and forced to live in relocation (internment) camps.

The most dramatic changes in education resulting from U.S. participation in the Second World War took place on college campuses. In 1942, the armed forces developed three programs for training officers in key areas of science and engineering, using the resources of thousands of colleges and universities. The Army Specialized Training Program, V-12 Navy College Training Program, and Army Air Forces College Training Program brought needed funds to colleges that had been hurt financially by the loss of large numbers of students to military service.

"Your colleges and universities are being turned into military academies and technical institutions," warned Archibald MacLeish, then librarian of Congress.[9] Yet these programs made higher education accessible to many young people who might never have afforded it otherwise, and although military programs were active only during the war, they permanently changed the public's perception of who went to college. The Serviceman's Readjustment Act of 1944, widely known as the G.I. Bill or G.I. Bill of Rights, had an even greater equalizing effect. This law provided tuition and other expenses for more than 2 million veterans of World War II to attend college between 1944 and 1956.

Postwar Growth

Veterans were not only going to college in 1945, when World War II ended; they were marrying and starting families as well. The resulting demand for housing fueled the growth of suburbs and, with them, suburban school systems that were soon straining their resources to accommodate the surge in enrollment of the baby boom.

Children born in the postwar period grew up during the years when African Americans won important legal victories in their quest for civil rights. In 1954, the U.S. Supreme Court ruled in the cases known collectively as *Brown v. Board of Education* that segregated schooling, as required by law in the southern states, violated the

Farm children walk home from school in Mobridge, South Dakota, February 1942. *(Library of Congress, Prints and Photographs Division, LC-USF347-064652-D-C)*

Constitution. This decision led to the desegregation of southern schools, which occurred peacefully in some communities and forcibly in others, including Little Rock.

The children of the baby boom also felt the philosophical chill of the cold war, the long-running ideological conflict between the United States and the Soviet Union. The perceived need to stay ahead of the Soviets scientifically broke down objections to federal aid to education, something long considered to be in opposition to the Constitution. With the National Defense Education Act of 1958, the federal government supported education at all levels and gained a permanent voice in what and how young Americans learned.

Legislation enacted during the presidency of Lyndon Baines Johnson furthered the national effort to improve education. Among the provisions of the Civil Rights Act of 1964 was one empowering the U.S. commissioner of education to oversee school desegregation; the commissioner would use this authority to link federal aid to integration efforts. Another law, the Economic Opportunity Act of 1964, addressed the learning needs of poor children in several ways, such as by creating Head Start, a program to prepare disadvantaged preschoolers for kindergarten. Speaking of Head Start in 1965, the president said that hope had "entered the lives of more than a half-million youngsters who needed it most."[10]

At least as significant as these pieces of legislation was the Elementary and Secondary Education Act of 1965 (ESEA), which gave more than $1 billion to schools in low-income communities. Many of these schools were in major cities and served minority populations.

Most African Americans who migrated north throughout much of the 20th century settled in cities, where discriminatory practices limited their choice of neighborhood. The flight to the suburbs of many white city residents and employers left black communities increasingly isolated and impoverished. Thus, even with federal aid, the predominantly minority students in inner-city schools faced challenges to learning that were all but unknown in suburbia: crime and violence in the community; a lack of hope; and rundown, poorly funded, badly run schools. In 1960, the psychologist Martin Deutsch published a report of his visit to a school where nearly all the students were African American. There he saw teachers whose "aim was mainly to keep order, and their expectation was not in terms of the children actually learning."[11] This finding was not unusual.

In some northern cities, public officials had manipulated school-district boundaries, the choice of construction sites, and other factors to keep white and minority students in different schools. The Supreme Court addressed such underhanded efforts in the 1970s by ordering cities to use busing and other methods to achieve a racial balance in the schools that reflected the city as a whole. Busing met with resistance in many places, most notably in Boston, but it generally achieved its objective.

College Students Demand to Be Heard

The 1960s were a time of turmoil on college and university campuses, as students staged strikes, marches, and takeovers, seeking a voice in administrative decisions and addressing broader social and political issues. The protests began in 1964 at the University of California at Berkeley, with the formation of the Free Speech Movement, an organized effort to assert students' right to free political expression. Many student demonstrations across the nation were against the escalating war in Vietnam, however, either explicitly or indirectly. For example, in April 1968, students at Columbia University took over campus buildings to protest the school's affiliation with the Institute for Defense Analyses, an organization devoted to weapons research and development. Many institutions of higher learning responded to student demands by liberalizing academic requirements and expanding course offerings to include programs acknowledging the heritage and concerns of groups within the student population. These included black, American Indian, Chicano, and women's studies.

The same willingness to reassess conventional practices persuaded some elementary school administrators and teachers to alter significantly classroom procedure. One result was open education, with rows of pupils seated at desks giving way to a less-structured environment, where children moved at will from one inviting learning center to another. The teacher left the front of the room and assumed a facilitator's role, unobtrusively aiding pupils' self-directed learning. Tests, grades, and formal lessons virtually went out the window.

This mood of openness and acceptance brought many children with disabilities into regular classrooms. Education of the disabled had progressed greatly since the 19th century, when residential facilities prevailed. The states gradually had passed laws either allowing or providing for the education of children with disabilities, and over the years instruction took place most often in special classes, with those who faced similar challenges grouped together. In 1975, with passage of the Education for All Handicapped Children Act, the federal government affirmed the right of all children with special needs to receive a free public education in the least restrictive environment possible. The resulting policy of inclusion, or mainstreaming, brought thousands of children out of special classes to learn alongside their nondisabled peers, usually with specialized assistance. Inclusion proved to be a lasting innovation, although open classrooms largely succumbed to the conservatism that arose in the wake of high inflation in the 1970s.

Students at New York University react to the shooting by the Ohio National Guard during protests at Kent State University that left four students dead, May 1970. *(New York University Archives, Photograph Collection)*

In 1983, a committee acting on behalf of the U.S. Department of Education—the newest cabinet-level department, established in 1980—issued *A Nation Risk*, a report on the state of U.S. education that identified several areas of concern. Among them were the failure of U.S. students to surpass or even match youths from other developing countries on academic assessments, a high level of functional illiteracy, and an all-too-common need for remedial instruction in school and work settings. "Our goal must be to develop the talents of all to their fullest," wrote the authors of the report.[12] The states responded by instituting changes that included more stringent graduation requirements, a longer school day or year, and dropout-prevention programs. Although some states, such as California, measured impressive gains, most fell short of their intended objectives.

The federal government offered strong incentives for improvement in 1994 and 2002, with reauthorization of the Elementary and Secondary Education Act. The 1994 version linked eligibility for Title I funds (aid to schools in disadvantaged areas) to demonstrated progress toward a set of goals put in place by President Bill Clinton. These ranged from preparing preschoolers for formal learning to graduating 90 percent of students from high school. The 2002 law, the No Child Left Behind Act (NCLB), called for all children to achieve optimal academic proficiency by 2014 and required the states to monitor progress through regular testing. State departments of education were obliged to give technical assistance to schools that were repeatedly performing poorly. NCLB gave options to students attending failing schools that included funds for supplemental instruction and the right to transfer to a better-performing public school.

Other alternatives to traditional public education had also gained popularity by the turn of the 21st century. These included charter schools, which are public schools founded by parents, teachers, and others; vouchers, or grants from a state or local government (or the federal government, in the case of the District of Columbia) enabling qualifying students from poorly performing schools to attend private schools; and home schooling. Families choosing these alternatives are veering from the well-worn course in the hope that their choice will yield great results.

Daunting Tasks Remain

The great and complex educational system that Americans have developed over the course of their history continues to encounter hurdles. African-American and Hispanic high school students consistently demonstrate lower levels of achievement in reading and mathematics than their white peers and have dropout rates exceeding 50 percent. School segregation has increased since 1992, when the U.S. Supreme Court first released cities from judicial oversight. Immigration, much of it from Latin America, has contributed to a significant rise in the number of school-age children who speak a language other than English at home. American Indian students very often endure great poverty and face additional obstacles to learning, such as limited proficiency in English and a high incidence of disability. Too many adults—44 million—are barely able to read or write English.

Meeting challenges leads to growth. American schools are continually developing, and teachers, students, parents, and, in fact, all people have the capacity to learn. Thus, roadblocks can become opportunities, and overcoming them can bring the goal of an equitable educational system, one that helps each person achieve his or her aspirations, into view.

CHAPTER ONE

"That Our Schools May Flourish": Education in Colonial America
1636–1782

"It is hard work to keep a school; but it is God's work, and it may be so managed as to be like the work of angels," observed the Reverend Cotton Mather, minister to Boston's North Church, in 1710.[1] Like their Puritan forebears, who settled Massachusetts Bay Colony just a few generations earlier, Mather and other pious New Englanders accepted it as their life's task to earn salvation through great effort—through hard work and study. It was constantly necessary to battle ignorance, which left mortals prey to evil; even children as young as seven, who were old enough to distinguish right from wrong, had to work for acceptance in the eyes of God. Children therefore needed to know how to read in order to study the Scriptures. The Puritans had set out to create a model colony in the wilderness, so children, as future citizens, also had to be taught to obey the law. According to the Puritan ideal, parents and apprentices' masters looked after children's education, either instructing their charges at home or sending them to school.

As in Europe, many boys were bound by contract as apprentices to master craftsmen, traditionally for seven years. Coastal cities such as Boston supported many of these artisans, who included printers, coopers, carpenters, tailors, hatters, and silversmiths. They all employed apprentices in their shops, teaching them the craft and benefiting from their labor. Opportunities for apprenticeship in rural areas were limited, although small communities depended on the services of local blacksmiths, wheelwrights, and the like. A small number of girls were apprenticed to dressmakers, milliners, embroiderers, and hairdressers, and some girls did learn to be governesses or midwives; to run "dame schools" for small children in their homes; or to fill other traditionally female occupations, but most prepared at home for the role of housewife.

Masters were legally obligated to provide apprentices with minimal schooling, but labor shortages in the colonies often led to long workdays, shorter periods of indenture, and neglect of educational responsibilities—by many masters and parents

1

The artist Jacob Maentel painted this early Pennsylvania schoolmaster instructing two pupils in the Ten Commandments. *(The Colonial Williamsburg Foundation. Gift of Dr. Alexander H. O'Neal)*

alike. A law enacted by the General Court of Massachusetts Bay Colony in 1642 therefore gave town selectmen the power to monitor children's literacy. If a child failed to demonstrate the ability "to read and understand the principles of religion and the capital laws of the country," then the parent or master could be fined and the child removed from his or her custody.[2]

In 1647, the General Court passed a more stringent law, the first in North America to mandate the establishment and support of schools. Known popularly as the "Old Deluder, Satan Act," this law required towns of 50 or more families to appoint an instructor for "all such children as shall resort to him to write and read."[3] Towns of 100 or more households were required as well to maintain a Latin grammar school.

The New England colonists modeled their educational system on European schools and traditions. As in Europe, schools were class-centered. Town primary schools provided the children of farmers and laborers with basic knowledge of reading, writing, arithmetic, and religion, and Latin grammar schools prepared the sons of clergymen, lawyers, and well-to-do merchants for positions of leadership in the church and community and possibly for college. The grammar schools' emphasis on the teaching of Latin and classical Greek, thereby imparting the wisdom of great lost civilizations, was based on an ideal image of the educated person formed during the Renaissance.

In 1648, Dedham, Massachusetts, became the first community in North America to collect a tax to support its schools, and in 1693 New Hampshire required towns to provide for their own schools. Tax funds in both Dedham and New Hampshire covered the cost of building a school and the schoolmaster's salary. Thus, by the start of the 18th century, the framework for the U.S. public school system—community schools paid for with local revenues—was already being instituted.

Also by 1700, there were 39 grammar schools in New England that typically offered a seven-year course of study in Latin conversation, composition, and literature and, to a lesser degree, Greek and Hebrew grammar and literature. These grammar schools faced competition from academies, which were private secondary schools. Most academies offered a classical education to young men, and many were boarding schools. Some were for girls and taught needlework and musicianship in addition to reading, writing, and arithmetic. The teachers in Latin grammar schools and academies tended to be college-educated ministers.

The Schoolmaster's Role

Town schoolmasters needed no specialized training, and their qualifications varied greatly. In thriving towns such as Dorchester, Massachusetts, most were college graduates, but in less desirable rural areas some were barely literate. A willingness to "keep" school and skill at mending quill pens made an individual fit to teach in certain remote places. "It is a general plague and complaint of the whole land that for one discreet and able teacher you shall find twenty ignorant and careless," remarked one writer of the period, probably with some exaggeration.[4] There is evidence that teaching employed a disproportionate number of men with physical disabilities, who were unfit for other forms of labor.

Schoolmasters had to pass an examination by the local minister before being hired, earned very little, were often boarded with nearby families. In 1760, the governor of New Jersey required schoolmasters there to be licensed and ordered magistrates "to inform themselves sufficiently of the Character of the School-Masters in the Province; to administer the Oaths to them, and give them . . . a Certificate of Approbation, by which they may obtain a License. . . ."[5] Other colonies then licensed schoolmasters too, and because teaching was considered less than full-time work, communities frequently assigned their schoolmasters religious or civic duties. Town pedagogues led choirs, swept churches, rang church bells, conducted prayer services in the minister's absence, and dug graves. Beginning in 1661 the schoolmaster in Portsmouth, New Hampshire, delivered messages for the court and served summonses. Elsewhere the teacher doubled as a grand juryman, town clerk, or registrar of probate.

A large number of colonial schoolmasters were indentured servants from England who were bound by contract to teach in a community for a period of years in return for their passage to the New World. Although the indentured population consisted largely of the poor, convicted felons, and people of questionable character, it also included debtors and adventurers considered qualified to teach. Most indentured servants fulfilled their contractual obligations, but some ran away, either to avoid serving out their period of indenture or to escape intolerable conditions, with the result that colonial newspapers frequently contained advertisements for runaways. In 1777, a Connecticut town offered a reward of up to 20 pounds for the return of two runaways, one of whom was "a schoolmaster, of a pale complexion, with short hair. He has the itch very bad, and sore legs."[6]

Complaints of drunkenness against schoolmasters were common as well. One such offender was the first teacher hired in Francestown, New Hampshire, a man named Burke who made "a rather free use of cider and rum."[7] Frequent alcohol abuse was usually grounds for dismissal, although a John Sullivan of Dublin, Ireland, worked for many years as a schoolmaster in Thomaston, Maine, and surrounding communities despite "habitual intervals of intemperance."[8]

Schoolmasters taught lessons heavily laced with religion, relying on texts such as the *New England Primer*, probably first published in 1690, which reminded young scholars that life was brief and the sufferings of hell were eternal, and led them in the path toward salvation. The primer began with instruction in the alphabet and advanced to a series of verses such as these, which were to be read and memorized:

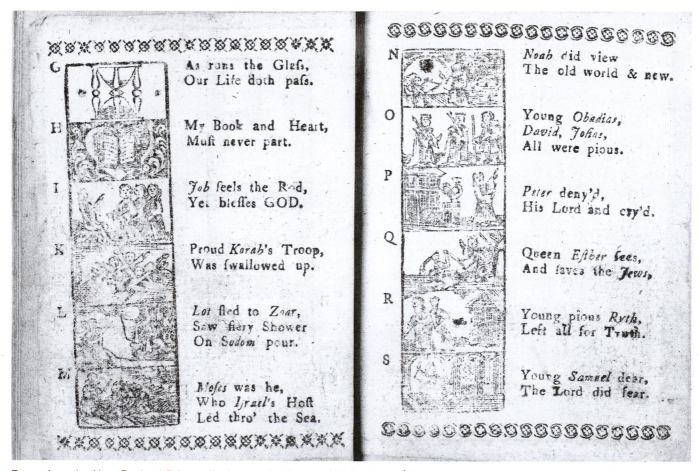

Pages from the *New England Primer* offer lessons in virtue and biblical lore. *(Library of Congress, Prints and Photographs Division, LC-USZ62-60943)*

This colonial-era hornbook is now in the collections of Columbia University. *(Plimpton Hornbook Collection, Rare Book and Manuscript Library, Columbia University)*

> I will fear GOD, and honour the KING.
> I will honour my Father & Mother.
> I will Obey my Superiours. . . .
> I will forgive my Enemies, and pray to God for them.
> I will as much as in me lies keep all God's Holy Commandments.[9]

There followed religious and moral readings, as well as a catechism to be committed to memory. Pupils spent hours praying and studying the Bible and memorizing lessons to recite before the master.

A child's school supplies might have included a slate, quill pen, and hornbook, which was a primer that took the form of a small board with a handle. Affixed to the board was a printed sheet of paper protected by a transparent layer of cow's horn, because paper was scarce and of poor quality. A boy or girl learning from a hornbook progressed from the alphabet to pairs of letters representing sounds, and then to sacred verses, such as the Lord's Prayer.

The typical colonial school was a cabin built of logs or covered with clapboard, with benches for seating, shelves for writing, and a stove for warmth. A number of the furnishings that became standard in American classrooms were lacking: there was no blackboard, globe, or map, and there were few, if any, books. The schoolroom held a chair and lectern for the master and, near the door, a whipping post. The master, whose work Mather compared to that of the angels, beat the devil out of children who broke the rules, acted up, or questioned his authority. Sometimes flogging seemed too lenient a punishment: accounts have survived of children being forced to kneel on gravel, wear a heavy yoke intended for a hard-laboring adult, or keep a wooden bit between their teeth as though they were horses.

By the age of 12, 13, or 14, a youth not headed for college typically left school to learn how to earn a living, possibly through apprenticeship but more likely at home.

The Middle and Southern Colonies

The educational system that developed in the middle colonies reflected the region's greater religious, ethnic, and linguistic diversity. New Netherland was a Dutch colony until 1664, when it was seized by the British and renamed New York. The Dutch West India Company, the organization of merchants that founded the colony for trade and profit, had established schools in 11 of the colony's 12 Dutch settlements. The company covered the schoolmasters' salaries, but communities paid for the schoolhouses and teachers' lodging, and local governments supervised the schools. School administration at the local level continued in most of New York under English rule, although a system of private schools developed in New York City to cater to various religious and cultural groups living in the busy port.

Neighboring Pennsylvania was established as an English colony in 1681, under a royal patent granted to Quaker William Penn. Penn's written contract between himself and the colonists, called the Frame of Government, guaranteed freedom of worship. In the 1700s, the colony therefore attracted not only English Quakers and Anglicans, but also German immigrants belonging to the Moravian, Mennonite, Dunker, and other religious sects.

By midcentury, as much as one-third of Pennsylvania's population was German, and there was concern among the English colonists that the German language and way of life would predominate. The English attempted to use schools as instruments for suppressing German influence and unifying the population, beginning in 1755 with English-language charity schools that educated poor English and German children together. The German population protested against these schools, claiming they presented a biased view of German culture, and the schools, which never served more than 600 to 750 children, were deemed a failure less than a decade after they opened. The Germans maintained their own schools throughout the colonial period, although they gradually adopted English.

The first school supported by public funds in Queen Anne's County, Maryland, opened in 1724. It measured 35 feet by 20 feet, had glazed windows, and was covered with cypress shingles. A few acres adjacent to the school were available to the schoolmaster for farming, in order to supplement his income of 20 pounds a year, although he was forbidden to grow tobacco. Like most colonial schools, this one was in session six days a week, all year long. There is no mention of holidays or vacations in the school's records until 1775.

The Maryland Assembly appointed a group of community leaders to act as "visitors" of the Queen Anne's County school. It was the visitors' responsibility to appoint schoolmasters who were "members of the Church of England and of pious and exemplary lives and capable of teaching well the grammar, good writing and the mathematics if such can conveniently be got."[10] True to the title of their position, the visitors paid occasional visits to the school to monitor the pupils' welfare and the quality of instruction.

In 1767, the visitors engaged a graduate of the College of New Jersey (later Princeton University) named Luther Martin as schoolmaster. On a visit to the school later that year, "observing the scholars shooting at marks with guns [the visitors] had them called together and admonished them and ordered them not to bring guns to school again and also in their presence order[ed] the master to have strict attention to them during their playtime, and to punish any who shall be catched contrary to this order."[11] Hearing "most of the scholars pronouncing badly," the visitors ordered the master "to be particularly attentive to make them express their words and syllables as distinct and clear as possible," and admonished the pupils "to use their utmost endeavors to break themselves of the bad habit which they have heretofore contracted in uttering their words in a thick confused manner."[12]

Luther Martin continued as schoolmaster for another two years. Whether he resigned by choice or was asked to leave is unknown. He studied law and later served as attorney general of Maryland, and in 1807 he defended Aaron Burr at his trial for treason.

School development lagged in the South, the region most segregated by class and race. Young whites living on plantations practiced at home to be gentleman farmers and managers or ladies and household mistresses. Many were also schooled at home by governesses and tutors trained in England. After the mid-18th century, a growing proportion of tutors were graduates of colonial colleges. Parents chose these teachers carefully and treated them less as paid servants than as esteemed members of the household. In addition, dancing and music masters called regularly at plantation homes to convey a degree of refinement. The most elite families sent their children to private schools in England, often entrusting them to the care of relatives or friends residing in the mother country. Some boys remained abroad to continue their studies at Oxford or Cambridge before returning home.

Here and there, tobacco farmers formed cooperative schools for their children, either building a one-room schoolhouse in a farmed-out field or converting an unused tobacco shed for this purpose. While some white children attended these "old field" schools, a small number of poor white southern children were trained through apprenticeship or charity schools. The majority of the poor, however, learned from their elders to subsist by farming, hunting, and trapping. Enslaved African-American children were trained in the agricultural and vocational skills necessary for a life spent in drudgery and servitude.

Slavery was permitted in all 13 colonies. Some enslaved Africans—and American Indians—worked as household servants in the North, but the majority of enslaved Africans labored in the South, and most of these were field hands.

Some slaves learned to read and write through the efforts of the Society for the Propagation of the Gospel in Foreign Parts, an evangelical group established by royal charter on June 16, 1701. The society's missionaries accepted slavery as an institution, but they considered it "a great Reproach to the Christian Name, that so many Thousands of persons should continue in the same State of Pagan Darkness, under a Christian Government, and living in Christian Families; as they lay before under, in their own Heathen Countries."[13] Literacy was essential, because it enabled the enslaved to study the Scriptures and convert to Christianity.

Slaveholders proved to be the greatest obstacle facing the society's missionaries. Most masters saw no need to educate their slaves or bring them into the Christian faith. It was commonly argued that slaves had no souls, or that turning them into Christians made them harder to control—or made it wrong to own them. Masters worked their slaves from the predawn hours until dusk, allowing them free time in the evenings, on Sundays, and possibly for half-days on Saturdays. Most slaves needed this time to feed their families, care for their children, and prepare for the work ahead, and not for study.

In 1704, the society's leaders decided to open a catechizing school for slaves in New York City, where they estimated that 1,500 Africans and Native Americans were enslaved. Hired to conduct this school was Elias Neau, a French Protestant who had been imprisoned in France for his beliefs. Neau began by going from house to house, teaching slaves where they lived. He prepared lessons that were easily memorized, so that even illiterate slaves could learn Bible stories and Christian doctrine, and eventually he persuaded masters to permit their slaves to attend classes in the second story of his lodgings, which he converted into a schoolroom. Teaching had to be done at night, though, when most of the students were tired. "I am obliged to receive them every night by Candle because they work all day long, except on Sundays at which time they come after the Second Sermon, altho' in the Winter, that is also by Candlelight," Neau reported.[14]

In 1712, the public blamed Neau and his school when a number of slaves set fire to a house in New York City as part of a planned uprising. Although only two of the several conspirators had attended the school, support for Neau and his work declined. The society had better success operating between five and 10 schools for whites in New York throughout much of the 18th century.

In Charleston, South Carolina, in 1743, the Society for the Propagation of the Gospel in Foreign Parts opened a school at which a series of teachers were slaves owned by the society. This school trained other African Americans as teachers and offered night classes for the enslaved population. The Charleston Negro School accommodated between 50 and 70 students a year until it closed in 1764, following the death of the teacher.

Colleges Are Established

The first institute of higher learning in the New World was Harvard College, founded in the village of Newtowne (later Cambridge) by the General Court of Massachusetts Bay Colony in 1636. It was named for John Harvard, recently deceased, a minister in nearby Charlestown who had bequeathed to the college half his estate of 1,500 pounds and his library of 320 books. Harvard ensured that the region would have a literate corps of ministers in years to come. The church leaders who had helped to found the colony had been educated in England, and it was doubtful that learned clergymen would come from England to replace them.

Proclaiming that its purpose was "To advance Learning and perpetuate it to Posterity," and "dreading to leave an illiterate Ministry to the Churches, when our present Ministers shall lie in the Dust," Harvard College offered a curriculum emphasizing theological and classical studies as well as instruction in Aristotelian logic and physics, arithmetic, geometry, astronomy, grammar, rhetoric, and other subjects thought to strengthen the mind.[15] The curriculum also included "disputes," or the development of debating powers. Undergraduates regularly debated such philosophical, ethical, religious, and scientific questions as "Did the reptiles of America originate from those preserved by Noah?"; "Does the heart make blood?"; "Is it lawful to subject Africans to perpetual bondage?"; and "Does dancing produce softness and urbanity of manners?"[16] Advanced students delved into classical Greek and Hebrew, and there were lectures in history and the natural sciences for students at all levels to attend.

Harvard quickly demonstrated its efficacy. Of 368 men who completed their studies at the college between 1642 and 1689, 180 were ordained as ministers, 42 entered public service, 27 became physicians, and 13 became teachers or tutors. The occupations of 68 are unknown, 27 died young, and the remaining 11 pursued various other lines of work.

Yale College, founded in New Haven, Connecticut, by the Congregationalist Church in 1701, offered a similar course of study, as did the College of New Jersey, founded by the Presbyterian Church in 1746.

The first college in the South, the College of William and Mary, was founded in Williamsburg, Virginia, in 1693, by virtue of a royal charter issued by King William III and Queen Mary II of England. The college, which was destroyed by fire in 1705 and immediately rebuilt, had schools of grammar, philosophy, and divinity, the latter to prepare ministers for the Church of England. Like the other colonial colleges, William and Mary accepted only men. At the time, most people thought that women should learn to read the Bible but that further study drew their attention away from domestic duties and strained their brains, which were ill-equipped for intellectual work.

The College of William and Mary educated between one and 24 American Indians every year, mostly by force. Enrollment was highest during periods of conflict between Indians and settlers, because it was thought that the presence of Indians at the college protected Williamsburg from attack.

Dartmouth College was founded in Hanover, New Hampshire, in 1769, by the Reverend Eleazar Wheelock, a Congregational minister who had operated a school for Native Americans in Lebanon, Connecticut. The royal charter granting Wheelock land on which to build Dartmouth established the college "for the education and instruction of Youth of the Indian Tribes in this Land . . . and also of English Youth and any others."[17] A Mohegan Indian named Samson Occom, who had been one of Wheelock's first students, raised substantial funds for the college, which was named for William Legge, second earl of Dartmouth, who strongly supported Wheelock's efforts.

The founder of Dartmouth College, Eleazar Wheelock, speaks to some of the college's first students in this woodcut by Samuel E. Brown. *(Courtesy of Dartmouth College Library)*

Learning among the Indians

Formal schooling, or education that occurred in a specific setting, apart from the activity of community life, was foreign to the Native people who occupied North America at the time of European colonization. From infancy, Indian children absorbed the accumulated knowledge of their people from immediate and extended family members and the other adults of the tribe. The group's survival depended on the effort of every able individual, so it was essential for young people to master those skills that were basic to subsistence and transmitting the culture.

The specific skills to be learned varied among tribal nations and geographic regions, but they commonly included hunting, fishing, raising crops, fashioning tools and household objects, constructing shelters, making clothing, and gathering, preparing, and preserving food. Many peoples in diverse locations grew maize, beans, and squash; the Plains Indians hunted the buffalo for its meat and its hide, which they used to make tipis and clothing. The peoples living between the Sierra Nevada and coastal ranges of present-day California had elevated basket making to an art form, and the Navajo (Dineh) and Hopi of the Southwest excelled as silversmiths. Some tasks were assigned according to sex, so that both boys and girls gathered nuts, berries, or shellfish, but boys typically learned to hunt, and girls sewed moccasins and leather garments.

Adults rarely resorted to corporal punishment to correct children's behavior. Public humiliation for misdeeds and praise and rewards for tasks completed well were the preferred methods because in a society in which people viewed themselves foremost as members of the group, public opinion was a powerful motivator.

Native Americans made no distinction between the spiritual and material worlds: The former was present in the latter. Elders passed on tribal history, mythological tales, and religious beliefs through storytelling. At puberty, young people were initiated into secret societies or took part in coming-of-age rituals, such as the vision quest, in which a boy on the cusp of manhood fasted in the wilderness, awaiting a vision of his guardian spirit, which often appeared as an animal. Young men commonly chose a new name based on this vision.

A Preference for the Secular

The drive toward independence in the colonies coincided with calls for secularism in education. Benjamin Franklin, Thomas Jefferson, and other leading thinkers were influenced by the ideology of the Enlightenment, an intellectual movement originating in western Europe that relied on reason and science to understand human culture and the natural world. In 1776, ideas central to the Enlightenment— that human beings have inalienable rights and that a contractual relationship exists between a government and the governed—provided a theoretical foundation for the Declaration of Independence.

An Enlightenment philosopher whose teachings affected the course of education in America was the Englishman John Locke. Locke taught that the human mind, at birth, was a blank slate, or *tabula rasa*, ready to record knowledge gained through the experience of the senses. Every idea sprang from experience, Locke said, and the measure of the truth of an idea was how well it corresponded with concrete, observable reality. In contrast to the Puritans, Locke said that people were born good and did not have to earn God's approval.

As early as 1749, Benjamin Franklin advocated a grammar school for Philadelphia at which English, and not Latin, was the language of instruction. The practical-minded Franklin advocated instruction in mathematics and science and the teaching of languages based on future professional needs.

In 1779, while serving in the Virginia Assembly, Thomas Jefferson proposed a statewide system of elementary and secondary schools. Jefferson's plan called for schools that were state-sponsored but locally controlled and a curriculum that was free of religion and emphasized literature, mathematics, and history. The proposal included a system for identifying the most promising students and giving them access to higher education. Jefferson's plan was rejected by the assembly, but it succeeded in planting the issues of state responsibility for schooling and equal opportunity for education in the national consciousness.

With America at war with Great Britain, suggestions of educational reform were speculative at best. Throughout the colonies, money that would have supported schools was used to fund armies. Books became scarce once printers could no longer get supplies from England. Town schools closed, and Latin grammar schools and colleges struggled along short-staffed as teachers left their posts to fight in the war—often for the British. Plundering redcoats burned schoolhouses and destroyed their contents; when the British occupied lower New York, in 1776, schools throughout the region closed. The great disruption of war resulted in something the Puritan forebears had hoped to prevent: a rise in illiteracy in America.

Chronicle of Events

1636
- The General Court of the Massachusetts Bay Colony founds Harvard College in the village of Newtowne (later Cambridge).

1642
- The General Court of Massachusetts Bay Colony authorizes town selectmen to monitor children's literacy and remove from their homes children whose education is being neglected.

1642–1689
- During this period, 368 men complete their studies at Harvard; of these, 180 are ordained as ministers.

1647
- The General Court of Massachusetts Bay Colony requires towns to establish and support schools.

1648
- Dedham, Massachusetts, is the first community in North America to support its schools through local taxes.

1664
- The British seize the Dutch colony New Netherland and rename it New York.

1681
- Pennsylvania is established as an English colony under a royal patent granted to William Penn.

1690
- It is thought that the *New England Primer* is first published in this year.

1693
- Towns in New Hampshire are required to build and support their own schools.
- The College of William and Mary is established by royal charter in Williamsburg, Virginia.

This statue of benefactor John Harvard, by sculptor Daniel Chester French, sits outside University Hall on the Harvard University campus. *(Library of Congress, Prints and Photographs Division, LC-USZ62-89107)*

1700
- There are 39 Latin grammar schools in New England.

1701
- Yale College is founded in New Haven, Connecticut, by the Congregationalist Church.
- *June 16:* A royal charter establishes the Society for the Propagation of the Gospel in Foreign Parts.

1704
- The Society for the Propagation of the Gospel in Foreign Parts decides to open a catechizing school for slaves in New York City.

1705
- Fire destroys the College of William and Mary; the college is immediately rebuilt.

1712
- Slaves in New York City set fire to a house in an attempted revolt; the catechizing school for slaves and its teacher are wrongly blamed.

1724
- The first publicly supported school in Queen Anne's County, Maryland, opens.

1743
- The Society for the Propagation of the Gospel in Foreign Parts opens the Charleston Negro School in North Carolina, and it trains African Americans to teach.

1746
- The College of New Jersey (later Princeton) is founded by the Presbyterian Church.

1749
- Benjamin Franklin proposes for Philadelphia an English grammar school with a curriculum that emphasizes science and mathematics.

1755
- English colonists in Pennsylvania establish English-language charity schools for poor English and German children; in less than a decade these schools cease operation.

1760
- The governor of New Jersey requires schoolmasters to be licensed.

1764
- The Charleston Negro School closes following the death of its African-American teacher.

1769
- Dartmouth College is founded by royal charter in Hanover, New Hampshire, to educate Indian and white men.

1775
- Holidays and vacations have become regular parts of the school year in Maryland and elsewhere.
- *April 18–19:* British and colonial forces exchange fire at Concord and Lexington, Massachusetts, in the first armed encounters of the American Revolution.

1776
- Thomas Jefferson authors the Declaration of Independence, a document influenced by the thinking of the Enlightenment.

1779
- Thomas Jefferson proposes to the Virginia Assembly a statewide educational system; the assembly rejects Jefferson's plan.

1781
- *October 19:* British general Charles Cornwallis surrenders to General George Washington, ending the hostilities of the American Revolution.

Eyewitness Testimony

Mr. Hopkins, the governour of Hartford upon Connecticut, came to Boston, and brought his wife with him, (a godly young woman, and of special parts,) who was fallen into a sad infirmity, the loss of her understanding and reason, which had been growing upon her divers years, by occasion of her giving herself wholly to reading and writing, and had written many books. Her husband, being very loving and tender of her, was loath to grieve her; but he saw his errour, when it was too late. For if she had attended her household affairs, and such things as belong to women, and not gone out of her way and calling to meddle in such things as are proper for men, whose minds are stronger &c. she had kept her wits, and might have improved them usefully and honourably in the place God had set her. He brought her to Boston, and left her with her brother, one Mr. Yale, a merchant, to try what means might be had here for her. But no help could be had.

John Winthrop, first governor of Massachusetts Bay Colony, 1645, The History of New England from 1630 to 1649, *vol. 2, pp. 216–217.*

. . . 6. We press [children's] Memory too soon, and puzzle, strain, and load them with Words and Rules; to know Grammer and Rhetorick, and a strange Tongue or two, that it is ten to one may never be useful to them; Leaving their natural Genius to Mechanical and Physical, or natural Knowledge uncultivated and neglected; which would be of exceeding Use and Pleasure to them through the whole Course of their Life.

7. To be sure, Languages are not to be despised or neglected. But Things are still to be preferred.

8. Children had rather be making of Tools and Instruments of Play; Shaping, Drawing, Framing, and Building, &c. than getting some Rules of Propriety of Speech by Heart; And those also would follow with more Judgment, and less Trouble and Time.

9. It were Happy if we studied Nature more in natural Things; and acted according to Nature; whose rules are few, plain and reasonable.

William Penn, founder of Pennsylvania, 1693, "Some Fruits of Solitude in Reflections and Maxims," in S. Alexander Rippa, ed., Educational Ideas in America: A Documentary History, *p. 41.*

The senses at first let in particular ideas, and furnish the yet empty cabinet: and the mind by degrees growing familiar with some of them, they are lodged in the memory, and names got to them. Afterwards the mind, proceeding farther, abstracts them, and by degrees learns the use of general names. In this manner the mind comes to be furnished with ideas and language, the materials about which to exercise its discursive faculty; and the use of reason becomes daily more visible, as these materials, that give it employment, increase. But though the having of general ideas, and the use of general words and reason, usually grow together, yet I see not how this any way proves them innate. The knowledge of some truths, I confess, is very early in the mind; but in a way that shows them not to be innate. For, if we will observe, we shall find it still to be about ideas not innate, but acquired; it being about those first, which are imprinted by external things, with which infants have earliest to do, which make the most frequent impressions on their senses. In ideas thus got, the mind discovers that some agree, and others differ, probably as soon as it has any use of memory, as soon as it is able to retain and receive distinct ideas. But whether it be then or no, this is certain, it does so long before it has the use of words, or comes to know that which we commonly call "the use of reason." For a child knows as certainly, before it can speak, the difference between the ideas of sweet and bitter, (that is, that sweet is not bitter,) as it knows afterwards, when it comes to speak, that wormwood and sugarplums are not the same thing.

John Locke, English philosopher, 1693, An Essay Concerning Human Understanding, *pp. 17–18.*

A child knows his nurse and his cradle, and, by degrees, the playthings of a little more advanced age; and a young savage has perhaps his head filled with love and hunting, according to the fashion of his tribe. But he that from a child untaught, or a wild inhabitant of the woods, will expect . . . abstract maxims and reputed principles of sciences, will, I fear, find himself mistaken. Such kind of general propositions are seldom mentioned in the huts of Indians; much less are they to be found in the thoughts of children, or any impressions of them on the minds of naturals. They are the language and business of the schools and academies of learned nations, accustomed to that sort of conversation or learning where disputes are frequent: these maxims being suited to artificial argumentation and useful for conviction; but not much conducing to the discovery of truth or advancement of knowledge.

John Locke, 1693, An Essay Concerning Human Understanding, *p. 25.*

A grammar school he would always have upon the place, whatever it cost him: and he importuned all other places to have the like. I cannot forget the ardor with which I even heard him pray, in a synod of these churches which met at Boston, to consider "how the miscarriages which were among us might be prevented." I say with what fervor he uttered an expression to this purpose: "Lord, for schools everywhere among us. O that our schools may flourish. That every member of this assembly may go home and procure a good school to be encouraged in the town where he lives. That before we die we may see a good school encouraged in every plantation of the country." God so blessed his endeavors, that Roxbury could not live quietly without a free school in the town; and the issue of it has been one thing which has made me almost put the title of Schola Illustris upon that little nursery: that is, "The Roxbury has afforded more scholars, first for the college and then for the public, than any town of its bigness, or if I mistake not, of twice its bigness, in all New England."

Cotton Mather, Congregational minister, writing about the Reverend John Eliot of Roxbury, Massachusetts, 1702, Magnalia Christi Americana, *in Walter Herbert Small,* Early New England Schools, *pp. 2–3.*

PARENTS! How much you ought to be devising for the good of your *children!* Often consider how to make them "wise children;" how to give them a desirable education, an education that may render them desirable; how to render them lovely and polite, and serviceable to their generation. Often consider how to enrich their minds with valuable knowledge; how to instil into their minds generous, gracious, and heavenly principles; how to restrain and rescue them from the "paths of the destroyer," and fortify them against their peculiar temptations. There is a world of good that you have to do for them. You are without the natural feelings of humanity, if you are not in a continual agony to do for them all the good that lies in your power. It was no mistake of an ancient writer, in saying, "Nature teaches us to love our children as ourselves."

Cotton Mather, 1710, Essays to Do Good, Addressed to All Christians, Whether in Public or Private Capacities, *in S. Alexander Rippa, ed.,* Educational Ideas in America: A Documentary History, *p. 49.*

I would be solicitous to have my children expert, not only at reading with propriety, but also at writing a fair hand. I will then assign them such books to read, as I may judge most agreeable and profitable, obliging them to give me some account of what they read; but will keep a strict eye on what they read, lest they should stumble on the devil's library, and poison themselves with foolish romances, novels, plays, songs, or jests, "that are not convenient."

Cotton Mather, 1710, Essays to Do Good, Addressed to All Christians, Whether in Public or Private Capacities, *in S. Alexander Rippa, ed.,* Educational Ideas in America: A Documentary History, *p. 49.*

The late barbarous Massacre attempted by the Slaves April 1712 gave strength at first to this clamour which had a full run for many days. The School was charged as the cause of this Mischief, the place of Conspiracy and that instruction had made them cunning and insolent.

The Catechist and all that were known to favour this design were reproached, and the flagitious villany was imputed to the Catechumens yet upon the strictest inquiry and severest tryal, where the bare affirmation of infidel Evidence who are not capable of any other tye to veracity was sufficient to fix the guilt, there were not found any other Actors or Accomplices in the Conspiracy who had duly attended the Catechetical instruction, but two were accused one of which had been formerly baptised and he dyed protesting his innocence, and was, (but too late for him) pityed and declared guiltless even by the Prosecutors. The other had made some proficience, but was not admitted to Baptism thro' the reluctancy of his Master whom he had often solicited for it. He was an eminent Merchant and with his son were both murdered in the Streets. This Negro was hung in chains alive. I went to see him after he had hung five days he declared to me he was innocent of the murder with a seeming concern for his Masters misfortune. He was often delirious by a long continuance in that painful posture thro' hunger thirst and pain but he then answered directly to what I enquired and called me by my name so that I might conclude he had some intervals of the exercise of his reason.

One would believe that such a happy instance as the innocency of the few who frequented the School should take away this prejudice but it still remains and was last winter improved by imaginary plotts contrived on purpose by some ill men to hinder the good work which was by amusing the people to keep them within the Evening which is the only time they are at Liberty from their Masters employ to attend on the School. The Devil finds his kingdom of darkness invaded and rages because his time is but short, 'tis no wonder therefore that he stirs up his instruments to oppose it.

John Sharpe, chaplain of the King's Forces, New York, 1713, in William Webb Kemp, The Support of Schools in Colonial New York by the Society for the Propagation of the Gospel in Foreign Parts, *pp. 240–241.*

The City is so conveniently Situated for trade and the Genius of the people are so inclined to merchandise, that they generally seek no other Education for their children than writing and Arithmetick. So that letters must be in a manner forced upon them not only without their seeking, but against their consent, and there is no doubt but as the youth are very ingenious, Subtile and of quick Capacities, it would in a short time gain upon their inclinations. The Improvement of a few would stir up Emulation not only in the Children but in their parents, and the happy influence would reach the most distant parts of the province.

John Sharpe, chaplain of the King's Forces, New York, 1713, in William Webb Kemp, The Support of Schools in Colonial New York by the Society for the Propagation of the Gospel in Foreign Parts, *p. 68.*

I have set my hand to a Testimonial of one Edward Fitzgerald who kept School in Mr. Forster's absence one Year at West Chester; in the Summer he had upwards of twenty-five scholars, in the winter under 12, but attended the whole Year. I think he deserves a half Years allowance.

The Reverend John Bartow of the Society for the Propagation of the Gospel in Foreign Parts, August 1720, in William Webb Kemp, The Support of Schools in Colonial New York by the Society for the Propagation of the Gospel in Foreign Parts, *p. 149.*

Here is one *Edward Fitzgerald* who, during the time I was absent in England which was about twelve months, kept school in this Town, and he has by pleading poverty prevailed with Mr. Bartow and some others to signe a Certificate in his favour for a Salary for that Year: Which Certificate as I am informed only setts forth the time he kept School and that he instructed in the principles of the Church of England, neither mentioning the Number of his Scholars nor his diligence. But that you may not be in the dark as to this man's true character I give them this acct. which if desired shall be sufficiently testifyed: he is much given to drink and don't attend the Church, for Mr. Bartow does not remember he saw him above once there in the time he kept y^e school here. On his request Mr. Bartow let him have some of the Books that were sent to me but I cannot find, tho' I have Examined all the Scholars, that he gave them any save one

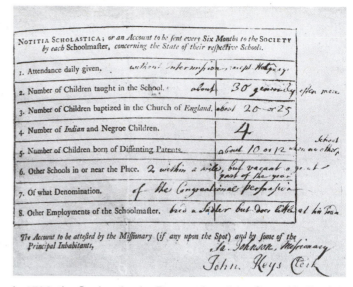

In 1738, the Society for the Propagation of the Gospel in Foreign Parts developed a form, called the *Notitia Scholastica,* for its teachers to fill out and submit twice yearly. A completed form is shown here. *(Library of Congress, General Collection)*

to a child where he lodged, and what use he put them to is not known; as to the Encouragm^t he gave by his dilligence it was such that, from near thirty Scholars, they were before my Arrival reduced to six.

William Forster, schoolmaster, Westchester County, New York, August 1720, in William Webb Kemp, The Support of Schools in Colonial New York by the Society for the Propagation of the Gospel in Foreign Parts, *p. 149.*

The front, which looks due east, is double, and is 136 feet long. It is a lofty pile of brick building, adorned with a cupola. At the north end runs back a large wing, which is a handsome hall, answerable to which the chapel is to be built; and there is a spacious piazza on the west side, from one wing to the other. It is approached by a good walk, and a grand entrance by steps, with good courts and gardens about it, with a good house and apartment for the Indian master and his scholars, and out-houses; and a large pasture inclosed like a park with about 150 acres of land adjoining for occasional uses. The building is beautiful and commodious, being first modeled by Sir Christopher Wren, adapted to the nature of the country by the gentlemen there; and since it was burned down it has been rebuilt, and nicely contrived, altered and adorned by the ingenious direction of Governor [Alexander] Spotswood, and is not altogether unlike Chelsea Hospital [London].

Hugh Jones, professor of mathematics at the College of William and Mary, describing the college, 1724, in Present State of Virginia, *p. 25.*

There are some private schools within my reputed districts which are put very often into the hands of those who are brought into the country and sold for servants. Some school masters are hired by the year, by a knot of families who, in their turn entertain him monthly, and the poor man lives in their houses like one that begged an alms, more than like a person in credit and authority. When a ship arrives in the river it is a common expression with those who stand in need of an instructor for their children, *let us go and buy a school master*. The truth is, the office and character of such a person is generally very mean and contemptible here, and it cannot be other ways 'til the public takes the Education of Children into their mature consideration.

> *The Reverend George Ross of the Society for the Propagation of the Gospel in Foreign Parts, New Castle, Delaware, 1725, in* Lyman P. Powell, History of Education in Delaware, *p. 36.*

As to those ministers who have Negroes of their own, I cannot but esteem it their indispensable duty to use their best endeavors to instruct them in the Christian religion in order to their being baptized; both because such negroes are their proper and immediate care, and because it is vain to hope that other masters and mistresses will exert themselves in this work, if they see it wholly neglected or but coldly pursued in the families of the clergy; so that any degree of neglect on your part, in the instruction of your own Negroes, would not only be withholding from *them* the inestimable benefits of Christianity, but would evidently tend to the obstructing and defeating the *whole design* in every other family.

I would also hope that the school masters in the several parishes, part of whose business it is to instruct youth in the principles of Christianity, might contribute somewhat towards the carrying out of this work, by being ready to bestow upon it some of their leisure time; and especially upon the Lord's day, when both they and the Negroes are most at liberty, and the clergy are taken up with the public duties of their function.

> *Edmund Gibson, bishop of London, May 19, 1727, in* Charles C. Jones, The Religious Instruction of the Negroes in the United States, *p. 26.*

The *Negroe* Slaves even in those Colonies, where the Society send Missionaries, amount to many Thousands of Persons, of both Sexes, and all Ages, and most of them are very capable of receiving Instruction. Even the grown Persons brought from *Guinea*, quickly learn *English* enough to be understood in ordinary Matters; but the Children born of *Negroe* Parents in the Colonies, are bred up entirely in the *English* Language.

> *David Humphreys, secretary of the Society for the Propagation of the Gospel in Foreign Parts, 1730,* An Historical Account of the Incorporated Society for the Propagation of the Gospel in Foreign Parts, *p. 232.*

[W]hat is the instruction of a few Hundreds, in several Years, with respect to the many Thousands uninstructed, unconverted, living, dying, utter *Pagans*. It must be confessed, what hath been done is as nothing, with Regard to what a true Christian would hope to see effected. But the Difficulties the Clergy meet with in this good Work are exceeding great. The first is, the *Negroes* want Time to receive Instruction. Several Masters allow their *Negroes* Sundays only, for rest; and then the Minister of a Parish is fully employed in other Duties, and cannot attend them: Many Planters, in order to free themselves from the Trouble and Charge of Feeding and Cloathing their Slaves, allow them one Day in a Week, to clear Ground and plant it, to subsist themselves and Families. Some allow all Saturday, some half Saturday and Sunday; others allow, only Sunday. How can the *Negroe* attend for Instruction, who on half Saturday and Sunday is to provide Food and Rayment for himself and Family for the Week following?

> *David Humphreys, secretary of the Society for the Propagation of the Gospel in Foreign Parts, 1730,* An Historical Account of the Incorporated Society for the Propagation of the Gospel in Foreign Parts, *p. 234.*

I endeavor, for beginners, to get Primers with syllables, viz., from one to 2, 3, 4, 5, 6, 7 or 8. I take them several times over them till they are perfect, by way of repeating according as I find occasion, and then to some place forward according to their capacity and commonly every two or three leaves. I make them repeat perhaps two or three times over, and when they get the Primer pretty well I serve them so in the Psalter, and we have some Psalters with the proverbs at the latter end. I give them that to learn, the which I take to be very agreeable, and still follow repetitions till I find they are masters of such places. Then I move them into such places as I judge they are fit for, either in the New or Old Testament, and as I find they advance I move them not regarding the beginning nor ending of the Bible, but moving them where I think they may have benefit by. So making of them perfect in the vowels, consonants and dipthongs, and when they go in their reading clean without any noising, singing or stumbling, with deliberate way, then I set them to begin the Bible in order to go throughout. And when I begin writing I follow them in the letters till they come to cut pretty clean letters and then one syllable and so to 2, 3, 4, and to the longest words, and when they join handsomely I give them some sweet pleasing verses, some perhaps on their business, some on behaviour, and some on their duty to parents, etc., of such I seldom want them to command, and when they come to manage double copies readily I give them some delightful sentences or Proverbs or some places in the Psalms or any part of the Bible as they are of forwardness and also to other fancies that may be for their benefit. And when I set them ciphering I keep them to my old fancy of repeating and shall go over every rule till they are in a case to move forward and so on. . . . I also give them tasks, when able, to learn out of books according to their ability, but one girl exceeded all. She had a great many parts in the Bible by heart and had the whole book of St. John and hardly would miss a word. I put them to spell twice a week and likewise to Catechism, and likewise I catechise every Saturday and often on Thursdays. Sometimes I set them to sing Psalms.

Rowland Jones, Pennsylvania schoolmaster, ca. 1730, in J. P. Wickersham, ed., A History of Education in Pennsylvania, *p. 214.*

When Youth are told, that the Great Men whose Lives and Actions they read in History, spoke two of the best Languages that ever were, the most expressive, copious, beautiful; and that the finest Writings, the most correct Compositions, the most perfect Productions of human Wit and Wisdom, are in those Languages, which have endured Ages, and will endure while there are Men; that no Translation can do them Justice, or give the Pleasure found in Reading the Originals; that those Languages contain all Science; that one of them is become almost universal, being the Language of Learned Men in all Countries; that to understand them is a distinguishing Ornament, &c. they may be thereby made desirous of learning those Languages, and their Industry sharpen'd in the Acquisition of them. All intended for Divinity should be taught the Latin and Greek; for Physick, the Latin, Greek, and French; for Law, the Latin and French; Merchants, the French, German, and Spanish: And though all should not be compell'd to learn Latin, Greek, or the modern foreign Languages; yet none that have an ardent Desire to learn them should be refused; their English, Arithmetick, and other Studies absolutely necessary, being at the same Time not neglected.

Benjamin Franklin, statesman and scientist, 1749, "Proposals Relating to the Education of Youth in Pensilvania," p. 415.

The Revd. Mr. Zouberbuhler and the Inhabitants of this Town having made repeated Complaints to this Board, that Mr. Peter Joubert Schoolmaster had for some Time past neglected to give proper Attendance to his Scholars, and likewise that He has been of late so much addicted to Drinking, that He gives great offence to the Inhabitants, and what is more pernicious sets a bad Example to their Children.—The Board being too sensible of this Complaint, and with concern finding that, their repeated Admonitions have not been duly regarded They are now obliged to discharge him.

Governor's Council of Georgia, December 20, 1749, in Willard S. Elsbree, The American Teacher, *p. 19.*

Our Colledge has lain under reflections for some Time, but of late has somewhat retrieved its Character, altho' it does not answer the Expectations that might be had from so great a foundation and noble an Endowment. There are at Present not above 70 Scholars in it, but that is in a great Measure owing to the Gentlemen of the Country who generally prefer private Schools, and from our personal Acquaintance with all the Masters of the Colledge, we have reason to believe that the reflections that are thrown on them are unjust, and that they are Sufficiently capable to lay the foundations of a Youth's Knowledge.

Charles Stewart, Virginia merchant, writing about the College of William and Mary, September 23, 1751, in Susan H. Godson et al., The College of William and Mary: A History, *vol. 1, 1693–1888, p. 84.*

One thing, I think, has not been sufficiently attended to. . . . As mothers have the principal direction in bringing up their young children, it will be of little use that the father can talk English, if the mother can speak nothing but Dutch to them; in that case the children will speak their mother-tongue. It therefore seems to me quite necessary that there should be English schoolmistresses as well as schoolmasters; and the girls should be taught something of the use of the needle, as well as to read and write, if writing should be thought necessary for girls.

William Parsons, school director of Easton, Pennsylvania, October 19, 1754, in James Pyle Wickersham, A History of Education in Pennsylvania, *p. 71.*

If the child is designed for any of the learned professions, some care indeed is taken to find out a Master qualified to teach him Latin and Greek; but if he be only designed for the common offices of life, it is thought sufficient if he be taught to read and write and a little arithmetic, and that often but very imperfectly, no matter by whom, but the cheaper the better. Thus it happens that persons every way unqualified both in learning and morals, are, for the sake of having it done cheaper, entrusted with the education of children.

For it is an undoubted truth, confirmed by fatal experience, that children catch the manners of those with whom they converse, and that impressions made on their tender minds are deep and lasting. Now what children are to learn from the generality of those entrusted with their education in this country, I shall not venture to say; I only wish it were a love of God and good will towards men.

But while an ill-timed formality prevails in the education of youth, while men are preferred for country schoolmasters for their cheapness, not their abilities, and while virtue is neglected in the choice of a tutor, little is to be expected.

It is a foolish and most absurd piece of thrift, for the sake of adding forty or fifty pounds to a child's fortune, to deprive him of such an education, under the care of a proper tutor.

Christopher Sower, a founder of the Germantown Academy, Germantown, Pennsylvania, 1758, in James Pyle Wickersham, A History of Education in Pennsylvania, pp. 171–172.

[The schoolmaster] must be qualified in Reading, Writing, Arithmetic, and Singing; and must undergo an examination in these branches.

He must be one that takes a lively interest in, and helps to build up the Christian Church; and must also be a God-fearing, virtuous man, and lead an exemplary life, and must himself be a lover of the Word of God, and be diligent in its use as much as possible, among the children of the school; and he must set a good example, especially before the young children, and must avoid exhibitions of anger.

He shall willingly and heartily seek to fulfill the duties obligatory upon him, with love to God and to the children; to the performance of which the Lord, their Maker, and Jesus, their Redeemer, have so strongly bound him.

Elders and deacons of the Reformed Church, Philadelphia, 1760, in James Pyle Wickersham, A History of Education in Pennsylvania, p. 141.

Whereas many of the Students of this College have run greatly into Debt with the Merchants, Tavern keepers and others, for unnecessary Things, whereby they have involved themselves with their Parents in great Difficulties.

VOTED, That no Undergraduate Student of this College, be allowed to buy, sell, or exchange any Thing whatsoever in New Haven, without the express Direction of their respective Parents or Guardians, or the consent of the President or a Tutor. And in as much, as the President and Tutors have not Time enough minutely to inspect the Expences of the Scholars: We Do hereby recommend it to the Parents and Guardians of the Scholars to appoint some discreet Person in New-Haven to have the Oversight of the Expences of their Children: And that all Money they expend here pass through their Hands. And the Law of College respecting Scholars Debts shall be understood of such Debts only as are contracted with the Consent of their respective Parents, Guardians, Overseers, on the Authority of College as aforesaid.

President and fellows of Yale College, July 31, 1762, in the Connecticut Gazette, *in Vera M. Butler, ed.,* Education as Revealed by New England Newspapers Prior to 1850, p. 50.

The EDUCATION of YOUTH being the most important Duty of all Societies, comprehending their present Honour and future Prosperity; it must therefore afford great Satisfaction to all who are unfeignedly regardful of the Prosperity of this Colony, that we can inform the Public, that DARTMOUTH COLLEGE is established in this Province, for the free Education of Indian Youth—and for instructing all others in the Arts and Sciences, upon the most liberal and public-spirited Plan; and endowed with very ample Incomes, from the Benevolence of charitable People of all Denominations, both in Europe and America.—We hear the EDIFICE will be built next Summer, and hope by the ensuing Autumn, to inform the Public, it is ready to receive Students.

Boston News-Letter, March 22, 1770, in Vera M. Butler, ed., Education as Revealed by New England Newspapers Prior to 1850, p. 82.

This Day, Mr. Silvanus Ripley, and his Companion, and Interpreter, Lieut. Joseph Taylor, returned from their Mission to the Indian Tribes in Canada, and brought with them ten Children from those Tribes, to receive an Education in this School [Dartmouth College]; two of which are Children of English Captives, who were taken by the Indians in former Wars, while they were young and naturalized; and these Children are brought up in the Language, and Customs of the Indians. The great forwardness and unanimity of their chief Men, when they were called in Council on the occasion, to have their Children come, and their final resolution to send them, notwithstanding the most forceable opposition their Priest made to it, the Chearfulness, orderly and good Behaviour of the Lads on their Way, the intire satisfaction on their arrival Home (as they called it) and the Accounts they gave of Numbers of their Acquaintance, which they have left behind, who desired to come with them for an Education and may be expected in due time, and all this from a Thirst for Learning, founded partly on a Conviction of the Utility of it, which they have got by observing the great Advantage which the Learned have, above others they have lived amongst, and only thro' their superior Learning, also the great and general Veneration the Chiefs expressed towards the benevolent, and charitable Design of this Indian School, exhibit a truly encouraging Prospect that God yet mercifully designs something shall be done in that Quarter for the Honor of his great Name. Among these Children, is a Grandson about 8 years old, of Mr. Tarbull, who was taken from Groton in the Province of the Massachusetts-Bay about 68 years ago, when he was about 10 years old; he greatly rejoiced to see them on this Occasion, and earnestly encouraged his Grandson's coming; the old Gentleman is hearty, and well, and is the eldest Chief of that Village,—he expressed great Affection to his Relations in New-England, and desired they might be informed of his Welfare, and also that he had a Grandson at this School,—also a Grandson of Mrs. Eunice Williams; who was Captivated with her Father, the Rev. Mr. Williams of Deerfield, in the year 1704, would have come with them; but was sick with the Measels; but may be expected in the Spring; if they meet with nothing discouraging.

> Boston News-Letter, *October 15, 1772, in Vera M. Butler, ed.,* Education as Revealed by New England Newspapers Prior to 1850, *pp. 86–87.*

I set out from home the 20th of Octr and arrived at the Hon: Robert Carters, of Nominy, in Westmorland County, the 28th I began to teach his children the first of November. He has two sons, and one Nephew; the oldest Son is turned of seventeen, and is reading Salust [Gaius Sallustius Crispus, a Roman historian] and the greek grammer; the others are about fourteen, and in english grammer, and Arithmetic. He has besides five daughters which I am to teach english, the eldest is turned of fifteen, and is reading the spectator; she is employed two days in every week in learning to play the Forte-Piana, and Harpsicord—The others are smaller, and learning to read and spell.

> *Philip Vickers Fithian, Virginia plantation tutor, December 1, 1773, in Hunter Dickinson Farish, ed.,* Journal and Letters of Philip Vickers Fithian, 1773–1774, *p. 34.*

In the morning so soon as it is light a Boy knocks at my Door to make a fire; after the Fire is kindled, I rise which now in the winter is commonly by Seven, or a little after, By the time I am drest the Children commonly enter the School-Room, which is under the Room I sleep in; I hear them round one lesson, when the bell rings for eight o-Clock (for Mr Carter has a large good Bell of upwards of 60 Lb. which may be heard some miles, & this is always rung at Meal times;) the Children then go out; and at half after eight the Bell rings for Breakfast, we then repair to the Dining-Room; after Breakfast, which is generally about half after nine, we go into School, and sit til twelve, when the Bell rings, & they go out for noon; the dinner-Bell rings commonly about half after two, often at three, but never before two.—After dinner is over, which in common, when we have no Company, is about half after three we go into School, & sit til the Bell rings at five, when they separate til the next morning; I have to myself in the Evening, a neat Chamber, a large Fire, Books, & Candle & my Liberty, either to continue in the school room, in my own Room or to sit over at the great House with Mr & Mrs Carter—We go into Supper commonly about half after eight or at nine & I usually go to Bed between ten and Eleven.

> *Philip Vickers Fithian, Virginia plantation tutor, December 15, 1773, in Hunter Dickinson Farish, ed.,* Journal and Letters of Philip Vickers Fithian, 1773–1774, *p. 41.*

CHAPTER TWO

Schooling a New Nation
1783-1859

On September 9, 1783, less than a week after the United States and Great Britain signed the Treaty of Paris, officially ending the American Revolution, Benjamin Rush, a prominent physician and signer of the Declaration of Independence, prepared the charter for Dickinson College, the first institution of higher learning established in the new United States. Named for the statesman John Dickinson, who was Rush's friend, the college was located in the frontier town of Carlisle, Pennsylvania, in a building that had housed a struggling grammar school.

Rush believed that education, and nothing else, would "render the American Revolution a blessing to mankind."[1] Like the Puritans of the early colonial period, he understood that an educated citizenry was essential to building a cohesive society. "We have changed our forms of government, but it remains yet to effect a revolution in our principles, opinions, and manners so as to accommodate them to the forms of government we have adopted," he said.[2]

In 1786, he put forward a plan for public schools in Pennsylvania that called for instruction in English and German. Jefferson and other thinkers influenced by the Enlightenment wanted to remove religion from the public-school curriculum, because of their conviction that religious teachings inhibited scientific inquiry, but Rush opposed any separation of church and state and advocated using the Bible as a textbook. He was convinced that scientific principles revealed the hand of God at work and argued that removing Latin and Greek from the curriculum, rather than religion, would further scientific progress. Classical studies belonged to aristocracies, he said, and not to the developing United States.

Rush also proposed a national system of education, but like his plan for Pennsylvania, such a program would never come to be. The Tenth Amendment to the Constitution, ratified on December 15, 1791, as part of the Bill of Rights, gave to the states all powers not delegated to the federal government by the Constitution, and the power to establish schools fell into this category. Massachusetts already had an education law, enacted in 1789. Similar to the colonial law of 1647, this legislation required towns of 50 households to support schools and employ a teacher for six months of every year. Towns of 100 or more households were obligated to support their schools for the entire year, and towns of 200 or more households also had to hire a grammar-school instructor.

The question of how best to educate the people of a free republic occupied many of the nation's leading minds. So important was this issue that in 1797 the American Philosophical Society, an organization of American and European intellectuals, offered a prize for the best essay on a "system of liberal Education and literary instruction, adapted to the genius of the Government of the United States"; entries were to include as well "a plan for instituting and conducting public schools in this country, on principles of the most extensive utility."[3] Two essayists shared the prize: Samuel Harrison Smith, a Philadelphia journalist, and Samuel Knox, a physician, Presbyterian minister, and principal of an academy at Frederick, Maryland.

Smith, in his essay, asserted that freedom and economic and social opportunity depended on an educated populace. He proposed mandatory education for boys between the ages of five and 18 in public schools supported by a property tax. As they progressed through the two grades of primary school, the boys would learn to read and write; master arithmetic; practice recitation; study history, geography, science, agriculture, and mechanics; and memorize the Constitution and fundamental laws of the United States. Those demonstrating the highest level of talent and industry would continue their education at one of several colleges or at a single national university.

Smith's plan included no instruction in classical languages, but Knox, a more traditional thinker, argued in favor of Latin, which offered insight into the origins of many English words. Knox advocated a public-education system that was the same for every male. "The course of education, instituted in the public seminaries, should be adapted to youth in general, whether they be intended for civil or commercial life, or for the learned professions," he wrote.[4] Knox's system emphasized reading as the foundation for all other learning.

Knox deplored the great lack of suitable textbooks for beginning and more advanced readers. His ideal reading text would contain brief excerpts from the works of esteemed historians and articles from current journals, arranged in order of difficulty. Poetry was to be placed among the most challenging selections, because it was appropriate only for those children who had mastered reading prose.

Popular Textbooks of the Era

Between 1783 and 1785, a teacher in Goshen, New York, published a three-part textbook series for use in U.S. schools. Noah Webster's *A Grammatical Institute of the English Language* consisted of a spelling book, a grammar text, and a reader. Believing that uniformity in language would contribute to a national identity, Webster called for conventions in spelling and grammar that were shaped by the usage and pronunciation of educated and literary Americans and that were free of British influences.

Webster's spelling book, known popularly as the "blue-backed speller," became a standard text in 19th-century American schools and remained in print for more than a century. An estimated 15 million copies had been sold by 1837, and an estimated 19 million had been sold by 1843, the year of Webster's death. This extraordinary volume of sales occurred at a time when the public could be expected to buy 25,000 copies of a top-selling book over the course of its years in print. The speller's principal publisher, Hudson and Goodwin, issued two editions of the book in 1784 and at least one edition each year thereafter for the next several decades.

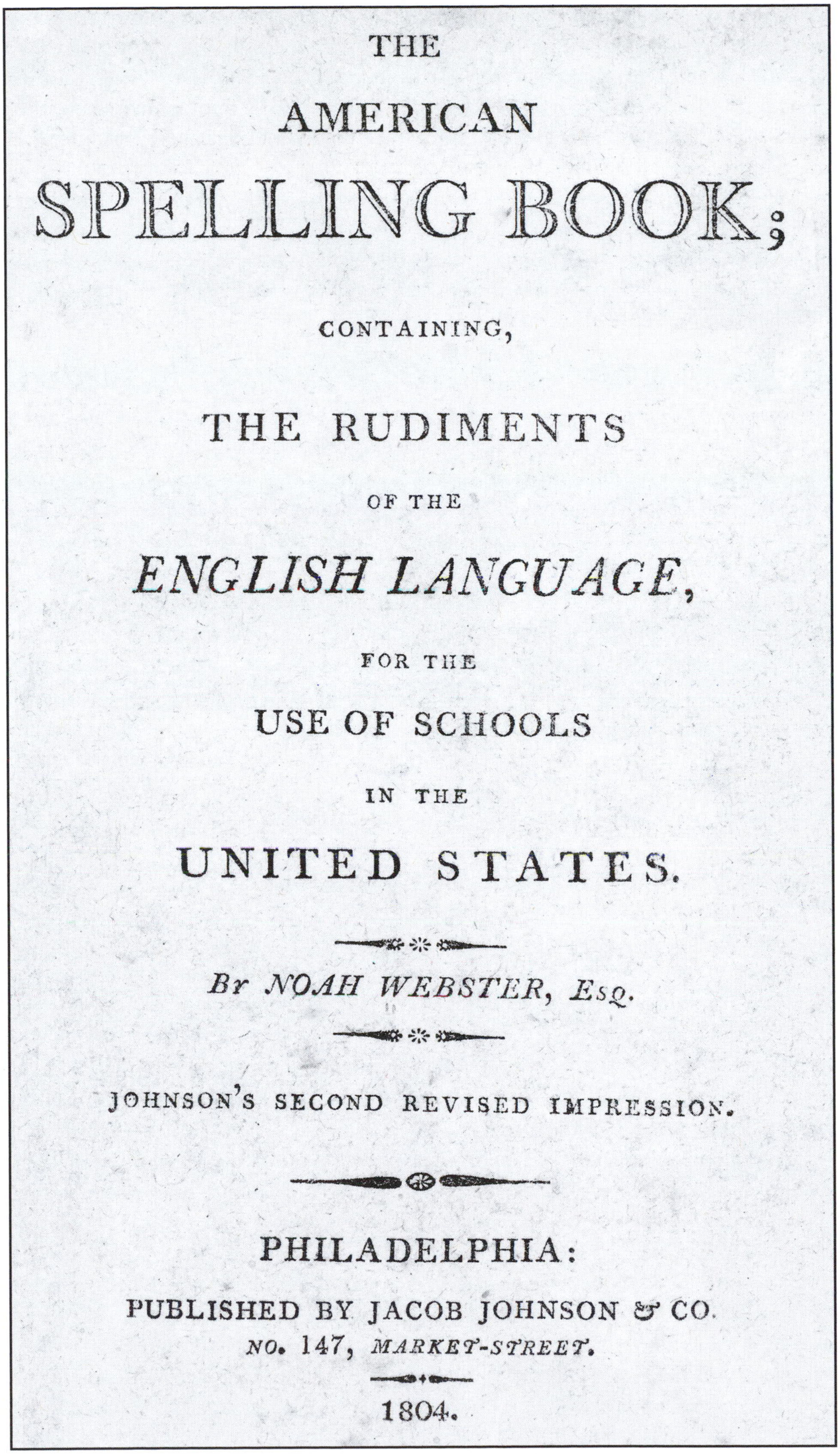

THE
AMERICAN
SPELLING BOOK;

CONTAINING,

THE RUDIMENTS

OF THE

ENGLISH LANGUAGE,

FOR THE

USE OF SCHOOLS

IN THE

UNITED STATES.

⸺✱⸺

By NOAH WEBSTER, Esq.

⸺✱⸺

JOHNSON'S SECOND REVISED IMPRESSION.

⸺❋⸺

PHILADELPHIA:

PUBLISHED BY JACOB JOHNSON & CO.
NO. 147, *MARKET-STREET.*

⸺⸺

1804.

This is the title page of an 1804 edition of Noah Webster's popular text, *The American Spelling Book. (Library of Congress, Prints and Photographs Division, LC-USZ62-51905)*

The main purpose of spelling books in the 18th and 19th centuries was to teach children to read. According to the "alphabet method," the only system for teaching reading employed in most American schools, children learned to spell and pronounce words one syllable at a time as the initial step in reading. The great majority of educators assumed that children only learned by rote, by memorizing and reciting lessons.

Spelling books facilitated this kind of drill. They proceeded from the letters of the alphabet to a syllabarium, which consisted of lists of paired vowels and consonants that presented short and long vowel sounds: ab, eb, ib, ob, ub; ba, be, bi, bo, bu. Next came tables of words with similar spellings or pronunciations listed alphabetically, followed by brief prose selections that included these words.

Webster divided words into syllables in keeping with pronunciation rather than standard practice. "In English books words are thus divided, ha-bit, le-mon, va-lor, te-nor. In this case, the learner, at first, gives to the vowel of the first syllable its long sound. . . . Webster's division, hab-it, lem-on, val-or, ten-or put an end to this difficulty," Webster wrote, referring to himself in the third person.[5] He also treated the suffixes *-tion* and *-sion* each as a single syllable rather than as two, contrary to common practice.

Despite the success of his language texts, Webster stated in 1787, "A selection of essays, respecting the settlement and geography of America; the history of the late revolution and of the most remarkable characters and events that distinguish it, and a compendium of the principles of the federal and provincial government, should be the principal school book in the United States."[6] Such a work would enlarge students' understanding of their nation and promote their attachment to it. Between 1802 and 1812, he therefore published the four-volume series *Elements of Useful Knowledge*, which surveyed U.S. history and scientific progress.

In 1825, Webster completed the contribution for which he is most remembered, the *American Dictionary of the English Language*. He spent 25 years compiling the dictionary, which contained 70,000 entries—significantly more than Samuel Johnson's dictionary, which, with 58,000 entries, was the largest English-language dictionary to date when published in London in 1824. Webster's additions consisted of terms commonly used in science, the arts, commerce, the professions, and "the ordinary concerns of life," thereby reflecting the American bias toward practicality in education.[7] In the years between the publication of Johnson's dictionary and his own, "a complete revolution has taken place in almost every branch of physical science," Webster said.[8]

Another extraordinarily popular series of schoolbooks, the McGuffey readers, was published for the first time in 1836. Developed by William Holmes McGuffey, then a professor of languages at Miami University in Oxford, Ohio, the readers progressed in difficulty, with each volume building on the skills introduced in the previous one. The first volume, which was intended for beginners, taught reading through phonics. The second volume offered simple stories for children who had mastered the fundamentals of reading, and the subsequent volumes presented new vocabulary in the context of increasingly challenging passages to be read. These included stories, poems, essays, and excerpts from works by writers such as Milton and Lord Byron. The McGuffey readers permitted a teacher to work with children at different skill levels, which made them a valuable tool in the one-room schoolhouses of the 19th century.

Common Schools Develop

The constitutions of eight of the 16 states mentioned education by 1800, and public school systems took shape in the decades that followed. Called common, elementary, or district schools, these institutions were controlled in some places by the state and in others by local officials.

In 1795, Governor De Witt Clinton of New York asked the state legislature to give financial aid to the common schools. The lawmakers responded with an act that for the next five years divided $50,000 annually among county schools that matched at least half their allotment with local funds. By 1799, the sources of revenue used to support state funding of schools—land sales and interest on surplus capital—were proving insufficient, and the senate voted against renewing the law. At the time nearly 58,000 children, or 37 percent of those from birth through age 19, attended state-assisted schools in those counties receiving state funds (16 of 23 counties).

Connecticut raised $1.2 million by selling its land in the Western Reserve and in 1795 used this money to create a permanent school fund. The interest earned by this fund paid teachers' salaries throughout the state. Until 1820, when the fund began to generate sufficient interest, the state supplemented it with a property tax of $2 per $1,000 of assessed value. In 1813, Connecticut passed the nation's first compulsory education law. Addressing the needs of child laborers employed in the textile mills that were proliferating throughout New England, this law required manufacturers within the state to provide the children on their payrolls with instruction in reading, writing, and arithmetic.

As in the past, school development advanced more rapidly in the North than in the South. In 1803, Washington, D.C., which was culturally and geographically a southern city, formed a board of education but restricted its role to opening and operating schools for the district's poor white children.

The federal government built a framework for public education in the unsettled territory west of the Appalachian Mountains with the Land Ordinance of 1785. This legislation called for government surveyors to divide the land into townships measuring six miles by six miles. They were then to divide each township into 36 numbered sections of 640 acres, with section 16 of every township set aside for education. A school could be located there, or the land could be sold and the profit used to support education.

One-Room Schoolhouses

A common school might sit next to a swamp, close to a heavily traveled road, or on a rocky hill. Some social critics said that the undesirable locations of so many common schools reflected a lack of public interest in education, but often a school was centrally situated to make access as equal as possible.

The typical one-room country schoolhouse had desks built into three walls. These were for the older children, who sat on backless benches that allowed them to face their desks or turn and give their full attention to the teacher. The younger children sat on smaller benches in the center of the room, close to the stove or fireplace. Toddlers of two or three frequently attended school, more to give their families a break from child care than to study. With children of all ages learning together, a country schoolhouse could be crowded, especially in winter, when there was little work for the older ones to do on a farm.

Disorder reigns in the New England one-room school painted by Charles Frederick Bosworth, ca. 1852. *(Courtesy of the Massachusetts Historical Society)*

Greater acceptance of schooling for girls also increased enrollments. Many Americans continued to believe that women's intellectual powers fell short of men's, but they recognized that it did girls no harm to acquire a common-school education. And, increasingly, those who could afford it sought secondary schooling for their daughters. Benjamin Rush and others pointed out that educated women were better equipped to raise children who would contribute to the new republic than those who were unschooled and that husbands would place more value on the companionship of wives who understood the issues that interested men. In addition, educating women helped to meet the growing demand for female common-school teachers; it was cheaper to hire a woman than a man.

In keeping with the new ideas about women's intellectual capabilities, in the 1820s and 1830s female academies added science to their curriculums. Whereas, between 1800 and 1820, the typical girls' school taught reading, writing, grammar, arithmetic, geography, and such refinements as needlework, painting, and drawing, by 1840 many female scholars were studying natural philosophy (the precursor of modern physics), astronomy, chemistry, and especially botany, which brought students outdoors and was therefore thought to benefit their health.

Classical education remained the province of boys and young men, however. A classical education conveyed prestige among men that parents sought for their sons but not for their daughters. Proficiency in Latin and Greek was a requirement for college, and U.S. colleges and universities admitted only men until 1836, when the first institution in the United States to grant baccalaureate degrees to women, the Georgia Female College, opened in Macon.

Advances in Higher Education

Oberlin College, founded in Oberlin, Ohio, by progressive Christians in 1833, was the first coeducational institution of higher learning in the United States. In 1835, taking another step toward inclusiveness, Oberlin admitted black students alongside whites. In 1841, three female graduates of Oberlin became the first American women to earn bachelor of arts degrees by studying the same curriculum as male students.

Opportunities for higher education for African Americans were severely limited. Wilberforce University, an institution affiliated with the African Methodist Episcopal Church, opened near Xenia, Ohio, in 1856, and was the first private college for African Americans in the United States.

Most of the colleges and universities established before the Civil War admitted only men, and in most cases only white men. These included the University of Virginia, which was founded by Thomas Jefferson. The former president called this state institution, which opened in March 1825, "the future bulwark of the human mind in this hemisphere."[9] It exemplified his conception of a modern university, one that contributed to scientific knowledge and was free of religious influence. Planning the university drew on Jefferson's talents as a statesman, architect, and forward thinker. Not only did he secure funding for the project from the Virginia legislature, but he also designed the college buildings, surveyed the site in Charlottesville, supervised construction, established the curriculum and admission standards, and organized the administration.

This early engraving of the University of Virginia was based on a drawing made in 1824. *(University of Virginia Library)*

There never would be a national university, but U.S. leaders did establish academies to train officers for the armed forces. On March 16, 1802, President Thomas Jefferson signed the legislation that created a school to train army officers, the U.S. Military Academy at West Point, New York. The academy opened on July 4, 1802, in a structure that had served as a fort during the Revolution. Colonel Sylvanus Thayer, superintendent of the academy from 1817 until 1833, did much to shape its standards and course of study. He imposed stiff academic requirements, instituted strict military discipline, and placed great importance on honor. He made engineering the core of the curriculum, with the result that through the first half of the 19th century, West Point graduates engineered many of the nation's railroad lines, bridges, roads, and harbors.

Secretary of the Navy George Bancroft oversaw the creation of a naval school that welcomed its first 50 midshipmen on October 10, 1845. Bancroft established this school without congressional funding on a 10-acre army post in Annapolis, Maryland, a "healthy and secluded" spot that was far from "the temptations and distractions that necessarily connect with a large and populous city," he said.[10] In 1850, by an act of Congress, the naval school at Annapolis became the U.S. Naval Academy, with a course of study that included four years of academic work and summers spent training aboard ships.

Science and technology formed the basis of study at the Rensselaer School (later Rensselaer Polytechnic Institute), founded in 1824 in Troy, New York, to apply scientific advances to agriculture, mechanics, and home economics. Soon the school offered degree programs in civil engineering, topographical engineering, mining, and architecture. Amos Eaton, the innovative senior professor at Rensselaer, instituted laboratory instruction, enabling students to pursue science and engineering actively, through experimentation, rather than passively, by attending lectures.

United States Naval Academy midshipmen train aboard the USS *Constitution* in 1853. *(Library of Congress, Prints and Photographs Division, LC-USZ62-48040)*

John Randolph, U.S. senator from Virginia (1825–27), lived in this spartan room while attending the College of William and Mary in 1792. *(Special Collections Research Center, Earl Gregg Swem Library, College of William and Mary)*

Advocates of technical and professional programs such as those offered at Rensselaer thought that colleges should offer courses that prepared students for their professional lives, whether they intended to be engineers, architects, bankers, or industrialists. Opposition came from many university faculty members who favored the traditional approach to higher education. Prominent among these was James L. Kingsley, president of Yale University, who in 1828 defended in writing the general classical education that Yale and other long-established universities were providing. Titled "Original Papers in Relation to a Course of Liberal Education," but known better as the Yale Report, this document affirmed Yale's goal of producing graduates who shared a common body of knowledge that included Latin and Greek, who were thus prepared to take their places in all professions. This statement of the conservative view of education influenced the curriculum at universities throughout the United States for the next several decades.

College students earned a reputation for violent rioting in the first half of the 19th century. At colleges and universities throughout the United States, students broke windows, smashed furniture, set fire to buildings, and harassed professors. The Conic Section Rebellion at Yale in 1830 erupted in response to a change in the teaching of mathematics, but riots occurred to protest the quality of meals or for no discernible reason. The underlying cause for all the disorder could have been discipline that was too strict or an overabundance of the Revolutionary spirit. Administrators at the College of New Jersey suspended more than half the student body after a riot that broke out on campus in 1807, and such mass punishments were not unusual.

Charity Schools for Poor Children

Industrialization was making urban poverty an increasingly visible problem at the start of the 19th century. It was widely believed that poverty bred laziness, drunkenness, and dishonesty, and that children who grew up poor were at risk of acquiring bad habits from their parents. Social reformers advocated mass schooling as an antidote, and Protestant and Catholic churches responded by opening charity schools. Because they were intended to protect children from a life of vice and crime, charity schools emphasized religion in a curriculum that also included reading, writing, and arithmetic.

Ensuring that indigent children devoted the Sabbath to uplifting pursuits rather than "the worst of purposes" was the aim of Sunday schools, which offered instruction twice on Sundays, in the morning and afternoon.[11] Laypeople taught the children prayers and hymns; also, young pupils studied the alphabet from printed cards, and older ones read and memorized passages from the Bible.

The first American Sunday school opened in Philadelphia in 1790. By 1800, there were enough Sunday schools in the city to accommodate more than 2,000 children. There was a Sunday school for the children of factory workers in Pawtucket, Rhode Island, and one for African-American children in New York City. Beginning in the 1830s, Sunday schools became agencies of denominational education for children at all economic levels.

At this time, northern cities had a growing population of free African Americans whose children needed schooling. Many male slaves had gained their freedom in return for service in the American Revolution, settled in northern communities, and started families. Also, once the United States achieved independence, the belief that slavery was contrary to the revolutionary ideals of freedom and equality took hold in the North. Some masters responded by releasing their slaves from bondage voluntarily, and by 1804, all the northern states had passed manumission acts.

In 1787, the Manumission Society, a largely Quaker organization, established a school for African Americans in New York City, "in hopes that by an early attention to their morals they may be kept from vicious [vice-ridden] courses and qualified for usefulness in life."[12] As with charity schools for whites, students' intellectual gains were less important than social control. By 1810, similar schools for African Americans had been opened in Baltimore; Burlington, New Jersey; and Wilmington, Delaware. Boston established schools for African Americans in 1817 and 1822.

Black and white children in the North attended separate schools by custom rather than by law, because many whites objected to racially integrated schooling and even to black children being educated in their communities. The citizens of Canterbury, Connecticut, were outraged in 1832 when Prudence Crandall, a Quaker who conducted a school for local girls and young women, admitted 20-year-old Sarah Harris, an African American who planned to be a teacher. So many parents withdrew their daughters that Crandall closed her school temporarily. On April 1, 1833, she announced that the school would reopen as an institution for "young Ladies and little Misses of color."[13] The state legislature reacted by making it illegal for anyone in Connecticut to educate an African American from out of state. Crandall was arrested for violating this law, jailed, and brought to trial. The case against her was dismissed in July 1834 due to a lack of evidence, but the people of Canterbury took the matter into their own hands. A mob attacked the school on

Students escape through a side door as rioting whites destroy Prudence Crandall's school for African-American girls, September 9, 1834. *(Library of Congress, Rare Books and Special Collections Division)*

September 9, and Crandall was at last forced to close it for good. The law that led to her arrest was repealed in 1838.

In 1846, the Primary School Committee of Boston rejected a petition submitted by African Americans demanding the abolition of separate schools for their children, stating that "the true interests of both races require, that they should be kept distinct."[14] Foreshadowing the separate-but-equal rhetoric with which the U.S. Supreme Court would in 1896 sanction two social systems in the South, the committee continued, "Let them not come to us with the humiliating confession, that they cannot make their separate schools as good as those for the white children; and tell us that their children, if put by themselves, even under the best instruction, must sink, unless they have white children to pull them up."[15] In 1855, however, the Massachusetts legislature outlawed segregation by race.

Missionaries Teach African Americans and American Indians

White missionaries operated schools for free blacks in the South, but only a small percentage of the targeted population benefited from their efforts. Gradually, state legislators made it illegal for African Americans, whether free or enslaved, to attend school in the South, because keeping them illiterate locked them into a subordinate position and prevented them from reading abolitionist literature. A number of states passed such legislation in reaction to the 1831 insurrection led by Nat Turner, a Virginia slave, in which 60 whites and more than 100 blacks died violently.

There were people who broke the rules: Some masters defied the law and taught a few trusted slaves to read, and some enslaved boys and girls learned from the master's children, who were their playmates. The most famous slave to be schooled was Frederick Douglass, the abolitionist writer and orator who escaped from slavery in 1838. Douglass learned to read from his mistress as a boy in Baltimore.

Plantation owners commonly provided their slaves with religious instruction to give them the opportunity for salvation and to reinforce their subservient status. Whether slaves attended church services with the white plantation family or listened to white or black preachers hired by their masters, they heard sermons based on biblical passages that countenanced slavery. The preachers taught, for example, that the slaves had descended from Ham, a son of Noah who had moved into Africa. According to the Bible, Noah had cursed Ham's son Canaan and ordered him to serve his uncles—Noah's other sons. Therefore, God had ordained the inferiority of Africans and wanted the slaves to serve their masters.

Enslaved adults exchanged information during clandestine prayer meetings held at night in "hush harbors," secret spots in the woods or swamps. There they might learn news of the world outside the plantation or hear escape plans. At home in their quarters, parents imparted to their children knowledge that would aid them in life. Not only did they pass on songs and folktales that contained traditional wisdom, but they also taught the youngsters some of the tasks they would perform when they embarked on their lives of work, which typically began between the ages of seven and 10.

Control was also a motivating factor when the white population endeavored to educate the American Indians. In this case, however, the stated goal was amalgamation, or indoctrination in the ways of the dominant culture. The American Board of Commissioners for Foreign Missions (ABCFM), organized in 1810 by graduates of Williams College in Williamstown, Massachusetts, sent missionaries to teach the American Indians, to make them "English in their language, civilized in their habits, and Christian in their religion."[16]

In the first half of the 19th century the ABCFM sent missionaries to the Iroquois in New York and Vermont, the Cherokee in Tennessee, and the Choctaw in Mississippi. These spreaders of faith and culture set up day schools near tribal villages and boarding schools in regions settled by whites. They primarily taught children at these schools, but they also instructed adults in reading, religion, and the agricultural and household-management practices of the settler culture. Other missionaries, including Moravian and Presbyterian groups, established schools among the Cherokee in the early 1800s with the tribe's permission.

The ABCFM funded its work with private contributions and money from the federal government. In 1819, Congress created the Civilization Fund, which made available $10,000 every year "to employ capable persons of good moral character, to instruct [the Indian tribes] in the mode of agriculture suited to their situation; and for teaching their children reading, writing and arithmetic. . . ."[17]

The Lancasterian System

In 1805, DeWitt Clinton, then mayor of New York City, founded the New York Free School Society to educate the children of the city's poor. The society employed the Lancasterian, or monitorial, system of schooling, which had recently been invented by a British educator, Joseph Lancaster. Lancasterian schools were great factories of learning that seemed to meet the needs of burgeoning industrial cities like New York. They employed a staff of monitors, or teaching assistants, to allow one schoolmaster to oversee the education of 500 or more pupils at once. The master selected monitors from among the advanced students and assigned them tasks, such as teaching reading or arithmetic to younger children. Pupils learned largely by recitation and progressed at their own pace.

There were also monitors to maintain discipline and take care of supplies, because, like factories, Lancasterian schools thrived on order and efficiency. Children hung up their coats in unison, sat behind desks in long rows, and folded their hands when listening. The monitorial system appealed to municipal leaders at a time when the poor were growing in numbers and visibility and when most states gave no support to public schools. It was efficient, and it was easy and inexpensive to implement. Lancaster's cost-cutting innovations included a sandbox in which pupils traced letters with their fingers, which reduced expenditures for paper and pens.

In theory, the monitorial system trained a new generation of teachers and guaranteed competent instruction, something all too rare in the schools of the early United States. This and other perceived benefits made monitorial schooling the most popular educational reform in North America and Europe in the first decades of the 19th century. Within 20 years, there were Lancasterian schools throughout New York State and in Philadelphia, Baltimore, Detroit, and other U.S. cities.

By the 1840s, monitorial education was already losing popularity, however. Not only was it impractical for use in small towns and rural communities, but also it gave children a rudimentary education at best and offered motivated students no opportunity for in-depth learning.

Teaching the Disabled

Prior to the Civil War, Americans founded residential schools for children who were blind, deaf, or developmentally disabled. In 1819, the American School for the Deaf became the first U.S. institution of any kind to receive state aid to education when the Connecticut legislature appropriated $5,000 for its support. This private school had been established in a Hartford hotel in 1817, with Thomas Hopkins Gallaudet, a teacher of the deaf who had been trained in Europe, as its first principal. Using sign language, the instructors presented a curriculum that emphasized literacy, religious salvation, and ways to earn a living.

The first state school for the deaf, the Kentucky Asylum for the Tuition of the Deaf and Dumb (later the Kentucky School for the Deaf) opened in Danville on April 10, 1823. An 1827 federal land grant financed the school's growth and

The "General Monitor of Order" stands front and center in the 1837 British monitorial school depicted here. Subordinate monitors stand to the left of each row, ready to take orders from the master, right. *(Syracuse University Library)*

maintenance for the next hundred years. In 1857, Congress incorporated the Columbia Institution for the Instruction of the Deaf and Dumb and Blind. Edward Miner Gallaudet, son of Thomas Hopkins Gallaudet, served as the first superintendent of this school in northeast Washington, D.C., and his deaf, widowed mother, Sophia Fowler Gallaudet, became the school's matron.

The New England School for the Blind, the first institution of its kind in the United States, began operation in 1829, in Watertown, Massachusetts, in the home of its director, Samuel Gridley Howe, the husband of writer Julia Ward Howe. Six years later, 65 students were enrolled, and the school had moved to the mansion of vice president and trustee Thomas Perkins, for whom it was later named. Perkins sold his home in 1839 and donated the proceeds to the school, to fund the takeover and conversion of a hotel. In the school's workshops, students manufactured for sale such items as mattresses, pillows, floor mats, and brooms. Howe also added a printing department to produce embossed-letter books. (Louis Braille had published his raised-dot Braille alphabet in 1834, but it had not yet come into popular use.) A well-known and successful student of the Perkins School was Laura Bridgman, the first blind and deaf person to be educated, who was admitted in 1839. At the time, most people thought that anyone with Bridgman's disabilities could not be taught at all.

During this period, Americans made their first efforts toward educating the developmentally disabled. In 1851, the New York State legislature made available $6,000 to support a two-year program for the "feebleminded," and the following year Pennsylvania appropriated funds for this purpose. In 1859, the first U.S. residential school for the developmentally disabled, the Massachusetts School for Idiotic and Feebleminded Youth, was established.

New Ways of Thinking about Education

Two influential thinkers, Johann Heinrich Pestalozzi and Horace Mann, had a lasting influence on educational practices in the United States, beginning in the first half of the 19th century.

The Swiss educator Pestalozzi taught that children had an inborn inclination to learn and that education ideally was the natural development of innate abilities. Children needed to learn about their environment, using their five senses, before proceeding to academic subjects—to reading, writing, and arithmetic. They benefited from examining the forms of familiar objects, learning their names, and counting them, Pestalozzi said. He used the word *Anschauung* to mean direct perception of the material world.

With children's minds actively seeking information rather than passively receiving it, learning proceeded from the particular to the general, Pestalozzi said, from the simple to the complex, and from the concrete to the abstract. There was no place for corporal punishment in a system that had pupil and teacher working together in a spirit of cooperation and mutual respect.

These ideas arrived in the United States in 1806, with Joseph Neef, who had taught in Pestalozzi's school in Burgdorf, Switzerland. Neef wrote the first American book on Pestalozzi's methods, *Sketch of a Plan and Method of Education*, which was published in 1808, and in 1809, he opened a school for boys in Schuylkill, Pennsylvania, the first of several schools he would establish before turning to farming in 1821.

Mann, who was secretary of the Massachusetts Board of Education from 1837 until 1848, did much to elevate the quality of public education and the professionalism of teachers nationwide. To Mann, who was philosophically opposed to the two-tiered structure of education in Europe, the term *common schools* implied sharing, or a system that brought together all levels of society by imparting a body of knowledge that had value to all. Students therefore were to pursue academic subjects that benefited them in daily life, including reading, writing, arithmetic, history, and geography, in an atmosphere that stressed hard work, honesty, thrift, and respect for others and their property.

By persuading the state legislature to raise taxes in support of schools, Mann increased teachers' salaries and attracted better-qualified people to the field. He pushed for improvements in school construction, and he advocated graded instruction as an effective way for municipalities to educate growing numbers of children. Largely because of Mann's recommendation, in 1847 school authorities introduced grading in the Quincy, Massachusetts, grammar school, which was divided into 12 classrooms for this purpose. Graded education worked so well in Quincy that the Boston School Committee adopted the system, and by 1855, the large study halls in every grammar school in the city had been partitioned into classrooms. Graded learning would quickly become the norm in U.S. cities, but it would be adopted much more slowly in rural America.

In 1839, Mann was a founder of the first public normal school in the United States, located in Lexington, Massachusetts. This institution and others like it produced competent teachers for the nation's public schools. The *Common School Journal,* which Mann founded in 1839 and edited until 1852, encouraged school improvements and professionalism among teachers, as did his many lectures throughout the United States.

"I believe in the existence of a great, immutable principle of natural law, or natural ethics—which provides the absolute right of every human being that comes into the world to an education," Mann stated; "and which, of course, proves the correlative duty of every government to see that the means of that education are provided for all."[18]

Educators took a further step toward professionalism in 1857, with the founding of the National Teachers Association (NTA; later the National Education Association). The NTA united teachers who were "ready to devote their energies and their means to advance the dignity, respectability and usefulness of their calling," and who believed "that the time has come when the teachers of the nation should gather in one great educational brotherhood."[19] The NTA restricted its membership to "gentlemen," although its leaders named two women as honorary members and permitted them to sign the organization's constitution.

Chronicle of Events

1783
- *September 9:* Benjamin Rush prepares the charter for Dickinson College.

1783–1785
- Noah Webster publishes the three-part *Grammatical Institute of the English language.*

1784
- The publisher Hudson and Goodwin issues two editions of Webster's "blue-backed speller."

1785
- The federal land ordinance passed in this year divides the land west of the Appalachian Mountains into townships with 36 numbered sections, and with section 16 of each set aside for education.

1786
- Benjamin Rush proposes a public school system for Pennsylvania offering instruction in English and German; the plan is rejected.

1787
- The Manumission Society opens a school for African Americans in New York City.

1789
- A Massachusetts law enacted this year requires towns of 50 or more households to support a teacher for six months of every year. Towns of 100 households or more must support their schools all year, and towns of 200 or more households must hire a grammar-school teacher.

1790
- The first American Sunday school opens in Philadelphia.

1791
- *December 15:* The Tenth Amendment to the Constitution, ratified on this date, gives the states all powers not delegated to the federal government in the Constitution, including the power to establish schools.

1795
- New York State makes $50,000 available annually for counties that match at least half their allotment.

- Connecticut sells its land in the Western Reserve to fund education and until 1820 supplements this with a property tax.

1797
- The American Philosophical Society offers a prize for the best essay proposing an educational system for the United States.

1799
- The New York State senate votes against renewing the 1795 law giving $50,000 annually to the public schools. At the time nearly 58,000 children (37 percent of those from birth through age 19) attend state-assisted public schools.

1800
- The constitutions of eight states mention education.
- Girls' academies typically offer instruction in basic academic subjects and needlework, painting, and drawing.
- Sunday schools in Philadelphia accommodate more than 2,000 children.

1802
- President Thomas Jefferson signs legislation creating the U.S. Military Academy at West Point, New York.

1802–1812
- Noah Webster publishes the four-volume series *Elements of Useful Knowledge.*

1803
- The District of Columbia creates a board of education for the purpose of schooling poor white children.

1804
- Slavery has been outlawed in all northern states.

1805
- Mayor DeWitt Clinton of New York City founds the New York Free School Society to educate the city's poor children.

1807
- The College of New Jersey suspends more than half the student body for rioting.

1808
- Joseph Neef publishes *Sketch of a Plan and Method of Education,* the first American book on the educational philosophy of Johann Heinrich Pestalozzi.

1809

- Joseph Neef opens a school for boys in Schuylkill, Pennsylvania.

1810

- There are schools for free African Americans in Baltimore; Burlington, New Jersey; and Wilmington, Delaware.
- The American Board of Commissioners for Foreign Missions (ABCFM) is organized. The ABCFM will found schools for American Indians.

1813

- Connecticut requires manufacturers to provide the children in their employ with instruction in reading, writing, and arithmetic.

1817

- Boston establishes a school for African Americans.
- The American School for the Deaf begins operation in a Hartford, Connecticut, hotel.

1819

- Congress establishes the Civilization Fund, making available $10,000 per year for the education of American Indians.
- The Connecticut legislature appropriates $5,000 for the support of the American School for the Deaf, making it the first U.S. school to receive state aid for education.

1820

- Girls' academies begin adding science to their curriculum.

1822

- Boston establishes a second school for African Americans.

1823

- *April 10:* The Kentucky Asylum for the Tuition of the Deaf and Dumb (later the Kentucky School for the Deaf) opens in Danville.

1824

- The Rensselaer School, a technical college, opens in Troy, New York.

1825

- Noah Webster's *American Dictionary of the English Language* appears, containing 70,000 entries.

- Children attend Lancasterian schools throughout New York State and in cities including Philadelphia, Baltimore, and Detroit.

1827

- The Kentucky School for the Deaf receives a federal land grant.

1828

- James L. Kingsley authors "Original Papers in Relation to a Course of Liberal Education," better known as the Yale Report.

1829

- The New England School for the Blind (later the Perkins School for the Blind) opens in Watertown, Massachusetts.

1830

- In an uprising known as the Conic Section Rebellion, students at Yale protest a change in the method of teaching mathematics.
- The purpose of Sunday schools shifts to denominational education for children at all economic levels.

1831

- Nat Turner leads a violent slave uprising in Virginia. Southern states respond by making it illegal for African Americans to attend school.

1833

- Oberlin College opens in Oberlin, Ohio, and admits both men and women.
- Prudence Crandall is arrested for opening a school for African-American girls in Canterbury, Connecticut.

1834

- A Connecticut court dismisses the charges against Prudence Crandall due to a lack of evidence.
- Louis Braille publishes the Braille alphabet for the blind.
- *September 9:* A mob attacks Crandall's school, forcing her to close it.

1835

- Oberlin College admits both black and white students.

1836

- The McGuffey readers are published.
- Wesleyan Female Seminary, the first college for women in the United States, opens in Macon, Georgia.

1837

• An estimated 15 million copies of Webster's spelling book have been sold.

1837–1848

• Horace Mann serves as secretary of the Massachusetts Board of Education.

1838

• The law that led to Prudence Crandall's arrest is appealed.

1839

• Horace Mann founds the first normal school in the United States, at Lexington, Massachusetts.
• Mann founds and edits the *Common School Journal.*
• Laura Bridgman, the first blind and deaf person to be educated, is admitted to the Perkins School for the Blind.

1840

• Lancasterian schools are falling out of favor.

1841

• Three graduates of Oberlin College are the first American women to earn bachelor of arts degrees by studying the same curriculum as men.

1843

• Approximately 19 million copies of Webster's spelling book have been sold.

1845

• The naval school at Annapolis, Maryland, established by Secretary of the Navy George Bancroft, admits 50 midshipmen.

1846

• The Primary School Committee of Boston rejects a petition from African Americans demanding an end to school segregation.

1847

• Students attending the Quincy, Massachusetts, grammar school are divided into grades.

1850

• By an act of Congress the naval school at Annapolis becomes the U.S. Naval Academy.

This 1850 group portrait is the earliest known photograph of students at the University of Virginia. *(University of Virginia Library)*

1851

• The New York State legislature appropriates $6,000 to support a two-year education program for the developmentally disabled.

1852

• The Pennsylvania legislature makes funds available to educate the developmentally disabled.

1855

• Massachusetts outlaws segregation by race.
• All Boston grammar schools have adopted graded education.

1857

• The National Teachers Association is founded in Philadelphia.
• Congress incorporates the Columbia Institution for the Instruction of the Deaf and Dumb and Blind.

1859

• The Massachusetts School for Idiotic and Feebleminded Youth, the first U.S. school of its kind, is founded.

Eyewitness Testimony

What are the objects of a useful American education? Classical knowledge; modern languages, chiefly French, Spanish, and Italian; mathematics; natural philosophy; natural history; civil history; and ethics. In natural philosophy, I mean to include chemistry and agriculture, and in natural history, to include botany, as well as the other branches of those departments. It is true that the habit of speaking the modern languages cannot be so well acquired in America; but every other article can be as well acquired at William and Mary College as at any place in Europe.

Thomas Jefferson, 1785, "Letter to John Banister: Advantages of an American Education," in Andrew J. Milson et al., eds., Readings in American Educational Thought: From Puritanism to Progressivism, *p. 69.*

It would require a lively imagination to describe, or even to comprehend, the happiness of a country where knowledge and virtue were generally diffused among the female sex. Our young men would then be restrained from vice by the terror of being banished from their company. The loud laugh and the malignant smile, at the expense of innocence or of personal infirmities—the feats of successful mimicry and the low priced wit which is borrowed from a misapplication of scripture phrases—would no more be considered as recommendations to the society of the ladies. A *double-entendre* in their presence would then exclude a gentleman forever from the company of both sexes and probably oblige him to seek an asylum from contempt in a foreign country.

The influence of female education would be still more extensive and useful in domestic life. The obligations of gentlemen to qualify themselves by knowledge and industry to discharge the duties of benevolence would be increased by marriage; and the patriot—the hero—and the legislator would find the sweetest reward of their toils in the approbation and applause of their wives. Children would discover the marks of maternal prudence and wisdom in every station of life, for it has been remarked that there have been few great or good men who have not been blessed with wife and prudent mothers.

Benjamin Rush, 1787, "Thoughts on Female Education, Recommended to the Present State of Society, Manners, and Government in the United States of America," in Frederick Rudolph, ed., Essays on Education in the Early Republic, *p. 28.*

This flourishing institution [Dartmouth College] is situated on a beautiful plain, about half a mile east of the Connecticut river, in the township of Hanover, in the western parts of the state of New Hampshire. It was founded by the late Rev. ELEAZOR WHEELOCK, D. D. who obtained a royal grant of the same from the crown of Great-Britain in 1769, with the most ample privileges and immunities, for the purpose of disseminating knowledge among the natives. Soon after it was obliged to conflict with the greatest difficulties, situated in an infant country and exposed to hostile invasions during the late war which prevented its receiving that encouragement which might reasonably have been expected in favour of an institution of this nature.

Since the conclusion of the war, it has continued in a flourishing condition; it consists at present of about 130 students, under the direction of a President, two Professors and two Tutors. The distinguished character and real abilities of the president are too well established to require a particular description.

This institution is furnished with an elegant library, containing a large collection of the most valuable authors, and has a curious apparatus, consisting of a complete number of useful instruments for making mathematical and philosophical experiments.

There are two buildings for the use of the students at present, and sometime in October, 1786, a new edifice was erected—said to exceed for magnitude any building in New-England, being 150 feet in length, and 50 in breadth, three stories high, constructed in the most elegant manner, perfectly agreeable to the most refined taste of modern architecture, it is divided through the middle lengthways by a large space, which is intersected by three others, and is situated to the best advantage to command a beautiful prospect, on a piece of ground somewhat elevated, in front of a large green encircled with elegant houses: it will speedily be fitted for the reception of students.

It is worthy of remark, that the climate is so favourable, and the air so salubrious, that there has not happened an instance of mortality among the students since its first establishment.

Connecticut Gazette, July 20, 1787, in Vera M. Butler, ed., Education as Revealed by New England Newspapers Prior to 1850, *pp. 89–90.*

Our constitutions of civil government are not yet firmly established; our national character is not yet formed; and it is an object of vast magnitude that systems of education should be adopted and pursued which may not only diffuse a knowledge of the sciences but may implant in the minds of the American youth the principles of virtue and liberty and inspire them with just and liberal ideas of government and with an inviolable attachment to their own country. It now becomes every American to examine the modes of education in Europe to see how far they are applicable in this country and whether it is not possible to make some valuable alterations, adapted to our local and political circumstances.

Noah Webster, 1790, "On the Education of Youth in America," in Frederick Rudolph, ed., Essays on Education in the Early Republic, *p. 45.*

What advantage does a merchant, a mechanic, a farmer derive from an acquaintance with the Greek and Roman tongues? It is true, the etymology of words cannot well be understood without a knowledge of the original languages of which ours is composed. But a very accurate knowledge of the meaning of words and of the true construction of sentences may be obtained by the help of dictionaries and good English writers, and this is all that is necessary in the common occupations of life. But suppose there is some advantage to be derived from an acquaintance with the dead languages, will this compensate for the loss of five or perhaps seven years of valuable time? Life is short, and every hour should be employed to good purposes. If there are no studies of more consequence to boys than those of Latin and Greek, let these languages employ their time, for idleness is the bane of youth. But when we have an elegant and copious language of our own, with innumerable writers upon ethics, geography, history, commerce, and government—subjects immediately interesting to every man, how can a parent be justified in keeping his son several years over rules of syntax, which he forgets when he shuts the book, or which, if remembered, can be of little or no use in any branch of business? This absurdity is the subject of common complaint; men see and feel the impropriety of the usual practice, and yet no arguments that have hitherto been used have been sufficient to change the system or to place an English school on a footing with a Latin one in point of reputation.

Noah Webster, 1790, "On the Education of Youth in America," in Frederick Rudolph, ed., Essays on Education in the Early Republic, *p. 46.*

[T]he principal defect in our plan of education in America is the want of good teachers in the academies and common schools. By good teachers I mean men of unblemished reputation and possessed of abilities competent to their stations. That a man should be master of what he

A cartoon from the *Common School Journal* of 1839 lampoons the incompetent rural schoolmaster. *(Library of Congress, General Collection)*

undertakes to teach is a point that will not be disputed, and yet it is certain that abilities are often dispensed with, either through inattention or fear of expense.

To those who employ ignorant men to instruct their children, permit me to suggest one important idea: that it is better for youth to have *no* education than to have a bad one, for it is more difficult to eradicate habits than to impress new ideas.

Noah Webster, 1790, "On the Education of Youth in America," in Frederick Rudolph, ed., Essays on Education in the Early Republic, *p. 57.*

The rod is often necessary in school, especially after the children have been accustomed to disobedience and a licentious behavior at home. All government originates in families, and if neglected there, it will hardly exist in society, but the want of it must be supplied by the rod in school, the penal laws of the state, and the terrors of divine wrath from the pulpit. The government both of families and schools should be absolute. There should in families be no appeal from one parent to another, with the prospect of pardon for offenses. The one should always vindicate, at least apparently, the conduct of the other. In schools the matter should be absolute in command, for it is utterly impossible for any man to support order and discipline among children who are indulged with an appeal to their parents. A proper subordination in families would generally supersede the necessity of severity in schools, and a strict discipline in both is the best foundation of good order in political society.

Noah Webster, 1790, "On the Education of Youth in America," in Frederick Rudolph, ed., Essays on Education in the Early Republic, *pp. 57–58.*

[E]ducation ought to begin with the beginnings of understanding. At this eventful period of life the little folks are in the arms of their mothers. Has the mother been well-educated, is the tender parent a good preceptress, the fortunate child is at the best school in the universe while in its mother's lap. As the faculties of the young mind expand, she will with a delicate and skillful hand nurture and direct it to knowledge and virtue. The pupil, being constantly with and strongly attached to the mother, will assume her as an example of perfection and imitate her every look, word, and gesture. These imitations will soon grow into habits and probably fix traits upon the child's mind, speech, and manners which will be durable as life. Hence the maxim, as is the parent so is the child; and hence the inconceivable consequences of female education.

Beside, such is the happy constitution of nature that wherever ladies are highly improved by a well-directed and refined education, there the gentlemen will soon become so. It is an aphorism, which it must be confessed carries much truth with it, that the fair part of creation rules the world. Would they, guided by the wise dictates of a virtuous education, give their approbation only to those who were (considering their circumstances) duly informed and virtuous, we might venture to affirm [that] scarcely an uneducated, irregular man would be seen in society. Permit me, then, ladies, to say, on

you it very much rests to fix the boundaries of human improvement.

Simeon Doggett, Unitarian minister and principal of the Bristol Academy, Taunton, Massachusetts, July 18, 1796, "A Discourse on Education, Delivered at the Dedication and Opening of Bristol Academy, the 18th Day of July A.D. 1796," in Frederick Rudolph, ed., Essays on Education in the Early Republic, *pp. 158–159.*

As the period of education will, it is probable, in most instances be protracted till the child shall be engaged in preparing himself for some employment in life, it would be important to confine his attention in a considerable degree to the acquisition of that kind of knowledge which would be of the greatest practical use in the profession for which he is destined. Give the mind an object worthy of its efforts and you may rely upon their being made. In this case the child would realize the connection between its present pursuits and its future prosperity, and this impression could not fail to kindle new ardor in its youthful breast.

Samuel Harrison Smith, journalist, 1798, "Remarks on Education: Illustrating the Close Connection Between Virtue and Wisdom. To Which Is Annexed a System of Liberal Education," in Frederick Rudolph, ed., Essays on Education in the Early Republic, *p. 199.*

Education is the training up of the human mind by the acquisition of sciences calculated to extend its knowledge and promote its improvement. According to the attention paid to it and the plan on which it is conducted, it becomes more or less useful to society but seldom fails to improve and elevate the powers of the mind above their natural state.

Samuel Knox, physician, Presbyterian minister, and educator, 1799, "An Essay on the Best System of Liberal Education, Adapted to the Genius of the Government of the United States. Comprehending also, an Uniform General Plan for Instituting and Conducting Public Schools, in This Country, on Principles of the Most Extensive Utility," in Frederick Rudolph, ed., Essays on Education in the Early Republic, *p. 298.*

It is a hackneyed argument by many against a classical education that all the authors in the dead languages of any eminence have been translated into English and consequently that the scholar's time has been ill applied in translating what has already been done to his hand. Such, however, must neither have attended to these considerations, nor duly weighed the advantages which the tender mind receives by such exercises, as well as with regard to things as words, and that too at an age not well adapted to more arduous literary studies.

Indeed in the very pronunciation and phraseology of our language the ingenious mind, prone to literary acquisitions and researches, could not be satisfied without some knowledge of the original languages. Let a youth, never introduced to any knowledge of Latin, be asked why his collection of books is styled a *library*, and the answer, it is presumed, will amply justify this observation.

Samuel Knox, physician, Presbyterian minister, and educator, 1799, "An Essay on the Best System of Liberal Education, Adapted to the Genius of the Government of the United States. Comprehending also, an Uniform General Plan for Instituting and Conducting Public Schools, in This Country, on Principles of the Most Extensive Utility," in Frederick Rudolph, ed., Essays on Education in the Early Republic, *p. 302.*

It is certainly laudable to pay due regard to those sciences that tend to enlarge the sphere of worldly interest and prosperity and without which the various and complicated business of human life cannot be transacted. This, however, by no means ought to check the exertion of that refined and sublime knowledge on which the improvement of genius, science, and taste, rather than worldly circumstances, chiefly depends. Indeed, it might be justly observed that a narrow or illiberal system of education from lucrative views would not ultimately tend to the prosperity or happiness of any nation. Were the human soul taught to cultivate only the sordid dictates of avarice or the knowledge of lucrative speculations, soon must that community lose a taste for whatever is most excellent in science or best calculated to refine and improve the faculties of the mind. Where such a taste hath become prevalent in any state, it is rather an evidence of its degeneracy than reformation and is commonly the forerunner of whatever may tend to enervate the patriotism, corrupt the virtue, or contaminate the morals of the community.

Samuel Knox, physician, Presbyterian minister, and educator, 1799, "An Essay on the Best System of Liberal Education, Adapted to the Genius of the Government of the United States. Comprehending also, an Uniform General Plan for Instituting and Conducting Public Schools, in This Country, on Principles of the Most Extensive Utility," in Frederick Rudolph, ed., Essays on Education in the Early Republic, *p. 313.*

[Noah Webster's] spelling-book has done more injury in the common schools of the country than the genius of ignorance herself could have conceived a hope of, by his ridiculous attempts to alter the *syllable* division of words and to *new model* the spelling, by a capricious but utterly incompetent attempt of his own weak conception.

Philadelphia Aurora, 1800, in E. Jennifer Monaghan, A Common Heritage: Noah Webster's Blue-Back Speller, *p. 119.*

The old School-house, in District No. 5, stood on the top of a very high hill, on the north side of what was called the County road. The house of Capt. Clark, about ten rods off, was the only human dwelling within a quarter of a mile. The reason why this seminary of letters was perched so high in the air, and so far from the homes of those who resorted to it, was this:—Here was the center of the district, as near as surveyor's chain could designate. The people east would not permit the building to be carried one rod further west, and those of the opposite quarter were as obstinate on their side.

The edifice was set half in Capt. Clark's field, and half in the road. The wood-pile lay in the corner made by the east end and the stone wall. The best roof it ever had over it was the changeful sky, which was a little too leaky to keep the fuel at all times fit for combustion, without a great deal of puffing and smoke. The doorstep was a broad unhewn rock, brought from their neighboring pasture. It had not a flat and even surface, but was considerably sloping from the door to the road; so that, in icy times, the scholars, in passing out, used to snatch from the scant declivity the transitory pleasure of a slide.

Warren Burton, who attended school in Wilton, New Hampshire, from 1804 until 1818, The District School as It Was, *pp. 1–2.*

[The teacher] had nothing particularly remarkable about him to my little mind. He had his hands too full of the great things of the great scholars to take much notice of me, excepting to hear me read my Abs four times a day. This exercise he went through like a great machine, and I like a little one; so monotonous was the humdrum and regular the recurrence of *ab, eb, ib, ob, ub,* &c., from day to day, and week to week. To recur to the metaphor of a ladder by which progress in learning is so often illustrated, I was all summer on the lowest round, as it were, lifting first one foot and then the other, still putting it down in the same place, without going any higher; and all winter, while at school, I was as wearily tap-tapping it on the second step.

Warren Burton, who attended school in Wilton, New Hampshire, from 1804 until 1818, The District School as It Was, *p. 16.*

[P]unishments were sometimes rendered doubly painful by their taking place directly in front of the enormous fire, so that the pitiable culprit was roasted as well as racked. Another mode of punishment—an anti-whispering process—was setting the jaws at a painful distance apart, by inserting a chip perpendicularly between the teeth. Then we occasionally had our hair pulled, our noses tweaked, our ears pinched and boxed, or snapped, perhaps, with India-rubber; this last the perfection of ear-tingling operations. There were minor penalties, moreover, for minor faults. The uneasy urchins were clapped into the closet, thrust under the desk, or perched on its top. Boys were made to sit in the girls' seats, amusing the school with their grinning awkwardness; and girls were obliged to sit on the masculine side of the aisle, with crimsoned necks, and faces buried in their aprons. . . .

[The master] had so many regulations, that he could not stop at all times to notice the transgressions of them. The scholars, not knowing with certainty what to expect, dared to run the risk of disobedience. The consequence of this procedure on the part of the ruler and the ruled was, that the school became uncommonly riotous before the close of the season.

Warren Burton, who attended school in Wilton, New Hampshire, from 1804 until 1818, The District School as It Was, *pp. 44–45.*

The whole school is arranged in classes; a monitor is appointed to each, who is responsible for the cleanliness, order, and improvement of every boy in it. He is assisted by boys, either from his own or another class, to perform part of his duties for him, when the number is more than he is equal to manage himself.

The proportion of boys who teach, either in reading, writing, or arithmetic, is as one to ten. In so large a school there are duties to be performed, which simply relate to order, and have no connexion with learning; for these duties different monitors are appointed. The word monitor, in this institution, means, any boy that has a charge either in some department of tuition or of order, and is not simply confined to those boys who teach.—The boy who takes care that the writing books are ruled, by machines made for that purpose, is the monitor of ruling. The boy who superintends the enquiries after the absentees, is called the monitor of absentees. The monitors who inspect the improvement of the classes in reading, writing, and arithmetic, are called inspecting monitors; and their offices indeed are essentially different from that of the *teaching monitors.* A boy whose business it is to give to the other monitors such books, &c. as may be wanted or appointed for the daily use of their classes, and to gather them up when done with; to see all the boys do read, and that none leave school without reading, is called the monitor-general. Another is called the monitor of slates, because he has a general charge of all the slates in the school.

Joseph Lancaster, 1805, "Improvements in Education as it Respects the Industrious Classes of the Community," in Carl F. Kaestle, ed., Joseph Lancaster and the Monitorial School Movement, *pp. 66–67.*

True it is that charity schools, entitled to eminent praise, were established in this city [New York]; but they were attached to particular sects, and did not embrace children of different persuasions. Add to this that some denominations were not provided with these establishments, and that the children most in want of instruction were necessarily excluded, by the irreligion of their parents, from the benefit of education.

New York governor DeWitt Clinton speaking at the opening of a new school by the New York Free School Society, 1809, in Carl F. Kaestle, ed., Joseph Lancaster and the Monitorial School Movement, *p. 156.*

What a master says should be done; but if he teaches on this system he will find the authority is not personal—that when the pupils, as well as the schoolmaster, understand how to act and learn on this system, the system, not the master's vague, discretionary, uncertain judgment, will be in practice. A command will be obeyed by any boy, because it is a command, and the whole school will obey the common, known commands of the school, from being merely known as such, let who will give them. In a common school the authority of the master is personal, and the rod is his scepter. His absence is the immediate signal for confusion and riot; and in his absence, his assistants will rarely be minded. But in a school properly regulated and conducted on my plan, when the master leaves school, the business will go on as well in his absence as in his presence, because his authority is not personal. This mode of ensuring obedience is a novelty in the history of education.

Joseph Lancaster, British educator, 1810, in David Hogan, "The Market Revolution and Disciplinary Power: Joseph Lancaster and the Psychology of the Early Classroom System," pp. 409–410.

I am fully satisfied—and every skeptical man who visits this school and examines the scholars will be convinced—

that the Negro is as capable of mental improvement as any white man in the creation of God. An African prince was there in one corner attentively copying the alphabet; a young man—say a boy about fourteen—reciting passages from the best authors, suiting the actions to the words; another answering difficult questions in geography &c &c. In fact, let the enemies of these neglected children of men perform a pilgrimage to New York and at this shrine of education recant their principles and confess that the poor despised African is as capable of every intellectual improvement as themselves.

Benjamin Shaw, visitor to the New York African Free School, May 1817, in Carl F. Kaestle, Pillars of the Republic: Common Schools and American Society, *pp. 38–39.*

Soon after our arrival in the [Cherokee] nation, we opened our doors to receive children into our family, to teach them the rudiments of the English language, the principles of the Christian religion, and the industry and arts of civilized life. The present number is twenty-six; of different ages, from four to eighteen years. Some are full blooded Cherokees; others three fourths white. Six of the native children had been at school before, and regularly read a portion of Scripture at our family worship. On the whole, we must say, that our children give us great satisfaction; they labor when out of school much more cheerfully and constantly than we had reason to expect: and could the friends of this mission look into our school, and see these tawny sons and daughters of the forest listening to our instructions, sitting at our table, and bowing around our family altar, we do not believe they would grudge the money they have given to commence this establishment. . . .

Besides this school we have on the Sabbath a school for black people, in which there are generally from twenty to thirty, mostly adults, two Cherokee men, and three white men. The conduct and improvement of all these is very pleasing; making in all fifty-six, that are either constantly or occasionally pupils.

Cyrus Kingsbury, missionary, June 30, 1817, in "Eighth Annual Report," in First Ten Annual Reports of the American Board of Commissioners for Foreign Missions, with Other Documents of the Board, *p. 155.*

It had two distinct departments, one comprising the common English branches, on the ground floor, the room divided in the center, like church pews. The sexes on separate sides, and seated in classes of ten or twelve, facing each other at a double desk. Beginning with the sand scratchers, each class presided over by a scholar taken from a higher class seated at the end of the desks to preserve order and give instruction for the day or week. There were broad aisles on the outsides, in which around half circles the classes recited their lessons to the instructor, standing within the circle with a pointer. The lessons for the juveniles, on placards upon the wall; all the classes reciting at the same time, being a school graded into classes. At the entrance end, between the doors, upon a raised platform, were seated two monitors, a young gentleman and a lady from the high school, with desks and chairs, overlooking the whole room, keeping order, giving instruction, and receiving reports from those presiding over the classes, and probably receiving pay. The principal, Mr. Shattuck, over all; quietly entering the room, passing around, giving instructions, sometimes carrying a small rattan, or raw-hide, but seldom used, except to tap a pupil on the shoulder when found playing or dozing.

Benjamin Shaw, who attended a monitorial school in Detroit, ca. 1818, "My Recollections of the Early Schools of Detroit that I Attended from the Year 1816 to 1819," in Carl F. Kaestle, ed., Joseph Lancaster and the Monitorial School Movement, *pp. 167–168.*

There is economy in expense, because *one* teacher is paid where *ten* are necessary, and are actually *employed*: but it is a striking and interesting fact, that, in this system, those who are themselves ignorant, may, in some instances, become the instructors of others; Yet this, by no means, is the case in every instance, and the fact is, that the most active and intelligent are generally selected for this office; and with bitter regret have I seen such, hindered in their studies they ought to have been pursuing, by their being appointed Monitors. Having attempted to remedy this evil by instituting what I call a Class of Merit, of which I was Monitor myself, and into which they who had well discharged the duties of Monitor, rose by certain gradation; I found myself imperceptibly reverting to the old system; and felt a conviction that the nature and degree of the information which can be communicated by one child to another, is circumscribed to narrow bounds; and though *to teach* is an effectual way *to learn*, Monitors, in the discharge of their duty, do not generally reap themselves much essential advantage. . . .

J. G. Hutton, Albany, New York, schoolmaster, criticizing the monitorial system, 1818, in Carl F. Kaestle, ed., Joseph Lancaster and the Monitorial School Movement, *p. 177.*

When the Golden rule is daily and hourly practised before a child it imbibes its influence in the same manner as it does the rays of Summer Sun—and finds as much internal warmth from the one, as external from the other. That the head the heart and the hands must be taught to act and assist each other, that the entire Man Soul and Body conjointly must be develloped, not in parts, or in an isolated manner, that every School master must first learn *to know himself* before he attempts to instruct youth, that they must consider their occupation as a religious one, as a holy duty, as a sacred duty that they have bound themselves to perform, and not as is now the custom to look upon it only as a means of livelyhood.

That mothers must resume their places in nature and become what heaven designed them to be, instructresses of their children, as well as companions and bosom friends of man. Number and form are the first means used in this Institution to cause reflection in the mind and the simplicity with which this is done is the great beauty of the System; The Boys are interested and instructed at one and the same time, they are acting and acted upon in a manner that pleases both master and Scholars, the faculties are always kept awake ready to receive the impression and delighted to communicate it, to learn is agreeable to them, to explain it is more. To hear them give their reasons why 6 times 4 is 24 is interesting to all who are present, that is why 2 quantities multiplied together produce a third, and when they explain why 2 lines will only make one point of reunion, or one of intersection and will do no more, the anxious mind then begins to observe that a child is an intellectual being and not altogether a sensible one, that he is a tender, but dear, and heavenly plant well worth watering with care, that the seed of the eternal nature may burst its prison of sense and be refined in the heat of the celestial Sun, that Sun which sheds its divine rays on every mind that is open to its influence, and in due time makes it blossom and bring forth fruit.

Johann Heinrich Pestalozzi, Swiss educational theorist, August 18, 1818, in Kate Silber, Pestalozzi: The Man and His Work, *pp. 320–321.*

That nature designed for our sex the care of children, she has made manifest by mental as well as physical indications. She has given us, in a greater degree than men, the gentle arts of insinuation to soften their minds and fit them to receive impressions; a greater quickness of invention to vary modes of teaching to different dispositions; and more patience to make repeated efforts. There are many females of ability to whom the business of instructing children is

The influential educator Johann Heinrich Pestalozzi taught that the ideal school nurtured children's natural propensity to learn. *(Library of Congress, Prints and Photographs Division, LC-DIG-pga-00128)*

highly acceptable; and who would devote all their faculties to their occupation. For they would have no higher pecuniary object to engage their attention; and their reputation as instructors they would consider as important. Whereas, whenever able and enterprising men engage in this business, they consider it merely as a temporary employment to some further object, to the attainment of which their best thoughts and calculations are all directed. If, then, women were properly fitted by instruction, they would be likely to teach children better than the other sex; they could afford to do it cheaper; and those men who would otherwise be engaged in this employment might be at liberty to add the wealth of the nation, by any of those thousand occupations from which women are necessarily debarred.

Emma Willard, educator and writer, 1819, "An Address to the Public: Particularly to the Members of the Legislature of New York, Proposing a Plan for Female Education," in Andrew J. Milson et al., eds., Readings in American Educational Thought: From Puritanism to Progressivism, *p. 117.*

Ages have rolled away; barbarians have trodden the weaker sex beneath their feet; tyrants have robbed us of the present light of heaven, and fain would take its future. Nations calling themselves polite have made us the fancied idols of a ridiculous worship, and we have repaid them with ruin for their folly. But where is that wise and heroic country which has considered that our rights are sacred, though we cannot defend them? That though a weaker, we are an essential part of the body politic, whose corruption or improvement must effect the whole? And which, having thus considered, has sought to give us by education that rank in the scale of being to which our importance entitles us?

History shows not that country. It shows many whose legislatures have sought to improve their various vegetable productions and their breeds of useful brutes; but none whose public councils have made it an object of their deliberations to improve the character of their women. Yet though history lifts not her finger to such a one, anticipation does. She points to a nation which, having thrown off the shackles of authority and precedent, shrinks not from schemes of improvement because other nations have never attempted them; but which, in its pride or independence, would rather lead than follow in the march of human improvement: a nation, wise and magnanimous to plan, enterprising to undertake, and rich in resources to execute. Does not every American exult that this country is his own? And who knows how great and good a race of men may yet arise from the forming hand of mothers, enlightened by the bounty of that beloved country, to defend her liberties, to plan her future improvement, and to raise her to unparalleled glory.

Emma Willard, educator and writer, 1819, "An Address to the Public: Particularly to the Members of the Legislature of New York, Proposing a Plan for Female Education," in Andrew J. Milson et al., eds., Readings in American Educational Thought: From Puritanism to Progressivism, *pp. 120–121.*

[The] antiquated schoolhouse stood on "Clark Hill," in the town of Acworth, New Hampshire. It was built upon a rock, and surrounded by boulders which the icebergs of another age had scattered there. The only shade-trees that adorned the playground were those which the sturdy woodman had spared in clearing the forest. The building was rude and simple in its construction. It has three small windows on as many sides, each of which had a heavy board shutter to keep out the light during vacations, and to conceal the bats in term-time. They served both purposes well. The bats, however, were easily captured by the roguish boys, and sometimes made trouble for the master. The inside arrangements of this schoolhouse were unique. On one side was a large open fireplace, which with its entrance door occupied the whole space. In this great heater, in the cold winter, not less than half a cord of green wood was consumed each day, roasting half the

school and leaving the other half nearly frozen during the process. The seats and benches were made of half-planed hemlock or spruce boards, and were arranged on three sides of the house, in amphitheatre style. The back seats were designed for the older boys and girls, and the front seats for the little ones sent to school to relieve the mothers of their care at home. These seats were so wide that the child's back could not be supported, and so high that his feet could not touch the floor. A more complete rack of torture and machine for making cripples could hardly be invented. Yet these children were kept upon these hard benches all day long, relieved only by short recesses, with nothing to do but play, if they dared.

Hiram Orcutt describing the school he attended ca. 1820–23, Reminiscences of School Life, *pp. 13–15.*

The teachers employed in this district—a Young man in the winter and a young woman in the summer—deserve a passing notice. They "kept school" one term each, but were seldom re-elected. As a matter of fact these teachers were incompetent. They had enjoyed no opportunity for culture and professional training. It was not their fault. There were no training schools in those days, no examinations, no opportunities nor inducements to gain the necessary preparation for their important work. The parents of the pupils had inherited the *idea* of education for their children, but knew little or nothing of its nature or importance. Economy was the main concern with them. Hence the scanty outfit for school purposes, and the cheap teachers. The question as to the candidate's qualifications for the teacher's office was seldom raised, but rather how small a compensation would be accepted for the service required. In fact, the school was "struck off" to the lowest bidder. That was not economy, but a ruinous waste.

Hiram Orcutt describing the district school in Acworth, New Hampshire, ca. 1820–23, Reminiscences of School Life, *pp. 16–17.*

[T]he teaching of composition in any form was never attempted. Writing in copy-books was allowed, but not *taught*. In reading, the pupil acquired the habit of uttering improper sounds mispronouncing words, and the incorrect expression of sentences. In arithmetic, he was required only to "do the sums," without understanding the principles or reasons. It was never suggested that a correct knowledge of this or any other branch of study would be of any practical benefit in the business of life. The study of geography consisted of committing to memory long lists of names and figures, to be forgotten before the next recitation. Grammar was, and continued to be, one of the seven wonders of the world. As a result, the best graduates from this school could not have estimated the measure and value of a pile of wood, could not have expressed correctly a simple sentence, or written a creditable letter to their mothers.

Hiram Orcutt describing the district school in Acworth, New Hampshire, ca. 1820–23, Reminiscences of School Life, *pp. 20–22.*

There are now many among our most active and valuable citizens, merchants, mechanics, manufacturers, and masters of ships, who were poor boys, without other means of instruction, and who owe their present standing, and in some instances large property, entirely to the education and manners acquired in the public schools.

Two schools, on the Lancasterian plan, are now in operation in this town, by individuals from abroad, without any support from the town. This is matter of experiment; they are well spoken of, and I think will be useful for children who have been altogether without instruction. In these they can commence the first rudiments, and be prepared to take their places in the other schools to more advantage. A committee appointed by the town at April meeting, made a report (highly favorable to the plan) in June. They were continued, and probably will, at a future meeting, recommend one school on the plan of Lancaster, for the support of the town.

John Howland, Providence, Rhode Island, tradesman and proponent of public education, September 20, 1824, in Thomas B. Stockwell, ed., A History of Public Education in Rhode Island, from 1636 to 1876, *p. 41.*

As children, beginning at the age of two or three years, my brother, four sisters, and myself were taught and trained by private teachers, young women whom my parents employed. They gradually admitted some of the neighbors who desired to enjoy the same opportunity for home instruction, and our little family school, kept in the second story of our country farmhouse, grew to be a school of eight or ten pupils, and later reached about twenty. This instruction lasted, for me, until I was about twelve years of age, when I was sent—for two years—to a public school of some forty pupils, a short distance from home.

Edward Hicks Magill, Pennsylvania educator, recalling his own education, ca. 1827–37, Sixty-Five Years in the Life of a Teacher, *pp. 1–2.*

By the new State law [of 1828], for the encouragement, or rather for the *discouragement* of schools, each town is to receive a small sum, annually, from the State treasury, and are allowed to assess a small sum, I don't recollect how much, in a town tax for the same purpose. This limitation, beyond which the towns are prohibited from assessing, was passed in the General Assembly by the influence of members who were opposed to the general instruction of the children throughout the State, and wished to confine it to paupers. But the town of Providence insisted on their right to assess as much as they pleased, or thought necessary for the support of their schools, and sufficient for the education of all the children in the town, and this privilege was reserved to us in the State law, but it is allowed to no other town in the State. The rich men of Providence are and always have been in favor of all the children being educated at the town's expense, and if a representative of this town, in the general Assembly, should oppose this system, he would never be sent to the Assembly again. But it does not altogether depend on rich men in this town. The Mechanics' Association consists of three hundred members, most of whom are voters, and all in favor of the schools. The number of children at the last quarterly visitation in our public schools, was twelve hundred and seventy-seven.

John Howland, Providence, Rhode Island, tradesman and proponent of public education, 1828, in Thomas B. Stockwell, ed., A History of Public Education in Rhode Island, from 1636 to 1876, *p. 46.*

When I reflect upon the enormities which continue to be practised in many parts of our otherwise favored country, on the ill-fated Africans, and their descendants, who are torn by the hands of violence from their native country, and sold like brutes to tyrannical slaveholders in different countries . . . I ought to feel myself greatly blessed for enjoying the many privileges I do; while there are so many in the southern states chained in slavery, who perhaps, have left mothers, fathers, sisters and brothers, to mourn their loss. I feel myself greatly blessed in belonging to a school which has been established for many years by the Manumission Society. The different branches that are taught in this school, are reading, writing, arithmetic, geography, navigation, astronomy, and map drawing. Our schools which now contain 700 male and female scholars, continue to be conducted on the Lancasterian system, and the improvement of the scholars is such, as to be satisfactory to the Trustees, and all visiters who come to the school.

Isaiah G. Degrass, age 15, student at the New-York African Free School, October 21, 1828, in Charles C. Andrews, The History of the New-York African Free Schools, *pp. 67–68.*

A middling standard is fixed in America for human knowledge. All approach as near to it as they can; some as they rise, others as they descend. Of course, a multitude of persons are to be found who entertain the same number of ideas on religion, history, science, political economy, legislation, and government. The gifts of intellect proceed directly from God, and man cannot prevent their unequal distribution. But it is at least a consequence of what I have just said that although the capacities of men are different, as the Creator intended they should be, the means that Americans find for putting them to use are equal.

Alexis de Tocqueville, French visitor to the United States, 1835, Democracy in America, *vol. 1, p. 55.*

It is an indisputable fact, that, for years past, far more attention has been paid . . . to the construction of jails and prisons, than to that of schoolhouses. Yet, why should we treat our felons better than our children? I have observed in all our cities and populous towns, that, wherever stables have been recently built, provision has been made for their ventilation. This is encouraging, for I hope the children's turn will come, when gentlemen have taken care of their horses. I implore physicians to act upon this evil. Let it be removed, extirpated, cut off, surgically.

Horace Mann, secretary of the Massachusetts Board of Education, 1837, "Means and Objects of Common School Education," in Andrew J. Milson et al., eds., Readings in American Educational Thought: From Puritanism to Progressivism, *pp. 158–159.*

Education must be universal. It is well, when the wise and the learned discover new truths; but how much better to diffuse the truths already discovered, amongst the multitude! Every addition to true knowledge is an addition to human power; and while a philosopher is discovering one new truth, millions may be propagated amongst the people. Diffusion, then, rather than discovery, is the duty of our government. With us, the qualification of voters is as important as the qualification of governors, and even comes first, in the natural order. Yet there is no Sabbath of rest, in our contests about the latter, while so little is done to qualify the former. The theory of our government is,—not that all men, however unfit, shall be voters,—but that every man, by the power of reason and the sense of duty, shall become fit to be a voter. Education must bring the practice as nearly as possible to the theory. As the children now are, so will the sovereigns soon be. How can we expect the fabric of the government to stand, if vicious materials are daily wrought into its frame-work?

Education must prepare our citizens to become municipal officers, intelligent jurors, honest witnesses, legislators, or competent judges of legislation,—in fine, to fill all the manifold relations of life. For this end, it must be universal. The whole land must be watered with streams of knowledge. It is not enough to have, here and there, a beautiful fountain playing in palace-gardens; but let it come like the abundant fatness of the clouds upon the thirsting earth.

Horace Mann, secretary of the Massachusetts Board of Education, 1837, "Means and Objects of Common School Education," in Andrew J. Milson et al., eds., Readings in American Educational Thought: From Puritanism to Progressivism, *p. 176.*

It was in the early autumn of [1841], at the age of sixteen, that I first stood before a class as their appointed teacher. The scene was the unceiled low room of the wagon-house loft on my father's farm. In my early years the free-school system had been adopted, and I was appointed teacher by the board of managers of my native township, and to these managers, and not to the parents, I must look for my monthly payments. . . .

Of the work in the schoolroom, I may say that such work would astonish and confound any young teacher of the present day. Arithmetic was "ciphered" individually, on slates, without any instruction or use of blackboards or charts, and the chief aim was to "get the answer," without much attempt at reasoning as to the process employed to obtain it. In penmanship, the copies were "set" by the teacher's hand, at the top of each page of the copy-book, and without any aid from printed or engraved slips or copies. Steel pens, too, were not yet in common use; quill pens were almost universally employed. As teacher of the art of penmanship, I see myself now, walking about the small, low-ceiled room, criticising the forms of the letters, keeping the pens mended, penknife in hand, with a bunch of new-made pens sticking behind my ear.

Edward Hicks Magill, who began teaching in Bucks County, Pennsylvania, in 1841, Sixty-Five Years in the Life of a Teacher, *pp. 8–9.*

I followed the usual practice of that time, working on the farm in the summer, teaching only in the late fall and winter months, and closing in time for corn-planting and other farm work in the spring. From the opening of the school I engaged with my pupils in games of ball, snow-balling, etc., during the recess, just as one of them, but was careful to put on the serious and resolute schoolmaster's face when I rang the bell for them to reassemble. This acting a double part, as master and student, was made all the more difficult because my pupils were my own personal friends, relatives, and near neighbors, and a number of them, both boys and girls, were my seniors by several years.

Edward Hicks Magill, who began teaching in Bucks County, Pennsylvania, in 1841, Sixty-Five Years in the Life of a Teacher, *pp. 10–11.*

A change in the course of study in the Institution [Harvard College] has been proposed by the Corporation, consisting of the president and Fellows, and submitted to the Overseers for their consideration. This proposed change consists in the introduction of what is termed the Voluntary or Elective System; i. e. allowing the students, after the close of Freshman year, to take their choice of studies to be pursued for the remainder of their College courses. It is intended,—and to be made a condition, on which the elective privilege depends—that the student shall, in his preparatory studies and by the close of his first Collegiate year, become acquainted, to a certain extent, with Latin, Greek, Mathematics, Natural and Civil History, and the French language. From this point as a foundation, he may pursue, at his option, any one or more of the branches taught in the College, till the close of his courses, according as he shall judge most useful in his future occupation in life. A committee of the Board of Overseers have had the subject under advisement, and in their report, recommended that the change proposed by the Corporation be approved by the Board, and that the Corporation be authorized to carry the same into effect.

Salem, Massachusetts, Gazette, *February 23, 1841, in Vera M. Butler, ed.,* Education as Revealed by New England Newspapers Prior to 1850, *p. 33.*

Dr. Webster has probably done less for the English language in our country by his dictionary than by his spelling book. But for the all-prevailing presence of this book throughout our wide extended country, nothing could have saved us from as great a diversity of dialects as there is in England. . . . And this is principally owing to the fact that nearly every one who has learned to read, has acquired his rudiments from Webster's Spelling Book, or some other spelling book compiled from Webster's.

New Haven Daily Herald, *January 4, 1842, in E. Jennifer Monaghan,* A Common Heritage: Noah Webster's Blue-Back Speller, *p. 39.*

There is a wide-spread dissatisfaction with the schools as they are: with the inefficient manner in which the system is administered; with the shortness of time for which the schools are kept,—although they are quite long enough, unless they can be kept by better teachers; with the amount of money which is now appropriated by the State without calling forth any corresponding efforts and appropriations from the towns and districts; with the want of any suitable regulation as to books and studies; with the defective methods of instruction, and the harsh, unnecessarily harsh, discipline pursued by many of the schools; in fine, with the entire organization and administration of the system, as far, at least, as the great mass of towns are concerned. True, there are good schools in Providence, Bristol, Warren and Newport, and in some of the eastern towns of Providence county, but the returns to the secretary of state, and the report of your school commissioner, will show that the public schools are not kept in the country districts, on the average, three months in the year; that there are a great variety of textbooks in every school, and that this variety is made greater every year through the activity of book agents, authors and publishers.

Wilkins Updike, lawyer and Rhode Island legislator, 1845, in Thomas B. Stockwell, ed., A History of Public Education in Rhode Island, From 1636 to 1876, *pp, 63–64.*

[The public schools] are, almost universally, badly located, exposed to the noise, dust and danger of the highway, unattractive, if not positively repulsive in their external and internal appearance, and built at the least possible expense of material and labor.

They are too small. There was no separate entry for boys and girls appropriately fitted up; no sufficient space for the convenient seating and necessary movements of the scholars; no platform, desk, or recitation-room for the teacher.

They are badly lighted. The windows were inserted on three or four sides of the room, without blinds or curtains to prevent the inconvenience and danger from cross-lights, and the excess of light falling directly on the eyes or reflected from the book, and the distracting influence of passing objects and events out of doors.

They are not properly ventilated. The purity of the atmosphere is not preserved by providing for the escape of such portions of the air as had become offensive and poisonous by the process of breathing, and by the matter which is constantly escaping from the lungs in vapor, and from the surface of the body in insensible perspiration.

They are imperfectly warmed. The rush of cold air through the cracks and defects in the doors, windows, floor and plastering is not guarded against. The air which is heated is already impure from having been breathed, and made more so by noxious gases arising from the burning of floating particles of vegetable and animal matter coming in contact with the hot iron. The heat is not equally diffused, so that one portion of a school-room is frequently overheated, while another portion, especially the floor, is too cold.

They are not furnished with seats and desks, properly made and adjusted to each other, and arranged in such a manner as to promote the comfort and convenience of the scholars, and the easy supervision on the part of the teacher. The seats are too high and too long, with no suitable support for the back, especially for the younger children. The desks are too high for the seats, and are either attached to the wall on three sides of the room, so that the faces of the scholars are turned from the teacher, and a portion of them at least are tempted constantly to look out at the windows,—or the seats are attached to the wall on opposite sides, and the scholars sit facing each other. The aisles are not so arranged that each scholar can go to and from his seat, change his position, have access to his books, attend to his own business, be seen and approached by the teacher, without incommoding any other. . . .

They are deficient in all of those in and out-door arrangements which help to promote habits of order, and neatness, and cultivate delicacy of manners and refinement of feeling. There are no verdure, trees, shrubbery and flowers for the eye; no scrapers and mats for the feet; no hooks and shelves for cloaks and hats; no well, sink, basin and towels to secure cleanliness; and no places of retirement for children of either sex.

Henry Barnard, Rhode Island commissioner of public schools, 1845, in Thomas B. Stockwell, ed., A History of Public Education in Rhode Island, from 1636 to 1876, *pp. 76–77.*

By what spirit are our schools animated? Do they cultivate the higher faculties in the nature of childhood,—its conscience, its benevolence, a reverence for whatever is true and sacred? or are they only developing, upon a grander scale, the lower instincts and selfish tendencies of the race,—the desires which prompt men to seek, and the powers which enable them to secure, sensual ends,—wealth, luxury, preferment,—irrespective of the well-being of others? Knowing, as we do, that the foundations of national greatness can be laid only in the industry, the integrity, and the spiritual elevation of the people, are we equally sure that our schools are forming the character of the rising generation upon the everlasting principles of duty and humanity? or, on the other hand, are they only stimulating the powers which lead to a base pride of intellect, which prompt to the ostentation instead of the reality of virtue, and which give augury that life is to be spent only in selfish competitions between those who should be brethren? Above all others, must the children of a republic be fitted for society as well as themselves. As each citizen is to participate in the power of governing others, it is an essential preliminary that he should be imbued with a feeling for the wants, and a sense of the rights, of those whom he is to govern; because the power of governing others, if guided by no higher motive than our own gratification, is the distinctive attribute of oppression; an attribute whose nature and whose wickedness are the same, whether exercised by one who calls himself a republican, or by one born an irresponsible despot. In a government like ours, each individual must think of the welfare of the State, as well as the welfare of his own family, and, therefore, of the children of others as well as his own. It becomes, then, a momentous question, whether the children in our schools are educated in reference to themselves and their private interests only, or with a regard to the great social duties and prerogatives that await them in after-life. Are they so educated, that, when they grow up, they will make better philanthropists and Christians, or only grander savages? For, however loftily the intellect of man may have been gifted, however skillfully it may have been trained, if it be not guided by a sense of justice, a love of mankind, and a devotion to duty, its possessor is only a more splendid, as he is a more dangerous barbarian.

Horace Mann, 1845, "Challenges to a New Age," in Louis Filler, ed., Horace Mann on the Crisis in Education, *pp. 87–88.*

Like all the other children of the neighborhood I was kept steadily in school both winter and summer until I was about twelve years of age; after that I helped on the farm in summer and went to school in winter. In *our* home there was always a school atmosphere and in winter the great kitchen was turned into an evening school-room, the older children helping the younger ones in their studies. Sometimes in the spring when the land was not yet fit for tilling and my brothers' schools were closed, the carpet was removed from the parlor and a cousin of ours—a graduate of Yale—was employed to teach us all. This extra home school continued for a month or more but it was always closed as soon as the land was fit for the plow.

Isaac Phillips Roberts, who attended the district school in Varick, New York, and turned 12 in 1845, Autobiography of a Farm Boy, *p. 60.*

Look now into this small school-room, where are assembled a collection of children, with a teacher unskillful in her art. What noise and disorder!—What indolence, and discontent, and misrule! The children hate school and all that belongs to it, and the teacher regards the children as little better than incarnate imps!

Look, again, into another, where the teacher, fitted by nature or trained by instruction and experience, is qualified for her office. See that little happy group around their best-beloved friend—their beau ideal of all that is good, wise, and lovely! How their bright eyes sparkle as she opens the casket of knowledge and deals out its treasures! How their young hearts throb with generous and good emotions, as she touches the thrilling chords she has learned so skillfully to play! What neatness and order in all her little dominion! What ready obedience, what loving submission, what contrite confession, what generous aspirations after all that is good and holy! She spends the pleasant hours of school in the exercise of the noblest powers of the intellect and feeling. She goes to rest at night, reviewing with gratitude the results of her toils; and as she sends up her daily thanks and petitions for her little ones, how does the world of peace and purity open to her vision, where, by the river of life, she shall gather her happy flock, and look back to earth, and on through endless years, to trace the sublime and never-ending results of her labors. Oh, beautiful office!—Sublime employment! When will it attain its true honors and esteem?

Catharine Beecher, 1846, "Remedy for Wrongs to Women," in Andrew J. Milson et al., eds., Readings in American Educational Thought: From Puritanism to Progressivism, *p. 145.*

As far as the facilities of education go, the slave is secured at least from physical want, the great temptation to crime, from idleness, and from excessive labor. And the growing spirit of religious teaching secures him from that dependence upon immoral influences, which the mind unaided can so rarely resist. This growing spirit of religious teaching is a far safer reliance than the uncertain influences surrounding the poor laborers of other countries. It is

fostered by a sense of responsibility in the master, by his Christian feeling, by the dependent condition of the slave, and by all the kindness that grows out of the relation. At the North, it has been thought a fanciful notion that the white man should regard himself as the natural protector of the black. At least it will be granted that such an opinion will have its influence upon the moral education of the slave. An answer to much of this is ready for us in the taunt that we should not boast of the education of the slave as long as the reading of the Bible is shut out from him by our laws. We shall be content to say on this point, that this furnishes us with another instance of the insufficiencies of legislation being corrected by what we have called the *vix medicatrix* [healing power] of nature. The slave's inability to read has given rise to a more kindly feeling, and to a closer connection between the races, than if each slave could read his own Bible. It has induced oral teaching; and the effect of this upon both races no man in the North can conceive. . . . We are sure that we need not repeat what has been so often said on this subject,—that the laws against reading were the only barrier we could devise against the flood of incendiary publications that threatened our safety. The responsibility must rest on other shoulders than ours.

Edward J. Pringle, "a Carolinian," defending southern laws against teaching slaves to read, 1852, in Edgar W. Knight, ed., A Documentary History of Education in the South before 1860, *vol. 5:* Educational Theories and Practices, *pp. 490–491.*

"Have you seen our popular schools?" is one of the first questions addressed to the stranger in the United States, by young and old, by men and women, and this question in itself speaks volumes. But when the stranger finds, that in reality the popular schools are one of the most prominent subjects of national pride and satisfaction; that the question of popular education is not only of interest to some few philanthropists and thinkers, is not only discussed in legislative assemblies, but that it forms part of the national life, and is considered an important, nay, the most important concern of the nation—then he feels that in the depths of American society there are forces at work, which in Europe have as yet produced but very mediocre results. This is, I think, the highest praise that can be bestowed on the United States. This constitutes the true greatness of the nation, and the best guarantee of its stability.

P. A. Siljestrom, Swedish visitor to the United States, 1853, Educational Institutions of the United States, *p. v.*

The teachers in the coloured schools are, I believe, generally persons of colour, but there are exceptions to this rule, and there have been instances of coloured teachers being appointed in white schools. The judgment of a person in authority, given in one of these cases, which has come to my knowledge is so remarkable, that I shall quote it as one of the strongest expressions of official prejudice against the negro race which I have experienced. The trustees of a school district in the State of New York had engaged a coloured person as a teacher in the district school. Complaints were in consequence made to the State Superintendent, whose judgment was to the effect, that although there was nothing contrary to law in the act of the trustees, provided the teacher was duly qualified, and that consequently no legal proceedings could be entered against them, yet he could not otherwise than express the highest disapprobation of their conduct in this matter, which he looked upon as highly improper. Now, although there may be good reason for having separate schools for white and for coloured children, it is more difficult to comprehend why, in any particular case, a coloured man, if he be otherwise qualified, should not be tolerated as a teacher in a white school. It is certain, however, that in the city of New York no trustees would venture to make such an appointment, were the individual in question even a black Pestalozzi.

P. A. Siljestrom, Swedish visitor to the United States, 1853,
Educational Institutions of the United States,
pp. 136–137.

In the rural districts it is generally the thinness of the population that forms the greatest obstacle to the establishment of an efficient system of popular schools. If the school be situated at a distance from the homes of the pupils, it may almost be considered as non-existent, particularly as regards very young children, and more especially in a country with a climate so cold as that of the northern parts of the American Union. These natural impediments either entirely prevent many children from attending school, or cause them to attend very irregularly, and it is difficult to say from which of these circumstances the greatest amount of evil arises; for if the one causes a certain number of individuals to grow up in total ignorance, the other introduces so much confusion in the course of instruction, that none of the pupils can derive as much benefit from it as they ought.

P. A. Siljestrom, Swedish visitor to the United States, 1853,
Educational Institutions of the United States, p. 157.

West Point is exclusively occupied by the military academy and its appurtenances, and must in every respect be considered a military establishment. In addition to the *personnel* of the academy, it has a garrison of about 200 men. Military discipline, of course, prevails, and the inhabitants lead altogether a garrison life. . . .

I have reason to think that the military knowledge acquired at West Point is of a very satisfactory character; but as the study of the preparatory branches, such as mathematics, natural philosophy, chemistry, &c., and also the military sciences, take up a great deal of time, there is but little left for the actual technological instruction, and this little is chiefly devoted to engineering. The lessons in chemistry are not accompanied by manipulation or experiments, and it will therefore be admitted that, however excellent the academy at West Point may be in other respects, as a technological institution it cannot pretend to any very high rank.

P. A. Siljestrom, Swedish visitor to the United States, 1853,
Educational Institutions of the United States,
pp. 400–401.

CHAPTER THREE

Adversity and Increase: The Civil War and Its Aftermath
1860-1880

By 1860, about 60 percent of white children between the ages of five and 19 were in school. The average white child attended school for nine years and for 50 days in each of those years. Although the ages for starting and leaving school varied, the great majority of white children attended school between the ages of nine and 12. Once they reached 13, young people began having to choose whether to remain in the classroom or enter the working world.

A number of factors influenced whether a child attended school. Living in a household headed by a widowed or deserted mother, or having a mother who worked, increased the chances that a child, particularly a boy, would be employed rather than enrolled in school. In contrast, young people living in affluent families, especially in communities with high levels of home ownership, were more likely than others still to be in school in their late teens. School attendance was lower among the children of immigrants than among the children of U.S. citizens in most places, but in the burgeoning city of Chicago it was the birthplace of a child, rather than of his or her parents, that made the difference. A higher percentage of children born in the United States than those born overseas attended school in Chicago, regardless of where their parents were born. It is thought that poor English skills acted as a barrier to education for foreign-born youth.

Burgeoning Chicago was the eighth-largest city in the United States in 1860, with a population of 110,000, which was up from 30,000 in 1850. Much of this phenomenal growth had resulted from immigration, with most of the foreign born coming from Germany, Ireland, and England. In 1860, 50 percent of Chicago residents and 70 percent of the city's adults had been born outside the United States. School attendance was higher among immigrants in Chicago than in eastern cities because those in Chicago tended to be more financially secure. Also, Chicago had a strong Catholic school system that served immigrant communities, especially the German and Irish. "Wherever possible a school is to be set up in each parish," decreed the Catholic Diocesan Synod of Chicago in 1860.[1]

Illiteracy in the United States remained constant between 1800 and 1860, with approximately 6 percent of white males' age 20 and older classifying themselves as illiterate, according to U.S. Census figures. This is an indication that publicly financed education had been reaching a large proportion of American youth throughout the 19th century. It should be noted, however, that some of those who called themselves literate could only read a few words or recognize the letters of the alphabet.

Low levels of literacy were more prevalent in the South, where school development lagged, than in the North. In 1860 the constitutions of all the southern states but one, South Carolina, contained provisions for public primary education, and public education remained in the planning stage in four southern states: Mississippi, Florida, Texas, and Arkansas.

Despite its shortcomings, the U.S. educational system was firmly established by 1860; but it was about to face a great test. Would it survive the enormous disruption of a war fought on American soil?

War's Impact in the North

The Civil War began on April 12, 1861, when southern artillery opened fire on U.S. forces attempting to supply Fort Sumter, a federal installation in the harbor at Charleston, South Carolina, in Confederate territory. The war, which was to last four years, interfered with education throughout the North and South. Declining revenues and the loss of teachers and students to the armed forces caused a number of schools to close or suspend operations, and others adjusted to the changed circumstances with varying degrees of success.

Private schools in northern states bordering the Confederacy lost their southern students at the start of the war, and they soon lost quite a few northern students as well. Not only were worried parents reluctant to have their children attending school so close to the theater of war, where there was a high risk of being killed or wounded or contracting a disease, but also economic depression during the first two years of the war made paying tuition a financial strain for many families.

The Reverend John B. Kerfoot, rector of the College of St. James, an Episcopal school in Washington County, Maryland, kept his institution open despite serious setbacks, including the loss of students. The school had an enrollment of 113 at the start of the 1860–61 academic year, but by June, just 81 students remained. Enrollment was lower still the following fall, and it never again topped 50. In 1863, Confederate soldiers retreating after the Battle of Gettysburg raided the school for food, clothing, and other supplies, but Kerfoot hung on. He at last closed the school in 1864, when Confederate general Jubal A. Early led a division across the Potomac River and into Washington County and instruction became impossible.

The depressed economy in 1861 and 1862 caused a large number of students to leave public schools and go to work to help their families. The economic outlook improved in 1863, but by then many children between the ages of 12 and 15 were taking jobs left vacant by men who had joined the army. At least former private-school students seeking a more affordable education partially offset the lost enrollment in public schools and helped keep them operating.

Municipalities encouraged—and sometimes enforced—patriotism among teachers and students. In August 1862, the Baltimore City Council required all teachers to take an oath of allegiance to the United States, but two principals and

Army regiments drill on the grounds of the U.S. Naval Academy at Annapolis, Maryland, in 1861. *(Naval Historical Center)*

26 teachers refused to comply, some on ethical grounds rather than because they had Confederate leanings. In July 1863, the City Council ordered all music teachers to teach patriotic songs and threatened to expel any students who refused to sing them.

The outbreak of war transformed Annapolis, Maryland, into a Union military base. In April 1861, General Benjamin Butler established temporary army headquarters at the U.S. Naval Academy and quartered his troops on the grounds. Concerned about a possible Confederate attack on the academy, the superintendent, Captain George Blake, relocated the school to Fort Adams in Newport, Rhode Island, for the duration of the war. Staff, furniture, books, navigational equipment—the navy shipped everyone and everything to Rhode Island. Removal of the academy had an immediate economic impact on Annapolis, causing businesses to lose revenue, workers to be fired, and property values to plummet. City leaders appealed to the secretary of the navy, Gideon Welles, to return the academy to Annapolis, but he denied their request.

Planning for an Educated Confederacy

In the Confederate states, the aged and women took over teaching duties in schoolrooms abandoned by teachers who went off to war or returned to the North, and many schools stayed open for shorter terms. In October 1861, the *Atlanta Daily Intelligencer* stressed the importance of keeping schools open and running. "The opportunity for instruction, if now lost by the boys and girls who are soon to be our men and women, will be irrevocably lost," the editors wrote.[2] Such sentiments may have prevailed in Atlanta and throughout the South, but hundreds of schools were forced to close. Private boarding schools for girls fared better than most other institutions, because many parents believed their daughters were safer away at school than at home, especially if the family lived near an area of heavy fighting or Union occupation.

Most southern colleges and universities also closed, because the war robbed them of students, faculty, and the public and private funds that kept them operating. South Carolina College (later the University of South Carolina), for example, closed in early 1862 as a result of declining enrollment. The University of North Carolina (UNC) at Chapel Hill remained open throughout the war, however, despite the occupation of the campus and village of Chapel Hill by 4,000 Union soldiers. Shut-down colleges throughout the South sheltered troops, either Union or Confederate, and served as military hospitals.

Like U.S. educators in the early national period, southern teachers and policy makers thought about how best to prepare the young citizens of their new nation. They devoted a great deal of attention to creating schoolbooks that met the educational needs of young Confederates, because once the war began and the North was the enemy, the South lost its principal source of textbooks. Yet even before the war, many southerners had found fault with textbooks printed in the North, books they claimed presented a biased view of their region and unfairly criticized the institution of slavery. Southern educators wanted books that employed regional place names in model sentences and word problems rather than the names of towns and cities in New England, New York, and Pennsylvania. They also objected to the northern emphasis on rote learning, or "short-cuts to knowledge" and the "superficial clap-trap of effect and show," and called for texts that inspired critical thinking.[3] "We must exclude from our schools all those productions of Yankee pretension and superficiality," commented a writer for the *Charleston Mercury* in February 1864.[4]

The Confederacy produced 93 textbooks by the end of the war, excluding revised editions. Some bore such titles as *The Confederate Spelling Book, The First Dixie Reader,* and *Southern Grammar,* and few differed substantially from books produced in the North. In fact, one enterprising compiler simply republished Noah Webster's spelling book, making some revisions to Webster's pronunciation guide and adding passages from the Bible that purportedly upheld slavery.

The new textbooks treated the ongoing war as part of Confederate history, glossing over the sectional issues that had divided the United States and instead listing major battles, military leaders, and the Confederate states and territories. Arithmetic texts asked students to calculate the productivity of slaves picking cotton and the number of Yankees captured by a Confederate soldier. The *First Book in Composition,* published in Raleigh, North Carolina, in 1863, asked students to fill in the appropriate pronouns in sentences such as, "Abraham Lincoln led ____ people into war," and, "Jefferson Davis defended ____ country bravely, and deserves great applause for ____ patriotism."[5]

North Carolinians concerned about textbooks and financial support for schools established the Educational Association of the Confederate States of America, which held its first convention on April 28, 1863, in Columbia, South Carolina. Sixty-nine teachers and school administrators—all men—representing South Carolina, North Carolina, Georgia, Virginia, Alabama, and Louisiana attended. The delegates spoke of plans to create a "Child's History of the War," a series of educational books on the Confederate states, and a Confederate dictionary.[6] Thinking of the many disabled veterans, they called on communities to consider as teachers the "worthy young men, who by the misfortunes of war, are rendered unfit for manual

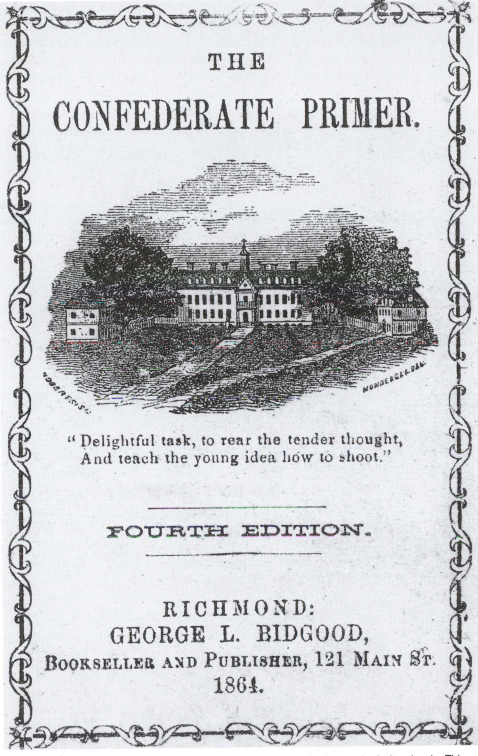

During the Civil War Southern educators developed textbooks for use in their schools. This is the title page to one such book, *The Confederate Primer*. *(Library of Congress, Prints and Photographs Division, LC-USZ62-60428)*

labor."[7] The association convened once more, on November 9, 1864, in Charlotte, North Carolina, but the Civil War ended five months later, and most of the group's plans were never carried out.

During the war, some forward-thinking Southerners called for equal education-al opportunities for women and men. The prevailing system of educating women, which the textbook author A. M. Scott called "one for *show* and not for use," had its origin in the North, he and others claimed.[8] Not only were women needed in the classrooms of the South to replace male teachers lost to war, but also well-educated, liberated women were a desired result of Confederate independence, an aspect of the new and loftier nation that many envisioned. Yet whether women would have taken their places beside men in the universities and public forums of the Confed-eracy, had the South won the war, cannot be known.

Former Slaves Were Eager to Learn

As Union forces captured territory and established bases in the South, thousands of slaves fled the region's plantations and appealed to the Northern soldiers for protection. The Union men referred to the fugitives as contrabands, as if they were enemy property that had been seized. The federal government lacked a policy for caring for these uprooted people, so military leaders did what they thought best or most expedient. The Militia Act of 1862 gave the president the power to employ African Americans "for any military or naval service for which they may be found competent," and this allowed Union generals to put African-American men to work clearing roads, building bridges, and burying the dead.[9] Many other men became soldiers in the newly formed U.S. Colored Troops, in units led by white officers.

Contraband camps near Union army posts in the South held great numbers of women, children, and old men. Conditions varied from one camp to another, with some presenting scenes of deprivation, disease, and death. In the worst camps, people of all ages begged, sold rags, and did whatever they had to do in order to survive. Life was better for the 15,000 people who sought shelter in camps on the Sea Islands of South Carolina, where the army required the able-bodied among them to work on the islands' plantations in exchange for food, shelter, protection, and small wages. Even children had jobs to do, just as they had under slavery. Boys as young as 12 labored in the fields for part of the day, and other youngsters took care of small boys and girls whose mothers worked.

Northern charitable groups, missionaries, and the army established schools for the formerly enslaved people, or freedmen. In the last year of the war, some 1,400 teachers staffed 975 schools in the South for African-American children and adults. Most of these teachers were white, but blacks opened the first freedmen's schools in Nashville and several other Tennessee cities and towns. African Americans also taught in a few schools in Virginia, North Carolina, and Washington, D.C. The northern teachers often found it necessary to present some basic instruction, such as counting or naming the days of the week and months of the year before embarking on the academic curriculum. Even more fundamental were lessons in classroom be-havior, which children who had never seen the inside of a school needed to learn.

The American Missionary Association (AMA), an organization of Congrega-tionalist and Presbyterian ministers dedicated to preparing African Americans to enjoy the privileges of citizenship, began its educational work among newly freed slaves in coastal Virginia. The missionaries, most of them young whites from New England, New York, or Ohio, opened their first two schools in Norfolk in April 1863. These schools met initially in black churches, but they soon moved into whites' schoolhouses that were sitting unused.

The former slaves hungered for education. Even when faced with hardship and the tasks required of them, most contraband children attended school for a time. Children talked about going to college, and adults confided their dream of being a teacher or minister. Open just three days, the AMA school housed in Norfolk's Brute Street Baptist Church had 550 day students. A month later, 700 children were enrolled; roughly 1,100 adults had registered for night classes, but attendance averaged 375. The AMA coped with the demand for education by opening additional schools wherever there was space: in nearby Portsmouth and Hampton and even in the empty farmhouse of former Virginia governor Henry Wise.

In many places, southern whites who were determined to impede the efforts of northern educators refused to sell or rent property to the AMA and similar organizations for use as schools. Typical of rural schools for blacks therefore was the schoolhouse at Fort Totten, North Carolina, which was a tumbledown, unheated barn with unglazed windows. The children had "to be *chilled* as well as *lighted* by opening the board shutters," an AMA educator complained.[10] Vandals set fire to schools for African Americans, including the AMA school at Clumfort's Creek, North Carolina, which burned in 1864. Throughout Union-occupied territory, whites tossed rocks through the windows of freedmen's schools, tore up books, defaced furniture, and threw dirt at teachers in an unsuccessful effort to stop them from educating blacks. Many whites in southern communities knew who had committed these outrages, but no one would provide names.

The northern teachers, too, were capable of cruelty. There are anecdotal reports of teachers in the freedmen's schools treating African Americans with overt prejudice and administering brutal whippings to youngsters they viewed as inferior to themselves. Generally, however, teachers avoided corporal punishment, which reminded both blacks and whites of the cruelties of slavery. Threatening expulsion, giving praise and rewards for good conduct, and evoking shame proved to be more effective methods of discipline.

AMA educators modeled their schools on the northern common schools with which they were familiar. The curriculum included reading, writing, basic arithmetic, and geography. Because classes were quite large, with one teacher instructing 60 to 100 children in a single room, some schoolmasters and mistresses adopted the monitorial system, having older students teach some of the younger ones and keep order.

Instructors and students never forgot that they were pursuing knowledge in close proximity to war. The firing cannons of nearby battles rattled schools and obscured the landscape with rising smoke. More than once, the Union army took over the AMA school at Beaufort, South Carolina, to shelter wounded men. Especially in North Carolina, Confederate raids forced teachers to close their schools temporarily and flee to safer ground. Teachers in North Carolina and elsewhere became caught in skirmishes between Union and Confederate snipers, and some were wounded or killed. "Under military sway we must live chiefly in the present for our educational interests & plans for promoting them, are liable at any moment to be disturbed & defeated," reported the Reverend William T. Briggs, the AMA's superintendent of education for North Carolina.[11]

The missionaries distributed primers to adults willing to master reading on their own or with help from their children, and they issued a call for more teachers. By September 1863, the AMA had 21 teachers instructing more than 3,000 people in 11 day and evening schools. Many more people would have sought instruction if they had adequate clothes to wear. "We are obliged to clothe many of the children before they can come to school," said the Reverend W. S. Bell of the school at Wise Farm. The teachers appealed to the North for clothes and books, but too often they received boxes of religious tracts instead.[12]

Poverty presented a great obstacle to education. Children with no shoes or warm clothes stayed out of school in cold weather, and those who were hungry lacked the energy to learn. Destitution caused numerous children to withdraw from school and go to work. One innovative teacher in Beaufort addressed her students' dire want by purchasing straw and teaching them to weave hats for sale. The teacher used a portion of the profit to buy more straw, and she gave the rest to her students for food and other necessities.

Most U.S. military leaders welcomed the northern teachers, believing that education would prepare the contrabands for their new lives as citizens and contribute to the success of a plantation system based on free, paid labor. "[I]t is indispensable to the cultivation of the soil that schools for colored children shall be maintained," stated General Nathaniel Banks, who, beginning in December 1862, commanded the Gulf Department, which encompassed New Orleans and the parishes in southern Louisiana that were under Union control. "Unless laborers are assured that the education of their children will be provided for, they become discontented, and will . . . remove to Parishes where such provisions are made."[13] Under Butler's leadership, the army established a system of elementary education for the African-American children of New Orleans.

Banks gave the job of organizing and staffing the schools to Lieutenant William Stickney of the 8th Vermont Regiment, a man considered an outstanding teacher by northern abolitionists. Preferring not to turn the schools over to teachers who answered to northern freedmen's aid and missionary societies, Stickney hired young white women from New Orleans. Soon seven schools staffed by 16 teachers were accommodating 576 children. Four of the schools met in churches, and the others held classes in private homes. By the end of the academic year, enrollment had doubled.

Much of the white population of the Gulf Department opposed the education of blacks and resented the property tax that had been forced on them to support the freedmen's schools. They refused room and board to the teachers employed in these schools, forcing the young women to pay for their lodging out of their limited earnings. Banks responded with an order that all teachers were to have proper accommodations and attached their living expenses to the unpopular property tax.

The army transferred oversight of the schools to a newly established board of education in March 1864. By that time 1,422 children were attending. Under the board's supervision, the number of schools for African Americans in the Gulf Department grew to 126, and the teaching staff numbered 222 and included 27 teachers from the AMA.

Contributions of the Freedmen's Bureau

In March 1865, with the war all but won, the federal government created the Bureau of Refugees, Freedmen and Abandoned Lands, known popularly as the Freedmen's Bureau, to provide emergency aid to the former slaves and help them adjust to freedom. At the close of the war, the South was a devastated region. Its landscape had been burned, its livestock slaughtered, and its system of labor broken down. The bureau distributed food, clothing, and medicine to needy people regardless of race, and it established schools for blacks. In 1865, when just 3 percent of southern blacks could read and write, 71,000 African Americans attended the bureau's schools; in 1869 enrollment reached 114,000.

Like the missionaries who taught contrabands during the Civil War, most teachers employed by the Freedmen's Bureau were white northerners who followed the New England tradition in education. They presented a curriculum that emphasized reading, writing, grammar, and geography as well as such Yankee virtues as thrift, diligence, and punctuality, and they employed Noah Webster's spelling book, McGuffey's readers, and other familiar textbooks. Some used texts prepared for the freedmen by the American Tract Society (ATS), an evangelical group. These included the first textbook prepared for freedmen, *The Picture Lesson Book*, which was published in 1862; *The United States Primer;* and *Tracts for Beginners.* The latter was a set of cards on which were printed, in large type, simple words and short sentences, most drawn from the Bible. *The Freedman's Spelling-Book*, another ATS publication, contained sample sentences rich in moral content, such as "It is a sin to sip rum," and "A lazy man can not get a job."[14] In 1864, the ATS estimated that 24,000 copies of its primer and 300 sets of cards were in use in freedmen's schools.

The New England writer and reformer Lydia Maria Child authored *The Freedmen's Book*, a text intended for advanced pupils and adults, which was published in 1865. Child's book was a treasury of poems, essays, biographical portraits of outstanding African Americans, and advice on varied topics: raising children, practicing good hygiene, caring for the home, and working diligently. She hoped it would give "fresh strength and courage" to people who had suffered through the subjugation of slavery and the disorder accompanying its abolition.[15] As an act of charity, Child donated thousands of copies of her book to the schools for African Americans.

The bureau also offered industrial training, which prepared students for lives as manual laborers—as farmers, mechanics, and laundry workers. In 1870, when the Freedmen's Bureau terminated its educational work, 247,333 students attended 4,329 bureau schools, and Congress had amended the Constitution to protect the rights of African Americans. The Thirteenth Amendment, ratified on December 6, 1865, abolished slavery in the United States; the Fourteenth Amendment, ratified on July 9, 1868, conferred citizenship on the former slaves; and Fifteenth Amendment, ratified on February 3, 1870, guaranteed all male citizens the right to vote, regardless of race. The bureau had spent $16 million on its schools and had taught roughly 10 percent of African Americans of school age.

Progress in Public Education

The U.S. Bureau of Education, created on March 2, 1867, gathered information on school development in the United States and trends in educational progress and thought. The commissioner of education, who oversaw the bureau's activities, prepared an annual report of its findings for the members of Congress and other interested people. The commissioner briefed lawmakers on such topics as the state of education in the southern states and the value of secondary education in the workplace.

By 1873, many state legislatures had passed laws to organize their public school systems. These laws imposed taxes to support schools and established some form of control, often by creating the position of state superintendent of schools. In addition, the public high school had gained popularity as a secondary institution of learning. The first American high schools opened earlier in the 19th century in Massachusetts, to meet the educational needs of boys who were not going on to college but who required more than the basic literacy acquired from a common-school education for careers in industry. After the war, the growing factory system was drawing people to Chicago, New York, Philadelphia, and other cities. As technology became more sophisticated, manufacturers sought better educated, more highly trained workers. Also, urban merchants and artisans wanted their sons to receive a practical secondary education that would prepare them for business careers and that could be acquired close to home at little or no cost.

Industrialization and the increase in urban population that accompanied it created a tax base large enough to support public secondary education, yet many people objected to paying taxes to finance high schools. They asked whether the community should be forced to pay for a high school that only a minority of students attended. This issue spawned several lawsuits, with the most notable occurring in Kalamazoo, Michigan, in 1873, when three of the city's taxpayers filed a suit against school authorities in order to stop them from collecting taxes to support the local high school. Instead, they argued, high schools were to be supported by tuition to be "paid for by those who seek them, and not by general tax."[16] Michigan school superintendent Oramel Hosford countered that a tuition system would lead to the demise of high schools and would amount to a step backward in public education. Judge Charles R. Brown ruled in favor of the school board, stating that the legislature had the power to require taxpayer support of schools that contributed to the welfare of the state.

In July 1874, the Michigan Supreme Court reaffirmed the decision of the lower court. Associate Justice Thomas Cooley stated that high schools were common, or public, schools, and that they acted as a necessary link between elementary schools and the state university. High schools provided equal opportunity, he said, because without them a college education would be available only to the wealthy. This case set a precedent, persuading other states to sanction taxation to fund public high schools. The number of high schools in the United States had increased from 325 in 1860 to 800 in 1870, but they served a small minority of the public-school population. In 1875, high school enrollment was below 25,000.

While some educators addressed the needs of older students, others turned their attention to the deaf or to young children. In 1867 the Clark School for the Deaf in Northampton, Massachusetts, and the New York Institution for the Improved Instruction of Deaf Mutes opened as the first schools to rely exclusively on oral communication to teach the deaf. Sign language had come under fire from proponents of various oral methods, who insisted that deaf students should rely on speech and speech reading to communicate.

Reports of the deaf learning to speak amazed many people, but success with the oral method varied widely and depended on the age at which a person lost his or her hearing and the degree of loss. Also, as champions of manual instruction pointed out, reliance on the oral method created a barrier to communication among the deaf. Other schools, including the American School for the Deaf in Connecticut, therefore, took a more flexible approach. There, students unable to master the oral method moved into classes employing manual communication. Despite the shortcomings, one of the leading promoters of the oral approach, the inventor Alexander Graham Bell, began a program in Boston to train teachers of the deaf in this method in 1872.

Kindergarten was another 19th-century innovation. In 1860, a Concord, Massachusetts, teacher named Elizabeth Peabody opened a private kindergarten in Boston. One of the first schools of its kind in the United States, Peabody's kindergarten was modeled on the teaching philosophy of Friedrich Froebel, a German educator.

Froebel believed that children had an inborn urge to learn and that they taught themselves through play. This was a novel concept for the many northern Europeans and Americans who thought that good things came only through hard work. Froebel first put his ideas into practice in 1837, at a school for small children in Blankenburg, Prussia. A lover of botany, he called his school a *Kindergarten*—a children's garden, or a place where he nurtured budding young minds. In 1867, Peabody traveled to Europe to observe kindergartens there and learn more about Froebel's methods, and in 1873 she began publishing the *Kindergarten Messenger,* a journal that encouraged American women to form neighborhood kindergartens.

St. Louis established the first citywide kindergarten system in the United States after an 1868 survey uncovered serious disparities in the municipal school system. Children living in slum neighborhoods in the factory and levee districts of St. Louis spent an average of three years in school, starting at age seven and leaving at 10 to go to work, but children whose families were better off financially stayed in school longer.

To increase the time poor children spent in school, the superintendent of education in St. Louis, William Torrey Harris, first tried to lower the age of admission to the public schools, to accept pupils younger than six. The school board rejected this plan, but in 1873 Harris persuaded its members to approve an experimental kindergarten program for children ages three through six. St. Louis had a large population of German immigrants who had been familiar with kindergartens in Europe, so as soon as the program was implemented in 1873, it gained favor. By 1876, proponents of kindergarten pointed to St. Louis as an exemplary system.

Resistance lingered in other parts of the country, however. Millions of people believed that children's early education should take place at home, within the family, and that formal schooling properly began with mastery of the three R's. To enlighten the public and overcome these obstacles, the Froebel Society of Boston, an advocacy group, created a model kindergarten at the Philadelphia Centennial Exposition of 1876, the great world's fair celebrating the nation's hundredth birthday. Before a crowd of curious visitors, Ruth Burritt, a primary-school teacher from Wisconsin, led 18 boys and girls from a local orphanage, the Northern Home for Friendless Children, through a full day of kindergarten activities: games, songs, and handwork intended to improve dexterity. For many onlookers, the demonstration was a revelation. "The blessing of Kindergarten training is one of the great discoveries of our day," wrote a reporter covering the event for the *Philadelphia Ledger.*[17]

The exposition glorified the achievements of artists and manufacturers, including toymaker Milton Bradley, who had produced a line of educational toys for use in schools, including the Kinder-Garten Alphabet and Building Blocks, which were small wooden blocks decorated with letters, numbers, and pictures of animals, and came in sets of 38 or 85. Bradley was one of 23 manufacturers exhibiting toys and educational equipment that middle-class parents could buy to challenge their children intellectually and keep them entertained.

Such innovations as kindergartens and high schools came later to the far western states and territories, where school development followed a course similar to that pursued in the East a century earlier. By 1860, pioneers had established homesteads and communities across North America, and children were growing up on the open range, often in remote locations, and needing schooling. Initially parents taught their children at home to read, write, and solve simple arithmetic problems, but as soon as several families lived close enough together and could afford to do so, they pooled their resources and hired a teacher. The intrepid easterners—women

The teacher and pupils of the first school to serve the Custer-Bonanza mining communities of Idaho moved their furniture and books outdoors to be photographed in the 1880s. *(Idaho State Historical Society, 73-215.1)*

as well as men—who responded to newspaper advertisements for frontier teachers often conducted school in a shack, abandoned sod house, or private home until the community could afford to construct a schoolhouse.

Because lumber, furniture, and supplies all had to be transported long distances, school building was much costlier in the West than in the East. In 1870, there were 38 schools in Nevada, or roughly seven for every 1,000 children. (In Massachusetts the ratio was 14 schools per 1,000 children.) Arizona had no schools at all, and New Mexico had five. By 1880, thousands of one-room schools dotted the plains and prairies.

The pupils, who likely ranged in age from five to 20, wrote their lessons with chalk on slates, because paper was scarce. Primers, spellers, and other textbooks were rare commodities, too, so children brought their own reading material from home and learned from well-worn copies of classic novels and treasured volumes of poetry that had survived the long trek west. The school year was shorter in western schools than in the East, because families depended on the labor of all members to get by. In 1880, two-thirds of schools in the western states and territories were open less than half a year, leaving pupils free to tend the family's crops from planting time in early spring until harvest in the fall.

Trends in Higher Education

Throughout the Civil War, the U.S. government continued to address the many concerns of the population, including education. There had been important technological advances in agriculture, manufacturing, and mechanization in the first half of the 19th century, but states lacked the necessary resources to prepare young people for careers in these fields. In 1862, Congress responded to this need by creating the land-grant college system with passage of the Morrill Act, named for Representative Justin Morrill of Vermont, a strong supporter of education. Thirty-four years earlier, the Yale Report had argued for the continuation of classical learning at colleges and universities, but this act transferred federally held land to the states for the support of agricultural and mechanical colleges. Each state received 30,000 acres of public land in the distant West for each of its U.S. senators and representatives, according to the apportionment of 1860, and was to use the proceeds from the sale of this land to endow and maintain at least one college for the teaching of agriculture, mechanical arts, and military science and tactics. The states were free to determine the balance of the curriculum, and they were to administer the schools. The first land-grant colleges appeared after the war, with some states redeveloping existing colleges and others constructing new universities.

Immediately these schools faced challenges. There were too few textbooks on American agriculture and too few adequately prepared students. Often land-grant colleges had no choice but to accept young men and women directly from the common schools. (The land-grant colleges and universities were coeducational from the start.) Furthermore, many farmers complained about the academic courses in the curriculum, explaining that they wanted strictly vocational training. The colleges responded by offering short practical courses in various aspects of farming, and their leaders remained undaunted. "We will teach the science of high production. Our college shall be a living and ever multiplying power to make the farms prosperous and happy and enable them to compete with the cities for the best talent of the land," said George C. Swallow, the first dean of the College of Agriculture at the University of Missouri, in 1872.[18]

Whether denominational or nonsectarian, most colleges, in the decade after the Civil War, offered nonclassical courses of study leading to degrees, an array of elective classes, and coeducation of the sexes. Charles W. Eliot, who became president of Harvard University in 1869, gradually instituted the elective system at the nation's oldest college. Prior to his presidency, all freshmen at Harvard studied Greek, Latin, mathematics, French, elocution, and ethics, and there were similar requirements for sophomores, juniors, and seniors. All class members were required to study the same curriculum, with every freshman studying French, for example, at the same level, regardless of proficiency. By 1874, students at Harvard could complete most of their required coursework in their freshman year and choose from a broad range of classes in the years that followed.

Increasingly, universities diversified further by adding schools of education, engineering, and agriculture, and by affiliating with schools of medicine, law, and theology. In 1870, the Bureau of Education identified 369 colleges in the United States, with many of the newest located in the West. With the extension of railroads, western towns and cities competed for new residents and welcomed institutions such as colleges, which drew people to them.

The progress that occurred in higher education in the 1860s and 1870s bypassed the South. The Civil War, through death and poverty, had robbed southern colleges of students and professors; occupying Union forces had set fire to their buildings and made off with equipment; and endowments had been lost.

That the University of Alabama had served as a training camp for Confederate troops during the war made it a target for Union soldiers, who burned the campus in

1865, leaving only seven buildings standing. The university tried to reopen later that year, but the attempt failed after a lone student showed up for classes. A reorganized University of Alabama resumed instruction in 1871 with an enrollment of 107.

Reconstruction governments dismissed antebellum faculty for political rather than economic reasons from colleges throughout the South, including UNC Chapel Hill. This school, which had remained open throughout the war, began its fall 1868 term with a small faculty selected by the state government; however, with debts in excess of $100,000 and inadequate revenues, it closed in 1870. Following a change in the political leadership of the state, UNC Chapel Hill opened successfully in September 1875 with seven professors and approximately 70 students.

Because nearly all U.S. colleges and universities accepted only white students, agents of the Freedmen's Bureau addressed African Americans' need for higher education. Working in cooperation with the AMA and other religious and charitable groups, they founded a number of colleges for African Americans, including Atlanta University, which was established in 1865; Fisk University, which opened in Nashville, Tennessee, in 1866; and Howard University, created in Washington, D.C., in 1867 and named for General Oliver Otis Howard, commissioner of the Freedmen's Bureau.

The Hampton Agricultural and Normal Institute, a coeducational school for African Americans, opened in Hampton, Virginia, in April 1868. This agricultural, mechanical, and academic school was established by the Freedmen's Bureau, with help from the AMA, under the direction of General Samuel C. Armstrong, the son of missionaries in Hawaii and a commander of African-American troops in the Civil War. In contrast to Howard University, where the curriculum was strongly academic, Hampton offered a course of study that reflected Armstrong's faith in manual labor as the means to achieving financial security and social acceptance for African Americans.

Students gained admission by demonstrating the ability to read and write at a fifth-grade level, presenting evidence of good character, and being between the ages of 15 and 25. The great majority of Hampton graduates pursued careers in education, and by 1880 they were teaching 10,000 children.

American Indians: Education for Assimilation

On April 13, 1878, 62 Native Americans arrived at the Hampton Institute

John Mercer Langston was dean of the Howard University School of Law from 1869 until 1876. *(Library of Congress, Prints and Photographs Division, LC-BH83-3736)*

to begin receiving instruction. They represented five western tribal nations: the Cheyenne, Kiowa, Comanche, Arapaho, and Caddo, but to reach Hampton they had traveled north from Fort Marion in St. Augustine, Florida, where they had been imprisoned for crimes committed in the Indian Wars.

Escorting the men was an army lieutenant, Richard Henry Pratt, who had served for eight years on the frontier and who had accompanied the prisoners east by train. Having seen the American Indians lose their autonomy and most of their land, Pratt believed that the Native people could flourish only by adopting the predominant language and culture. His thinking was in line with the policy of the federal government, which advocated schooling to wean young Indians from their traditional way of life.

By the 1860s, the U.S. Indian Service had established 48 day schools adjacent to Indian encampments. In these schools Indian children received instruction in reading, writing, spelling, recitation, and arithmetic. Industrial training constituted a major part of the curriculum, with boys learning carpentry and farming skills and girls practicing sewing, cooking, and cleaning. In theory, the cultural lessons children learned would rub off on their families, but interaction with parents and elders had the opposite effect: Children who returned home at night reverted to their traditional ways. A federal Indian agent stated in 1878 that "to place these wild children under a teacher's care but four or five hours a day, and permit them to spend the other nineteen in the filth and degradation of the village, makes the attempt to educate and civilize them a mere farce."[19]

Reservation boarding schools, which proliferated in the 1870s, held promise, although they were costlier to operate than day schools. It was hoped that children kept in school for eight or nine months a year would more easily break their ties with Indian traditions than those who returned home daily. Located at agency headquarters, where adult Indians came to collect rations and conduct business with the government, these schools offered graded instruction, both academic and industrial. Still, however, the culture into which they were born exerted a strong pull on the young people. The sight of smoke rising from Indian encampments, easily visible from boarding-school windows, made the children desperately homesick. Also, children who returned home in summer or at Christmas quickly shed the veneer of "civilization" acquired at school. Educators built higher fences and considered founding schools farther away, perhaps in the East.

Congress appropriated funds to create these boarding schools soon after Lieutenant Pratt delivered his charges to the Hampton Institute. For a while, Pratt stayed on at Hampton to oversee the Indians' education; he also journeyed to Indian agencies in the Dakotas and Nebraska to recruit more students for Hampton. Then, eager to carry on his own experiments in Indian education, he traveled to Washington, D.C., where he persuaded the Congress and the commissioner of Indian affairs, Carl Schurz, to place him in charge of a new school for Native American youth to be located in abandoned army barracks at Carlisle, Pennsylvania, the home of Dickinson College.

Pratt acted quickly. By September 1879, he had hired a staff and acquired students, drawing 60 boys and 24 girls from the Pine Ridge and Rosebud Reservations in the Dakota Territory and 38 boys and 14 girls from the Indian Territory (present-day Oklahoma). Some parents and tribal leaders let children go willingly, but others consented only under pressure. Most of the original 136 children spoke no English

Wearing uniforms and hair cut in the style of non-Indians, boys of the Sioux (Dakota, Lakota, Nakota) nation pose for a photograph at Carlisle, Pennsylvania, ca. 1880. *(National Archives)*

upon their arrival and had a poor understanding of what was happening to them. Some worried that the whites had taken them away to kill them.

The prisoners Pratt had taken to Hampton moved to Pennsylvania to continue their education, and on November 1, 1879, the Carlisle Indian Industrial School opened. Three and a half months later, Commissioner Schurz and members of the House Committee on Indian Affairs visited the new school at Carlisle. They reported to U.S. Commissioner of Education John Eaton that what they saw was "astonishing": The staff at Carlisle had cut the boys' long hair, replaced the children's buckskin clothes with uniforms, and given them new names that reflected a European, rather than an Indian, heritage.[20]

Chronicle of Events

1860

- Approximately 60 percent of white children ages five to 19 are in school, with those ages 9 to 12 most likely to be enrolled.
- The average white child attends school for nine years and for 50 days in each of those years.
- School attendance is related to income and nation of birth, with children from affluent families and those who were born in the United States or whose parents were born in the United States more likely to attend school than poor and immigrant children.
- With a population of 110,000, Chicago is the eighth largest city in the United States.
- About 6 percent of white males age 20 or older classify themselves as illiterate.
- The constitutions of all southern states except South Carolina provide for public education.
- There are 325 high schools in the United States.
- Elizabeth Peabody opens the first private kindergarten in the United States, in Boston.
- Many pioneers on the western frontier educate their children at home.

1861

- *April 12:* Confederate forces open fire on Union soldiers attempting to supply Fort Sumter in Charleston, South Carolina, starting the Civil War.
- *April 21:* General Benjamin Butler establishes temporary headquarters on the grounds of the U.S. Naval Academy in Annapolis; the academy relocates to Newport, Rhode Island, for the duration of the war.

1861–1862

- Economic depression in the North forces numerous young people to leave school and go to work.

1862

- South Carolina College is one of many southern colleges and universities forced to close because of declining enrollment.
- The Militia Act passed in this year gives the president the power to employ African Americans for military purposes.
- The American Tract Society (ATS) publishes *The Picture Lesson Book*, the first textbook for freedmen.

- With passage of the Morrill Act, Congress creates the land-grant college system, which will make agricultural and mechanical instruction available to students nationwide.
- *August:* The Baltimore City Council requires teachers to swear allegiance to the United States. Two principals and 26 teachers refuse to do so.
- *December:* General Nathaniel Banks takes command of the Gulf Department, which encompasses New Orleans and several southern Louisiana parishes.

1863

- The economic outlook improves; now, however, young people fill jobs vacated by men who have gone to war.
- *April:* The American Missionary Association (AMA) opens its first two schools in Norfolk, Virginia.
- *April 28:* The Educational Association of the Confederate States of America (EACSA) holds its first convention, in Columbia, South Carolina.
- *July:* The Baltimore City Council requires all music teachers to teach their students patriotic songs.
- *September:* The AMA operates 11 day and evening schools in the South, employing 21 teachers to instruct more than 3,000 African Americans.
- *December 6:* The Thirteenth Amendment to the Constitution is ratified, abolishing slavery in the United States.

1864

- White hoodlums destroy the AMA school at Clumfort's Creek, North Carolina.
- The ATS estimates that freedmen's schools are using 24,000 copies of its primer and 300 sets of its instructional cards.
- *March:* The army transfers oversight of its 126 schools for African Americans in the Gulf Department to a new state board of education.
- *November 9:* The EACSA holds its second and final convention in Charlotte, North Carolina.

1865

- The Confederacy has produced 93 original textbooks.
- Approximately 1,400 teachers are instructing African Americans in 975 schools in the South.
- Three percent of African Americans in the South can read and write.
- Lydia Maria Child publishes *The Freedmen's Book* and distributes it at her own expense.
- Union soldiers burn the campus of the University of Alabama.

- Atlanta University, a historically black school, opens.
- *March:* The federal government establishes the Bureau of Refugees, Freedmen and Abandoned Lands, known popularly as the Freedmen's Bureau; by year's end, 71,000 African Americans attend the bureau's schools.

1866

- Fisk University, a historically black school, opens in Nashville.

1867

- Howard University, a historically black school named for General O. O. Howard, commissioner of the Freedmen's Bureau, opens in Washington, D.C.

- The first schools to teach the deaf with oral methods exclusively, the Clark School for the Deaf and the New York Institution for the Improved Instruction of Deaf Mutes, open.
- *March 2:* The U.S. Bureau of Education is formed to report to Congress on progress in school development and educational thought.

1868

- A survey uncovers alarming disparities in public education in St. Louis.
- *April:* The Hampton Agricultural and Normal Institute, a coeducation school for African Americans, opens in Hampton, Virginia.

A lithograph printed in Baltimore and "dedicated to the colored Citizens of the U.S." celebrates the 1870 ratification of the Fifteenth Amendment to the Constitution. Its artist imagined fine educational opportunities for African-American children resulting from the voting power of the men of their race. *(Library of Congress, Prints and Photographs Division, LC-USZ62-22396)*

- *July 9:* The Fourteenth Amendment to the Constitution is ratified, conferring citizenship on the former slaves.

1869
- Enrollment in Freedmen's Bureau schools reaches 114,000.
- Charles W. Eliot becomes president of Harvard University and begins instituting the elective system.

1870
- The Freedmen's Bureau terminates its educational work; 247,333 students are attending 4,329 bureau schools.
- High schools in the United States number 800.
- The Bureau of Education counts 369 colleges in the United States.
- Understaffed and inadequately funded, the University of North Carolina at Chapel Hill closes.
- There are 38 schools in Nevada, five in New Mexico, and none in Arizona.
- *February 3:* The Fifteenth Amendment to the Constitution is ratified, guaranteeing all male citizens the right to vote.

1871
- The University of Alabama, destroyed by fire in 1865, reopens with 107 students.

1872
- In Boston, Alexander Graham Bell begins training teachers of the deaf in oral communication.

1873
- Laws are in place in many states to organize a public school system and support it through taxation.
- Ruling in a suit brought by taxpayers in Kalamazoo, a Michigan court confirms the right of the legislature to require support of public high schools through taxation.
- Elizabeth Peabody begins publishing the *Kindergarten Messenger.*

- The St. Louis school board approves an experimental kindergarten program.

1874
- *July:* The Michigan Supreme Court upholds the decision of the lower court in the Kalamazoo case.

1875
- Fewer than 25,000 students are enrolled in U.S. high schools.
- *September:* The University of North Carolina at Chapel Hill successfully reopens with seven professors and about 70 students.

1876
- The kindergarten system in St. Louis serves as an example to other cities.
- The Froebel Society of Boston creates a model kindergarten at the Philadelphia Centennial Exposition.

1878
- Sixty-two American Indians enroll in the Hampton Institute.

1879
- *September:* Lieutenant Richard Henry Pratt has assembled a staff and students for a new boarding school for American Indians in Carlisle, Pennsylvania.
- *November 1:* The Carlisle Indian Industrial School opens.

1880
- Two-thirds of western schools are open less than half a year.
- Graduates of the Hampton Institute are teaching 10,000 African-American and American Indian children.
- The U.S. commissioner of Indian affairs and several members of Congress visit the Carlisle Indian Industrial School and admit to being astonished at the changes in students' appearance and behavior that have occurred in three and a half months.

Eyewitness Testimony

Can it be expected . . . that we, the representatives of the sovereign States, will agree here, at the seat of Government, to assemble and hear the question argued as to the equality of the races, and whether children are to be put upon the same footing; to see a policy instituted, violative of every principal of the Constitution of the United States and the history of its foundation, which confounds the difference between the races, and makes ours an institution which shall be mongrel white and negro? From what race of these States have the men descended who make this argument? Not from the old Puritan blood, which asserted its supremacy both against the negro and the Indian; asserted its supremacy under Catholics, nor the severest trials to which the colonists were ever subjected; not the cavaliers, nor the Quakers, nor the younger sons of noble families, who peopled different colonies; for in all of them they asserted their supremacy as a race, and only permitted emancipation within their limits when the negro slave had ceased, to them, to be profitable. . . .

Do gentlemen need more to convince them of the distinction between the races? Do they hope, offending against all the teachings of history; against the marks of God; in violation of the Constitution; and by trampling upon the feelings of the southern representatives here, to found in the District of Columbia an experimental establishment to disprove the inequality of the races? . . . I am not answered by saying they may go to different schools. What right have you to take charge of [the Negro] race at all? Where do you get your authority? The Government was not made for them. They were not represented in the formation of the Government save as property, now holding that joint relation of persons and property which establishes a three-fifths representation for the southern States.

Senator Jefferson Davis of Mississippi arguing in the U.S. Senate against a proposed amendment to allow African-American children in the District of Columbia to attend school, 1860, in Edgar W. Knight, ed., A Documentary History of Education in the South before 1860, *vol. 5:* Educational Theories and Practices, *pp. 506–507.*

On the title page, a neat vignette presents a colored child and a white teacher. Turning the leaf, and before an open cabin door, we see seated a white teacher and his black pupil. . . . This book is the initial volume of a reform that turns a new page in history. It is the first book ever printed for the elevation and education of the black race,—the American slave. It is designed for the use of the contrabands at Fortress Monroe and Port Royal and Kansas. In its general aspects, it is just such a stepping-stone to knowledge as you would throw down before the feet of your pet child,—neat and bold in typography, ornate with wood cuts, elegant in embossed muslin. But, in its purpose and intent, it is eloquent with suggestions of the era now opened.

A description of The Picture Lesson Book, *the first textbook for freedmen, from the* Chicago Tribune, *1862, in "Introduction," Robert C. Morris, ed.,* Freedmen's Schools and Textbooks, *vol. 1:* Semi-Annual Report on Schools for the Freedmen, *n.p.*

This quiet close of this year, our not quite half-full roll of students, our graduating class of less than half of even our usual number, are to us, and to all who know our work and history, signs of the *times,* effects of changes *external* to us. . . . We have no thought of letting St. James's even suspend its living action. With that countenance and help from GOD, which we humbly but, we think, rationally count upon, we announce our purpose to re-open the College in all its departments, and in their full undiminished efficiency, at the regular day—the last Wednesday in September next. We are prepared to expect, it may be, no larger a roll next year than we have had this. There *may* be on it more names, or there may be fewer names than this year. We shall give Maryland and the region adjacent full chance to show whether the times leave means, leisure and will enough to educate the youths of our community as has hitherto been done. We shall offer the same full advantages; though the half-roll of this, and perhaps of a year or two to come, may demand somewhat less work than of old, and must of course yield far less income. The College, therefore, will not need and cannot retain quite so many officers as before. The wonted facilities and duties, however, shall none the less be vigorously maintained. Still, we who are to do the work for the future, must now anticipate our own great personal deprivation in the withdrawal of some of our working corps who have so long, so lovingly and so efficiently shared our College offices and their toils. It will be very strange and sometimes very sad to me, and to us all who work on here—to miss the friend and companion of early and of later life; the pupils, co-workers and reliable friends and counsellers who have so long mingled in all the associations and duties of our College life. But here again the stern sobriety of the times bids every one suppress every regret of such personal sort, in the recollection of the heavy woes and cares that press the thousands all over the land.

John B. Kerfoot, rector, College of St. James, July 9, 1862, An Address Delivered at the Commencement of the College of St. James, Washington County, Maryland, in 1862, pp. 3–5.

[Kindergarten] presupposes gardeners of the mind, who are quite aware that they have as little power to override the characteristic individuality of a child, or to predetermine this characteristic, as the gardener of plants to say that a lily shall be a rose. But notwithstanding this limitation on one side, and the necessity for concurrence of the Spirit on the other,—which is more independent of our modification than the remote sun,—yet they must feel responsible, after all, for the perfection of the development, in so far as removing every impediment, preserving every condition, and pruning every redundance. . . .

A teacher leads children in a game called "the windmill" in this kindergarten scene from 1878. *(Library of Congress, General Collection)*

If every school-teacher in the land had a garden of flowers and fruits to cultivate, it could hardly fail that he would learn to be wise in his vocation.

Elizabeth Palmer Peabody, proponent of kindergarten, November 1862, "Kindergarten—What Is It?" pp. 586–587.

Order is the child of reason, and in turn cultivates the intellectual principle. To bring out order on the physical plane, the Kindergarten makes it a serious purpose to organize *romping*, and set it to music, which cultivates the physical nature also. Romping is the ecstasy of the body, and we shall find that in proportion as children tend to be violent they are vigorous in body. There is always morbid weakness of some kind where there is no instinct for hard play; and it begins to be the common sense that energetic physical activity must not be repressed, but favored. Some plan of play prevents the little creatures from hurting each other, and fancy naturally furnishes the plan,—the mind unfolding itself in fancies, which are easily quickened and led in harmless directions by an adult of any resource. . . . Children delight to personate animals, and a fine genius could not better employ itself than in inventing a great many more plays, setting them to rhythmical words, describing what is to be done. Every variety of bodily exercise might be made and kept within the bounds of order and beauty by plays involving the motions of different animals and machines of industry. Kindergarten plays are intellectual exercises; for to do anything whatever with a thought beforehand develops the mind or quickens the intelligence; and thought of this kind does not try intellect, or check physical development, which last must never be sacrificed in the process of education.

Elizabeth Palmer Peabody, proponent of kindergarten, November 1862, "Kindergarten—What Is It?" p. 589.

No better Spelling-book than Dr. Webster's has ever been presented to the American people. The unparalleled extent of its circulation furnishes ample proof of the high estimation in which it is held by an enlightened public. For many years it has been almost the only Spelling-book used in the Southern States, as well as in other sections of the old Union; and his Dictionary may be found in almost every family, occupying, as it deservedly does, a pre-eminence over all others. But those friendly relations which once existed between the Northern and Southern States have been severed by a protracted, unjust, and oppressive federal legislation, and thus we have been driven from them, and the channel through which we have, hitherto, been accustomed to obtaining our supplies is now closed by blockade; the offspring of an unjustifiable and tyrannical war which is waged against us by those who should have continued to be our friends. Driven from them never to return, we ask, what must now be done to meet the wants of our Schools? This is an important question.

Robert Fleming, Confederate textbook author, 1863, The Elementary Spelling Book, Revised and Adapted to the Youth of the Southern Confederacy, Interspersed with the Bible Readings on Domestic Slavery, *p. 3.*

The Bible readings on the subject of Domestic slavery, which are introduced into this book in various places, are given the exact verbiage of the sacred page. The people of these Confederate States of America will not henceforth withhold from their school-books, the teachings of the Scriptures on this subject. They have no higher law than Holy writ. It is their standard in religion and morals. . . .

It is the object of the Spelling book to teach orthography and orthoepy [pronunciation]; and the various tables of spelling are so constructed as to condense into the smallest compass a complete system of teaching the elements of the language. However small this book may appear, it may be considered as the most important classbook, not of a purely religious character, which the rising generation of the Southern Confederacy are destined to use.

Robert Fleming, Confederate textbook author, 1863, The Elementary Spelling Book, Revised and Adapted to the Youth of the Southern Confederacy, Interspersed with the Bible Readings on Domestic Slavery, *pp. 4–5.*

This eve. Harry, one of the men on the place, came in for a lesson. He is most eager to learn, and is really a scholar to be proud of. He learns rapidly. I gave him his first lesson in writing to-night, and his progress was wonderful. He held his pen almost perfectly right the first time. He will very soon learn to write, I think. I must inquire who w'ld like to take lessons at night. Whenever I am well enough it will be a real pleasure to teach them.

Charlotte L. Forten, African-American teacher in the freedmen's school, St. Helena Island, South Carolina, November 13, 1863, The Journals of Charlotte Forten Grimke, *p. 398.*

Just one year has elapsed since the first free day school was opened and instructors sent from the North for the express purpose of teaching. In review, we can not repress the exclamation: "Behold what God hath wrought!"

After surveying this district, (North Carolina,) and traversing the field for more than six months, I confess to an agreeable surprise at the success of this grand educational work. . . . Schools have multiplied, and more than forty different teachers have been sent into this district. With a full share of difficulties always incident to a new enterprise, coupled with those peculiar to this, it is a marvel that there have been such steady progress and enlargement of the work. Of course, much is due to the teachers, who, as a body, have proved worthy of the societies under whose auspices they have been sent. They are a noble band; and whatever the future may yield, it must be a lifelong satisfaction to have been identified with this year of labor. Should the present prospects continue or brighten, no doubt the number of schools may be doubled before the first of January. Even this will not nearly meet the demand. This work has not been begun a moment too soon; it could not be. Wherever colored children can be found in sufficient numbers, there it is time to begin a school. I can not for my life see how one who has at heart the welfare of his country can fail of deep interest in the work of elevating the negro race; it bears vitally on our national prospects; we must not be indifferent to it. The freedmen are providentially thrown upon our hands, and the simple question is, whether they shall be an element of strength or weakness. The humble efforts of teachers now scattered through the rebellious States within our lines, will tell mightily on the future of this nation; especially if, in connection with their proper work of training the intellect, they couple efforts for the moral and religious improvement of these benighted ones. . . .

On the whole, my faith in the negro, in his capacity for improvement, in his ability to support himself and become a worthy and honored citizen, has been wonderfully strengthened by the observations of the past six months. There is something grand in the lifting of a race from servitude to the enjoyment of liberty and equality, and opening to them a fair field in which to rise or fall. The American Missionary Association, the Freedman's Association, and the Educational Commission, are doing a noble work. . . . In a quiet way, they are solving the greatest problem of the age, and preparing the highway whereby this nation may pass safely through her final struggle.

The Reverend William T. Briggs, superintendent of the American Missionary Association schools in North Carolina, 1864, in The Eighteenth Annual Report of the American Missionary Association, *pp. 15–16.*

The country schools are prosperous and thronged, and although they have been in being but a few months, they are rapidly demonstrating the capacity of the African to receive our civilization. Children who eight weeks ago were beginning the alphabet are now reading in First readers, and solving with facility problems in the primary rules of arithmetic.

The more intelligent of the planters are comprehending that whatever dignifies their laborers is a reciprocal benefit to themselves; and the instances are continually increasing where the planters not only willingly, but cordially, aid the Board in the location of schools on their plantations. . . .

Three years ago it was a crime to teach their race. Now they read the testament and the newspaper. They are learning the geography of the world. They are gaining the knowledge of figures, with which to do the business of labor and life. They are singing the songs of the Union and freedom. They show a healthy mentality, and have made it appear to reasonable minds that they are very much like the rest of mankind, and are thus entitled to a fair chance in the world.

The result of this new chapter of human experience will be a general resurrection of buried mind through the worn and wasted South. Our military expeditions do the pioneering work of blasting the rock and felling the forest. Education follows to sow the grain and raise the golden harvest. The most glorious work is now opening—to lift up the freedmen with instruction, counsel, and culture. The day of antagonism is over, and that of befriending begins. Behind the advancing lines of our forces follows the small pacific army of teachers and civilizers; and the school-house takes the place of the whipping-post and scourge.

Lieutenant Edwin M. Wheelock of the 4th Regiment, Corps d'Afrique, and member of the Board of Education, Gulf Department, 1864, in The Eighteenth Annual Report of the American Missionary Association, *pp. 18–19.*

The Yankee teacher, or author of school-texts, attempts to give the "worth of his money" to his pupil, or his reader, in terms as tangible as possible. He stuffs his pupil with scraps and dates and facts, producible on the greatest possible number of occasions, or he crams his book with the greatest possible amount of information—with a number, as nearly as possible, approaching the magic "One Thousand Facts Which Everybody Ought to Know." Thus, the New England ideal of a textbook, is a book with as much information in it as it can contain.

Now, the opposite system of education would direct all its methods towards inducing *thought* in the student; and this system, modified by a due attention to imparting sufficient information for a reliable foundation for thought, seems to us to embody the true theory of education. A real education is not a catch-penny exercise of memory, but a thorough discipline of the whole mind.

William Burwell, editor of the Richmond Age, *January 1864, in Christopher Clausen, "Some Confederate Ideas about Education," p. 240.*

You have no idea of the state of things here. Go out in any direction and you meet negroes on horses, negroes on mules, negroes with oxen, negroes by the wagon, car and buggy load, negroes on foot, men, women and children . . . all hopeful, almost all cheerful, every one pleading to be taught, willing to do anything for learning. They are never out of our rooms, and their cry is for "Books! Books!" and "when will school begin?" . . . Every night hymns of praise to God and prayers for the Government that oppressed them so long, rise around us on every side—prayers for the white teachers that have already come—prayers that God would send them more.

Letter from a Presbyterian minister in Louisiana to the Liberator, *January 8, 1864, in William F. Messner, "Black Education in Louisiana, 1863–1865," p. 45.*

In addition to the day-schools were eight flourishing night-schools. In the largest of these, fifteen teachers have been employed instructing one hundred and seventy pupils. The pupils attending these feel the importance of their time, and are very eager to make the most of it. After a hard day's work they return to their homes, take their frugal meal, change their dress when they can make a change—come to the school and devote an hour or an hour and a half to earnest study. In one respect the evening-schools have a stronger claim for support than the day-schools, as with most who attend them, it is about the last chance. The privilege *is* prized—the good seed is scattered broadcast, and in due time the harvest will appear.

The Reverend William T. Briggs, superintendent of the American Missionary Association schools in North Carolina, 1865, in The Nineteenth Annual Report of the American Missionary Association, *p. 22.*

It is really wonderful how quickly these untutored children will wheel into line and approach the high standard in our Northern schools. There is, moreover, a genuine

Students holding their books line up outside a contraband school, ca. 1865. *(National Archives, ARC ID 529344)*

love for school. Repeatedly the vote has been unanimous to dispense with holidays for the sake of attending. In fact, they will endure almost any penance sooner than be deprived of this privilege. In one of our schools, two of the larger pupils, a girl and boy, for a very grave offense were ordered to leave the school or receive a whipping. They might take their choice. The boy instantly came forward and was whipped. The girl gathered up her books, left the room, and the teacher supposed, of course, that was the end of it. She was much surprised the next morning to see this girl enter, and walking straight up to the teacher, said, "Missus, I've come for my whippin'." Such was her love for the school, that after a night's reflection, she had rather be whipped, old as she was, than stay away. The children seem quite ambitious to improve. Frequently they carry their books home. In passing through the camps I have often been assailed by little urchins holding out their slates, "Please, sir, set me a copy," and it is no uncommon thing for children, "just let loose from school," to gather in groups and go through with a spelling exercise in fine style, and close off with—"Hail Columbia."

The Reverend William T. Briggs, superintendent of the American Missionary Association schools in North Carolina, 1865, in The Nineteenth Annual Report of the American Missionary Association, *pp. 22–23.*

Here is seated a middle-aged man, intently studying the first principles of arithmetic; yonder is his wife, as diligently poring over her primer. Here, a mother just commencing to read; there, her son of sixteen, trying to conquer the multiplication-table. In this class is a man just learning his letters; by his side are children five years old at the same lesson; and so on.

Some who had families could attend school but three or four days in the week, the rest of the time being spent in "earning something to eat." Many refused to go out to work for *high wages,* preferring to work for their board and go to school while there was opportunity. I have often been asked if colored children learned as rapidly as the whites. Taking all their circumstances into consideration, I never saw any school, that *as a whole,* advanced more rapidly.

One old woman said she was willing to work as long as she *could stand,* if by so doing she would be able to read the Bible; when, about three months afterward, she was able not only to read her Bible, but *write* a little, her cup of happiness was full; she thought she could never thank the Lord *enough* that he had placed her where she "could *learn* beautifully."

An American Missionary Society teacher, Missouri, 1865, in The Nineteenth Annual Report of the American Missionary Association, *p. 27.*

The scholars were all beginners, a few knowing the alphabet, while none were able to read. Most of them were ignorant of any restraint, and the order and discipline of the school-room were entirely new. Not a day passed without two or three fights among the pupils when at their plays, and these were often severe and bloody. The prospect before us was discouraging. Our scholars, numbering from one hundred and fifty to two hundred, were crowded into one room in which were two or three recitations at the same time. We entered upon our labors strongly determined to see what could be done, and as we look at our school to-day, and think what it was nine months ago, the change seems incredible.

We now have an average of one hundred and eighty scholars daily. These are divided into three apartments. A class of sixteen read quite well in the "National Third Reader," a very hard reader of that grade; about fifty read in the Second Reader of the same series; fifty more are in the First Reader; and the remainder are in the Primer, or yet learning their letters. Those in out first department all write, some of them a very fair hand; they also study Arithmetic; and have nearly completed "Monteith's First Lessons in Geography." Nine months ago, many of these did not know a letter. In order and application to study, this department, composed mostly of scholars who have been in school from the first, will compare favorably, with any of our best white schools in the North. . . .

We are *now* fully convinced that the colored children can learn.

An American Missionary Association teacher, Baton Rouge, Louisiana, 1865, in The Nineteenth Annual Report of the American Missionary Association, *p. 32.*

In former times, the country was overrun with an endless number of competition School Books in every line of instruction. The present condition of the country has delivered us from this evil. Will that last hereafter? That is the question. "To be, or not to be?" . . .

Under the present circumstances, the scarcity of materials is in itself a safeguard against a fruitless competition in the publishing business; but it is not the publisher's mission to depend upon physical incidents. He should rest safe upon public opinion.

S. H. Goetzel, Confederate textbook publisher, 1865, in A. de V. Chaudron, Chaudron's Spelling Book, Carefully Prepared for Family and School Use, *p. 5.*

The University buildings are all burned. Nothing was saved but the private residence of the officers. The most valuable part of my library . . . was consumed. This is a great loss to me just now.

I do not know that the University of Alabama will be rebuilt—if at all, it will be several years hence. I cannot await the final results, but must look for some employment.

Landon C. Garland, president of the University of Alabama, May 30, 1865, in Joseph M. Stetar, "In Search of a Direction: Southern Higher Education after the Civil War," p. 237.

The first want of the negroes is instruction by devoted and cultured teachers. . . . The tyranny under which they have been ground was nursed by ignorance. Upon intelligent people it would have been powerless. Send out teachers then, and especially female teachers. Let them follow in the track of every conquering army. Let them swarm over the savannas of the South. Bring hither the surplus of females in New England, greatly increased by the bereavements of war, for here it can essentially contribute to the national wealth and honor. No more beautiful resolution of a difficult and delicate social dilemma can be conceived of.

Horace James, U.S. district superintendent of Negro affairs, North Carolina, June 1865, in Robert C. Morris, Reading, 'Riting, and Reconstruction: The Education of Freedmen in the South, 1861–1870, *p. 22.*

We found the school-house (a barn-like frame structure), a little removed from the cluster of negro huts, and took the school fairly by surprise. Passing up a long hall, wide enough for double rows of desks, in the center, with seats for about ten or twelve boys in each, and an aisle on either side, with benches for the class recitations against the walls, we came to an elevated platform, from which led off, in opposite directions, two other precisely similar halls. The fourth, completing the cross, was designed for girls, and was yet unfinished. Down these three long halls were ranged row after row of cleanly-clad negro boys, from the ages of six and seven up to sixteen or seventeen.

All seemed attentive; and though the teachers complained that the sudden entrance of visitors always led to more confusion than usual, there was certainly no more than one would expect from any school of equal extent anywhere, under any management. The rolls contained the names of three hundred and seventy-four pupils, of whom about two hundred were present. The Superintendent, who seemed an earnest, simple-minded man, enthusiastically convinced that he had a "mission" here, spoke of this as about the average attendance. The parents, he said, were themselves so uncertain, and so little accustomed, as yet, to the habits of regularity, that they could not well bring up this average to a better point. It seemed to me surely not so far behind our ordinary public schools at the North as to suggest any unfavorable contrasts.

Whitelaw Reid, journalist, visiting a freedmen's school in Norfolk, Virginia, 1866, After the War: A Southern Tour, *pp. 15–16.*

Several classes were called up to exhibit their proficiency. . . . It was strange to see boys of fourteen or fifteen reading in the First Reader; but stranger to observe how intelligently scholars in the First Reader went about their work, and with what comparative rapidity they learned. I passed among the forms and conversed with a good many of the soldier-teachers. They all united in saying that on the average the raw negro boys admitted to the school would learn their letters and be able to read well in the First Reader in three months; while some of them, who were originally bright, and who were kept in regular attendance, made considerably more rapid progress.

Whitelaw Reid, journalist, visiting a freedmen's school in Norfolk, Virginia, 1866, After the War: A Southern Tour, *pp. 16–17.*

The first school-house to which we were conducted was an old store-room, the second story of which had been used as a hall for the Knights of the Golden Circle, and still bore on its walls the symbols of that hollowest and most insolent of southern humbugs. Rude partitions divided the store-room, and separated the three different grades of the primary school.

In the first we were received by a coarse, ill-dressed, rude-looking man, who evidently sprang from the poor white trash. Ranged along the wall as we entered were a dozen or more boys, reading as boys do read, in the Third Reader—with many a pause and many a tracing of hard words with a great fore-finger that blurs everything it touches. . . .

The next room was ruled by a woman as coarse and slatternly as became the neighbor of the man whose school we had just left. A little fellow made some noise to displease her as we entered, and she bowled him against the wall as one would bowl down a ten-pin alley. Children were at work mumbling over charts hung against the wall, and professing, with much noisy show of industry, to be spelling out simple sentences. But their zeal did not prevent surreptitious pinches, when the slatternly school-mistress's back was turned, nor a trade of "five alleys [marbles] for a bright-colored glass one," on the sly. I think such scenes are not unknown even in model Northern schools.

The teacher in the third room was as great a contrast to the two we had just seen as was her school to theirs. . . . This teacher seemed capable of giving an intelligent opinion as to the capacities of her scholars. She had taught in the North, and she saw no difference in the rapidity with which whites and blacks learned to spell and read. There were dull scholars and bright scholars everywhere. Some here were as dull as any she ever saw; others were bright as the brightest.

Whitelaw Reid, journalist, visiting a school for African Americans in New Orleans, 1866, After the War: A Southern Tour, *pp. 246–248.*

Judging, both from personal observation and from the testimony of the teachers and the Board of Education, I should say that the negro pupils are as orderly and as easily governed as any corresponding number of white children, under similar circumstances. There is, I think, a more earnest desire to learn, and a more general opinion that it is a great favor to have the opportunity. There is less destruction of books, less whittling of school furniture, less disposition to set up petty revolts against the teacher's authority. The progress in learning to read is exceptionally rapid. I do not believe that in the best schools at the North they learn the alphabet and First Reader quicker than do the average of these slave children. The negroes are not quicker-witted, but they are more anxious to learn.

Whitelaw Reid, journalist, 1866, After the War: A Southern Tour, *p. 255.*

At no future period will education be so much needed as it is at present; nor will [African Americans] at any other time lay hold of the pearl of great prize in the same good earnest they do now. Of course, the assistance if they are to have any must come from the North; and at this time persons coming from there and showing their friendly feelings for them command a powerful influence among them. Now their enthusiasm is aroused. Let it be suppressed without feeding it, and it will never be so active again. There is another incentive to them for learning that they will not have in the future, though it must be confessed it is not a very laudable one in itself. They delight in doing any thing, that, in ante bellum days, they were disallowed, and the white people allowed, to do. So some will learn *now* just for the sake of doing it.

Jacob E. Yoder, assistant superintendent of the freedmen's school at Lynchburg, Virginia, May 3, 1866, in Samuel L. Horst, ed., The Fire of Liberty in Their Hearts: The Diary of Jacob E. Yoder of the Freedmen's Bureau School, Lynchburg, Virginia, 1866–1870, *p. 8.*

We are reliably informed that a white-skin teacher of a Negro school, was hung in Tarrant County last week, by a colored mob, for procuring a license to marry one of the pupils. His license was tacked to the trunk of the tree on which he was hung, as a warning to the rest of the whites. It seems the negroes apprehended that if miscegenation was not checked, the whites would soon get all the best-looking wenches.

Denton [Texas] Monitor, *1869, in Robert C. Morris,* Reading, 'Riting, and Reconstruction: The Education of Freedmen in the South, 1861–1870, *p. 232.*

In education, the individual traits of different minds have not been sufficiently attended to. Through all the period of boyhood the school studies should be representative; all the main fields of knowledge should be entered upon. But the young man of nineteen or twenty ought to know what he likes best and is most fit for. If his previous training has been sufficiently wide, he will know by that time whether he is most apt at language or philosophy or natural science or mathematics. If he feels no loves, he will at least have his hates. At that age the teacher may wisely

Julia Hayden, a 17-year-old African-American teacher, was murdered in Hartsville, Louisiana, in 1874, by the White Man's League, a white supremacist group. *(Library of Congress, Prints and Photographs Division, LC-USZ62-55606)*

abandon the school-dame's practice of giving a copy of nothing but zeros to the child who alleges he cannot make the figure. When the revelation of his own peculiar taste and capacity comes to a young man, let him reverently give it welcome, thank God, and take courage. Thereafter he knows his way to happy, enthusiastic work, and, God willing, to usefulness and success. The civilization of a people may be inferred from the variety of its tools. There are thousands of years between the stone hatchet and the machine-shop. As tools multiply, each is more ingeniously adapted to its own exclusive purpose. So with the men who make the State. For the individual, concentration, and the highest development of his own peculiar faculty, is the only prudence. But for the State, it is variety, not uniformity, of intellectual product, which is needful.

These principles are the justification of the system of elective studies which has been gradually developed in this College during the past forty years. At present the Freshman year is the only one in which there is a fixed course prescribed for all. In the other three years, more than half the time allotted to study is filled with subjects chosen by each student from lists which comprise six studies in the Sophomore year, nine in the Junior year, and eleven in the Senior year. The range of elective studies is large, though there are some striking deficiencies. The liberty of choice of subject is wide, but yet has very rigid limits. There is a certain framework which must be filled; and about half the material of the filling is prescribed. The choice offered to the student does not lie between liberal studies and professional or utilitarian studies. All the studies which are open to him are liberal and disciplinary, not narrow or special. Under this system the College does not demand, it is true, one invariable set of studies of every candidate for the first degree in Arts; but its requisitions for this degree are nevertheless high and inflexible, being nothing less than four years devoted to liberal culture.

Charles William Eliot, 1869, "Inaugural Address as President of Harvard," in Richard Hofstadter and Wilson Smith, eds., American Higher Education: A Documentary History, *vol. 2, pp. 608–609.*

People who think vaguely about the difference between a good college and a good polytechnic school are apt to say that the aim of the college course is to make a rounded man, with all his faculties impartially developed, while it is the express object of a technical course to make a one-sided man—a mere engineer, chemist, or architect. Two truths are suppressed in this form of statement. First, faculties are not given by God impartially,—to each round soul a little of each power, as if the soul were a pill, which must contain its due proportion of many various ingredients. To reason about the average human mind as if it were a globe, to be expanded symmetrically from a centre outward, is to be betrayed by a metaphor. A cutting-tool, a drill, or auger would be a juster symbol of the mind. The natural bent and peculiar quality of every boy's mind should be sacredly regarded in his education; the division of mental labor, which is essential in civilized communities in order that knowledge may grow and society improve, demands this regard to the peculiar constitution of each mind, as much as does the happiness of the individual most nearly concerned. Secondly, to make a good engineer, chemist, or architect, the only sure way is to make first, or at least simultaneously, an observant, reflecting, and sensible man, whose mind is not only well stored, but well trained also to see, compare, reason, and decide. The vigorous training of the mental powers is therefore the primary object of every well-organized technical school.

Charles William Eliot, president of Harvard University, February 1869, "The New Education," p. 218.

Our three years' courses, with but little preliminary training, cannot be expected to furnish much. Our students could never become advanced enough in that time to be more than superficially acquainted with Latin and Greek: their knowledge would rather tend to cultivate their conceit rather than to fit them for faithful educators of their race, because not complete enough to enable them to estimate its true value. . . .

An English course, embracing reading and elocution, geography, mathematics, history, the sciences, the study of the mother tongue and its literature, the leading principles of mental and moral science and of political economy, would, I think, make up a curriculum that would exhaust the best powers of nineteen-twentieths of those who would, for years to come, enter the institute. Should, however, any pupil have a rare aptitude for the classics and desire to become a man of letters in the largest sense, it would be our duty to provide special instruction for him or send him where he could receive it. For such the Howard University at Washington offers a broad and high plane of intellectual advantage.

Samuel Chapman Armstrong, director of the Hampton Institute, 1870, "General Armstrong's First Annual Report," in Armstrong's Ideas on Education for Life, pp. 52–53.

Here, especially in the city of Washington, there should be a model system of elementary and secondary training for the resident youth, complete in its buildings, grounds, apparatus and in its opportunities for research in literature, science and art. . . . Alas! What a contrast with facts! How reluctant, nay, how imperfectly, the general government has provided common schools for the children of the District! The system struggles under four different boards—one for the white schools of Washington, another for those of Georgetown, the third for those of the rest of the district, and another for the colored schools of the whole district; in spite of the excellence of some of the school buildings, others in use are utterly unfit for the assembly of children; no provision has yet been made for the training of teachers, and no exact or thoroughly arranged method for development by grades into higher school instruction; and nearly one-half of the children of school age are growing up unbenefited by the system of public instruction.

John Eaton, Jr., U.S. Commissioner of Education, The Relation of the National Government to Public Education: An Address Delivered before the National Teachers' Association, at Cleveland, Ohio, Aug. 17, 1870, pp. 8–9.

The clear sighted and far-seeing educator, justly looking at the defects in the best city and State systems, giving amplest credit for all excellencies, yet perceiving the need acknowledged by the educators of Massachusetts, for progress there, and the failure in New York and nearly all our large cities to reach the tens of thousands of degraded youth, marks everywhere the resistance offered by ignorance, self-interest, vice and crime to the enlightenment and culture of the people, and knows that the battle has to be renewed in a measure for every generation. He finds Delaware without State school supervision, leaving all educational questions to the counties, and having no provision for the blacks; Maryland, though recently revising her laws, educating colored children only in Baltimore; Virginia but just putting a free school law on her statute book; West Virginia upon the point of striking from her system its right arm, county supervision; Kentucky just enacting a new school law, but giving no opportunity for colored youth; Tennessee, after establishing free schools and assembling in them nearly two hundred thousand children, reversing her course and providing only for the most inefficient county action outside her largest cities; North Carolina with a school law upon her statute books, but at the close of the last year not a school in the country districts directly under the auspices of the State law; South Carolina but slightly in advance; Georgia with her legislation where it was before the war; Alabama, though with a free school system and one hundred and sixty thousand pupils enrolled, yet with the whole so connected with the old order of private schools as to rob it of much of its freedom of action and prevent its highest usefulness; Florida with a system partly organized, the Legislature adjourning after its late winter session without making any provision for the levy of the school tax; Mississippi just writing its school law; Arkansas with an efficient system, but the schools only partially organized; Louisiana with a system adapted for efficiency, but not more than seventy-five schools reported outside of New Orleans at the date of the last report; Texas without legislation, the Senate refusing to confirm the Superintendent nominated by the Governor—all over this Southern section not only lack of educational sentiment but positive hostility to instruction and instructors.

John Eaton, Jr., U.S. Commissioner of Education, The Relation of the National Government to Public Education: An Address Delivered before the National Teachers' Association, at Cleveland, Ohio, Aug. 17, *1870, pp. 12–13.*

Discipline is itself the great educational process. The well disciplined alone are well educated. It is the teacher's chief business, therefore, to discipline his pupils. He cannot "add to their stature one cubit," nor their mental or moral capacity one new power; but he can bring them under such a process of training as will subdue their wild and untamed impulses, develop the latent energies of the body, mind, and soul, and direct them to a course of right action, so that the future citizen and lawgiver may be fitted for his great work and high destiny.

School discipline has reference to all the regulations and prohibitions, restraints and stimulants, which are calculated to regulate the habits of study and deportment, through the interesting and important period of school life.

The object to be secured is twofold: viz., school vices must be prevented or cured, and school virtues must be cultivated.

Among the school vices, as they have been classified, are idleness, whispering, disorderly movements in the schoolroom, injury to property, and rudeness of speech, or act, in the intercourse of every-day life.

The school virtues to be cultivated are suggested as the opposites of these; viz., regularity of attendance, promptness, obedience, truthfulness, earnestness, diligence, kind-

ness, neatness, and thoroughness in the preparation and recitation of lessons.

Hiram Orcutt, educator and writer, 1871, The Teacher's Manual; Containing a Treatise upon the Discipline of the School, and Other Papers upon the Teacher's Qualification and Work, *pp. 12–13.*

Much has been said and written upon corporal punishment and moral suasion; but their appropriate use in school discipline is seldom understood, as it seems to me.

Moral suasion is not the remedy for bold and defiant violations of law, if you mean by that term the *persuading* of the culprit to return to obedience, or the *purchase* of his allegiance by a promised reward.

Rebellion should be met by stunning, crushing blows, such as will vindicate and re-establish authority, and deter others from committing the same crime.

Mildness is cruelty under such circumstances. All such cases demand instant and determined action. The time for conciliation is after the rebels are subjugated and the authority of the government is restored.

Hiram Orcutt, educator and writer, 1871, The Teacher's Manual; Containing a Treatise upon the Discipline of the School, and Other Papers upon the Teacher's Qualification and Work, *p. 59.*

The amount of latent and dormant power; of wealth-discovering and wealth-producing energy; of beauty-loving and beauty-inspiring taste and skill, that lie concealed and slumbering in the brains and hearts and hands of the keen, shrewd, capable, but untutored millions of our youth, is beyond computation. Now over all this unreclaimed but magnificent intellectual and moral territory, over all these minds and souls and bodies, with their untold possibilities of good, the State has, in my opinion, a sort of *right of eminent domain* and not only may, but should exercise it in the interest of her own prosperity and dignity.

Newton Bateman, state superintendent of public instruction of Illinois, on the state's obligation to support public high schools, 1871, in Edgar B. Wesley, NEA: The First Hundred Years, *p. 63.*

The school must seize the pupil, and train him by a strict discipline to obedience, before it can do much with him in an intellectual point of view. A lax school allows the weeds of selfishness, indolence, and insolence to grow up and choke the fair virtues that spring from self-restraint and renunciation.

It is therefore especially important that we in this country extend the school-life of the child during the most plastic period of his growth. Moral education requires time—far more than theoretical education. Where we must do both—give the child theoretical and practical education—we should require the maximum of time in school. In one word, our whole education should aim to give the pupil directive power. He must therefore be practised for a long time in self-government, and he must be thoroughly initiated into the social necessity that underlies moral action; he must see principles. Upon such, and such forms alone, is the combination of man with man based, and this combination is the necessary condition for the ascent of one and all above the life of mere animals.

William Torrey Harris, superintendent of schools, St. Louis, 1872, The Early Withdrawal of Pupils from School: Its Causes and Its Remedies, *p. 3.*

We have in all our States many special conditions that enhance the importance of . . . early schooling. There is the call for youth to enter the fields of productive industry, at an age closely bordering upon infancy. In our manufacturing population, now growing far more rapidly than any other population, this is a very serious evil. Various devices, such as statute laws, requiring a certain number of months per year, or a certain number of days per week, have been tried. Evening schools have been established, libraries and reading rooms opened; still the problem is but indifferently solved. Looking at this phase of the subject, and considering the fact that in such communities the family life at home is mostly pernicious to the child, and his life on the street still more so, I think it necessary to modify the character of our lowest primary schools, allowing the entrance of pupils at the age of four years, and making the exercises less severe, and more entertaining to the pupil. Large changes, looking in the direction of the kindergarten system of Froebel, can probably be made to advantage.

Pupils thus received and nurtured at an early age will be at least made to love school, and to form good habits. They will be likely to continue at school to a far greater age than otherwise, for two reasons; first on account of the fact that having learned to love school life, their preference will go far to determine the consent of the parents. The child in this country has so much self assertion that he, as a rule, prevails over the will of his mother; and the two combined—what father can resist? Great power lies in the hands of school managers, there-

fore, to control school attendance by making schools attractive to children.

William Torrey Harris, superintendent of schools, St. Louis, 1872, The Early Withdrawal of Pupils from School: Its Causes and Its Remedies, *p. 4.*

The family and the school are inseparably connected in the great work of education; yet much the larger share of the labor and responsibility necessarily belongs to the parents. Teachers are only their assistants and employes, having delegated authority and power; and their success and usefulness depend largely upon the wisdom and cooperation of their employers. Hence the discipline of the family embraces the discipline of the school, and should be based upon the same principles, and studied with equal care and earnestness by both parents and teachers.

Hiram Orcutt, educator and writer, 1874, The Parents' Manual; or, Home and School Training, *p. 1.*

An examination of our schools shows that reading, spelling, penmanship, arithmetic (mental and written) and geography are taught in all the schools of the State of an intermediate and grammar grade. United States history and English grammar are taught in most of our grammar schools. Vocal music is practised in many of our schools, and taught in a few, particularly in those of all grades in Providence and Newport. Drawing is taught in the intermediate and grammar grades of Providence and Newport. Sewing is taught in a few of the schools of Providence.

In the high schools we find the pupils pursuing the studies of natural philosophy, chemistry, astronomy, botany, algebra, trigonometry, bookkeeping, general history, mental and moral philosophy, English literature, Latin and Greek.

Thomas B. Stockwell, Rhode Island commissioner of public schools, January 1875, in A History of Public Education in Rhode Island, From 1636 to 1876, *p. 93.*

[U]pon the basis of finance depends the building of school houses, and how many will be erected in Colorado in the immediate future! What kind of a house? How expensive? What its interior arrangement? What its external appearance? . . . An architect will plan the house, the Board will accept the plans, and the teacher who occupies his proper position will be permitted materially to advise. What shall we advise? A building with two floors, never more, staircases open and every stair in sight from either floor, ample heating and ventilating apparatus, comfortable seatings, ample wardrobe and proper light. The people sometimes call for towers and elaborate belfries; the architect will insist upon a proper architectural effect and display, while we will say, give us a comfortable, reasonable house with good teachers; never mind the sky-scrapers, long flights of stairs and magnificent exteriors. Beautiful buildings will never make effective schools.

Aaron Grove, president of the Colorado State Teachers' Association, January 2, 1877, in Education in Colorado: A Brief History of the Early Educational Interests of Colorado, Together with the History of the State Teachers' Association, and Short Sketches of Private and Denominational Institutions, *p. 57.*

Some [African Americans] are very anxious to have their children educated, but again the greater number think they must make farmers of their sons and daughters before they educate them. Many very often say to me, when I tell them they can be better workers with an education, "O, no they will think themselves above working when they get a little learning and leave us, and our farms." And thus some of the country people are really afraid to send their children to school.

An American Missionary Association teacher in Dalton, Georgia, October 1877, in Jacqueline Jones, Soldiers of Light and Love: Northern Teachers and Georgia Blacks, 1865–1878, *p. 203.*

It is true that not all the pupils of the elementary schools will attend the high schools, but the latter are open alike to all who choose to avail themselves of their advantages. There will be more educated people in a town maintaining a high school than there would be without it, and the more educated people there are the greater will be the development of material resources, the more perfect the security of property and of persons, the higher the civilization, and the more complete the facilities for the unmolested enjoyment of all the objects of our natural rights.

A further argument in favor of maintaining high schools at the public expense may be made by showing, first, that they serve to give increased efficiency to the elementary schools below them. From the fact that the higher education is within the reach of *all,* pupils in the lower schools are stimulated to remain in them until they have learned all that is required to be known and have obtained all the discipline of mind required as a preparation for high school work. . . . The influence of one grade of schools upon another grade is from

above downward, in so far as courses of study, amount of work done, and methods of teaching are concerned; it is from below upward just in proportion as that from above downward has succeeded in leading the elementary schools to prepare their pupils thoroughly for higher courses of study.

By the standards of admission to their classes which they establish, and the opportunities for a higher education which they offer, the high schools determine what the lower schools shall do, and they everywhere stimulate pupils to remain in the lower schools until what is required has been accomplished.

Again, the lower schools, on account of the age and attainments of their pupils, can only teach elementary knowledge, a knowledge of facts. If the high school is taken away, the opportunity to obtain free instruction in somewhat higher knowledge is taken away also. The elementary and the high school courses are parts of one whole. No system of schools would be complete without both.

John W. Dickinson, secretary of the Massachusetts Board of Education, 1877, in "Proceedings of the Department of Superintendence of the National Education Association for 1877," p. 161.

My little friends—for so I have learned to call them—are moving in couples to the sound of a lively air played on a piano by the principal of the school; several assistant teachers, walking before, instruct the "little men and women" in the figures of the marching exercise, two hundred tiny feet keeping time with vigorous tread, two hundred chubby hands clapping in unison, and all their baby voices piping merrily:

"Let us march without a blunder,
Right and left we part asunder,
Till we meet in pairs again,
Following our leading men."

Up and down the long room, now in single, now in double file, passes the mimic procession, till, halting before their respective tables, the music ceases, and the little companies seat themselves with a merry babble of speech and laughter that, for the time, converts the room into a very Babel of silvery sound. Presently this subsides into a low murmur of expectation, the Kindergartners are seen approaching with their "gifts," some bringing boxes of colored balls for the tiniest scholars; others boxes of blocks, steel rings, piles of colored papers, worsteds, card-board, strips of wood, and slates; receiving which, the little ones fall to work.

F. E. Fryatt, journalist, November 1878, "A Free Kindergarten," p. 801.

The Twenty-second Ward [New York City] "Free Kindergarten," the subject of our sketch, is intended for the poor only, and owes its support mainly to the contributions of the children of the "Religious School" and members of the "Society of Ethical Culture." It was formally opened by Professor Felix Adler [founder of the Society for Ethical Culture] on the second day of the present year, with a view to reaching and benefiting the children of the extremely poor, and more especially those of the workmen in the Forty-second Street gas factory, in whose neighborhood it was purposely planted. A large, well-kept, well-ventilated room is devoted to the purposes of the school, which, under the intelligent management of its founder and principal, has attained an attendance of one hundred scholars. To the right stands a moderately good grand piano, a fine upright blackboard, and a long table on which are arranged a few books and piles of Froebel's "gifts;" to the left a cupboard for lunches, towels, etc., and six long, low tables of polished wood, with comfortable settees on either side. Rows of pegs, just high enough for little hands to reach, dot the wall at one end of the room, and gayly colored prints of birds, animals, and plants hang above for the instruction and amusement of the children. Potted plants fill the ledges and flourish in the sunshine that finds free entrance through the spacious windows, while the luxurious vines clambering around the casements give the nearest approach to the garden which Froebel considered indispensable in his institutions.

F. E. Fryatt, journalist, November 1878, "A Free Kindergarten," p. 802.

"A republican government needs the whole power of education." These words of Montesquieu have, perhaps, never found a more striking application than in the subject which we are about to consider. If there be a nation which has expected everything from this power of education, which has intimately united its national destinies with the development of its schools, which has made public instruction the supreme guarantee of its liberties, the condition of its prosperity, and the safeguard of its institutions, that nation certainly is the people of the United States.

The peculiar position assigned to the school in American social life has always been one of the first points to attract the attention of foreigners.

The great zeal for the education of the young which grows as the population increases, penetrates into the public mind more and more, and manifests itself in more and more decided ways. What may have seemed at first a transient glow of enthusiasm, a generous impulse, has in time assumed all the force of a logical conviction or rather of a positive certainty. It is no longer a movement of a few philanthropists or of a few religious societies, but it is an essential part of the public administration, for which the States, the cities, and townships appropriate every year more money than any other country in the world has hitherto devoted to the education of the people. Far from limiting this generosity as much as possible to primary instruction, it goes so far as to declare free for all not only primary but even secondary schools.

Ferdinand E. Buisson of the French Commission on American Education, 1879, "The Free School System," p. 9.

The new energy given to the perceptive and reflective powers by study in the schools remains a permanent possession after the period of education shall have ceased, even though the lessons may have been forgotten. The boy in his plays abroad, men and women in all their pursuits, find ceaseless occasion for their use and pleasure as well as profit in their exercise. The eyes are opened; the dull vision becomes keen; the educated boy or girl becomes an observer, and sees things which the unawakened eye and untrained mind pass by without notice.

The reasoning faculty is also quickened, and the nature, relations, and purposes of things are studied. Thus people become unconscious philosophers, in their several ways, with various depths of insight into the character of the matters that come before them.

Life is a perpetual opportunity of study presented to our attention. The earth and all surrounding objects, the world and its circumstances, are or may be unceasing subjects of observation and reflection. People and animals, and their conditions and relations, are ever offered for our thought. The mind perceives these with more or less care and accuracy, according to its education and habit; one that is developed and trained to activity sees more than another that has not been quickened nor accustomed to action.

"The Value of Common School Education to Common Labor," 1879, p. 3.

An engineer at our blast furnace near Wheeling—a man who had previously been intrusted with important machinery and run an engine successfully when all was right, a temperate and well meaning man, but without education, except to read and write and make the simplest arithmetical calculations—was directed to place a hand forcepump at the river and have water driven up to the tanks, located 60 feet above the river level; a half day, with two assistants, was spent in fixing the pump on the river bank 40 feet above the water, with a soft hose from the pump to the water and another from the pump to the tanks. He did not know why he was unsuccessful in getting the water into the tanks. . . .

Now for another kind of a man. In a part of the country where the services of a railroad engineer were very difficult to procure as well as very expensive, it was necessary to construct two or three curves to a definite radius in a short railroad extending from the coal mine to the main line of railroad. An employe who knew nothing of engineering but had mastered the first six books of Euclid, by an evening's study and application of the geometrical principles involved, discovered the very rule and method used by the best engineers, and next day, with the aid of a transit, located the curves with correctness and dispatch. How much was such a man worth above an ordinary hand!

Cyrus Mendenhall, president of the Kenton Iron Company, Newport, Kentucky, 1879, in "The Value of Common School Education to Common Labor," pp. 30–31.

Educated workingmen live in better houses, have better surroundings, and are in all respects superior to those whose education is limited and defective. They are less idle and dissipated than the untaught classes. As regards economy, morality, and social influence, educated laborers are preeminent among their fellows. I may add one general observation, that, while I was foreman of a shoe factory employing forty hands, I always got better work, had less trouble, and, as a general rule, paid better wages to the more intelligent workmen. The more ignorant hands were continually giving me trouble, either by slighting their work or failing to appear in a fit condition to work after pay day. They were, many of them, coarse and vulgar, drank liquor, grumbled, and were in all respects disagreeable.

I am so well satisfied of the inestimable value of education to the laborer that I would make it compulsory.

S. P. Cummings, secretary of the Massachusetts Grand Lodge of the Order of St. Crispin [a shoemakers' union], 1879, in "The Value of Common School Education to Common Labor," p. 31.

The people of the South have consented to give up the old and try the new; they have studied the philosophy of the modern educational system, and many have studied with approval; they have dismissed speculative theories and have accepted what they now consider accomplished facts. The most convincing proof of these declarations is found in the fact that constitutions conforming to the new ideas are generally being adopted throughout the South by conventions in which men of the old school hold absolute sway, and an honest effort is being made everywhere throughout that entire section to educate all the children, irrespective of race. The greatest obstacle of all . . . still remains . . . our poverty and the vast number of the helpless thrown upon our hands. Out of this hard, stern fact grows the great, the overshadowing need of the South at this time, viz, more means. True, there are other needs. We need a deeper and more general public interest in education than can be excited among a partially educated population. We need a more intelligent comprehension of our educational situation than can be found among our rulers. We need a much larger and more enterprising body of thoroughly qualified teachers for both our white and colored schools, and especially for the latter. We need very much an adequate number of well endowed, well manned normal schools for keeping up this supply of well trained teachers.

Gustavus J. Orr, state school commissioner of Georgia, 1879, "The Needs of Education in the South," p. 55.

We have now in school at this Agency 170 Arapahoe children and 162 Cheyennes. We ought to have 500 more children receiving the same advantages. The children *must* be taken *from* the camps if we expect them to advance from savage life, and I count it money wasted to continue the large annual appropriations to feed and clothe these children *in camp* and under camp influence.

Congress may go ahead from year to year and appropriate means to supply the youth *in camp* and they will still be the same dirty, ignorant, camp Indians; while if it would increase the appropriation just sufficient to clothe and support them *in school* (Industrial schools) and make it available while in attendance at school, either on their reservations or at "Training Schools" similar to the Carlisle School, then we might expect a decided forward movement from our present Indian status.

John D. Miles, U.S. Indian Service agent, Darlington, Indian Territory, February 12, 1880, in Richard Henry Pratt, Battlefield and Classroom: Four Decades with the American Indian, 1867–1904, p. 242.

The child, left to itself amidst the natural environments of country life, teaches us true and deep lessons. As soon as by contact with nature through the senses the mind is awakened, he discovers beauty in the flower, is pleased with the green landscape and laughs with Nature's cheerful moods. Before the reason is employed or the intuitions defined, he is attracted by the beauty of natural objects and is lulled by the soothing influence of music. He soon weaves fanciful pictures in his mental world, builds strange castles, peoples the air with impossible beings, and dreams of wonderful climes. He longs for legend and fairy tale and listens to them with pleased credulity. He chases the butterfly by a natural instinct.

This tendency of childhood to thrill with the inspirations of Nature, and to love fanciful creations is innate.

Were man never burdened with absorbing cares and selfishness this tendency would never leave him. We find here the rudiments of that principle which grows into the ideals, purpose and enthusiasm of manhood, and which controlled by reason moves the world. Happy the man whose childhood has taken him through lessons in the first school of life.

James H. Baker, president of the Colorado State Teachers Association, December 1880, in Education in Colorado: A Brief History of the Early Educational Interests of Colorado, Together with the History of the State Teachers' Association, and Short Sketches of Private and Denominational Institutions, *pp. 65–66.*

CHAPTER FOUR

Meeting Diverse Needs
1881–1916

The teachers at the Carlisle Indian Industrial School used to say that they taught their pupils to do everything except swallow, walk, and sleep, although the new arrivals did need to be shown how to sleep in a bed. The staff also taught the young Indians tasks as basic as caring for their newly issued clothing and practicing hygiene as white Americans did. Academic instruction remained basic, because many school administrators considered Indians incapable of challenging intellectual work. In the classrooms at Carlisle, the students learned to speak English and to read and write. They mastered addition, subtraction, multiplication, division, and measurement, to prepare themselves to handle money, build houses and barns, and calculate the worth of a crop; they memorized the names of the states and the English names of rivers and mountain ranges; and they were made to understand that phenomena such as lightning and eclipses could be explained by science rather than religion, and that God had willed the spread of U.S. settlement from the East to the West.

Vocational education received greater emphasis. Boys at Carlisle and other Indian boarding schools practiced carpentry, masonry, harness making, blacksmithing, and printing. Girls received training in domestic science, or the application of scientific knowledge to such aspects of household management as preventing disease, planning meals, and budgeting. School administrators thought that girls needed this training to be suitable wives for Indian men entering white society and to prevent them from raising children according to "heathen rites and superstitions."[1]

To strengthen acculturation and, it was hoped, help students resist the lure of Indian life, Pratt developed the "outing" program, arranging for boys and girls to spend a summer with a Pennsylvania or New England farm family. Some students stayed with their foster families longer, for one to two years. Home tugged at the children's hearts, however. Many students grew depressed, and some were said to have died of homesickness. The Bureau of Indian Affairs kept no record of student mortality prior to 1904, but the staff at Carlisle minimized deaths at the school by returning sick children to the reservations.

The government continued its educational efforts, constructing 24 additional off-reservation boarding schools between 1880 and 1902. Unlike the Carlisle school, these institutions were situated in the West and Midwest, closer to the reservations.

Students march on the grounds of the Phoenix Indian School, ca. 1910. *(Arizona Historical Foundation/Barry Goldwater Photograph Collection, G-38)*

Not only did choosing western locations reduce the cost of sending children to school, but also the planners in the Bureau of Indian Affairs (BIA) had tried to strike a balance, educating children away from the reservations but close enough for them to maintain family ties. With schools in places such as Pierre, South Dakota; Mount Pleasant, Michigan; and Fort Bidwell, California, "the parents may often visit their children, and thus grow accustomed to their improvement, and . . . the children may spend each year a long vacation at their homes," said the superintendent of the Albuquerque school in 1885.[2]

One boarding school, the U.S. Industrial Training School, opened in Lawrence, Kansas, in 1884, with 15 students. In 1887, administrators changed the school's name to the Haskell Institute, to honor Dudley Haskell, the U.S. representative from Kansas who was responsible for locating the school in Lawrence. By 1894, 606 students from 36 states were in attendance, and the institute had added a normal school. Two years later, young women could study stenography, bookkeeping, and the new skill called typewriting.

Despite their training, female graduates of the Indian schools found it nearly impossible to secure employment in any other field than domestic service. Even those who went to work for the U.S. Indian Bureau held lowly government jobs, doing laundry, cooking, and sewing. The bureau employed some Indians as teachers in its schools but none as administrators.

Off-reservation schools benefited developing western communities by giving residents jobs, serving as a market for provisions, and supplying farm labor and domestic help through the outing program. By 1900, 21,568 Indian students—about half of all Indian children—attended school. More than 80 percent of these young people were in schools operated by the Bureau of Indian Affairs, and about 15 percent studied in schools run by religious groups.

Public Schools in the West

The traditional Indian way of life for which the children yearned belonged to the past. Irresponsible white hunters had nearly wiped out the bison that had provided food, shelter, and spiritual sustenance to generations of plains people. War and disease had drastically reduced the Native American population, and the remaining Indians had been forced onto reservations.

By 1890, the continental United States had assumed its present boundaries. The states carved from the plains and prairies had established school districts to educate the children of the growing settler population. More than 6,800 districts had been formed in one of these states, Nebraska. Roughly 4,400 of Nebraska's districts conducted school for at least six months of the year, 2,000 kept schools open for shorter periods, and 444 were districts in name only and offered no instruction at all.

Schools in Nebraskan cities and towns bore little resemblance to those in rural parts of the state. They were frame, brick, or stone structures that looked like the schools in thriving eastern communities. They typically were divided into classrooms, each with the U.S. flag and portraits of George Washington and Abraham Lincoln at the front. Classrooms also featured a map of the United States or the world, a blackboard of slate or painted wood, and possibly a piano. The teacher's wooden desk faced rows of manufactured desks for the students, each with an inkwell cut into its wooden top and cast-iron scrollwork on its sides. Many classrooms held desks for more than 50 pupils.

In villages and remote counties, the one-room schoolhouse prevailed. It was likely to be a wood-frame or brick structure, although an 1890 survey conducted by the state superintendent's office counted 792 sod schoolhouses in use. In 1895, children in Scotts Bluff County, in western Nebraska, attended a school constructed of bales of hay. Most of the state's rural districts had low enrollments. In 1903, 4,282 of Nebraska's approximately 7,000 school districts

The teacher, pupils, and two male visitors stand outside the last remaining sod schoolhouse in Decatur County, Kansas, in 1907. *(Library of Congress, Prints and Photographs Division, LC-USZ62-112792)*

educated between five and 20 children, and 489 districts had enrollments of four or fewer.

Rural western districts had trouble attracting and keeping teachers for a number of reasons. Their locations were remote; salaries were meager, around $40 per month; and both the school board and the community kept a close watch on the teacher's behavior, in and out of school. People expected the teacher to be a model of virtue and to embody the values they wanted instilled in their children. Also, the teacher, who doubled as the school custodian, worked hard. It is hardly surprising that in some districts the only job candidate was a girl of 14 or 15 with an eighth-grade education who was looking to escape drudgery on the farm.

By 1907, all states but seven in the South had made schooling compulsory, requiring children to attend school from age seven or eight through age 12 to 16, but the various state laws were poorly and unevenly enforced. In many rural places, the truant officer was the teacher, who overlooked absences because she understood that families needed their children's help planting and harvesting.

Child-labor laws had reduced the number of working children and improved job conditions for those who were employed; still, advocates for children expressed concern that working-class children commonly left school after the sixth grade to begin full-time employment, thus limiting their options. Owen R. Lovejoy, secretary of the National Child Labor Committee observed that "the child of sixteen goes from school so much better equipped as a wage-earner that in two years his earnings aggregate more than those of the child who left school at fourteen and has been working four years."[3] The solution, according to Lovejoy and others, was better and earlier vocational training.

The state governments had also standardized public education, so that offering eight years of elementary school and four years of high school was the norm. Increasingly, states required new teachers to pass competency examinations, which tested their knowledge of curriculum content and pedagogical technique. Under its first certification law, which was in effect from 1881 through 1910, Nebraska offered testing for three levels of competency. Most teachers attained only the lowest level, demonstrating knowledge of spelling, reading, writing, geography, arithmetic, physiology, and English composition and grammar.

Immigration Strains Resources

New York City in 1897 established a Board of Examiners to certify all applicants for teaching positions. The board created a list of qualified individuals that public schools in the city's five boroughs used for hiring. The city was striving to raise the quality of instruction as it strained to cope with a burgeoning student population, caused largely by immigration from southern and eastern Europe. "Sometimes as many as 125 children are admitted to the school in a single day, usually the day following the arrival of the steamer, Jewish or Italian," observed a former student at P.S. [Public School] 110, located on the Lower East Side of Manhattan.[4] In 1914, the city was educating nearly 300,000 more children than it had in 1899, but it had added only 38 schools.

Out of necessity, many buildings in disgraceful condition remained in use. Children attended schools wedged between tenement buildings that were dark and lacked space for outdoor play. They crowded in classrooms where plaster fell from the ceiling and rats ran behind the walls. Ventilation was poor, toilets few and unsanitary, and fire escapes hard to find. In some schools, nearby elevated trains periodically rattled windows and drowned out teachers' voices. Sixty or more children tried to learn in some crumbling classrooms, frequently sitting two to a desk. In a school on Henry Street, in lower Manhattan, 80 children squeezed into a classroom intended for 40.

In 1881, the New York City public schools simply turned away 9,000 children because they had no space for them, and the following year Philadelphia refused to admit 60,000 for the same reason. The Milwaukee and Boston school systems erected temporary structures to accommodate the influx of students at this time; in Buffalo, New York, school hallways, basements, and coat closets doubled as classrooms; and in Minneapolis in 1893, children in grades one through three attended school for half a day, some in the morning and some in the afternoon.

The foreigners streaming into U.S. cities seeking political and religious freedom and economic and social opportunity encountered a native population that was largely Protestant and of northern European descent and that watched the current wave of immigration with alarm. The newcomers were Jewish, Roman Catholic, and Eastern Orthodox; they wore exotic clothes, had strange tastes in food, and practiced mysterious customs and rites. Many Americans worried that the immigrants would corrupt the prevailing way of life. Once again, public schools served as the great purveyors of culture.

According to the U.S. Census of 1890, 80 percent of school-age children in New York City and Chicago had foreign-born parents. The percentage was high in other eastern and midwestern cities as well. Upon entering school, often just days after arriving in the United States, these children found themselves thrust into a system that forced them to communicate in English. Teachers, often with little or no awareness of the values and traditions with which these children had been raised, tried clumsily to wipe out all traces of foreignness in their charges and replace them with American practices and ideals. As a result, some children from families that followed the Jewish dietary rules had their mouths washed out at school for speaking Yiddish—with soap that was not kosher. Convinced that the level of cleanliness in the children's homes fell short of U.S. standards, teachers stressed the need for frequent bathing and laundering, thereby placing a burden on immigrant mothers, many of whom had to carry water up several flights of tenement stairs.

Catholics and Jews frequently objected to a perceived Protestant bias in the public schools of New York, Chicago, Boston, and other cities. When possible, urban immigrant families wishing to preserve the faith and traditions of their countries of origin sent their children to parochial schools. Roman Catholic parishes tended to be organized along ethnic lines, which meant that a parish school was likely to serve a community that shared a common cultural heritage, possibly Irish, German, Polish, Bohemian, or Slovak. Instructing the children in these schools were nuns, members of teaching orders, who more often than not came from the same European country as their pupils' families. Ethnic homogeneity among the students and faculty ensured that the language and customs families had carried over from their homelands remained central to the children's education.

In 1884, the Third Plenary Council of Baltimore, a conference of archbishops and bishops that met to decide issues concerning the Catholic Church in the United States, called for Catholic parents to give their children "an education which is truly Christian and Catholic," and to "defend them throughout infancy and childhood from the perils of a purely secular education and place them in safe-keeping"—in a

Catholic school.[5] The council also ordered all parishes to provide schools for Catholic children within the next two years. In 1884, the number of Catholic schools in the United States approached 3,000. The expansion of parochial education was evident in cities such as Boston, where the percentage of children attending Catholic schools grew from 8 percent in 1888 to 15 percent in 1894. Jews, Lutherans, Quakers, and other religious groups also opened schools, but these were fewer in number than the Catholic schools.

During this period, settlement-house workers assisted the foreign-born of all ages, giving people the skills they needed to be self-sufficient and improve their communities from within. The settlement movement began in Victorian London and moved to the United States in 1886, when reformer Stanton Coit established the Neighborhood Guild (later called University Settlement) on the Lower East Side of Manhattan. The social activists Jane Addams and Ellen Gates Starr founded the best-known U.S. settlement, Hull-House, in Chicago in 1889, and by 1900, Hull-House was one of a hundred settlement houses located throughout the United States.

A settlement house was both a home for its staff and a community center that offered such services as vocational training, child care, health care, after-school recreation, English classes, and instruction in art, music, and drama. Hull-House and other settlements also operated kindergartens and conducted classes for the older neighborhood children.

Schools Serve the Broader Community

The progressive spirit that spawned the settlement movement also inspired administrators in many U.S. cities to make the local school a center of community life by keeping it open after the hours of instruction for social and civic groups. The New York City Board of Education took this step in 1897. It was a move, said Jacob Riis, a noted activist for the poor, that would "develop a social spirit and an enthusiasm among young and old," and make "the school truly the neighborhood house and soul."[6] City residents participating in the after-hours recreation program played games such as checkers, chess, dominoes, and lotto; attended classes in etiquette, grooming, and folk or social dancing; and joined clubs devoted to hobbies or politics. The school building also offered quiet space for study, something lacking in most tenement homes.

Increasingly, municipalities were building high schools and some elementary schools with auditoriums, gymnasiums, playgrounds, and libraries that served pupils and the community alike. In 1907, the Rochester, New York, Board of Education opened the city's public schools during off hours for adult civic clubs, boys' and girls' clubs, and public lectures and entertainments. By 1910 Boston, Cincinnati, and Newark, New Jersey, were among the cities that had made their school facilities available for recreation and for public lectures on topics as varied as dental hygiene and American customs and institutions.

Evening classes at public schools in New York and other cities offered elementary, secondary, and vocational instruction to students who generally were age 14 or older. There were also English classes for the foreign-born in cities with high immigrant populations. To meet the needs of adult learners, the evening elementary curriculum in Buffalo, New York, included academic classes and vocational training, especially in trades that largely employed women, because women objected less than men did to learning alongside youngsters. Therefore, in addition to reading, writing, spelling, arithmetic, history, and geography, evening elementary students could acquire dressmaking, millinery, and clerical skills. Evening high school curriculums emphasized vocational training for both sexes, and many also held classes that prepared adults to take civil service examinations.

Vacation schools in many places enriched children's lives and kept them off city streets in summer. These programs featured arts and crafts, with the most popular classes including basketry, singing, drawing, sewing, cooking, and sloyd (a way of teaching woodworking, developed in Sweden and popular roughly from 1866 to 1910, that was designed to improve dexterity and problem-solving skills). Vacation schools also provided remedial academic work and playground activities.

High Schools Come of Age

By the close of the 19th century, most cities and towns east of the Mississippi River and many in the West had built high schools. In 1900, there were 6,055 public high schools in the United States, educating 915,061 students, or 82 percent of the young people enrolled in U.S. secondary schools. Still, only a small percentage of 14- to 17-year-olds attended high schools or academies. From 6 percent to 7 percent of people in this age group had enrolled in secondary schools in 1890, and 11 percent had enrolled in 1900. A minority of these students—between 10 and 20 percent—completed the four-year course and graduated.

Some city high schools had become quite large, accommodating 1,500 or more students. One of the largest and most up-to-date was Joliet Township High School in Illinois. Completed in 1901, it had been built to hold 1,400 students. Its facilities included an assembly hall with 1,500 seats; gymnasiums; physics, chemistry, and biology laboratories; an internal telephone system; thermostatically controlled heating; and a ventilation system capable of supplying 60,000 cubic feet of fresh air per minute.

After 1900, some high schools offered something additional: cafeteria service. Town and city high schools drew students from a larger area than elementary schools did, making it impractical for many youths to return home at lunchtime, and student bodies were too large to eat lunches packed at home in classrooms or the schoolyard. One school that pioneered lunch service, Englewood High School in Chicago, sold such fare as beef stew, chicken pie, and ham sandwiches for five cents and plain cake, milk, or cocoa for three cents, beginning in 1903. The Englewood Woman's Club prepared and served the food, setting an example of "unselfish desire to be useful to the community at large," according to a teacher at the school.[7]

The high school curriculum had developed haphazardly, as school administrators added courses to their curriculums with no uniformity. It seemed that every new principal or superintendent knew of an additional subject that needed to be taught. "Undue congestion is the most serious malady from which our high-school courses of study are suffering today—a congestion arising both from the amount of class work and from the number of different subjects embraced in the course," said E. W. McCoy, principal of Cincinnati's Hughes High School, in 1897.[8] Some communities offered a high school program that was largely academic and intended to prepare students for college, while elsewhere the high school curriculum stressed vocational training for students planning to end their education with grade 12. The Jesuits and other Catholic orders had begun establishing high schools that offered

Students and their teacher gather in the manual training room of the Emerson School in Gary, Indiana, in 1910. *(Library of Congress, Prints and Photographs Division, LC-USZ62-88536)*

a curriculum emphasizing English grammar and literature, Latin, and religion and minimizing vocational training. By 1910, there were more than 300 Catholic high schools in the United States.

To encourage consistency in secondary education and clarify its goals, on July 9, 1892, the National Education Association (NEA) appointed the Committee on Secondary School Studies, commonly known as the Committee of Ten. Its members included William T. Harris, the former St. Louis school superintendent who had been named U.S. commissioner of education; Charles W. Eliot, president of Harvard University; four other college presidents; two private-school headmasters; one high school principal; and one college professor. The NEA charged the committee with establishing advisory groups to report on the principal subjects taught in high schools and recommend how students could best be prepared in each subject for college.

In 1893, the committee issued its findings, acknowledging the importance of both academic and vocational education in high schools but, in keeping with its mission, endorsing a strong academic curriculum for all students, whether or not they intended to go on to college. The committee's recommendations, which were to influence course offerings at high schools nationwide, therefore echoed the conservative viewpoint of the 1827 Yale Report. Yet the 10 committee members sought, not merely to uphold tradition, but to keep the doors of academia open for those high school students whose desire to attend college developed after they began their secondary studies. "Their parents often do not decide for them, four years before the college age, that they shall go to college," they noted, "and they themselves may not, perhaps, feel the desire to continue their education until near the end of their school course."[9]

To introduce vocational and college-preparatory subjects to younger students, some school districts established junior high schools. Junior highs opened first in the

United States in 1909, in Columbus, Ohio, and Berkeley, California, and gradually spread to other locations. They gained the support of forward-thinking educators because they made the transition from elementary school and childhood to high school and young adulthood less abrupt. In districts with junior high schools, students typically attended six years of elementary school, three years of junior high, and three years of high school.

Evaluating College Applicants

The proliferation of high schools was enabling more students to apply to college, and colleges needed a more efficient method for evaluating applicants' academic achievements. Colleges traditionally administered their own entrance examinations, usually in Latin, Greek, mathematics, geography, and English grammar, and by 1900 the established eastern colleges also required applicants to demonstrate proficiency in modern languages (French and German) and the natural sciences. Faculty devoted a great deal of time and effort to preparing and grading these essay tests. A number of midwestern and western colleges had also developed an accreditation system, whereby faculty members evaluated the quality of instruction at secondary schools within their state. Schools that met the professors' standards received accreditation, which meant that the college would automatically admit the school's graduates. (At the time, the number of qualified applicants rarely exceeded the available space in the freshman class.)

Also, high schools needed some guidance on preparing students for college. Each college or university required something different from the others, such as knowledge of a specific Latin work. Helping a minority of students meet the varied criteria of different colleges challenged the resources of most high schools. In 1891 one high school principal complained of admission standards that varied "from Babylonian and Assyrian history, specially designated in the requirements of one college, and of Persian history, in those of another, down to the history of Texas and North Carolina, the former required by three, the latter by two colleges."[10]

On November 17, 1900, therefore, representatives of 11 colleges and five high schools held the first meeting of the College Entrance Examination Board (CEEB), an organization formed to standardize college admission by developing common entrance examinations (later known as the Scholastic Assessment Tests or SAT program). The board endeavored to distinguish applicants who were likely to succeed in college from those who clearly were unqualified. In so doing, the application process was democratized by creating a criterion that applied to all students, regardless of background.

The CEEB administered its first tests, in a variety of academic subjects, in June 1901, at 67 sites in the United States and two in Europe. That year, 973 candidates from 237 schools completed 7,889 CEEB tests. Proctors sent their exam books to Columbia University, to be marked by 39 readers chosen for their academic expertise, and the candidates learned their results by mail. Only three schools—Columbia, Barnard College, and New York University—discontinued their own entrance exams that first year, and 35 schools, primarily in the East, agreed to honor the board's exams as well as their own. In 1911, when Harvard, Yale, and Princeton abandoned their own entrance exams, the board examined 3,731 applicants, still mainly for eastern schools.

The NEA's Committee on College Entrance Requirements, established in 1895, recommended measuring high school courses in units based on hours of instruction offered during the academic term. Further refinement of this suggestion came from the Carnegie Foundation for the Advancement of Teaching, an organization created by the steel tycoon and philanthropist Andrew Carnegie in 1905. Carnegie had launched the foundation with $10 million to fund retirement pensions for college teachers, but its administrators wanted a systematic method for determining eligibility. One way to evaluate institutions of higher learning was to look at the caliber of incoming students. The administrators favored the unit plan for admission and in 1909 defined a unit as a course taught for 120 one-hour sessions, or the equivalent amount of time, during one year of high school. Colleges wishing to qualify for the pension program adopted the "Carnegie unit" for evaluating applicants, and by 1910 most states were already using it to plan high-school course requirements.

Meeting state-imposed curriculum requirements made large high schools more efficient, but it strained the resources of small and rural high schools. Young, inexperienced teachers often relied heavily on textbooks in the classroom, but the books available to them fell short of what was needed. Also, states based their requirements on a nine-month academic year, but some rural high schools were only open five months a year. The average high school operated 145 days, or roughly seven months, in 1900. State universities helped close the gap by offering preparatory work for students from high schools that fell short of accreditation standards who wanted to attend college.

Higher Education Diversifies

In 1881, the University of Pennsylvania founded the nation's first undergraduate business school, the Wharton School of Finance and Commerce. Clark University, established in Worcester, Massachusetts, in 1889, opened strictly for graduate study. The total enrollment at U.S. colleges and universities more than doubled between 1890 and 1910, increasing from 157,000 to 355,000.

In 1890 Congress bolstered the land-grant college system by passing a second Morrill Act, one that made $15,000 available annually to each of the original land-grant colleges and universities and spurred great expansion. The act denied appropriations to any state that restricted admission on the basis of race, unless the state created separate colleges for the races. Seventeen states, most of them in the South, established separate land-grant colleges for African Americans, and by 1900, the 48 states had founded 65 colleges and universities with funding from the two Morrill Acts. With the development of medical, law, and other professional schools, some of these institutions were developing into major centers of higher learning.

The Hatch Act of 1887 supported agricultural experiment stations at one land-grant college in each state, thereby making agricultural research a function of the land-grant system nationwide. Researchers in agriculture and home economics used demonstrations to deliver their findings to the rural population, and in 1906, Smith County, Texas, hired the first extension agent to serve the population of a single county.

On May 8, 1914, President Woodrow Wilson signed into law the Smith-Lever Act, providing funds to the states to support education of the rural population in subjects related to agriculture and home economics, thus creating the Cooperative Extension Service. County extension agents, who were usually affiliated with land-grant colleges and universities, traveled the countryside teaching farmers how to increase production through such methods as building silos for storage of grain and fodder and terracing hillsides to prevent erosion. They also led 4-H Clubs to educate rural youth in farming and homemaking. In addition, counties employed specialists in such fields as dairying, animal husbandry, agronomy, and farm management to meet specific educational needs. In 1914, 928 counties in the United States employed agricultural agents.

Debating the Education of African Americans

In 1896, in deciding the case *Plessy v. Ferguson,* the U.S. Supreme Court sanctioned segregated public services, including the segregated school systems that had been developed in the South, as long as the facilities provided were "separate but equal." Schools for southern black children remained inferior to those for whites, however, and supporting two school systems—one for white children and one for blacks— wasted precious funds. Largely because of financial limitations, the South continued to lag behind other regions of the nation in its ability to educate the young. The rural South could offer only scant tax support, and funding was inadequate as well in economically depressed southern cities. At the start of the 20th century, poor administration, ill-trained teachers, and short school terms characterized public education in the South. Southern teachers earned half as much as northern teachers did, on average, with southern black teachers being paid the least.

In the late 19th century, Booker T. Washington emerged as the leading spokesperson for African-American education. A former slave and an 1875 graduate of the Hampton Institute, Washington espoused Samuel C. Armstrong's doctrine of vocational education for African Americans. In 1881, Armstrong recommended Washington to head a new vocational school in Alabama for African Americans, the Tuskegee Normal and Industrial Institute. This school prepared its students to be teachers or to perform manual labor such as carpentry, mechanical repairs, farming, mattress making, and food preparation.

Advising the people of his race to "Cast down your bucket where you are," to "Cast it down in agriculture, mechanics, in commerce, in domestic service," Washington called on African Americans to reconcile themselves to playing a useful but subservient role in the community, at least temporarily.[11] By demonstrating diligence and high moral standards, he said, they would gradually gain acceptance from whites. According to Washington, it remained for future generations to pursue higher learning and give the nation its great African-American scientists, scholars, writers, and political leaders.

Washington assured white southerners that blacks could live and work among them yet remain apart socially. He expressed this view most famously and controversially at the Atlanta Exposition of 1895, when he said, "In all things that are purely social we can be as separate as the fingers, yet one as the hand in all things essential to mutual progress."[12]

Not every African American agreed with what he said. "[I]f we make technical skill the object of education, we may possess artisans but not, in nature, men," claimed the loudest challenger of Washington's ideas, W. E. B. DuBois. A professor of sociology at Atlanta University who had earned a doctorate from Harvard, DuBois believed that "intelligence, broad sympathy, knowledge of the world that was and is, and of the relation of men to it—this is the curriculum of that Higher Education which must underlie true life."[13] He demanded educational equality for African Americans, to allow them to participate fully in the political, social, and professional life of the nation. Education was essential to the group he called the "Talented Tenth"—the brightest young African Americans, those destined to become leaders and role models.[14] Washington's ideology was harmful, DuBois said, because it kept blacks at the lowest socioeconomic levels. He also criticized Washington's leadership, insisting that the Tuskegee educator had achieved prominence not because blacks supported his opinions, but because whites approved of what he had to say.

The Educational Progressives

While Washington and DuBois debated the role of schooling in furthering racial equality, other thinkers tackled broader educational issues, including the nature of learning itself. The United States had entered the Progressive Era, a period stretching from the 1890s into the first decades of the 20th century, when technological development and social change caused many people to consider the direction the nation was to take, whether in managing natural resources or in controlling big business. Reform became the Progressives' watchword, and educational reformers sought to update curriculums and teaching methods, to replace the passive learning-by-rote that had been handed down from the small-town schoolhouse with active methods better suited to the needs of an increasingly industrialized urban society.

The foremost American educational philosopher of the Progressive Era, John Dewey, taught that experience sharpened the human mind and made it a more accurate tool for problem solving. Dewey formulated a philosophy of learning-by-doing that he called instrumentalism. Knowledge results from problem solving, he said, because problems force people to think. When a problem acts as a barrier to activity, the individual gathers information, formulates a possible solution, tests it, and, in so doing, learns. Learning was not preparation for future life, but part of the process of living. According to Dewey, teachers best served students by involving them in meaningful activity that matched their interests and encouraged inquiry, communication, and artistic expression.

To test his ideas, Dewey developed the Laboratory School at the University of Chicago. This experimental school opened in 1896 with 16 pupils and two teachers, and by 1902, it served 140 children and employed 23 teachers. Learning usually occurred during group activities targeted to the children's stage of development. These ranged from field trips, nature study, and cooperative building projects for the younger children to food preparation, scientific experimentation, and club membership for the older ones. Dewey's work had a lasting impact, persuading many teachers to abandon the role of authoritarian and wielder of the rod and to act more as their students' guide and partner in learning.

Psychologist G. Stanley Hall, who in 1889 became the first president of Clark University, identified adolescence as a distinct stage between childhood and adulthood and taught that each stage had unique properties and was essential to human development. Because of this, educators needed to place as much emphasis on students' emotional growth as on their acquisition of knowledge. Hall urged high schools to concentrate on the complete education of adolescents rather than on college or vocational preparation. His 1904 book *Adolescence* led to a greater awareness among educators and the public of the complex transition from childhood to maturity.

During the Progressive Era, there were also attempts to treat intelligence as something to be measured. In 1905, two French psychologists, Alfred Binet and Theodore Simon, produced a test to identify those children who were struggling academically and might benefit from placement in a class for slow learners. This test presented a series of tasks, in order of increasing difficulty, that were designed to measure innate intelligence rather than anything learned in school. Binet and Simon were more interested in measuring reasoning ability, for example, than reading proficiency. An age level assigned to each task indicated the youngest age at which an average child should first have been able to complete it. Subjects proceeded from one task to the next until the tasks became too difficult. The tester then compared the age assigned to the last completed task, the subject's "mental age," with his or her actual age to determine if the subject's performance equaled or was above or below what was typical for children of that age.

In 1916, Lewis Terman, a Stanford University psychologist, increased the number of tasks and extended the level of difficulty to include some that could only be performed by adults of superior ability. Terman's test, the Stanford Revision of the Binet-Simon Scale, became commonly known as the Stanford-Binet test. It was widely used to measure subjects' intelligence quotient, or IQ, which was the product that resulted from dividing the mental age by the chronological age and multiplying the quotient by 100. The Stanford-Binet test made it possible to identify individuals of seemingly superior intelligence, thus calling attention to the educational needs of children whom Terman labeled "gifted." It also attracted the interest of U.S. military leaders, educators, and business people.

Chronicle of Events

1881

- Nebraska requires teachers to pass competency examinations and offers three levels of testing.
- The New York City schools turn away 9,000 children.
- The University of Pennsylvania founds the Wharton School of Finance and Commerce, the nation's first undergraduate business school.
- Samuel C. Armstrong of the Hampton Institute recommends Booker T. Washington to head the Tuskegee Normal and Industrial Institute, a vocational school for African Americans in Alabama.

1882

- The Philadelphia schools turn away 60,000 children.

1884

- The U.S. Industrial Training School opens in Lawrence, Kansas, with 15 students.
- There are nearly 3,000 Catholic schools in the United States.
- The Third Plenary Council of Baltimore advises Catholic parents to send their children to Catholic schools and orders all parishes to provide schools by 1886.

1886

- Stanton Coit establishes the first settlement house in the United States, the Neighborhood Guild in Lower Manhattan.

1887

- The U.S. Industrial Training School is renamed the Haskell Institute to honor Dudley Haskell, a U.S. representative from Kansas.
- The Hatch Act supports agricultural research at land-grant colleges in every state.

1888

- Eight percent of Boston's children attend Catholic schools.

1889

- Jane Addams and Ellen Gates Starr found Hull-House, the best known U.S. settlement house.

- Clark University opens in Worcester, Massachusetts, for graduate-level study with psychologist G. Stanley Hall as president.

1890

- The continental United States has assumed its present boundaries.
- In Nebraska, 4,400 school districts offer instruction for at least six months each year; 2,000 districts conduct school for shorter periods; and 444 districts offer no instruction.
- Between 6 percent and 7 percent of 14- to 17-year-olds are enrolled in secondary schools.
- The Nebraska state superintendent of education counts 772 sod schoolhouses in use in the state.
- Eighty percent of children in New York City and Chicago have foreign-born parents.
- The second Morrill Act makes $15,000 available annually to each of the original land-grant colleges and universities but denies funding to any state restricting admission on the basis of race.
- Enrollment at U.S. colleges and universities totals 157,000.

1892

- *July 9:* The National Education Association (NEA) appoints the Committee on Secondary Schools Studies (Committee of Ten) to report on the subjects taught in high schools and recommend how students should be prepared in each.

1893

- Children in Minneapolis attend school for half a day.
- The Committee of Ten endorses an academic curriculum for all high school students.

1894

- The Haskell Institute has added a normal school and has enrolled 606 students from 36 states.
- Fifteen percent of Boston's children attend Catholic schools.

1895

- A school in Scotts Bluff County, Nebraska, is noted as being constructed of bales of hay.
- The NEA forms its Committee on College Entrance Requirements, which recommends measuring high school courses in hours of instruction.

- Speaking in Atlanta, Booker T. Washington calls for the races to interact economically but remain apart socially.

1896
- In deciding the case *Plessy v. Ferguson*, the U.S. Supreme Court sanctions "separate but equal" public facilities, including schools.
- John Dewey opens the Laboratory School at the University of Chicago, with 16 pupils and two teachers.

1897
- New York City establishes a Board of Examiners to certify applicants for teaching positions.
- New York City opens its schools after hours for community activities.

1899–1914
- The New York City school system gains almost 300,000 children and adds 38 schools.

1900
- Settlement houses in the United States number 100.
- In the United States, 6,055 public high schools educate 915,061 young people, or 82 percent of secondary-school students.
- Eleven percent of 14- to 17-year-olds are enrolled in secondary schools. Between 10 percent and 20 percent will graduate.
- Some high schools begin to offer food service.
- The established eastern colleges require applicants to demonstrate proficiency in modern languages as well as Latin, Greek, mathematics, geography, and English grammar.
- Most high schools are open for 145 days, or roughly seven months, every year.
- The 48 states have established 65 land-grant colleges and universities.
- *November 17:* The College Entrance Examination Board (CEEB) holds its first meeting.

1901
- Workers finish constructing Joliet Township High School in Illinois, which can accommodate 1,400 students.

- *June:* The CEEB administers its first exams at 67 sites in the United States and two in Europe, to 973 candidates from 237 high schools.

1902
- The Laboratory School at the University of Chicago has 140 pupils and 23 teachers.

1903
- Of Nebraska's 7,000 school districts, 4,282 educate between five and 20 children, and 489 educate four or fewer children.

1904
- G. Stanley Hall publishes *Adolescence*, a book that increases awareness of the psychological changes that accompany the transition from childhood to maturity.

1905
- Andrew Carnegie creates the Carnegie Foundation for the Advancement of Teaching.
- In France, psychologists Alfred Binet and Theodore Simon produce a test to assess the mental ability of children.

Girls at the Perkins School for the Blind take part in a physical education class in 1904. *(Courtesy of the Perkins School for the Blind)*

1906
- Smith County, Texas, hires the first county extension agent.

1907
- All states but seven in the South have made education compulsory.
- Rochester, New York, allows the community to use public-school facilities after hours.

1909
- The nation's first junior high schools open in Columbus, Ohio, and Berkeley, California.
- The Carnegie Foundation for the Advancement of Teaching defines a Carnegie unit as one high school course taught for 120 one-hour sessions or their equivalent in an academic year.

1910
- Boston, Cincinnati, and Newark, New Jersey have made schools available for community recreation and lectures.

- There are more than 300 Catholic high schools in the United States.
- Most states have adopted the Carnegie unit as a standard for high school instruction.
- Enrollment at U.S. colleges and universities totals 355,000.

1911
- Harvard, Yale, and Princeton abandon their own entrance examinations and use the CEEB exams.

1914
- *May 8:* President Woodrow Wilson signs into law the Smith-Lever Act, creating the Cooperative Extension Service. In this year, 928 counties employ agricultural agents.

1916
- At Stanford University, psychologist Lewis Terman refines Binet and Simon's test of mental ability to develop the Stanford Revision of the Binet-Simon Scale, or the Stanford-Binet test of intelligence.

Eyewitness Testimony

We have had four or five Indian students from the Creek Nation with us for the last five years, three having left meanwhile with others taking their places. They were all from schools in the nation where they have been trained some years before coming here. With but one exception they have been quite as bright as the average white students who have had no more opportunities than they have enjoyed. Some of them are very bright and able to think deeply. They are quiet and very studious, giving us never the least trouble. One or two of them have had great taste for mathematics, while one took the Latin prize in the 3rd preparatory year, in a class of over 60 who were entering Freshmen. We see no difference and make no distinction between them and others. So far as we have had experience we have every confidence in their ability to acquire an education as well as any other human beings. In my judgment their education and that alone, will solve the problem of the future preservation of the tribes from obliteration and the elevation of their people to the position of useful members of society. To make them educated, Christianized citizens, will solve the Indian problem, and I cannot see what else would do the same.

Archibald Alexander Edward Taylor, president of Wooster University (now the College of Wooster), Ohio, January 19, 1881, in Richard Henry Pratt, Battlefield and Classroom: Four Decades with the American Indian, 1867–1904, *p. 262.*

[T]he boys returned to this agency with a three years' training at Hampton have thus far proved a failure. At the start they promised well, but they have all returned to their old ways, having learned just sufficient of the vices of the whites to make them worse than at the beginning. I am exceedingly mortified to make this admission, but if the truth be not told the evil will go on, and both time and money be expended, and little or no good result from the expenditure. Of the five boys returned from Hampton, one was placed in the blacksmith shop, three in the carpenter shop, and the other employed as assistant teacher in the boarding-school; all of the five have left their positions, and are no longer employed in any department.

Indian agent at Lower Brulé, Dakota Territory, August 1882, in Samuel Chapman Armstrong, The Indian Question, *p. 31.*

I don't think the boys stopped working for their own fault. They lived far from the shop. Sometimes they came late, and all little things like that. I know of the Hampton boys who went home; all about them. He (the Agent) didn't talk to them and try to help them. I tell you he is not a right man. I know this; the people are changing towards the good, and if no one is to help them how can they get it? I am an Indian and don't know anything.

Phillip Councilor, Lower Brulé Lakota Sioux, responding to the Indian agent's report of August 1882, in Samuel Chapman Armstrong, The Indian Question, *p. 31.*

At Hampton there are now ninety, (soon to be one hundred and six) and at Carlisle there are over three hundred Indians—boys and girls—who are learning civilization as an object lesson, and are themselves an object lesson to the centres of intelligence and wealth where is the sentiment that inspires and the means that provides for the combined practical and spiritual teaching of the red man. They suffice, perhaps, for a tangible proof of the Indian's capacity, of which the need was great; their effect upon public sentiment has been marked. The result with Indians has, so far, proved satisfactory. Scattering these pupils among the farmers of Massachusetts and Pennsylvania for a portion of the year, has had such a good effect mutually, that five hundred more might well be so placed in various states under the care of special agents, with proper rendezvous, where the sick or unsatisfactory might be kept with a view of returning home, say ten per cent. of the entire number.

Samuel Chapman Armstrong, director of the Hampton Institute, 1883, The Indian Question, *pp. 14–15.*

Let there be in a community a Negro who by virtue of his superior knowledge of the chemistry of the soil, his acquaintance with the most improved tools and best breeds of stock, can raise fifty bushels of corn to the acre while his white neighbor only raises thirty; and the white man will come to the black man to learn. Further, they will sit down on the same train, in the same coach and on the same seat, to talk about it. Harmony will come in proportion as the black man gets something that the white man wants, whether it be of brains or of material. Some of the country whites looked at first with disfavor on the establishing of a normal school in Tuskegee. It turned out that there was no brick yard in the county; merchants and farmers wanted to build, but bricks must be brought from a distance or they must wait for one house to burn down before building another. The Normal School with student labor started a brick yard. Several kilns of bricks were burned; the whites came from miles around for bricks.

From examining the bricks they were led to examine the workings of the school. From the discussion of the brick yard came the discussion of Negro education—and thus many of the "old masters" have been led to see and become interested in Negro education.

Booker T. Washington, African-American educator, speaking before the National Education Association, July 16, 1884, in Louis R. Harlan, ed., The Booker T. Washington Papers, *vol. 2, 1860–89, p. 257.*

English speaking is pushed in every way, from first to last. It is the law of the school, and, at roll call every night, each reports on his or her adherence to it. Rewards, and marks leading to penalties, such as loss of half a holiday, are used to emphasize the rule. Admission to the "Fancy Work Class," which the girls esteem a great pleasure, depends on their fidelity to English speech. A visitor who had been much among the Indians in the West, recently reported that he had addressed an Indian boy that he met on our grounds, in his own tongue. The boy's face brightened, but he answered in English, that "there is no Indian talk here." The daily associations with English speaking schoolmates of kindly natures, with whom they feel at their ease, is a very great help to them in acquiring the language. Not a good, but a "usable" knowledge of it can be acquired, on an average, in three years. After that the progress is more rapid. There are great individual differences of course.

Managers of the Hampton Institute, 1888, Ten Years' Work for Indians at the Hampton Normal and Industrial Institute at Hampton, Virginia, *p. 31.*

As soon as I came home, I applied for work, but the agent told me there was no work. I then went over to the Missionary and applied for work. He hired me as an interpreter for two or three months, when, through his influence, I obtained position as teacher in a day school among the Pottawatomies, where I taught one term of 8 months. In the summer of 1883 I was transferred to the Shawnees' boarding school of this place [Shawneetown, Indian Territory], where I taught from year to year until the time of my removal last fall. Since then I have been working about home first at one thing and then another. My savings have enabled me to own a little house of two rooms, beside outbuildings, a team of ponies, a wagon and a buggy, and about 45 head of cattle.

There are a great many obstacles in the way of returned Indian students which no one can enumerate. In the first place the returned student has still his natural propensities which were only made dormant, as it were, for the time being that he was surrounded by the comforts of civilization in a school. As soon as he is brought in contact with his people these forces are alive, being aroused by arguments of his people and other ways, and are at work in direct opposition to the principles he has just learned in school, and, unless the student has something to do to direct his thoughts, or is uncommonly decided in his convictions (but 3 years are hardly long enough for that) or receives sympathy or encouragement, no one can fail to see which of these two forces will come out a conqueror. *Work* is the great remedy in this case, as I found out, and perhaps the only deliverance the students have, and as students in general, especially those of Hampton and Carlisle are willing to work. But here we come to the worst feature of the case. There is not enough work for them at the Agency or at home.

Thomas Wildcat Alford, Absentee Shawnee and graduate of the Hampton Institute, February 6, 1888, in Ten Years' Work for Indians at the Hampton Normal and Industrial Institute at Hampton, Virginia, *p. 49.*

Two points have always impressed me in the criticisms I have heard upon returned students of Indian training schools off the reservation, and particularly those situated in the East.

First: The notion that youths, after three or five years' training should be able to at once revolutionize their native customs, irrespective of environment, local prejudice and poverty of resources.

Second: That the individual character of each pupil is not taken into account, but every boy and girl is supposed to be equally capable of absorbing new ideas, acquiring a new language, and developing a mental power equal to creating new conditions, and enabling him or her to become a leader while still almost a child in years.

Such hard lines are never laid upon our own children. Boys and girls are not expected in a few years to master a foreign language and studies unfamiliar to their parents, and upon this basis revolutionize the accustomed methods of living and speaking, and become successful workmen and farmers. Yet this is what is demanded of Indian boys and girls by those who are called on to report upon returned students, and by those who await the stories of the travelers or observers upon these young folk.

Alice C. Fletcher of the Winnebago Agency, Nebraska, February 8, 1888, in Ten Years' Work for Indians at the Hampton Normal and Industrial Institute at Hampton, Virginia, *p. 61.*

Samuel Baxter is doing well. He is married to a Carlisle girl. He has a team and a wagon, and is doing work on his farm. He tries to keep up what he has learned. Goes to night school whenever he can.

Noah and Lucy La Flesche, Philip and Minnie Stabler, are doing excellently. They are living on their farms near the town of Bancroft [Nebraska], and the young men are on an equal footing with the white men they have dealings with. Their influence and examples are doing a great deal, especially among the young men. They are often referred to, and too much cannot be said about the help they are to the people.

The two women keep their houses as neat and clean as anyone would wish. Both families are of good standing among the white people, and they have been a help to the Indians in general, by doing away with the prejudices of the whites against the Indians.

David Wells is doing very well. He has married into a nice family. He has seven horses, and has done well on his farm. He is always neat in his appearance, and goes to night school when he can. He told me he did not want to lose the little he had gained in school.

Henry Stabler did well while at home, doing the work of a man. He is now at school in Genoa, Neb. From all accounts he is doing well there also.

Irish Leaming did well while he lived. He took special pride in telling where he had been, and said if he lived he would go back to Hampton.

Stella Leaming is at home. She is doing the best she can. She uses what she learned while away as far as she can. The family is very poor, and it is hard for her to do as she likes. She has not gone back to Indian ways. . . .

Milton Levering has not done well. For a while he returned to Indian ways, but had the grace to be ashamed of himself when he met any of the students. He is off with a show, but said he wished he had done better, just before he left.

Marguerite La Flesche, American Indian graduate of the Hampton Institute, reporting on former Hampton students living near Omaha, March 3, 1888, in Ten Years' Work for Indians at the Hampton Normal and Industrial Institute at Hampton, Virginia, *pp. 52–53.*

In order to reach the highest results, the use that is to be made of education should be kept constantly in mind. If education is of any practical value it should serve to guide us in living, in other words, to fit us for the work *around* us and demanded by the times in which we live. It should aid us in putting the most into life in the age, country, and

into the position we are to fill. Perhaps all of us agree that training is best which gives the student the broadest and most complete knowledge of the arts, sciences, and literature of all the civilized nations, ancient or modern, but where the want of time and money prevents this broader culture and this choice must be made (and a choice must be made by most), let us choose to give the student that training in his own language in the arts and sciences that will have special bearing on his life, and will thus enable him to render the most acceptable worship to God and the best service to man.

Booker T. Washington, African-American educator, addressing the Alabama State Teachers' Association, April 11, 1888, in Louis R. Harlan, ed., The Booker T. Washington Papers, *vol. 2, 1860–89, p. 432.*

The *how* of punishment often intrudes itself unbidden before the mind of the teacher, demanding immediate consideration. It may seem strange that out of the teeming list of punishments that our profession has developed, the teacher should experience any difficulty in selecting just the one for any offense. Pulling the ears, pulling the hair, slapping about the face, whipping in the hand, standing on the floor for hours at a time, sitting on the floor, bending over, standing on one foot, standing on the desk, holding out the arm with a weight in the hand, pointing the finger at a mark, and a multitude of others are to be condemned, many of them as silly and others as dangerous. Punishment about the head is especially to be condemned as barbarous and unfit for the school room.

Popular opinion seems to have declared exterminating war against the rod, yet, in spite of the trend of sentiment against it, I am not made to blush when I express a firm belief that this may yet serve some good purpose in many a school room. Young America is sometimes rash, mischievous, and impulsive, and under mild influences brought to bear upon him, he often remains obstinate, defiant; but how quickly he becomes a humble penitent when standing in the majestic presence of the gad [stick].

G. M. Castor of Hampton, Nebraska, April 1891, "Punishments," p. 251.

The very term "high school" has too little of definite meaning. Its use is applied to all grades from the higher room of a school of two departments to the school having a course of study approaching in number of subjects that of the university. The term "high school," first year, should give every superintendent information as to whether the pupil is studying arithmetic or geography, whether English composition or Latin verse. It should not be inferred that every city and village must have the same rigid course of study, without variation in any particular and neither more nor less in quantity, but that there is a certain order of study upon which school men should be able to agree in every essential respect. While a high school course should lead a pupil toward the college, the high schools in the larger cities do a small part of the college work. The public sentiment and the number of high school pupils should determine the grade of the high school, whether it shall have a course of one, two, three, or four years. A small city with a small teaching force in the high school cannot do the work of a four-year course, and the sooner superintendents and boards of education realize this fact, the better will it be for the schools of the state.

W. H. Gardner of Wymore, Nebraska, April 1891, "High Schools—Suggestions for Their Improvement," p. 253.

When I walked home afternoons, with the great big geography book under my arm, it seemed to me that the earth was conscious of my step. Sometimes I carried home half the books in my desk, not because I should need them, but because I loved to hold them; and also because I loved to be seen carrying books. It was a badge of scholarship,

and I was proud of it. I remember the days in Vitebsk when I used to watch my cousin Hirshel start for school in the morning, every thread of his student's uniform, every worn copybook in his satchel, glorified in my envious eyes. And now I was myself as he; aye, greater than he; for I knew English, and I could write poetry.

Mary Antin, whose family came to Boston from Russia in 1894, when she was 13, At School in the Promised Land, p. 51.

How long would you say, wise reader, it takes to make an American? By the middle of my second year in school I had reached the sixth grade. When, after the Christmas holidays, we began to study the life of Washington, running through a summary of the Revolution, and the early days of the Republic, it seemed to me that all my reading and study had been idle until then. The reader, the arithmetic, the song book, that had so fascinated me until now, became suddenly sober exercise books, tools wherewith to hew a way to the source of inspiration. When the teacher read to us out of a big book with many bookmarks in it, I sat rigid with attention in my little chair, my hands tightly clasped on the edge of my desk; and I painfully held my breath, to prevent sighs of disappointment escaping, as I saw the teacher skip the parts between the bookmarks. When the class read, and it came my turn, my

The high school senior class of Springfield, Massachusetts, studies in one large classroom in 1899. While some students read their textbooks, others solve geometry problems on the room's extensive blackboards. *(Library of Congress, Prints and Photographs Division, LC-USZ62-39319)*

voice shook and the book trembled in my hands. I could not pronounce the name of George Washington without a pause. Never had I prayed, never had I chanted the songs of David, never had I called upon the Most Holy, in such utter reverence and worship as I repeated the simple sentences of my child's story of the patriot. I gazed with adoration at the portraits of George and Martha Washington, till I could see them with my eyes shut. And whereas formerly my self-consciousness had bordered on conceit, and I thought myself an uncommon person, parading my schoolbooks through the streets, and swelling with pride when a teacher detained me in conversation, now I grew humble all at once, seeing how insignificant I was beside the Great.

Mary Antin, Russian-Jewish immigrant, who began school in Boston in 1894, At School in the Promised Land, *pp. 52–53.*

The secondary school should grow, not by crowding new studies into its course, but simply by organizing new subjects of instruction side by side with the old ones, as so many new opportunities of culture. No school should have to wait for another school, or be required to follow the example of another school. Nor should a school maintain lines of instruction which the community obviously does not want. What a community wants experiment will soon show. Perhaps the public will grow cool towards a subject because the subject is ill taught. No wholesomer influence can be exerted on the schools than this practical and effectual criticism, expressed by withdrawal of favor from branches not made attractive and interesting by their teachers. Precisely this tonic the schools seem to need. The rigid course is the paradise of inefficiency.

S. Thurber of the Girls' High School, Boston, April 1895, "Rigid Courses versus *Optional Studies," p. 210.*

[T]he teacher . . . must be a sturdy and persistent worker, but he must not be overworked. The schoolmaster who allows his nervous system to be upset and his spirits broken by carrying too heavy and unreasonable burdens, commits a wrong, not only against himself, but also against his school. No remuneration is great enough to compensate a man for loss of health; and no teacher whose blood lacks oxygen or whose nerve centres lack what Dr. Hall calls "euphoria" is qualified to instruct or train a healthy and vigorous youth. The teacher should have time for abundant physical exercise in the open air, and for such recreation as affords him needful rest and pleasure. This is not only his right but his duty. Children are as soft as clay

in the hands of a teacher who possesses an abundance of vitality and good nature. But how many teachers in the village high schools of New England can even approximate such a condition? As a class they are seriously overwrought. They spend their days in the most harassing kind of labor in the school room and their nights in tutoring some ambitious pupil, or in preparing for the six, seven, eight or more recitations that must be conducted the next day. The debilitating effects of such a life are easily discernable. No one should wonder that such teachers are nervous, irritable, and despondent. If young men of ambition and ability are to be induced to enter the small high schools and remain in them, this stress and strain of overwork that depresses the spirits and impairs the health of conscientious and faithful teachers should be removed.

Edward J. Goodwin of Newtown, Massachusetts, May 1895, "The Curriculum of a Small High School," p. 269.

[I]f the village high school does not prepare its pupils for college, the brightest and most ambitious boys and girls are frequently withdrawn and sent away to other schools. This alienates the patronage and, naturally, the sympathetic support of the most influential families of the community and deprives the school of its natural leaders, girls and boys who have inherited intellectual and studious tendencies, and whose attendance would establish the confidence of the community in the school, and exercise a beneficent influence upon other pupils who may be less richly endowed and less aspiring.

Furthermore, to be able to send boys and girls directly from the local high school to college is a source of gratification to any community, and this reacts to the advantage of the school, especially when the graduates return from college and take their places as men and women among those who patronize and support the school.

On the contrary . . . there are weighty reasons why the small high school should not expend its valuable time and strength upon a curriculum designed primarily for pupils preparing for college. The greatest good to the greatest number is quite generally recognized as a sound policy in the management of public schools. If there be one curriculum containing Greek for the few who prepare for college, and another for the many who do not, even if the two curricula are identical in several important subjects, justice cannot be done to the many while so much attention is given to the few.

Edward J. Goodwin of Newtown, Massachusetts, May 1895, "The Curriculum of a Small High School," pp. 275–276.

The thing we need to secure a uniform standard of enforcement by subject is an examining board, authorized to act for a large number of institutions, and conducting through agents appointed by itself examinations all over this country; the examinations being held, not primarily at colleges, unless they are conveniently situated for the purpose, but at railroad centers, and the actual examiners being drawn not only from the institutions represented in the board, but from a great variety of colleges and scientific schools. On the central board there should be some representatives of secondary education. The results should be given by subject for every candidate; and these results might be accepted and used by any college or scientific school in the country, just as that college or school chose. The different colleges would undoubtedly use the results in different ways—one college demanding more subjects for admission than another, or a better record on the same number, or a different selection or grouping of subjects. The actual record of each candidate, as certified by the board, would be taken at its face value wherever it should be presented. In that way we should gradually obtain a uniform standard of enforcement by a method fair to all institutions; and, in my judgment, we should also obtain an admirable instrumentality for promoting uniformity in general, and a closer connection between the secondary schools of the country and the colleges and universities.

Charles W. Eliot, president of Harvard University, February 1896, in College Entrance Examination Board, The Work of the College Entrance Examination Board, *1901–1925, pp. 21–22.*

We are apt to look at the school from an individualistic standpoint, as something between teacher and pupil, or between teacher and parent. That which interests us most is naturally the progress made by the individual child of our acquaintance, his normal physical development, his advance in ability to read, write, and figure, his growth in the knowledge of geography and history, improvement in manners, habits of promptness, order, and industry—it is from such standards as these that we judge the work of the school. And rightly so. Yet the range of the outlook needs to be enlarged. What the best and wisest parent wants for his own child, that must the community want for all of its children. Any other ideal for our schools is narrow and unlovely; acted upon, it destroys our democracy. All that society has accomplished for itself it puts, through the agency of the school, at the disposition of its future members. All its better thoughts

of itself it hopes to realize through the new possibilities thus opened to its future self. Here individualism and socialism are one. Only by being true to the full growth of all the individuals who make it up, can society by any chance be true to itself.

John Dewey, philosopher of education, 1899, The School and Society, *pp. 15–16.*

When we turn to the school, we find that one of the most striking tendencies at present is toward the introduction of so-called manual training, shop-work, and the household arts—sewing and cooking. . . .

If we were to cross-examine even those who are most favorably disposed to the introduction of this work into our school system, we should, I imagine, generally find the main reasons to be that such work engages the full spontaneous interest and attention of the children. It keeps them alert and active, instead of passive and perceptive; it makes them more useful, more capable, and hence more inclined to be helpful at home; it prepares them to some extent for the practical duties of later life—the girls to be more efficient house managers, if not actually cooks and sempstresses; the boys (were our educational system only adequately rounded out into trade schools) for their future vocations. I do not underestimate these reasons. . . . But the point of view is, upon the whole, unnecessarily narrow. We must conceive of work in wood and metal, of weaving, sewing, and cooking, as methods, not as distinct studies of life on its active and social sides. We must conceive of them in their social significance, as types of the processes by which society keeps itself going, as agencies for bringing home to the child some of the primal necessities of community life, and as the ways in which these have been met by the growing insight and ingenuity of man; in short, as instrumentalities through which the school itself shall be made a genuine form of active community life, instead of a place set apart in which to learn lessons.

John Dewey, philosopher of education, 1899, The School and Society, *pp. 22–23.*

As one enters a busy workshop in which a group of children are actively engaged in the preparation of food, the psychological difference, the change from more or less passive and inert recipiency and restraint to one of buoyant outgoing energy, is so obvious as fairly to strike one in the face. Indeed, to those whose image of the school is rigidly set the change is sure to give a shock. But the change in the social attitude is equally marked.

The mere absorption of facts and truths is so exclusively individual an affair that it tends very naturally to pass into selfishness. There is no obvious social motive for the acquirement of mere learning, there is no clear social gain in success thereat. Indeed, almost the only measure for success is a competitive one, in the bad sense of that term—a comparison of results in the recitation or in the examination to see which child has succeeded in getting ahead of others in storing up, in accumulating the maximum of information. So thoroughly is this the prevalent atmosphere that for one child to help another in his task has become a school crime. Where the school work consists in simply learning lessons, mutual assistance, instead of being the most natural form of cooperation and association, becomes a clandestine effort to relieve one's neighbor of his proper duties. Where active work is going on all this is changed. Helping others, instead of being a form of charity which impoverishes the recipient, is simply an aid in setting free the powers and furthering the impulse of the one helped.

John Dewey, philosopher of education, 1899, The School and Society, *pp. 24–25.*

The object of the high school is to take the boys and girls who have reached a certain stage of advancement—at present, those who have acquired a reasonable knowledge of grammar, history, geography, and arithmetic—and to engage their energies in the master of advanced studies which will discipline their several faculties, develop their individual powers, give them a general survey of the inviting fields of knowledge and effort, furnish them with tools and motive power to extend their conquest of the material and spiritual universe to the limit set by their native endowments; withal to excite in them an insatiable thirst, an undying love, for the true as discovered in science, or philosophy, or religion; for the beautiful as disclosed in nature, or literature, or art; for the good as revealed in history or ethics; to enkindle in them, I say, an absorbing passion for the true, the beautiful, the good; the true—the real, our environment material and spiritual; the beautiful—the ideal, to be realized in personal life, in the home, in society, in the nation, in the world; the good—the means of uniting the real and the ideal, the marriage of the beautiful and the true.

William J. S. Bryan, principal of the Normal and High School of St. Louis, Missouri, 1900, in Neil R. Fenske, A History of American Public High Schools, 1890–1990: Through the Eyes of Principals, *p. 15.*

Mr. [Booker T.] Washington distinctly asks that black people give up, at least for the present, three things—first, political power; second, insistence on civil rights; and third, higher education of Negro youth—and concentrate all their energies on industrial education, the accumulation of wealth, and the conciliation of the South. This policy has been courageously and insistently advocated for over fifteen years, and has been triumphant for perhaps ten years. As a result of this tender of the palm branch, what has been the return? In these years there have occurred:

1. The disfranchisement of the Negro.
2. The legal creation of a distinct status of civil inferiority for the Negro.
3. The steady withdrawal of aid from institutions for the higher training of the Negro.

W. E. B. DuBois, professor of history and economics at Atlanta University, 1903, The Souls of Black Folk, *p. 40.*

Until the September of 1903 the lunch problem was a serious menace to the welfare of the school. Some of the pupils brought sandwiches, cake, and fruit from home. Some purchased waffles at a wagon on the street. Some rushed two blocks to a bakery where pie, dill pickles, and cream puffs were sold. Others refreshed themselves at an inconvenient soda-water fountain. Still others patronized a restaurant which it took them five minutes to reach, and where they waited ten before they were served with a repast which they consumed in five in order to get back to their classes on time. The result of these conditions was often, as one student put it, "a pain in the stomach, an ache in the head, a zero in the teacher's class-book, and a great daub of blueberry pie on the shirt waist." The afternoon classes were lifeless; the school building, during the afternoon session, was foul and slippery with remnants of lunch; and the school yard, to say nothing of adjacent streets and lawns, was so bestrewn with paper bags, banana peels, fragments of broken meats, and decadent bones that the residents and owners thereof were shaken by a chronic palsy. . . .

Edwin L. Miller of Englewood High School, Chicago, describing the school's lunchtime situation prior to the September 1903 opening of the cafeteria, March 1905, "The Lunch-Room at the Englewood High School," p. 202.

In a college town in the middle West, not many months ago, I looked down from my hotel window upon a football field in which the teams of two coeducational

This photograph shows the teacher and pupils of a rural Massachusetts school in the first years of the 20th century. The author's grandfather, David Deeley, is seated in the first row, third from the right. *(Author's collection)*

colleges were contending. On the side lines were a host of shrieking young women, and after the game was over the young women of the victorious college marched with the young men in procession down the street, under my window, screaming and waving their banners. If this is what coeducation means, I said to myself, I want none of it. This is coeducation, but coeducation of a crude and vulgar type. It is not the form it necessarily takes. But it certainly will take this form so long as the student body is left free of restraint to work out its own salvation or its own destruction. How to steer between an iron constraint and an unregulated freedom that degenerates into license, is . . . the most difficult of the problems of the coeducational college. The problem can be solved, but only by those who recognize its difficulty and its far-reaching scope, and who are willing to bring to its study not only a calm and clear-headed judgment, an unsubduable patience, an inflexible persistence, but also a tactful and

generous sympathy which never for a moment forgets its own college days.

Edward S. Parsons, Colorado College, May 1905, "The Social Life of the Coeducational College," pp. 388–389.

[T]he first eight weeks in the high school are the most important in the course. The psychological moment has come to endear the pupil to the school, and to put him on such a firm foundation that the floods of discouragement and the winds of bad preparation will not shake him. Never again will he be so impressionable, never again will he slave so willingly, never again will the mere novelty of mastering things hard and dry seem like such a glorious victory. The majority of teachers begin a new subject too rapidly and give the pupils too little time to find themselves. In many cases a third of the class is so far behind at the end of eight weeks that their doom is already sealed. A horse- or a dog-trainer who failed with such a large percentage of animals would be speedily asked to change his occupation.

Reuben Post Halleck, principal, Boys' High School, Louisville, Kentucky, September 1905, "Why Do So Many Pupils Leave the Public High School During the First Year?" p. 555.

Ought a woman to receive a liberal education, or ought she to spend the usual college years in a school for matrimony?

My conviction is all for the college education. Matrimony is only one of a large number of possible occupations for women. In the ministry, in law, in medicine, in teaching, in journalism, in scientific research, in civil engineering, in insurance, in business of many kinds, women have worked successfully and contentedly. Although it will always be true that the greater number of women will elect the domestic career, yet I cannot but think that the superlative fascination of that estate has been by recent writers a trifle overworked. Sentiment aside for the moment, is not matrimony the most precarious business in the world? The material returns—not to mention the vagaries of affection—are notoriously disproportionate to a woman's efficiency. If it be the business of a domestic woman to rear a large family of children, we must acknowledge that her reward in worldly goods is inversely proportional to her success; for with every additional child the same income must be made to reach farther. . . . We must remember that reproduction is too often a vain repetition. Why repeat, until we find something worth while? Indeed, I would almost say that a woman had no business to be a mother until she can demonstrate her ability to be something else.

Kate Gordon, Mount Holyoke College, December 1905, "Wherein Should the Education of a Woman Differ from That of a Man," p. 791.

[F]rom the teacher's point of view, the most frequent and troublesome fault in children is inattention and lack of application. Trying enough to the overworked teacher, no doubt, but from the child's point of view there is something to be said in regard to subjects to which he is required to pay attention. A child's attention is chiefly of the passive or involuntary sort, and active or voluntary attention is a later development. It is easy for a child to attend to the things which interest him, but too often he is required to pay attention to things in which he has no interest whatever. Voluntary attention is a much more complex matter and, even in adults, unstable and dependent upon nervous conditions. It is easily fatigued, and to expect a child to continue a voluntary exertion throughout school hours without an appeal to his natural interests is irrational. . . . Voluntary attention is a complex development involving an effort of will and dependent upon the natural or involuntary attention, and the best educational methods demand a study of children's interests, and an adaptation of the school routine to them, so that full advantage may be taken of the simpler and earlier development.

G. Stanley Hall and Theodate L. Smith, psychologists, 1907, "Curiosity and Interest," in G. Stanley Hall, Aspects of Child Life and Education, *pp. 107–108.*

Many of us feel that, splendid as the public schools are in their relation to the immigrant child, they do not understand all of the difficulties which surround the child—all of the moral and emotional perplexities which constantly harass him. The children long that the teacher should know something about the lives their parents lead and should be able to reprove the hooting children who make fun of the Italian mother because she wears a kerchief on her head, not only because they are rude but also because they are stupid. We send young people to Europe to see Italy, but we do not utilize Italy when it lies about the schoolhouse. If the body of teachers in our great cities could take hold of the immigrant colonies, could bring out of them their handicrafts and occupations, their traditions, their folk songs and folk lore, the beautiful stories which every immigrant colony is ready to tell and translate; could get the children to bring these things into school as the material from which culture is made and the material upon which culture is based, they would discover by comparison that which they give them now is a poor meretricious and vulgar thing. Give these children a chance to utilize the historic and industrial material which they see about them and they will begin to have a sense of ease in America, a first consciousness of being at home. I believe if these people are welcomed upon the basis of the resources which they represent and the contributions which they bring, it may come to pass that these schools which deal with immigrants will find that they have a wealth of cultural and industrial material which will make the schools in other neighborhoods positively envious.

Jane Addams, social reformer, 1908, in Daniel Calhoun, ed., The Educating of Americans: A Documentary History, *p. 423.*

"Because you get paid for what you do in a factory," "Because it's easier to work in a factory than 'tis to learn in school." "You never understands what they tells you in school, and you can learn right off to do things in a factory." "They ain't always pickin' on you because you don't know things in a factory." "You can't never do t'ings right in schools." "The boss he never hits yer, er slaps yer face, er pulls yer ears, er makes yer stay in at recess." "It's so hard to learn." "I don't like to learn." "I couldn't learn." "The children don't holler at ye and call ye a Christ-killer in a factory." "They don't call ye a Dago." "They're good to you at home when you earn money." "Youse can eat sittin' down, when youse work." "You can go to the nickel show." "You don't have to work so hard at night when you get home." "Yer folks don't hit ye so much." "You can buy shoes for the baby." "You can give your mother yer pay envelop." "What ye learn in school ain't no good. Ye git paid just as much in the factory if ye never was there. Our boss he never went to school." "That boy can't speak English, and he gets six dollars. I only get four dollars, and I've been through the sixth grade." "When my brother is fourteen, I'm going to get him a job here. Then, my mother says, we'll take the baby out of the 'Sylum for the Half Orphans."

Chicago teenagers explaining why they prefer working in a factory to going to school, 1909, in Helen M. Todd, "Why Children Work: The Children's Answer," p. 216.

As things stand at present, It is my unwilling judgment that while the factory may become a sweat shop, the average school in the United States to-day is little better than a mental treadmill for the average boy of the working classes after twelve years of age; and the education is so purely formal, so bookish, so ladylike, so irrational and impractical in a word, that it stunts his mind, bewilders his senses and fills him with a dislike for real education and training, which warps him mentally as badly as the factory does physically. Many a boy of this class and age, as our antiquated curriculum stands at present, is better off working six hours a day, in a well-ventilated, thoroughly sanitary workshop, conducted on kindly and intelligent principles, than he would be in the schoolroom droning and day-dreaming over classical absurdities, in which he can find no interest nor profit. The motto of the school is "By books ye are saved." But it is a case of "the letter that killeth." In total, the school is doing more physical damage to our children than the factory.

Woods Hutchinson, physician and writer, March 1909, "Overworked Children on the Farm and in School," p. 114.

The visitor entering one of the New York vacation schools will be struck with the atmosphere of happy relaxation which pervades the class rooms. Systematic, diligent work is carried on, but the children enjoy it so thoroughly that very little discipline is required. The children receive instruction in chair making, basketry, bench work and fret sawing, elementary woodwork, Venetian ironwork, knitting, elementary sewing, dressmaking, millinery and embroidering. They are also instructed in the domestic arts and cooking. The very small children are given kindergarten work.

As a rule, these classes are held only during the morning, and as the session is short the child generally spends the whole morning in one class. At the end of the term the pupils are allowed to take home the things they have made.

Clarence Arthur Perry, urban planner, 1910, Wider Use of the School Plant, p. 7.

The boys were so busy making things, putting themselves into broom-holders, brackets, candlesticks, that represented their ability which they could show to others,—they were so intent on all this that it did not occur to them to annoy their neighbors or the teacher. The girls were so occupied in learning how to make dresses and hats that they forgot to talk loudly or laugh boisterously. When the teacher helped them over a difficult step in their work their faces gleamed with gratitude; when she gave some general directions they all listened intently. On entering the school their countenances reflected the satisfaction felt at home over the fact that they were neither in the street nor under foot in the house impeding the work that had to be done. Aside from the joy of making things, the children were glad to escape from their hot stuffy apartments into the cool, well ventilated school rooms. In a word, both teachers and pupils were happy because they were doing what they liked to do. Teachers taught and pupils attended this school because it was a "school of play."

Clarence Arthur Perry, urban planner, describing a New York City summer school, 1910, Wider Use of the School Plant, pp. 120–121.

The excuse made for not including domestic science in trade schools now existing is that girls do not desire to go into domestic service. It is preposterous that only those girls who are willing to enter such employment should receive this training. For every girl there should be adequate instruction in the subjects that vitally affect the home. She should receive some knowledge of productive processes in general hygiene, decorative art in its relation to the home and domestic science. Society, in order to serve its own ends, should expect each girl to be mistress in her own home, and if industrial training is provided at all, should embody domestic science not as a fitting for remunerative occupation, but as preparation for home-making. When it does not mark a girl as having chosen to be a domestic servant, undoubtedly many will choose such instruction and go out with loftier ideals of a home and with preparation for its responsibilities. The stigma now resting upon domestic science as being something necessary to be understood only by domestic servants should be removed.

Owen R. Lovejoy, secretary of the National Child Labor Committee, June 1910, "Will Trade Training Solve the Child-Labor Problem?" p. 95.

In the city system, school affairs are on the whole well managed, the schools are supervised by trained educators, and are taught by well-educated and professionally trained teachers. The schoolhouses are modern, sanitary, and well equipped with adequate furnishing and facilities for teaching. On the other hand, it is generally true for the United States as a whole that rural schools lack intelligent and economical management, adequate supervision, and efficient teaching. The majority of them are housed in uncomfortable buildings unsuitable from almost every standpoint, without proper furniture or facilities for heating, ventilating, and lighting; without adequate provisions for guarding the health and morals of the children, and with comparatively little equipment for teaching.

The attention of our best educators has during the past half century been devoted to the development of the city school. The country school has been left largely to itself. The development of the city school has in a measure retarded the country school, as the city has drawn, and continually is drawing, the best teachers away from the country. A program, course of study, system of grading, and textbooks have been developed for city schools, all

City schoolchildren benefited from the nearness of museums and other cultural sites. In this picture, some Washington, D.C., students view exhibits at the Smithsonian Institution as part of an 1899 field trip. *(Library of Congress, Prints and Photographs Division, LC-USZ62-4544)*

in large measure for the schools whose conditions caused their development. In too many instances those courses and methods have been thrust upon the country school, which exists under conditions entirely different from those surrounding the city school; it is needless to say that they have proved unsatisfactory.

A. C. Monahan of the U.S. Department of Education, 1913, The Status of Rural Education in the United States, pp. 9–10.

The following extracts from publications of the various State departments of education or from statements of the State superintendents of public instruction referring largely to one-teacher schools . . . contain statements of facts relative to conditions true not only in the State indicated but also in large measure in nearly every other State.

Arkansas.—The State includes 4,796 common-school districts, with 6,295 schools, of which 5,050 are one-room buildings. Of this number, 120 are log buildings. The average value of the one-room school building and grounds is $352. The average cost of maintaining the 6,295 country schools, including the teacher's salary, was in 1911 $286 each. The length of the school year was 100 days. There were 110 schools with 10 or fewer pupils; 179 with from 11 to 16; and 636 with from 16 to 26 pupils. . . .

Illinois.—The State has 10,615 ungraded schools, with an average enrollment of 27 pupils in each school, and an average annual session of 7.5 months. Ten of these ungraded schools were in 1910 in log buildings. There were 99 schools with an enrollment of 5 or less; 568 with 10 or less; and 1,512 with 15 or less. There were employed 3,063 teachers who were teaching in 1910 their first year. In these ungraded schools in that year there were 3,448 teachers who had less education than the equivalent of a complete high-school course. . . .

Iowa.—The State department classifies the rural school buildings as, approximately, 60 per cent "good," 30 per cent "fair," and 10 per cent "poor"; 5 per cent are without suitable and separate outhouses. There were 12,640 one-room country schools in 1910. The State superintendent reports that in January of that year 257 of these had an enrollment of 5 or fewer pupils; 1,814 from 6 to 11; 2,986 from 11 to 16; and 2,453 from 16 to 21. He secured reports from 10,350 of these schools, giving the actual attendance for the best day in the third week of January, 1910. Ten schools reported 1 pupil each; 35 reported 2 pupils each; 73 reported 3 each; 160 reported 4 each, and 244 reported 5 each. There were altogether 522 schools with an actual attendance of 5 or less; 2,498

with attendance of from 6 to 11; 3,127 with from 11 to 16; and 2,168 with from 16 to 21. In these country schools were 4,676 teachers teaching their first year, and 2,500 who began the year with less than 1 year's experience. . . . Owing to the great number of changes in teachers during the year, the average number of months each teacher was employed was, approximately, 5.

A. C. Monahan of the U.S. Department of Education, 1913, The Status of Rural Education in the United States, pp. 27–28.

The four years spent in college comprise the formative period of a man's life. The habits formed and the faculties developed then are the foundation for future usefulness. These four years of college are not an isolated period during which the individual may give himself up entirely to fun and play and after which he may turn suddenly to professional or business endeavor with the guarantee of success. Those who have neglected their economic opportunities always find themselves handicapped in the real competition of life. The community supports a college because its function is to teach men to think, to foster learning, and to add to the store of human knowledge accumulated through the ages. This being the purpose of a college, no such institution can thrive unless scholarship is its main concern. Therefore, through loyalty to college and duty to community, the young men who have the opportunity for a higher education should understand and improve it.

Students come to Harvard with diverse notions as to what they want to do. A great many come to study; a larger number win distinction in the various activities of college life; and, unfortunately, too many intend to enter merely to enjoy the "best time ever." It is well to come to Harvard with the determination to do something; it is better to come with mind set on studies before all else; it is despicable to come to loaf.

D. E. Dunbar, senior at Harvard, 1913, in John Brett Longstaff, ed., Harvard of Today from the Undergraduate Point of View, p. 21.

What working children need is what all children need, but these especially—love from some one who has the time and intelligence to love, work from some one who knows what kind of work will be most possible and useful to them; but, above all, play, music, stories, pictures, and the personality of a teacher who is joyful, tender, intelligent. Discomfort, anxiety, and privation make their faces old at ten years. They stand, little shabby creatures, between the mockery of what our civilization has made of their homes, and the wreckage that machinery and speeded-up industry will make of their lives. Meantime, there is our school here. Would it not be possible to adapt this child of foreign peasants less to education, and adapt education more to the child?

Helen M. Todd, social researcher and writer, April 1913, "Why Children Work: The Children's Answer," p. 218.

Harvard University has great possessions. It has more than twenty-five millions of dollars well invested for yielding a cash income. It has more than eighty acres of land in Cambridge, with numerous buildings of brick and stone. In southwestern Boston it owns three hundred acres of land devoted to agricultural and horticultural purposes, including an admirable Arboretum of over two hundred acres. It has in Cambridge an admirably equipped Observatory, a Botanic Garden and Herbarium, a great Museum of Natural History, Geology, and Archaeology, a Semitic Museum, a Germanic Museum, and laboratories of all sorts for the study of the natural and physical sciences. It has in Boston a Medical School equipped with every facility for teaching medicine and for conducting medical research; and this Medical School is surrounded by a group of hospitals which furnish the Professors of the School with ample and varied opportunities for giving clinical instruction. Associated with this Medical School is a perfectly equipped Dental School. The University possesses good Laboratories for Engineering and Mining, and a large estate at Squam Lake, New Hampshire, which is devoted to the use of an Engineering Camp for three months of the summer. In Petersham, Massachusetts, it possesses two thousand acres of forest, where practical forestry is taught under highly favorable conditions. But the greatest possessions of Harvard University, considered as a permanent place of academic and professional instruction during an indefinite future, are its great collections of books. The three most important libraries are in Cambridge at the central seat of the University—the General Library, for the accommodation of which a new building is now being erected with every possible convenience for the storage and ready use of millions of books; the Law Library, which is certainly the most comprehensive and serviceable in the country, and the two Libraries of Theology, that of the Harvard Divinity School and that of the Andover Theological Seminary, now united under one direction in the new Andover building.

Charles W. Eliot, former president of Harvard University, August 7, 1913, in John Brett Langstaff, ed., Harvard of Today from the Undergraduate Point of View, *pp. 8–9.*

Harvard University undertakes to prepare young men for all the professions, including the traditional liberal professions, all the new scientific professions, and all the higher walks of business. It maintains courses of instruction both elementary and advanced in all subjects of learning, both in subjects for which there is an active demand, and in those which interest but a few students. In 1912–13 it maintained seven hundred and seventy-four teachers, of whom one hundred and forty-two were full Professors. In that year it employed one teacher for every seven students, not counting as teachers preachers, curators, and library officers, or administrative officers. . . .

Harvard University attracts more than four thousand regular students each year, exclusive of Extension students and students in the Summer Schools. Of this total, four-sevenths come from New England. The other three-sevenths are distributed among all the other States of the Union and twenty-nine foreign countries. The foreign countries include eight Eastern countries, Far and Near; and from these countries there came in 1912–13 thirty-seven students. It is an advantage to the University that four-sevenths of its students come from New England; because that is the part of the United States in which good systems of education have been longest established, and in which literature, science, and art have been longest cultivated; but it is also a great advantage to the University that students come to it in large numbers from all parts of the United States and from many other parts of the world. To belong to a selected body of youth representing such a variety of religions, governments, and industrial and social conditions is a useful part of the education of any young American between eighteen and twenty-five. The sons of Harvard come from all parts of the earth, and they scatter to all parts; and wherever they live, east or west, north or south, they can establish connections with other Harvard men, older or younger than themselves, and find in such connections welcome support in their own undertakings and aspirations.

Charles W. Eliot, former president of Harvard University, August 7, 1913, in John Brett Langstaff, ed., Harvard of Today from the Undergraduate Point of View, *pp. 9–10.*

[S]uccessful teaching is represented by the development of not less than a certain minimum of intelligence and efficiency in the pupils. This, of course, commits me to the stand that the school is primarily an institution of learning, or, rather, an institution for the training of the mind and the hand, which is evidently out of harmony with the doctrines of large numbers of present-day educators, who are apparently firmly pledged to the stand that the school is intended primarily as an institution for the training of character, while learning is only of secondary importance. Therefore, in a great many quarters, the suggestion that the efficiency of a school must be gauged, in the first instance, by the intelligence and efficiency of the pupils will be looked upon as entirely too realistic, and forthwith ruled out of court. To prove that I am in earnest, I need only call attention to the fact that no topic is more widely discussed in educational circles to-day than that concerning the ways and means of estimating the efficiency of a teacher, and to the further fact that, while all sorts of methods are suggested, few who value their reputations seem to have the courage to say that the efficiency of a teacher must be judged by what her pupils can do.

J. M. Rice, educational researcher, 1914, Scientific Management in Education, *pp. 254–255.*

The building is 81 feet, 6 inches long, 54 feet, 6 inches wide, and one and one-half stories high, with basement. The basement is faced with Hytex brick, the main story is first-class pressed brick, while the roof is of galvanized steel shingles.

In the basement in the southeast and northeast corners are two rooms, each 21 by 23 feet, which can be used for classrooms or laboratories. In the other corners are the toilet rooms, the building being equipped with a modern sanitary incinerating system. In the center of the basement is the furnace room. This also includes a small room in which is located an electrically-driven fan forcing heat and ventilation to all the rooms.

On the main floor are all the classrooms, consisting of primary and intermediate rooms to the north, main high school in west central, with adequate recitation room in the southwest and the grammar room in southeast. There are cloakroom facilities and a large corridor also on this floor. In each room is a large wall case 58 inches wide by 69 inches high for books and apparatus. Between the grammar room and the high school recitation room are folding doors, making it possible to throw the room together for meetings of various kinds.

Above all is the assembly room, built in what might be called the attic. It is a nice room, 31 by 36 feet, well lighted. A new piano has been secured and paid for by popular subscription. All seats are new except in two

rooms, and they were purchased only last year. The building is electric lighted throughout. Just to the south of the school building is the house this district has provided for the principal.

Missouri Department of Education, description of the consolidated school building at Bigelow, Missouri, 1915, in Sixty-sixth Report of the Public Schools of the State of Missouri, *p. 38.*

Several causes combined to make popular a movement to reorganize our school system in such a way as to provide for the junior high school. In the first place, there was a desire on the part of many patrons that the work in the seventh and eighth grades be more efficiently done; in the second place, there was a demand for the introduction of more work of a vocational nature in the upper grades and high school; and, in the third place, the grade schools were crowded and, to relieve the grade buildings of the seventh and eighth grades, helped materially to solve the problem of crowded conditions in the grade schools, as well as provided additional room for vocational work in the high school. And hence, when the arguments that are usually advanced in favor of the junior high school were clearly set before the people, the idea at once met with such popular approval that the voters willingly voted the board the necessary funds with which to provide the room required to carry out the plan. An addition, which complete is costing about $25,000.00, was added to the high school building, a structure which was erected some four years ago at a cost of $35,000.00. This addition has provided ample room for several new courses as well as for the junior high school work.

Our junior high school, then, is housed in the same building with the senior high school, a fact which so far as I can see, has, under local conditions at least, more advantages than disadvantages. . . .

So far as possible the two schools are separated, with exception of the laboratory courses, the seventh and eighth grades being confined to their part of the building. Each school has separate assembly exercises except on Friday when they occasionally assemble together.

G. W. Diemer, superintendent of schools, Excelsior Springs, Missouri, 1915, in Sixty-sixth Report of the Public Schools of the State of Missouri, *pp. 56–57.*

In grades seven and eight we condensed reading, language, grammar, and spelling into one English course for each grade. Writing and drawing were included in one course, alternated by days. The same arrangement was made for music and manual training. The conventional four-year history course in the upper four years was organized into a three-unit course, beginning in the ninth grade. . . . We eliminated German from the program.

This reorganization enabled us to introduce courses in music, manual training, and bookkeeping with the same number of teachers formerly employed in the upper six grades. We offer music one day and manual training the next in the seventh grade. The same arrangement holds for the eighth grade. The boys take manual training while the girls take drawing. Both boys and girls take music. We have a sophomore manual training class composed of both boys and girls and a junior-senior music class of boys and girls. The bookkeeping course is offered to the juniors and seniors. The music and manual training are taught by the same teacher (a man) while the bookkeeping teacher has also most of the mathematics.

The content of the writing, drawing, mathematics, geography, hygiene, and history courses has so far remained much the same as it formerly was. We are working out a definite system of library reference work for the seventh and eighth grade history and English courses. More laboratory work has been done in connection with the seventh grade geography-hygiene course. We plan to terminate this course at the end of the first semester and substitute general science for it. We also plan to terminate the eighth grade arithmetic course at the end of the first semester and introduce something in the way of general mathematics.

A. L. Threlkeld, superintendent of schools, Unionville, Missouri, describing the curriculum of the upper six grades, 1915, in Sixty-sixth Report of the Public Schools of the State of Missouri, *p. 55.*

I think without doubt the thing that has resulted best this year, while an outgrowth of several years' work, was our harvest home festival. This was started four years ago with the purpose of encouraging the boys of the county to learn to raise corn, and to awaken an interest in the parents toward the capability of their children and a greater interest in educating them to fill their place in our great working world. Four years ago there were about two dozen people present at the meeting. Three years ago about 200; two years ago, 500, and last year 1,000 were estimated to be present, and this year we had between 4,500 and 5,000. It was so great in every way that we had to hold it at the fair grounds as the only place large enough. Almost every school in the county had on exhibit the work of its

children. Everything from paper cutting in the first grades to the splendid map drawing, water-color painting and very fine needle work in the eighth grade. Vegetables of all kinds were exhibited, each school having a booth of its own to decorate and fill as it might plan. We had very little money to use for this purpose, but used what we could get, giving over a hundred dollars in premiums and equipment. . . . The double quartette from our State Normal School at Kirksville aided us in our musical program, and with the local band we furnished music which I think was appreciated by all. Our purpose in this "big day" was to awaken the country people to the work that our children are doing, and we think that this was accomplished in a large measure. Numerous offers of help have come in for our festival for next year, and the children are now working for next year's exhibit, so a number of teachers report. . . . The teachers, children and parents are waking up, and that is a long stride toward better conditions in our individual districts.

Helen F. M'Kee, superintendent of schools, Clark County, Missouri, 1915, in Sixty-sixth Report of the Public Schools of the State of Missouri, *pp. 358–359.*

A new department of Geography has been organized, thus enabling the school to take care of this phase of instruction in a way hitherto impossible. The advanced courses in this department are proving very interesting and attractive. The department of Agriculture and Biology have been strengthened by the addition of another faculty member, thus enabling each subject to be organized into a department of its own. A new course in the department of Home Economics including Home Economy and Sanitation is being given this year which is required of all students seeking the Elementary Certificate or Diplomas. This course is proving highly efficient and satisfactory. It deals with fundamental issues of the home, the school and the individual. Much additional equipment has been added to the departments of Science, Manual Training and the department of Education, thus rendering them more efficient in their work.

During the past year this school has changed its conception of student teaching in the Training School to the extent that all student teachers give an entire day for one quarter to their practice in the Training School. They thus secure a fundamental and satisfactory type of experience, being placed in charge of a room or grade and made responsible for all work of the day. They may not actually teach the entire day, but when not teaching, they are concerned with conferences, preparation of material and other duties with immediate contact with the Training School.

In the Department of Education we have added courses in Educational Sociology and Primary-kindergarten Methods. There are yet a few departments not properly organized in the school which we hope to have before the close of another year. This will then give the school an equal rating of work with any other complete school.

Ira Richardson, president of the Fifth District Normal School, Maryville, Missouri, describing progress at the school, January 6, 1915, in Sixty-fifth Report of the Public Schools of the State of Missouri, *p. 122.*

[The elective system] is based on the valid principle that different individuals have different aptitudes and abilities, and was designed to give those aptitudes freer play. But with the consequent gain there follow dangers. Our old, fixt course had one great asset: it taught pupils to fight and conquer obstacles in such a way that they knew the joy of difficulties overcome; the elective system frequently shows an easy way round the obstacle, allows the pupil to follow the line of least resistance, and leaves him weak and without the spirit of determination. We find naturally capable boys choosing "snap" courses, intended for those of weaker mental caliber, and shunning those which mean hardest work and highest achievement.

Furthermore, the offering of election to pupils of high school age presupposes ability to choose wisely. This assumption, particularly in cases of pupils just passing from elementary to secondary school, is at least a matter of doubt. . . .

My final criticism of the elective system is that unless under good control it may develop "rolling stones," pupils with no concentration, shallow and without definite aim.

Carleton E. Preston of the English High School, Boston, March 1916, "Are Our Schools Hitting the Mark?" pp. 277–278.

The practical value of the commercial high school course calls for consideration. What business men most wish is young men to come into their businesses who are prepared to be intelligent apprentices, who have some facility which will enable them to take hold in the business and to develop themselves with this as a starting point. The chief value of the commercial high school course to the future business man is in the orientation which it gives him. By such a course he may be inducted into business. He has an interest in it and comes to its problems with an intelligent devotion to their solution. Too often the business man has felt that business was only a last resort, that a profession or some other calling would have been more honorable but that business is a cruel necessity. The commercial high school course as conceived by this paper creates an attitude of respect towards and an interest in the business calling and teaches a man to like the particular thing which he has to do in life.

Cheesman A. Herrick, president of Girard College, Pennsylvania, a school for orphaned boys, March 11, 1916, "Commercial Education in Secondary Schools," p. 260.

The following are some of the main assimilative activities of the public school:

a. The school at once throws the children of various nationalities into mutual relationships. This breaks up the standards and habits of any one nationality and in order to progress the child finds that he must adopt a common way of thinking and acting, which means that he must adopt the American standard. . . .

b. The public school teaches the children the English language which enables him to associate with Americans and various other nationalities, even outside of the school and his own district.

c. The schools tend to break up hostilities between nationalities. The teacher prevents hostilities in the schoolroom and this does away with strife on the playgrounds.

d. It teaches American traditions and the history of our institutions under which comes a growth of patriotism. Race ties are broken up and a social solidarity is secured.

e. The public schools by the introduction of manual training, not only give the child some idea of American industrial methods, but teach him that manual work is here the universal rule and not a stamp of inferiority.

Frank B. Lenz of the Young Men's Christian Association, San Francisco, May 1916, "The Education of the Immigrant," p. 475.

CHAPTER FIVE

Scientific Management
1917–1929

"I am a citizen of America and an heir to all her greatness and renown. The health and happiness of my own body depend upon each muscle and nerve and drop of blood doing its work in its place."[1] During World War I, in obedience to state laws, public school students throughout the United States recited a lengthy loyalty pledge that began with these sentences.

By declaring war on Germany on April 6, 1917, the United States had for the first time involved itself in a major conflict among European nations. Seeking to create oneness of thought and effort, the federal government and many in society tried to gag those voices insisting that the United States was fighting this war for commercial interests, or that the nation needed first to solve its problems at home.

U.S. colleges and universities, which traditionally encouraged the free exchange of ideas, took steps to silence dissenters. In 1917, Columbia University president Nicholas Murray Butler made headlines when he fired Professor Henry W. L. Dana, an expert on Russian theater, for working with peace organizations, and Professor James M. Cattell, a noted psychologist, for protesting the draft. Cattell insisted, "I have done nothing except exercise the constitutional right and fulfil the duty of a citizen to petition the Government to enact legislation which I believe to be in the interest of the nation." He warned, "Professors in every university are terrorized so that they dare not exert their influence for peace and good-will."[2]

Public schools required their employees to sign oaths of allegiance, and many communities removed from classrooms any textbooks containing passages that might present Germany in a positive light or be construed as supporting autocratic government. The California Council for National Defense dealt with a music book containing German folk songs and other pieces labeled "from the German" by cutting out the offensive pages. "Never before has there been such a widespread and determined effort to make . . . schools the means of inculcating the ideals of democracy," concluded Thomas H. Briggs, a professor of education at Columbia University Teachers College.[3]

German became a dirty word, as Americans tried to rid their culture of Germany's influence and their schools of the German language, the "language that disseminates the ideals of autocracy, brutality and hatred," according to the California State Board of Education.[4] In summer 1918, Washington became the first of several states to ban German classes in its public high schools, despite Commissioner of Education P. P. Claxton's appeal to reason. "The fewer hatreds and antagonisms that get themselves embodied in institutions and policies the better it will be for us when the days of peace return,"[5] he said. A number of teachers of German, accused of trying to replace English with German as the predominant language in the United States or of promoting German imperialism, began teaching Spanish instead, and Spanish gained popularity as an academic subject.

The Government's Wartime Curriculum

The war that curbed instruction of some subjects also invigorated curriculums as teachers incorporated world events into lessons in history, civics, English and science. With Claxton's reluctant support, the U.S. Bureau of Education cooperated with the Committee on Public Information, a propaganda agency created by President Woodrow Wilson, and the National Board for Historical Service, a group of war-supporting history professors who had offered their services to the nation, to draft a war-study curriculum for the public schools. The lessons created and distributed by these groups explained the war as the Wilson administration wanted the public to understand it and promoted patriotism, heroism, and democratic ideals.

Elementary school pupils learned that the Americans fought to prevent the Germans from overrunning the United States, burning homes, and murdering citizens. They read about Joan of Arc, the Marquis de Lafayette, William Pitt, and other heroic figures from the Allied countries, and they studied the differences between autocratic government in Germany and democracy in their own country. The war-study curriculum listed ways for children to help the national effort, such as hoarding their pennies to buy thrift stamps, eating less candy and otherwise conserving food, taking care of their clothing and shoes to save cloth and leather, and practicing healthy habits to avoid using medical resources. The curriculum also instructed teachers to model an appropriate attitude toward the war: "Above all, the teacher should in her whole personality express an enthusiastic and patriotic interest in her topic; the contagion of her spirit will be of more value than the facts she is trying to impart."[6]

Some 800,000 secondary school students and teachers received a survey of the war and its roots that had been prepared for recruits in training camps. Written by Samuel B. Harding, a professor of history at Indiana University, it was a propaganda piece rather than an accurate historical account, portraying the Germans as cruel, militaristic, and totally responsible for the war. There was room for neither ambiguity nor opposition in the curriculum for secondary schools, as in the one for elementary schools.

At the request of the Committee on Public Information, the U.S. Bureau of Education compiled a mailing list that included virtually every school in the United States. The government used this list to distribute information to communities via their schoolchildren. The list allowed the U.S. Food Administration, directed by future president Herbert Hoover, to pass out literature on food conservation, as part of a national effort to ensure adequate provisions for the men fighting overseas and divert rail transportation from domestic to wartime needs.

During World War I, physical education became a standard offering at public schools. By 1918, 11 states—North Dakota, Ohio, Idaho, Delaware, Maryland, Rhode Island, New York, New Jersey, Illinois, Nevada, and California—had made it mandatory, largely in response to the alarming condition of military recruits. The army had rejected nearly half the 2.7 million men aged 21 to 31 examined during the first wartime draft because they were physically or mentally unfit.

Military drilling for boys, previously available at a few public and private secondary schools, became a common high school course offering as well. Schools intended this regimen to improve physical fitness, moral development, and military preparedness. The skills taught varied widely and included marching in formation, tactics, signaling, marksmanship, map reading, and field engineering. While the United States was at war, one in seven high school boys underwent military training, although only one state, New York, made it mandatory for all boys ages 16 to 19.

Instruction in agriculture, industrial skills, and home economics for students age 14 and older received greater emphasis in public schools following passage of the Smith-Hughes Act, which Wilson signed into law on February 23, 1917. This federal legislation made funds available to states that created a board for vocational education and submitted a plan for a statewide vocational-education program. The states were required to file annual reports with the newly established Federal Board for Vocational Education, in which they summed up the work accomplished in the previous year and explained how the government's money—which had to be matched with state funds—had been spent. A state received funds to pay teachers of agriculture, home economics, and industrial arts and to educate teachers for these subjects, although Congress limited support to schools under public supervision. Within 10 months of the bill's passage, 41 states had created agricultural courses with federal aid, 32 had established industrial programs, and 29 had begun courses in home economics.

Helping to Win the War

Schoolchildren engaged in extracurricular activities in support of the war effort. They bought and sold war bonds and thrift stamps and gathered books for soldiers' libraries. Both girls and boys knitted scarves and socks for the men in uniform, and these were collected and sent overseas by organizations such as the Young Men's Christian Association (YMCA) and Junior Red Cross. In school kitchens, sewing rooms, and industrial shops, students canned food and made patients' garments, surgical dressings, furniture, and other items needed in military hospitals and training camps and on the battle lines. Older students serving as volunteers for civic groups drew posters, addressed envelopes, and did filing and other clerical work.

In cooperation with a government agency, the U.S. School Garden Army, 1.5 million children helped feed the nation by raising vegetables on plots carved from school property, backyards, golf courses, tennis courts, and vacant lots. As of July 10, 1918, children wearing armbands emblazoned with the letters U.S.S.G. had turned 20,000 unproductive acres into crop-yielding land in the after-school hours and on Saturdays. Their efforts attracted hundreds of thousands of parents to the home-gardening movement, including 5,200 mothers in Salt Lake City alone.

The U.S. Department of the Interior, in its evaluation of this project, reported that 300,000 of the children's gardens failed, thereby calling into question the effectiveness of the School Garden Army in adding to the food supply. The project had other benefits, though. "One and one-half million children were given something to do last summer," said J. H. Francis, director of the U.S. School Garden Army, in 1919; "something that helped carry the burden of their country in the struggle for freedom, something that helped them to build character, and something that appealed to and developed their patriotism."[7]

Tending schoolyard gardens let children feel that they were contributing to winning the war, but with the loss of 1.1 million farm laborers to the armed forces

JOIN THE
UNITED-
STATES
SCHOOL
GARDEN
ARMY

ENLIST NOW

Write to The United States School Garden Army,
Bureau of Education, Department of Interior, Washington, D.C.

A government-issued poster promoted the U.S. School Garden Army during World War I.
This organization encouraged schoolchildren to raise vegetables in support of the war effort.
Library of Congress, Prints and Photographs Division, LC-USZC4-10321)

and war industries, the nation needed real help raising its crops. Much of this aid
came from high school boys. Schools in rural sections of the United States excused
youths in 1917 and 1918, in both spring and fall, to serve as volunteers with the
U.S. Boys' Working Reserve, an agency of the U.S. Department of Labor, which
enrolled 250,000 boys before the war's end. So important was the boys' assistance
to the economic well-being of one state, North Dakota, that on May 16, 1917, the
state board of education passed a resolution requiring schools to postpone opening

in the fall until after October 1. In 1918, more than 7,000 boys in another state, Michigan, harvested a beet crop worth $5 million.

In many states, the boys completed brief courses at local colleges of agriculture before beginning their work; elsewhere they received instruction from retired farmers, farm-implement dealers, or cooperative extension agents. County agents also recruited and trained volunteers from other nontraditional sources of farm labor, including women and businessmen. African-American agents in southern states organized Uncle Sam's Saturday Service League, whose members pledged to work on farms throughout their states until the war ended. Agricultural agents, employed by 2,435 counties in 1918, also taught farmers how to increase their production of wheat and other grains, meat, poultry, and eggs. County home economists showed women how to can and dry fruits and vegetables and make substitutions for foods that were scarce. In Allegheny County, Pennsylvania, for example, home economists gave more than 125 demonstrations of food preservation to 6,000 women. These efforts contributed to a 15 percent decline in U.S. food consumption during the war, without rationing, and a surplus large enough to feed U.S. troops and send food to postwar Europe.

The nation also faced a shortage of school personnel as male teachers and principals signed up to serve overseas. Both the U.S. Bureau of Education and the U.S. Employment Service created agencies to place teachers at schools that needed them, and they encouraged retired teachers to return to work. In addition, many school districts waived longstanding rules against hiring married women and welcomed back teachers who had left the profession to marry and have children.

Some of the older high school boys also joined the fighting force, but a larger number of high school students withdrew to take paid employment, filling jobs left vacant by men in uniform, as schoolchildren had done during the Civil War. High wages attracted many, and rising prices induced others to contribute to their fami-

Extension agents demonstrate food preparation in 1926. *(Library of Congress, Prints and Photographs Division, LC-USZ62-114695)*

lies' welfare. School officials in New Bedford, Massachusetts, reported that 23 percent of the high school student body withdrew during the academic year ending in June 1917, and of these 62 percent went directly to work. Most losses were smaller, from 1.4 percent to 7 percent of the high school population. Quite a few districts actually reported increased enrollment because of the continued rise in popularity of secondary education, but nearly all the new students were girls.

Educational Efforts for the Armed Forces

With the coming of war, the U.S. government initiated ambitious training programs to meet a sudden, great need for skilled workers.

The Students' Army Training Corps (SATC), a program directed by the Committee on Education and Special Training of the U.S. War Department, prepared officer candidates and technicians to meet various needs of the military. Most of the participants were volunteers, men age 18 or older who were in college or who met college-acceptance criteria. The uniformed young men undergoing training lived for two months in units of 200 to 2,000 at colleges, universities, and professional and vocational schools. As soldiers of the U.S. Army, they received tuition, board, and a private's pay of $30 a month.

By August 1, 1918, 144 schools in 46 states and the District of Columbia housed 52,025 soldiers pursuing 35 different professions or trades. In addition to their other studies, all men in the SATC completed a required course called War Issues that was based on a list of 100 questions provided by the National Board for Historical Service. Like the public school curriculums that the group developed, this overview of 19th- and 20th-century European history painted an entirely negative portrait of Germany.

Subject to military discipline and a call to active duty that could come at any time, the men adhered to a strict daily regimen such as that imposed at the University of Colorado, where reveille sounded at 6:45 A.M. It was followed by mess at 7:00 and drill from 7:30 to 9:30. The officers-in-training then attended classes until noon, when they broke for mess, and continued their classes from 1:30 to 4:40 P.M. They devoted the hour from 4:30 to 5:30 to exercise, attended mess at 6:00, enjoyed a free hour from 6:30 to 7:30, and studied under supervision from 7:30 to 9:30. They heard the notes of taps at 10 P.M.

College-based SATC programs, like other military and civilian educational efforts, felt the impact of the 1918–19 influenza pandemic, which killed 675,000 Americans and was deadliest for those age 20 to 40. SATC trainees had just arrived at Middlebury College in Vermont, in October 1918, when army officers discovered that several were ill with influenza. Twenty-six cases developed within two days, and two fraternity houses became infirmaries. As the number of cases reached 100, an academic building also housed the sick. Public health officials placed the college under quarantine, instruction halted for almost a month, and the army postponed the examination and induction of more men. Physicians and nurses from nearby towns cared for the ill recruits, and all but two recovered.

While the army trained officers at colleges and universities, naval recruits took a wide variety of industrial courses. In the electrical schools at the Brooklyn Navy Yard in New York and the Mare Island Naval Shipyard in California, men learned to operate and repair steam engines, internal-combustion engines, and generators; at the Norfolk, Virginia, Navy Yard, others learned to be shipwrights, ship fitters, painters, and plumbers. At bases along the East and West Coasts, navy men practiced clerical skills, musicianship, and aeronautics. "The man who does not wish to go to school ought not to knock at any door in the naval service," stated Secretary of the Navy Josephus Daniels.[8]

The government provided more than 100 types of vocational training, such as automobile repair, carpentry, telegraphy, typewriting, and gardening, to the wounded men convalescing in military hospitals. Any man capable of limited duty and equipped with a skill who could replace an able-bodied man behind the lines made one more soldier available for combat. Although many of the wounded returned to the front, many others were eligible for discharge. It was the responsibility of the Federal Board for Vocational Education to reeducate disabled veterans who were unable to return to their former occupations, to give them an employable skill in civilian life.

In the months leading up to U.S. entry into the war, German submarines sank more than a thousand U.S. and Allied commercial vessels, severely impairing the shipping industry. On April 16, 1917, the federal government established the Emergency Fleet Corporation (EFC), a temporary agency within the U.S. Shipping Board, to repair and equip for commercial use ships owned wholly or in part by corporations or citizens of enemy nations that had been seized in U.S. waters and ports. The EFC also had the responsibility for building new ships and dry docks and was given jurisdiction over private shipyards.

Facing a shortage of mechanics and other laborers with knowledge of shipbuilding, the EFC immediately increased its workforce by drawing thousands of skilled and semiskilled workers from related trades and putting them through intensive six-week courses in various aspects of shipbuilding. The fact that in October 1918 the EFC called for 60,000 workers in the Philadelphia district alone reveals the great scope of the need for skilled labor.

National Goals for High Schools

On November 11, 1918, the warring nations signed an armistice, and in the months that followed, the United States emerged as a political and economic power. Young Americans were coming of age in a changing world, one in which U.S. citizens would tackle difficult problems at the local, national, and international levels. The workplace had become more complex, with sophisticated machinery replacing manual labor, yet in 1918 only about one-third of the children who began elementary school entered high school, and only a third of these students graduated. At the same time, more and more fathers commuted from suburban homes to big-city offices and were therefore largely absent from their children's lives, and urbanization continued to strain the bonds of extended families. It seemed to many educators that children and adolescents had lost key supports as they developed mentally and emotionally.

Deciding that it was time for the nation to reassess its goals for high schools, the National Education Association (NEA) appointed the Commission on the Reorganization of Secondary Education, which in 1918 published a list of seven objectives, its "cardinal principles" of education for students ages 12 to 18. These included, first, "Health," which encompassed instruction in good health habits and safety as well as physical education; second, "Command of fundamental processes," or instruction and practice in reading, writing, arithmetic, and oral expression; third, "Worthy home-membership," which the commission defined as development of the qualities that enable a person to contribute to family life, such as appreciation of the arts, interpersonal skills, and a willingness to assume responsibility; fourth, "Vocation," or the ability to earn a living and get along with coworkers; fifth, "Civic education," or loyalty to the community, concern for its welfare, and awareness of social agencies and institutions; sixth, "Worthy use of leisure," or the ability to use one's free time in ways that refresh the mind and body and offer opportunities for growth; and seventh, "Ethical character," which the commission defined as the cooperative spirit and moral values essential for achieving the previous six objectives.[9] As educators throughout the nation adopted these seven objectives, they contributed to the standardization of the high school curriculum.

School Consolidation

By 1920, when high school enrollment totaled 2.2 million, all the states had passed compulsory education laws, and more than 85 percent of the young people required to attend were enrolled in school. Education for the younger generation had growing public support. Not only did technological advancement demand an educated workforce, but also schooling furthered the Americanization of the immigrant population and curbed child labor. State governments became protectors of children's right to education through such measures as hiring truant officers, gathering school census data, and basing financial aid to schools on attendance figures.

Despite the growth of towns and cities, 70 percent of schools were of the one-room, rural variety. This concerned U.S. Bureau of Education officials and state school superintendents, because one-room schools were expensive and inefficient to operate, and they lacked the modern equipment and specialized classes available at graded town and city schools. They were also poorly supervised and failed to attract well-qualified teachers. "It is well known to all school board members that capable young women with high school education and two years of professional training, which should be required of any one teaching in an elementary school, cannot commonly be hired to teach in the remote rural school," reported researchers in educational administration from the Teachers College at Columbia University in 1919.[10]

The quality of instruction in one-room schools also worried the urban college professors, writers, ministers, and business people who were behind the Country Life movement, which was an effort in the early 20th century to stem the flow of rural people to towns and cities, especially in the Midwest. Many in the Country Life movement had themselves grown up on farms, and they subscribed to the agrarian ideal, the belief prevalent in North America since the time of Thomas Jefferson that the family farm nurtured democratic values. As paved roads, automobiles, telephones, and radios made country people more aware of city customs and morals, rural life appeared increasingly dull and old-fashioned to farm youth seeking jobs, intellectual challenges, and cultural enrichment. The Country Life movement endeavored to forge a new kind of rural community, one that combined the best of city and country living and would entice the brightest and most talented youths to stay on the farm.

Educational leaders and Country Lifers alike saw the consolidated school as a means of achieving their goals. If several districts pooled their resources to support one larger school instead of separate small ones, then the population benefited from state-of-the-art facilities, graded classes, better teachers, and an expanded curriculum matching anything offered in a city.

A shining example was the Unionville Consolidated and Vocational School, which opened in Chester County, Pennsylvania, in September 1923, with 700 elementary and high school students. This two-story brick building replaced 16 one-room schools, one two-room school, and one four-room school. It featured 21 classrooms, a gymnasium that converted to an auditorium, flush toilets, electric lighting, and laboratories for instruction in chemistry, physics, biology, and agriculture. The cafeteria

Students in all grades, from kindergarten through high school, attended the Greenbank Consolidated School in Pocahontas County, West Virginia, one of the largest consolidated schools in the United States when it was photographed in October 1921. *(Library of Congress, Prints and Photographs Division, LC-DIG-nclc-04373)*

was equipped to serve 700 hot lunches daily. Many of the pupils traveled to school on "auto trucks," or buses provided for this purpose, but in spring, when thawing snow and ice turned the unpaved roads to mud, they rode in horse-drawn buggies to shelters along one of the few macadam roads, where the auto trucks picked them up.

Proponents of the consolidated school at Unionville hoped that the modern, sanitary building would attract a more experienced, less transient teaching force to the region, and that the improved opportunities for learning and the stimulation provided by a larger student body would induce more students to stay in school and graduate. The academic curriculum offered adequate preparation for the minority of young people going on to college, but agriculture and homemaking constituted vocational training, because most of the students would one day be farmers or farmers' wives.

Consolidated schools gradually replaced one-room schools in the Midwest and elsewhere, although not without opposition from farmers. Cost was a concern, both the potential added expense of transporting daughters and sons to and from school, and the threat of higher taxes to support a more ambitious educational system. Many rural people resented losing control of the district school to professionals, and some objected to the forced integration of young people from common schools that previously had been segregated by religion, ethnicity, or economic level.

Private Support for Schools for African Americans

Modern, consolidated schools were luxuries impossibly out of the reach of most African Americans, especially those living in the rural South. Their children continued to attend dilapidated, inferior schools, where low salaries attracted minimally qualified teachers. White male teachers in one southern state, Alabama, earned $431 in 1917, on average, and white female teachers earned $363. In the same year, black male teachers in Alabama earned $161, and black females earned $152. Of

These employees of the Julius Rosenwald Fund posed for a photograph around 1916. *(Library of Congress, Prints and Photographs Division, LC-USZ62-134343)*

the 2,551 African-American teachers required to hold state certificates, the great majority—1,802—held the lowest of four possible grades of certification.

The desire for educational opportunities for the young was a major reason for the relocation to northern cities of approximately 250,000 African Americans annually during World War I. People moved to find jobs in industry and escape the South's brutal racism, but northern schools drew them as well. Even if these schools were segregated by custom rather than by law and located in economically depressed parts of town, they were better than the ones the people had left behind.

Meanwhile, private philanthropic groups supported most secondary schools for African Americans in the South and worked generally to improve the education of southern African Americans. The Jeanes Fund, founded by Anna T. Jeanes, a wealthy Quaker from Philadelphia, sent vocational teachers to schools for blacks in the South. In the academic year ending in June 1918, these teachers visited 5,717 schools in 14 states. In addition to their regular teaching duties, they conducted classes in sanitation and hygiene and organized gardening and homemaking clubs. The Julius Rosenwald Fund, formed in 1917 for the benefit of humankind, built schools for African Americans throughout the rural South, and the Phelps-Stokes Fund, working through the U.S. Bureau of Education, helped these schools improve their curriculums and record keeping. This agency also established two university fellowships for the study of racial problems.

Deteriorating Conditions at Indian Boarding Schools

During the 1920s, reformers protested federal policies that kept many Indians living in poverty and allowed non-Indian speculators to acquire reservation land. They aimed harsh criticism at the federal boarding schools, which had degenerated since the start of the 20th century. In 1921, Congress cut appropriations for food and clothing at these schools by 25 percent, and further cuts followed, resulting in the children devoting increasing amounts of time and energy to keeping their schools up and running. Children cooked meals, washed dishes, sewed uniforms, laundered clothing and linens, and repaired buildings. Meanwhile, they ate a diet deficient in calories and nutrients, and they slept in crowded dormitories where tuberculosis, measles, and trachoma (an eye infection that can lead to blindness) spread easily.

Typical of these institutions was the Rapid City Indian School, established by the U.S. Bureau of Indian Affairs in 1898 for the assimilation of Lakota people from South Dakota, Montana, and Wyoming. The students, in grades four through 10, spent half the day on academic work and half in vocational training, which for the girls meant sewing the boys' trousers and operating heavy laundry equipment—dangerous work that violated child labor laws in many states. Two girls lost fingers while operating the school's mangle (mechanical clothes wringer).

In one ordinary year, 1920, 38 boys and 12 girls ran away from the Rapid City school, knowing that if captured they would endure severe punishment. At the very least, runaways had their heads shaved and their ankles chained together. Some teachers forced them to march on the school grounds until they had covered the same distance they had run away, and then placed them in solitary confinement. Nearly all Indian boarding schools had locked rooms or outlying buildings where rule breakers were incarcerated.

In 1926, Secretary of the Interior Hubert Work commissioned the Institute for Government Research, an independent nonpartisan group, to look into federal management of Indian affairs. The investigators spent seven months examining records and visiting Indian reservations as well as agencies, clinics, and schools that served the Native population. They published their findings in 1928, a year when more Native American children were enrolled in public schools than in government institutions. Titled *The Problem of Indian Administration,* this book was often called the Meriam Report, after its principal author, Lewis Meriam.

The report called for improvement of services provided to Indians, better protection of Indians' property, and more involvement of Indians in overseeing their affairs. The section on education criticized the discrepancy between the vocational curriculum offered in many boarding schools and the work available on reservations, where most of the students would later live. Why teach boys to operate printing presses and make shoes, the authors asked, when Indians have no paper and generally wear moccasins? In addition, the report stated, "The Indian children taken away from families and communities got no training in Indian family life, and many of them never had any experience in white family life. Thus the moral force of traditional community opinion was seriously weakened if not destroyed."[11] The schools were creating a generation of young Indians who felt at home in neither culture.

The investigators also faulted the severe punishments administered in the schools and the meager, monotonous food that was served. At one school they inspected, the Rice Station Boarding School in Arizona, the children had black coffee, bread, and syrup for breakfast every day, bread and boiled potatoes for dinner and supper, and a quarter cup of milk with each meal.

Overall, boarding-school administrators ignored the current thinking in education and social work. The investigators therefore favored sending elementary school-age children to reservation day schools instead of boarding schools. They urged the Bureau of Indian Affairs (BIA) to abandon the Assimilation policy and adopt a curriculum that would prepare children to function in both the Indian and predominant cultures. They called for the hiring of better-qualified teachers; the serving of adequate, nutritious meals; and the cessation of child labor. Their recommendations would influence federal Indian policy in the decade to come.

The Mental-Testing Movement

During World War I the U.S. Army administered intelligence tests to approximately 1.75 million incoming soldiers. Heading the Committee on the Psychological Examination of Recruits, and therefore overseeing this effort, was Robert M. Yerkes, a Harvard psychologist and one of the developers of the group test that was used. The Stanford-Binet test, designed to be administered to one subject at a time, was unsuitable, although Lewis M. Terman, its developer, also served on the committee. Ostensibly screening the men to find the best candidates for officer training, the psychologists welcomed the opportunity to gather intelligence data on a large population.

The draftees included a significant number of immigrants from southern or eastern Europe and African Americans, young men who generally had grown up in poverty and had had little or no schooling, so the psychologists administered two tests, labeled Alpha and Beta. The Alpha test included written instructions, whereas the Beta test employed pictures and required no reading. The examiners scored the tests according to a point scale and then converted the point scores to letter grades, from A through E. At one extreme, an A indicated "a high officer type when backed by other necessary qualities"; at the other extreme, an E suggested that the subject was unfit for military service.[12] Based on these tests, Yerkes's committee concluded that the average adult American male had a mental age of 14, and some immigrant groups and African Americans had lower average mental ages. Many people found these results disconcerting, because the advocates of testing insisted that attempting to educate a person beyond his or her mental age was futile. Rarely did anyone consider the possibility that a test might be culturally biased.

The army stopped testing recruits once the war ended, but the belief that tests could measure intelligence took root in the academic community during the prosperous 1920s. Lewis Terman was among those who recommended regular testing of all schoolchildren in order to place them in the appropriate grade and in a track for fast, slow, or average learners. "All the pupils in the fourth grade and beyond should be given a test by the group method every year, and those whose scores are either very high or very low in the group examination should be given a Binet test," Terman advised, adding, "it is highly desirable that every pupil be given a mental test within the first half-year of school life."[13] Researchers and marketers filled the demand by developing and selling tests of intelligence, reading ability, and skill in arithmetic. Terman, Yerkes, and others authored the National Intelligence Tests for the group testing of schoolchildren, which were first published in 1920, and grew wealthy from the royalties they earned.

Testing had its critics, of course, among them the journalist Walter Lippmann, who insisted that the idea of a fixed mental age resulted from wishful thinking rather than objective science. "If the impression takes root that these tests really measure intelligence, that they constitute a sort of last judgment on the child's capacity, that they reveal 'scientifically' his predestined ability, then it would be a thousand times better if all the intelligence testers were sunk without warning in the Sargasso Sea," Lippmann said.[14]

One problem that educators hoped to remedy with testing was the number of children held back at the end of the school year when their classmates were promoted to the next grade. To see boys and girls three or four years older than their classmates was common in the first decades of the 20th century. In Toledo, Ohio, for example, more than one-fifth of pupils enrolled in the public elementary schools in the year ending in June 1923 had repeated one or more grades.

Oakland, California, addressed this problem by instituting a three-track system for its public-school students in 1918, and Berkeley, California, did the same in 1920. Before long, similar plans had been adopted throughout the United States, and children found themselves placed in a track based on test results or according to the teacher's judgment of their ability, as in the Susan B. Anthony School in Rochester, New York, which in 1922 was "face to face with the foreign problem in seemingly its most intensive form."[15] In other words, nearly all its pupils were the children of Italian immigrants. Immigrant children in Rochester and elsewhere often ended up in classes for slow learners.

Children who achieved high scores on intelligence tests earned the label "gifted." By 1920, classes for gifted children were up and running in Cleveland, Los Angeles, and other cities, and the Columbia University Teachers College was preparing teachers for them.

At this time, the states had begun taking responsibility for the education of children who were intellectually or developmentally disabled. In 1918, Wyoming appointed a state director of special education, and the Massachusetts State Department of Education assumed oversight of schooling the developmentally disabled and the blind. J. E. Wallace Wallin, a professor of clinical psychology at Miami University in Ohio, called for respectful treatment of children in special classes when speaking before the Department of Special Education of the Ohio State Teachers Association in 1923. "[T]he practice of applying the terms 'feeble-minded,' 'mentally defective,' 'imbecilic,' and 'moronic' to the children in the special classes of special schools," Wallin said, "should be abandoned."[16] Yet the students championed by Wallin continued to face discrimination. By 1929, 23 states had legalized the involuntary sterilization of the developmentally disabled, and approximately 7,000 people had been surgically sterilized as a result.

A Modern Educational System Takes Shape

During the First World War, both public schools and institutions of higher learning adapted their programs to support the national cause. In the decade that followed, the educational system moved toward uniformity, with elementary and secondary schools attempting to train students according to their abilities and needs. There were public and private efforts to school people with physical and mental disabilities and classes created for the intellectually gifted. Effective methods of student accounting encouraged regular attendance.

State certification requirements and the founding of college departments of education elevated the teaching profession so that, typically, elementary school teachers had completed courses at normal schools and high school teachers had graduated from college. The College Board, which in 1925 tested approximately 20,000 applicants at 316 examination centers, had secured its place in the system as well. In June 1925, more than 600 readers gathered in New York City to review and grade the tests.

There were shortcomings, to be sure, but this generally was the state of American education when the stock market crash of October 29, 1929, signaled the collapse of the U.S. economy. Over the next decade schools, like other institutions, would face great challenges.

Chronicle of Events

1916–1917

- Twenty-three percent of high school students in New Bedford, Massachusetts, withdraw from school; 62 percent of these go to work.

1917

- Columbia University fires Professors Henry W. L. Dana and James M. Cattell.
- In Alabama, on average, white male teachers earn $431 per year, white female teachers earn $363, black male teachers earn $161, and black female teachers earn $152. Of the 2,551 black teachers in the state, 1,802 hold the lowest level of certification.
- The Julius Rosenwald Fund is established; it will build schools for African Americans in the rural South.
- *February 23:* President Woodrow Wilson signs the Smith-Hughes Act, providing federal support to the states for vocational education.
- *April 6:* The United States declares war on Germany.
- *April 16:* The U.S. government establishes the Emergency Fleet Corporation (EFC) to repair and equip for commercial use enemy ships that have been seized.
- *May 16:* The North Dakota Board of Education passes a resolution requiring schools to delay opening in the fall until after October 1, to allow boys to help with the harvest.
- *Spring:* High school boys first are excused from school to serve as volunteer farm laborers for the U.S. Boys' Working Reserve.

1917–1918

- Vocational teachers employed by the Jeanes Fund visit 5,717 schools for African Americans in 14 states.
- The U.S. Army administers intelligence tests to 1.75 million recruits.

1918

- Physical education is mandatory in 11 states.
- More than 7,000 boys in Michigan harvest a beet crop worth $5 million.
- The number of counties employing agricultural extension agents reaches 2,435.
- The Commission on the Reorganization of Secondary Education of the National Education Association publishes its cardinal principles of education.

- Oakland, California, institutes a three-track system in its public schools.
- Wyoming appoints a state director of special education.
- The Massachusetts State Department of Education assumes responsibility for educating the developmentally disabled and the blind.
- *July 10:* Children in the U.S. School Garden Army have cultivated 20,000 acres of previously unproductive land.
- *August 1:* The army is educating 52,025 officer candidates at 144 institutions of higher learning.
- *summer:* Washington becomes the first state to ban the teaching of German in public high schools.
- *October:* The EFC calls for 60,000 workers in the Philadelphia district.
- *November 11:* The armistice ending World War I is signed.

Two smiling New York City girls hurry to greet their classmates on the first day of school, ca. 1920. *(Library of Congress, Prints and Photographs Division, LC-USZ62-70859)*

1920
- High school enrollment totals 2.2 million.
- Compulsory education laws are in place in every state.
- More than 85 percent of the young people required by law to be in school are enrolled.
- One-room schoolhouses account for 70 percent of U.S. elementary schools.
- Fifty children—38 boys and 12 girls—run away from the Rapid City Indian School.
- The National Intelligence Tests, intended for group testing of schoolchildren, are published.
- Berkeley, California, institutes a three-track system in its public schools.
- Cleveland, Los Angeles, and other cities offer classes for gifted students.

1921
- Congress cuts by 25 percent appropriations for food and clothing for children in Indian boarding schools.

1922
- Children attending the Susan B. Anthony School in Rochester, New York, are placed in academic tracks according to a teacher's assessment of their potential.

1922–1923
- More than 20 percent of pupils in the Toledo, Ohio, public schools have repeated at least one grade.

1923
- The Unionville Consolidated and Vocational School opens in Chester County, Pennsylvania.
- J. E. Wallace Wallin calls for an end to the use of derogatory names for students in special classes.

1925
- The College Board tests approximately 20,000 applicants at 316 examination centers.

1926
- Secretary of the Interior Hubert Work enlists the Institute for Government Research to investigate federal management of Indian affairs.

1928
- More American Indian children attend public schools than federal Indian schools.
- The Institute for Government Research publishes its findings as *The Problem of Indian Administration* (The Meriam Report). The researchers call for an end to the Assimilation policy and a curriculum in Indian schools that equips students for the lives they will lead.

1929
- Involuntary sterilization of the developmentally disabled is legal in 23 states; 7,000 people have undergone forced surgical sterilization.
- *October 29:* The stock-market crash occurring on this date signals the start of the Great Depression.

Eyewitness Testimony

In our zeal to teach patriotism, we are often teaching disrespect for the history and the traditions that the ancestors of the immigrant parent had their part in making. This often means disrespect for the parent himself. Some teachers, with a quick appreciation of the difficulty the family is meeting in the sudden change of national heroes and standards, are able to avoid mistakes of this sort by making it clear that, for example, the story of the achievement of Italian nationalism is a thrilling one to us and that we are all indebted to the Bohemians because of their long struggle for religious liberty. A little Greek boy who is a friend of mine explained, "My teacher likes me because I tell her stories of the Athens." Whether Miss O'Grady really cared for the stories he told of the city from which so few of our Greek immigrants come and whose history and traditions are yet so intimately loved by them all, I cannot say; but I do know that both the school and Athens occupied a different place in the eyes of the boy because of the seeming interest of the teacher.

Grace Abbott, pioneering social worker, 1917, The Immigrant and the Community, *pp. 226–227.*

This eagerness on the part of the foreign parents to have their children learn to read and write in their native language is difficult for many Americans to understand, but the explanation is simple. In addition to the cultural value of knowing two languages, it should be remembered that the peculiar isolation of the mother keeps her from learning English and often leaves her in almost complete dependence on her native language; and so for the sake of the family life, a knowledge of that language by the children is necessary. The devotion to their own language is strongest among the Bohemians, Poles, Slovaks, Lithuanians, and others who come from countries in which, because they have struggled for years to resist the efforts of the government to stamp out their language and to substitute German, Russian, or Magyar, freedom of language has come to be regarded by them as an evidence of liberty. Not to teach their children the language for which they and so many of their friends have made great sacrifices would be a supreme act of disloyalty.

Grace Abbott, pioneering social worker, 1917, The Immigrant and the Community, *pp. 230–231.*

The present war has brought a peculiar opportunity to American teachers of European history, and at the same time it has laid upon them a great responsibility. Their subject is more vital to Americans than ever before. By proper selection and emphasis of topics, they can instruct their pupils so that they will have a better understanding of present-day conditions and therefore of the reasons why the United States is taking part in the war. Through the pupils they will reach many parents, and if the teaching is sound, they may be an effective factor in the country's political development. Two dangers, in particular, must be avoided. In the first place, the war has not changed history; the methods of treatment and presentation that have proved to be sound in the past are not necessarily to be abandoned. In the second place, and as a corollary of the first, the teacher needs to be on guard against the perversion of history in the interest of any particular creed, whether that creed be pacifism or militarism, nationalism or internationalism. He should not follow the German practice which has used the teaching of history in the public schools as a means for inculcating "love of the reigning Hohenzollern family" and the "need of a strong navy."

National Board for Historical Service, 1917, Opportunities for History Teachers, *pp. 9–10.*

For many years old-fashioned textbooks have been criticized for giving too much space to war and military operations, and so crowding out the less spectacular but at least equally important achievements of peace. These objections became still stronger as the belief prevailed that history is not wholly a record of governments, whether at war or peace, but that it should take more account of other forms of social activity, including industry, education, and religion. War history was considered objectionable not only because there was too much of it relatively, but also because it seemed to be so presented as to stimulate the war spirit, perpetuating popular prejudices, and suggesting to each succeeding generation that kind of patriotism which consists largely of hatred for some other nation. . . .

War can not be left out of American history, but that part of the record should be approached with a different perspective and a different set of questions from those of the old textbook histories. The simple problems of strategy may be suggested, and typical battles, like Yorktown and Gettysburg, may be studied in detail for the purposes of illustration; but after all the citizen, young or old, needs to think most of what happens before the Army and Navy get to their stations and what has to be done at home to enable them to fight at all.

National Board for Historical Service, 1917, Opportunities for History Teachers, *pp. 17–18.*

The one agency which touches the life of all the country people is the rural school. But this school has not kept pace with modern progress. It has not adjusted itself to changed conditions. It is not rendering its fullest service. The course of study must be changed to help solve the farmers' economic problems, to point the way to a new era of health and sanitation in country communities, to place before boys and girls new ideals of citizenship. The rural school must have a more definitely recognized and recognizable purpose, a more direct connective with life problems and activities.

The social problems of the country are large, and here, too, the rural school must do its part. We shall always have a country-minded people living in the country. Any agency which does not recognize this fact must fail to get results in the country. In the country school must be sympathetic understanding and foresight; a knowledge of boys and girls, and of men and women and the forces which move them and lead to success or failure. Inside this school there is a reflection of the spirit and life of the community. The shortcomings of parents, the petty jealousies and sympathetic friendships of the small community, the impulsiveness of adolescence, the foolishness of youth, the rowdyism so difficult to control, the extremes of rural independence, the capacity for doing things, the willingness to respond to wise leadership—all these are a part of the school and must be reckoned with for good or for evil.

Henry Jackson Waters, president, Kansas State Agricultural College, 1917, in Marion G. Kirkpatrick, The Rural School from Within, *pp. 5–6.*

With the country at war and with President Wilson asking of all colleges and universities a most thorough rallying to the cause of democracy, this is not the time when the much-abused term, "academic freedom," can be invoked to cover offenses which, if they were wide-spread, would mean the downfall of all Governmental activity and the defeat of the great cause of the people. Columbia has led the way in a clarion call to the patriotic, and the actions of its officers in the matter of the dismissal of the professors is the logical outcome of a grave situation, in which it behooves all to remember that their sacred duties are of more value in promoting freedom and democracy than are their "rights."

Editors of the Philadelphia Ledger, *1917, in "Columbia's Dismissed Professors," p. 24.*

Some of life's best lessons are taught by the simplest and most obvious illustrations, as in the case of the sluggard who was advised to observe the unrecognized ant; and so we may say that if any man will observe the work of the colored demonstrators or supervising teachers—men and women whose services have been almost thrust upon the State by private generosity—he can not hesitate for a moment in deciding what is the next step in the development of our work among the white children. These colored leaders have increased teachers' salaries; they have also lengthened the term and have brought into the schools so many new children that the taxpayer has found the per capita cost materially reduced.

Virginia superintendent of public instruction writing at the close of the school year ending in 1917, in Thomas Jesse Jones, Recent Progress in Negro Education, *p. 6.*

One of the first weaknesses a stranger would detect in the high-school system in South Carolina would be our small number of four-year schools in places amply able to support them, and the attempt of a few small places to support four-year schools with too few pupils and too little money. The number of the latter class is small, but of the former class there are too many. To maintain a four-year school there are three things necessary: Enough pupils to justify its existence, enough money to employ the teachers and to equip the school, and a community that appreciates such a school.

From the point of view of attendance it seems reasonable to hold that any three-year school with as many as 75 pupils is well able to maintain a fourth-year class. Seventeen of our schools last year had enrolled 1,816 high-school pupils going out with a three-year high-school education. Admittedly, those going to college are not prepared as they should be, and certainly those leaving school are entering life with meager equipment. . . .

The people of this State have had so little practical experience with well-equipped four-year high schools that they do not appreciate their value. For long years we have known nothing higher than a three-year high school resting upon a seven-year elementary school, and the people have come to look upon such a school as ideal. In fact, one occasionally hears the argument that such a school is enough for any people. . . . If the study of pedagogy has taught us anything, it has convinced us that we can not force the growth of the human plant. It requires time for the human plant to grow and mature. When we consider the comparatively small number of men and women with a college education, and the even smaller number with a four-year high-school education, we begin to understand the limitations of our people intellectually, industrially, and economically. South Carolina's having more college graduates than four-year high-school graduates furnishes amusement for everybody but us.

W. H. Hand, state inspector of high schools for South Carolina, 1918, in Thomas H. Briggs, Secondary Education, pp. 5–6.

To anyone familiar with the conditions that obtain in many places throughout the State, it is simply amazing to see the absolute indifference of the people as to the qualifications of those who teach their children and fleece them of their money. Men and women innocent of any charge of education, without any aptitude to teach, and without any experience are put in charge of schools, in the face of the fact that they are to have little, if any, supervision. It is safe to say that there are in South Carolina 500 white teachers holding legal certificates to teach who could not make a grade of 50 per cent on the studies of the eighth and ninth grades of our public schools, if examined as rigidly as are the pupils of these grades in the best schools of the State. It would be unsafe to say how many white teachers are holding certificates granted on all manner of pretexts, from long experience (successful or unsuccessful) down to two weeks' enrollment at some summer school. Notwithstanding the fact that almost anybody can get a certificate to teach school, there are in the public schools not fewer than 100 white teachers drawing salaries without any semblance of legal authority to teach. Some of them have been teaching from 10 to 20 years without a certificate of any kind.

W. H. Hand, state inspector of high schools for South Carolina, 1918, in Thomas H. Briggs, Secondary Education, p. 22.

In many ways the high school is doing excellent work, for which both principal and teachers deserve full credit. There are, however, in my judgment, some weak points that ought to be strengthened. One weakness is in the organization of the high school. The general attitude of faculty and students seems to be that children are sent to the school to do a certain amount of work, and that the teachers are there for the purpose of testing the children to find out whether or not they have done their work and to grade them accordingly. Both parties seem to feel that when each has performed his work individual responsibility ends. It does not seem to be the prime motive of the high-school faculty as a whole to bring out the best that is in the pupil, but rather to permit the delinquent to eliminate himself from his class or school through repeated failures. The character of this kind of discipline is negative and repressed instead of positive and directive. . . . Throughout the high-school course there should

be continuous growth in self-reliance, willing and cheerful obedience, and closer cooperation between the student body and faculty, and also like relations should exist between the principal and faculty.

Superintendent of schools, Williamsport, Pennsylvania, 1918, in Thomas H. Briggs, Secondary Education, p. 32.

While, in any circumstance, war is a most deplorable thing, in my judgment it has been a most wonderful factor in the development in the secondary school of the spirit of citizenship, honor, integrity, and loyalty. The various war activities which the schools have been doing during the year have been wonderful factors of education. There is no other one influence which has so emphasized the responsibility of even the high-school boy or girl as a citizen, and demonstrated beyond the question of a doubt the fact that no individual can live in a community and be part of the community without being responsible to the community, and that no person, even a high school boy or girl, can live in modern society as an individual entirely independent of the other individuals in the community.

Superintendent of schools, La Crosse, Wisconsin, 1918, in Thomas H. Briggs, Secondary Education, pp. 34–35.

Some one has well said that one of the great defects of American life to-day is slouchiness—slouchiness of physique, slouchiness in the appearance of our towns and villages, slouchiness in the application of mind and body to the tasks of the day, slouchiness in discipline and responsiveness to orders in cooperative efforts of all kinds. Compulsory military training enforces on a boy promptness in obeying orders, and he must apply himself to a given task until it is satisfactorily finished. His mental and physical being must always be at the best. All of these phases are being introduced and emphasized when military training is taught. It must be introduced in a spirit of civic service, and the cadets must be taught that this is a part of their training for citizenship.

Our experience with military training for several years in the Rochester High School leads me to say that it is one of the very best courses that we have offered. The discipline of the school is very much better, the boys are seeing the value of self-control and decent restraints. The cadets are interested in civic problems and their responsibilities. Citizens of Rochester will testify to the value of this training for their boys. I have yet to hear a complaint on the cadet organization in the Rochester High School from the parents of the boys taking this work. . . .

Finally, I wish to say that here is an organization in which the physical welfare of practically every high-school boy can be cared for. Football takes care of about 15 or 20, basketball about 10 or 15, baseball about 12 or 13; but in drill, setting up exercises, and rifle practice, every high-school boy may compete. Where the cadet movement has been tried, it is a success. . . . Those who have tried the experiment can speak from experience, others can only guess, and those who oppose the movement are mostly guessers and mothers who did not raise their sons to be soldiers but want them to be mollycoddles.

State superintendent of public instruction for Minnesota, 1918, in Thomas H. Briggs, Secondary Education, *p. 41.*

All the arguments that have prevailed in peace times for vocational education of secondary grade are intensified by the war. Every school that has facilities for trade training or can secure such facilities has an opportunity to serve the Nation in a definite way and with a sense that a permanent service is being rendered from which the community will later benefit many times over. The need for skilled workers in every occupation is felt to-day as never before. Every school that can teach agriculture, either on a school farm or by the home project plan, or both, owes it to itself and to the community to do it. Home economics for girls offers a similar unexampled opportunity.

U.S. Bureau of Education, January 1918, Secondary Schools and the War, *p. 1.*

[T]here are several things which we have come upon recently which seem to those of us who have not been wise to be discoveries. The first is that we have a great body of our own people, five and a half millions, who can not read or write the language of this country. That language is English. And these are not all of foreign birth. A million and a half are native born. The second is that we are drafting into our Army men who can not understand the orders that are given them to read. The third is that our man power is deficient because our education is deficient. The fourth is that we ourselves have failed to see America through the eyes of those who have come to us. We have failed to realize why it was that they came here and what they sought. We have failed to understand their definition of liberty.

To be an American is not to be the embodiment of conceit as to all things that are fundamental in America, or to be satisfied with things as they are or to let things drift. Germany has made herself a composite, compact, purposeful nation by methods of education as well as by authority. We can make ourselves a composite, purposeful nation and impose no authority other than the compel-

ling influence of affection, sympathy, understanding, and education.

Franklin K. Lane, secretary of the Interior, April 13, 1918, in Americanization as a War Measure: Report of a Conference Called by the Secretary of the Interior, and Held in Washington, April 13, 1918, *pp. 18–19.*

If you will suppress or prohibit the teaching of German, or any other foreign language—you can include all of them—below the high school, that is one step; and then when you do this, require the educational forces and the schoolbook companies to get out German American textbooks that shall not advertise the Kaiser and kaiserism and the royal family. I doubt if there is a man here that has read the textbooks used in his own State in teaching the German language. I have, and when I read them I wanted to get a gun and go right to the trenches regardless of age or distance. It is a part of the demoralization of American life and has been for the past 40 years. . . .

They are undermining the hearts and souls of the little boys and girls on our farms, not in the cities only, but everywhere else. I can take you to religious schools in which there is nothing taught but German. The religious preacher who preaches in German is perpetuating discord for the United States, and the reason he does it is because he will not learn English and does not want his people to learn English; if they learned English, he would be out of a job.

We could throw German out of a good many of the public schools except for the good-hearted board of trustees that dislikes to throw a nice lady out of the business of teaching German. We have not got to the place where patriotism overrules affection.

Lafayette Young, Sr., chairman, Iowa State Council of Defense, April 13, 1918, in Americanization as a War Measure: Report of a Conference Called by the Secretary of the Interior, and Held in Washington, April 13, 1918, *p. 34.*

We have one public school in one district in our State where there are but two pupils, while within a stone's throw there is a German school having 33 pupils, teaching nothing but German. Of the 339 teachers investigated, less than 2 per cent are certified, and in nearly all instances, with respect to these graded and private schools that come in such competition with our public schools, they drive many of them out. As a rule, though not entirely without exception, but as a rule, they train the children up to the sixth grade, and do not bring them to the eighth grade, where they could enter the high school. Of 379 teachers investigated, 350 were Germans. In three counties where

German schools predominated the German national hymn was generally sung until our State Council of Defense protested. In 100 of these schools the American national hymn, up to 30 days ago, had never been sung. It needed this war to uncover the situation in which our country is rapidly drifting. We have in our State passed many years ago a measure locally known as the "market law," that was passed at the behest of the German Alliance. That law requires that whenever 12 patrons of a school district shall indicate a certain foreign language to be taught the chosen one shall be taught, and the school board has no choice. The result of that is that the German language is taught generally throughout our public schools. . . .

To-day our legislature is in special session. A few days ago the house, without a dissenting vote, passed a bill to repeal that so-called market law. It is absolutely necessary that we protect ourselves from this private grade school, as well as to provide that there shall be nothing but the language of the country taught in the public graded schools.

Richard L. Metcalfe, member, Nebraska State Council of Defense, April 13, 1918, in Americanization as a War Measure: Report of a Conference Called by the Secretary of the Interior, and Held in Washington, April 13, 1918, *pp. 38–39.*

We have organized an appeal to the patriotism of the people of the State. It has not been necessary to call the legislature together. We appealed to the Germans to stop German in their private schools. We appealed to the Lutheran ministers to stop it in the parochial schools, and we have succeeded in doing that without resorting to the rule of force. We have felt that this was the wise way. We treat fairly the men of foreign birth and German parentage; we draw them to our country in this way. If we do not succeed by an appeal to reason, then would be the time for force, but in this great contest for democracy reason and patriotism should be the first recourse.

Robert L. Williams, governor of Oklahoma, April 13, 1918, in Americanization as a War Measure: Report of a Conference Called by the Secretary of the Interior, and Held in Washington, April 13, 1918, *p. 56.*

The crisis through which we are now passing has called our attention to the weakness and the dangers that spring from our neglect of the education of our own people and the proper instruction of those who come to us from abroad. The Secretary of Agriculture is sending out millions of dollars worth of bulletins, urging farmers to produce more food and telling them how to do so; but two and a half million farmers can not read a word of them, and nearly twice as many read with such difficulty that they make little or no use of these bulletins. We are drafting men into the Army who can not understand a word of the commands, and others who can not read any order, direction or sign, or make any memorandum of anything which they are told or which they see. Until April of last year such men were not admitted into the Army for the reason that it requires an unusual amount of time to drill and train them, and the further reason that most of them can not be made into good and intelligent soldiers. The first draft brought more than 40,000 of them, and in every cantonment one is told the same story of the difficulty of training them, their inefficiency, and the attempts to shift them from one command to another.

P. P. Claxton, U.S. commissioner of education, April 13, 1918, in Americanization as a War Measure: Report of a Conference Called by the Secretary of the Interior, and Held in Washington, April 13, 1918, *p. 60.*

If an alumnus of even the most recent years should suddenly find himself on the Vanderbilt campus, he would rub his eyes in complete bewilderment as he saw the changes that have taken place in the University this year. He would find West Side Row, once the center of University life but so long depleted except for a student here and there living in isolation, now the home of Company C—a jolly, vigorous group of American soldiers. He would find Kissam Hall, with all its rooms and hallways freshly plastered and painted, filled from top to bottom, with the men of Company B, and the dingy old dining hall transformed into an attractive mess hall and study hall for all the companies. Strangest of all, he would find the top two floors of Wesley Hall crowded with the members of Company A—a crowd somewhat different from the theologues of former years.

The alumnus would be even more surprised to see the contrast between the life heretofore and that now led by the 500 students who make up the unit of the Students' Army Training Corps on the West Campus. Called from their cots at 5:45 to setting up exercises at 6:00, to breakfast at 6:30, to drill from 7:15 to 9:00, to retreat at 5:30, to supper at 6:00, and to study hall from 7:30 to 9:30, they have all the appearance of men living in an officers' training camp. It would even seem that the college has been transformed into a camp, with its men in khaki, now parading along the reconstructed roads of the campus, now drilling on Dudley Field, now marching in squads to their classrooms.

"The Students' Army Training Corps: Entire University Reorganized as Army Post—Soldiers in Khaki March to Class," November 1918, p. 5.

The insistence on English as a prerequisite to Americanization is one thing, but the sudden and radical suppression of all foreign languages by city or State command is another, and is likely to defeat the very ends that are sought for. Presenting American ideals and customs is one thing, but attempting to *command* immediate and utter forgetfulness of the old country is another, and perhaps the very way to insure in this country unassimilable foreign groups after the model of those existing in such countries as Austria, Hungary, Russia, and Germany where repression has marked the treatment of alien groups. The normal course of Americanization in many parts of the country with respect to English has so far been from the uni-lingualism of the immigrant to the bilingualism of the second generation, to the uni-lingualism (English) of the third generation. Whenever the process is slower, there is the likelihood that there is maintaining itself a distinct racial unit that may be holding too vigorously to all of its foreign habits and customs. Such a state of affairs demands the attention of immigrant and welfare experts. An analysis may prove that a great deal of responsibility for it may rest on the American of older generations who by his indifference and social exclusiveness has thwarted the initial impulses toward Americanization. It is difficult to see, however, how this normal process can be greatly accelerated without detriment to the immigrant and to his new country. Competent observers have remarked the deterioration that is evident in that immigrant who has contemptuously stripped himself overnight of all the customs and habits of his old country, for in their stead he has too frequently appropriated a shoddy Americanism of the streets. The problem that confronts those who would deal intelligently with the immigrant is how to transmute the real value that the foreigner brings with him into the new Americanism. The common assumption that the foreigner has nothing to lose and everything to gain in the transition; that he has nothing of himself, his

Members of the Students' Army Training Corps stationed at Vanderbilt University, in Nashville, attend a lecture in 1918. *(Vanderbilt University Special Collections and University Archives)*

background, his country to give in exchange for what he receives, makes both him and the new country losers.

J. H. Van Sickle, John Whyte, and W. S. Deffenbaugh of the U.S. Bureau of Education, 1919, Public Education in the Cities of the United States, *p. 7.*

I have been asked repeatedly concerning the attitude the Portland schools will take regarding the teaching of German and French. Some have asked if we expect to do away with the former and increase the work in the latter. Now, it is well known that Americans are deficient in language study. Europeans have been stimulated to understand the tongues of their near neighbors; but separated as we have been by great oceans, we have lived on without feeling the need of mastering any language save our own. But now comes the present stimulus. We are concerned as never before in our national life with events and developments in Europe. We wish to gain for ourselves the fine literature, art, and science of the Old World. We confidently trust that a time is near at hand when all nations will be united in a compact of enduring peace; and when such a time comes we all shall need to know the languages of other nations. The boys and girls in the high school will be the leaders of the coming age. They must be prepared to meet the requirements at that time. Spanish must be learned, French must be learned, German must be learned, and learned with more enthusiasm than ever before.

L. R. Alderman, superintendent of schools for Portland, Oregon, 1919, in J. H. Van Sickle, John Whyte, and W. S. Deffenbaugh of the U.S. Bureau of Education, 1919, Public Education in the Cities of the United States, *pp. 8–9.*

[Our] enthusiasm for education will necessarily be colored by the experiences through which we have passed, and will reflect the new spirit of patriotism and service. Education must continue to provide for culture and self-development, but from now on it must do more. It has been shown that it is possible for education to develop efficiency of the most rigorous and exacting type, and at the same time to generate idealism and nobility of motive. Even the educational program of our training camps, which many thought of only in terms of inexorable military discipline and short cuts to well-defined objectives, made definite provision for the humanistic element—the "morale" of the troops.

It has been discovered that education can be vocational *and* cultural; henceforth we shall not be satisfied with education that is not both. The new point of view

that seems to be making definite headway suggests again the essential unity of the thing we call education.

William T. Bawden, specialist in industrial education, U.S. Bureau of Education, 1919, Vocational Education, *p. 26.*

In the past this country has suffered and been handicapped by the lack of engineers, scientists, and skilled mechanics, and took no adequate action. During the war the point was reached where measures for remedying this lack became an imperative necessity, and hence schemes for vocational and technical training were developed on an unheard-of scale. We came to realize that we must make a more determined effort to secure for a much larger proportion of our people a serviceable amount of technical and scientific training. In the accomplishment of this purpose we must vitalize the work of the elementary and secondary schools, as well as the higher engineering and scientific schools, and stimulate them to do their part in this great program.

William T. Bawden, specialist in industrial education. U.S. Bureau of Education, 1919, Vocational Education, *p. 27.*

[I]n some sections of the State the Negro is not receiving for the education of his race the direct school taxes that he contributes. To fail to grant him this amounts to confiscation. Segregation of funds or taxes for the two races is undesirable, but let us not take from the negro, by throwing all tax money into a general fund, what he is clearly entitled to. Surely this includes a just share of State taxes, a just share of corporation taxes, all fines that his race pays, and the indirect school taxes that he pays as renter and as laborer in helping to produce the wealth of the State. In dealing with this question we must learn to apply the same standards of honesty and fairness that we use in dealing with the different white schools and white communities. Only through the exercise of justice and fair play may we expect justice and fair play in return, and as a result of this, good feeling and good citizenship.

Louisiana Department of Education, 1919, in Thomas Jesse Jones, Recent Progress in Negro Education, *p. 14.*

It is obvious to anyone who knows the school situation in Delaware or elsewhere that a teacher who is required to teach children from the first to the eighth grade can give relatively little time or attention to any one group or to any individual. It is customary to find from eighteen to thirty recitation periods per day in these schools. The usual length of recitation is from five to ten minutes. The teacher has literally no time to teach the children, and not enough time even to hear them recite what supposedly they have been studying during the greater part of the day, without attention or guidance from the teacher.

Children work to best advantage when approximately the same age groups and those of the same intellectual attainment are put in classes together. The one room rural school, because of the range of work to be covered, often places children varying widely in age or in attainment in the same class. In the larger school, with the better grading of pupils, every pupil has a better chance to advance as rapidly as his intellectual equipment and his industry permit.

George D. Strayer, N. L. Engelhardt, and F. W. Hart, Department of Educational Administration, Teachers College, Columbia University, 1919, Possible Consolidation of Rural Schools in Delaware, *p. 3.*

Education will be more expensive wherever children are given better education. Instead of the dreary day during which the pupil has had only thirty or forty minutes with the teacher, there is substituted in the consolidated school an opportunity for instruction multiplied by anywhere from two to eight times. Instead of a very restricted course of study consisting almost entirely of the three R's, with a very minimum of geography and history, the pupil in the consolidated school should have opportunity for music and drawing, for work in the manual and household arts, and should, above all, learn, because of the instruction which he received from a superior teacher, to be a student. Surely the difference between a partial literacy, gained in a miserable one room school, and the significant education which is now commonly provided in the consolidated school, is enough to convince any one of the desirability of making a somewhat larger investment.

George D. Strayer, N. L. Engelhardt, and F. W. Hart, Department of Educational Administration, Teachers College, Columbia University, 1919, Possible Consolidation of Rural Schools in Delaware, *p. 5.*

Schools for rural children should be developed in terms of the rural life which they are leading and which they may normally be expected to continue to lead. Their education should look in the direction of making them more efficient farmers and housekeepers rather than to converting them into clerks, stenographers or trade workers.

George D. Strayer, N. L. Engelhardt, and F. W. Hart, Department of Educational Administration, Teachers College, Columbia University, 1919, Possible Consolidation of Rural Schools in Delaware, *p. 6.*

In the case of a physical trait such as height, perhaps few would deny that the differences found represent in the main differences in original endowment. That the progress children make through the grades of a school system is also chiefly dependent upon original endowment is neither so obvious nor so generally believed. The common opinion seems to be that nearly all children are capable of satisfactorily accomplishing eight grades of school work in eight years, and that if they fail to do so it is because of faulty school management. The remedies most often proposed for the prevention of retardation [holding children back from promotion to the next grade] are better attendance laws, school census reform, extension and improvement of medical inspection, flexible grading, and adaptations of the course of study.

That reform in all these lines is needed, for other reasons as well as for the reduction of retardation, will be admitted by all. We are beginning to learn, however, that all of these measures combined are powerless to reduce greatly the number of over-age children in the grades. Notwithstanding the persistent campaign which has been waged against the evils of retardation for the last dozen years, the number of retardates remains to-day much the same as it was when the campaign began. We are justified in raising the question whether the most important cause of retardation has been located, and whether it can be removed.

Lewis M. Terman, psychologist and developer of the Stanford-Binet intelligence test, 1919, The Intelligence of School Children, *pp. 21–22.*

The first grade is the most critical in the school system. It is the place above all others where the raw material with which the school is to work should be correctly evaluated. Success or failure for the child's school career hangs often upon his success or failure in the first grade. In a way school administrators appreciate this fact. Effort is usually made to place the best teachers in charge of the entering pupils. School doctors, school nurses, and school dentists are commonly urged to give special attention to the younger children. Nevertheless, it is in the first grade that retardation scores its worst record. *In the average city approximately a fourth of the pupils fail of promotion at the end of the first year.*

Schools for backward children ordinarily do not draw from classes below the third grade. By this time the dull pupil is already a lost cause. Special classes for superior children, when they exist at all, are too likely to confine their efforts to bright pupils whose intellectual progress has already been retarded by several years spent in the educational lockstep. By this time their intellectual ardor has cooled and the edges of their mental faculties have been dulled.

Lewis M. Terman, psychologist and developer of the Stanford-Binet intelligence test, 1919, The Intelligence of School Children, *pp. 42–43.*

In almost every city there are schools to which the children come from homes that are foreign, with little or no English spoken, where the parents are generally illiterate and endow the child with little mental inheritance. In such cases the child's experiences have been limited to those he encounters in the street or in the squalor of his own backyard. There are other schools attended by children coming from homes of affluence and plenty—children who possess the finest type of mental inheritance and a stock of experiences which are in direct antitheses to those of the less fortunate children to whom reference has just been made.

In the democracy of our public schools these children figuratively, and often literally, are put side by side. At the end of the first year they are promoted to the second grade, theoretically equally well prepared to go on with their work. But when their capacities for doing school work are measured in a scientific manner, it is found that there is wide variation, not only among those from different strata of society, but also among those from the same stratum who have had similar opportunities.

Theodore A. Zornow of the Susan B. Anthony School, Rochester, New York, and L. A. Pechstein, professor of psychology, University of Rochester, October 1922, "An Experiment in the Classification of First-Grade Children through the Use of Mental Tests," pp. 136–137.

It is no secret that the rural school is in bad repute. The building is old, poorly arranged, and poorly equipped. The teaching personnel is relatively immature, inexperienced, and untrained. Supervision is meager and often inefficient. The curriculum attempts to provide little more than so-called bare essentials, and these are presented without much relation to the child's experience or to the issues he is likely to face. In achievement in the fundamental subjects the rural child is approximately one year behind the urban child of the same grade. The rural people themselves are far from satisfied with the present conditions. In fact, to criticize the rural school has been the easy and popular thing to do. Judging from reports, people are quite unanimous in calling it the black sheep of the educational family. On the other hand, suggestions for its improvement are many.

Orville G. Brim, professor of rural education, Cornell University, April 1923, "The Curriculum Problem in Rural Elementary Schools," p. 586.

The teacher is held responsible for building civilization in every part of the [rural] community. She must be able to conduct a Sunday-school, to run a woman's cooking club, a better baby contest, and club work for boys, to develop community co-operation in buying and selling, to entertain them all, to tell the farmer a better way to fertilize his crops, and to tell the age of his horses by their teeth. In addition, she must paint the glories of the open country and the wickedness of the city so that the attractiveness of the city will fade and rural life will become supreme. Through her ministration all rural boys and girls will want to stay at home, and through her leadership they will create in their simple, rustic way the perfect life in its rustic simplicity. City girls cannot hope to do this.

Orville G. Brim, professor of rural education, Cornell University, April 1923, "The Curriculum Problem in Rural Elementary Schools," p. 591.

For boys and girls who find themselves most "at home" in the shop, drafting-room, kitchen, or sewing-room of the school, a special curriculum has been arranged—the technical course. This course prepares boys for industrial occupations, such as automobile repairman, cabinet-maker, carpenter, draftsman, electrician, machinist, printer, sheet-metal worker or wood-worker; and girls, for such occupations as dressmaking, millinery, and cooking.

Many pupils believe that education is not needed for work of this kind. This is a false and mistaken idea. The boy who has a high-school education on which to base his trade will go much farther and will be promoted much earlier to positions of responsibility in the trade than he can ever hope for without it.

Boys who elect this course are assigned to a shop for a ten-week course in the work of that shop. At the end of this shop course, they are assigned to a second shop for another ten-week course. By means of this plan of rotation of shops, the boys are given a chance to become somewhat acquainted with the work of four different trades in a year. They are thus able to make a more intelligent choice of the trades they wish to follow.

Boys enrolled in this course are required to take English, general mathematics, general science, social science, shop, mechanical drawing, and physical training. There are no electives.

Girls who elect the technical course do not follow the rotation plan but are scheduled to take cooking, sewing, and millinery throughout the year, with English, mathematics, social science, and physical training as additional required subjects.

The parents of a boy choosing the technical course are required to sign a card, indicating their willingness to have the boy operate such machines as are a part of the shop equipment of the course of instruction.

C. R. Foster, associate superintendent of schools, Pittsburgh, describing the technical course at Latimer Junior High School, December 1923, "The Latimer Junior High School," *p. 282.*

That there are physical differences among children need hardly be pointed out. Not only are there such crude deviations as are represented by total blindness and deafness; by physical deformities that handicap future usefulness unless compensation is provided by special education; tubercular, anemic, and other debilitating factors such as weak heart; there are also physical differences more difficult to discern and to measure, differences in the rate of development toward maturity. Physiological and anatomical age, when we have learned to measure them with exactness, will be more reliable as an index of physical status than chronological age, in the same measure as mental age has already demonstrated itself to be more reliable in the determination of intelligence than the mere lapse of time since birth.

John Louis Horn, associate professor of education, Mills College, 1924, The Education of Exceptional Children: A Consideration of Public School Problems in the Field of Differentiated Education, *p. 5.*

The law requires that all children present themselves for education; the need for meeting the problem of educating large numbers makes the practice of individual instruction, which might automatically take care of many deviates, an impractical process; the method of simultaneous instruction is devised to meet the situation. Simultaneous instruction is based on the assumption of some, even though crude, homogeneity. This homogeneity is found in the most obvious characteristic,—approximate similarity of age. The children are grouped in this manner, and minor variations of every kind, such as slight deafness, blindness, dullness, are taken care of in a variety of modifications of the procedure, in frequent reclassification of the groups, and in the common agreement that perfect evenness of progress and equality of ultimate attainment are not to be expected.

A teacher trains a mute child to speak in 1917. *(Library of Congress, Prints and Photographs Division, LC-DIG-nclc-05254)*

But some children are totally deaf or totally blind or completely lacking in intelligence. No amount of resiliency in the prescribed procedure can take care of these children. They cannot be subjected to the process of instruction at all, as it is organized for the typical group. And yet they cannot be disregarded. Democracy means equality of opportunity. We should not be acting in accordance with our ethical and social ideals if we failed to educate these children who are not susceptible of treatment in the standard manner devised for the group.

John Louis Horn, associate professor of education, Mills College, 1924, The Education of Exceptional Children: A Consideration of Public School Problems in the Field of Differentiated Education, *p. 7.*

The belief that differences in capacity are illusory is without foundation in fact. This does not mean that we can always determine with precision what the individual's capacity is. An intelligence test is only a somewhat better measure than is the actual accomplishment of the student in his school work. The verdict which they give must be taken as provisional, and must be subject to revision as the pupil's accomplishment rises above or falls below the prediction which is based upon the test. This is only to say that our measure of capacity is not a perfect one. It does not imply that the differences in capacity do not exist and are not large in extent. Wherever freedom of opportunity and proper stimulus to accomplishment are given, differences in achievement manifest themselves which are as marked as the differences in the test scores.

Frank N. Freeman, professor of education, University of Chicago, November 1924, "Sorting the Students," p. 169.

It is probably true that, because of its definiteness, an intelligence test score makes distinctions a little clearer than they would otherwise be. It may also be true that classification into ability groups make distinctions more obvious. Let it be noted, however, that neither the test nor the classification creates distinctions. Distinctions have always existed and there seems no immediate prospect that they will be done away with. A much more harmful mode of recognizing distinctions than homogeneous grouping has existed for generations in the school. Failure of promotion is a more serious form of branding than is classification in a low ability group. It can hardly be regarded as kind to allow the child to undertake work which we know he cannot accomplish and then to make his failure in the work conspicuous by forcing him to fall behind his companions. It is much better to attempt to measure his ability and to set him at the work in which he can succeed.

Frank N. Freeman, professor of education, University of Chicago, November 1924, "Sorting the Students," p. 170.

Counterbalancing the possible disadvantage from the student's recognition that he is in a low section, or that he is in a high section, and his consequent depression or elation, is the relief from unduly marked contrasts which arise when pupils of widely different capacities are in the same class. If slow pupils are in a class with others whose ability is of the same order, they are not subject to the discouraging comparison between their own attainments and those of gifted pupils. On the other hand, if the bright pupils are in classes which are composed of others of similar ability they do not have the opportunity to shine so brightly by contrast with dull companions. They are brought into keener competition and are forced to exert themselves in order to show superiority. On the whole, then, homogeneous grouping provides rather less cause for discouragement and for undue elation, due to the contrast with the attainments of one's companions, than does mixed grouping.

Frank N. Freeman, professor of education, University of Chicago, November 1924, "Sorting the Students," pp. 170–171.

There are those who criticize, and who criticize severely, the College Board. These critics may be divided into two broad general classes, those who hold that the Board's examination standards are unreasonable, and those who hold that any examination standard, as a test of fitness for college entrance, is unreasonable. To the critics of the first class the reply is easy. The Board has no standards of its own. It is simply the instrument which brings together representative groups who in cooperative action frame requirements, set papers, and interpret results. The so-called Board standards are those of the most representative teachers that the Board is able to collect. They are primarily the standards of those who are closest to the problem, those who are teaching the boys and girls in the school, and those who are dealing with the result of that teaching in college.

The second class of critics, those who protest against any examination as a test of fitness for college entrance, offer two chief objections. The first is that the record of a boy or girl in school offers a better prognosis of success or failure in college than any examination can give, and the second is that the thought of the examination looming up ahead restricts the freedom of the teacher, and leads to placing the emphasis on preparing for an examination instead of on teaching the subject, and thus tends to lower the general standard of secondary education. . . . [L]et me simply say in passing that a large, I fear a very large, proportion of the secondary schools of the country have not attained a sufficient degree of thoroughness in their work, and have not a sufficient comprehension of what is needed for success in college to make the record of their pupils an adequate criterion of preparation for college work, and that in our better schools, the examinations have proved an incentive rather than a hindrance, and have raised rather than lowered the standard of attainment. A fair examination is no hindrance to good teaching. It does restrict undue freedom, and it is a check to vagaries, but at the same time it is an incentive to thoroughness and with a good teacher the examination is an incident rather than an end.

Wilson Ferrand, headmaster, Newark Academy, New Jersey, November 6, 1925, in College Entrance Examination Board, The Work of the College Entrance Examination Board, 1901–1925, pp. 10–11.

We are now moving steadily toward the time when every candidate for college entrance will first of all submit his complete school record, and the opinion of his teacher as to his qualifications for going on with advanced work. These will not be treated mechanically, but will be given the weight that experience has shown the records of that school and the judgment of that teacher to deserve, and they will be supplemented by a written examination, and in all probability by an intelligence test. All four will be taken into account in arriving at the final decision.

Probably the character of the examinations will undergo a gradual change. They will become less of content examinations, and more tests of method and power. The school record will show the ground covered, while the examination will test the way in which the work has been done. The machinery of the Board is organized to bring about such a change as rapidly as the judgment of the teaching world decides it to be desirable. In fact such a change is already in progress, and has advanced further than many of us realize.

Wilson Ferrand, headmaster, Newark Academy, New Jersey, November 6, 1925, in College Entrance Examination Board, The Work of the College Entrance Examination Board, 1901–1925, p. 12.

The first point to be clearly recognized is that the Indian boy or girl leaving school is under a tremendous handicap as compared with the typical white boy or girl, in that he or she is not a member of a family already fairly well adjusted to the existing economic civilization. These young Indians leaving school cannot look to the older generation for advice, guidance, and assistance in getting established on a sound economic basis. Often they cannot make their homes with their parents in the first few trying years after leaving school, as can many a white boy who shifts about from job to job in an effort to get a suitable place in the industrial world. Their earnings in such a period are frequently low, especially in jobs which offer possibilities for the gradual acquisition of skill and ultimately the larger earnings that come to skilled workers. Having no homes where they may stay without cost or with such payment as they can afford to make from their earnings, they are obliged to shift for themselves and direct themselves, although they are not as well equipped as white children with knowledge of the industrial life of the communities where work is to be found.

Institute for Government Research, 1928, The Problem of Indian Administration, p. 434.

The first constructive step . . . in aiding the Indians to be self-supporting, should be definite improvement in their educational equipment and the devising of a suitable system for placing Indian youths in the industrial world in positions that afford them a reasonable opportunity to achieve economic independence.

Increased efforts, however, must not be confined to the schools and the placement of the youths just leaving school.

Far more must be done than in the past for the economic advancement of adult Indians on the reservations. The persons engaged in this work should be recognized as teachers and their duties as primarily educational. Every activity must be planned with major consideration for the educational result. Control and conservation of Indian property that does not educate the Indians in the use and management of their own property, merely postpones the ultimate solution of the Indian problem. The task of employees of the Indian Service is the humanitarian task of the teacher, as rapidly as possible to train the pupils so that they will cease to require the services of the teacher. The standards of employment in the Indian Service and the standards of work must be at least on a par with that of other agencies doing like work, so that fairly satisfactory progress can be made in teaching and stimulating the Indian to be self-supporting and to maintain a reasonable standard of living.

Institute for Government Research, 1928, The Problem of Indian Administration, p. 435.

When in the year 2000 the historian writes his account of the period through which we are now passing, how, I often wonder, will he appraise the various educational tendencies of our generation. He will no doubt have something to say about the extraordinary extension of educational opportunity, the structural reorganization of the educational system, the almost universal concern with curriculum making, the differentiation of the program of higher education, the so-called progressive education movement, the development of teachers' colleges, the tremendous growth in educational expenditure, the widespread interest in the scientific study of education, and numerous changes in the structure and procedure of our schools and colleges. From his vantage point in time he will be able to assess in terms of their fruits that vast medley of currents and movements which now disturb the educational consciousness.

George S. Counts, professor of education, Teachers College, Columbia University, 1929, Secondary Education and Industrialism, pp. 1–2.

Why have boys and girls crowded into the secondary schools in such multitudes? This is not a question of purely theoretical interest. On the contrary, it is a question of crucial importance, because the answer that we give to it will largely determine our attitude towards numerous problems which we face in the secondary school today. If we find that the expansion of the high school is a product of the efforts of our own profession [teaching], we may assume that what we have done we can at least in part undo. If such an

Children enjoy the playground at the Robert E. Lee School, a modern facility in Okmulgee, Oklahoma, in 1917. *(Library of Congress, Prints and Photographs Division, LC-DIG-nclc-05234)*

explanation is supported by the facts, we might, after deciding that the admission of boys and girls from the less favored social classes and from the lower levels of ability is undesirable, proceed to restore the selective secondary school of tradition. If, on the other hand, we conclude that the movement is the fruit of the operation of forces over which we have relatively little control, then for better or for worse we must accept a *fait accompli*. In this latter event our major task would be that of adjusting programs and policies to the new conditions which have been set by society.

George S. Counts, professor of education, Teachers College, Columbia University, 1929, Secondary Education and Industrialism, *pp. 18–19.*

Among the most obvious of the characteristics of the American elementary school are the following:

(1) It is the elementary school which establishes first contact with the child so far as his formal education is concerned. The kindergarten, which in many well-organized school systems precedes the first grade, does not regard itself as a part of the formal schooling. Its function appears rather to be a better and more systematic accomplishment of that part of the child's pre-school training which is ordinarily left to the home.

(2) The typical American elementary school is a non-specialized institution, offering the same type of training to all throughout the period of their attendance. It is a single-curriculum school.

(3) The American elementary school is an eight-grade school, each year corresponding to one grade. Typically, it undertakes the training of the child from age six to age fourteen.

(4) It is a fundamental characteristic of the American elementary school that it seems to assume that it is providing the only education that its children are to receive. While it is impossible for it to be unaware of the fact that numbers of its graduates are to go on with their education and to attend secondary schools, it is by tradition, and, indeed, by theory, bent upon giving a sense of completion in order to equip for life as well as possible those of its pupils who may end their formal schooling with the eighth grade. It conducts graduation exercises; it grants diplomas; and, as a matter of fact, it was, until well into the second half of the last century, the only school attended by a large majority of the American people.

John Louis Horn, professor of education, Mills College, 1929, Principles of Elementary Education, *pp. 17–18.*

CHAPTER SIX

The Hardest of Times:
Schools Withstand the Great Depression 1930–1940

The year 1930 began with one great shiver. January of that year was the coldest month in Denver and the coldest January in San Antonio since the federal government began keeping records. As snow piled up in Los Angeles and Louisiana, people throughout the United States felt another kind of chill, one that reached deep into their pockets. Banks were closing, businesses folding, and jobs disappearing. One in 10 able-bodied workers in Buffalo, New York, and one in four in Detroit were unemployed, and the American Federation of Labor (AFL) reported that one-fifth of the members of its affiliated unions had lost their jobs.

By the end of the year, an estimated 4 million U.S. workers were unemployed, and by 1931 the word *depression* had taken on a concrete and timely meaning. It stood for breadlines wrapping around city blocks, household furnishings piled on sidewalks, and despondent wage earners who had lost their livelihoods and their pensions.

For a time it seemed as though the nation's schools might bear up against the economic hard times. A comparison of national statistics for 1930 and 1931 revealed small increases in school enrollment, staff, and teachers' salaries. Only capital outlay—money spent to improve school property and equipment—declined. The figures were deceiving, though, because they obscured the fact that schools in many urban areas and in the most prosperous states were minimally affected, while those in poor districts suffered. Not until the depression worsened and the number of unemployed grew to an estimated 12 million in 1932, causing states and municipalities to lose significant tax revenues, did the financial crisis in education become evident.

Many school districts coped by retrenching: cutting budgets, services, and staff. In Chicago, for example, the school board announced in 1933 that cost-saving measures would include closing the city's junior high schools, operating fewer kindergartens, and eliminating classes in art, music, and physical education. In addition, many central-office workers and half the elementary school principals would lose their jobs. With teachers' salaries already in arrears, the board hoped to cut expenses by $9 million.

Other districts saved money by eliminating vocational courses, summer-school programs, and evening classes and by postponing purchases, construction projects, and building maintenance. Budget cuts for the 1932–33 academic year ranged from 3 percent, on average, in the Northeast to 16 percent in the cities of the southern and central states. Nationwide, sales of textbooks declined 30 percent between 1930 and 1933, which meant that as the depression wore on, students learned from books that were increasingly out of date, dirty, and damaged. Reference books fell apart from use and were not replaced, limiting students' opportunities for independent research.

In Ohio, schools in Findlay and Cuyahoga Falls, cities that each had a population of about 20,000, closed in spring 1933 after being open seven months. Akron kept its schools open a little longer but closed them when teachers' unpaid salaries totaled $330,000. Dayton avoided cutting short the academic year by having schools open three days a week instead of five. The legislature of another midwestern state, Iowa, no longer required high school students to take courses in agriculture, home economics, and mechanical training, and they made kindergarten attendance optional for younger children. Iowa's lawmakers also cut appropriations for the state's department of public instruction by 30 percent.

Many Americans, including most educators, bemoaned the changes, which appeared to undo much of the progress made in education during the previous decades. Others, especially the members of taxpayers' associations, called the

This 1930 cartoon depicts the effects of school closings: illiteracy, depreciation of school property, and idle, unproductive children. *(Library of Congress, General Collection)*

cutbacks beneficial and claimed that they eliminated wasteful "fads and frills" education.[1]

The cutbacks most hurt schools that were financially strained before the depression. These were schools that were already paying low salaries to poorly trained teachers; were operating for the shortest terms; had the most rundown, ill-equipped buildings; and had the highest dropout and truancy rates. Many of these were rural schools.

Rural communities generally had higher birth rates than cities, which resulted in fewer taxpayers supporting the schools per child enrolled. In 1930, the farm population, which received 9 percent of the nation's income, was responsible for educating 31 percent of its children. The 11 states with the highest birth rates and lowest expenditures per pupil formed a belt across the South and Southeast, from Texas to Virginia, that included Arkansas, Louisiana, Mississippi, Tennessee, Kentucky, Alabama, Georgia, South Carolina, and North Carolina.

Thousands of schools in these and other states were forced to close. By spring 1932, school closings had halted the formal education of about 330,000 children. Of these, 170,790 had attended the 1,318 elementary and secondary schools in Georgia that had closed. By spring 1933, 85 percent of public schools in Alabama had closed, including every school in 50 of the state's 67 counties. This was a serious setback for Alabama, the state with the fifth highest illiteracy rate and one that had been working to raise the number of years children spent in school. "As far as education is concerned," said A. F. Harmon, state superintendent of schools, "we are facing the worst situation that has confronted us since the reconstruction period."[2] Of the small number of teachers still working in Alabama, few had received their full salary during the 1932–33 school year. Some were paid partly in scrip that was all but useless, and others worked only in return for room and board.

The depression affected children's well-being in other ways that interfered with learning. Many repeatedly went to school hungry, including the one-fifth of schoolchildren examined by the New York City Health Department in 1932 who showed signs of malnutrition. In Chicago, teachers regularly fed 11,000 of their students. Throughout the country, children from the poorest families stayed home from school because transportation, books, and other supplies cost more than their families could afford. "Shoes seem the insurmountable obstacle to school attendance in many impoverished families," observed Betty Lindley and Ernest K. Lindley, journalists who reported on educational issues in the 1930s. "Underwear can be made from sugar sacks. Clothes can be patched and remade."[3] Shoes, however, needed to be bought.

Thousands of older children and teens left their impoverished homes to wander from town to town, hitching rides on freight trains or along highways, searching for work and handouts. Not only did these young people cut short their schooling, but they also put themselves at risk for accidents and assaults. Meanwhile, thousands more who remained in school endured significant chronic stress caused by economic uncertainty, upheaval, and discord at home.

Libraries Suffer Too

In this time of hardship, people of all ages turned to a traditional resource for learning, the public library. The number of books circulated in 1933 was 23 percent higher than in 1929, and the number of patrons with library cards increased

19 percent over the same period, as people sought reading matter than would help them understand the economic and social issues of the day, prepare them for a new line of work, or teach them how to earn money from home.

Ironically, this upsurge in interest coincided with a 23 percent drop in library funding. In some places, such as the industrial city of Birmingham, Alabama, reductions were more severe. In 1933, Birmingham's libraries were operating on half their 1930 budget. The cuts were especially painful, in Birmingham and elsewhere, because even before the depression, public libraries generally were inadequately funded. "There was no water to squeeze out," commented Julia Wright Merrill, chief of the Public Library Division of the American Library Association, in 1934.[4]

Many libraries initially economized by forgoing purchases of new books and periodicals, thus making unavailable the materials that would most have benefited patrons interested in current events. Declining purchases also left gaps in collections that might prove difficult to fill later on. A survey of 60 libraries in select cities conducted by the American Library Association revealed that spending for new books had declined from a collective total of $2,340,000 in 1931 to $957,000 in 1933. Detroit's book fund shrank from $175,000 in the 1930–31 fiscal year to $72,000 in 1931–32. There was even less to spend the following year, although $80,000 had been budgeted, because the city simply did not have the money. Whenever possible librarians steered patrons toward older books, but when these wore out, there were no funds to rebind or replace them, and collections were further depleted.

Limiting hours of operation also curbed expenses. Public libraries in many cities closed one day a week. The Minneapolis library system closed for two weeks in summer and a week at Christmas. Minneapolis also eliminated evening library service, keeping only the newspaper and technology reading rooms open after daytime business hours. Also, librarians throughout the nation had their salaries cut by as much as 50 percent. Job vacancies went unfilled as thousands of library workers were moved to part-time status or laid off. In 1930 the demand for librarians was greater than the supply, but in 1934 about 10 percent of U.S. librarians were out of work.

Dissatisfied Voters

President Herbert Hoover, a Republican, believed that the economy would correct itself, given time. He was philosophically opposed to using federal funds for welfare purposes, but as production declined and unemployment rose, he sanctioned greater government spending for public works. In 1932, he established the Reconstruction Finance Corporation, a government agency that made loans to business firms, in the hope that injecting capital into corporate America would speed recovery at all levels of the economy. Also in 1932, Hoover acknowledged the urgent needs of education, stating that "the very first obligation upon the national resources is the undiminished support of the public schools."[5] Because he made no federal aid available to education, when referring to national resources the president apparently had in mind private charities and state and local coffers. Yet public and private sources of aid were already being exhausted by the immediate needs of the poor and hungry.

In 1932, the United States faced a financial crisis that was more severe and persistent than any depression or panic of previous years, and no one knew how to remedy it, including the president. Yet as suffering and despair worsened, the people expected their leaders to take decisive action. The president was pursuing a course that seemed intended to aid large corporations, and the public perceived that he was out of touch with their needs.

In that presidential election year, voters rejected Hoover's bid for a second term and chose instead the Democratic candidate, Franklin Delano Roosevelt. As governor of New York, Roosevelt had established the Temporary Emergency Relief Administration (TERA), an agency that created jobs for the unemployed and gave food, clothing, and housing to needy state residents. Americans responded to Roosevelt's promise to help "the forgotten man at the bottom of the economic pyramid."[6] With their votes they endorsed his willingness to experiment with new and untested economic remedies, and they would elect him to an unprecedented four terms.

Roosevelt's principal curative approach was to create a complicated mix of government agencies and programs to regulate the economy and put people to work that became known as the New Deal. New Deal legislation brought about the Federal Deposit Insurance Corporation (FDIC), for example, to insure bank deposits, and the Social Security system, to provide the old and disabled with pensions that were supported by employer and worker contributions. New Deal initiatives also included the Agricultural Adjustment Act (AAA), which was intended to boost prices for agricultural products by reducing surpluses, and the Tennessee Valley Authority (TVA), which implemented measures to control flooding in the impoverished Tennessee Valley basin and brought electricity to the region.

Some New Deal programs had educational components. Foremost among these were two that targeted out-of-work young people: the Civilian Conservation Corps (CCC), established on March 31, 1933, and the National Youth Administration (NYA), created by executive order on June 26, 1935.

Jobs and Education for Young Men and Women

The CCC initially employed young men between the ages of 18 and 25 on conservation and civic-improvement projects. In 1935, legislation extended the program for two years and expanded the age range to include young men age 17 to 28; additional legislation in 1937 extended the CCC for another three years and lowered the upper age limit to 25. To be eligible, a young man had to be a U.S. citizen in a family receiving public assistance, single, and neither working nor in school. Enrollment was just over 250,000 in 1933 and reached its highest level, 505,872, in 1935.

Participants lived in military-style camps, often in wilderness areas, that were organized and staffed by personnel from the Departments of War, Labor, Agriculture, and the Interior. They were employed on approximately 200 kinds of projects that were as varied as planting trees, constructing roads through remote areas, fighting forest fires, controlling insects, and creating bird sanctuaries and wildlife refuges. Each enrollee received $30 a month—roughly a dollar a day—as well as meals, clothing, and lodging, for his six to nine months of service, and $23 to $25 of each month's earnings went directly to his family.

The CCC began strictly as a conservation and employment program, but its leaders added an educational component in December 1933, after screening

James J. McEntee, director of the Civilian Conservation Corps (CCC), looks on as CCC enrollees learn to assemble an automotive engine. *(Library of Congress, Prints and Photographs Division, LC-USZ62-107724)*

determined that 84 percent of participants had never finished high school, 44 percent had failed to complete elementary school, and some were illiterate. Furthermore, nearly half had never held a steady job, and many of these were looking for vocational guidance and training. Each camp employed an education adviser and staff to carry out a program of instruction intended to further understanding of social and economic conditions, deepen appreciation of the natural world, teach vocational skills or basic literacy, and offer outlets for self-expression. The curriculum varied from one camp to another, but popular course offerings included citizenship, English, history, botany, zoology, geology, forestry, surveying, bookkeeping, music, and painting. By 1938, 62,000 young men had learned to read and write while enrolled in the CCC, nearly 500,000 had completed classes at the elementary level, and more than 400,000 had done some high school work.

The CCC offered a place in society and an income to a large number of youths in need. Yet it failed to aid many others, especially girls and young women, students struggling to stay in school, and boys and young men who were physically unfit for CCC service. Seeing such a great number of Americans coming of age without prospects created fear in the minds of many adults that these young people would grow disillusioned with democracy and join revolutionary political movements. At the very least, an enormous amount of human potential was going to waste. One person who worried about the nation's youth was First Lady Eleanor Roosevelt. "I live in real terror when I think we may be losing this generation," she said in 1934. "We have got to bring these young people into the active life of the community and make them feel that they are necessary."[7]

Eleanor Roosevelt successfully lobbied her husband to sign an executive order establishing the NYA. This agency addressed the problem of out-of-work youth by granting financial aid to high school and college students in return for work, thereby helping young men and women stay in school. The NYA also gave jobs and training in marketable skills to many between the ages of 18 and 24 who were unemployed. These participants were divided almost equally by sex, and the proportions of whites, blacks, American Indians, and other racial groups among them reflected those of the general population.

Participants took advantage of an array of educational opportunities. Eight young people employed through the NYA in the Merrick County, Nebraska, surveyor's office attended weekly classes in the mathematical and practical skills basic to surveying. Others, working in a Cleveland department store, received instruction in operating elevators, making and altering draperies, upholstering, and selling merchandise. Meanwhile, young women in Salt Lake City attended a waitress-training course sponsored by the NYA at the local civic center.

Educational Efforts of the Works Progress Administration

It was common for young people in the NYA to receive instruction from teachers employed by the Works Progress Administration (later the Work Projects Administration; the WPA), the largest New Deal agency and the most visible. The WPA gave work to millions of adults, from construction workers and plumbers, to biologists and physicians, to writers, musicians, and artists.

In Kentucky, WPA teachers in 1937 instructed approximately 2,000 young men and women enrolled in the NYA in masonry, metalworking, home nursing, home economics, child care, first aid, and elementary school subjects. In Ohio, teachers on the WPA payroll were among the many adults who led a variety of classes for NYA participants in 1938. Some of these courses had vocational content, promoting proficiency in automobile mechanics, domestic service, practical nursing, shorthand, typing, and the like. Others covered academic subjects, such as French, history, reading, and basic arithmetic, because in Ohio and elsewhere, an alarming number of the teenagers and young adults aided by the NYA needed remedial academic work. Of 26 boys employed on one small project in Kentucky, for example, 17 were unable to read or write when they signed on with the NYA. These boys were typical of the young people in the region who were depending on government assistance.

A survey of 35,638 NYA youth in nine states revealed that only half had attended school beyond the eighth grade and most of the others had left high school before graduating, primarily because of financial need, boredom, or discouragement. Only 3 percent had ever been to college. None of the young people surveyed came from southern states, where educational attainment was lowest.

Schools reached out to NYA youth in their communities, although classrooms were overcrowded, teachers were heavily burdened, and many of the young people being served had formed negative attitudes toward formal education. In 1937,

Juanita Coleman, a teacher employed by the National Youth Administration, instructs adults at Gee's Bend, Alabama, in May 1939. An 82-year-old student reads to the class. *(Library of Congress, Prints and Photographs Division, Lc-USF34-051530-D)*

the Minneapolis Board of Education cooperated with the NYA to give a year of training to 450 boys and girls at the Millar Vocational School, a public secondary school, while in Missouri, public school teachers teamed up with WPA instructors and social-service workers to provide part-time classes in vocational and elementary school subjects to 65 percent of NYA enrollees.

Teachers employed by the WPA also served adult learners. In New York City, on a typical day in 1937, about 70,000 men and women over age 17 received instruction through the efforts of the WPA. Their classes met in public schools kept open after hours and in settlement houses, community centers, churches, and private homes, and they covered academic, vocational, cultural, social, and political topics, with the goal of benefiting both the individual and society. "It is the adults of today who are going to solve our problems," said Gustav A. Stumpf, director of the WPA adult education program for the New York City Board of Education; "adequate education can enable them to make intelligent decisions."[8] The WPA also produced "People's Forum of the Air," a weekly program offering dramatizations and discussions of controversial social problems, for a New York radio station.

In New York and other cities, WPA educators taught illiterate residents to read and write English. One WPA official estimated that a million people learned to read through the program between 1933 and 1938. The WPA helped immigrants—including many who had fled Nazi persecution—prepare for naturalization. It also addressed the educational needs of children by operating 1,500 nursery schools throughout the country and offering summer remedial classes for high school students and summer study programs for boys and girls ages eight to 14.

In October 1933, the Federal Emergency Relief Administration (FERA), another New Deal agency, instituted its Emergency Education Program to provide work relief to unemployed teachers. State departments of education drafted their own program plans, which were then approved by the state relief administrator and FERA. States could plan programming in any or all of five categories: general adult education, adult literacy, vocational education, vocational rehabilitation, and nursery schools for preschoolers from disadvantaged homes. To qualify for this program, teachers had to meet their state's educational requirements and be on relief. The Emergency Education Program reached its height in March 1935, when it employed more than 44,000 teachers to instruct more than 1,724,000 adults and children. In addition, FERA's Emergency Work Relief Program employed men and women to clean, repair, and catalog books at public libraries.

In 1934, FERA created 28 residential summer programs for women, offering instruction in a variety of academic, vocational, and recreational skills. Located in schools, other public buildings, and summer-camp facilities in 27 states and the

Unemployed women practice typing at the Federal Emergency Relief Administration camp in Arcola, Pennsylvania, ca. July 1934. *(Franklin D. Roosevelt Library, Hyde Park, New York)*

District of Columbia, these programs gave four to eight weeks of training to women drawn from relief rolls who showed a desire to learn. Most participants were between the ages of 16 and 24, but women as old as 45 were admitted. The NYA took over the program in its second and final year and maintained 47 camps in 27 states; roughly 3,000 women between the ages of 16 and 25 participated.

This experiment in education had mixed results. Most of the women arrived hungry and stressed, with some on the verge of suicide. They therefore benefited from the regular meals, camaraderie, and respite that camp life provided. Many also began the program believing it would lead to steady, paid employment and for this reason left disappointed. In 1934, FERA placed about 20 percent of participants in jobs at the end of their period of instruction; the rest returned home, still unemployed. The percentage placed in 1935 is unknown.

Help for College Students

FERA also aided college students. In the rough year 1932, college attendance dropped for the first time since World War I. Because of declining incomes, many parents could no longer pay tuition for their sons and daughters. Also, the dearth of job opportunities meant that fewer students than in the past could work their way through school. In fall 1933, FERA implemented an experimental program at the University of Minnesota, allowing students to work at jobs generated by the school. This work-study program proved so successful that in February 1934 it was extended to colleges and universities nationwide. Each state received $15 per month for each student employed part time, although the number of students participating could not exceed 12 percent of the state's college enrollment in October 1934. In March 1935, the college student aid program employed 104,000 young men and women who otherwise would have been forced to drop out.

For young people whose families could afford it, college offered an appealing alternative to unemployment. Enrollment in colleges and universities eventually climbed during the depression, so that by 1937 the student population of U.S. campuses totaled 1,250,000, or roughly a million more than in 1917. College undergraduates represented 1 percent of the U.S. population and 15 percent of Americans in their age group.

With support from the states, alumni, and other private donors, institutions of higher learning grew in size and number. Great lecture halls accommodated enormous classes, such as the economics course at the University of Wisconsin, which, with 845 students, was one of the largest offered in the nation.

Philanthropy created schools such as Duke University, which opened in Durham, North Carolina, in 1930. A gift of $20 million from tobacco tycoon James B. Duke transformed tiny Trinity College into the 5,000-acre Duke campus, a showplace of Gothic architecture with a $2 million chapel, a medical school, and a hospital.

Reaching the Children of the Dust Bowl

Children in families uprooted by drought conditions in the Southwest formed another group whose educational needs were addressed by the federal government. Beginning in 1931, a lack of rainfall afflicted portions of Oklahoma, Texas, Kansas, New Mexico, and Colorado, states in which poor farming practices had left the earth vulnerable to erosion. By 1934, the drought had become severe, and winds carried the dry, fine-grained soil aloft, forming blinding, smothering dust storms that made farming impossible.

Thousands of farmers and their families tied their belongings onto old cars and trucks and fled the dust bowl, as the region came to be called. As many as 200,000 of these refugees made their way to California, where agriculture was big business, hoping to gain employment. Instead, with too many workers competing for a limited number of seasonal jobs, growers turned most of the desperate applicants away. Those who did find work labored for steadily shrinking wages. The southwesterners roamed north and south on California's highways, covering up to 3,000 miles a year. Families camped beside roads or on the outskirts of towns, barely surviving on dwindling resources, and creating a social crisis. By June 1934, 1,225,000 California residents were receiving some kind of economic relief. How could the state possibly feed, house, and care for so many thousands of newcomers?

Public education in California faced a crisis, too. Between 1935 and 1940, public-school enrollment in agricultural Kern County, increased 300 percent. Teachers in Bakersfield, the county seat, often used their own money to feed hungry migrant children at lunchtime. Throughout California, dust-bowl children in public schools

Children attend school at a government camp for migrants in Caldwell, Idaho, in 1941. *(Library of Congress, Prints and Photographs Division, LC-USF34-039130-D)*

endured ridicule from classmates because they wore dirty, ragged clothes and spoke with unfamiliar accents; and frequent moves made it hard for them to learn. Nearly half the children enrolled in public schools in and around Bakersfield in 1935 changed schools at least once that year.

Responding to the need, the Resettlement Administration, a federal agency, established camps in California's San Joaquin Valley to shelter the migrant population. The first two opened in 1935, at Marysville, in Yuba County, and at Arvin, in Kern County. The camps offered one-room cabins or tents on platforms; clean water for washing and drinking; toilets, showers, and laundry tubs; low-cost food; a clinic with a resident nurse; recreational facilities; and a school where the children were welcomed and treated with respect. The U.S. Farm Security Administration (FSA) assumed oversight of the camps in 1937, and by 1939 the FSA was operating 10 camps in California and several in other states, aiding about 20 percent of the migrants.

The Advisory Committee on Education

Despite the extraordinary use of government funds for employment and education during his administration, by 1936, Roosevelt felt growing pressure to increase federal aid to schools. He therefore appointed a committee of leading educators, labor leaders, businesspeople, and government officials to study conditions in U.S. education and recommend a course of action. The committee's report, published in 1938, found glaring inequalities in the opportunities for schooling available throughout the nation. In some places, the quality of school buildings and instruction were so low that they threatened the stability of democratic institutions, the committee warned.

Although schools in all communities felt the impact of retrenchment during the depression years and were endeavoring to bounce back, the committee observed the most rapid improvement in suburbs. Conditions were less satisfactory in major urban areas, if only because large city school systems adjusted slowly to changing conditions. Rural schools, for the most part, remained the most inadequate.

The continued use of one-room schoolhouses contributed to rural inefficiency. In 1934, nearly 44,000 U.S. schools had an average attendance that was between three and 17. Rural communities spent from $80 to $200 in 1934 to provide inferior instruction to a single pupil in a small school; in the same year, larger town and village schools had an average operating cost of $40 per pupil and offered wider and better opportunities for learning. In 1935, researchers employed by the Kansas State Planning Board counted 8,217 one-room schools still in use in the state. Of these, 3,949 had been built before 1900, 1,355 had no source of fresh water, and 832 had no playground equipment. Old country schoolhouses in Kansas and other states went without repairs during the depression because of economic need.

Almost nothing was being done to educate children with special needs who lived in rural places. In 1938, 26 states had laws requiring specialized instruction for children with impaired hearing, sight, or speech or other disabilities, but in no state were these classes adequately funded. The president's advisory committee estimated that of the 2.5 million children with special needs in the United States, 325,000, at most, were being properly taught.

The committee noted that approximately 12,000 private elementary and secondary schools were operating during the 1933–34 academic year. Nearly two-thirds of these were Catholic schools, and another sixth were affiliated with other churches. Private schools, which educated one-tenth of elementary school pupils and one-sixteenth of high school students, held tax-exempt status as nonprofit institutions in most states.

At the time the committee issued its report, the federal government had spent more than $2.4 billion on education since the start of the depression, for the instructional programs of the CCC, NYA, and WPA, and as emergency aid to keep schools open and build additional school buildings. In its conclusion, the committee called for still more: It recommended that an additional $855 million in federal funds be earmarked for education over the next six years and distributed to the states according to need. Most of the money would support existing elementary and secondary schools, and the remainder would pay for school construction, teacher training, adult education, rural libraries, educational research, and administration at the state level. In its most controversial recommendation, the committee asked that states be permitted to allocate some of the money to parochial schools, if they so chose.

As soon as it was published, the report generated negative comments. "I think it is a very dangerous and vicious recommendation, an entering wedge to destroy the public-school system," said Professor George S. Counts of the Teachers College at Columbia University.[9] Proponents of the committee's recommendations failed to find the support in Congress that would have been needed to turn them into law. Roosevelt, too, was against such a high level of federal involvement in education and refused to back any bill to increase federal aid to schools. The recommendations therefore never were implemented.

Continued Disadvantages for African Americans

The president's advisory committee noted that in states where racial segregation existed, schools for black children received about half the state funding that white schools did, and that even with their greater support, white schools were functioning at a level below the national average. In addition, black teachers in the South taught larger classes and had less formal education than their white counterparts.

The agent for Negro education in Mississippi reported that between 1933 and 1935, 3,753 schools for African Americans operated in his state. Of these, 2,313 were housed in buildings owned by public school districts, and the remainder met wherever teachers and students could find space: in churches, abandoned stores, and tenant farmhouses. All the schools for African Americans, and many for whites, in Mississippi and other southern states, lacked furniture and such basic equipment as books, blackboards, and maps. Four empty walls, crude benches, an old wood-burning stove, and painted boards serving as a chalkboard were the norm in African-American schools.

In Kentucky, where state law mandated school segregation, district superintendents defended the inferior schools provided for black students and the smaller salaries paid to black teachers by arguing, first, that blacks in Kentucky had a lower standard of living than whites, and second, that blacks in all fields earned less than whites performing the same work, and the public would disapprove of equal pay for black and white teachers. Despite the inequities, Leonard Ephraim Meece, an educational researcher with the University of Kentucky, felt confident enough to

Barely literate herself, a Transylvania, Louisiana, woman teaches her sons letters and numbers at home in January 1939. *(Library of Congress, Prints and Photographs Division, LC-USF34-031938-D)*

comment in 1938, "It appears that Kentucky may be justly proud of progress made in Negro education."[10]

African Americans benefited from the educational provisions of the New Deal, especially those of the NYA. In 1935, African-American youths in the targeted age group suffered disproportionately because of the depression. They represented 13 percent of Americans in this age range but 15 percent of young people in families on relief. Most had received inferior educations and minimal vocational training in the segregated schools of the South, and opportunities had diminished in the lines of work typically open to them—agriculture and domestic service—because out-of-work whites were taking some of these jobs.

When the NYA was established in 1935, Roosevelt appointed to its National Advisory Committee two African Americans: Mordecai Johnson, president of Howard University, in Washington, D.C.; and Mary McLeod Bethune, a founder and the first president of Bethune-Cookman College, a school for African Americans in Daytona Beach, Florida. In 1936, the president chose Bethune to head the NYA's Division of Negro Affairs. In this position, she worked unceasingly to bring NYA training and employment to African Americans. In 1939, as a result of her efforts, six traditionally black colleges participated in the NYA's Civilian Pilot Training

Program (CPTP). Created ostensibly to increase the civilian flying force, the CPTP also boosted military preparedness in the years leading up to World War II. The pilot training conducted at the Tuskegee Institute, the Hampton Institute, Howard University, Delaware State College, North Carolina Agricultural and Technical State College, and West Virginia State College enabled African Americans to break down a barrier of discrimination and enter civilian and military aviation.

American Indian Culture in Government Schools

On April 21, 1933, John Collier, a social worker dedicated to securing self-government for Native peoples and protecting their cultures, took office as commissioner of Indian Affairs. Collier's influence led to passage of the Indian Reorganization Act of 1934, also known as the Wheeler-Howard Act, which permitted tribal self-government on a limited basis, restored to the Indians the right to manage their own assets, especially their land, and halted the sale of reservation land to non-Indians.

Under Collier's leadership, Native American history and traditions entered the curriculums of federal Indian schools. Collier introduced bilingual education for Indian children, basic instruction for adults, and ongoing training for the teaching staff. Beginning in the 1930s, the Indian Service required its teachers to have college degrees. During Collier's tenure, education in the federal Indian schools became more progressive, with teachers basing lessons on their students' culture and experiences. Writing assignments focused on Indian family life, customs, and legends and on village economic life. Children received instruction in crafts appropriate to their heritage, including blanket weaving in Navajo (Dineh) schools. Emphasizing active rather than rote learning, some teachers experimented with such innovations as using lunch as an opportunity for teaching English vocabulary.

In the 1930s the Haskell Institute and the boarding schools at Carlisle and Phoenix began offering more advanced courses of study. Students at the Phoenix school enjoyed a variety of extracurricular activities that included Boy Scouts, Campfire Girls, instrumental and choral music groups, sports teams, and literary and home economics clubs. The school also regularly sent a bookmobile to 23 surrounding day schools. By 1937, the faculty had cut back on athletics in order to stress academics and made the outing program optional.

Collier estimated that it cost three times as much to educate a child in a boarding school than in a day school near his or her home. The number of federal Indian boarding schools, which had dropped from 77 to 65 between 1928 and 1933, declined further under his leadership, and the number of day schools grew, despite the reluctance of some members of Congress to close boarding schools that benefited communities economically.

In 1935, when just 15 percent of Indian children were enrolled in school, Collier used $1.5 million in WPA funds to build 40 modern day schools with Indian labor. Four of the schools were intended to serve the Navajo population and were built to resemble outwardly the sacred Navajo home, or hogan, a five-sided structure that was often covered with adobe. For a number of reasons, the Navajo and other Native peoples failed to make the best use of the new schools, however. Not only were families on many Indian reservations dispersed, but also buses and other vehicles got stuck on unpaved and occasionally muddy reservation roads. In addition, buses and other modern equipment were of little value without personnel trained to operate and repair them.

Some Indian children attended public schools. Between 1934 and the end of the decade, four states—California, Washington, Minnesota, and Arizona—used federal funds made available by the 1934 Johnson-O'Malley Act to educate American Indian children in public schools, with less than optimal results. "Schools which they are attending rate from 'excellent' to 'very poor,'" stated Assistant Commissioner of Indian Affairs A. C. Monahan.[11] As state administrators resisted pressure from the Bureau of Indian Affairs to offer courses in Indian culture in schools that had eliminated vocational and enrichment classes, Indian students endured mistreatment and neglect by teachers and communities that resented their presence. Many children who entered school speaking little or no English had to fend for themselves, without tutors or interpreters. They immediately fell behind their classmates, and after a few years were too far out of step ever to catch up. The faculty in some schools sequestered Indian pupils and gave them busywork rather than lessons. These children received no report cards, made no progress, and left school when they came of age.

In 1935 Monahan spoke optimistically about young Indians attending college, supported by loans made available through the Indian Reorganization Act and other federal funds that might one day be appropriated for this purpose. He was obliged to admit, though, that "The number that can be thus taken care of is, of course, limited."[12]

Education for Democracy

In 1939, war again broke out in Europe. Nazi Germany had forcibly annexed Austria in March 1938 and Czechoslovakia in March 1939. When Adolf Hitler's forces moved into Poland, on September 1, 1939, Great Britain declared war on Germany. Across the Pacific Ocean, Imperial Japan was eager to take over territory in Southeast Asia, to seize petroleum and other resources. Roosevelt reaffirmed the neutrality of the United States, but, with an eye on events overseas, he issued a declaration of limited emergency, and he submitted to Congress a $1.319 billion defense budget.

If the Americans were to be drawn into another international conflict, this time they would be prepared. Increased spending for defense did what no federal jobs program had been able to do: It lifted the nation out of the depression. Many thousands of unemployed men and women went to work building military tanks, planes, ships, and weaponry. Colleges and universities responded to the changing political climate by instituting programs of defensive preparedness, such as the Civilian Pilot Training Program, that could easily be turned into wartime training if the need arose. Elementary and secondary schools modified their curriculums to include such concepts as totalitarianism and civil defense.

Chronicle of Events

1930s

- The Haskell Institute and the federal boarding schools for American Indians at Carlisle and Phoenix offer more advanced courses of study. The Phoenix school expands the range of its extracurricular activities.

1930

- The farm population receives 9 percent of the nation's income and is responsible for educating 31 percent of schoolchildren.
- The 11 states with the highest birth rates and lowest expenditures per pupil span the South and Southeast.
- The demand for librarians is greater than the supply.
- Duke University, developed with a gift of $20 million from James B. Duke, opens in Durham, North Carolina.
- *January:* Record cold temperatures are recorded in Denver and San Antonio.
- *January:* One in 10 able-bodied workers in Buffalo, New York, and one in four in Detroit are unemployed.
- *January:* One-fifth of the members of AFL-affiliated unions have lost their jobs.
- *December:* An estimated 4 million U.S. workers are unemployed.

1930–1931

- Nationwide, school enrollment, staff, and teachers' salaries increase slightly; capital outlay declines.
- The book fund of the Detroit public libraries totals $175,000.

1931

- Sixty public libraries surveyed by the American Library Association (ALA) spend $2,340,000 on new books.
- A large section of the Southwest begins to experience drought.

1931–1932

- The book fund of the Detroit public libraries totals $72,000.

1932

- Approximately 330,000 children are not being educated because their schools have closed.
- In Georgia, 1,318 schools accommodating 170,790 children are forced to close.
- One-fifth of schoolchildren examined by the New York City Health Department show signs of malnutrition.
- Chicago teachers are feeding 11,000 students.
- President Herbert Hoover establishes the Reconstruction Finance Corporation to lend money to businesses.
- College attendance drops for the first time since World War I.

1932–1933

- School budget cuts for this academic year average 3 percent in the Northeast and 16 percent in the cities of southern and central states.

1933

- The Chicago School Board closes junior high schools; reduces the number of kindergartens; cuts art, music, and physical education from the curriculum; and fires many central-office workers and half of elementary school principals.
- Textbook sales decline 30 percent from 1930.
- The circulation of books at public libraries increases 23 percent from 1929.
- Birmingham, Alabama, public libraries operate on half their 1930 budget.
- The 60 libraries surveyed by the ALA spend $957,000 on new books.
- Federal boarding schools for Indians, of which there were 77 in 1928, now number 65.
- *March 4:* President Franklin Delano Roosevelt is inaugurated.
- *March 31:* The Civilian Conservation Corps (CCC) is established for young men ages 18 to 25. Enrollment will top 250,000 this year.
- *spring:* Schools in Findlay and Cuyahoga Falls, Ohio, close following seven months of instruction.
- *spring:* In Alabama, 85 percent of public schools have closed.
- *April 21:* John Collier assumes the duties of commissioner of Indian Affairs.
- *October:* The Federal Emergency Relief Administration (FERA) establishes its Emergency Education Program to give work to teachers on relief.
- *fall:* FERA implements an experimental work-study program at the University of Minnesota.
- *December:* The CCC adds an educational component.

1933–1934

- Approximately 12,000 private elementary and secondary schools are in operation. Private schools educate one-tenth of elementary school pupils and one-sixteenth of high school students.

1933–1935
- Of the 3,753 schools for African Americans in Mississippi, 2,313 are housed in buildings owned by public school districts. The remainder meet in any available space.

1934
- One in 10 U.S. librarians is unemployed.
- The Federal Emergency Relief Administration (FERA) establishes 28 educational camps for women. FERA places about 20 percent of the 2,000 participants in jobs.
- The drought in the dust bowl of the Southwest has become severe.
- Nearly 44,000 U.S. schools have an average daily attendance between three and 17.
- Rural communities spend between $80 and $200 to educate a pupil in a small school; larger towns and villages spend $40 per child and offer superior instruction.
- The Indian Reorganization Act permits limited tribal self-government and protects Indians' rights to manage their own assets.
- The Johnson-O'Malley Act funds the education of Native American children in public schools.
- *February:* FERA extends its work-study program to colleges and universities nationwide.
- *June:* Some 1,225,000 Californians receive economic relief.

1935
- Federal legislation extends the life of the CCC for two years and expands its age range to include young men ages 17 to 28.
- CCC enrollment reaches its highest level, 505,872.
- Nearly half the children enrolled in school in the Bakersfield, California, area change schools at least once.
- The first two federal migrant camps open in Marysville and Arvin, California, under the direction of the Resettlement Administration.
- The Kansas State Planning Board counts 8,217 one-room schools in the state; 3,949 were built before 1900, 1,355 have no source of fresh water, and 832 have no playground equipment.
- African-American youths constitute 13 percent of their age group and 15 percent of young people in families on relief.
- Fifteen percent of American Indian children are enrolled in school.

- John Collier uses WPA funds to employ Indians to build 40 day schools.
- The NYA takes over from FERA the summer education program for women. About 3,000 women live and learn at 47 sites.
- *March:* FERA's Emergency Education Program employs more than 44,000 teachers to conduct classes for more than 1,274,000 adults and children.
- *March:* FERA college student aid finances the employment of 104,000 young men and women.
- *June 26:* Roosevelt creates the National Youth Administration by executive order.

1936
- Roosevelt appoints a committee to study the state of U.S. education and make recommendations on federal aid.
- The president chooses Mary McLeod Bethune to head the NYA's Division of Negro Affairs.

1937
- Federal legislation extends the CCC for three more years and lowers the upper age limit to 25.
- In Kentucky, teachers employed by the Works Progress Administration (WPA) instruct approximately 2,000 NYA enrollees in vocational and academic subjects.
- The Minneapolis Board of Education cooperates with the NYA to give a year of training to 450 young people at the Miller Vocational School.
- Public school teachers, WPA instructors, and social service workers instruct NYA youth in vocational and elementary academic subjects.
- On a typical day in New York City, the WPA instructs 17,000 adults.
- Roughly 1,250,000 students are enrolled in U.S. colleges and universities. College undergraduates account for 1 percent of the population and 15 percent of Americans in their age group.
- The U.S. Farm Security Administration (FSA) assumes control over the federal migrant camps in the West.
- The faculty of the federal Indian boarding school at Phoenix emphasizes academics over athletics and makes the outing (work on farms) program optional.

1938
- While enrolled in the CCC, 62,000 young men have learned to read and write, nearly 500,000 have completed elementary-level classes, and more than 400,000 have completed some high school work.

Teacher Lois Slinker eats lunch with her pupils on the grounds of their one-room school in Grundy County, Iowa, in October 1939. *(Library of Congress, Prints and Photographs Division, LC-USF34-028425-D)*

- WPA teachers in Ohio are among the adults who teach classes for NYA participants.
- WPA teachers have taught an estimated 1 million adults to read since 1933.
- The federal government has spent more than $2.4 billion on education since the start of the depression.
- Twenty-six states require specialized instruction for children with impaired sight, hearing, or speech or other disabilities.
- The President's Advisory Committee on Education publishes its report. The committee finds disturbing inequality in U.S. education and recommends federal funding for public and private schools.
- The advisory committee estimates that 325,000 of the 2.5 million children with special needs in the United States are being properly taught.
- The advisory committee recommends $855 million in federal spending for education over the next six years. This recommendation is never implemented.
- *March:* Germany annexes Austria.

1939
- The FSA manages 10 migrant camps in California and several more in other states.
- Roosevelt reaffirms U.S. neutrality, but he also declares a state of limited emergency and drafts a $1.319 billion defense budget.
- Six traditionally black colleges and universities participate in the NYA's Civilian Pilot Training Program.
- *March:* Germany annexes Czechoslovakia.
- *September 1:* Germany invades Poland; France and Great Britain declare war on Germany.

1940
- Public school enrollment in Kern County, California, has increased 300 percent since 1935.

Eyewitness Testimony

In some school systems, the administration of an intelligence test to each child yearly is rated as in itself a significant accomplishment, demonstrating the "scientific" basis of the system. In collegiate and university departments of education an enormous number of "courses" have as their content some form of mental testing. To some departments, the growth of mental testing has been a veritable god-send, enabling them to greatly expand their staff, to promulgate the satisfying news that education (pedagogy) is now on a "scientific" basis, just like physics and psychology. . . .

Knight Dunlap, professor of psychology, Johns Hopkins University, 1930, "Mental Tests," p. 123.

At one time viewed as the people's college, the high school is apparently coming to be a place where an increasingly large segment of American youth can get a little knowledge of almost every imaginable subject, practical, often in the most trivial sense, or cultural, sometimes in the best sense. Subject-matter, like Latin, mathematics, or history, and skills, like typewriting and cooking, are ingeniously combined on an utterly fallacious theory into "units," "points," and "counts"; and when by a simple arithmetical process enough "points" have been accumulated and enough hours and years have been consumed in the process, the pupil has received "a four-year high school education." Calculation by means of arithmetically added "points" serves, unintentionally, greatly to reduce intellectual effort. The four-year course is at first broken up into bits; it is easier to master bits than to master a whole; the credits accumulate from year to year. . . . The prevailing philosophy of education tends to discredit hard work. Individuality must be respected. Undoubtedly. The child's creative possibilities must be allowed to unfold. Certainly. But by the time several such considerations have come into play, discipline through effort has been relegated to a very subordinate position.

Abraham Flexner, founder of the Lincoln School, a laboratory school at Columbia University, 1930, Universities: American English German, *pp. 46–47.*

[A] student of Columbia College may study serious subjects in a serious fashion. But he may also complete the requirements for a bachelor's degree by including in his course of study "principles of advertising," "the writing of advertised copy," "advertising layouts," "advertising research," "practical poultry raising," "secretarial booking," "business English," "elementary stenography," "newspaper practice," "reporting and copy editing," "feature writing," "book reviewing," "wrestling, judo and self-defence." If an advanced student in the School of Practical Arts, he may count towards a Columbia degree courses taken in Teachers College—an independent corporation belonging to Columbia—"in cookery—fundamental processes," "fundamental problems in clothing," "clothing decoration," "family meals," "recent research in cookery," "food etiquette and hospitality," "principles of home laundering," "social life of the home," "gymnastics and dancing for men including practice in clog dancing," and "instruction (elementary or advanced) in school orchestras and bands."

Is not this an appalling situation?

Abraham Flexner, founder of the Lincoln School, a laboratory school at Columbia University, 1930, Universities: American English German, *pp. 55–56.*

To my thinking, the greatest and the fundamental weakness in American education comes from the fact that the brightest minds are withdrawn from it. I do not mean to convey the idea that individual great minds are not in education, but that, on the one hand, the great imaginative and creative genius of America is not in it, and on the other, that the machinery and the range of higher education have outgrown completely the minds of the men available to direct it.

It may be questioned whether an important innovation in educational practice has been made in this country except as a result of pressure or compulsion from without. In the motor, airplane, or radio industries, executives design next year's machines this year. They do not wait for the public to demand improvements; they anticipate wants. In education, however, vision has been lacking to foresee and prepare for the social structures of the future. Those who might have proved to be the commanding educational statesmen of our day, and of future days, have been enticed into commerce or industry or other professions than education and the ministry, neither of which has been offering adequate inducements that are necessary in order to command the services of the brightest minds.

Matthew Lyle Spencer, president, University of Washington, June 1930, in "Think Straight," p. 5.

Sixty-five per cent of the total expenses of operating the public schools of the United States goes for teachers' salaries. The reasons for this are the increase in the number of children taught, the increase in the cost of living, and increased demands made upon the modern teacher. A parent now wants his child's mind developed, he wants him to know how to think, to desire knowledge, to have self-confidence, and to have initiative; and he expects these to be acquired in school. His acquiring these valuable traits in school depends upon the kind of teacher he gets, and the kind of teacher depends upon the salary paid. Society each year places increasing burdens upon the school. Each decade demands a higher type of training for successful living. Each year the school calls for teachers with greater capacity and better training. Such teachers cannot be obtained at the rate paid unskilled labor because training costs money and must be paid for. The statement is sometimes made that teachers are paid all they are worth. That is only a recognition of the economic law that the price paid regulates the quality. It is equally true that what teachers are paid largely determines their worth.

Clyde Duncan, member of the Texas State Teachers Association, June 1930, "Salaries of Public School Teachers," p. 10.

The teacher who has a standard of living which permits her to live in comfortable quarters, where her evenings are not always spent mending clothes, doing her laundry, or something to add to her low salary, brings to her classroom vigor, enthusiasm, self-respect, and initiative. She brings to her pupils life more abundant. To do this she herself must so live that she has self-respect and the respect of the community. Can a community expect a teacher to interpret life correctly to children when her standard of living is below that of the majority of the people of ability and culture in the community?

Clyde Duncan, member of the Texas State Teachers Association, June 1930, "Salaries of Public School Teachers," p. 10.

Train for citizenship! This Exhortation comes to the teacher in increasing volume both from outside sources and from inner compulsion. Se far as the schools are concerned, they are now committed to the idea of having the child live his citizenship in the every-day situations of school, neighborhood, and home. This, I take it, we are all agreed is properly so. Analogies and experiences to support this position are readily found, and efforts to refute it are scarcely attempted.

Supplementary methods to aid this plan must be resorted to, however, just as the melody in a composition, the thing we carry away with us, whistling or humming it

gladly, is most effective when supported by a fitting harmony. Chief among these helps is good literature. We have no more effective antidote against the undesirable impressions that may come to him from the conversation and the acts of cynical adults, against the false admiration of people whose unsocial conduct has given them temporary publicity, against the lurid appeal of sordid lawlessness which unfortunately in the daily papers is often fitted out in heroic dress, than may be found in the record of the noble people of history and the best characters of fiction. These writers put into the pages of their books men and women who have lived lives of service, who have met hard circumstances and overcome them, who have sacrificed personal gain or pleasure for community good, who have placed at their country's command their abilities of heart and body and mind, and the boy or girl takes from these pages an impetus toward emulation which is sure in its power.

George F. Cassell, principal of the Penn School, Chicago, August 1930, "English and Its Value to Our Schools," p. 43.

After my four years in high school I began to wonder about this college idea and to mull over in my mind its practical value. Realizing that after graduation I was to face the world on whatever equipment the schools had given to me, and realizing that such would be my sole aid in earning my way, I coldly weighed the values that a college education would impart—and found them wanting!

However, because my reluctance to enter college was indefinitely formed and because it was the accepted thing to do in my community, I entered the Freshman college class in the university at my home. At the end of the second quarter I had definitely crystallized my thoughts and I left school, to work in a foundry. After a few months of this I saw the need for more education of some kind and so I returned to school to learn a trade. This I learned and then, upon the advice of others, I reentered and finished the college course. This is all, of course, auto-biographical, yet is indicative of the train of thought of any average student of college rank.

Since leaving college I have found my former beliefs justified—that I earn my living by the use of my trade and that my college degree is of use to me only in a social way!

John Louis Clarke, African-American college graduate, October 1930, in "Students Answer the Professor," p. 336.

If the Indian Service were starting afresh on the task of Indian education, with what is now known of the processes of change and adjustment through schools and other agencies, it would undoubtedly begin with the Indian people in their own environment or in some comparable environment in which they could develop their own resources. It would employ other methods than some of those that have been employed—it would not use to any extent the reservation, "rations," or distant boarding schools for young children. But we are not starting afresh, and cannot; one kind of philosophy and one kind of system have been established for a long time. The basic Indian Service educational problem, therefore, is to work over from a more or less conventional institutional conception of education to one that is local and individual. It means abandoning boarding schools wherever possible, eliminating small children from the larger boarding schools, setting up day schools, or making arrangements with the local public schools to receive these children, providing the necessary family follow-up for such children, and directing the boarding schools into specialized purposes, at least partly vocational; in the meantime all these boarding schools . . . [need] to be made as effective educationally as it is possible to make them, utilizing Indian arts and crafts and Indian culture generally wherever these exist or can be revived, and developing throughout the service at all levels a staff of workers who understand the new point of view.

Charles Rhodes, commissioner of Indian affairs, 1931, in W. Carson Ryan, Jr., and Rose K. Brandt, "Indian Education Today," pp. 83–84.

A group of University of Chicago faculty members warns against the ravages of undernourishment among children in the public schools. It appears that principals and teachers in many schools have for several months been contributing from their salaries in order to provide free lunches for hungry children. Allowances have been made to the schools from the fund raised by the Governor's Commission on Unemployment, but the money has been insufficient to meet the need.

Meantime, the [Chicago] Board of Education announces that it has exhausted its fund for the payment of teachers and other educational purposes.

New York Times, April 8, 1931, in Sol Cohen, ed., Education in the United States, vol. 4, p. 2527.

Looking over the recent catalogues of the leading Negro colleges, I find their courses drawn up without much thought about the Negro. Invariably these institutions give courses in ancient, mediaeval, and modern Europe, but they do not offer courses in ancient, mediaeval, and

A girl prepares a hot lunch donated by a farm family for herself and her schoolmates in Walmouth County, Wisconsin, in the 1930s. *(Wisconsin Historical Society, WHi-43904)*

modern Africa. Yet Africa, according to recent discoveries, has contributed about as much to the progress of mankind as Europe has, and the early civilization of the Mediterranean world was decidedly influenced by the so-called Dark Continent.

Negro colleges offer courses bearing on the European colonists prior to their coming to America, their settlement on these shores, and their development here toward independence. Why not be equally as generous with the Negroes in treating their status in Africa prior to enslavement, their first transplantation to the West Indies, the Latinization of certain Negroes in contradistinction to the development of others under the influence of the Teuton, and the effort of the race toward self-expression in America?

Carter G. Woodson, historian, August 1931, "The Miseducation of the Negro," p. 267.

There can be no good individual apart from some conception of the character of the *good* society; and the good society is not something that is given by nature: it must be fashioned by the hand and brain of man. This process of building a good society is to a very large degree an educational process. The nature of the child must of course be taken into account in the organization of any educational program, but it cannot furnish the materials and the guiding principles of that program. Squirm and wriggle as we may, we must admit that the bringing of materials and guiding principles from the outside involves the molding of the child.

> *George S. Counts, professor of education, Teachers College, Columbia University, 1932,* Dare the School Build a New Social Order? *pp. 15–16.*

The world is changing with great rapidity; the rate of change is being accelerated constantly; the future is full of uncertainty. Consequently the individual who is to live and thrive in this world must possess an agile mind, be bound by no deep loyalties, hold all conclusions and values tentatively, and be ready on a moment's notice to make even fundamental shifts in outlook and philosophy. Like a lumberjack riding a raft of logs through the rapids, he must be able with lightning speed to jump from one insecure foundation to another, if he is not to be overwhelmed by the onward surge of the cultural stream. In a word, he must be as willing to adopt new ideas and values as to install the most up-to-the-minute labor saving devices in his dwelling or to introduce the latest inventions into his factory. Under such a conception of life and society, education can only bow down before the gods of chance and reflect the drift of the social order. This conception is essentially anarchic in character, exalts the irrational above the rational forces of society, makes of security an individual rather than a social goal, drives every one of us into an insane competition with his neighbors, and assumes that man is incapable of controlling in the common interest the creatures of his brain. Here we have imposition with a vengeance, but not the imposition of the teacher or the school. Nor is it an enlightened form of imposition. Rather it is the imposition of the chaos and cruelty and ugliness produced by the brutish struggle for existence and advantage. Far more terrifying than any indoctrination in which the school might indulge is the prospect of our becoming completely victimized and molded by the mechanics of industrialism.

> *George S. Counts, professor of education, Teachers College, Columbia University, 1932,* Dare the School Build a New Social Order? *pp. 26–27.*

Here is a young engineer who wants everything on subway building, for a civil service examination. Next a woman is making scarfs to sell and needs some attractive designs. Next a man experimenting at home with a new varnish formula. Next, one who is trading his city equity for a farm, and wants to know all about the soil, climate, and so on, of the locality. Some want to study foreign languages, others to pick up their education where they left off when they went to work. They are not working now and might as well do that. One young man had to have the lives of famous clowns. A few weeks later one of our branch librarians recognized him on the stage in a local show, where he had a job as a clown.

> *Carl Roden, Chicago librarian, 1932, in Robert L. Duffus,* Our Starving Libraries: Studies in Ten American Communities during the Depression Years, *p. 35.*

It is pitch dark and forty below zero when we start the fire that modifies the temperature in our one-room school plant. The big cannonball heater glows like a red moon. Noiselessly, dark forms begin to congregate although the first bell has not sounded.

At eight thirty we ring the bell and light the gas lamps. Most of the school children have arrived and are in their places although school does not commence until nine. It is still ten below zero in the schoolroom when the flag is saluted and school opens. A fourteen-year-old boy in deerskin mukluks, parka and sealskin trousers goes to the humble organ and plays with gloved hands. Rich voices rise in melody and a thick fog rises in the room; the frozen desk tops become white with frost. As they sing, the children hold their ink bottles in their hands, alternately blowing on them and singing.

We watch the bottles. When sufficient ink has thawed we start the penmanship class.

> *Edward L. Keithahn, public school principal, Kake, Alaska, February 1932, p. 136.*

There are two extremes represented in the attempts of a Navajo child learning to read. On the one hand, he reads fluently and with good expression but has not the slightest conception of what it is all about; on the other hand, if he is interested, he comprehends the subject matter but seems to have very little mechanical memory for the words used in the context. "Neither would you," said a teacher with whom I was discussing this problem. "Don't you keep a dictionary at hand when learning a foreign language?"

> *Helen E. Lawhead, teacher, Theodore Roosevelt School, Fort Apache, Arizona, February 1932, "Teaching Navajo Children to Read," p. 131.*

[I]n a democratic country such as ours ideally is, the ultimate end of racial segregation in all branches of our society should be to destroy the need for its own existence. Put differently, this means that segregation should be regarded by Negroes as a means to an end rather than as an end in itself. When so conceived the function of the Negro college, for example, should be to equip itself according to the standards of the best white colleges, so as to provide its students *pari passu* with the mere tools of living. But, at one and the same time, it should orient its students to the need for a continuous, critical examination of the soundness of the principle underlying segregation, to the end that they will accept it merely as an immediate condition, and not as an ultimate fact. The ultimate problem of the separate Negro school, therefore, is that of the American race problem in general: to see to it that whilst the Negro improves himself intraracially, that he also remain ever sensitive to the need for preserving and propagating the ideal of freedom in all social relationships.

J. St. Clair Price, Howard University, July 1932, "General Summary and Conclusions," pp. 334–335.

Vocational and "hobby" reading took a spurt in Detroit, as in other cities. An excellent technological department, including what is probably the best collection in the country dealing with the automobile industry, and a downtown business library, helped to meet this demand. The unemployed worker, eager, at least during the first months of his idleness, to prepare himself for a better job or to catch up with reading he "had always meant to do when he had time," was a familiar figure. The class of visitors described by some rather unfeeling observers as "bums" did not become a serious problem in Detroit. "Bum" is, in fact, a difficult word to define. If it signifies the externals of abundant leisure, ragged clothes, and an appearance of undernourishment it may be applied to those who in happier times were considered desirable patrons.

Robert L. Duffus, journalist, 1933, Our Starving Libraries: Studies in Ten American Communities during the Depression Years, *p. 25.*

Our school system is in the throes of an agony induced by the State-wide, nation-wide and world-wide financial panic. The shafts of light which have begun to shine through the nation's financial clouds have not reached the doors of the schools of this State. The sacrifices made by teachers, though great, have not proved sufficient, nor can they ever be sufficient, nor should they be expected to be sufficient, to carry through the complete school program without help. . . .

The boasted free school is no more. If a normal term is to be conducted, advancing children a grade each year, it must be maintained as a private or subscription school, the expenses falling heaviest upon those least able to pay, and from which those unable to pay are often excluded.

The very existence of higher institutions is threatened. Their teachers have been patient but have in many cases reached their limit of credit. Merchants are notifying college professors that they must pay something on account or stop buying food. Few teachers of elementary, high school or college rank have been paid their entire salaries to date and most of them are three to eight months behind in pay. Many others have had no checks for virtually an entire year.

A. F. Harmon, state superintendent of schools, Alabama, April 23, 1933, in F. Raymond Daniell, "Crisis Threatens Alabama Schools," p. 1.

If any particular building were to be selected to accompany the bellicose-looking eagle on the national seal, that building undoubtedly would be a schoolhouse. Both logic and sentiment would dictate the choice, for the public school is a peculiarly American institution. It is the social service and political unit which most closely touches the lives of us all. From the highest officials down to the ordinary citizen most Americans have reserved for it a special brand of loyalty which has been far more than lip service. Perhaps only the word "mother" is wrapped in a thicker fold of sentimentality than that which has enveloped "the little red schoolhouse."

In observing the contemporary scene one must continually remind oneself of this traditional American attitude toward the public schools, otherwise one misses some of the deepest shades and most significant lines in the picture. For the school system is being deflated with a thoroughness, I almost said savagery, which no one a few years ago could have imagined possible in the hardest of hard times.

Avis D. Carlson, writer, November 1933, "Deflating the Schools," p. 705.

On the whole, consolidation in Negro schools has not brought the desired benefits to all Negro scholastics. The greatest handicap to the development of consolidation of Negro schools is the lack of transportation for the children, and the whites take no interest in the matter. Excepting the county training schools, there is little or

A teacher guides a pupil at the blackboard in Lakeview Project, Arkansas, in December 1938. Lakeview Project was one of about 200 planned communities established by the U.S. Resettlement Administration during the depression in an attempt to lift families out of poverty. *(Library of Congress, Prints and Photographs Division, LC-USF34-031873-D)*

no transportation provided for Negro children. Where consolidation has occurred many Negro children are cut off from school because the distance to school is too great for them to walk, and no means of transportation is provided. In one community there are five families of Negroes who do not send their children to school at all. The nearest school is seven miles away. Apparently no effort has been made to provide educational advantages for the children of these Negro families. In another community where the white schools have consolidated, one of the districts included in the consolidation has fourteen Negro scholastics who have no school. No provision is made for these children to have a school in their community, and no means of transportation is provided for them to attend school elsewhere. . . .

It is not unusual for Negro children to walk five miles to school. In one community where five white schools have consolidated into one system, the Negro schools of these districts have also joined together in a consolidated system, with three teachers. A Rosenwald building is being used. The Negroes worked out their own consolidation plans, without aid, and with little encouragement. . . .

William R. Davis, professor of history, Stephen F. Austin State College, 1934, The Development and Present Status of Negro Education in East Texas, *p. 69.*

The building was a crude box shack built by the Negroes out of old slabs and scrap lumber. Windows and doors were badly broken. The floor was in such condition that one had to walk carefully to keep from going through cracks and weak boards. Daylight was easily visible through walls, floor, and roof. The building was used for both church and school. Its only equipment consisted of a few roughhewn seats, an old stove brought from a junk pile, a crude homemade pulpit, a very small table, and a large water barrel. All the children drank from the open barrel which was refilled with fresh water only when it became empty. Water was hauled to the schoolhouse and poured through a window into the barrel. There was no blackboard and there were no desks. When the children wrote, their knees served for desks. Fifty-two children were enrolled. All these crowded into a single small room, with benches for but half the number. The teacher and pupils had tacked newspapers on the walls to keep the wind out. Rain poured through the roof, and school was dismissed when it rained. No supplies, except a broom, were furnished the school by the district during the year.

A student's description of a school for African Americans in East Texas, 1934, in William R. Davis, The Development and Present Status of Negro Education in East Texas, *p. 56.*

When I joined the CCC I was still all hopelessness and despair. My viewpoint had become so distorted that life and law were all wrong to me, and there seemed no such thing as justice. The long tramp from coast to coast, looking for the job I never found, hadn't improved my temper any. But there is something soul-satisfying about good hard labor, especially when you've ached for something to do for three long years. The CCC became a kind of game—one that kept challenging the best that was in me. It caused me to take stock of my shortcomings and to set up a standard of mental and physical perfection.

The Civilian Conservation Corps has regenerated me mentally, physically, and spiritually. It has given me practical knowledge about camp life, plumbing, carpentry, bookkeeping; but more than that, it has taught me to appreciate the good things in life. I have learned to appreciate what Thoreau calls "the beneficence of nature." In the deepening twilight my eyes stray up until they rest upon the last tall pine on the hills, etched against the afterglow of the sun. And as it fades, a flood of memories closes in upon me—memories of the boy who wearily tramped the streets and sought death in the bitterness of despair. Happiness to him was something out of reach, somewhere beyond the stars. I know now the serenity of soul that comes from a busy, well-ordered life. And happiness—well, happiness, is here, not beyond but beneath the stars.

A CCC enrollee, 1934, in C. S. Marsh, "The Educational Program of the Civilian Conservation Corps," p. 405.

A thin little youngster stops at the desk to have her "admit slip" signed after absence. "Feeling better?" you ask. "Oh, I wasn't sick," she answers in a thread of a voice. "It was my mother. She fainted on the street and they brought her home. We didn't know she was so tired." Your heart gushes out of you like water running waste in a gutter. You go down the aisle to a girl who is not working. "Something the matter, Olga?" She doesn't move; she doesn't speak for a long minute—"Yesterday afternoon," she says breathlessly, "I saw—my mother—jump out the window. . . . She's dead. My father thought—I'd best be—in school." . . .

There are girls out six, eight, even ten weeks, whose note from home about the absence concludes, "I'll appreciate it if the teachers will cooperate to help her make up the work she has missed." There are others whose attendance record is fairly perforated with absence.

Fannie B. Biggs, New York City, teacher, February 2, 1934, "The Teacher's Side of It," p. 16.

What are our obstacles? Obviously these: Great variety of study interests; dearth of suitable text material for adults; lack of comfortably furnished and adequately lighted discussion and classrooms; lack of ample library books, though each camp has a library; lack of laboratory facilities; fatigue on the part of enrollees after a day of labor; sufficient teacher-training of the advisers directed toward this particular task.

What are our advantages? In the first place, enrolment is voluntary. No one has to study anything. Only those who want to learn will continue in a class. Moreover, the men themselves decide what they want to be taught. Then, too, no credits are at stake. For the most part the work is informal and the plan flexible. We shall get ingenious and virile teaching. The teacher or discussion leader who can not hold the attention of a group of men, under conditions which the camp presents, simply is not the right man for the job. He may have been an able administrator, or he may have been an acceptable teacher of formal classes, but if he can not do this job under conditions as they are, he must give place to some one who can. But our great advantage is that here is comradeship in quest of knowledge. Learners and teachers live together under camp conditions. A teacher or discussion leader confronted by a student's baffling question can not well retreat behind a Jovian frown. His success will largely depend upon the extent to which in genuine comradeship he and those who help him can lead these young men along the paths of knowledge.

C. S. Marsh, educational director, Civilian Conservation Corps, March 31, 1934, "The Educational Program of the Civilian Conservation Corps," p. 404.

"Shorter hours when people need longer hours, few new books when people want to study and need up-to-date books, fewer assistants when new patrons are crowding our reading rooms and needing personal assistance"—a summary of the effect of the depression on the Minneapolis Public Library by its librarian, now president of the American Library Association, applies equally well to libraries the country over.

If hundreds or thousands of public libraries had closed their doors completely, as rural schools have done, their communities would at least have realized what they were losing and quite possibly would have found some alternative. But librarians have been ingenious in stretching greatly reduced funds to provide as much service as possible. They may not have made clear to their readers or to public officials that more was at stake than temporary curtailments of hours of opening or of book buying—that the backbone of their book collection was wearing out.

Julia Wright Merrill, chief, Public Library Division, American Library Association, May 1934, "What the Depression Has Done to Public Libraries," p. 135.

In a democratic society, dependent upon a general high level of intelligence, provision for continuing self-education of adults is an essential. The free public library is an important agency for adult education, and has been one of America's contributions to democracy. If the "new deal" is to bring increased leisure and added social responsibility, library service, with its educational side more emphasized, will be of greater rather than of less importance, and will warrant generous financial support. It is to be hoped that increased appropriations can come in time to save the service already developed.

Julia Wright Merrill, chief, Public Library Division, American Library Association, May 1934, "What the Depression Has Done to Public Libraries," p. 139.

It has been pathetic to watch the tremendous deterioration of our book supply under the strain of constant use. The very heart of our collections has been in danger.

But even this has not been an unmixed evil. People have turned to older titles which were as good if not better than the newer ones. Librarians have become expert in displaying their wares with interesting labels, and have deliberately guided the way to good literature. The new readers who came were often unacquainted with books or library ways and took readily the advice of library assistants. Conscientious assistants have all become readers' advisers to good purpose. We have learned much about the guidance of readers; we have increased our attention to individual men and women, through the very necessity of making our book stock carry the demands upon it and through sympathy for each reader.

Gratia A. Countryman, librarian, Minneapolis Public Library, May 1934, "Value of Library Must Be Sold to City Officials," p. 140.

The municipal government in most cities has not felt that the library was an essential part of the government. It has had no political significance, nor have its patrons been organized or vocal. I believe this depression, during which libraries have received more than their share of cuts, has taught library trustees, librarians, and friends of libraries that they must be aggressive and more insistent in presenting their needs to the tax-levying bodies. If we believe in

adult education and opportunity through books, why not fight earnestly for support as do other city departments?

Gratia A. Countryman, librarian, Minneapolis Public Library, May 1934, "Value of Library Must Be Sold to City Officials," p. 140.

More than three hundred of the best citizens of this community gathered at the Brown schoolhouse Sunday for a regular good old time picnic. If everyone present did not have a good time it was nobody's fault but their own, as everyone apparently came with but one idea in view and that was to have a good sociable time. Cars began to roll in about eleven o'clock and unload baskets and in a short time, two tables 30 feet long were filled with all the good eats you could think of. To look at those tables you would not think there were any hard times around here. While the ladies prepared dinner, men played horseshoes and softball to work up an appetite and they were sure ready to do justice to the fine dinner. After the dinner an excellent program was put on by old and young.

Report of a "Grand Picnic" held on school grounds from the Argenta, Illinois, Register, August 3, 1934, in Wayne E. Fuller, One-Room Schools of the Middle West: A History, p. 111.

Last year we thought we were hard up because school closed April 1. This year I guess we aren't going to have school at all. Eighth graders from our school and from Turtle River are trying to keep up our work. Pastor T's wife has us at the parsonage Friday mornings to hear our lessons. But most of the time is taken up with her asking how we do things and comparing with the ways in Norway. Well, I guess I'll have to give up my plan to take highschool. With the school closed (I feel like crying every time I see it with the doors and windows boarded up) I'll be too old before I am ready to go to highschool. Do you think you could get on without a school or even a set of books? Grace has the Arithmetic VIII and I have the grammar. Teacher let us borrow them when school closed. I guess she had a hunch how this year was going to be. For all of us that go to the parsonage there is one history book. It's the one the Swanson's oldest boy had the year he went to town. It stops before the War but I guess there hasn't been much since then except trouble and I don't need a book to learn about that.

Anna, 14, Minnesota student, 1935, in Charles A. Beard and William G. Carr, "The Schools Weathering a Storm," p. 149.

Picture how you would feel with two or three children headed for school, almost barefoot, with ragged or ill-fitting clothing. You see them going down the road with a paper bag in their hands, with two baking-powder biscuits, maybe, and some beans in-between. And if you were a little child, how would you feel going to school that way—and when it comes noon you sit down in your little bunch and drag out those two sandwiches full of beans, when the rest of the little ones are sitting around you there, children of more fortunate people? How do the children feel?

A dust bowl emigrant, a father, ca. 1935, in Jerry Stanley,
Children of the Dust Bowl: The True Story of the
School at Weedpatch Camp, *p. 39.*

Public education in Harlem has been . . . long and grossly neglected. The facts are notorious.

Dirt and filth and slovenliness have no more educational value for our children than for yours. . . . new school-houses with ample grounds and appropriate modern facilities are urgently needed to supplement or replace overcrowded and outmoded structures, to provide for the large increase in our population during the past decade or more. . . .

Teachers, principals and superintendents are needed who have abiding faith in our children and genuine respect for the loins and traditions from which they have sprung. . . .

So far as public education is concerned, we beg you to dispel by concrete action the widespread conviction that this region is neglected because its people are comparatively poor in the world's goods and in social and political influence, because many of them are of African descent.

*Petition submitted to the New York City Board of Education
by Harlem residents, March 1935, in Cheryl Lynn Greenberg,*
"Or Does It Explode?" Black Harlem in the Great
Depression, *p. 190.*

The school plant as a whole is old, shabby . . . in many instances not even sanitary or well-kept and the fire hazards . . . are great. The lack of playgrounds and recreational centers . . . is all the more serious when it is considered that some of the schools are surrounded by . . . corrupt and immoral resorts of which the police seem blissfully unaware. Four of the schools lack auditoriums: one endeavors to serve luncheons to 1,000 children when there are seats for only 175. Most of all, no elementary school has been constructed in Harlem in 10 years. . . .

Prejudicial discrimination appears from the fact that the Board of Education, asking funds from the federal government for 168 school buildings, asked for but one annex for Harlem.

*Conclusion of the Mayor's Commission on Conditions in
Harlem, April 1935, in Cheryl Lynn Greenberg, "Or Does
It Explode?" Black Harlem in the Great Depression,
p. 189.*

In the Government day schools for Indians exists an excellent opportunity for breaking away from the so-called formalized or stereotyped curriculum, and developing an active program in which the "Three Rs" may be correlated with life training through prevocational activities, home making activities, health activities, and cultural activities. The importance of reading, writing and arithmetic should not be underestimated, but it must be remembered that these subjects are but tools to a full education and have relatively slight value unless they are made useable and continued in use during the entire lives of the pupils. The mere ability to read, for instance, has little value unless the ability is used in after life. Reading for pleasure is, of course, an asset. Reading for information is a greater asset. However, ability to read and interpret printed instructions and to put into operation the instructions in life improvement is a much greater asset. There is available in the United States a great deal of instructive literature in the form of Government, State and other bulletins which have direct application to the improvement of living. Such bulletins have to do with all phases of life, but particularly with agriculture, home making and health. If Indians in their lives after school are going to make use of such available printed instructions, they will have to be taught in the school how to do so.

*A. C. Monahan, assistant commissioner of Indian Affairs,
August 15, 1935, "The Indian Education Program," p. 11.*

A deeper reach of effort is seen in the day schools among some of the tribal Indians. Here, the problem of conserving and using the natural resources is an overwhelming one, and the schools build their activity around this pressing problem. Conserving the soil; breeding up the sheep; flood-water farming, and the use of irrigated land; the use and increase of native plants; marketing of produce and the buying of commodities; these are natural elements in the curricula of these schools. The school life of necessity is bi-lingual, because the schools serve adult and child needs alike and most of the Indians as yet do not talk English. English is learned more genuinely and more rapidly than it ever was in the segregated boarding schools, and it becomes a living language, into which the personality of the child molds itself. But the native language is not frowned on.

John Collier, commissioner of Indian Affairs, in an untitled introduction to the August 15, 1935, issue of Indians at Work, *pp. 5–6.*

In every camp one was immediately struck with the overwhelming need of constructive assistance for unemployed women. To see a group of girls assemble on the first night of any school, was to receive an immediate and tragic impression of the results of unemployment. Thin, emaciated girls (most of them under twenty-one years of age), they were overwhelmed at the sight of a simple supper on that first night. One Director wrote "great was my bewilderment at the polite but unresponsive meal crowds until I realized that they were there to eat. Singing or even casual conversation marred the flavor of corn bread dripping in butter and the crackle of bacon and made questionable the assurance of a second helping."

Many girls showed symptoms of long fatigue, exhausted nerves, and mental strain; many expressed tense anxiety in leaving husbands, fathers, or brothers unemployed; thankful, however, to relieve them of the burden of another person to feed for the summer. All were bewildered in trying to understand what was happening in their own lives;—why they were out of work, what the government could do to help them, but above all, what they could do to help themselves. All expressed a strong desire in all discussions for reliable advice on occupations for which they might qualify, vocational training, and the first steps they might take in trying to secure a job. Above all one was impressed with their courage, almost the courage of desperation, in facing an uncertain future, for themselves and their dependents.

U.S. Federal Emergency Relief Association, May 1936, Report of Resident Schools and Educational Camps for Unemployed Women, *p. 5.*

It seemed obvious in many places that the directors and staff were filled with enthusiasm in the opportunity to have a place in the camp and take part in a pioneer experiment. It was equally obvious to anyone familiar with the educational needs of unemployed women that in many cases the staff was not equipped to meet these needs. This apparent lack of special qualifications in many teachers was easily explained when one realized the rapidity with which the camps had been organized, the necessity of choosing teachers from among those eligible for relief, and the fact that the plan itself led teach-

ers into new and untried fields of social and educational experiment.

Added to these deficiencies in the educational program, was the fact, reiterated by many students and expressed in their letters, that they had not been informed accurately as to the type of instruction they might expect. They were not always interested, therefore, in the courses which they found open to them. Many girls held the illusion that the camps would prepare them for immediate jobs, and were disappointed to find that they could not find employment after they left.

U.S. Federal Emergency Relief Association, May 1936, Report of Resident Schools and Educational Camps for Unemployed Women, *pp. 7–8.*

When I went to camp, my particular problem had become one of acute mental depression—the trip to camp was simply welcomed as a possible temporary escape from my troubles. However, it wasn't long before the delightful contact with my camp-mates, all of whom seemed to have in common problems much the same as mine; the refreshing and invigorating camp life; the understanding, sympathetic helpfulness of the counsellors, all conspired to change completely the dark aspect of my mental outlook. I attained new courage, new determination, new confidence in myself, in short a reconstructed mental outlook on life. Nor was this confined to my case alone. It was apparent in the uplifted heads, the steady gaze, the smiling countenances of each individual at the close of camp.

A FERA women's educational camp participant, May 1936, in Report of Resident Schools and Educational Camps for Unemployed Women, *pp. 8–9.*

The white school [near Shelby Post Office, Virginia] has three large rooms, three teachers, ninety children, with four buses to bring them to school. The equipment inside is excellent, with desks, and small tables and chairs for special activities. . . .

The colored school has one room, one teacher, fifty-three children, who must walk if they get to school. The children have to sit on uncomfortable homemade benches. With no equipment whatever, the teacher was trying to do a progressive job of teaching. On a rickety table in one corner of the room were some dishes and bowls, for which the teacher apologized, because it was lunch time, for which she was trying to give the children hot lunches. A well had been dug four years ago, but efforts to get a pump put in had failed, and the school was getting its water from a neighbor's spring.

"'Equal' Schools in Virginia," November 1936, p. 333.

A typical Harlem school is like a prison, and a badly run one at that. Even the most diligent scrubbing cannot really clean a building built in the 70's or 80's; that there is not diligent scrubbing the odor of ages in the lunchrooms and the rubbish accumulated under benches testify. The children have none of the *joie de vivre* popularly associated with their age, and tuck their rachitic legs under benches too small for them in rooms unadorned, bleak and dingy. Teachers, trying to cope with classes whose numbers average slightly more than even those in other overcrowded sections, with children who have eye defects and toothaches and empty stomachs, suffer from frayed nerves and give way to harsh-voiced impatience.

Few teachers would make a Harlem appointment first choice. The Board has a ruling that new teachers will not be granted transfers until three years after appointment, and the inexperienced undergo a three years' purgatory at the expense of pupils who need the most experienced. Some bring with them indifference, some prejudice. Discriminatory practices are supposedly dealt with by the authorities; yet one teacher who snapped, "How dare you talk like that to a white woman?" was still teaching in the same school weeks after the incident.

Edith M. Stern, writer, July 1937, "Jim Crow Goes to School in New York," pp. 201–202.

[T]he Florida Negro realizes that the money spent on the public education of all children in Florida is just about one-half of the average for the country, [and] that the money spent in Florida for Negro public education is just one-sixth of the general state average. This means to the Florida Negro that roughly one-twelfth as much money is spent to educate his child as is spent on the average child in the country. . . .

[T]here are 1,494 school buildings for white children in the state, with an assessed valuation of seventy million dollars. The 1,029 buildings for Negroes have cost the good folk who spend education money only five million. If the white school buildings are such that several local politicians are elected each year by promising to improve them, imagine the shacks the Negroes must go to school in!

Martin D. Richardson and Le Roy M. Washington, writers, September 1937, "A Picture of Florida's Schools," p. 270.

Some of the unemployed youth would like to return to school or to continue with the studies which by ne-

cessity they may be forced to terminate. But either the school program has nothing more to offer that interests them, or the costs of further schooling are prohibitive. Although the facilities for free education have been provided, the costs of maintenance are such that many youth cannot afford to avail themselves of these facilities. It has been the common experience of social workers and school principals that children who drop out of school come most frequently from families in the lower income brackets; and it is the general impression that the representation of students in college is directly related to the income of their families. Various ways of providing for needy youth, such as low tuition fees, scholarships, and the cooperative plan of alternative periods of study and gainful employment, were in fairly common practice at the college level even before the depression; and the inadequacy of these provisions was recognized. That similar need existed and still exists among high school students was not fully appreciated until the depression made it obvious.

Palmer O. Johnson and Oswald L. Harvey, educational researchers, 1938, The National Youth Administration, pp. 4–5.

Unemployed youth out of school are caught between the upper and lower millstones of necessity. On the one hand, without training or experience they are of little or no value to an employer; current laws relating to accident liability and insurance influence employers to give preference, if any, to the older youth; and the

A boy employed by the National Youth Administration in Washington, D.C., teaches younger boys to sculpt with clay. *(National Archives)*

demand for higher educational qualifications has grown more and more insistent. On the other hand, without resources to prolong their schooling, or without confidence in the programs offered by the schools, these unemployed youth cannot prosecute that period of further preparation conducive to adequate participation in gainful employment. As a result, unless they are given direct encouragement and considerable rehabilitation, they almost inevitably constitute a focus of social maladjustment. Upon them is the curse of not being wanted, with all its concomitants of apathy or resentment and of personality disintegration. The possibilities of their engaging in antisocial behavior under such circumstances are obvious.

Palmer O. Johnson and Oswald L. Harvey, educational researchers, 1938, The National Youth Administration, *p. 6.*

Before her NYA employment, Margaret worked for one year in a shirt factory which closed and threw her out of work. She then worked in another sweat-shop shirt factory, which she was forced to leave because of an injury to her finger. When assigned to NYA, Margaret was placed in one of the city hospitals in the laundry department, where she did fine hand-pressing and operated a mangle. She satisfactorily participated in classes offered by the WPA Adult Education Department. She was self-assured, had a pleasing personality, and a neat appearance. After nine months with NYA, her own abilities, together with the intercession of the NYA supervisor, brought Margaret a permanent job in the hospital which put her in charge of all fine laundry work.

Betty Lindley and Ernest K. Lindley, journalists, 1938, A New Deal for Youth, *p. 133.*

George, age 21, was passionately fond of music. He had graduated from high school, taking academic subjects and music, but could not continue with studies because his stepfather insisted he "get a job."

The youth applied for NYA assistance in September 1936 and was placed on a project where he was very satisfactory as a messenger and was encouraged to keep on with his studies. During this period, George attended night classes in musical composition and played a saxophone in a small orchestra. His ambition was to go to the Boston Conservatory of Music. He took every odd job that he could find, canvassing the office force for any sort of work, and whenever he had a spare moment he kept busy transcribing musical notes.

George did so well in his work in class that he was awarded a scholarship to the Boston Conservatory of Music in September 1937. He has since written asking for a work reference, stating: "But for the help of NYA I could never have made it."

Betty Lindley and Ernest K. Lindley, journalists, 1938, A New Deal for Youth, *pp. 133–134.*

In the recent years of depression, the schools have been on trial. Although the influx of pupils into the high schools has continued at an undiminished rate, for several years the programs both in elementary and in secondary schools were greatly disrupted. In many areas school terms were curtailed, entire sections of the curriculum were dropped, crowding in schools increased, fewer teachers were provided, and the salaries of those remaining were drastically reduced.

In most cases, the worst injuries of the depression have now been repaired, and there is a general disposition to build anew on a sounder foundation. The tests of the depression have demonstrated, however, that the general pattern of the tax-supported school has been firmly established and will not soon be changed. In the years that lie ahead there must be many new developments and some expansion of educational programs, but the coming decades are not likely to be marked by so great an expansion as occurred during the half century closed in 1930. . . . [I]t may well be that America is now entering upon a period of evaluation—a period in which will be determined more accurately what educational policies are best suited to a modern democracy and how best they may be realized in practice.

Report of the Advisory Committee on Education, *1938, p. 4.*

In most of the States where there are separate schools for Negroes, the schools for white children are below the national average, yet Negro schools are only about half as well supported as white schools. Because of the intimate economic relations that necessarily exist between the two races, the low level of education among Negroes is a severe burden not only on themselves but on all who must employ them or have dealings with them. Even in Northern States, the large influx of Negroes from the South makes the quality of their previous training a matter of vital importance to the localities where they live and work. All the statistics for length of school term, average attendance, educational qualifications of teachers, type of school buildings, and other factors indicate that a wasteful neglect is characteristic of the treatment of Negro school children in most of the areas where they are required to attend separate schools.

Report of the Advisory Committee on Education,
1938, p. 7.

The possibility that Negro teachers are less efficient than white teachers with equal training should challenge school administrators to investigate the reasons for the difference. If it is because of lack of proper training, the Negro teacher-training institutions should be strengthened so that they will provide the necessary training. If it is because Negro teachers have more limited facilities with which to work, these conditions should be remedied. If the reason is lack of cultural background of the Negro teachers, then better educational and economic advantages are needed in order to enable them to overcome this condition. In any case, the solution demands increased support and interest in Negro education. The problem cannot be solved by invoking penalties against the Negro teachers or the Negro pupils.

Leonard Ephraim Meece, Bureau of School Service,
University of Kentucky, March 1938, Negro Education in
Kentucky, *p. 175.*

Probably no events in the past quarter-century have so profoundly stirred the American people as those connected with the present European war. Youths and adults are eager to share in appraising the significance of these happenings, anticipating their outcomes, and developing a policy for the American people with reference to them.

In such circumstances there are several courses of action open to those in charge of the educational program. One possibility is to forbid discussion of such issues in the school and in other activities under the control of the teacher. Another possibility is to give free rein to the discussion of this question with neither guidance nor stimulation on the part of the teacher.

An adequate sense of professional responsibility will not approve either of these extremes. Neither repression of discussion nor abdication of responsibility is an appropriate policy for American education. At such a time as this, the schools should serve as centers of community deliberation with reference to the pending issues. They should not evade any question which is pertinent to a better understanding of the international situation and of America's relation to it. The education of a free people should know no undebatable propositions.

Educational Policies Commission of the National
Education Association and American Association of School
Administrators, October 1939, American Education and
the War in Europe, *p. 1.*

The schools and other educational institutions should do everything possible to prevent the disastrous activities which occurred during the last war when some reputable scholars joined with uneducated demagogs in a mad rush to decry and malign the cultural contributions of entire peoples. All the belligerent nations have made significant cultural and human contributions to American life. These contributions should be emphasized in the discussion of appropriate topics. For example, it is unwise and unfair to undervalue the contributions of a nation to music, art, literature, and science merely because the government of that nation is waging an unjust war.

Educational Policies Commission of the National
Education Association and American Association of School
Administrators, October 1939, American Education and
the War in Europe, *p. 10.*

CHAPTER SEVEN

"Every Life Is Affected":
Education for Victory in World War II
1941–1946

The Japanese attack on the U.S. naval base at Pearl Harbor, Hawaii, on December 7, 1941, left 2,403 Americans dead and 1,178 wounded. It destroyed most of the Pacific Fleet and influenced public opinion so strongly that virtually no one opposed U.S. entry into World War II. On December 8, President Franklin D. Roosevelt asked Congress to declare war on Japan, and on December 11, Germany and Fascist Italy declared war on the United States. Americans were again involved in a global conflict, and they were determined to do battle to the finish.

Fear of further attacks on American soil was widespread in the early months of U.S. participation, so preparedness took on greater import within the educational system. Elementary and secondary schools throughout the nation conducted air-raid drills, requiring frightened students to hunker down beneath their desks or sit tight and low against hallway or basement walls.

Children in Gary, Indiana, returned to their classes in January 1942, following the winter holidays, to encounter stricter school discipline. The administration believed this change was necessary to keep the students under control in an emergency. The farther west a community lay, the more vulnerable to Japanese bombardment its residents felt, which is why San Francisco officials issued numbered tags to the city's children that matched a list held by the local civil defense office. In case of emergency, this numbering system would identify those who might be evacuated, wounded, or killed. Hawaiian schools remained closed until February 1942, and when they reopened, the children received gas masks to be worn during periodic drills in which they were exposed to tear gas.

Schooling for Total War

School systems nationwide altered their educational priorities to help students meet the demands of "modern total warfare."[1] Classroom discussions centered on such immediate issues as rationing, production problems, and price controls. In keeping with recommendations from the U.S. Office of Education and leaders in the armed forces, curriculums stressed aviation and the related fields of geography, mathematics, and physics. Children in the public schools of Denver learned two-flag semaphore signaling and practiced the international Morse Code for wireless, two specialized skills that local school administrators considered essential in wartime.

The Baltimore Department of Education formed a War Issues Committee that in 1943 identified eight areas of preparedness to be emphasized in classrooms: the differences between democracy and totalitarianism; maintaining healthy public morale, which the committee defined as an "unyielding, unrelenting, unfearing, unbeatable determination to win"; economic aspects of war and peace; the armed forces and civilian mobilization; physical fitness; preparation for peace; changes in Baltimore resulting from the war; and, not least, education for life in the age of aviation.[2] In Baltimore and throughout the United States, people proclaimed that global war had ushered in the air age, an era in which air travel was making the world smaller and transforming the upper levels of the atmosphere into a familiar environment. "Air power is not merely pilots and planes," explained N. L. Engelhardt, Jr., of the Newark, New Jersey, Board of Education. "It demands new world maps and a new geography. It stimulates rethinking of international relations. It requires the sloughing off of many mores and traditional concepts of social and economic patterns."[3]

Schools also organized children's participation in home-front efforts in support of the war: selling war bonds and stamps, making cookies and useful gifts for the

In 1942, children in San Juan Bautista, California, parade on school grounds with scrap metal they have collected for the war effort. *(Library of Congress, Prints and Photographs Division, LC-USF34-072473-D)*

servicemen, and collecting scrap. In 1942, Chicago's public school students gathered 1.5 million pounds of tin, rubber, and scrap metal that they carried to their schools by hand, in wagons, or in family cars and trucks. All this rapid change and added activity created heavy workloads for teachers and caused Ernest O. Melby, president of the University of Montana, to declare that a "new concept and practice of education" had been adopted.[4]

High school teachers saw their students' interest shifting from classroom studies to opportunities in the community and the chance to play a role in events overseas. "By April 1943, it was apparent that every high school in the State was affected by the war, and that as the war continued, its effects on schools would be more pronounced," observed Ethel L. Cornell, a research associate with the New York State Education Department.[5] Many students in New York and other states were already working in agriculture or the defense industries, either full- or part-time, and many others were about to enter the armed forces. By early 1944, 4.6 million boys and girls ages 14 to 19 held jobs, and 1.43 million of these were enrolled in school.

High schools responded to their students' needs by making military training mandatory for boys. Recognizing that students planning to go to work or enlist might cut short their education, many high schools created accelerated programs, permitting these students to graduate early. Lengthening the school day and allowing students to carry a heavier course load proved to be the most popular methods of acceleration, but some schools expanded their summer programs; offered short, intensive courses; or gave students credit for attending less than a full term. High schools also offered flexible schedules for those already working or whose help was needed on local farms.

In addition, high schools developed new academic and vocational courses to fill perceived wartime learning needs. They updated the syllabuses of existing classes, purging them of content that had come to seem irrelevant and substituting topics with possible value to military service or civilian defense efforts. Chemistry teachers therefore taught lessons on explosives, emergency water purification, and waste disposal; trigonometry classes included maritime and aerial navigation; biology now involved such practical issues as public health, camp sanitation, and first aid; and history students read aloud patriotic poems and historic documents. "Every lesson stressing the courage and fortitude of our forefathers against much greater odds than our own, will develop civic responsibility and confidence in our national leaders," advised A. H. Bryan, a science instructor at Baltimore City College.[6]

The most popular new course offerings included aeronautics, nutrition (a concern because of rationing), and vocational training for war industries. Beginning in February 1943, junior and senior high school boys in Chicago took required courses in fundamental shop work, basis of electricity, and pre-flight training. Girls could enroll in these classes, too, on an elective basis. A small-town high school in New York State developed a comprehensive pre-induction course for boys who were subject to the draft that covered the military background of the war, deciphering codes and reading maps, colloquial French and Italian, a review of arithmetic, first aid and hygiene, sewing and laundry skills, and aircraft identification.

High schools in every state intensified physical training, especially for boys, to "harden" them for service in the armed forces.[7] Chicago's high schools, which reputedly had more swimming pools than any other school system in the world, required their students to learn to swim underwater, fully clothed, after the faculty

Two Los Angeles girls, members of the High School Victory Corps, practice first aid. *(Library of Congress, Prints and Photographs Division, LC-USE6-D-007723)*

heard reports that servicemen had drowned in the attack on Pearl Harbor because their uniforms and gear weighed them down.

On September 25, 1942, U.S. Commissioner of Education John W. Studebaker established the High School Victory Corps, a voluntary organization that encouraged students to participate in the war effort while in school and prepared them for war service after graduation. Within a year, more than 70 percent of U.S. high schools had embraced the program. Participating students completed a physical-fitness program and a war-training class. They also volunteered for at least one extracurricular wartime activity, such as collecting scrap metal or selling war stamps or bonds. In June 1944, with the war drawing to a close, the government began phasing out the High School Victory Corps.

Learning under Duress in Relocation Camps

"Teachers of foreign languages should do everything possible to prevent cultural vandalism directed against the language, literature, music, and art of the peoples with whom we are at war," the office of the Los Angeles County superintendent of schools advised principals and teachers in March 1942.[8] Like educators in other places, the superintendent and his staff hoped to prevent the kind of nationalistic fervor that had led to the purging of many things German from U.S. culture during World War I. Ironically, their state was one of four in which U.S. citizens and longtime residents of the United States were having their basic rights stripped away because of their ancestry.

Along the West Coast, where the majority of Japanese Americans lived, prejudice fueled suspicion that spies and saboteurs might be hiding in plain sight. On February 19, 1942, Roosevelt used his power as commander in chief—or abused it, as critics said—to issue Executive Order 9906, confining Japanese Americans from Washington, Oregon, California, and western Arizona to internment camps. The evacuation of 120,000 Japanese Americans, including 77,000 U.S. citizens and 30,000 schoolchildren, began on March 31. The government transported the evacuees to relocation centers in harsh, inhospitable parts of the West, to live in crowded barracks under armed guard and surrounded by barbed wire. Each center was an austere city unto itself. For a time, the Heart Mountain Relocation Center was the third largest city in Wyoming.

For the first months in places such as the Manzanar Relocation Center, in the high desert of eastern California, the government provided no school facilities, textbooks, supplies, or teachers. College-educated evacuees taught youngsters who sat on the bare earth or the floors of barracks, often reading from a single copy of a book. On September 15, 1942, nursery schools, elementary schools, and a high school opened at Manzanar, although furniture and supplies remained scarce. Considered part of the California educational system, these schools were required to offer the state-prescribed curriculum, which for high schools included foreign languages, mathematics, and laboratory science.

Only 26 of the 59 white teachers hired for Manzanar showed up for work in September. The rest had changed their minds about living and working in the remote desert or had taken more lucrative jobs in the defense industries. The government compensated by hiring qualified evacuees as teachers' aides, paying them $16 a month—much less than the teachers' salary of $1,620 a year—to do comparable work. The barrack-schoolrooms lacked insulation and became frigid in winter, forcing classes to be canceled, and morale plummeted. Many children and teens stopped caring about grades, acted out aggressively, retreated into themselves, or learned to hate their white fellow citizens.

Approximately 3,000 students of college age had help that was unavailable to the other evacuees. This group included nearly all the 2,500 who had been enrolled in West Coast colleges until they were forced to evacuate, as well as graduates of the internment-camp high schools. The National Japanese American Student Relocation Council, a private organization founded on May 29, 1942, by the American Friends Service Committee, a Quaker group, and sanctioned by the U.S. War Relocation Authority, worked to place the students in colleges and universities in other parts of the country, far from the West Coast.

Students had to pass a background check conducted by the Federal Bureau of Investigation before placement, and until January 1944, when restrictions were eased, the schools accepting them had to be cleared by the Departments of War and the Navy. More than 500 approved colleges, universities, and vocational schools welcomed the students, who were often the first nonwhites to enroll and the first people of Japanese ancestry their professors and classmates had ever met.

Because the suddenness of the evacuation had left their families without assets and income, the majority of students placed by the council worked part-time to cover their expenses. Through December 31, 1944, the council distributed $188,972 in scholarship funds that were contributed by churches and other organizations, and 741 students received grants from their colleges and other sources. In 1943, the residents of the Central Utah Relocation Center in Topaz, Utah, gave $100 toward the further education of each of 31 graduates of the camp high school. "It was not the amount of money they received, but it was the spirit of encouragement which was given to them that caused them to fight for higher education," said the chairman of the fund.[9] Apathy and apprehension deterred many of the young people from pursuing admission to college and had to be overcome.

On December 19, 1944, noting a "substantial improvement in the military situation," Major General H. C. Pratt, commander of the Western Defense Command, rescinded the civilian exclusion orders that had kept Japanese Americans forcibly confined.[10] Along with their families, those of school age returned home and began the difficult work of rebuilding their lives.

Great Social Changes

Many other Americans relocated voluntarily during the war. The demand for labor in the defense plants of Baltimore and other coastal and northern industrial regions drew people from rural Appalachia and the Deep South. Accommodating the newcomers' needs strained existing housing supplies and infrastructures, and put enormous stress on school systems. Rapid population increases led to overcrowded classrooms, cafeterias, and playgrounds, and dangerously congested corridors. Teachers worked harder to maintain control, contagious diseases spread rapidly, and standards of cleanliness declined.

San Diego, a West Coast manufacturing center, saw its population double between 1940 and 1944, rising from 289,000 to 609,000, but the changes in small towns could be even more profound. The farming community of Seneca, Illinois, experienced unanticipated growth when the Chicago Bridge and Iron Company built a shipyard there. Seneca's population skyrocketed, increasing from 1,200 in spring 1942 to between 8,000 and 10,000 a year later. Families lived wherever they could: in crowded apartments, dormitories, or trailers supplied by the Federal Public Housing Authority.

Seneca's high school, built in 1922 to accommodate 90 students, had a student body numbering 130 in the 1941–42 academic year and 200 the following year. The public elementary school, completed in 1884, had an enrollment of 170 and employed five teachers in 1941–42. In 1942–43 enrollment topped 425, and the teaching staff numbered 12. The student body had outgrown the old school, so grades one through five met in the building that had served as the contractor's office while the shipyard was being constructed.

The new pupils came from 28 states and Canada. Like the children of migrant defense workers in other towns and cities, many had left regions where academic standards lagged behind other parts of the nation. They therefore entered their new schools with deficiencies in learning and appeared culturally deprived in contrast to their classmates.

Rural Schools Fail to Keep Up

Despite the advances in technology and teaching methods that had been made in the first 40 years of the 20th century, many rural schools remained largely unchanged and generally paid low salaries that failed to attract well-trained teachers. Because people were leaving rural areas to enter urban labor markets, the quality of the education they received had taken on national importance. The state of country schools concerned Roosevelt, who convened a White House Conference on Rural Education in October 1942. Two hundred experts—educators, community leaders, representatives of farmers' organizations, editors of agricultural magazines, and university extension agents—came together to discuss the place of rural education in American life.

The conference issued a list of goals for rural school districts that included providing community members of all ages with educational opportunities on a par with those available elsewhere; offering young people a curriculum broad enough to permit complete personal development; encouraging a democratic way of life; securing well-paid, certified teachers; and creating larger school districts for improved efficiency and financial support.

Yet as World War II came to an end, 96,000 one-room schools were still in use in the United States, and 54,000 of these were in the Midwest. Enrollments had fallen off with the decline in rural population, and hundreds of midwestern one-room schools had nine pupils, five, or even fewer. Some communities kept their schools open with no pupils at all in the hope that some would register.

Schools Offer Child Care

Not only did whole families relocate during the war, but also women—many of them mothers of young children—entered the workforce to fill jobs vacated by men in the military or to earn money in war-related industries. The altered pattern of family life left large numbers of children inadequately supervised. The children's well-being was a concern, because youngsters left with less-than-vigilant caregivers were getting into mischief, some of it dangerous and destructive.

Organized day care seemed an imperfect solution to the many people who worried that it would weaken family ties, but it appeared to be a necessary one. "Boys and girls should not be allowed to go cold and hungry and lonesome just because their mothers are working in war-production plants," stated Sallie B. Marks, an instructor in education at the University of Chicago.[11] Until February 1, 1943, when the president directed that its activities be terminated, the Works Progress Agency (WPA) provided nursery schools and day-care centers for the children of working mothers, often in cooperation with public schools and community agencies. Three such nursery schools operated in Cincinnati elementary schools. Open from 7 A.M. to 5:30 P.M., Monday through Friday, and from 7 A.M. to noon on Saturday, these centers cared for children aged two to five whose mothers were employed in war industries or held jobs that released others for war work. The centers charged a fee based on family income.

In July 1943, the Federal Works Agency took over for the WPA, equipping and staffing day-care centers for the preschool children of working women. By February 1944, 2,243 centers were in operation, offering a full day's activity and supervision to 65,772 children aged two to five. Some school districts pitched in, extending the hours of kindergarten and serving the children a meal, and some cooperated with community groups to offer nursery-school classes.

Another federal program, Extended School Services, addressed the care needs of elementary school children. ESS functioned under the direction of the U.S. Office of Education for the 1942–43 academic year, employing librarians, college students, and others to lead children in organized recreation in the hours when school was closed but parents were still at work. Approximately 320,000 children benefited from ESS activities before funding ran out and the program was terminated. ESS had proved so popular, however, that Kansas City, Cleveland, and other municipalities secured alternate funding to keep it going.

Teens needed attention as well. A lack of supervision, the absence of many fathers and other male authority figures, and extra spending money earned from employment appeared to be responsible for a perceived rise in juvenile delinquency. During World War II, more young people than in the past became ungovernable at home, chronically truant, or runaways, and arrests of juveniles for offenses ranging from theft to assault rose alarmingly. In 1942, Gary, Indiana, addressed the problem of unsupervised youths with too much free time with an expanded summer-school program that included civil-defense training for high school students and a home-nursing and child-care class for junior and senior girls. Teens could enroll as well in an elementary aeronautics course and popular cooking classes, including one on preparing meals in wartime. For younger children, Gary offered model-airplane building, which interested a great many boys during World War II; music lessons; arts and crafts; and playground recreation.

Higher Education and the War

Financial as well as patriotic incentives drove colleges and universities to seek a military presence on campus, because as male students were called to active duty or enlisted, schools lost revenues from tuition. Yet many college administrators recalled with resentment the seeming takeover by the military of campus buildings and facilities during World War I. Although ready to offer their resources to the armed forces for education and training, they wanted to maintain some control over how those resources were used. For these reasons, the American Council on Education (ACE), a coordinating body for U.S. institutions of higher learning, responded to the nation's entry into the war by forming jointly with the National Education Association (NEA) the National Committee on Education and Defense. This group protected the interests of colleges and universities while facilitating their cooperation with the federal government.

In January 1942, the National Committee on Education and Defense and the U.S. Office of Education brought together in Baltimore a thousand professionals: college and university presidents, representatives of educational organizations, and government officials. The academic presidents collectively offered their faculties, student bodies, and physical plants to Roosevelt, commander in chief of the armed forces, with recommendations. They asked that the federal government study how colleges and universities might best serve the war effort; that selective service take into account the interests of existing social institutions, including colleges and universities; and that their schools receive federal financial aid during wartime. The presidents also came out in favor of accelerated programs, academic credit for military instruction and experience, and increased training in physical fitness.

The War Manpower Commission, a federal agency, determined in August 1942 that the responsibility for preparing students destined for military service belonged to the army and navy. Roosevelt asked the secretaries of war and the navy to study how to use the resources of the nation's colleges, and on December 12, 1942, their departments announced plans for three training programs to be carried out

Men in the V-12 program at Bates College, Lewiston, Maine, train to be physically fit. *(The Edmund S. Muskie Archives, Bates College)*

on college campuses: the Army Specialized Training Program (ASTP), V-12 Navy College Training Program, and Army Air Forces College Training Program.

The new specialized college programs produced technologically trained personnel for active duty and therefore differed from existing courses of study leading to reserve-officer status, such as the Reserve Officers' Training Corps (ROTC), which focused solely on military preparedness. Most college students belonged to the age group that traditionally carried the heaviest burden in war, and the leaders of the armed forces hoped to avert a shortage of officers with college education in the key areas of science and engineering, especially after the government lowered the age of eligibility for the draft from 21 to 18, on November 13, 1942.

The new training programs drew largely from the pool of active-duty soldiers. High school seniors who scored high on qualifying exams were accepted as well. Those admitted were on active, rather than reserve, status, which meant that they wore uniforms, received the regular pay of enlisted men, and were subject to strict military discipline. They pursued intensive courses of study: With the exception of those working toward degrees in medicine, dentistry, or veterinary science, who fulfilled requirements at the same rates as their civilian counterparts, ASTP personnel completed 25 credit hours per quarter, cramming four years of college into a year and a half.

V-12 students attended school year-round, carrying 17 credit hours, and underwent 9.5 hours of physical training each week. Most then attended an additional four-month course at a reserve midshipmen's school; those in the Marine Corps V-12 section completed boot camp and a 12-week officer-candidate course at Quantico, Virginia.

ASTP enrollment had reached a high of 145,000 in February 1944, when the army announced that it would be cut to 35,000 by April 1, to supply men for the ground forces in Europe, and then disbanded. The V-12 program had a longer life. It trained more than 125,000 college-age men at 131 colleges and universities by June 30, 1946. Sixty thousand of these men received commissions as navy ensigns or Marine Corps lieutenants.

The navy permitted African Americans to enroll in the V-12 program in 1943, almost a year before the first African-American naval officers were commissioned. (There had been African-American army officers since the Civil War.) Among the V-12 midshipmen was Samuel Gravely, who in 1971 became the first African-American admiral in the history of the navy. "The V-12 program was a turning point in my life," Gravely said. "It gave me an opportunity to compete on an equal footing with people I had never competed with before. It gave me an opportunity to prove to myself that I could succeed if I tried."[12]

The Army Air Forces College Training Program was briefer and narrower in scope than either ASTP or V-12 training in order to produce qualified pilots and support personnel as quickly as possible. It responded to a great and sudden need for meteorologists by offering three levels of instruction: a six-month pre-meteorology course at 11 colleges and universities, a 12-month basic course at 12 institutions, and an advanced course at five schools. The army air forces also offered air-crew training to prepare students for the air forces flight schools. The intense air-crew course compressed a year of college into five months, covering such technical knowledge as civil air regulations, medical first aid, and hands-on flight training, and including several academic courses.

The military training brought needed funding to institutions coping with lost students and revenues. The Departments of War and the Navy entered into contracts with participating colleges and universities, agreeing to pay for instruction in academic and technical subjects but requiring faculty members to teach larger classes and for more hours per week than in peacetime. The government paid the schools to feed the military personnel on campus at rates that varied from one region to another and reflected actual costs. For the use of classrooms, dormitories, and other buildings, schools received 2 percent of an established rental value and another 2 percent to cover depreciation. "It is anticipated that no institution utilized for war training will make a profit and that the only financial advantage will be in keeping facilities busy and physical plants in operation," explained Raymond Walters, president of the University of Cincinnati, in 1944.[13]

The military programs were a stroke of good fortune, especially for small colleges. Just 50 civilian students were attending Hobart College, a small men's school in Geneva, New York, in fall 1943. The 323 V-12 students who came to campus that summer kept the school afloat. Hobart, like most institutions of higher learning, toughed out the war. In fall 1941, 1,756 colleges and universities were registered with the U.S. Office of Education; four years later, 1,685 were registered.

Military participation on college campuses during World War II would change forever the nature of higher education in the United States and Americans' ideas about who should go to college. The emphasis on science and technology persisted, and purely academic study lost ground to knowledge with industrial and business applications in many disciplines. College professors learned from military instructors the effectiveness of visual aids such as films, slides, and filmstrips. The navy, for example, had produced 2,000 training films for various educational programs by January 1944. Civilian instructors also observed how rapidly students acquired the ability to speak foreign languages through the military's oral method. Conversation received greater emphasis in the teaching of foreign languages after World War II, although academicians deplored the neglect of literature in this approach—some called it training rather than study.

Perhaps what was most significant, millions of Americans had stopped viewing college as something beyond their financial or intellectual resources. "For the first time on any large scale, men are allowed to go to college, not on the basis of social prestige or financial ability, but upon their own merit," said Rear Admiral John Downes, commenting on the V-12 program in July 1943.[14]

Meeting the Need for Nurses

Another federal educational initiative, the U.S. Cadet Nurse Corps, changed the public's perception of nursing as a suitable career for middle-class women. The government began the program on July 1, 1943, to meet an increased demand for nurses in civilian and military settings. Women between the ages of 17 and 35 who were in good health and had graduated from an accredited high school with satisfactory grades were eligible to receive a subsidy covering nursing-school tuition, books, and uniforms, as well as a small stipend. In return, they agreed, once they completed their training, to practice nursing wherever they were needed most for the duration of the war.

In 1943, although nursing was an overwhelmingly female profession, many parents discouraged their daughters from pursuing it in the belief that a young woman could choose a profession or marriage, but not both. Also, some parents worried that nursing might be too physically demanding, that it might strain their daughters' backs or otherwise harm their health. The Division of Nurse Education of the U.S. Public Health Service therefore launched an ambitious and successful advertising campaign to persuade young women to enlist in the Cadet Nurse Corps. One magazine advertisement showed a cadet nurse admiring her engagement ring and demonstrating that marriage and a career were both within her reach.

The Cadet Nurse Corps accepted young women of all racial backgrounds, including 3,000 African Americans, 40 Native Americans, and a number of Japanese Americans, many of whom had been placed by the National Japanese American Student Relocation Council. The cadets completed their training in 30 months rather than the standard 36 and spent the final period of training in hospitals or public or rural health centers that needed their services. The corps stopped admitting students in October 1945 but permitted candidates in the program to complete their training.

Thousands of Veterans Enroll

Possibly the most democratizing effect on U.S. colleges at this time came from the educational provisions of the Serviceman's Readjustment Act of 1944, better known as the GI Bill of Rights, or simply the GI Bill. This federal legislation gave World War II veterans access to loans for buying businesses or homes, vocational and educational counseling, and financial support for higher education. Congress passed and the president signed the GI Bill in appreciation of the veterans' sacrifices in the war and in the hope that having educational opportunities would cause the returning servicemen to enter the job market gradually and allow the economy to accommodate them.

The law provided a monthly allowance for living expenses of $50 for a single veteran enrolled in college and $75 for a married veteran. On December 19, 1945, these amounts increased to $65 and $90, respectively. Students also received up to $500 a year for tuition, fees, books, and other supplies. This allotment exceeded the costs of attending many schools, and its availability led to widespread tuition increases. Despite this negative consequence, the program was enormously successful. By the fall 1944 semester, 12,864 men and women who had been discharged from the armed forces were enrolled in colleges, universities, and other institutions under the GI Bill, and by fall 1946 the number had grown to a million. By 1956, when the program was terminated, 2,232,000 veterans had been to college on the GI Bill.

With so many veterans enrolling, colleges grappled with the questions of whether and how to award academic credit for military training and experience. Not only had valuable learning taken place in the armed forces, but also schools wanted to show their gratitude. In 1944, the New York State university system allowed 10 academic credits for six months or more military service and five credits for service of less than six months. Other colleges and universities developed similar plans.

To aid colleges desiring a more accurate and individualized way to award credit, in 1946 a committee of the American Council of Education, chaired by University of Illinois registrar George P. Tuttle, published *A Guide to the Evaluation of Educational Experiences in the Armed Forces*. Commonly referred to as the Tuttle Guide, this book had been delivered to 17,000 military offices and 7,000 colleges and universities by year's end.

War Ends

By then, the war was over. Germany had surrendered unconditionally on May 7, 1945, and Japan had done the same three months later, on August 14. Victory against Japan followed the explosion of two atomic bombs, one over the Japanese city of Hiroshima, on August 6, and the second over the city of Nagasaki, on August 9. The knowledge that they lived in a world where atomic war could occur again overshadowed the consciousness of every person aware of the momentous events of August 1945. The air age had become quaint to a population jolted into the atomic age.

Chronicle of Events

1941

- *fall:* In this year 1,756 colleges and universities are registered with the U.S. Office of Education.
- *December 7:* A surprise attack on the U.S. naval base at Pearl Harbor, Hawaii, by the military forces of Japan virtually destroys the U.S. Pacific Fleet and leaves 2,403 Americans dead and 1,178 wounded.
- *December 8:* President Franklin D. Roosevelt asks Congress to declare war on Japan.
- *December 11:* Germany and Italy declare war on the United States.

1941–1942

- In Seneca, Illinois, 130 students attend the high school, and 170 attend the public elementary school. The elementary school employs five teachers.

1942

- Chicago's public school students collect 1.5 million pounds of scrap material for the war effort.
- *January:* At a conference convened by the National Committee on Education and Defense and the U.S. Office of Education, the nation's colleges and universities offer their personnel and facilities to the president, as commander in chief.
- *February:* Schools in Hawaii, closed since the December 7, 1941, attack on Pearl Harbor, reopen.
- *February 19:* Roosevelt signs Executive Order 9906, mandating the internment of 120,000 people of Japanese ancestry.
- *spring:* Seneca, Illinois, has a population of 1,200.
- *March:* The superintendent's office of the Los Angeles County Public Schools cautions teachers against disparaging the cultures of enemy nations.
- *March 31:* The evacuation of people of Japanese ancestry begins.

In 1941, white children in Greene County, Georgia, attend a graded school that has a desk and chair for each child, blackboards, and adequate books and supplies. *(Library of Congress, Prints and Photographs Division, LC-USF34-046146-D)*

In the same year, 1941, black children in Greene County, Georgia, attend a falling-down one-room school lacking desks and supplies. *(Library of Congress, Prints and Photographs Division, LC-USF34-04628-D)*

- *May 29:* The American Friends Service Committee establishes the National Japanese American Student Relocation Council to place Japanese-American college students in schools that will accept them.
- *summer:* Gary, Indiana, expands its summer-school program to reduce the number of unsupervised youngsters.
- *August:* The War Manpower Commission determines that it is the responsibility of the army and navy to prepare college students for military service.
- *September 15:* Schools open at the Manzanar Relocation Center.
- *September 25:* Commissioner of Education John W. Studebaker establishes the High School Victory Corps.
- *October:* Roosevelt convenes a White House Conference on Rural Education. The conference calls for improved educational services in rural communities and continued school consolidation.
- *November 13:* The federal government lowers the age of eligibility for the draft from 21 to 18.
- *December 12:* The secretaries of war and the navy announce plans for the Army Specialized Training

Program (ASTP), V-12 Navy College Training Program, and Army Air Forces College Training Program.

1942–1943
- In Seneca, Illinois, 200 students attend the high school and more than 425 attend the public elementary school. The elementary school employs 12 teachers.
- Extended School Services, an agency of the U.S. Office of Education, provides organized recreation after school to 320,000 children.

1943
- The Baltimore Department of Education lists eight areas of preparedness for teachers to emphasize, ranging from discussions of totalitarianism to physical fitness.
- The navy permits African Americans to enroll in the V-12 program.
- *February:* Junior and senior high school boys in Chicago are required to take classes in fundamental shop work, fundamentals of electricity, and pre-flight training.

- *February 1:* Roosevelt directs the Work Projects Administration (WPA) to terminate its activities, which have included operating nursery schools and day-care centers for the children of women working in defense plants.
- *spring:* The population of Seneca, Illinois, is now between 8,000 and 10,000.
- *July:* The Federal Works Agency equips and staffs day-care centers for the preschool children of working women.
- *July 1:* The federal government launches the U.S. Cadet Nurse Corps to train nurses to meet civilian and military needs.
- *fall:* Fifty civilian students and 323 V-12 trainees attend Hobart College in Geneva, New York.

1944

- Some 4.6 million Americans age 14 to 19 are employed; of these, 1.43 million are enrolled in school.
- San Diego's population is 609,000, up from 289,000 in 1940.
- The Serviceman's Readjustment Act (GI Bill) provides tuition, other educational expenses, and a monthly living allowance of $50 for a single person and $75 for a married person for World War II veterans wishing to attend college.
- The New York State university system gives veterans 10 academic credits for six months or more of military service and five credits for service of less than six months.
- *January:* The navy has produced 2,000 training films.
- *February:* The Federal Works Agency is operating 2,243 day-care centers attended by 54,772 children.
- *February:* The army begins scaling down the ASPT.

- *June:* The government begins phasing out the High School Victory Corps.
- *fall:* Thanks to the GI Bill, 12,864 veterans are enrolled in institutions of higher learning.
- *December 19:* Major General H. C. Pratt of the Western Defense Command rescinds the orders keeping Japanese Americans confined.

1945

- Ninety-six thousand one-room schools are still in use in the United States; of these, 54,000 are in the Midwest.
- *May 7:* Germany surrenders unconditionally.
- *August 6:* The United States explodes an atomic bomb over the Japanese city of Hiroshima.
- *August 9:* The United States explodes a second atomic bomb, over the city of Nagasaki, Japan.
- *August 14:* Japan surrenders unconditionally.
- *fall:* In this year 1,686 colleges and universities are registered with the U.S. Office of Education.
- *October:* The U.S. Cadet Nurse Corps stops admitting students.
- *December 15:* The monthly living expenses paid to veterans attending college increase to $65 for a single person and $90 for a married person.

1946

- A committee of the American Council of Education develops *A Guide to the Evaluation of Educational Experiences in the Armed Forces* (the Tuttle Guide), which is distributed to 17,000 military offices and 7,000 colleges and universities.
- *fall:* One million veterans are enrolled in institutions of higher learning under the GI Bill.

Eyewitness Testimony

If we are true humanists, if we are truly democratic, we teachers—you and I—must prop ourselves from within. With the great humane tradition behind us, the great books recording what the race has esteemed as the highest values, with the great basic words to be kept clear and clean, with the threat of the overthrow of those values, the reversal of the meaning of those words, so imminent, with boys and girls, serious-minded, looking to us for leadership, it is for us teachers of English to supply not only the prop, but the vision to see, the will to endure, the security of mind to meet all change, to accept and to fulfill all responsibility.

Allan Abbott, professor of English, Teachers College, Columbia University, January 1941, "'In These Bad Days,'" p. 339.

A few short months ago many [rural] youth were asking: Why can't I get a job? What can I do in a world that does not want me? How can new jobs and new resources for jobs be developed? Today they are asking: When will I be called to camp? How can I prepare for camp life? How can I make the most of camp life? What branch of the army am I best fitted for? Should I go into a defense industry? Where can I get vocational training? How can I keep physically fit? Why is democracy worth defending? What kind of an America will emerge when the war is over? What will happen to me when the war is over? These questions of rural youth must be answered. They will be answered. The success with which they are answered will depend largely on the effectiveness of the public school. The public school is the one educational agency which reaches into *all* communities and to which the individual attending devotes the major portion of his time.

Frank W. Cyr, associate professor of education, Teachers College, Columbia University, May 1941, "Looking Ahead in Rural Education," p. 700.

We have taught the ways of peace to find our students forced by exigencies to become soldiers, and our leaders demanding greater speed in preparation for war. We have taught the ways of thrift and diligence to find the thrifty and diligent in dire need in the midst of plenty. We have taught democracy to find our own democracy adopting autocratic methods in the hope of preserving that democracy. The depression and the war have left us baffled. Changes have occurred and are occurring so rapidly that we cannot predict the kind of world that the children in our classrooms will find in 1970, or even in 1950. What

are the underlying causes operating to produce such drastic transformations? Can we make youth more intelligent concerning these underlying causes?

Although we do not know what the future holds for our boys and girls, we may be certain that we should strive to assist them to attain an intelligent equipment to cope with the emergencies of the years that lie before them.

Gerald S. Craig, professor of natural science, Teachers College, Columbia University, November 1941, "Childhood Education and World Crisis," pp. 118–119.

There is a possibility that today we are in the midst of a world-wide struggle to determine whether humanity is to enter into the age of science or another dark age. The present World War should be viewed as but a by-product of this larger struggle. We need to make certain that the youth leaving our schools has learned to distinguish between the gadgets of invention and the scientific method. Youth can gain hope and a constructive attitude, as opposed to an attitude of fatalism, through the realization that science is still a new tool, one with which man is still experimenting, one with which man is far from expert.

Gerald S. Craig, professor of natural science, Teachers College, Columbia University, November 1941, "Childhood Education and World Crisis," p. 110.

With no exceptions, schools at the centers opened in unpartitioned barracks meant for other purposes and generally bare of furniture. Sometimes the teacher had a desk and chair; more often she had only a chair. In the first few weeks many of the children had no desks or chairs and were obliged to sit on the floor—or stand up all day. Linoleum laying and additional wall insulation were accomplished in these makeshift schoolrooms sometime after the opening of school. At some centers cold waves struck before the winterization could be started.

By the [end of 1942] . . . it was no longer necessary for many pupils to sit on the floor, but seating was frequently of a rudimentary character. Text books and other supplies were gradually arriving. Laboratory and shop equipment and facilities, however, were still lacking. No center had been able to obtain its full quota of teachers.

War Relocation Authority report on schools in the wartime relocation camps, 1942, in Personal Justice Denied, *p. 170.*

I recall sitting in classrooms without books and listening to the instructor talking about technical matters that we could not study in depth. The lack of qualified evacuee

Girls at the Manzanar Relocation Camp learn from volunteer evacuee teachers, July 1, 1942. They sit on the ground in the shade of a building, because school equipment has yet to reach the camp. *(National Archives, ARC ID 537961)*

intelligent democratic action can be secured during and especially following the war. It is important, too, that a thorough understanding of the third dimension in which we are beginning to live be brought about among teachers and pupils. Aerography must supplement geography. The study of the air, winds, clouds, troposphere, and stratosphere should be commonplace. Every individual will wish to understand the realities of flight. This does not imply a technical education in aerodynamics for all, but it does mean that all people need basic knowledges and skills.

N. L. Engelhardt, Jr., acting director of research, Newark, New Jersey, Board of Education, 1942, Education for the Air Age, *pp. 2–3.*

teachers, the shortage of trained teachers was awful. I remember having to read a chapter a week in chemistry and discovering at the end of a semester that we had finished one full year's course. There was a total loss of scheduling with no experiments, demonstrations or laboratory work.

A Japanese-American evacuee remembering his high school chemistry class in a wartime relocation camp, 1942, Personal Justice Denied, *p. 171.*

Education should teach people how to do—that is how to work. It should provide the training an individual needs in order to be able to earn his living. Encouraging preparation for a given job implies that opportunity will be available to use such preparation. Possibility of getting a job, as well as interest and ability, must be considered in choosing a field for specialized training.

There is now, and during the post-war period there will be, urgent need for much more opportunity for education which prepares one specifically for earning a living. Specialized education should be made more widely available on a national, State, and local basis.

John Guy Fowlkes, professor of education, University of Wisconsin, 1942, Planning Schools for Tomorrow: The Issues Involved, *p. 6.*

The education of Americans for world citizenship in the air age is the responsibility of the schools. This responsibility resolves itself into two parts. First, the responsibility for aviation training rests, in large measure, on the public school system. Air supremacy demands planes, pilots, service personnel, and the support of an educated citizenry that understands air power. The schools of America are training boys and girls for aviation jobs. Two million youths in high school and college should be given basic pre-flight training in addition to millions more who are receiving vocational training useful in the manufacture and maintenance of aircraft. The American teachers will wish to accept a large part of the responsibility for this program. Second, the schools should accept the responsibility for air-conditioning the children, youth, and adults to develop complete awareness of the social, economic, and political impacts of air power. This understanding must be brought about as rapidly as possible in order that

Full human development is the major objective of a school. Therefore, the essential offerings in a school program must be wide and varied. The list of minimum essentials for an adequate educational program is much longer than is now found in the majority of our schools. At least the following pupil services and experiences should be available: Necessary formally organized teaching; educational and vocational guidance; library services; extracurricular activities; work experience; junior placement services; transportation facilities; lunch facilities; health services, including nutritional, medical, dental, nursing, and psychiatric; and camp experience.

The only item in this list of minimum essentials that is now universally provided is formally organized teaching. Furthermore, the nature of much of the organized teaching at present within both elementary and secondary schools and institutions of higher learning leaves much to be desired. It was recently observed that the "lecture textbook memorizing type of learning" does not occur in any life experience except in the school. Teachers at all levels would do well to become familiar with, and utilize, the methods by which people learn outside school.

John Guy Fowlkes, professor of education, University of Wisconsin, 1942, Planning Schools for Tomorrow: The Issues Involved, *pp. 6–7.*

When the schools closed on Friday, December 5, they had many purposes and they followed many roads to achieve those purposes. When the schools opened on Monday, December 8, they had one dominant purpose—complete, intelligent, and enthusiastic cooperation in the war effort. The very existence of free schools anywhere in the world depends upon the achievement of that purpose.

It is already clear that many educational adaptations are required. Many aspects of education will need to be strengthened and extended. Other aspects, very important ones in times of peace, may be redirected or otherwise modified in order that the total expanded efforts of wartime education may be applied at the points of greatest need.

Educational Policies Commission, February 1942, A War Policy for American Schools, *p. 3.*

[T]eachers should be vigilant to protect loyal Americans of Axis descent and their children against discrimination and maltreatment in the schools. The enemy doubtless will stir up our suspicions of these people, will spur us on to alienate them, and will seek to make them feel unwanted, insecure, resentful. It is in his interest to do so. Let us repel the enemy's strategy by looking beyond names and faces for the essential loyalty in people's hearts. The fundamental civil liberties of all citizens should be protected against unreasonable restrictions. The crucial test for such liberties as freedom of speech, freedom of the press, and freedom of assembly is our ability to use them with a sense of public obligation in a time of national crisis. The schools therefore should stress the responsibilities which accompany the enjoyment of civil liberties, both in the study of civil liberties and in their practice in the school.

Educational Policies Commission, February 1942, A War Policy for American Schools, *pp. 18–19.*

Educational leaders have turned their attention increasingly to the ways in which the schools can best serve the war effort. Neither indifference nor lethargy have characterized the contribution of the teaching profession toward the common task of winning the war.

It is only to be expected, however, that under the necessity for immediate action, ill-considered plans will be proposed and a certain amount of hysteria will prevail. Nor is it unlikely that reactionary forces will take advantage of the fluid nature of the times to forward their own concerns.

Already there are evidences of such trends. During the air-raid alarms on the East Coast immediately after the declaration of war, a great variety of unfortunate regulations were instituted by school administrators. Children were forced to carry outdoor clothing throughout the school day, air-raid drills were organized in such a way as to increase fear and insecurity, and teachers were ordered on all-night patrols of school buildings. Plans for wholesale acceleration of educational programs have been hastily proposed and as hastily withdrawn. . . . Men with outstanding names in the field of education are demanding that school programs be centered largely around one or another specific wartime need. Nor have those who oppose the further development of public education been idle at such a strategic time. State aid has been reduced, class size has been increased, teachers' salaries have been cut, various educational services have been curtailed, all in the name of patriotism and the necessity for increased war effort.

Ernest G. Osborne, associate professor of education, Teachers College, Columbia University, April 1942, "Education's Task in a World at War," *pp. 538–539.*

Our schools, public and private, have always been molds in which we cast the kind of life we wanted. Today, what we all want is victory, and beyond victory a world in which free men may fulfill their aspirations. So we turn again to our educators and ask them to help us mold men and women who can fight through to victory. We ask that every school house become a service center for the home front. And we pray that our young people will learn in the schools and in the colleges the wisdom and forbearance and patience needed by men and women of good will who seek to bring to this earth a lasting peace.

President Franklin D. Roosevelt, August 28, 1942, in Baltimore Department of Education, Educational Adjustments to War and Post-War Conditions, *p. 9.*

The high school as well as the elementary school must prepare for after the war. Every future citizen should spend at least an hour and a half every school day preparing to do his part in the years to come as an intelligent citizen. We may expect after the war widespread bitter clashes between labor leaders and capitalists, between new dealers and antis, who have not yet learned enough and have not yet recognized the basic attitudes and appreciation of cooperation. Unless the American schools, pulpit, and press build an intelligence which will surpass that of the previous generation, we are in great danger of depression and misery and poverty of dimensions unheard of, if not complete economic collapse and revolution.

Harl R. Douglass, director, College of Education, University of Colorado, Boulder, September 1942, in "Highlights from Denver Speeches," p. 17.

One cannot help being alarmed over a trend appearing prominently during the past few months in our schools and in the national education program of our country. There seems to be a definite trend toward an educational program which is based on central authority and procedure; which emphasizes the caste system of rank, uniforms, insignia, and military discipline; which is moving toward the development of intolerance and hatred; and which is confined solely to the achievement of narrow and restricted objectives. It might be well for us to read again the descriptions of the educational programs of Nazi Germany, Fascist Italy, and militaristic Japan and to compare the trends appearing in our own educational programs with the important characteristics of the educational programs developed by these countries to achieve their ends. Must we forget democracy in order to preserve its essential elements for posterity? Must we forget all that we have learned about democratic procedures and the basic elements of democracy in order to meet the present emergency?

Virgil E. Herrick, assistant professor of education, University of Chicago, November 1942, "Educational News and Editorial Comment," p. 132.

[T]he teachers would exhort us with shouts and occasional slaps to finish all of our wieners and sauerkraut or our bologna and blackeyed peas. It was our small contribution to the war effort, to eat everything on our plate. Once the third-grade teacher, known as the cruelest in the school, stood over me and forced me to eat a plate of sauerkraut, which I did, gagging and in tears, wishing I could leave . . . and never come back.

Writer Willie Morris remembering his childhood in Yazoo City, Mississippi, 1942–45, North Toward Home, p. 20.

Hatred only perpetuates the causes of war for generations to come. Teaching children to hate means descend-

ing to the level of much German education, resorting to the methods of barbarism. If American schools adopt some of the worst features of the German methods, then that is a moral victory for Germany. War conditions may breed a callousness toward suffering and a contempt for human life; the schools must counteract this if one of the permanent values of civilization is to be maintained. The schools probably cannot effectively teach children to love their enemies but they can give them an understanding and appreciation of the lives of other children over the world. . . . One of the most practical applications of true internationalism exists in the place in school activities accorded to children of enemy alien descent, the second or third generation Italians, Germans and Japanese. As someone has put it, "What a loss for us if others should lose their ships but we should lose our hearts." We should not teach hatred.

David H. Russell, professor, Graduate School of Education, University of California at Berkeley, 1943, "The Elementary School Child and the War," p. 150.

We must take more seriously the task of rendering our young people in school intelligent regarding all people who appear superficially to be different from us. We must study the peoples of Asia and Africa with keener insight and more intelligent appreciation. Specifically, we must break down the unscientific prejudice that the white peoples are innately superior to others. More generally, we must in our schools attack the whole problem of subgroups in our midst and help to cultivate a positive democratic treatment of all groups. We cannot any longer allow our young people to grow up either ignorant or careless as to what is involved in this question. Our inherent honesty in professing democracy and ethics is at stake.

William H. Kilpatrick, philosopher of education, 1943, "Racial and Minority Problems," in Ernest O. Melby, ed., Mobilizing Educational Resources for Winning the War and the Peace, *p. 117.*

The winning of the war and the peace is far more than a military matter. It is far more than an economic or political matter. It is also a matter of our character as a people; of our discipline, our loyalties, our faith; of our capacity to sacrifice comfort, to endure hardship, to remain steadfast in the face of adversity and suffering. It is a matter of the fullest development of our military talents, our technical and productive energies. It is a matter of achieving a more adequate understanding of the world in which we live and of developing in highest degree our inventive, our creative, and our staying powers. In a word, in the winning of the war and the peace we are confronted with a vast and far-reaching educational task.

George S. Counts, professor of education, Teachers College, Columbia University, 1943, "Needed New Patterns of Control," in Ernest O. Melby, ed., Mobilizing Educational Resources for Winning the War and the Peace, *pp. 223–224.*

The surest safeguard against the regimentation of education by either national or local authorities is an independent, powerful, and informed body of teachers. Such a body of teachers, whatever the forms of control, is also the most dependable guarantee of the maintenance of a spirit of freedom in the processes of education. The dictators, seeing this clearly, make every effort to man their schools and other educational agencies with a staff of thoroughly docile and subservient professional workers.

Unfortunately ... the teaching profession in the United States does not enjoy a status equal to the responsibility which we would place upon it. Many of our teachers are inadequately trained, the majority of them are poorly paid, and most of them feel insecure in their posts. Although the situation has improved greatly during the past generation, they are still for the most part reared in a tradition of acquiescence and servility—acquiescence respecting inherited practices and servility toward the more powerful and vocal persons and groups in the community.

George S. Counts, professor of education, Teachers College, Columbia University, 1943, "Needed New Patterns of Control," in Ernest O. Melby, ed., Mobilizing Educational Resources for Winning the War and the Peace, *p. 225.*

The general increase in juvenile delinquency over the Nation is attributed in part to the inability of working mothers to provide proper supervision for their children. In times of severe labor shortages and attendant high wages, there is a tendency for both parents to seek employment and leave small children in the care of an older child or entirely without supervision during working hours. Again, a depleted labor market is often responsible for the employment of indigent parents, a condition which leaves children of low-level moral and spiritual background unsupervised and free to spread their previously acquired undesirable habits among other children in the community. Congested living conditions, inadequate entertainment and recreational facilities, tardy development and coordination of child welfare services, and the character-

istic sagging of human moral fibre in times of national crises, all contribute to the urgent need for child-care in a world at war. . . .

The Extended School Services program is designed to meet the needs of working mothers by providing a rich environment, wholesome companionship, and guidance of trained adults. The all-day extended school program may include many interesting activities, meals, out-door play, reading and storytelling, dramatics, arts, crafts, excursions, gardening and canning, caring for pets, and other natural experiences. Specially trained teachers are engaged to carry on the program with the help of volunteers, including high school boys and girls interested in community service. These volunteers are given training courses.

The school is considered the most desirable location for both the nursery-kindergarten unit and the all-day school-age program.

Roy Scantlin, state superintendent of schools, Missouri, 1943, War Problems and Responsibilities of Missouri Schools, *pp. 44–45.*

Sometime recently an educator said, "When is the Navy going to take over your college?" A naval officer, hearing that question, said, "My good friend, the Navy is not taking over any college, but the educators are taking over a job that the Navy is not equipped to do at this time, and they are doing a job that only they can do." The job of educating America still remains in the hands of the educators. God grant that it will always remain there, as the job of fighting the enemy still remains in the hands of the military! The two, working together as they have in the past and as they will continue to do in the future, will be a winning combination.

Ralph A. Sentman, lieutenant commander, U.S. Navy (Ret.), 1943, "The Problem of Voluntary Education in the Armed Forces," in John Dale Russell, ed., Higher Education under War Conditions, *p. 12.*

There is widespread concern over the decline of general and liberal education during the emergency. Education for war emphasizes applied mathematics, applied science, and technology at the expense of the humanities and the social sciences. Although history, geography, English, and, in some instances, psychology appear in the Army and Navy college military training programs, these subjects play a relatively minor role, except in the case of such advanced curriculums as those in the Army Specialized Training Program concerned with foreign language and area study. Many persons fear that the current stress on technical training will put it in such a dominant position that liberal education will never be restored.

T. R. McConnell, acting dean, College of Science, Literature, and the Arts, University of Minnesota, 1943, "A Program of General Education for Members of the Armed Forces," in John Dale Russell, ed., Higher Education under War Conditions, *p. 13.*

Only a few weeks ago, a boy in uniform walked into a Middle West high school. He wore on his shoulder the insignia of the Army Air Forces, and there was pride in his step. He was home on 10 days' leave, and he was visiting the high school from which he had recently graduated. The principal gave the boy a warm welcome and of course asked how he was getting on in the Army. The young soldier replied, "I'm getting along fine. I'm a sergeant in the air force mechanic service, and, believe me, Mr. Jones, the math course I took from you certainly helped a lot."

Everywhere in our Nation, soldiers and sailors on leave are calling on their former teachers with stories like that. These little incidents bring home to us the new relation of education to a new kind of war. Very few soldiers visited their high schools in the first World War, because only 4 percent of the doughboys of 1917 had completed high school. . . . In 1917 a high-school mathematics course was no particular help to a man carrying a rifle.

Paul V. McNutt, federal security administrator, 1943, "Schools in Wartime," in Handbook on Education and the War, *p. 1.*

I am becoming convinced that if the war we are now fighting continues for another year, as it doubtless will, every American over the age of 3 and this side of senility will be enrolled in some kind of school.

Elbert D. Thomas, U.S. senator from Utah, 1943, "What Education Is Doing to Help Win the War," in Handbook on Education and the War, *p. 72.*

Just as it is true that a soldier cannot fight unless he knows what he is fighting for, it is equally true that a child cannot be expected to give his best to the war effort unless he knows what we are fighting for. He should understand the meaning of the four freedoms and the advantages of living in a country possessing these ideals. He should learn that freedom must be *earned* and *appreciated,* even *fought for.* He must be brought to understand that with the winning

of freedom comes *responsibility,* which each individual must assume if he is to enjoy the privileges of freedom. It must be remembered that these and other democratic ideals can be developed, not through indoctrination, but only through democratic procedures and through democratic living.

Maud Frothingham Roby, principal, Shepherd Elementary School, Washington, D.C., January 1943, "Implications of the Present World Situation for the Elementary School," p. 270.

With the colleges and secondary schools geared to serve in an all-out effort to meet war needs, the elementary school, in its eagerness to serve, is asking that its contribution in this national and international conflict be clearly defined. This war vitally touches the elementary school and the life of each child in it. In modern mechanized warfare the people are not isolated, and there are no civilians as such. This is total war; every life is affected; and the complete energies and full participation of every person are required. . . .

We teachers must believe in the importance of our work. We must regard ourselves as full partners in the war effort and must do our work with an impelling sincerity and patriotic zeal.

Maud Frothingham Roby, principal, Shepherd Elementary School, Washington, D.C., January 1943, "Implications of the Present World Situation for the Elementary School," p. 267.

Teachers are intrusted with the most precious wealth of the nation, its children. The children in our schools today are the men and women of tomorrow, the carriers of democracy. What they are as men and women is, to a startling degree, our responsibility. For instance, children are going to need the basic skills if they are to be competent citizens. Teachers do this task competently, but our responsibility does not end there. We must also take account of the developing attitudes of these children. If they develop something better than mere tolerance—a genuine liking for peoples of different races, creeds, and colors—it may be the result of having spent a year with a teacher who kept alive this friendly appreciation of other peoples.

Children need a sense of courage and confidence in themselves these days when both parents may be out of the home. Teachers who have a real love for children and a calm sense of courage, can help their boys and girls face insecurity with intelligence.

Teachers who know the founding fathers of our country, not as a series of names and dates, but as troubled, earnest men, giving voice to the best expression of democratic principles ever formulated, can make those men live for their children. And if the youngsters value those democratic principles, it will be partly because their schools are living embodiments of those principles.

May Hill Arbuthnot, educator and children's literature scholar, January 1943, in Olga Adams, "Educational News and Editorial Comment," p. 565.

Art, like music, has a tremendously important contribution to make to the war effort, both in society and in the school. Enlightened educators realize that far from being a peacetime luxury, it is one of the most effective of the democratic weapons for fighting the war. Fascism, from the start, has always tried to destroy or restrict the arts.

Today, art serves wartime needs—in government, in industry, and in military and civilian life. The output of factories has been speeded up by the use of "production drawings," which are large, freehand, visual interpretations of blueprints. "Production charts," like school bulletin-board displays, use cartoons, posters, and slogans to transmit morale-building ideas to workers. Military recruitment and government information agencies have always relied heavily on the poster as having more direct effect upon action than does the printed word alone. Our allies have found, as we are finding, that art does its part in relieving the tensions of a war-torn society, and we know that it will have its therapeutic effect in rehabilitation after the war.

The situation poses a challenge to all art teachers. If they are alert they will seize every opportunity to have art function to meet wartime needs. If art contributes its share to victory, it will have won thereby the place it deserves in the postwar world.

National Education Association of the United States, January 1943, Wartime Handbook for Education, p. 27.

Teachers are favorably situated to see and understand the problems of children confronted by dislocations in family life. They can themselves feel the pull of necessitous home conditions and wage-earning opportunities by which many children are being drawn out of school for homemaking service on behalf of the family or for gainful employment in other homes or in industry. They witness the waning of interest on the part of pupils who are sensitive to the distracting force of an atmosphere of war, and they see these pupils desert the school in the search for satisfying excitement. They struggle with the growing restlessness of boys and girls released from the accustomed surveillance of parents whose normal pursuits have recently been interrupted by the war.

There are many manifestations of the concern with which teachers view the emerging problems of child welfare and education. Reports from all areas and from all types of schools give evidence of the teachers' untiring efforts to minimize the hazards to health, emotional stability, morality, and appropriate developmental experiences which beset the children under their care. Generous contributions in service and substance are being made by thousands of classroom teachers in daily ministrations both to the children and to their families in situations where critical conditions prevail. Such teachers suffer no little distress because of the limited reach of their endeavors, and they are alarmed by the certain knowledge that the war's demoralizing effects on schooling will be accentuated as more and more persons, particularly the women, are diverted from civilian to military occupations.

Nelson B. Henry, associate professor of education, University of Chicago, February 1943, "Educational News and Editorial Comment," p. 319.

Consider the problem of the American girl of Japanese ancestry, evacuated from the West Coast to a relocation center after war came, and denied the right to enrol in a school of nursing, or not permitted to return to complete the course which was interrupted when she was evacuated.

Provision has been made by the government to permit loyal Americans of Japanese ancestry to transfer to certain institutions of higher learning away from the West Coast, but students who wish to enter schools of nursing encounter resistance not met by ordinary university students. . . .

One girl, describing her inability to find a nursing school which would admit her, writes: "I am an American of Japanese ancestry and one cannot choose one's ancestors."

This young woman graduated from high school at fifteen, in the upper 20 per cent of her class. She worked for her board, laundry, and a salary at the same time. She has had some college—where she also worked for board, laundry, and a salary. She writes: "People don't know my nationality until I or someone else tells them. The United States is the only country I know. My friends are Caucasians."

"The Problem of Student Nurses of Japanese Ancestry," October 1943, p. 895.

Many aspects of the curriculum should be redirected toward victory. Classroom subjects, particularly at the higher secondary levels, should contribute directly to pre-induction training for the armed forces, industry, and community service. Curricular offerings at all levels should be modified so that students may be given an understanding of what issues are involved in this war and an opportunity to contribute toward the attainment of victory at home and abroad. Those aspects of the curriculum concerned with community relationships and so-called extra-curricular activities offer special opportunities for service. No phase of the curriculum can justly remain isolated from the impact of the war and the succeeding peace.

Baltimore Department of Education, November 1943,
Educational Adjustments to War and Post-War
Conditions, p. 9.

[T]he schools at Inkster, Wayne, and other small villages already have two or three sessions daily of three hours each. In Ypsilanti, although there are no double sessions, there is overcrowding of 170 per cent. A new school of six rooms was constructed in the township which was immediately filled with over 400 pupils. Even with the best teaching, education under such conditions is a farce. In Inkster the stove in the colored school was defective. This school had to be closed during cold weather. The truancy rate in some districts has gone up 300 per cent.

Agnes E. Meyer, journalist, describing school overcrowding in
the Detroit suburbs, 1944, Journey through Chaos, *p. 36.*

Our school has accepted the philosophy that in addition to the accepted and constant educational objectives there is also a necessity for the school to serve as a "war in-

Children attending a school for African Americans in segregated Washington, D.C., weigh scrap paper they collected for the war effort in March 1942. *(Library of Congress, Prints and Photographs Division, LC-USW3-000875-E)*

dustry". . . . In adjusting the school program to changed conditions an effort has been made to have pupils realize that they are making a contribution to the war effort by continuing their senior high school education. Courses have been adapted to include materials which serve this purpose. . . . It is probable that more than 50 per cent of the student body during the last year were employed either in full-time or part-time work. It was necessary for the school to give some attention to the effect this work schedule had upon their school work. Greater stress was placed upon the work done in the school, and home assignments were curtailed in most departments.

A metropolitan high school principal, New York State, 1944, in Ethel L. Cornell, High School Adjustments to War Needs, *pp. 25–26.*

Practically every child, teacher, bus driver and janitor who can and will work is in demand during the season for harvesting tomatoes, corn and potatoes. . . . This year we ran single sessions, closing at noon during two months and also on all days of suitable weather (at other times). . . . Add to this the piles of mimeographed information, printed pamphlets, and numerous questionnaires to be read and answered, and you may see why we have no time for organizing a Victory Corps.

A rural high school principal, New York State, 1944, in Ethel L. Cornell, High School Adjustments to War Needs, *p. 27.*

University officials were at a loss when Japanese from the West Coast colleges and high schools first applied for admission here, as they felt these people should be given educational advantages, yet were loath to make any move that might in any way endanger the security of the community. Subsequently the Army went on record as opposing Japanese at Minnesota because of the large number of secret, war-related research projects going on upon the campus. This has now been lightened. . . . University officials said they do not expect any large influx of Japanese students in the immediate future, as most of those who were seeking admittance in the autumn of 1942 entered other colleges and universities.

University of Minnesota News Service, 1944, in "Japanese Who Get Clearance May Attend the University of Minnesota," p. 136.

The United States Government . . . is underwriting *in full* the education of thousands, hundreds of thousands, of young men at the college level. That it is education for a restricted war purpose is aside from the point in so far as broad educational implications are concerned. It should be stressed, too, that this education is given without respect to the economic status of those who receive it. Rich and poor are treated alike. The only consideration is ability to profit from the instruction.

Here, in wartime, is a new conception of democratic education. It frankly raises the question of what the responsibility of government is to be once the war is over. Are the thousands of men who have had the advantages of the war program of higher education likely to forget the fact that a government which needed their services in war was willing to meet the costs that were involved in training them? Are these same men not likely to ask why there is not a parallel responsibility on the part of government to train them for peacetime service as well? It seems unlikely that our basic educational philosophies will remain untouched by the implications of the war programs. And it will be difficult to dismiss the argument that a nation that spends hundreds of millions in higher education for war should be willing and under obligation to spend at least equivalent amounts for higher education for peace.

Malcolm M. Willey, vice president, academic administration, and professor of sociology, University of Minnesota, January 1944, "The College Training Programs of the Armed Services," pp. 27–28.

Military conscription has swept the students from the campus so suddenly that there has been scarcely time to appraise the significance of the event. Is higher education in the present war situation confronted by a disaster or an opportunity, a blank period in its service to society or a cleared lull in which to take bearings and elevate vision?

If colleges may cease their quest for government subsidies to continue artificially "college as usual" and devote their efforts to establishing foundations for a more stable civilization in postwar years, they not only might attune themselves to the new world which lies on the other side of the war, but might indeed render a benefit to humanity that is beyond the powers of any other agency to confer. If this time of testing should prove that the mission of higher education is the betterment of civilization and that individual satisfactions are a by-product, war's conflagration will become not its pyre but a refining furnace.

Clement C. Williams, president, Lehigh University, June 3, 1944, "Higher Education Without Students," p. 385.

A trend that is cause for considerable concern is the tendency, which has become more and more prevalent, to promote and encourage in our high schools—and even in some of our junior high schools—the formation of "swing bands." While the "swing band" probably fills a need in the social life of the school, it cannot possibly take the place of the legitimate school orchestra as a vehicle for developing in our children a love for and appreciation of the highest and noblest in music. Swing-band activities, therefore, should be limited purely to the purpose for which the organization is meant, namely, to furnish music for school dances. This, however, is not the case. Swing bands, in some of our schools, are exalted to the rank of concert organizations and permitted to give assembly programs and to participate in various school affairs. Thus to a great majority of our pupils, "swing music" has become the only music worthy of the name. They have become so fascinated by this type of music that they have lost respect not only for good music and for their classmates who belong to the regular school orchestras and bands, but also for the instructors who direct these organizations. To the "swing" addicts, serious music is, as they put it, "corny," and meant for older "frogs" only.

Nino Marcelli, director of instrumental music, San Diego Public Schools, June 17, 1944, "An Unfortunate Trend in School Music," p. 428.

Today liberal education faces perhaps greater opportunity for reappraisal than it has had for a hundred years. We have been shocked by wartime adjustments which have taken half of our students out of their peacetime programs, and then have returned to us many hundreds for special wartime training. We have been forced to do many things which we should not have done voluntarily—to go on a 12-month year, to increase the number of contact hours, to accelerate the pace, to teach some subjects not heretofore considered in the realm of the colleges, and to conform in a dozen details to the demands of the military authorities.

But the war will end, and then what? Unless we give some thought to it, we shall go back to things as they were. We may do this anyway, but I propose that we take advantage of the upset conditions to examine critically some of our fundamental educational policies and procedures so that the university in the future may develop by the direct and thoughtful action of the faculty of today, accepting the ways of the past only after careful consideration of their present-day validity.

Deane W. Malott, chancellor, University of Kansas, June 17, 1944, "Will Liberal Education Survive?" p. 417.

The war has caused an upward trend in delinquency. . . . Everyone recognizes that there are many factors contributing to delinquency, such as broken homes, discordant family life, lack of space for play, immoral community conditions. We know, too, that in many communities the schoolroom is dreary; the school work, monotonous; the teacher, nervous or nagging; the school, isolated from home and community. Just as some wives drive their husbands to drink, some elementary schools drive children to delinquency. We know that there are certain factors in the biological, psychological, and sociological development of children that are still beyond our grasp. But there is much that we do know and more that the elementary school can do in removing the causes or the conditions of delinquency.

J. Cayce Morrison, assistant commissioner for research, New York State Education Department, September 1944, "Some Issues for Postwar Elementary Education," pp. 16–17.

What took me from our Morey farm in Kansas to the Cadet Nursing Corps was my sister. Thelma Morey Robinson entered nurses' training and became a cadet nurse. I was impressed with my tour of Lincoln General Hospital and nurses' residence. Attending her candlelight capping ceremony confirmed my decision that I wanted a nursing career. Mother had concern for my health, since the nurses she knew worked long hours, often around the clock. She told me that nursing could break my health. My parents, however, gave their sanction without question. Thelma had already convinced them that nursing was an acceptable and noble profession and the Cadet Nurse Corps made it affordable as well. Which school of nursing was for me? My sister's school, Lincoln General Hospital School of Nursing, of course!

Paulie M. Perry, who entered the U.S. Cadet Nurse Corps in 1945, in Thelma M. Robinson and Paulie M. Perry, Cadet Nurse Stories: The Call for and Response of Women During World War II, p. 30.

CHAPTER EIGHT

Toward Equal Educational Opportunity for All
1946–1963

The 16 million veterans of World War II came home to a society in which the educational and technological advances of the war years were enlarging the middle class. Long-awaited economic prosperity allowed couples to marry at younger ages than in the past, and in 1946 the marriage rate reached 118.1 per 1,000 unmarried females over age 14. Couples could afford larger families, and babies born in 1946 numbered 3.4 million. U.S. births reached a record 4 million in 1954 and hovered at that lofty level until 1964. In all, 76 million Americans were born in the 19 years from 1946 to 1964, and they became known as the baby-boom generation.

The soaring marriage and birth rates created a demand for housing, fueling the growth of suburbs that were largely populated by young, white, middle-class or upper-middle-class families. The need was so great that in 1955, suburban subdivisions accounted for 75 percent of new construction. Along with the houses came schools. Built low to the ground of brick, cinderblock, and glass, with sprawling corridors and sunny classrooms, suburban schools mirrored the ranches and split levels of the surrounding communities.

Many of these schools had been built in a hurry. When 38 percent more children entered kindergarten in 1951 than in 1950, suburban school districts rushed to accommodate the surge; but even the 50,000 classrooms added by September 1952—an astonishing increase—fell short of the number needed for all the children starting school that year. The growing state of California opened schools on the average of one per week throughout the 1950s, and still classrooms were overcrowded. Throughout the United States, children shared textbooks and went to school on split sessions, with half the pupils attending in the morning and half in the afternoon, to make limited resources meet the needs of all. Putting a teacher in every new classroom forced school districts to bend rules, and by 1959, approximately 100,000 of the 1.3 million teachers in U.S. public schools lacked the required credentials.

Despite these challenges, the new and growing towns surrounding U.S. cities generally had the necessary resources to support their schools and offer wide-

A teacher reads to a kindergarten class at the Pearl River School in Pearl River, New York, in 1950. This suburban classroom scene is typical of the postwar period. *(Library of Congress, Prints and Photographs Division, LC-G613-T-58378)*

ranging courses of study. Also, like suburbanites, the business and professional people who served these communities valued education as the path to career and social standing and therefore were committed to building high-quality school systems. Within just a few years, the suburban school was a familiar, established part of the American scene and a shining example of what American education ought to be.

The State of Rural Schools

Two midwestern states, Ohio and Indiana, had made significant progress in school consolidation, and the others had passed laws requiring the closing of one-room schools and the reorganization of school districts. Consolidation took time, though. Between 1945 and 1950, nearly half the one-room schools in Kansas closed; between 1944 and 1954, the number of these schools still in use in Illinois dropped from 8,000 to 800. Nationwide, nearly 75,000 one-teacher schools remained in use at mid-century, however. With a total enrollment of 1.5 million children, they represented 44 percent of all public schools.

Schools remained substandard in many rural places despite the recommendations of the 1942 White House Conference. The 1945–46 school census in Harlan County, Kentucky, an impoverished region of Appalachia, revealed that many of the schools there were poorly constructed, and most lacked such standard safety features as fire extinguishers and stairway handrails. One school met in an abandoned theater, and another was housed in an old warehouse. The schools—including one built relatively recently, in 1937—generally lacked indoor plumbing, and a number of the outdoor privies drained into streams. Classroom lighting tended to be inadequate, and libraries, lunchrooms, and auditoriums were largely missing.

Resistance to Federal Funding

The evident disparities in the quality of education in U.S. schools led President Harry S. Truman to propose federal funding for education. Aid to education was one of six major legislative initiatives known as the Fair Deal that Truman announced in January 1949. With the twin goals of distributing income more equitably and addressing social problems, the president also called for a national health insurance program, new civil rights legislation, a federal housing program, an extension of unemployment insurance benefits, and tax cuts for the poor.

Congress extended unemployment coverage slightly and passed a major housing initiative in 1949, but the nation's lawmakers rejected or postponed the rest of the Fair Deal package, including aid to education. Ever since the nation was founded, overseeing education had been a right and responsibility left to the individual states, and many Americans remained vehemently opposed to federal involvement. Also, southern whites in Congress feared that ending segregation might be a condition for the granting of federal aid, and with good reason: The President's Committee on Civil Rights, appointed by Truman in 1946, had recommended that aid be denied to states where segregation was mandatory, and African-American legislators vowed to support the president's bill only if it conformed to the committee's recommendation. While all this was happening, Catholic organizations lobbied for federal support of parochial schools, and the National Education Association (NEA) and National Congress of Parents and Teachers lobbied against it, arguing that federal aid to private, especially religious, schools would represent a violation of the traditional separation of church and state.

Life-Adjustment Education

At the same time, professional educators were reassessing the role of high schools. According to Charles A. Prosser, Ph.D., of the Federal Board for Vocational Education, U.S. high schools were meeting the needs of the 20 percent of students who entered skilled trades and the 20 percent who went on to college. The student population had grown larger and more diverse than in past decades, and schools needed to do more for the remaining 60 percent, those going on to lives as unskilled or semiskilled laborers, clerical workers, or homemakers—or so Prosser said. He called on high schools to expand their curriculums, to offer courses that prepared these students for satisfying lives as citizens, workers, and family members. Schools needed, too, to equip all students for life in a period of apparent social change, with divorce and delinquency rates rising and rapid suburban growth stressing the young. Prosser's call gave rise to the life-adjustment movement, which flourished in the decade after World War II.

In 1947, Secretary of Education John W. Studebaker formed the National Commission on Life-Adjustment Education for Youth, which sought "to promote in every manner possible ways, means, and devices for improving the life adjustment education of secondary school youth."[1] The commission defined this type of education in general terms, stating that "it recognizes the inherent dignity of the human personality," and "is concerned with ethical and moral living and with physical, mental, and emotional health."[2]

A strict definition remained elusive, because each community was to tailor its program to its students' particular needs. In many places, therefore, life adjustment remained a way of thinking about secondary education that never was fully put into practice. The Pennsylvania Program of Secondary School Curriculum Revision, for example, enlisted teachers, students, and laypeople to produce bulletins and participate democratically in planning, as Pennsylvania principals and teachers attended state and regional conferences and workshops. The West Virginia Steering Committee listed eight areas to receive emphasis: oral and written communication; literature; health, recreation, and fitness; social studies; the physical and biological sciences; applied arithmetic and elementary mathematics; fine and applied arts and handicrafts; and home skills and consumer education. High schools throughout the United States developed nonacademic elective courses in subjects ranging from social skills to career opportunities and core curriculums that were intended to meet the life-adjustment objectives.

Life adjustment had barely gained momentum when critics halted its progress. Chief among the faultfinders was Arthur Bestor, a professor of history at the University of Illinois, who in two influential books, *Educational Wastelands* (1953) and *The Restoration of Learning* (1955), called life-adjustment education trivial and unfocused. He blamed educational professionals—the "educationists"—for devaluing academic study. Not only had the educationists "undermined public confidence in the schools," he charged, but they had also distanced schools from the "disciplines of science and scholarship, which citizens trust and value."[3] In 1956, Bestor founded the Council on Basic Education, a think tank committed to reviving interest in academic instruction at the secondary level.

The Rise of Community Colleges

More lasting than the trend toward life-adjustment education were efforts to broaden the definition of higher education and make it accessible to a larger segment of the population. In 1948, the President's Commission on Higher Education, another group appointed by Truman in 1946, issued a report advocating greater enrollment in colleges and universities. The commission recommended that each state form a board to oversee the expansion of higher education and that community colleges be developed. Like junior colleges, community colleges offered the first two years of study toward a four-year bachelor's degree. Their mission extended beyond this, however, to include two-year professional and technical courses, adult education, and instructional, recreational, and social activities for people living within commuting distance. California, New York, and other states made community colleges key components of their systems of higher education to ease enrollment at four-year colleges and universities.

The president's commission also set a goal for college enrollment of 4.6 million in 1960; by that year, 3.6 million Americans—a million fewer—were attending institutions of higher learning.

A New Commitment to Academic Instruction

Attitudes changed, and changed again. Life-adjustment education passed in and out of fashion, and federal aid to education, considered too controversial in 1949, became acceptable by 1958. The National Defense Education Act, signed into law in that year, gave financial aid to public and private schools at all levels. The act was intended to advance education, especially in science, mathematics, and modern foreign languages, although it barred the government from directing, supervising, or controlling curriculum, instruction, administration, or staffing at any institution. It also provided colleges and universities with 90 percent of the capital funds for low-interest student loans.

The new willingness to let the national government support education had its roots in international events. Since the end of World War II, the United States and the Soviet Union had engaged in a tense, competitive, ideological conflict known as the cold war. This rivalry between nations bred mistrust at home, causing many Americans to eye one another suspiciously, wondering who might be a communist infiltrator. Concern that disloyal individuals might be employed by the federal government was so strong that in 1947, Truman signed an executive order authorizing a loyalty investigation to be conducted of every new employee of the executive branch. The order also established the Loyalty Review Board, a division of the Civil Service Commission that investigated workers suspected of subversive acts.

In the 1950s, some school administrators followed the president's example and required teachers and other staff to sign loyalty oaths. School officials pored over textbooks, alert for un-American sentiments expressed within their pages. During these years, high school and college students learned the dangers that communism posed, and students of all ages learned how to survive if they should see the blinding flash of light that signaled a nuclear explosion. The prevailing fears culminated in congressional investigations of alleged communist activities, begun in 1953 and led by Senator Joseph McCarthy of Wisconsin. The McCarthy hearings targeted government officials, intellectuals, educators, and people in the arts.

The threat of nuclear war and its destructive power prevented the cold war from erupting into a direct military confrontation, but the two world powers supported opposing sides in the Korean War (1950–53), in which communist North Korea and democratic South Korea reached an uneasy truce. The United States and Soviet Union also engaged in the "space race," a contest to prove scientific and technological superiority by taking the lead in space exploration.

The Soviets pulled ahead on October 4, 1957, with the launch of *Sputnik I,* the world's first artificial satellite, a metallic sphere weighing 183 pounds and orbiting the earth every 98 minutes. Then, on November 3, the Soviets launched *Sputnik II,* which carried a dog named Laika. Clearly, the United States, the nation whose technology had won World War II, had slipped into second place.

Stunned Americans, determined to catch up, focused attention on their schools, demanding higher academic standards and greater emphasis on science and mathematics. Admiral Hyman G. Rickover, the engineer who had developed the first nuclear-powered submarine, emerged as a leader in the call for educational reform. Rickover's comparisons of the U.S. and European educational systems demonstrated that U.S. schools lagged woefully behind. He said that the United States needed to do a better job of identifying the academically gifted and preparing them for leading roles in society, but he warned that rigorous training in science and mathematics was not enough. Echoing the Committee of Ten of 1893, Rickover insisted that talented students needed a well-rounded academic education, one that gave them a firm grasp of history, economics, literature, foreign languages, and other disciplines, if they were to use their "specialized training wisely."[4]

A more scholarly and dispassionate commentary was that of James B. Conant, a former president of Harvard University, who surveyed U.S. high schools in the

1950s and early 1960s. At each school, Conant evaluated the quality of general academic education according to course requirements in English and American literature and composition; social studies, including American history; science; mathematics; and foreign languages. He judged the adequacy of vocational programming by the courses offered to boys and girls and the opportunities for students to gain supervised work experience. He also looked at how the school met the learning needs of "very slow readers" and the academically talented.[5]

In the 1959 book based on his findings, *The American High School Today*, Conant made suggestions that influenced course offerings at secondary schools nationwide. He recommended a core curriculum that filled at least half a student's schedule and included four years of English, three or four years of social studies, and at least one year each of science and mathematics. Electives that matched a student's interests and career plans were to account for the rest of his or her course work. Balancing the goals of both the proponents and critics of life adjustment, Conant called for better academic counseling, more individualized instruction, grouping of students by ability, and a broader range of vocational studies that was geared to the local job market.

In *Slums and Suburbs* (1961), Conant presented a sobering contrast of high schools in prosperous suburban communities and impoverished urban ghettoes, some within half an hour's drive of each other. As whites moved to suburbs in the postwar years, cities increasingly became home to people of color. African Americans from the rural South had settled in northern industrial centers during both world wars, and they continued to migrate. Growing numbers of Puerto Ricans and Mexican Americans also made their homes in cities as part of their quest for economic and social opportunity. The urban minority population generally lacked the financial resources of the whites who had moved out, which meant that tax support for urban schools declined. No new schools could be built, and in the old ones children crowded together in deteriorating classrooms and tried to learn.

The spacious, new suburban schools that Conant visited spent as much as $1,000 per pupil each year and employed as many as 70 teachers and other professionals for every 1,000 pupils. The rundown, dismal, poorly equipped schools of the urban ghettoes spent less than half as much money per pupil and employed 40 professionals, at most, for every 1,000 pupils.

Children and teens attending inner-city schools coped with stressors, unknown to most suburban youth, that included, not only poverty, but also the absence of a father or other adult male relative from the home and frequent exposure to crime and gang violence. In New York and other cities, people recently arrived from Puerto Rico had formed their own ghettoes. Many of the newcomers spoke no English, and the children among them generally had received inferior schooling in Puerto Rico and therefore faced added obstacles to learning.

Conant reported the discouraging fact that in one large inner-city neighborhood, 59 percent of males between the ages of 16 and 21 were out of school and unemployed. He noted that the percentages were nearly as high in other poor urban communities and warned that allowing so many young men to exist without hope or purpose was to create breeding grounds for social unrest. "[W]e are allowing social dynamite to accumulate in our large cities," he wrote.[6] Although acknowledging the shortage of funding for urban education, he expressed his wish for school authorities to take responsibility for helping these young men return to school or find jobs.

Students use the library at Walter R. Dolan Junior High School in Stamford, Connecticut, in 1952. *(Library of Congress, Prints and Photographs Division, LC-G613-T-61178)*

Progress in Special Education

In 1948, most U.S. states and territories and the District of Columbia required children to attend school between the ages of seven and 16. In states and territories where the requirements differed, children entered school at six or eight and were permitted to leave at 14, 15, 17, or 18. By 1948, 25 states and the Territory of Hawaii had also passed compulsory education laws for deaf or blind children; by 1949, 34 states had laws allowing or requiring special education for children with impaired mobility, and 18 states provided for the education of the developmentally disabled. A few states had enacted similar legislation that applied to all "exceptional children," a group that Elise H. Martens of the U.S. Office of Education defined as "The blind and the partially seeing, the deaf and the hard of hearing, the crippled (including the cerebral-palsied), the delicate (including the tuberculous and the cardiopathic), the epileptic, the speech-defective, the mentally handicapped, the mentally gifted, and the socially or emotionally maladjusted and delinquent. . . ."[7] Some states began educating children with disabilities at younger ages than other children, because the disabled often needed an earlier start to make comparable progress.

Every state provided for children with disabilities to be educated at residential facilities or in special classes in their communities. Some states maintained their own residential schools, and others paid for students to attend private institutions or residential schools in neighboring states. The states offered residential schooling to children who were blind, deaf, developmentally disabled, or severely physically disabled, although the length of stay varied according to need. Residents could spend most of their lives in institutions for the developmentally disabled, which served people of all ages and offered custodial and protective care as well as education. In contrast, physically disabled children remained in hospital-schools only until they were medically stable and ready to return home. A number of states also operated residential schools for juvenile delinquents, where young people received clinical care and therapy intended to help them make a healthy psychological adjustment.

The majority of exceptional students attended special classes in their communities, however, and each state established methods for identifying children who qualified. States conducted screening tests of hearing, vision, health, and cognitive ability to identify exceptional children within the public school population and looked for them as well among those youngsters who were not enrolled in school, either because they were too young or because their parents kept them home, believing they had no place in the public school system. In most instances, students could only be placed in special classes following examination by a physician or psychologist and with the examiner's approval.

Another group to be identified was the gifted. Interest in the education of children with unusual ability grew after the publication in 1951 of *The Gifted Child,* a book edited by the child psychologist Paul A. Witty, who broadened the definition of giftedness to include more than those who scored highest on the Stanford-Binet Intelligence Scale. He recognized as gifted "any child whose performance, in a potentially valuable line of human activity, is consistently remarkable."[8]

Why place gifted children in special classes? Previously most school systems had moved rapid learners to a higher grade, but by the 1950s students of child development were cautioning that these children generally lacked the physical and social development of their older classmates and felt isolated. Yet to group them with average children of their own age was to sentence them to boredom and frustration and to inhibit the development of minds with the potential to benefit humankind. Offering enrichment within the regular classroom was another way to address the learning needs of the gifted.

Soon, educators also perceived that children with poor academic performance might not necessarily be "slow," but might instead have cognitive problems that prevented them from keeping up with the rest of the class. These were children with normal intelligence who were highly distractible or hyperactive, or who had difficulty learning to read. In 1963, Samuel A. Kirk, director of the Institute for Research on Exceptional Children at the University of Illinois, coined the term *learning disability* to describe "a discrepancy between the child's learning capacity (as indicated by aptitude tests) and his achievement. . . ."[9]

The federal government aided special education in 1947 by establishing an annual appropriation of $1 million for the Library of Congress to provide reading material for the blind. In 1958, the year the National Defense Education Act became law, the government made grants available to colleges, universities, and state educational agencies to advance the training of teachers for the developmentally disabled. In 1961, Washington allocated funds to train teachers of children with impaired hearing and speech and to distribute books and other educational materials for the blind, and a year later, the government also paid for the distribution of captioned films for the deaf and related training and research.

In 1962, an estimated 1.25 million developmentally disabled children attended classes. In 1963, approximately 1,666,000 children were enrolled in various special education programs offered by 5,600 school systems nationwide.

Segregated Schooling Is Unconstitutional

Educational opportunities improved for African Americans, especially in the South, on May 17, 1954, when the U.S. Supreme Court reversed its 1896 ruling on the constitutionality of separate public facilities for blacks and whites, at least as it affected public education. Reading the Court's opinion, Chief Justice Earl Warren famously declared that "in the field of public education the doctrine of 'separate but equal' has no place. Separate educational facilities are inherently unequal."[10] At the time, 40 percent of the nation's public school students attended segregated schools, and psychological tests had revealed that African-American children in these schools had lower self-esteem than did those in school with children of other races.

The justices reached this unanimous opinion in deciding five cases collectively titled *Brown v. Board of Education*. In the best-known of these cases, Oliver Brown of Topeka, Kansas, had brought suit against the board of education of his city on behalf of his daughter. Every school day, Linda Brown took a long and hazardous walk to the all-black elementary school that she attended; her father asked in his suit that she be allowed to attend the school in her neighborhood, which was for white children only. Among the other cases was a suit filed by students attending all-black R. R. Moton High School in Farmville, Virginia, calling for improvements to their school and an end to school segregation in their community; and another brought by the parents of Spottswood Thomas Bolling, Jr., a public-school student in Washington, D.C., who was denied admission to Sousa Junior High School in his city because of his race. Similar suits had been filed in federal court seeking an end to school segregation in Summerton, South Carolina, and Wilmington, Delaware.

The Court failed to impose a deadline, however. In a second ruling, on May 31, 1955, the justices left desegregation in the hands of local school authorities and ordered federal district judges to ensure not immediate school integration, but rather "a prompt and reasonable start toward full compliance."[11]

Across the South, most school districts took some steps to comply with the Supreme Court's ruling. Cities such as Louisville, Baltimore, San Antonio, and Washington, D.C., desegregated their schools rapidly and served as models for other municipalities. These and other compliant school systems desegregated by reconfiguring districts without regard to race and assigning children to the schools nearest their homes. Some also allowed students to transfer to the schools of their choice. Louisville's school board began formulating its desegregation plan immediately after the 1954 Supreme Court decision and implemented it in September 1956. At inception, 73.6 percent of the city's schoolchildren attended schools with at least some racial mixing.

Face-off in Little Rock

Some districts, especially in the Deep South, the region with the highest percentage of African Americans, resisted desegregation. The effort to integrate one southern school, Central High School in Little Rock, Arkansas, precipitated a showdown between the federal government and the forces determined to uphold the tradition of racial segregation.

The Little Rock school board had developed a plan for gradual integration of the city's schools, and in 1957, nine black students volunteered to attend all-white Central High School: Their names were Minnijean Brown, Elizabeth Eckford, Ernest Green, Thelma Mothershed, Melba Pattillo, Gloria Ray, Terrence Roberts, Jefferson Thomas, and Carlotta Walls. Yet on September 2, the day before schools were to open, Governor Orval Faubus ordered the Arkansas National Guard to surround Central High School. Faubus had permitted voluntary segregation to proceed in districts throughout the state, but that night he appeared on television to declare Central High School off limits to blacks.

None of the "Little Rock Nine" attempted to enter the high school on September 3. When Elizabeth Eckford tried to attend school the next day, guardsmen blocked the doors, their bayonets raised. Newspapers throughout the nation printed a photograph of the lone black teen maintaining her dignity as she was trailed by shouting, jeering, whites, their faces distorted by hatred. The nine students at last entered their school on September 23, through a side door, evading the thousand angry protesters gathered in front of the building. Knowledge that the students were inside triggered violence outside, including the beating of African-American reporters. As white students within Central High taunted their black peers, the principal closed the school, claiming he did so for the safety of the student body.

President Dwight D. Eisenhower responded to the events in Little Rock by federalizing the National Guard and sending the 101st Airborne Division to the scene to restore order and protect the African-American students. Each of the three boys and six girls had a soldier assigned to him or her, and on September 24, the students entered Central High School through the main doors. Even with this military presence, the African Americans endured cruel treatment, however. White students tripped them, spat on them, poured ink on their clothes, and shot them with water pistols. When the nine students appealed to school authorities for help, Superintendent Virgil Blossom trivialized their concerns and advised them not to respond to the attacks.

The white offenders went unpunished, and their assaults grew more violent. The nine blacks suffered kicking, name calling, and being pushed down stairs. White teens sprayed acid in Melba Pattillo's face; they hit Jefferson Thomas in the head, knocking him unconscious; and anonymous whites bombed the home of Carlotta Walls. The enemies of integration terrorized the black students and their families with menacing notes and telephone calls, and they made bomb threats in repeated attempts to disrupt education at Central High School.

Minniejean Brown, possibly the most outspoken of the nine, was expelled for standing up to her tormenters, but the remaining eight completed this long, torturous school year. On May 27, 1958, Ernest Green, the lone senior among the Little Rock Nine, became the first African American to graduate from Central High School.

That fall, Faubus closed Little Rock's four high schools in a further attempt to prevent desegregation from proceeding, but the nation had committed itself to school integration, and there would be no returning to legally sanctioned segregation. With their schools closed, nearly half of Little Rock's white high school students enrolled in private schools, and a third attended schools in other communities. The rest of the whites and most blacks received no formal education that year. When the high schools reopened, in August 1959, integration proceeded according to the federal mandate.

James Meredith Attends the University of Mississippi

The desegregation of public schools in the South was part of the larger, greater Civil Rights movement through which African Americans won important legal victories in the 1950s and 1960s. On November 14, 1956, the U.S. Supreme Court let stand the decision of a lower court outlawing segregation on public transportation, and by 1962, college students were staging sit-ins at lunch counters in southern towns, demanding that African Americans be served.

In that year as well, 23-year-old James Meredith broke the color barrier at the University of Mississippi, the first and largest public institution of higher learning in that southern state. Meredith was a student at Jackson State College (now Jackson State University), a school for African Americans in the Mississippi capital, in early 1961, when he applied for admission to the university. He met the academic criteria for admission, so when the university denied his application, he knew he had been rejected because of his race. With help from the Legal Defense and Educational Fund of the National Association for the Advancement of Colored People (NAACP), Meredith sued the state, and on September 3, 1962, a federal district court ordered the university to admit him.

The reaction in Mississippi was swift and negative. Governor Ross Barnett publicly promised to block Meredith from registering, and in a televised speech declared, "We must either submit to the unlawful dictate of the federal government or stand up like men and tell them, 'Never.'"[12] Privately, though, Barnett dropped the political posturing and was in communication with President John F. Kennedy and Attorney General Robert F. Kennedy to work out a plan for getting Meredith safely on campus. As the president directed, with deputy U.S. marshals, the U.S. Border Patrol, and federal prison guards in place, Meredith proceeded to his dormitory room under armed escort on September 30, at 6 P.M.

An hour later, rioting began. Throughout the night, a mob numbering 2,000 or more threw bricks and Molotov cocktails and fired guns at the forces of law and order. Federal troops, ordered to Oxford by the president, arrived in the early morning hours and gained control of the crowd with tear gas. The rioters at last withdrew, leaving two people dead and 160 marshals injured; 28 of them had been shot. At 8 A.M. on October 1, with the acrid smell of tear gas lingering, Meredith crossed the campus and registered. An hour later, he attended his first class. Meredith's years at the University of Mississippi did not pass without incident. Some

Flanked by U.S. marshals, James Meredith walks to class on October 1, 1962, his first day as a student at the University of Mississippi. *(Library of Congress, Prints and Photographs Division, LC-U9-8556-24)*

students persecuted him, but others courageously showed their support. On August 18, 1963, James Meredith received his diploma, becoming the first African-American graduate of the University of Mississippi.

His victory presaged others that were less violent but equally significant. On June 11, 1963, Governor George Wallace of Alabama stood in a doorway on the University of Alabama campus, blocking the entry of two African-American students. The governor who had vowed "segregation now, segregation tomorrow, segregation forever" stepped aside when ordered to do so by a general of the Alabama National Guard, however, and the students passed inside.[13] Wallace's action had been largely symbolic, but this incident, closely following the brutal treatment of civil rights demonstrators in Birmingham, caused the president to conclude that Americans faced "a moral crisis as a nation and as a people."[14] Eight days later, Kennedy sent to Congress a comprehensive civil rights bill, one that would outlaw discrimination on all forms of interstate transportation, deny funding to any federal program that practiced discrimination, establish a standard of literacy for voter registration, and empower the attorney general to initiate lawsuits to further school integration.

Chronicle of Events

1946
- The marriage rate is 118.1 per 1,000 unmarried females over age 14.
- Births in the United States total 3.4 million.
- Many schools in Harlan County, Kentucky, are poorly built and lack standard safety features.
- The President's Committee on Civil Rights recommends that the government deny any federal aid to education to states with mandatory school segregation.

1946–1964
- Children born in these years are known as the baby-boom generation.

1947
- Secretary of Education John W. Studebaker forms the National Commission on Life-Adjustment Education for Youth.
- President Harry S. Truman establishes the Loyalty Review Board and requires new employees of the executive branch of the federal government to undergo a loyalty investigation.
- The federal government establishes an annual appropriation of $1 million for the Library of Congress to provide reading material for the blind.

1948
- The President's Commission on Higher Education sets a goal for college enrollment of 4.6 million in 1960 and advocates the expansion of community colleges.
- Most states, territories, and the District of Columbia require children between the ages of seven and 16 to attend school. In the other states and territories, compulsory schooling may begin at age six or eight and end at age 14, 15, 17, or 18.
- Twenty-five states and the Territory of Hawaii require deaf or blind children to attend school.

1949
- As part of his Fair Deal legislation package, Truman proposes federal aid to education; Congress rejects this bill.
- Thirty-four states have laws allowing or requiring special education for children with impaired mobility; 18 states provide for the education of the developmentally disabled.

1950s
- California averages one new school per week.
- Many public school districts require employees to sign loyalty oaths.
- Child-development specialists caution educators against advancing superior students to higher grades.

1950
- Kansas has half as many one-room schools as in 1945.
- Nearly 75,000 one-room schools remain in use in the United States; these have a combined enrollment of 1.5 million and represent 44 percent of public schools.

1950–1953
- The United States and Soviet Union support opposing sides in the Korean War.

1951
- Kindergarten registrations are up 38 percent from 1950.
- Publication of *The Gifted Child,* by Paul A. Witty, stimulates interest in the education of children of higher-than-average ability.

1952
- *September:* Construction has added 50,000 new classrooms to the nation's schools.

1953
- Arthur Bestor publishes *Educational Wastelands,* the first of his books criticizing the life-adjustment movement in education.
- Senator Joseph McCarthy of Wisconsin begins investigations of alleged communist activities.

1954
- A record 4 million babies are born in the United States.
- There are 800 one-room schools in Illinois; in 1944 there were 8,000.
- *May 17:* The U.S. Supreme Court declares segregated schooling unconstitutional.

1955
- Suburban subdivisions account for 75 percent of new construction.
- Bestor publishes *The Restoration of Learning.*

Black students file past their white classmates at a newly integrated school in Clinton, Tennessee, December 4, 1956. *(Library of Congress, Prints and Photographs Division, LC-U9-657B-14)*

- *May 31:* Without setting a deadline, the U.S. Supreme Court leaves the responsibility for school desegregation with local authorities but orders federal district judges to ensure that a reasonable effort is made.

1956
- Bestor establishes the Council on Basic Education.
- *September:* Louisville implements a school-desegregation plan that is looked upon as a model for other cities.
- *November 14:* The U.S. Supreme Court lets stand the decision of a lower court outlawing segregation on public transportation.

1957
- Nine black students (the Little Rock Nine) volunteer to integrate all-white Central High School in Little Rock, Arkansas.
- *September 2:* Governor Orval Faubus of Arkansas sends the Arkansas National Guard to Central High School and declares the school off-limits to African Americans.

- *September 4:* The Little Rock Nine are prevented from entering Central High School.
- *September 23:* Entrance of the Little Rock Nine into Central High School spurs mob violence and the closing of the school
- *September 24:* The Little Rock Nine enter Central High School under military guard.
- *October 4:* The Soviet Union launches *Sputnik I,* the first artificial satellite.
- *November 3:* The Soviets launch *Sputnik II,* which carries the dog Laika.

1958
- The National Defense Education Act gives federal financial aid to public and private schools at all levels.
- The government provides grants for the training of teachers for the developmentally disabled.
- *May 27:* Ernest Green is the first African American to graduate from Central High School.
- *fall:* Faubus closes Little Rock's four high schools.

1959

- Some 100,000 of the 1.3 million teachers in U.S. public schools fall short of certification requirements.
- James B. Conant publishes *The American High School Today,* calling for more stringent academic standards in high schools.
- *August:* Little Rock's high schools reopen, and desegregation proceeds.

1960

- Approximately 3.6 million Americans attend institutions of higher learning.

1961

- Conant publishes *Slums and Suburbs,* in which he contrasts high schools in suburbs and inner-city neighborhoods.
- Suburban high schools spend up to $1,000 per pupil per year and employ as many as 70 teachers and other professionals for every 1,000 students; poor urban high schools spend less than $500 per pupil per year and employ 40 or fewer teachers and other professionals for every 1,000 students.
- In poor inner-city neighborhoods, up to 59 percent of males ages 16 to 21 are out of work and unemployed.
- The government provides funding for the training of teachers for children with impaired hearing and speech and for the distribution of books and other educational materials for the blind.
- An estimated 1.25 million developmentally disabled children are in school.
- James Meredith is denied admission to the University of Mississippi because of his race.

1962

- College students stage sit-ins at southern lunch counters.
- *September 3:* A federal district court orders the University of Mississippi to admit James Meredith.
- *September 30:* With an armed escort, Meredith occupies his dormitory room; rioting ensues on campus.
- *October 1:* Meredith registers and begins classes.

1963

- Samuel A. Kirk of the University of Illinois coins the term *learning disabilities* to describe cognitive problems that interfere with learning.
- Nationwide, 5,600 school systems offer special education classes in which 1,666,000 children are enrolled.
- *June 11:* Governor George Wallace tries and fails to block two African-American students from entering the University of Alabama.
- *June 19:* President John F. Kennedy sends Congress a comprehensive civil rights bill.
- *August 18:* Meredith becomes the first African American to graduate from the University of Mississippi.

Eyewitness Testimony

In a town in the Middle West, twenty miles from a large city, I visited a small, three-room rural school, containing 103 children. A seedy-looking man of forty-five served as principal. He disclosed that about twenty-five years ago he had finished high school but had not gone beyond. During the war he worked as a tool-and-die cutter in one of the factories. When the war ended, he became weary of machine-shop work. He heard that teachers were needed, and so:

"I saw the county superintendent and he hired me. I've been here a couple months now. Never taught a day before in my life. It was hard at first, not knowing how to make out a schedule and such things, but I figured out what to do. I done the whole thing without any help."

The ex-mechanic hushed his noisy children—he had thirty-four of them in grades six, seven, and eight. The room was a mess. Apple cores and dirty milk bottles were strewn over the floor. A potbellied stove gave off acrid smoke that brought tears to one's eyes.

"Quiet down there, keep quiet," he barked.

Then he continued: "I wasn't showed one thing how to conduct a school. But it just came natural to me as if I had taught all my life."

"Any discipline problems?" I asked.

"None at all," he boasted. "I use a stick. See it in the corner? Cut 'em up now and then. I try to appeal to their intellect. If I can't, I wham 'em. They don't fight back. I see to that."

Benjamin Fine, journalist, 1947, The Crisis in Education, *p. 27.*

I am deeply disturbed by this notion that by putting more money and better teachers into a segregated school system in the South you will thereby take an appreciable step toward the eventual elimination of segregation. You won't. Children don't learn from books, but from the life they are living, and the basic truth of a Southern educational system lies not in what you teach but in the fact that the white child knows that the colored child isn't good enough to go to school with him, and I don't care how much money you put into it, so long as you tell a white child, merely by implication, that the Negro child can't sit next to him in school, you are licked.

Rabbi Roland B. Gittelsohn, member, President's Committee on Civil Rights, 1947, in Diane Ravitch, Troubled Crusade: American Education, 1945–1980, *p. 23.*

The core of Washington's segregated society is its dual system of public education. It operates under congressional legislation which assumes the fact of segregation but nowhere makes it mandatory. The Board of Education and a white Superintendent of Schools administer two wholly separate school systems. The desire of Congress to insure equal facilities is implemented by a requirement that appropriations be allocated to white and Negro education in proportion to the numbers of children of school age. But this has not been successful. Negro schools are inferior to white schools in almost every respect. The white school buildings have a capacity which is 27 percent greater than actual enrollment. In the colored schools, enrollment exceeds building capacity by eight percent. Classes in the Negro schools are considerably larger and the teaching load of the Negro teachers is considerably heavier. Less than one percent of all white school children, but over 15 percent of colored children receive only part-time instruction. Similar inequalities exist in school buildings, equipment, textbook supplies, kindergarten classes, athletic, and recreational facilities.

The District Superintendent of Schools recently answered charges of inequality in school facilities with the statement that "Absolute equality of educational opportunity is impossible. Reasonable equality . . . is the goal." The conditions described above eloquently document the extent to which even "reasonable equality" is impossible in a segregated school system.

President's Committee on Civil Rights, 1947, To Secure These Rights, *p. 90.*

The Committee is not convinced that an end to segregation in education or in the enjoyment of public services essential to people in a modern society would mean an intrusion upon the private life of the individual. In a democracy, each individual must have freedom to choose his friends and to control the pattern of his personal and family life. But we see nothing inconsistent between this freedom and a recognition of the truth that democracy also means that in going to school, working, participating in the political process, serving in the armed forces, enjoying government services in such fields as health and recreation, making use of transportation and other public accommodation facilities, and living in specific communities and neighborhoods, distinctions of race, color, and creed have no place.

President's Committee on Civil Rights, 1947, To Secure These Rights, *p. 87.*

I don't like to be the only fourth grader. I been the only one in my grade ever since I come here and I don't like it that way. The sixth graders they're sure lucky—only one girl, too. They do everything together and they have lots more fun. Teacher says if there was anybody in the fifth grade she could maybe put me in the fifth grade, too, but there ain't. Sometimes she lets me work with the third grade kids, but I don't like that so well. . . . They're both girls. Goshee, I sure wish a fourth grade kid'd move out here.

A boy attending a one-room school in rural Chautauqua County, New York, 1948, in Lorene K. Fox, The Rural Community and Its School, *pp. 89–90.*

I think it's a crime against society to close down these country schools. Why, when you look for a place to live, you always try to get where the school will be close for your children . . . and to make these children ride all the way to Beamus Point over those icy roads in bitter cold weather . . . why, one of the little girls says when they go down some of those hills, you can just feel the back of the bus skidding across the road. . . .

All four of our boys [grandsons] went to that little school down yonder. . . . It was a good school, too, and they loved it. Then all these people came in from the outside and from other countries even. They didn't know what it was all about, but they all got together and voted us down. . . . One woman who voted for it, I actually heard her swear last winter when her children were having to ride the bus in such bitter weather. And I just said to her, I said, "It serves you just damn good, for bringing in all those people and voting us down the way you did."

"An older farm woman," Chautauqua County, New York, 1948, in Lorene K. Fox, The Rural Community and Its School, *p. 85.*

It is essential today that education come decisively to grips with the world-wide crisis of mankind. This is no careless or uncritical use of words. No thinking person doubts that we are living in a decisive moment of human history.

Atomic scientists are doing their utmost to make us realize how easily and quickly a world catastrophe may come. They know the fearful power for destruction possessed by the weapons their knowledge and skill have fashioned. They know that the scientific principles on which these weapons are based are no secret to the scientists of other nations, and that America's monopoly of the engineering processes involved in the manufacture of atomic bombs is not likely to last many years. And to the horror of atomic weapons, biological and chemical instruments of destruction are now being added.

But disaster is not inevitable. The release of atomic energy that has brought man within sight of world devastation has just as truly brought him the promise of a brighter future. The potentialities of atomic power are as great for human betterment as for human annihilation. Man can choose which he will have.

The possibility of this choice is the supreme fact of our day, and it will necessarily influence the ordering of educational priorities. We have a big job of reeducation to do. Nothing less than a complete reorientation of our thinking will suffice if mankind is to survive and move on to higher levels.

U.S. President's Commission on Higher Education. 1948, Higher Education for American Democracy, *pp. 6–7.*

The community college seeks to become a center of learning for the entire community, with or without the restrictions that surround formal course work in traditional institutions of higher education. It gears its programs and services to the needs and wishes of the people it serves, and its offerings may range from workshops in painting or singing or play writing for fun to refresher courses in journalism or child psychology.

If the health of the community can be improved by teaching restaurant managers something about the bacteriology of food, the community college sets up such a course and seeks to enroll as many of those employed in food service as it can muster. If the community happens to be a center for travelers from Latin America, the college provides classes in Spanish for salespeople, waitresses, bellboys, and taxicab drivers.

U.S. President's Commission on Higher Education. 1948, Higher Education for American Democracy, *p. 69.*

What was once winked at in California can now justly be called discrimination.

That an "Anglo" who was young and intelligent as a business man should be driven out of his new home in a Southern California city because his wife was of Mexican ancestry, although born in the same city and educated in its high school, is an evidence of discrimination. The neighbors waited upon him and he had to sell his home. That a schoolteacher who took her class to a motion picture theater had to divide them so that the "whites" sat in their proper sections and the "Mexicans" in theirs, is evidence of discrimination. When a probation officer finds on his hands a Mexican-American boy who is so brilliant that he gets ahead of his classes and gets into trouble and when this officer tries to place the boy in employment and finds the jobs that are suited to his caliber closed to him because he is a Mexican, there is evidence of discrimination. When a vice-principal of a high school admits that he does not urge Mexican boys to seek varied employment as other boys do because he knows they cannot do anything more than work in the groves, there is discrimination.

W. Henry Cooke, professor of history, Claremont Graduate School, June 5, 1948, "The Segregation of Mexican-American School Children in Southern California," p. 418.

The military use of audio-visual aids in wartime proved their effectiveness not only in imparting information but in the development of attitudes and understanding. As a result, since the war they have had a wave of popularity that has shown itself in a variety of ways. Many city systems have made large provision for equipment, including projectors and films. Commercial firms and educational organizations have promoted the production and use of these aids to teaching throughout the land. Some universities have established film centers that serve states or regions.

O. C. Carmichael, president, Carnegie Foundation for the Advancement of Teaching, September 25, 1948, "Some Educational Frontiers," p. 194.

Education is no longer considered an exclusively juvenile activity. Self-improvement is becoming a major drive. Night schools are overflowing. Correspondence education is booming. Industries are sponsoring general education as well as technical training. Social institutions, settlement houses, recreation clubs, labor organizations, trade associations, literary clubs, are engaging in adult education. The public-forum movement and war-training activities have introduced people to the joys of self-development. This movement is at once an opportunity for the demagogue and a challenge to the educator.

Dwayne Orton, director of education, IBM Corporation, December 11, 1948, "The Community College: Fad or Fundamental?" p. 404.

The diffused and "jumbled" pattern of adult education will go on. It is democracy in action. It is the democratic community of interest expressing itself. It is the genius of our way of life that the cultural, social, economic, and political aspirations of the people shall rise out of the interest groups in the local community. When America

stifles or loses this generic freedom, the American way of life will have lost its lungs.

However, here is a supreme opportunity for the community college to serve the needs of the people. It can be the center and service institution for the people's educational interests. As a supply station, it can be the visual-education center; the arts-and-crafts workshop for the hobby and cultural expression can find a home and studio there. The community college can give leadership and lay teacher-training service. Its staff should be able and ready to advise on program making and organization procedure to community groups. In co-operation with the libraries, it can develop home reading courses and stimulate the tastes of the people for good literature. Running inventories of population and business trends can serve the planning needs of the region. The principle of the rural home-and-farm demonstration service can be applied to the manifold needs of the American community by a genuine people's college.

Dwayne Orton, director of education, IBM Corporation, December 11, 1948, "The Community College: Fad or Fundamental?" p. 405.

Today, as never before, the American people are asking for an all-inclusive program for educable children who have all kinds and degrees of physical limitation. The people have a quickened sense of responsibility toward those children who are physically so different that they cannot attain maximum development without special educational as well as health services. The people of the United States are reaching out through local and State legislation, through organizations, popular articles, speeches and other means for a program which will meet the needs of *all* educable children. This means not only the children with cerebral palsy, orthopedic and cardiac conditions, vision and hearing defects, but also those who suffer from epilepsy, diabetes, malnutrition, and asthmatic and other below-par conditions. This "out-reaching" of the public extends to the young child and to the adolescent and youth, as well as to the child of elementary school age.

Romaine P. Mackie, specialist for schools for the physically handicapped, U.S. Office of Education, 1949, Education of Crippled Children in the United States, p. 9.

Life adjustment education is designed to equip all American youth to live democratically with satisfaction to themselves and profit to society as home members, workers, and citizens. It is concerned especially with a sizable proportion of youth of high-school age (both in school and out) whose objectives are less well served by our schools than the objectives of preparation for either a skilled occupation or higher education. Some leaders have for years been at work in secondary schools developing a guiding philosophy and bringing about program reorganization in the direction of life adjustment education for every youth. Under such leadership, many high schools have made considerable progress in building programs of study and providing educational services basically useful to each participating pupil.

Many high schools, however, continue to be dominated by traditional curriculum patterns which emphasize verbal and abstract learning or place undue emphasis on specialized courses useful to a relatively small number of pupils. As a result many pupils unable to benefit from either of these types of instruction are left to flounder or to leave the schools as soon as the compulsory education laws will permit.

U.S. Office of Education, February 1949, in Commission on Life Adjustment Education for Youth, Vitalizing Secondary Education, *p. 1.*

Boyd had recently won first prize in an essay contest open to elementary school children of metropolitan New York. The title of his essay had been "The Meaning of the Life of Theodore Roosevelt in the Development of the American Idea." Boyd had a library of more than one hundred books, largely science, history, and biography. After consultation with the town librarian, he had indexed them according to the Dewey decimal system.

In the basement of his home he had a physics laboratory and a machine shop. A large part of his time was spent in contriving and conducting experiments. He had written a book, *The A B C's of Electricity,* which he had presented to the school library. He had applied, through his father, for a patent on a new process for capping oil wells (it was not to his discredit that an engineer had been granted a patent on the same principle shortly before).

Boyd's father was a famous scientist, and fellow scientists were frequent visitors in the home. It was Boyd's delight to engage his father's distinguished guests in dinner table discussions of the influence of religion on the development of civilization. Boyd, in the fifth grade of a suburban school system, was completely bored with what went on in the classroom.

Harvey Zorbaugh, Rhea Kay Boardman, and Paul Sheldon of the School of Education, New York University, 1951, "Some Observations of Highly Gifted Children," pp. 86–87.

Expansion and diversification of the secondary school population demands more than the multiplication of offerings. The college preparatory curriculum does not fulfill the needs of newer elements among high school students. In fact, these students are undecided and inarticulate as to what kinds of learning they seek. Some are unconcerned and listless about the entire problem of education. Many attend school only because of the compulsory attendance laws. They know no other reason for attendance. They are some of the youth who are less well served by today's secondary school

The problem of selecting curricular experiences for these aimlessly drifting boys and girls is complex and difficult. Intelligent study of their characteristics, seen in the light of a clear understanding of societal needs and direction, must provide the foundation for a sound guidance program and enlightened instructional procedures planned to enhance life adjustment.

John W. McFarland, assistant professor of curriculum and instruction, University of Texas, April 1952, The Development of Life Adjustment Education in the United States with Special Reference to Texas, *p. 10.*

The rising tide of mental illness and the high rate of juvenile delinquency challenge us to a reconsideration of the secondary school program. Some educators contend that authoritarian and dictatorial methods of teaching, the marking system, and the rigid curriculum or the lack of adequate guidance in the selection of courses contribute to the spread of both mental illness and juvenile delinquency. Whether or not certain secondary school practices cause mental illness or juvenile delinquency, there is much that secondary school teachers can do to set up conditions that will combat the development of these troubles. Establishment of wholesome school conditions conducive to sound mental health, to good citizenship, and to effective clean living is one of the goals of life adjustment education.

John W. McFarland, assistant professor of curriculum and instruction, University of Texas, April 1952, The Development of Life Adjustment Education in the United States with Special Reference to Texas, *p. 11.*

Originality, reason, and common sense are at a discount; maxims, formulas, and rules (the most degraded kinds of book-learning) are at a premium. The nation should view with grave alarm the undermining of that self-reliance upon which our greatness was based. One can search history and biography in vain for evidence that men or women have ever accomplished anything original, creative, or significant by virtue of narrowly conceived vocational training or of educational programs that aimed merely at "life adjustment." The West was not settled by men and women who had taken courses in "How to be a pioneer." The mechanical ingenuity which is a proverbial characteristic of the American people owes nothing whatever to schoolroom manipulation of gadgets. I for one do not believe that the American people have lost all common sense and native wit so that now they have to be taught in school to blow their noses and button their pants.

A citizen today needs an *education*, not a headful of helpful hints. The problems of modern life are so complicated that a vast fund of knowledge and a developed skill in the use of intellectual processes are required to handle them. Engineering and medicine, for example, rest upon formal education—not, however, the kind that purports to satisfy immediate "real-life" needs, but the kind that consists in prolonged and systematic study of the basic disciplines of mathematics, chemistry, and biology. Statesmanship, which we need even more desperately, calls for education, and for something more substantial than high-school civics. The men who drafted our Constitution were not trained for the task by "field trips" to the mayor's office and the county jail.

Arthur Bestor, professor of history, University of Illinois, 1953, Educational Wastelands: The Retreat from Learning in Our Public Schools, *p. 64.*

Charged with the responsibility for recognizing giftedness in children, the teacher might well ask, "What constitutes reliable evidence or manifestation of giftedness?" The task of identification is not always easy. In earliest childhood, children learn to say and do those things that bring them approval and praise from adults. As they grow older, their greatest satisfaction is derived from acceptance by peers, who often resent superiority. Because of this, the gifted child sometimes conceals his ability to answer correctly, perform well, follow directions efficiently, or complete a task quickly. In seeking to attract the praise of adults, on the other hand, he may tend to imitate them in speech and mannerism and thus appear to be exceedingly mature and "advanced for his age." Actually, he has acquired easily and prematurely certain adult reaction patterns and vocabulary that are not based on real understanding.

In the classroom teachers are apt to overrate the intelligence of children who are neat, obedient, friendly, or talkative. The child who is independent in his thought or behavior or who asks embarrassing questions is sometimes irritating to the teacher and does not win her approval; yet originality and curiosity denote superior intellience.

Marian Scheifele, instructor, Teachers College, Columbia University, 1953, The Gifted Child in the Regular Classroom, *p. 4.*

A functional program in homemaking at the secondary level is primarily concerned with the growth of the individual as a person and his role in achieving satisfying home and family life for himself and the members of his family. The thinking and practices of educators have been influenced by changes in the family during the past few decades. Home economics educators have found it imperative to study basic social changes and to reconsider their concepts accordingly. The changing patterns of family life forced upon us by rapid social changes in our times have resulted in significant changes in the teaching of home economics. Recognizing that the family is the basic social unit and that democratic family living is essential to democratic government, many homemaking teachers are working toward making their classrooms laboratories for democratic practice. Through providing opportunities to work toward the solution of problems important to them and their families, homemaking teachers are helping pupils achieve a more satisfying and happier life.

Beatrice Paolucci, teacher trainer in home economics education, Michigan State College, East Lansing, October 1953, "A Look at Today's Homemaking Programs," p. 1.

The life activities of every adult person whether a ditch-digging laborer or a highly trained and educated specialist seem to vary in degree rather than kind. Nearly all persons, regardless of occupation, will be citizens, consumers of goods and services, workers in contact with other people; and a majority will be parents and homemakers, will have leisure time to use, will be in a position to conserve the natural and human resources of our country and desire to maintain good physical and mental health. Why, then, should not the outcomes of secondary-school efforts be to assist *all* youth to adjust in all areas of their present and future living more effectively than they would otherwise? It is not for sixty per cent but for one hundred per cent that education for life adjustment is intended.

Raymond J. Young, assistant professor of education at Oklahoma Agricultural and Mechanical College, November 1953, "Life Adjustment Education after Five Years," p. 66.

It is one thing to accept the lowering of standards as an unavoidable consequence of rapid expansion. It is quite another to accept lowered standards as a permanent and even desirable feature of a democratic educational system. To do the latter is to betray not only education but democracy itself. We perpetrate a fraud if we promise—for the first time in human history—to offer an education of adequate duration to every child in the nation, and then proceed to dilute it and vitiate its strength. If a man does not believe that thorough intellectual training is valuable and appropriate for every citizen, then he ought not to masquerade as a democratic educator, for he is in effect admitting that the opponents of democracy were right when they said that the masses of men were uneducable in the ordinary sense of the word and ought only to be "adjusted" to the mindless kind of life they were bound to lead.

If American education is to accomplish the high purposes to which it dedicated itself in the beginning, it must set a qualitative goal for the future and not settle down to smug contemplation of its past quantitative achievements. Our first task is to see whether we cannot make more effective use than we do of the educational system we already possess. Instead of prolonging the schooling of every young person, we ought to squeeze out the enormous quantity of water that has been injected into the elementary- and secondary-school curriculum. We ought to make the years of schooling that we already provide and already require into years of thorough and rigorous intellectual training, thus rendering the child's investment of time and society's investment of money productive of really high intellectual returns.

Arthur Bestor, professor of history, University of Illinois, 1955, The Restoration of Learning: A Program for Redeeming the Unfulfilled Promise of American Education, *p. 22.*

In our democracy it is sometimes difficult to avoid confusing the idea of "equality of opportunity" with the general principle of "equality" as applied to social conditions.

Our children are not born equal in natural abilities, and the longer the educative process is continued the greater these inequalities become. True education develops inequalities: the inequalities of individuality,

Girls line up in an integrated classroom at Barnard Elementary School in Washington, D.C., on May 27, 1955. *(Library of Congress, Prints and Photographs Division, LC-DIG-ppmsca-03119)*

the inequalities of work and production, the glorious inequalities of talent and genius that we find in many fields of creative endeavor. The true measure of progress in our country must lie in such variations in abilities as opposed to mediocrity—in the advantageous use of individual abilities as contrasted with stultifying standardization.

Theodore Hall, staff writer, Cleveland City Planning Commission, 1956, Gifted Children: The Cleveland Story, *p. 9.*

[The gifted child] certainly knows he is gifted—he would hardly be gifted if he didn't!—and here he is in a selected class, in a program of study with the imposing name of "Major Work," that is shared by only 2 per cent of Cleveland's school children. Many people ask, "Doesn't this make him conceited? Doesn't this give him a superiority complex?"

The Major Work teachers have a simple answer. They point out that the one surest way to make this gifted child conceited is to leave him in a class of average children, where chances are he will have no least rival, where he will finish his work far ahead of everyone else, where he will be the one child in the room who knows all the answers and who can speak up on almost any subject. *That,* they say, is the way to breed conceit.

Theodore Hall, staff writer, Cleveland City Planning Commission, 1956, Gifted Children: The Cleveland Story, *p. 38.*

Americans seem to have an instinctive dislike for the doctrine of formal discipline. They can never forget that Washington was a surveyor, that Lincoln split logs, that Eisenhower is an expert on tanks—or that theirs is a technological civilization which depends for its existence on

Students develop their drawing and painting skills in an art class at St. Albans School, a private boys' school in Washington, D.C., in the mid-1950s. *(St. Albans School)*

manual skills. In the course of time "The Great End and Real Business of Living," which the early academics professed to teach, has accordingly taken on a narrower and more utilitarian meaning. Running through the whole course of the high school's development, from Franklin's proposal that "it would be well if they could be taught everything useful" down to the present, the dignity of work has been a never-failing source of inspiration.

> W. Kenneth Richmond, instructor in education, University of Glasgow, 1956, Education in the U.S.A.: A Comparative Study, p. 148.

As the American sees it, there is no justification for the fear that Life Adjustment means the final abandonment of any new kind of intellectual standards. In theory it amounts to a new deal for the ordinary boy and girl who are the salt of the earth in any democracy. In practice it means the assumption by the Secondary School of certain responsibilities which have hitherto been regarded as none of its concern. It means teaching young folk how to get married, how to furnish a house and budget for its upkeep, how to develop efficient work habits, how to vote intelligently, how to drive a car, how to dress and make the best of themselves—in a word, how to "win out" in the free-for-all of American life. Modest and worldly-wise as they may appear, these are no unworthy objectives.

> W. Kenneth Richmond, instructor in education, University of Glasgow, 1956, Education in the U.S.A.: A Comparative Study, pp. 185–186.

As a child of thirteen growing up in Little Rock, I lived through the 1957 desegregation crisis with my eyes closed. My "Uncle Virgil" Blossom was superintendent of schools, but I was more interested in the fact that my cousin was a cheerleader and "popular" than that her father was instituting a dramatic social revolution in my city. I knew of course that Orval Faubus was governor of my state, but I was more impressed by the fact that my older brother made fun of [the governor's son's] socially unacceptable, "country" white socks and blue jeans than that the governor was resisting integration. "Brooks" was my father's old family friend Representative Brooks Hays, whom my congressman-grandfather had mentored in Washington, but no mention was ever made around our dinner table that Dad's friend was somehow involved in resolving one of the great crises of our time. . . .

It did not occur to me that I was being shielded purposely from affairs beyond my limited little world, although my father did explain often that girls should not think about "unhappy things." The carefully cultivated product of a patriarchal culture, I floated blithely through those days believing that if anything ever went wrong in my world, the men would fix it. A rigorously and self-consciously "good" little girl, I had always worked hard to fulfill my parents' expectations of me, which included being proper, pretty, and popular, in that order. It did not occur to me until many years later that I had been sealed in an airtight box because female questioning could somehow threaten the established order in worlds beyond my own.

> Elizabeth Jacoway, historian and writer, recalling Little Rock, Arkansas, in 1957, Turn Away Thy Son: Little Rock, the Crisis that Shocked the Nation, p. xi.

Like many southerners—a larger number than was at first evident—I felt that the decision of the Supreme Court on May 17, 1954, had been eminently fair and just; that no public school system segregated by law on the basis of race was consistent with democracy. The Christian ethic proclaimed by my father, a Presbyterian minister, had its foundation in a belief in the worth of the individual and in our common humanity. Having grown up in the South, I had never known any black well except those in household employ. I had an understanding of its prejudices; but as I grew into the recognition that they were just that, I had set about eradicating them from my thinking. I knew now that I would welcome our black pupils and was eager to play my proper role in the integration of Central High School.

> Elizabeth Huckaby, vice principal for girls at Central High School in Little Rock, Arkansas, during the 1957–58 school year, Crisis at Central High: Little Rock, 1957–58, p. 2.

The picture of the girl screaming after Elizabeth Eckford as she walked through the mob on the day the National Guard had turned back the black students had haunted me. No one seemed to be able to identify the girl—and small wonder. We were not used to seeing our students look like that. But by noon on Friday, I discovered she was someone I knew, and I sent for her in the afternoon. When she readily admitted she was the screaming girl I told her how distressed I was to hear it since hatred destroys the people who hate. She shrugged. Well, that was the way she felt, she said. Undeterred by her shrug, I said that I hoped I'd never see her pretty face so distorted again, that I never would have recognized that ugly face in the picture as hers. Wasted breath.

> Elizabeth Huckaby, vice principal for girls at Central High School in Little Rock, Arkansas, during the 1957–58 school year, Crisis at Central High: Little Rock, 1957–58, p. 24.

About twenty soldiers moved toward us, forming an olive-drab square with one end open. I glanced at the faces of my friends. Like me, they appeared to be impressed by the imposing sight of military power. There was so much to see, and everything was happening so quickly. We walked through the open end of the square. Erect, rifles at their sides, their faces stern, the soldiers did not make eye contact as they surrounded us in a protective cocoon. After a long moment, the leader motioned us to move forward.

Hundreds of Central High students milled about. I could see their astonishment. Some were peering out of windows high above us, some were watching the yard, others were on the landing. Some were tearful, others angry.

I felt proud and sad at the same time. Proud that I lived in a country that would go this far to bring justice to a Little Rock girl like me, but sad that they had to go to such great lengths. Yes, this is the United States, I thought to myself. There is a reason that I salute the flag. If these guys just go with us this first time, everything's going to be okay.

Melba Pattillo Beals, one of the Little Rock Nine, recalling the events of September 4, 1957, Warriors Don't Cry: A Searing Memoir of the Battle to Integrate Little Rock's Central High, *pp. 132–133.*

There is not general agreement concerning just who is gifted but this problem must be resolved by those who plan a specific program in a specific community. A program can not be planned until a decision is made concerning just who the program will serve. Perhaps the task will be easier if it is remembered that the gifted when out-numbered, as they clearly are in most programs, tend to adopt the pace and attitudes toward learning of their average age mates. When and if this adjustment process is completed, both the world and the gifted individual lose.

Indiana Department of Public Instruction, 1958, The Gifted Child, *p. 7.*

The fault for neglecting our talented children lies in deep-seated national attitudes and in faulty educational theories and practices. Unless these are changed, the much-needed contributions of many potential scientists, engineers, or other professional persons will be lost. There are not enough young people with above-average minds and we cannot spare any of them. We must make special provision for our talented children. Every American has a legitimate concern with our educational system. Our children are the nation's hostages to the future. Both as parents and as citizens we have no more important job than to insure that all are given the very best education they are capable of absorbing. Never has this been more important than today when we are in danger of being outdistanced in technological developments by Russia.

Vice Admiral Hyman G. Rickover, 1959, Education and Freedom, *pp. 111–112.*

The consequence of technological progress is that man must use his mind more and his body less. We still think in terms of a more primitive era; we overvalue physical prowess and undervalue intellectual competence. This has a profound effect on our attitudes toward education. The kind of school which prepares young people adequately for life in a less complicated environment is of little use today. Nor do we need schools that concentrate primarily on adjusting the children of immigrants to this new country; on helping them become Americans quickly and painlessly. Today we must have schools which develop in all children—talented, average, and below average—the highest level of intellectual competence of which they are capable; schools that help young people to understand the complex world of today and how it came to be what it is.

Vice Admiral Hyman G. Rickover, 1959, Education and Freedom, *pp. 17–18.*

The number of small high schools must be drastically reduced through district reorganization. Aside from this important change, I believe no radical alteration in the basic pattern of American education is necessary in order to improve our public high schools. If all the high schools were functioning as well as some I have visited, the education of all American youth would be satisfactory, except for the study of foreign languages and the guidance of the more able girls. Most of the schools which I found unsatisfactory in one or more respects could become satisfactory by relatively minor changes, though I have no doubt that there are schools even of sufficient size where major improvements in organization and instruction would be in order. If the fifty-five schools I have visited, all of which have a good reputation, are at all representative of American public high schools, I think one general criticism would be in order: The academically talented student, as a rule, is not being sufficiently challenged, does not work hard enough, and his program of academic subjects is not of sufficient range. The able boys too often specialize in mathematics and science to the exclusion of foreign languages and to the neglect of English and social studies.

The able girls, on the other hand, too often avoid mathematics and science as well as foreign languages.

James Bryant Conant, educational administrator, researcher, and statesman, 1959, The American High School Today, *p. 40.*

When a child enters school, certain abilities and certain degrees of skill in various types of activity are assumed. In arranging the prescribed series of experiences which represent the school curriculum, it is necessary that a starting point, a level of ability which can be used as a base, be agreed upon. Since the school is designed primarily for the so-called normal child, it is logical that this base should assume the abilities which the average child displays at the age when he begins the school experience.

This basic assumption of the school is tested and the extent to which each child meets the assumption is examined through the use of readiness tests and similar devices. The skills and abilities represented in the readiness test, however, do not represent the starting point of learning for the child as they do for the school. These abilities themselves are the result of a long series of learnings. They are the culmination of a very extensive and rapid period of learning throughout the pre-school years.

Under normal conditions, the child in our culture can be expected to assimilate these learnings before he reaches school age. However, when conditions are not normal, as when the environment is inadequate or the organism damaged or subjected to extreme emotional disturbances, these assumed learnings may not take place. The child will then enter the school with a lesser degree of skill and ability in one or more areas than the educational curriculum assumes. Since later learning is based in large degree upon these earlier learnings, such a child finds himself in ever-increasing difficulty as his school experience continues.

Newell C. Kephart, researcher and writer in education and psychology, 1960, The Slow Learner in the Regular Classroom, *pp. 19–20.*

I have walked through school corridors in slum areas and, looking into classrooms, have seen children asleep with their heads on their hands. Is this situation the result of poor teachers without either disciplinary control or teaching ability? No, the children asleep at their desks have been up all night with no place to sleep or else have been subject to incredibly violent family fights and horrors through the night. Checking into one case, a principal told one of my staff that after climbing six flights of a tenement he found the boy's home—one filthy room with a bed, a light bulb, and a sink. In the room lived the boy's mother and her four children. I might add that it is not unusual for teachers in these schools to take home with them children with no place to go at night. The social attitudes found in this kind of slum neighborhood are bound to affect the atmosphere of the school. As one Negro teacher said to me, "We do quite well with these children in the lower grades. Each of us is, for the few hours of the school day, an acceptable substitute for the mother. But when they reach about 10, 11, or 12 years of age, we lose them. At that time the 'street' takes over. In terms of schoolwork, progress ceases; indeed many pupils begin to go backward in their studies!"

James Bryant Conant, educational administrator, researcher, and statesman, 1961, Slums and Suburbs: A Commentary on Schools in Metropolitan Areas, *pp. 20–21.*

Nearly everyone has had school experience, and he generalizes from this experience. He may not have been in a classroom since his own student days, but he does not hesitate to use the memory of that experience as a basis for appraisal of what goes on today. He is humble in his appraisal of his business occupation; he does not measure his doctor by his childhood memories, or his pastor by his adolescent recollections. Yet he does not hesitate to assume authoritative judgment on educational matters because he has once been to school. . . .

Part of our difficulty in attaining public understanding arises from the knowledge that education perennially has had an imbalance between its aspirations and realizations, has never had enough resources to fully accomplish its mission. And there is the feeling that the problems now talked about are more of the same, with the familiarity of an old refrain.

David D. Henry, president, University of Illinois at Urbana, 1961, What Priority for Education? The American People Must Soon Decide, *p. 75.*

Adults are not alone managers of the present, but trustees of tomorrow. Thousands are on the march to the campus of the future. We must prepare for them. Even for those who do not attend, the college opportunity must be available, so that the decision not to attend is a free choice, not one of economic selection or limited alternatives. Whether or nor the child of today takes advantage of the opportunity of tomorrow, the existence of that opportunity is a major influence upon his own life, his attitudes, his hopes, his aspirations. It is a symbol of the public concern for the welfare of the individual. It is an index to the hope that he, too, may learn how to grow and develop and prepare for any task for which he is capable.

David D. Henry, president, University of Illinois at Urbana, 1961, What Priority for Education? The American People Must Soon Decide, *p. 84.*

"All men are created equal" has become trite, but it still has important meaning for education in a democratic society. Although it was used by the founding fathers to denote equality before the law, it has also been interpreted to mean equality of opportunity. This implies educational opportunity for *all* children—the right of each child to receive help in learning to the limits of his capacity, whether that capacity be small or great.

It is consistent with a democratic philosophy that all children be given the opportunity to learn, whether they are average, bright, dull, retarded, blind, deaf, crippled, delinquent, emotionally disturbed, or otherwise limited or deviant in their capacities to learn. Our schools have evolved, therefore, numerous modifications of regular school programs to adapt instruction to children who deviate from the average and who cannot profit substantially from the regular program. These modified programs have been designated as programs for exceptional children.

The programs for exceptional children in school systems have been found to benefit not only the deviant child but also other children. Handicapped or gifted children in a regular classroom sometimes require individual attention. It is inevitable that if a regular classroom teacher devotes adequate time to a deviant child he must curtail the attention which he ordinarily gives the other children. But when special services are offered the deviant child, the normal pupils benefit by having more of the regular teacher's time.

Samuel A. Kirk, director, Institute for Research on Exceptional Children, University of Illinois, 1962, Educating Exceptional Children, *pp. 3–4.*

An irate citizen storms into the educator's office, demanding that a "subversive" textbook be censored. An equally angry visitor insists that "money is being spent foolishly." A group descends upon the superintendent to plead for a "return" to the three R's. A minister lambastes the schools from his pulpit, while a politician builds his criticism into his platform. Patriotic organizations bemoan the lack of fundamental Americanism, and college professors decry the lack of fundamental learning.

Not only is American education under fire; the practice of criticizing our schools is well on its way to becoming a national pastime. For some, it is already a favorite armchair sport. For others, it has become a full-time career.

Mary Anne Raywid, professor of education, Hofstra University, 1962, The Ax-Grinders: Critics of Our Public Schools, *p. 1.*

What is needed now is some fresh approach to the discovery and cultivation of the talents that undoubtedly exist among millions of children from unpromising backgrounds. The usual tests won't identify these able pupils; the usual curriculum won't challenge them; the usual teachers won't inspire them. While additional research would be helpful, the more urgent need seems to be for creative teaching on the basis of a different set of assumptions. It won't do to parade excuses, or to blame the individual, or the neighborhood. These pupils may not score high on verbal tests, but they are clever about many other things. They may be "uncooperative" in carrying out traditional assignments, but they often show extraordinary loyalty to their families or their gangs. Their parents may not volunteer for P.T.A. committees, but it would be wrong to assume that these parents are not concerned about what their children are able to achieve. Even their preference for television and movie shows over storybooks may arise from authentic awareness that print is actually a devious and impoverished medium in comparison with the presence of speaking, acting persons.

Under-cultured children have much to learn from education, but educators could well take some lessons from some of these youngsters. Their language may not be grammatical, but it is often more vivid and expressive than is the turgid prose of textbooks. These children face some of the "facts of life" more realistically than many of their teachers do. Even their pugnacity might be worth attention by some long-suffering, overworked, underpaid teachers. When it comes to making friends and standing by their pals, some children from underprivileged neighborhoods far outshine their priggish teachers.

The starting point is respect.

Goodwin Watson, social psychologist and professor, Teachers College, Columbia University, 1962, in The Culturally Deprived Child, *by Frank Riessman, pp. x–xi.*

In the field of cultural attainments, and in this alone, the upgrading process which has been so marked in other areas of the [teaching] profession has been conspicuous by its absence. Our teachers, taken as a great totality, today know more about mental hygiene than those who went before, but less about the English language. They are far more at ease in the field of handicrafts, but far less so in discussion of historical figures or events. They have more instructional techniques at their disposal than did their forebears, but fewer resources in the realms of literature and art.

Too many educators can no longer write a paragraph correctly.

Too many cannot spell a variety of words in common use.

Too many make gross errors of grammar in their daily speech.

Too many are lost when the conversation turns to cultural subjects.

Max Rafferty, educator and critic of public education, 1962, Suffer, Little Children, *pp. 33–34.*

Words that America has treasured as a rich legacy, that have sounded like trumpet calls above the clash of arms and the fury of debate, are fading from the classrooms, and so from life itself. "Liberty and Union, now and forever, one and inseparable. . . ." "I only regret that I have but one life to give for my country. . . ." "Millions for defense, but not one cent for tribute. . . ." Search for these golden phrases in vain today in the textbooks of too many of our schools, in the hearts and minds of too many of our children. The golden words are gone, and in their place brain-numbing accounts of the nation's second-class mail service or units on the trucking industry and Highway 66. We must all, you see, grow up to be mailmen or truckers. We have no need of Websters, nor of Nathan Hales.

Max Rafferty, educator and critic of public education, 1962, Suffer, Little Children, *p. 24.*

Today, more than at any other time in our history, we need to develop our intellectual resources to the fullest. But the facts of the matter are that many thousands of our young people are not educated to their maximum capacity—and they are not, therefore, making the maximum contribution of which they are capable to themselves, their families, their communities, and the Nation. Their talents lie wasted—their lives are frequently pale and blighted—and their contribution to our economy and culture are lamentably below the levels of their potential skills, knowledge and creative ability. Educational failures breed delinquency, despair, and despondence. They increase the cost of unemployment and public welfare.

They cut our potential national economic output by billions. They deny the benefits of our society to large segments of our people. They undermine our capability as a nation to discharge world obligations. All this we cannot afford—better schools we can afford.

To be sure, Americans are still the best educated and best trained people in the world. But our educational system has failed to keep pace with the problems and needs of our complex technological society. Too many are illiterate or untrained, and thus either unemployed or underemployed. Too many receive an education diminished in quality in thousands of districts which cannot or do not support modern and adequate facilities, well-paid and well-trained teachers, or even a sufficiently long school year.

President John F. Kennedy, February 6, 1962, "Special Message to the Congress on Education," in John F. Kennedy on Education, *edited by William T. O'Hara, pp. 133–134.*

Now a veritable tidal wave of students is advancing inexorably on our institutions of higher education, where the annual costs per student are several times as high as the cost of a high school education, and where these costs must be borne in large part by the student or his parents. Five years ago the graduating class of the secondary schools was 1.5 million; five years from now it will be 2.5 million. The future of these young people and the nation rests in large part on their access to college and graduate education. For this country reserves its highest honors for only one kind of aristocracy—that which the Founding Fathers called "an aristocracy of achievement rising out of a democracy of opportunity."

President John F. Kennedy, 1963, Message from the President of the United States Relative to a Proposed Program for Education, *p. 5.*

The city schools today deal with pupils who represent the total range of academic ability and educational motivation. In all cities there are "good schools" and "difficult schools." The former are generally located in the areas away from the city centers, beyond the "gray" belt, or where there is a large concentration of higher income families in cooperative houses or in middle-income housing projects in downtown sections. The "difficult schools" are concentrated in the blighted and gray areas.

In general, the "good schools" differ little from schools in suburban areas, either in pupil population, stability of teaching staff, or parental drive for higher education. Largely fed by middle-class white families, these schools deal with pupils whose abilities and academic performances, as measured by intelligence, aptitude, and achievement tests, are above the national average. Although these schools have their share of retardates, slow learners, and even an occasional discipline problem, these are the exception rather than the rule.

Miriam L. Goldberg, associate professor of education, Teachers College, Columbia University, 1963, "Factors Affecting Educational Attainment in Depressed Urban Areas," p. 78.

Beginning with the family, the early pre-school years present the child from a disadvantaged home with few of the experiences which produce readiness for academic learning either intellectually or attitudinally. The child's view of society is limited by his immediate family and neighborhood where he sees a struggle for survival which sanctions behavior viewed as immoral in the society at large. He has little preparation either for recognizing the importance of schooling in his own life or for being able to cope with the kinds of verbal and abstract behavior which the school will demand of him. Although he generally comes to first grade neat and clean and with his mother's admonition to be a "good boy," he lacks the ability to carry out those tasks which would make him appear "good" in the eyes of his teacher.

Miriam L. Goldberg, associate professor of education, Teachers College, Columbia University, 1963, "Factors Affecting Educational Attainment in Depressed Urban Areas," p. 87.

Social pressures by her peers, and a preference by her superiors for complaisance and tractability over effort and accomplishment have helped to mold [the intelligent girl] into the stereotype of feminine charm. As a result she has . . . managed to escape the notice of the social critics who had, long before sputnik, already started clamoring for stricter mental disciplining, more rigorous academic drill, and stiffer competition in the classroom. Without a thought for what effect all this would have on girls, the critics said it was necessary for preparing "our best intellects" to take over their destined roles—leadership.

What they had inexplicably failed to notice was that the majority of "our best intellects," by which they meant those who excel in the classroom, were of a gender that is almost automatically barred from positions of leader-

ship. It shouldn't have taken much reflection on this fact to make them suspect that there is a missing element in the equation: natural intelligence, plus rigorous academic training, equals leadership.

Ethel Strainchamps, housewife and journalist, 1963, "The Plight of the Intellectual Girl," p. 139.

[S]omething went wrong with life adjustment education. Before the episode recedes too far into history or oblivion, it would be well to give this ill-named, ill-famed movement a parting glance. . . .

The term "life adjustment" is meaningless, and this fact surely contributed to the eventual discrediting of what it represented. "Adjustment" may be a useful concept to those concerned with mental health, but to many others it carries a connotation of blind and spineless conformity, and when prefaced with the adjective "life," it suggests a resignation to prevailing conditions and pressures and a lack of self-reliant aggressiveness in meeting challenges. Distasteful as this notion might have been a decade ago, it became positively obnoxious in the reaction against the "other-directed" organization man, which has of late brought on a renaissance of the individual.

Mauritz Johnson, Jr., professor of secondary education, Cornell University, 1963, "The Rise and Fall of 'Life Adjustment,'" pp. 52–53.

After taking my place among the graduates, I looked out at the curious and staring audience. Cameras were clicking in every direction. There in the audience was my seventy-two-year-old father with my three-year-old son. Throughout his life he had given his all in an effort to make Mississippi and the world free for his children and his children's children. He had lived to see the day that he had always longed for but had never really expected to see. Sitting on his knee was my son, not yet aware of the existence of the system of "White Supremacy" that would seek in every possible way to render him less than human. He seemed quite amused by the events. My gratification came from the hope that my son might be a future Governor or President.

James Meredith, first African American to attend the University of Mississippi, recalling his August 18, 1963, graduation, Three Years in Mississippi, p. 326.

CHAPTER NINE

Turbulent Years
1963–1980

Lyndon Baines Johnson, who ascended to the presidency on November 22, 1963, after the assassination of John F. Kennedy, came into office with ambitious social goals that had been formed during his years as a U.S. senator from Texas and then as Kennedy's vice president. He was committed to securing the civil rights legislation that Kennedy had called for and to addressing economic inequality.

The Civil Rights Act of July 2, 1964, the most comprehensive federal legislation of its kind to date, safeguarded the right to vote. It outlawed discrimination based on race, religion, or national origin in public facilities such as restaurants, hotels, theaters, and parks, and it empowered the attorney general to take legal action to enforce the desegregation of these accommodations. It also banned discrimination in employment and in any federally assisted program.

The Civil Rights Act charged the U.S. commissioner of education with monitoring the progress of school integration and assisting any community that was trying to desegregate its schools. The act defined school desegregation as "the assignment of students to public schools and within such schools without regard to their race, color, religion, or national origin," but said nothing about achieving a desired racial balance.[1]

Johnson also addressed the economic issues associated with inequality in education. With the Economic Opportunity Act of August 20, 1964, he made good on the promise contained in his first State of the Union address to wage "unconditional war on poverty in America."[2] Because the president considered education key to moving people out of poverty, some of the act's most significant provisions were intended to equip the poor with the knowledge they needed to be productive wage earners and citizens.

Title I, for example, created Job Corps, a program that provided vocational training, academic instruction, and work experience to people ages 16 to 21 who had dropped out of high school. A second-work training program gave economically disadvantaged teens jobs with state and local governments and nonprofit agencies. The latter program encouraged participants to complete high school and gave them experience that made them more employable upon graduation.

Title II of the Economic Opportunity Act targeted the youngest learners, because the children of the poor typically began their school years already at a disadvantage. They were more likely than other children to have had low birth weights, to be malnourished, and to have high blood levels of lead resulting from exposure to deteriorating paint in old, rundown housing. All these conditions put the children at risk for academic failure, learning disabilities, and possibly brain damage. Poor preschoolers also were less likely than more affluent children to have been read to by adults, to own books and educational toys, or to have visited museums and other centers of culture.

Title II therefore established Operation Head Start, which readied preschoolers for kindergarten. Head Start endeavored to prepare children academically and socially and improve their health and nutrition. The children who were enrolled took part in group games and unstructured play; learned songs; listened to stories; and went on field trips to zoos, farms, and suburban supermarkets—places many of them had never visited. They also received medical and dental checkups and were given nutritious snacks and meals.

A "Basic Floor" Supporting Education

Johnson's landslide victory over Republican nominee Barry Goldwater in his 1964 bid to be elected president in his own right gave him the mandate he needed to secure passage of additional federal legislation to aid education. "Education is primarily a State function," the president acknowledged, but in justification of the steps he was taking, he explained that "in the field of education, as in the fields of health, relief, and medical care, the Federal Government has a secondary obligation to see that there is a basic floor under those essential services for all adults and children in the United States."[3] Johnson hoped to see the government improve the education of disadvantaged youths, spur progress in educational methodology and teacher training, have all students benefit from the latest technological and pedagogical innovations in education, and give incentives to learners at every stage of life.

Accordingly, the Elementary and Secondary Education Act (ESEA) of April 11, 1965, marked the beginning of an expanded, lasting role in education for the federal government. The act made more than $1 billion available for building and instructional programs in schools and school districts where 40 percent or more of students came from low-income families, as defined by the U.S. Census Bureau, to improve educational opportunities for students in kindergarten through grade 12. ESEA offered grants to the states to upgrade school libraries and purchase textbooks and other educational materials, and it encouraged innovation through model schools, pilot programs, and grants to universities for research in educational techniques.

A companion piece of legislation, the Higher Education Act of November 8, 1965, was intended to build up the resources of colleges and universities and help students financially. It therefore supported cooperative extension programs, university-level research on urban social problems, the expansion of college libraries, and training and research in library science. The act gave financial incentives to faculty members willing to teach at small colleges, and it created the first federal scholarships, awarding up to $800 per year to students who otherwise could not afford to continue their studies beyond high school.

April 11, 1965: President Lyndon B. Johnson signs the Elementary and Secondary Education Act on the grounds of the former Junction Elementary School in Johnson City, Texas. Seated with the president is Kate Deadrich Loney, his first teacher. *(Lyndon Baines Johnson Library and Museum)*

Linking School Integration to Federal Aid

In 1964, a decade after the historic Supreme Court decision in *Brown v. Board of Education*, just 2 percent of African-American students in the 11 states of the former Confederacy attended racially mixed schools. Since 1954, the federal government had had the power to enforce federal court orders to desegregate, but it had been unable do anything more to advance school integration. The Civil Rights Act, because it linked federal aid with desegregation, gave the government—and specifically the U.S. Office of Education—a powerful, new weapon.

In April 1965, the Office of Education began requiring school districts that had been legally segregated before 1954 to demonstrate their eligibility for ESEA funds by attesting that they had eliminated segregation; alternatively, school districts could either file documents showing the progress made toward court-ordered desegregation or submit a voluntary plan for full desegregation by fall 1967. These requirements raised the percentage of African Americans attending school with whites in the 11 southern states to 6 percent and caused 1,563 school districts to begin desegregating, but the Office of Education wanted integration to proceed more rapidly. In 1966, it therefore gave school districts stricter objectives, requiring between 12 percent and 18 percent of African-American students to be attending integrated schools in the 1966–67 academic year.

The new requirement coincided roughly with the publication of *Equality of Educational Opportunity*, a report to the president and Congress prepared under the direction of James S. Coleman, a professor of sociology at Johns Hopkins University, at the request of U.S. Commissioner of Education Harold Howe II. This was one of the largest studies ever conducted, involving approximately 645,000 students, 60,000 teachers, and 4,000 schools. Coleman's group concluded that most American children attended schools in which the great majority of students were of the same race. Throughout the nation, schools serving minority groups had larger classes, inferior facilities and supplies, and less-qualified teachers than did schools for white students. When the researchers looked at achievement-test scores, they discovered that, with the exception of Asian Americans, minority students scored lower than whites did at all levels and that the difference increased with the number of years spent in school. Generally, however, minority students attending racially mixed schools scored better than those in segregated schools.

The Federal Courts Require Greater Desegregation Efforts

When schools opened in September 1968, 20.3 percent of school-age African-American children in the 11 states of the old Confederacy attended schools that could be considered fully integrated. The goal set by the Office of Education had been met, but in the same year, in their opinion in the case *Green v. School Board of New Kent County*, the justices of the U.S. Supreme Court stated that progress to date had been inadequate and called for school segregation to be cut down "root and branch."[4] Before 1954, New Kent County, Virginia, had maintained one school for blacks and another for whites. Under the county's freedom-of-choice desegregation plan, 15 percent of black students had elected to attend the formerly white school, but no whites had asked to attend the school for blacks. A number of factors, including prejudice, fear of retaliation, and the belief that the formerly all-black school was inferior, had kept students from mixing voluntarily. Desegregation plans such as this one, which did nothing to promote a racial balance in the schools, violated the court's interpretation of equal opportunity, the justices declared.

Yet how far did localities need to go to achieve a desired racial balance? In 1971, by upholding a lower-court decision in the case *Swann v. Charlotte-Mecklenburg Board of Education*, the Supreme Court directed school systems to "make every effort to achieve the greatest possible degree of actual desegregation."[5] The Charlotte-Mecklenburg School District of North Carolina was another in which the great majority of black students still attended all-black schools. The federal courts now sanctioned such extreme methods as establishing racial quotas, redistricting, and busing students from one part of a city to another for achieving integration.

Where blacks and whites were neighbors and children of different races attended separate schools, as in many parts of the South, including New Kent County, a segregated system clearly persisted and needed to be remedied. The issue was more complicated in some northern metropolitan areas, where schools had long been segregated by custom rather than by law. Most northern students were assigned to the schools nearest their homes without regard to race or ethnicity, but because they were likely to live among people of their own race or national origin, few attended racially integrated schools.

Social scientists theorized that the inferiority of urban schools serving minorities, coupled with the sense of isolation felt by students attending them, had contributed, along with high unemployment, poor housing, police brutality, and other factors, to the rioting and looting that erupted in northern urban ghettoes in the 1960s. The work of the National Advisory Commission on Civil Disorders, a group appointed by Johnson in 1967, supported this contention. The commission reported in 1968 that "for many minorities, and particularly for the children of the racial ghetto, the schools have failed to provide the educational experience which could help overcome the effects of discrimination and privation. . . . This failure is one of the persistent sources of grievance and resentment within the Negro community."[6] Some experts argued that if allowing children to attend schools that were segregated, either by law (*de jure*) or by circumstance (*de facto*), harmed both minority children and society, then the situation needed to be changed. Also, it was becoming apparent that some of the school segregation that existed in states outside the South might in actuality be *de jure*.

The U.S. Supreme Court first ordered northern schools to desegregate in 1973, when ruling in the case *Keyes v. School District No. 1, Denver, Colorado*. Lawyers for the African-American and Latino students who were the plaintiffs in this case claimed that the Denver School Board had chosen sites for new schools, amended zoning, and used other deliberate methods to keep white students separate from minorities. The justices agreed and upheld the order of the U.S. District Court for busing to achieve integration. This case was significant, too, because it extended to Hispanics the same right to equal educational opportunity that had been guaranteed to African Americans.

In the case *Morgan v. Hennigan*, lawyers representing African-American parents successfully demonstrated to the U.S. District Court of Massachusetts that the city of Boston had used illegal methods to maintain school segregation in violation of the 14th Amendment to the Constitution, which forbids the states to deny anyone equal protection of the law. In some instances, the Boston School Committee had assigned white students to overcrowded predominantly white schools rather than to underutilized largely black schools that were located nearby. The fact that, during the 1971–72 academic year, South Boston High School, which served white students, had an enrollment that was 676 over capacity while 92 percent-black Girls High School, in an adjoining district, had room for 532 students was evidence of this practice. The committee had used portable classrooms to accommodate more students at largely white schools but rejected their use to further integration as "educationally undesirable."[7] The committee also assigned most African-American teachers and principals to schools serving African Americans, with the result that 40 percent of schools had never employed an African-American on the faculty.

Judge W. Arthur Garrity, Jr., ruled on June 21, 1974, that the Boston School Committee had "knowingly carried out a systematic program of segregation affecting all of the city's students, teachers and school facilities."[8] Garrity ordered the committee to use busing, reassignment, and plant improvements to desegregate the city's schools.

Phase I of the desegregation plan affected 80 schools, or 40 percent of the system, and went into effect on September 12, 1974, the first day of the academic year. Under Phase I, 17,000 students were bused to schools in different neighborhoods with the objective of achieving desegregation. Most of the targeted schools accepted their new pupils without incident; the busing of students from the largely black neighborhood of Roxbury into staunchly white South Boston gave rise to anger and violence, however. Shouting racial slurs, outraged whites threw rocks, eggs, and rotting produce at buses coming from Roxbury. They injured nine African-American students and damaged 18 buses. There was trouble again on December 11, when a black student stabbed a white schoolmate inside South Boston High School. Racial tensions simmered for the rest of the term without boiling over, and the black students completed the year in their assigned schools, although a number of white parents withdrew their children in protest and instead sent them to night-time tutoring sessions conducted by sympathetic public school teachers, college students, and others.

A second, or Phase II, plan was implemented on September 8, 1975, and required the busing of 25,000 students to achieve a more uniform racial mix. This time busing occurred within newly created districts, and students had the option of attending one of 32 magnet schools that drew from all of Boston and had a racial composition that reflected the city as a whole.

Busing improved the racial balance in schools in Denver, Boston, and elsewhere, but the prejudice that had underlain the segregated school systems persisted and caused many whites to enroll their children in private schools or flee to all-white suburbs. Busing proved to be unpopular as well with black parents, who often objected to the long rides their children had to take and the fact that it was hard for their children to see friends or participate in extracurricular activities when they lived far away from their schools. According to a 1974 Gallup poll, less than 25 percent of the population, and 32 percent of African Americans, favored busing to achieve school integration.

Colleges and universities in the 1970s instituted affirmative action plans and quotas, two methods used by government and private employers to promote diversity in the workplace, to achieve racially and ethnically balanced student bodies. Thus, schools considered ethnicity—in addition to grades, test scores, and other criteria—when making decisions regarding admission. These policies generated controversy right from the start. Americans debated the ethics of trying to remedy past discrimination in this manner and asked whether it benefited minority students more to receive preferential treatment or to succeed on their own merits.

The U.S. Supreme Court brought some clarity to the issue on June 28, 1978, in its opinion in *Regents of the University of California v. Bakke*. This case involved Allan Bakke, a white applicant twice denied admission to the medical school at the University of California at Davis in years when minority candidates with lower test scores had been accepted to satisfy a quota. (The medical school set aside 16 spots in a class of 100 for disadvantaged minority applicants.) The justices upheld the decision of the California Supreme Court that Bakke be admitted to the medical school. They declared admissions quotas unconstitutional but stated that minority status could be considered in admissions, because diversity in education represented a compelling interest.

Activism on College Campuses

In 1964, colleges and universities had experienced a surge in enrollment as the children of the baby boom began to graduate from high school; the entering freshman class at the University of California at Berkeley, for example, was 37 percent larger than the class that entered in 1963. Students on college campuses in the 1960s had grown up during the years of the Civil Rights movement and generally were committed to bettering society. Some of the most dedicated spent summers in the South, perhaps working with organizations such as the Student Nonviolent Coordinating Committee (SNCC), the student arm of Martin Luther King's Southern Christian Leadership Conference, and registering African Americans to vote; or they might have participated in sit-ins and freedom rides. Many students rejected the rigid conformity of 1950s America, which for them was typified by the throngs of businessmen commuting daily between downtown office buildings and assembly-line suburban homes, with their eyes always on the bottom line. As students endeavored to turn their schools into forums where social issues could be addressed, they met resistance from administrators who seemed to represent the prevailing conservatism and unwanted parental supervision.

This was the climate on U.S. campuses at the start of the fall 1964 semester, when the administrators of the University of California at Berkeley declared the "Bancroft strip," a spot outside the university gates where students often gathered and exchanged information, off limits to political recruiters and fundraisers. On September 29, several students protested the ban by setting up tables and distributing political information in the proscribed area and refusing to leave. University officials ordered five students to appear at disciplinary hearings on September 30, but at the specified time, 500 students descended on the administration building, Sproul Hall, and demanded to be disciplined, too. As a result, eight students received suspensions that day: the five being disciplined and three protest leaders.

The next day, SNCC, the Congress of Racial Equality (CORE), and other political groups set up tables outside Sproul Hall. The arrest of one person at the CORE table, a sometime graduate student named Jack Weinberg, triggered a spontaneous demonstration that for 32 hours prevented the police car carrying Weinberg from moving. Clark Kerr, president of the University of California system, agreed to create a committee of administrators, faculty, and students to decide questions of political activity on campus, and the university dropped the charges against Weinberg.

Kerr had conceded too little, however. Still determined to secure the right to free political expression, a group of students established the Free Speech Movement, which staged demonstrations and organized graduate students in a strike. During a demonstration outside Sproul Hall on December 2, Mario Savio, a philosophy student and one of the movement's founders, gave voice to the determination to change the social system that was common to many of his generation. "There's a time when the operations of the machine become so odious, makes you so sick at heart, that you can't take part," he said. "And you've got to put your bodies upon the gears and upon the wheels, upon the levers, upon all the apparatus, and you've got to indicate to the people who own it that unless you're free, the machines will be prevented from working at all."[9] Between 1,000 and 1,500 students then occupied Sproul Hall.

Police officers arrested 773 students who refused to leave the building voluntarily, in what proved to be the largest mass arrest in California history. After being booked for trespassing and released on bail, the students returned to campus, and the strike continued. Meanwhile, the administration wavered in determining its course of action. On December 8, the academic senate voted to endorse the Free Speech Movement's position, but on December 18, the board of regents rejected the senate's recommendation. The strike ended on January 2, 1965, with the appointment of Martin Meyerson, dean of the College of Environmental Design and a supporter of the Free Speech Movement, as interim chancellor of the Berkeley campus. Meyerson immediately approved the students' demand to set up tables for distributing political material and raising funds on the Bancroft strip and on campus.

Antiwar Protests

Students were demonstrating on other college campuses as well. As the 1960s progressed, they spoke out increasingly against the escalating military conflict in Vietnam, a war that many considered morally wrong, but one that thousands in their age group were being drafted to fight. Across the United States, students marched, made speeches, and sang protest songs. Many, but not all, were affiliated with Students for a Democratic Society (SDS), a national activist organization. Colleges and universities held teach-ins, during which students and like-minded faculty spent several days discussing the war and domestic social problems. The young directed much of their anger against the president who had dramatically increased the U.S. presence in Vietnam and steadfastly defended U.S. involvement in the war, and this youthful dissatisfaction did much to persuade Johnson not to seek another term as president in 1968.

One of the most sensational demonstrations took place at Columbia University in April 1968. Led by SDS and the Student Afro Society (SAS), the Columbia protest had two causes: Columbia's affiliation with the Institute for Defense Analyses (IDA), which conducted weapons research and development for the U.S. Department of Defense, and the university's plan to construct a gymnasium on land owned by the City of New York in Morningside Park, adjacent to the campus. The gymnasium was being built on land that was to have been the site of low-cost housing for the residents of Harlem, a predominantly minority section of the city bordering the park. Also, although Harlem residents would be allowed to use the gym, the separate, lower-level entrance set aside for them reminded many students of Jim Crow segregation.

On April 23, 1968, after an unsuccessful attempt to halt construction of the gym, a group of protesters led by campus SDS chairman Mark Rudd took over Hamilton Hall, which houses Columbia College (the undergraduate school of arts and sciences) and barricaded Dean Harry Coleman in his office. The SDS and SAS then separated; the African-American students remained in Hamilton Hall to protest against the gymnasium while the others occupied the president's office and several other campus buildings.

The siege ended on April 30, when the New York City Police Department cleared the demonstrators from the buildings. The SAS members left Hamilton

Hall peacefully, but the police used rough tactics to evacuate the other buildings and injured 150 students seriously enough to require treatment at a hospital. Seven hundred protesters were arrested, and 30 were suspended by the administration, but they achieved their objectives. Columbia ended its affiliation with IDA and canceled plans for the unpopular gymnasium. Instead the university built an underground athletic facility in another location.

A campus protest turned deadly on Monday, May 4, 1970, the date of a national student strike held to protest the movement of U.S. forces into Cambodia, which President Richard M. Nixon had announced April 30 in a televised address. For days leading up to the strike, student demonstrators at Kent State University in Ohio had disrupted campus and community life, breaking store windows, setting fire to the school's Reserve Officers' Training Corps (ROTC) building, and obstructing the efforts of law enforcement to restore order. On May 4, Ohio governor James A. Rhodes ordered the National Guard to disperse demonstrators on campus. Met by a rock-throwing, uncooperative crowd, guardsmen opened fire, killing four students and wounding nine others. Two of those killed had simply been walking to class.

News of the bloodshed at Kent State triggered protests at colleges and universities throughout the nation, some peaceful and some confrontational. On May 4 and 5, for example, students at New York University forcefully occupied several buildings in the school's Washington Square Complex, including Warren Weaver Hall, which housed a $3.5 million computer owned by the Atomic Energy Commission. The strikers demanded a ransom of $100,000 for the computer and planned to use the money as bail for imprisoned members of the Black Panthers, a militant African-American organization. Facing forced removal, the students gave up their ultimatums and evacuated the occupied buildings on May 7, but they tried to blow up the computer upon departing. University employees extinguished the makeshift bomb moments before it was to explode. Violence next burst forth at Jackson State College in Mississippi, where a face-off between rioting student protesters and city and state police on May 14 and 15 left two students dead and at least 12 wounded.

On June 13, Nixon responded to the killings at Kent State and Jackson State by forming the President's Commission on Campus Unrest to study the ongoing disruptions on college campuses. The commission found no justification for the lethal force applied at Kent State. About the violence occurring at Jackson State, its members were less clear, concluding, "It is the duty of public officials to protect human life and to safeguard peaceful, orderly, and lawful protest. When disorderly protest exists, it is their duty to deal with it firmly, justly, and with the minimum force necessary; lethal force should be used only to protect the lives of officers or citizens and only when the danger to innocent persons is not increased by the use of such force."[10]

Student protests diminished as the 1970s progressed and the United States withdrew its forces from Vietnam. The SDS dissolved into splinter groups at its final convention, in 1969, and was defunct by 1972. Also, the high inflation that characterized the U.S. economy in the mid-1970s had a chilling effect, causing college students to focus on their studies with the aim of making themselves employable.

Acknowledging Diversity

The Black Power movement of the 1960s encouraged interest in African-American history and culture and gave rise to academic departments of black studies at colleges and universities in the 1970s. Similarly, the efforts of women, Hispanics, Native Americans, and other population groups to achieve economic and social equality led to the creation of college-level courses exploring the history, artistic contributions, and problems of these groups.

Educators and legislators were also seeking ways to address the learning needs of ethnic minority students at the elementary and secondary levels. With the Bilingual Education Act of 1968, the federal government encouraged innovative instruction of low-income children who had limited ability to speak English. School districts could apply for grants to fund the development of educational programs and materials, the training of teachers and teachers' aides, and the creation of projects that involved parents in their children's schooling. A successful program could be funded for five years; the school district was then expected to cover the cost.

The 1968 law made bilingual education voluntary, but in 1974 Congress amended the act and required schools to provide bilingual education that addressed students' deficiencies in English, whether or not the schools received federal funding for this purpose. Congress passed this amendment in response to the 1974 U.S. Supreme Court decision in the case *Lau v. Nichols*, filed on behalf of non-English-speaking Chinese students in the San Francisco school system. The justices determined that "there is no equality of treatment merely by providing students with the same facilities, textbooks, teachers, and curriculum; for students who do not understand English are effectively foreclosed from any meaningful education."[11] Congress eliminated the low-income eligibility requirement, and in the 1974–75 academic year funded bilingual education programs in 383 school districts for speakers of 65 languages, including those of American Indians and Native Alaskans.

In 1965, 48,000 children attended schools run by the Bureau of Indian Affairs (BIA), and another 4,200 lived in dormitories provided by the bureau while they attended public schools. Indian children, who were still arriving at government boarding schools without knowledge of English, generally were forbidden to speak their Native languages in school and were required to receive instruction in a non-Indian religion.

The continued disregard of Indian culture by people in authority contributed to the rise of Indian activism in the late 1960s. The American Indian Movement (AIM), founded in Minneapolis on July 28, 1968, used an aggressive approach to gain publicity and draw attention to its concerns. AIM members were among the people calling themselves "Indians of All Tribes" who occupied Alcatraz Island for 19 months, beginning November 20, 1969. AIM also briefly took possession of the Bureau of Indian Affairs headquarters in Washington, D.C., in 1972, and occupied the village of Wounded Knee, South Dakota, in 1973.

During these years, two major studies examined the state of Indian education in the United States. In 1969, an investigation by the Special Senate Subcommittee on Education measured a dropout rate for Indian youths that was twice the national average and higher than that for any other ethnic or racial group in the United States. Those in school lagged two to three years behind their non-Indian counterparts in achievement, and the longer they spent in school, the further behind they fell. This study also pointed out that just 1 percent of Indian children attended schools that had an Indian teacher or principal.

From 1969 to 1971, Robert J. Havighurst, a professor of education and human development at the University of Chicago, directed the National Study of American Indian Education, which concluded that schools for Indians needed to place greater emphasis on Native culture if their students were to succeed. "Many Indian children live in homes and communities where the cultural expectations are different and discontinuous from the expectations held by school teachers and school authorities," the researchers stated.[12]

These findings generated support for the Indian Education Act, which Nixon signed into law on June 23, 1972, and which funded supplemental cultural and bilingual programming for Indian children attending public schools both off and on reservations. To be eligible, a school had to have 10 or more Indian children enrolled and to include parents and community members in program planning. The act created the Office of Indian Education within the U.S. Office of Education, to help Indians and Alaska Natives who were working at the local level to raise students' achievement. It also established the National Advisory Council for Indian Education, a board of 15 Indians and Native Alaskans appointed by the president to report annually to Congress on the state of Indian education.

In 1974, the Bureau of Indian Affairs issued a set of regulations for its schools that clarified students' rights. The bureau guaranteed students the "right to freedom of religion and culture," as well as "to freedom of speech and expression, including symbolic expression, such as display of buttons, posters, choice of dress, and length of hair. . . ." In addition, students were assured the "right to freedom from discrimination."[13]

The Tribally Controlled Community College Assistance Act, which became law in 1978, gave greater government support to two-year postsecondary schools on Indian reservations. These community colleges received $4,000 per year for each full-time student enrolled as long as they had an Indian governing board and adhered to an educational philosophy and program of study that served the needs of the Native population.

Openness in the Classroom

The questioning of societal conventions and concern for free expression that in the late 1960s led many young Americans to experiment with communal living or consciousness-expanding drugs caused some educators to rethink traditional school procedures. The typical classroom came to be seen as a rigid, sterile place that wasted children's time and taught them little of value, and the standard method of instruction, a teacher standing at a blackboard and lecturing to a class of silent children, was dismissed as "talk and chalk."[14] A number of alternative educational approaches therefore gained popularity with teachers and school administrators who wished to create an atmosphere more conducive to informal learning and development. Among the best known was the open-education movement, which originated in Great Britain.

As in John Dewey's laboratory school, the teacher acted as facilitator in the open classroom, which might have been a large indoor space with moveable walls or a traditional classroom with the desks removed and the door left unclosed, allowing children to move freely around the room or venture into the hallway or other classes. The seemingly unstructured space was in reality carefully arranged, with appealing learning stations devoted to reading, writing, art, exploration of science or mathematics, and other activities.

The ideas that most influenced open education were not Dewey's, but those of the Swiss psychologist Jean Piaget, who taught that children construct knowledge from within as a result of observation and experimentation. According to this constructivist theory of learning, children first experience the world through their senses and developing motor skills and then gradually acquire the ability to think logically and handle abstract concepts. Based on the belief that children learn best when their interest is strong and they see relevance in the material to be mastered, educators encouraged students in open classrooms to choose their own activities and establish their own schedules. The children would not be tested or graded and could progress at their own pace.

By 1975, the widespread enthusiasm for breaking with tradition was already evaporating. Some teachers and children had adapted to open education better than others, and many parents wanted the evidence of their children's progress that traditional testing and grading had provided. In that year, when the College Entrance Examination Board announced that scores on the Scholastic Aptitude Test had dropped steadily for a decade and school districts faced a declining school-age population and soaring inflation, returning to tried and true methods seemed the most prudent course, although open education continues to be used successfully in numerous schools.

Despite strained school budgets and retrenchment in many places, in 1975 the federal government addressed the needs of children with disabilities through the Education for All Handicapped Children Act, commonly called the special-education law, which called for children with special needs to receive "a free appropriate public education which emphasizes special education and related services designed to meet their unique needs."[15] For the first time, parents who were dissatisfied with the school district's plans for educating their disabled children were entitled to have the matter resolved through mediation or litigation.

The act also required children with special needs to be taught in the least restrictive environment possible, which for many meant in a regular public school classroom, alongside children who were not considered disabled, for all or part of the day. This practice, called inclusion, or mainstreaming, was thought to give children with special needs a greater opportunity to develop their knowledge and talents and to interact with their peers. It was hoped that children with disabilities who were educated in this way would be better equipped to take their places in society as adults than those sheltered in the special classroom, although whether the disabled actually gained from inclusion was an open question. Inclusion was thought to benefit the rest of the class by increasing awareness of people with disabilities, even if teachers worried that meeting the educational needs of disabled students took their attention away from the rest of the class.

Segregating disabled pupils in special classes, probably unnecessarily, smacked of "separate but equal" discrimination. Not only was inclusion required for schools to be in compliance with the law, but also it was in harmony with ongoing efforts to achieve racial integration. By spring 1980, nearly 70 percent of children with disabilities were enrolled in regular classes.

Chronicle of Events

1963

- *November 22:* President John F. Kennedy is assassinated; Vice President Lyndon B. Johnson is sworn in as president.

1964

- Johnson defeats Republican Barry Goldwater in the presidential election.
- Two percent of African-American students in the 11 states of the former Confederacy attend racially mixed schools.
- Colleges and universities experience a surge in enrollment.
- The entering freshman class at the University of California at Berkeley is 37 percent larger than the entering class of 1963.
- *July 2:* The Civil Rights Act, signed into law on this date, empowers the U.S. commissioner of education to monitor the progress of school integration and assist school districts that are trying to desegregate.
- *August 20:* The Economic Opportunity Act creates several educational programs, including Job Corps, which gives vocational training and academic instruction to high school dropouts ages 16 to 21, and Head Start, which prepares economically disadvantaged preschoolers for kindergarten.
- *September:* The University of California at Berkeley administration bans political recruiting and fundraising on the Bancroft strip.
- *September 30:* Eight Berkeley students are suspended for political activity and protesting.
- *October 1:* Political groups set up tables outside Sproul Hall, the Berkeley administration building.
- *December 2:* The Free Speech Movement, the group that has organized a student strike, occupies Sproul Hall; police arrest 773 students.
- *December 8:* The academic senate at the University of California at Berkeley endorses the Free Speech Movement's position.
- *December 18:* The university's board of regents rejects the senate's position.

Mario Savio, a leader in the Free Speech Movement, addresses a crowd on the Berkeley campus in 1964. *(Courtesy of the Bancroft Library, University of California, Berkeley)*

1965

- Approximately 48,000 children attend Bureau of Indian Affairs (BIA) schools, and another 4,200 live in bureau dormitories and attend public schools.
- *January 2:* Martin Meyerson, a supporter of the Free Speech Movement, is appointed interim chancellor at Berkeley. The student strike ends.
- *April 11:* The Elementary and Secondary Education Act (ESEA) makes more than $1 billion in federal funds available to schools serving low-income students.
- *April:* The Office of Education begins requiring school districts that were legally segregated before 1954 to demonstrate eligibility for ESEA by documenting their desegregation efforts.
- *September 8:* The Higher Education Act bolsters the resources of colleges and universities and creates the first federal scholarships.

1966

- The Office of Education requires 12 percent to 18 percent of African-American students in formerly segregated school districts to attend integrated schools in the 1966–67 school year.
- A study directed by James S. Coleman of Johns Hopkins University finds that most American children attend school with students predominantly of their own race; that schools serving minority populations are inferior in terms of class size, facilities, and supplies; that most minority students score lower than whites on achievement tests, but those attending racially mixed schools have higher scores than those who are segregated.

1968

- In deciding the case *Green v. School Board of New Kent County,* the justices of the Supreme Court call for more rapid progress in school integration.
- The National Advisory Commission on Civil Disorders links rioting in northern inner cities to the poor schools available to urban minority children.
- Johnson announces his decision not to seek another term as president.
- Through the Bilingual Education Act, the federal government funds instructional programs for low-income children with limited knowledge of English.
- *April 23:* At Columbia University, members of Students for a Democratic Society (SDS) and the Student Afro Society protest the university's involvement with the Institute for Defense Analyses and the building of a controversial gymnasium by occupying several university buildings.
- *April 30:* The New York City Police Department clears demonstrators from the occupied buildings at Columbia.
- *July 28:* The American Indian Movement (AIM) is founded in Minneapolis.
- *September:* In the 11 states of the former Confederacy, 20.3 percent of school-age African-American children attend integrated schools.

1969

- SDS breaks into several factions.
- The dropout rate for Americans Indians is twice the national average and higher than for any other U.S. ethnic or racial group.
- Indian students are two to three years behind non-Indians in achievement.
- One percent of Indian children attend schools that have an Indian teacher or principal.
- *November 20:* Native Americans calling themselves Indians of All Tribes begin a 19-month occupation of Alcatraz Island.

1969–1971

- The National Study for American Indian Education finds that instruction in Native culture generally is lacking in schools educating American Indian children.

1970

- *April 30:* President Richard M. Nixon announces the entry of U.S. forces into Cambodia.

- *May 4:* Ohio National Guardsmen open fire on demonstrating students at Kent State University, killing four and wounding nine.
- *May 4 and 5:* Students occupy several buildings at New York University (NYU).
- *May 7:* Students end their occupation at NYU.
- *June 13:* Nixon creates the President's Commission on Campus Unrest.

1971

- In letting stand a lower-court decision in the case *Swann v. Charlotte-Mecklenburg Board of Education,* the Supreme Court endorses such methods for achieving a racial balance in schools as establishing quotas, redistricting, and busing.

1971–1972

- The enrollment of South Boston High School, which serves white students, is 676 over capacity; nearby Girls High School, which serves a black community, has room for 532 more students.

1972

- SDS is defunct.
- AIM briefly takes possession of the Bureau of Indian Affairs headquarters in Washington, D.C.
- *June 23:* Nixon signs into law the Indian Education Act, which supports cultural and bilingual education for Indian children and establishes the National Advisory Council for Indian Education.

1973

- In its ruling in the case *Keyes v. School District No. 1, Denver, Colorado,* the U.S. Supreme Court gives the first order for northern schools to desegregate.
- AIM occupies the village of Wounded Knee, South Dakota.

1974

- According to a Gallup poll, less than 25 percent of Americans, and 32 percent of African Americans, favor busing to achieve school integration.
- The U.S. Supreme Court rules in the case *Lau v. Nichols* that a failure to provide bilingual education to children with limited knowledge of English denies those children equality of educational opportunity.
- The Bureau of Indian Affairs issues guidelines for its schools.

- *June 21:* Judge W. Arthur Garrity, Jr., of the U.S. District Court of Massachusetts orders the Boston School Committee to desegregate the city's schools.
- *September 12:* Court-ordered busing begins in Boston; white residents of South Boston hurl rocks, produce, and epithets at buses carrying African-American children.
- *December 11:* A black student stabs a white schoolmate at South Boston High School.

1974–1975
- The U.S. government funds bilingual education programs in 383 school districts for speakers of 65 languages.

1975
- Enthusiasm for experimental teaching methods such as the open classroom is diminishing.
- The College Entrance Examination Board announces that SAT scores have dropped for the 10th straight year.

- The Education for All Handicapped Children Act becomes law, protecting the right of children with disabilities to a free, appropriate public education.
- *September 8:* Boston implements a new busing plan designed to achieve a more uniform racial mix in the schools.

1978
- The Tribally Controlled Community College Act supports two-year colleges on Indian reservations.
- *June 28:* In the case *Regents of the University of California v. Bakke,* the U.S. Supreme Court rules that schools may not apply rigid admissions quotas that ignore academic qualifications, although they may consider race in granting admission.

1980
- Nearly 70 percent of children with disabilities are enrolled in regular classes.

Eyewitness Testimony

Though the goal of the busing program was to integrate P.S. 183, the students there remained predominantly white and from high-income families. Thus I had to adjust to a whole new set of realities. On a regular basis I was forced to battle my white teachers' and classmates' low expectations and negative perceptions about blacks and Latinos. Meanwhile, as one of the relatively few minority faces in the classroom, I was routinely called on to serve as the white person's lens on the Negro experience.

Likewise, attending school in a well-to-do community aggravated my sense of my own poverty and forced me to engage in multiple, mostly futile attempts to mask it. Each September I dreaded writing about my summer "vacations" and cringed when we were asked if our parents might visit the class and talk about their careers and educational experiences.

To students like me, integration came to mean sending a small phalanx of mostly poor black and Latino children to attend schools in white neighborhoods. I never took the opportunity to learn what integration meant to my white classmates and teachers, but it certainly did not mean asking any of them to take my place at P.S. 121 in East Harlem.

Warren Simmons, executive director of the Annenberg Institute for School Reform at Brown University, who attended New York City public schools in the 1960s, "A Stranger in Two Worlds," pp. 21–22.

Americans are frequently accused of worshiping the normal or average. . . . Thus, to the casual thinker, it will seem just common sense that it is virtually impossible for an exceptional child to be well adjusted. Furthermore, such common sense thinking suggests that the greater the exceptionality the greater the deviation from the "idolized normal standard" and the more difficult it will be for persons with exceptionalities to obtain or maintain good adjustment.

In common sense terms, the "genius" is expected to be more maladjusted than average children, often being considered an "oddball," or at least a "bookworm," "egghead," or "non-conformist." Another widely held common sense notion is the "happy little moron theory" that assumes the retarded have relatively few adjustment problems because they don't have to come to grips with many of life's complexities. Similarly common-sense generalizations are often expressed about the physically disabled. In terms of common sense, the severely impaired are assumed to have more serious adjustment problems than the mildly impaired. The hard of hearing are expected to be better adjusted than the deaf; the partially seeing better adjusted than the blind; the am-bulatory cripple better adjusted than the wheelchair case. In other words, common sense suggests that the degree of maladjustment will be a relatively simple function of the degree of deviation from normal or the degree of impairment. . . .

[C]ommon sense alone fails to provide an adequate basis for understanding and dealing with adjustment to exceptionality. Common sense notions about adjustment of exceptional children frequently fail to be validated by careful research.

Samuel C. Ashcroft, associate professor of special education, George Peabody College for Teachers, 1963, "Exceptionality and Adjustment," pp. 521–522.

So, cries the overwrought Deep-Southern parent in areas of large Negro concentration, what will save us from the Federal wolves? Are our schools to be invaded and overrun by a mass of black children whose economic and social background—to say nothing of our own long-rooted folkways—makes them unacceptable as schoolmates and playfellows for our children?

The realistic answers ought to be reassuring to the fearful white Southerner, and disillusioning and disturbing to non-Southerners of both races who may believe that a real breakthrough is just around the corner. . . .

As in many cities of the North, school segregation will be maintained simply because of the segregation of residential districts. Except for consolidated rural districts, students generally attend the schools nearest their homes. Obviously, children in an all-Negro or nearly all-Negro residential area will go to all-Negro or nearly all-Negro schools—and in the latter case the handful of white children almost invariably will be transferred.

It does not seem likely that the Federal Government can do much about this. It most certainly follows that the school boards and other governing bodies, all of them composed of, or dominated by, white members, will build new schools well within the established white and Negro neighborhoods. Moreover, only the most naïve observer can doubt that most school boards will resort to the ancient political device of gerrymandering, whenever and wherever the carving out of new school districts or the reshaping of old ones becomes necessary to prevent anything but token integration.

Hodding Carter, editor of the Delta Democrat-Times, *Greenville, Mississippi, 1964, "Desegregation Does Not Mean Integration," pp. 136–137.*

Last summer I went to Mississippi to join the struggle there for civil rights. This fall I am engaged in another phase of the same struggle, this time in Berkeley. The two battlefields may seem quite different to some observers, but this is not the case. The same rights are at stake in both places—the right to participate as citizens in a democratic society and the right to due process of law. Further, it is a struggle against the same enemy. In Mississippi an autocratic and powerful minority rules, through organized violence, to suppress the vast, virtually powerless majority. In California, the privileged minority manipulates the university bureaucracy to suppress the students' political expression. That "respectable" bureaucracy masks the financial plutocrats; that impersonal bureaucracy is the efficient enemy in a "Brave New World."

Mario Savio, student at the University of California at Berkeley and a founder of the Free Speech Movement, 1964, "An End to History," p. 216.

The university is the place where people begin seriously to question the conditions of their existence and raise the issue of whether they can be committed to the society they have been born into. After a long period of apathy during the fifties, students have begun not only to question but, having arrived at answers, to act on those answers. This is part of a growing understanding among many people in America that history has not ended, that a better society is possible, and that it is worth dying for.

The free-speech fight points up a fascinating aspect of contemporary campus life. Students are permitted to talk all they want so long as their speech has no consequences.

Mario Savio, student at the University of California at Berkeley and a founder of the Free Speech Movement, 1964, "An End to History," p. 218.

I hated elementary school. The teachers were narrow-minded. The questions they asked were mundane, uninspired. I wanted the universe and they gave me a rectangle with four sides. I could understand the space within the rectangle, but what about the space beyond the sides? I asked the teachers questions, but the answers they gave me were pat, solved: *Case closed.* I doubted pat answers.

I sat in the back of the class with the trouble-makers. They would make funny noises or throw erasers to disrupt the class and disturb the teacher. I would occasionally raise my hand to point out a mistake the teacher had made on the board. The trouble-makers would be momentarily silenced and the entire class would turn around to stare at me. Then the whole class would burst into hysterics. After about two weeks of this, my fifth-grade teacher called my parents in to tell them that I would never be able to handle abstract math. As my parents suspected, and I knew, it was the teacher who was having difficulties with

abstract math. She stopped calling on me and passed me into the sixth grade.

John Aristotle Phillips, who designed a nuclear bomb from publicly available documents while an undergraduate at Princeton, recalling elementary school in North Haven, Connecticut, ca. 1965, Mushroom: The Story of the A-Bomb Kid, p.24.

Every child must be encouraged to get as much education as he has the ability to take.

We want this not only for his sake—but for the Nation's sake.

Nothing matters more to the future of the country: not our military preparedness, for armed might is worthless if we lack the brainpower to build a world of peace; not our productive economy, for we cannot sustain growth without trained manpower, not our democratic system of government, for freedom is fragile if citizens are ignorant.

We must demand that our schools increase not only the quantity but the quality of America's education. For we recognize that nuclear age problems cannot be solved with horse-and-buggy learning. The three R's of our school system must be supported by the three T's—teachers who are superior, techniques of instruction that are modern, and thinking about education which places it first in all our plans and hopes.

President Lyndon B. Johnson, 1965, "President Lyndon Johnson's Call upon Congress to Pass Elementary and Secondary Education Act (1965)," in Education in the United States: A Documentary History, edited by Sol Cohen, vol. 5, p. 3372.

Although disappointing, it is no surprise that the breakdown of communication across generations and between fragments of our society should also be evident in the universities. "The administration," hero of a generation ago when salvation seemed to lie in organization, is an obvious target; but the growth of administrative power, in any institution, is not a simple phenomenon. The students' complaint about being manipulated by a group of conspirators to serve the economic needs of business, or whatever, is naïve. On the other hand, their sense of alienation is painfully real and justifiable. The proxy-parent—the administration rather than the faculty seems everywhere to play this role—is more powerful and more impersonal than any mother and father, and less inclined than many parents to treat the students with the dignity and respect accorded adults. The reasonable-sounding suggestion that the students had avenues of appeal open to them is simply not true in practice. In this context, it should be clear, I think, that until the students are really given responsibility, they should not be charged with being irresponsible.

John F. Boler, visiting professor of philosophy at the University of California at Berkeley, February 1965, "Behind the Protests at Berkeley," p. 112.

[T]o what extent should academic freedom protect those who protest the war effort? I do not agree with those who sharply would curtail the right of dissent on our college and university campuses on the ground that such demonstrations give aid and comfort to the enemy. I do not question the patriotism of the protestors—I do not question their academic freedom to be against the war, to be against this war, to be against the way this war is conducted, to be against the inequities in the draft. I believe, also, that academic freedom should protect the right of a professor or student to advocate Marxism, socialism, communism, or any other minority viewpoint provided he does so openly and is not in violation of the law of the land.

But there is a far more difficult question: Should academic freedom protect a professor when he uses the forum of a state university to welcome victory for the enemy in a war in which the U.S. is engaged? I know that, in answering "no" to that question, I am expressing disagreement with many of the faculty and graduating class at this institution.

Former vice president Richard M. Nixon delivering the commencement address at the University of Rochester, June 5, 1966, "Academic Freedom Today," p. 453.

Enter the computer! What makes it a potentially important—perhaps revolutionary—educational instrument is precisely the fact that it offers a technology by which, for the first time, instruction really *can* be geared to the specific abilities, needs, and progress of each individual.

The problem is how.

Charles E. Silberman, social scientist and writer, August 1966, "Technology Is Knocking at the Schoolhouse Door," p. 125.

Obviously, a complex, highly technological society faced with serious international problems requires even greater numbers of persons with developed intellects. The United States faces a scarcity of academic talent, as numerous studies have shown; and the argument for better nurturing of the gifted, through distinctive courses, separate sections, and even special schools, is a powerful one.

Yet, the need to achieve a fully democratic and egalitarian society seems equally imperative, both on humanitarian and internationally political grounds. . . . There may be a very real danger of leveling, in the worst sense, in the one position; but there may also be a genuine danger of erecting a meritocracy—a 20th century form of enlightenment despotism—in the other.

Neither "equal treatment" in the schools nor "equality of opportunity" in the schools is a discardable ideal. Unfortunately, it is easier to celebrate them in the abstract than to reconcile them in practice. There is an inherent tension between equality and excellence—though not, one hopes, a contradiction. How the school systems cope with this tension is perhaps the fundamental issue in educational policy in our lifetime, as well as one of the key determinants of the future social arrangements of American society.

George C. Keller, editor, Columbia College Today, *summer 1966, "The Search for 'Brainpower,'" pp. 68–69.*

[W]hat is important is not to "equalize the schools" in some formal sense, but to insure that children from all groups come into adult society so equipped as to insure their full participation in this society.

Another way of putting this is to say that the schools are successful only insofar as they reduce the dependence of a child's opportunities upon his social origins. We can think of a set of conditional probabilities: the probability of being prepared for a given occupation or for a given college at the end of high school, conditional upon the child's social origins. The effectiveness of the school consists, in part, of making the conditional probabilities less conditional—that is, less dependent upon social origins. Thus, equality of educational opportunity implies, not merely "equal" schools, but equally effective schools, whose influences will overcome the differences in starting point of children from different social groups.

James S. Coleman, professor of social relations, Johns Hopkins University, summer 1966, "Equal Schools or Equal Students?" p. 72.

Berkeley is now a symbol in the full sense of the word, that is, an image which condenses a complete range of ideas and emotions and presents it for our contemplation. Berkeley is a symbol of the necessities and the possibilities which confront higher education in the United States today. In this sense, Berkeley is now a convenient shorthand name for the internal structural strains and the external social demands which trouble every university and college in the country. If it were not, if the explosion of student unrest and the painful grinding to a halt of one of the world's great universities were purely local phenomena, Berkeley would soon have passed from the front pages of the national press and soon been forgotten. But . . . Berkeley dramatized a national and not a local problem. Higher education in the United States is today—always granting the fond hope that the war will not obliterate all other social matters and make them inconsequential—the most important institution in American society as we enter the second half of the twentieth century. The claim is large but not extravagant. And Berkeley symbolizes the crucial fact that higher education is in trouble.

John William Ward, professor of history, Amherst College, summer 1966, "The Trouble with Higher Education," p. 76.

The slum child is known to come from physical home conditions ranging from a status of mere existence to almost tolerable. The suburbs? Johnny Suburban may live in the cleanest, classiest, and highest mortgaged house in the village—a house with all the plumbing conveniences that two and one-half baths can provide—yet a home which has what is loosely referred to as "wall-to-wall" indebtedness. . . .

The suburban child who has been conditioned to expect everything and who is unable to finish a task in school without an immediate extrinsic reward is likely to be personally blamed for his "overindulgence." For this child, overindulgence is as much an unhealthy aspect of his environmental conditioning as is the inability of the child from the low-income family to finish a task because he has learned, of necessity, to live from day to day and to worry about tomorrow if and when it comes. The end products seem disturbingly similar and dissimilarly disturbing to a society which is inherently committed to helping the "underdog."

William E. Kuschman, coordinator of research, College of Education, Northern Illinois University, November 12, 1966, "Education and Society in Disadvantaged Suburbia," pp. 386–387.

Stephen is eight years old. A picture of him standing in front of the bulletin board on Arab bedouins shows a little light-brown person staring with unusual concentration at a chosen spot on the floor. Stephen is tiny, desperate, unwell. Sometimes he talks to himself. He moves his mouth as if he were talking. At other times he laughs out loud in class for no apparent reason. He is also an indescribably mild and unmalicious child. He cannot do any of his school work very well. His math and reading are poor. In Third Grade he was in a class that had substitute teachers much of the year. Most of the year before that, he had a row of substitute teachers too. He is in the Fourth Grade now but his work is barely at the level of the Second. Nobody has complained about the things that have happened to Stephen because he does not have any mother or father. Stephen is a ward of the State of Massachusetts and, as such, he has been placed in the home of some very poor people who do not want him now that he is not

Students at St. Albans School in Washington, D.C., leave the Activities Building and head for class in the late 1960s. *(St. Albans School)*

a baby any more. The money that they are given for him to pay his expenses every week does not cover the other kind of expense—the more important kind which is the immense emotional burden that is continually at stake. Stephen often comes into school badly beaten. If I ask him about it, he is apt to deny it because he does not want us to know first-hand what a miserable time he has. Like many children, and many adults too, Stephen is far more concerned with hiding his abased condition from the view of the world than he is with escaping that condition.

Jonathan Kozol, writer, educator, and activist, 1967, Death at an Early Age: The Destruction of the Hearts and Minds of Negro Children in the Boston Public Schools, p. 1.

American education should shift from a system which prepares children in terms of specific information, skills, and goals to preparing children to adjust to our rapidly changing world. They need an education which will enable them to continue on their own so as to acquire the knowledge they will need. The worst we could do for our children would be to determine that there is one kind of training, mathematics or science, for example, to insure their preservation in the future.

Since we live in an age of innovation, a practical education must prepare youth for work that does not exist yet and can not be clearly defined yet. In other words, the most practical education has become the most theoretical. What should the goals of American education be in this complex world?

It is obvious that we must develop a global consciousness in individuals. There was a time when the U. S. adhered to a policy of isolation; however, those days are gone forever. It is very hard to learn to live with one's family, as evidenced by our increasing divorce rates, but today we must even learn to live with all the people of the world.

Billy J. Paschal, associate professor of educational psychology, University of Miami, October 28, 1967, "Goals for Space Age Education," p. 390.

The year 1967 will be referred to as the Year of Violence, not only in international affairs, but also in domestic matters, both in the U.S. and in the rest of the world. On the educational scene, demonstrations, interference with the rights of others, and riots have become the order of the day, an established fact that permits no contradiction—all in the name of academic freedom, civil rights, and liberalism. Respect for authority and tradition, discussion, and patience seem to have been discarded in favor of pressure and violence in order to gain one's ends. In the U.S., this type of behavior, which has roots as far back as the 17th century, has been gaining momentum from the beginning of Berkeley-itis in 1964 and has spread to campuses all over the country.

William W. Brickman, professor of educational history and comparative education, Graduate School of Education, University of Pennsylvania, January 6, 1968, "Student Power and Academic Anarchy," p. 6.

Teachers are overworked and underpaid. True. It is an exacting and exhausting business, this damming up the flood of human potentialities. What energy it takes to turn a torrent into a trickle, to train that trickle along narrow, well-marked channels! Teachers are often tired. In the teachers' lounge, they sigh their relief into stained cups of instant coffee and offer gratitude to whoever makes them laugh at the day's disasters. This laughter permits a momentary sanity-saving acknowledgment, shared by all, that what passes for humdrum or routine or boring is, in truth, tragic. (An hour, of which some 50 minutes are given up to "classroom control." One child's question unanswered, a hundred unasked. A smart student ridiculed: "He'll learn better." He learns.) . . .

How do teachers bear their tragic task? They learn to look away. They hasten to a way of talking that lets

them forget their problems. What cannot be solved is named. Once named, it does not seem to need a solution so urgently—perhaps never. James "acts out." (He is mad as hell at his teacher.) Melissa is an "underachiever." (So be it.)

George B. Leonard, senior editor, Look *magazine, September 17, 1968, "How School Stunts Your Child," p. 31.*

It started, perhaps, at Berkeley, then moved through Chicago, Ohio State, Howard, Columbia, and eventually may spread to the most remote and least notable Podunk State and Private University. It is misnamed the Battle for Student Power; it should be called more correctly the War of the Unstudent.

This War of the Unstudent is distinguished by forceable occupations of college buildings in the name of free speech and by demands in the name of academic freedom to dictate university policy, from course content to the hiring and firing of professors, to where and whether buildings shall be erected, and to the rules or absence of them in dormitories. The struggle for power is not to assert student power as much as it is to demolish the power of the establishment; the resolve is not to replace one program with another, but to destroy the existing program. The deficiencies of the old order are detailed simply for they surround one, but the new order is explained only in the broadest terms: love, equality, justice, and flower power.

John F. Ohles, associate professor of secondary education, Kent State University, October 26, 1968, "The University and the Unstudent," p. 361.

The fact of the matter is that large numbers of what once were called institutions of higher learning are in danger of demise through the revolutionary tactics of some student and faculty personnel. It appears unlikely that any college or university is safe—unless something substantial is done by the responsible elements of the institution.

In too many instances, administrators, faculty, and students have been immobilized by indecision, paralyzed by propaganda, and frozen by fear, while those bent on ruining the university as an agency of scholarship and society literally ran riot. Too many persons associated with higher education either kept silent or overtly or covertly supported the extremists. Such an attitude stemmed possibly from the conviction that any counteraction against violence toward university personnel or property was an infringement upon the students' academic freedom. Some professors, indeed, do not express disapproval of the hyperactivists because of their belief that they would not be considered "liberal."

William W. Brickman, professor of educational history and comparative education, Graduate School of Education, University of Pennsylvania, October 26, 1968, "Anarchy vs. Freedom in Academia," p. 356.

A teacher in an open classroom needs to cultivate a state of *suspended expectations.* It is not easy. It is easy to believe that a dull class is dull, or a bright class is bright. The words "emotionally disturbed" conjure up frightening images. And it is sometimes a relief to discover that there are good pupils in the class that is waiting for you. Not reading the report cards or ignoring the standing of the class is an act of self-denial; it involves casting aside a crutch when one still believes one can't walk without it. Yet if one wants to develop an open classroom within the context of a school which is essentially totalitarian, such acts of will are necessary.

What does it mean to suspend expectations when one is told that the class one will be teaching is slow, or bright, or ordinary? At least it means not preparing to teach in any special way or deciding beforehand on the complexity of the materials to be used during a school year. It means that planning does not consist of finding the class's achievement level according to the record cards and tailoring the material to those levels, but rather preparing diverse materials and subjects and discovering from the students as the year unfolds what is relevant to them and what isn't.

Herbert R. Kohl, educator and advocate of experimental teaching methods, 1969, The Open Classroom: A Practical Guide to a New Way of Teaching, *pp. 20–21.*

Two days after the liberation of the buildings began, I was asked, in the middle of a crowded faculty meeting, the following question by Professor Alan Silver, a good liberal who always considered himself a radical: "Mr. Rudd, is there nothing in the university worth saving?" Had I been as sure then as I was several weeks later, after much study, experience, and discussion, the answer *No* would have come readily. As it was, neither I nor any of the six or so SDS people present had any answer. We had to decide what is the value of a capitalist university, what is its function in society, and what are the contradictions which can possibly make it useful to a revolutionary movement?

Given that the capitalist university serves the function of production of technology, ideology, and personnel for business, government, and military (we had hit at these functions in our exposure of IDA [the Institute for Defense Analyses] and expansion), the question of "saving" the university implies capitulation to the liberal mythology about free and open inquiry at a university and its value-neutrality. Whatever "good" function the university serves is what the radical students can cull from its bones—especially the creation and expansion of a revolutionary movement.

Mark Rudd, leader of Students for a Democratic Society at Columbia University during the April 1968 demonstrations, 1969, "Columbia: Notes on the Spring Rebellion," pp. 300–301.

In schools run by humans, we have not succeeded in developing intensely humanistic learning environments—not in process, not in content, and not in perspective. The schools do not, in general, foster man's most creative traits, nor grapple with his great ideas, nor relate these ideas and talents to the contemporary environment where man's dramas are continuously re-enacted. The schools are bogged down with routine, trivialities, and the lesser literacies. In the rat race to cover what is in the textbook, schooling has lost sight of education as an end in itself and has become instrumental to the next textbook, the next grade, higher education, and the Gross National Product. And now—at a critical time in the history of schools, education, and man—an electronic teacher of great power, the computer, comes into this human-based environment. The instructional era now on the horizon is one of man-made interaction. Will the computer dehumanize learning and teaching even more? The choice is ours. . . .

Already it is clear that computers, unlike television, are more efficient by far than humans in performing routine instructional tasks and in assuring error-free performance on the part of learners in those basic skills to which teachers devote so much time. It is clear, then, that computers have a viable, albeit threatening, role in the schools. The critical problem is how computers and people are to live together productively in the school environment. If educators continue to confuse instruction in the basic skills with education, then teachers will merely monitor the computer and, in time, become its servant. Under such circumstances, in due time, there would be no need for schools as other than custodial agencies, since computer terminals might more readily and profitably be placed in homes.

John L. Goodlad, dean of the Graduate School of Education, University of California at Los Angeles, April 19, 1969, "The Schools vs. Education," p. 81.

A new kind of education is beginning to sweep across the plains of North Dakota and show signs of finding its way into schools across the nation. Children who used to be the last to trickle in to class each morning and the first to bound out, are arriving early and lingering late. Parents who once tried to drill multiplication tables into unwilling minds, now report that their children regard mathematics as a fascinating game. And veteran teachers exclaim that they are realizing the full satisfaction of their profession for the first time. . . .

The schools that are earning this devotion are vastly different from traditional public schools. Gone is the familiar classroom where the teacher stands up front, expecting all eyes to face her and all ears to listen as she pours identical information into rows of silent children. Gone are the rigid lines of forward facing desks, so arranged that the teacher can keep her eye on every child at the same time. In their stead are scatterings of lightweight desks or tables and chairs and home-made room dividers which create unexpected nooks and crannies where children can slip away for independent work.

At first glance it may seem that the teacher herself is gone, for she no longer dominates the room; the children and their activities do. But a second look will spot the teacher. She may be helping a few students in the math center, listening to a small group discussion in the social studies center or observing a youngster's experiment in the science center.

Arlene Silberman, educator and writer, 1970, "Excitement in North Dakota," p. 43.

Our democracy is not destroyed, but it is in danger. Not the least of the reasons is the fact that the community has not wanted for all its children what the best parent wants for his own child. As a result, the public schools are failing dismally in what has always been regarded as one of their primary tasks—in Horace Mann's phrase, to be "the great equalizer of the conditions of men," facilitating the movement of the poor and disadvantaged into the mainstream of American economic and social life. Far from being "the great equalizer," the schools help perpetuate the differences in condition, or at the very least, do little to reduce them. If the United States is to become a truly just and humane society, the schools will have to do an incomparably better job than they are now doing of educating youngsters from minority-group and lower-class homes.

Charles E. Silberman, social scientist and writer, 1970, Crisis in the Classroom: The Remaking of American Education, pp. 53–54.

Four second-grade children sit around a table containing four mail-order catalogues, four sets of advertisements from department stores, four pads, four pencils, and four "adding-multiplying" machines. For a time, the children select random items from the catalogues for the sheer fun of going "shopping" and then adding up costs. Then they follow a prepared "suggestion card" written by the teacher, directing each child to pretend that he has a forty-dollar budget with which to buy a complete Easter outfit, from hat to shoes, from underwear to lightweight coat. A furious amount of addition, subtraction and multiplication ensues as the children struggle to stretch the budget as far as possible. For these children, arithmetic has become "relevant."

Charles E. Silberman, social scientist and writer, 1970, Crisis in the Classroom: The Remaking of American Education, p. 309.

If one airplane in every four crashed between takeoff and landing, people would refuse to fly. If one automobile in every four went out of control and caused a fatal accident or permanent injury, Detroit would be closed down tomorrow.

Our schools—which produce a more important product than airplanes or automobiles—somehow fail one youngster in four. And so far we have not succeeded in preventing the social and economic fatalities every school dropout represents.

For each child thus failed by his school, all of us pay a price in taxes and in social unrest, and the child himself is deprived of his chance to develop his potential.

Leon M. Lessinger, Callaway professor of education, Georgia State University, 1970, Every Kid a Winner: Accountability in Education, p. 3.

Most of us can still recall the extraordinary dreariness of so much of the teaching to which we were exposed: the textbooks flat as old root beer, the boring assignments, the perfunctory explanations, the passive note taking, the mindless regurgitation of meaningless facts, and a scheme of grading that taught so many children to give up hope. Our schools have made some progress in these areas, but we have a long way to go. In many classrooms these boring practices still occur. . . . Young people almost swim in a mixture of media such as magazines and paperback books, recorded music, TV, and easy travel. They are exposed to a life that is exciting and exhilarating. They are eager to do, learn, taste, see.

What they are *not* eager to do is to serve time, to sit in a room as the world is sliced up into little units that the teacher serves up according to an invariable curriculum. How often do they slip away into half-sleep or escape to a world of daydreams? How many look forward solely to recess, snow days, and social get-togethers? If we were to sit through a typical school week as if we were students, with no hope of escape, we might begin to appreciate the terrible effects of boredom, redundancy, endless repetition.

Leon M. Lessinger, Callaway professor of education,
Georgia State University, 1970, Every Kid a Winner:
Accountability in Education, *pp. 123–124.*

What is at issue is the issue of racism versus humanity. We have been educated for 350 years to think first in terms of race and property and almost never in terms of human lives. What is the value of human personality in this country? What would you give for a man's life? These two young men shot down, they could have been my sons. Of what value are they to the American society? Hundreds have been shot down. What does it mean? Is it tragic to other people, to anyone but the mother or the sister or the wife? What is the value of human life in America today?

Margaret Walker Alexander, writer and professor of English at
Jackson State College, testifying before the grand jury investigating
the May 1970 shootings at Jackson State, August 1970, in The
Report of the Commission on Campus Unrest, *p. 444.*

A third-grade classroom opens off the corridor. At first our eyes are assailed by the apparent chaos of the scene—a profusion of movement, sounds, colors, shapes. Gradually, however, the organization of the class reveals itself. The room is perhaps a little smaller than is standard and has a class register of 30 children, a few of whom are in the corridor or visiting other classes. What is most striking is that there are no desks for pupils or teachers. Instead, the room is arranged as a workshop.

Carelessly draped over the seat, arm and back of a big old easy chair are three children, each reading to himself. Several other children nearby sprawl comfortably on a covered mattress on the floor, rehearsing a song they have written and copied neatly into a song folio.

One grouping of tables is a science area with equipment ranging from magnets, mirrors, a prism, magnifying glasses, a microscope, a kaleidoscope, batteries, wires, an electric bell, to various natural objects (shells, seeds, feathers, bones and a bird's nest). Also on nearby shelves are a cage with gerbils, a turtle tank and plants grown by the children. Several other tables placed together and surrounded by chairs hold a great variety of math materials such as shaped blocks known as "geo blocks," combination locks and Cuisenaire rods, rulers and graph paper. A separate balance table contains four scales.

Walter Schneir and Miriam Schneir, journalists, describing an
open classroom at P.S. 84 in Manhattan, April 4, 1971, "The
Joy of Learning—in the Open Corridor," *p. 72.*

A child playing with a pendulum may be engaged in music by beating time with the swing, or in art by making interesting patterns with a sand pendulum, or in math by timing the frequency as a function of string length. But the pendulum is placed in the science corner because the adult, at least, sees it as having intrinsic "science" value. It is puzzling that open educators continue to organize their materials by academic subject when they see such distinctions as having no meaning for children. We are left with an important and, as yet, unanswered question: To what extent and in what ways is it appropriate for the adult to *order* the environment in which children are exploring and learning?

Roland S. Barth, professor of education, Harvard University,
1972, Open Education and the American School, *p. 54.*

Open educators assume that children learn by exploring living things, inanimate materials, and quite animate persons—in short, by exploring the real world in all its richness and variety. Learning is not distinguished from living, nor living from learning.

Knowledge is the goal of open education, and the teacher and school are important means of reaching this goal; but the meaning of knowledge is radically changed. Knowledge is the child's personal capacity to confront and handle new experiences successfully, not the ability to verbalize the adult-known on demand. Knowledge is a system of strategies and processes—intellectual, personal, social—which an individual develops for handling the world.

Roland S. Barth, professor of education, Harvard University,
1972, Open Education and the American School, *p. 56.*

I just want to let you know how *opposed* I am to your *forced* busing order, but opposed though we are, my husband and I are trying so hard to be law abiding and set a good example for our 6 children, 3 of whom attend the South Boston-Roxbury District. We have silently protested and aloud to each other, but never marched or felt violent or even angry about your decision, so on Sept. 12 my children all went to school even though they were frightened, and among the very few in South Boston who did so.

[But] I haven't sent my 3 older children since that first day, why—because I'm terrified 24 hours a day. Living if that's what you can call it in a nightmare, helicopters over head, police everywhere (for which I'm thankful), but which are constant reminders, people so full of hate, I never dreamed possible. I guess I'm quite a fool, I never thought a lot of people I see in church so often were so unchristian like, it truly hurts, and makes the job of being a parent so much harder.

A South Boston mother writing to Judge W. Arthur Garrity, Jr., September 23, 1974, in Ronald P. Formisano, Boston against Busing: Race, Class, and Ethnicity in the 1960s and 1970s, p. ix.

Regardless of the school system they are in, Navajo students find themselves in an environment controlled and dominated by non-Indians. Most of the teachers and administrators in reservation schools are Anglo. Public school boards of education are dominated by non-Indians and those few Indians who do serve wield little authority. Parent advisory boards are the [Bureau of Indian Affairs] school equivalent of a board of education; while these are all Indian, their function is only advisory and they are essentially powerless.

Navajos, in fact, have been excluded from the decision-making process in these school systems. The result has been a variety of education policies unrelated to the Navajo community. The Navajo language and culture have been largely ignored in the curriculum offered to Navajo students.

U.S. Commission on Civil Rights, 1975, The Navajo Nation: An American Colony, pp. 126–127.

We adhere to two basic principles with regard to the issue of busing to achieve racial balance. First, educational systems which separate students on the basis of race violate the Constitution and therefore are unacceptable. We believe that the court decisions ordering the modification of such discriminatory systems should and will be upheld as the law of the land, and that it is imperative to direct our energies into their smooth implementation rather than into resistance. Citizens have the right to seek judicial redress without fear of harassment or legal sanction; once a court has rendered a decision, however, the only right that remains is the choice between obeying that decision and suffering the consequences of contempt of court. Court-ordered balancing of the schools must be seen as a fact, not an option.

Second, the issues surrounding the busing of school children for racial balance cannot be viewed simplistically, nor can people who support or oppose that busing or the details of its implementation be stereotyped. It is all too easy for some people to mistake the means by which individuals' control over their environment is equalized for the goal that it be equalized. It is all too easy for some people to confuse neighborhood cohesiveness with racism, or to assert that black students are prone to crime. We believe it will be impossible to understand the issues which busing for racial balance

invokes as long as simplistic or stereotypical views are taken as truth.

The editors of the Harvard Educational Review, February 1975, "Busing for Racial Balance," p. 3.

In the furor over the mythical evils of school busing and the purported inviolability of neighborhood schools, many Americans have overlooked four essential points. School desegregation is a necessary, viable, and important national goal. The Constitution requires it. Minority children will never achieve equal educational opportunity without it. And our children will never learn to live together if they do not begin to learn together now.

Marian Wright Edelman, director of the Children's Defense Fund, November 1975, "Winson and Dovie Hudson's Dream," p. 417.

Brown addressed the constitutional rights of black school *children*. The vagaries of public and parental opinion, black and white, cannot be permitted any more than the vagaries of social science data to govern the fulfillment of rights. The very reason for having a Constitution in this country is to transcend the views of the moment.

Our history of segregation and slavery is replete with the lesson that in a society in which the majority rules, a minority can have no equal opportunity if it is separated and denied the right—even if some choose not to exercise it—to associate and share with those who control the instruments of power. Even if a quality education were provided for every child tomorrow, it would not solve the problem of racial segregation in public education.

Marian Wright Edelman, director of the Children's Defense Fund, November 1975, "Winson and Dovie Hudson's Dream," p. 449.

[A] definition [of mainstreaming] which has general acceptance is necessary if we are to communicate with a reasonable degree of effectiveness and efficiency. Unless we reach some such meeting of the minds, we can expect the examples which follow to be all too common.

First, some friends of mine sent an inquiry to superintendents of a group of residential schools for handicapped pupils to learn the nature and extent of their moves toward mainstreaming. One superintendent spoke proudly about the extensive mainstreaming being practiced. In fact, he was referring to two things: a weekly Boy Scout troop meeting after school which integrated several handicapped youngsters and a nearby church Sunday school also attended by some handicapped youngsters from the residential school.

Under police escort, school buses head toward South Boston High School on September 19, 1976, as the third year of court-ordered busing begins. *(The Boston Herald)*

Second, in the name of mainstreaming I have been shown educable mentally retarded pupils being scheduled to regular shop, home economics, music, physical education or art teachers, either as separate sections or individually in with other children. That kind of arrangement is certainly a precursor of mainstreaming but far from what it is today.

I have heard itinerant speech clinician service referred to as mainstreaming and itinerant instruction for partially seeing children renamed mainstreaming too. The same is true of various resource room programs for other groups of exceptional pupils.

Jack W. Birch, president of the Council for Exceptional Children, 1976, in Teacher, Please Don't Close the Door: The Exceptional Child in the Mainstream, *edited by June B. Jordan, p. 16.*

Educators must understand the culture of inner-city groups. This is not the same thing as recognizing the economic difficulties and general life conditions of the poor. Most informed people are cognizant of the "deprived" side of the picture.

It is natural enough for educators to stress the liabilities of the underprivileged. These are the things that the teacher is confronted with all the time. From the teacher's point of view, the inner-city child clearly is not happy in school, does not read well, appears unmotivated, is antagonistic to the teachers, possesses few well-formulated career plans. These are the things that are easiest to see, because they are on the surface. To see the strengths and positive struggles requires a deeper, more penetrating look.

Frank Riessman, social psychologist and founder of the National Self-Help Clearinghouse, 1976, The Inner-City Child, *p. 5.*

What is special about the educational problems of inner-city children is the prevailing ignorance of the children's strengths. An important factor here is the attitudes, as well as the knowledge, of teachers and other educational personnel. The most obviously destructive attitude is that "inner-city children are incapable of learning, so why bother even trying to teach them." A more benign version is that "since these children have so many environmental problems and so many difficulties in learning, we must not set educational standards, we must be easy on them." Both attitudes result in nonlearning and reveal a lack of awareness of the coping strengths of inner-city children, particularly their resiliency and their sensitivity to other people's attitudes. More important than specific techniques and programs is the need for all educational personnel to understand the strengths of the inner-city child and to build upon these strengths.

Frank Riessman, social psychologist and founder of the National Self-Help Clearinghouse, 1976, The Inner-City Child, *p. 125.*

Several weeks ago, our CLOSER LOOK program, which provides information to parents and other persons about education for handicapped children, received a letter from a young girl, a seventh or eighth grader, asking if we could help find a special school for a retarded girl in her class. The letter went on to express her grievances that the retarded girl was given too much of the teacher's attention and that she received good grades for work for which the others would have received poorer grades. In all, the writer felt that this retarded youngster should be put somewhere else, a suitable place.

Her letter, while clearly understandable from a young, maturing person, summarizes in one short page the major historical response of our schools and our culture to the needs of handicapped people. They are different. They are quite different at times from us but they are also part of us. They trouble us in deep, inexplicable, irrational ways, and we would like them somewhere else, not cruelly treated, of course, but out of sight and out of mind.

If, in advocating mainstreaming, we do not plan today for these societal patterns of response to the handicapped, we will be painfully naive; and I fear that we will subject many children to a painful and frustrating educational experience in the name of progress. We cannot deny that prejudice toward the handicapped does exist, and we must deal with that prejudice.

Edwin Martin, deputy commissioner of education and director, Bureau of Education for the Handicapped, U.S. Office of Education, 1977, "Integration of the Handicapped Child into Regular Schools," p. 3.

The choice before the nation is not whether its urban schools should be desegregated—that issue has been settled by the findings of unconstitutional segregation in most cities, judicial recognition of the right to desegregation, and insistence by civil rights groups on enforcing this right. The choice is whether we will integrate in a peaceful, beneficial, and lasting way. Although there can be many disagreements about particular strategies, it should not be difficult to make the choice once the issue is honestly faced.

Political leaders must choose between accepting a process of spreading segregation, punctuated by isolated and bitterly controversial court orders in a few cities each year, and devising a positive policy for school integration and the eventual creation of integrated communities. The limited reach of the courts and private civil rights groups means that public officials can easily find ways to delay desegregation, to make it harder, and to make it less successful. If they choose to work for integration, on the other hand, positive change can be promoted with targeted aid programs, with the provision of better research and technical assistance, with policies for integrated housing, and with procedures that incorporate major local participation in designing plans.

Gary Orfield, professor of education and social policy, Harvard University, 1978, Must We Bus? Segregated Schools and National Policy, *p. 454.*

CHAPTER TEN

The Learning Society
1980-2008

On May 7, 1980, the brand-new U.S. Department of Education took over the federal programs that had come under jurisdiction of the old Office of Education as well as various educational programs that had been the responsibility of other government departments. President Jimmy Carter, a Democrat, predicted that the new cabinet department would "profoundly transform the quality of education in our nation," and he appointed Shirley Mount Hufstedler, a judge of the Ninth Circuit of the U.S. Court of Appeals, to be the nation's first secretary of education.[1]

Carter lost the November 1980 presidential election to Republican Ronald Reagan, a conservative who was philosophically opposed to having a cabinet-level department devoted to education. Although Reagan cut funding for many social programs, determined as he was to lift the United States out of the severe economic recession that was eating away at Americans' morale and national pride, he took no steps to dismantle the Department of Education. Schooling nevertheless remained low on his list of concerns.

Reagan's first secretary of education, Terrel H. Bell, affirmed the worthiness of his department and made education a national priority by establishing a commission to survey teaching and learning in the United States and make recommendations for their improvement. In 1983, this group, the National Commission on Excellence in Education, issued its sobering report, *A Nation at Risk*, which catalogued a decline in scholastic performance. The commission reported that the average achievement of high school students on standardized tests was lower in 1983 than it was in 1957, when the launch of *Sputnik* by the Soviet Union led to efforts to improve academic outcomes in science and mathematics. On 19 academic tests administered in the 1970s, American youths trailed students from other industrialized countries and were last in seven instances. In addition, approximately 23 million adults and 13 percent of 17-year-olds were considered functionally illiterate, which meant they were unable to read, write, or compute well enough to perform such common tasks as filling out a job application, understanding road signs, following printed instructions for taking medicine, and using a train schedule. Among minority youth, the rate of functional illiteracy was as high as 40 percent. The list of shortcomings continued and included gifted students whose achievement fell short of their ability, a continued decline is Scholastic Aptitude Test (SAT) scores, an increase in remedial mathematics courses at colleges and universities, and millions of dollars spent by corporations and the military on classes and training programs to bring employees and recruits up to minimal standards of competency.

The report attributed these failings to "disturbing inadequacies in the way the educational process itself is often conducted" and focused on four aspects of this process—curriculum content, expectations for student effort and accomplishment, time devoted to school and independent study, and teaching—especially as they affected the teenage population.[2] Secondary school curriculums, the commission reported, had become "homogenized, diluted, and diffused," offering students a more extensive choice of courses but fewer stringent academic requirements than in the late 1960s.[3] As a result, small percentages of students enrolled in such moderately challenging classes as intermediate algebra and beginning French.

In its consideration of lowered expectations, the commission noted, among other deficiencies, a decrease in the amount of homework required of high school seniors and an overall rise in the grades they received, both coinciding with a drop in average student achievement. Institutions of higher learning were accommodating the decline, with 23 percent of the top colleges and universities acknowledging that they had become less selective in admissions, and 20 percent of four-year public colleges having to accept every high school graduate within the state, regardless of his or her grades or the curriculum completed.

American students devoted much less time to schoolwork than did students in other countries, the commission reported, and the time they did spend in the classroom or on homework was often used ineffectively. The low salaries paid to teachers—an average of $17,000 after 12 years of teaching—deterred many of the ablest college students from entering the field, and collegiate education curriculums contained too many courses in teaching methods and too few in the subjects to be taught. Shortages of high school mathematics, physics, and earth science teachers meant that unqualified men and women were often teaching these subjects.

The commission called for more stringent requirements for high school graduation and proposed that curriculums be founded on the "Five New Basics": four years of English, three years of mathematics, three years of science, three years of social studies, and one-half year of computer science.[4] This change would necessitate more time devoted to academic study through a longer school year, a longer school day, or more effective use of the existing school day. The commission members recommended more rigorous, measurable standards, such as grades that accurately reflected achievement and higher college admission requirements. They said that teachers needed to be adequately prepared to meet the new standards and to demonstrate an aptitude for teaching and competence in their academic discipline. Also, they stated that teachers' salaries needed to be raised.

The authors of *A Nation at Risk* urged that educational reform "focus on the goal of creating a Learning Society." As they explained, "At the heart of such a society is the commitment to a set of values and to a system of education that affords all members the opportunity to stretch their minds to full capacity, from early childhood through adulthood, learning more as the world itself changes. Such a society has as a basic foundation the idea that education is important not only because of what it contributes to one's career goals but also because of the value it adds to the general quality of one's life."[5]

Washington, D.C., public school students and their families take part in a field trip to the Smithsonian Institution's National Museum of Natural History on July 14, 2007. The trip was sponsored by Turning the Page, an organization that brings together schools, families, and the community to enrich the education of children in the District of Columbia. *(Turning the Page)*

The States Take Action

Like the *Sputnik* launch, *A Nation at Risk* awakened Americans to the need to improve their schools. With prosperity returning, states had money to invest in education, and they responded to the report by raising standards. They added to the academic requirements for high school graduation, assessed students' progress more often, attached hours to the school day or days to the school year, and made teachers meet stiffer requirements for recertification.

Some states considerably changed the way they educated their children and youth, but perhaps none did so with more success than California. In January 1983 the Golden State launched an enormous effort to raise educational standards and outcomes. The state legislature lengthened the school year by the equivalent of 17.3 school days and also established high school graduation requirements that included three years of English, three years of social studies, two years of science, two years of physical education, and one year of foreign language or courses in the visual or performing arts. At the same time, a dropout prevention and recovery program encouraged at-risk teens to remain in school and graduate, and it offered remedial classes to those who had left school. Curriculum frameworks for all grade levels stressed reading, writing, and problem solving, and the state used its considerable buying power to demand better textbooks from suppliers. California also honored its outstanding schools and teachers, strengthened its teachers' knowledge and skills through state-funded training and mentoring programs, and encouraged top students to become teachers.

In 1993, when 5.2 million girls and boys were enrolled in California's public schools, 20 percent had limited knowledge of English, and the system was accommodating 100,000 new students annually. Ten years had passed since the California Department of Education had instituted its reforms, and significant improvements could be measured. Ninety-six percent more high school students enrolled in physics than in 1983, 87 percent more studied chemistry, and 60 percent more took advanced mathematics classes. The number of seniors taking the SAT was up by 14,500, although there were fewer seniors overall. What was more, the high school dropout rate had decreased by more than 27 percent.

Most states measured little change in student performance, however. Although they had beefed up their curriculums in the 1980s, adding more classes in science and mathematics, the new courses often were remedial rather than advanced and far from intellectually challenging. To help state education departments institute standards that promoted academic excellence, Congress passed the Goals 2000: Educate America Act, which President Bill Clinton signed into law on March 31, 1994. This act set eight educational objectives for the nation to reach by 2000. Chief among them was having all children start school ready to learn; that is, in good health and possessing the academic and social knowledge and skills that would enable them to succeed. Also among the goals were having a high school graduation rate of 90 percent or more; requiring demonstrated mastery of challenging academic material by all children progressing from grades four, eight, and 12; surpassing all other countries in achievement in science and mathematics; achieving 100 percent adult literacy; keeping schools free of drugs, violence, and guns; giving all teachers access to continuing education; and increasing parental involvement in children's education. The act provided for states that developed improvement plans to apply for grants, and it established the National Education Standards and Improvement Council to review and certify any standards for curriculum content or voluntary standards for student performance that might be developed at the national level, and to certify content or performance standards that states might wish to submit.

Clinton and his vice president, Al Gore, encouraged the use of computer technology in education. The Clinton administration erected four pillars, or foundations, of technology in education that included making up-to-date computers available to every student, creating electronic connections among classrooms and with the larger world, incorporating educational software in academic instruction, and preparing teachers to instruct with technology. In 1996, through the Technology Literacy Challenge Fund, the federal government allocated $2 billion for five-year grants to schools for computer technology.

In 1981, there was one computer in U.S. schools for every 125 students. In 1991, the year before Clinton was elected, there was one computer for every 18 students, and in 2000 the ratio had narrowed to one computer for every five students. By then, U.S. elementary and secondary schools were spending more than

$5.5 billion per year, or $119 per student, on computer equipment, the hardwiring of buildings, and technical support.

Leaving No Child Behind

Congress reauthorized the Elementary and Secondary Education Act in 1994, calling it the Improving America's Schools Act and linking aid provided to schools in disadvantaged areas under Title I to efforts to meet the standards set in Goals 2000. In 2001, with the goals unmet, Congress reauthorized the act again and renamed it No Child Left Behind (NCLB). Signed by President George W. Bush on January 8, 2002, this new incarnation of the federal education law called for all students in the nation's public schools to attain their optimal level of academic proficiency by 2014 (a goal that many educators consider impossible), and it held schools and state departments of education accountable for students' progress. Each state had to develop and put into use a system of tests to measure improvement in reading and mathematics in children in grades three through eight. The information gathered in this way formed the basis of annual reports on school performance and statewide progress.

Under NCLB, state officials had the authority to honor schools that met or exceeded their yearly improvement goals with academic achievement awards; they also had the obligation to step in and provide technical assistance to any school that

President George W. Bush signs the No Child Left Behind Act at Hamilton High School, Hamilton, Ohio, on January 8, 2002. Among those with the president are Representative George Miller of California, Senator Edward Kennedy of Massachusetts, and Representative John Boehner of Ohio. *(U.S. Department of Education Archives)*

Volunteers from Howard University read with children during a Community Night sponsored by Turning the Page in winter 2007. *(Turning the Page)*

continuously performed below expectations. Some state departments of education even had the power to take over poorly performing schools. In 2003, 8,600 U.S. schools were deemed in need of improvement by state departments of education following NCLB guidelines. This number equaled less that 10 percent of U.S. public schools.

On June 12, 2007, Mayor Adrian M. Fenty took control of the Washington, D.C., schools, with the goal of turning around one of the worst-performing systems in the nation. The public school system in the nation's capital, a city with a 40-percent functional illiteracy rate among the adult population, was notorious for deplorable student performance, deteriorating schools, and gun violence.

NCLB tripled federal funding for reading instruction, raising it from $300 million in 2001 to $900 million in 2002, and it linked this funding to the use of proven, established teaching methods. The act also contained provisions aimed at promoting facility in English among students with limited proficiency and improving the quality of learning by placing a qualified teacher in every classroom.

Finding and keeping qualified teachers has become a growing problem, however, especially in impoverished communities. Not only are teachers born in the baby-boom years starting to retire, but also new teachers are leaving the profession in record numbers. In 2007, nearly one-third of new teachers were seeking other lines of work within three years, and half were departing within five years. With teaching positions hard to fill, hundreds of school districts began offering cash bonuses to teachers willing to take jobs in low-performing schools. In 2007, the New York City school system—the nation's largest—offered $5,000 toward a housing down payment to any teacher certified in mathematics, science, or special education who accepted a position. Los Angeles, with the second-largest system, offered $5,000 to any teacher recruited for a low-performing school. Annually, U.S. schools spend $7 billion to recruit and hire teachers.

Unwilling to see any student trapped in a failing or poorly performing school and therefore held back academically, through NCLB the nation's lawmakers offered options to these children and their parents. One was supplemental services: Federal money given to the school under the provisions of Title I (funds made available because a significant portion of the student body was economically disadvantaged) could be used to pay for tutoring, after-school instruction, or summer-school programs. Another was school choice: As soon as a school was identified as failing, students had the right to transfer to a better-performing public school. In 2003, 15 percent of students in grades one through 12 attended a public school selected by their parents rather than the one to which they had been assigned, many because NCLB had made it possible to do so. This figure was up from 11 percent in 1993.

Choosing Charter Schools

To encourage innovation in public education and better responsiveness to students' needs, many states allow parents, teachers, and others to establish new schools or make over existing ones. States hold these institutions, known as charter schools, to the same standards for student progress as traditional public schools, and require them to hire teachers who meet state certification requirements. Charter schools have greater freedom, however, in deciding how to meet the goals mandated by law.

Charter schools exhibit great variety. The Princeton Charter School, in Princeton, New Jersey, groups children in small classes and emphasizes "drill and skill," requiring pupils to master a challenging body of knowledge.[6] Nueva Esperanza Academy, a charter high school serving a poor Latino community of north Philadelphia, offers classes taught in English but requires all students to study Spanish. It aims to prepare "critically thinking, socially capable, spiritually sensitive and culturally aware young adults who can use English, Spanish and technology as tools for success in the 21st century."[7]

Charter schools can be grass-roots ventures overseen by parents and community members, or they can be operated under contract by education management organizations such as Edison Schools, a profit-making company founded in 1992, or American Quality Schools, a not-for-profit agency running charter schools in the Midwest.

In 1992 Minnesota became the first state to allow dollars earmarked for education to be used in support of charter schools; by 2005 more than 3,400 of these schools were up and running throughout the United States. Many serve inner-city communities with large minority populations, but others have set up shop in rural places where most of the children are white. Urban or rural, these schools tended to serve low-income populations. In 2002, nearly 70 percent of charter school students in two states, Illinois and Ohio, came from families with incomes that fell below the federal poverty level. At the same time, 30 percent of students in the traditional public schools of these two states came from low-income families. Charter schools have proliferated in New Orleans since August 2005, when Hurricane Katrina flooded the city and damaged or destroyed many schools and their resources. Fifty-five charter schools were scheduled to open their doors in New Orleans in 2007.

Charter schools frequently fail to fulfill their promise. Eleven of the 23 charter schools educating children in another state, Maryland, during the 2006–07 academic year fell short of federal standards. Three in Baltimore, a city with a struggling public school system, received failing grades for the second year in a row, which put their charters at risk of being revoked. Nevertheless, nine new charter schools opened in Maryland in fall 2007, including six in Baltimore. In neighboring Washington, D.C., nearly one-fourth of the city's 75,000 public school students attended 55 charter schools in 2007.

The fact that parents choose to send their children to a charter school—and can choose to withdraw them—is thought to be a strong incentive for success. Limited data on the effectiveness of charter schools have been gathered, but a study published in 2005 of students in Chicago charter schools measured significant increases in reading and mathematics test scores. Also, the children in attendance and their parents generally report satisfaction with their school choice. Three-fifths of charter school students participating in a 1997 survey responded that they preferred their teachers to those in their old schools, and half found their schoolwork more interesting. The parents polled expressed happiness with their children's class size, the quality of instruction, the curriculum content, expectations for academic achievement, and the approach to discipline.

Opponents of charter schools assert that they siphon resources and support from public schools and that they contribute to racial and ethnic segregation. Critics also point out that private companies operating charter schools need to make a profit and might therefore trim costs by hiring nonunion teachers, substituting computer exercises for human instruction, or eliminating services.

Public Funds for Private Education

Some states and municipalities, including Florida, Colorado, Milwaukee, and Cleveland, experimented with voucher programs in the late 20th and early 21st centuries. Vouchers are grants provided by a state or local government that permit students from poorly performing schools in low-income areas to attend private or parochial schools.

In January 2004, President Bush signed legislation creating the first federally funded voucher program, targeting children in Washington, D.C. In this five-year trial that began in fall 2004, approximately 1,700 low-income students living in the District of Columbia each receive up to $7,500 a year to attend a private or parochial school.

Vouchers, like charter schools, have stirred up controversy: Proponents expect them to act as a catalyst for public school improvement, and opponents point out that vouchers help a relatively small number of students and divert money away from public education—money that could have supported measures to benefit larger numbers of students, such as reduced class size and dropout-prevention programs. The latter group predicted that rather than spurring improvement, vouchers would weaken public schools.

As is the case for charter schools, little data have been collected on the effectiveness of voucher programs. It is known that children using vouchers to attend private schools tend to show improvements in behavior, and they are more likely to complete their education than are students remaining in poorly performing public schools. Also, the children's parents report greater satisfaction with the private schools. Yet voucher programs have proven to be less popular than their supporters expected them to be. A typical experience is that of the largest voucher program in the United States, the Milwaukee Parental Choice Program, which provided for 15,000 children to receive vouchers to attend private or parochial schools during the 2002–03 academic year; fewer than 11,000 took part in the program. Vouchers have, however, benefited many traditionally white private schools by making them more racially and ethnically diverse.

The Home-Schooling Movement

A growing number of parents have elected to bypass public, charter, and private schools and educate their children at home. The U.S. Department of Education counted 850,000 home-schooled students in the United States in 1999 and 1.1 million in 2003, with the latter figure representing 2.2 percent of the student population. The number of home-schooled children in the kindergarten-through-grade-12 age range has been predicted to reach 3 million by 2010.

Parents take this step for a variety of reasons that range from a child's special learning needs to transportation obstacles. Many think they can provide a better education than the available schools, which they may perceive as fostering a poor learning environment or failing to offer challenging material, and many others want their children to have an education in keeping with the family's religious or moral beliefs. The exposure to drugs, precocious sexuality, bullying, and negative peer pressure that a large number of home-schooling parents consider part of school attendance are also strong motivators.

Home-school students in Maryland participate in a 1997 archaeological dig. *(Kimberley A. Reef)*

People's reasons for home schooling vary, and so do their approaches. Lessons can be traditional, with children seated at desks and using textbooks to complete formal assignments for grading, or unstructured, with youngsters following their own interests and parents giving minimal guidance. Approximately half of home-schooling families surveyed by the U.S. Department of Education in 2003 relied on prepared curriculums. Many also benefited from community resources, such as libraries, museums, science or nature centers, and home-schooling cooperatives.

Every state has laws governing home schooling. Some are as lenient as Idaho, which merely requires home-schooled children between the ages of seven and 16 to meet the state's attendance and curriculum requirements. Others, such as New York, have enacted a long list of regulations. New York State requires home-schooling parents to file an annual notice of intent, maintain an attendance record that is subject to inspection by state authorities, submit detailed progress reports four times a year, and file the results of annual standardized achievement tests demonstrating satisfactory progress.

Detractors have said that home schooling shortchanges children academically and that young people educated in this way miss out on the social interaction and exposure to differing points of view that going to school provides. They have said as well that home-schooled children are being denied their rights—or, conversely, that they are being given an unfair advantage. Studies have shown that the home schooled as a group perform well on standardized tests, and their parents frequently seek opportunities for them to interact socially with other youngsters.

On February 28, 2008, the California Second District Court of Appeal ruled that parents or tutors must be certified by the state to educate children at home. The three-judge panel based its ruling on a rarely enforced state law. California, the state with the most home-schooled students, held off on enforcing the ruling, pending appeals, but educational policy experts predicted that if the California supreme court declined to strike it down, then other states might follow the example set by this large and influential state and impose stricter regulation of home schooling.

Meanwhile, home-schooled students are seeking higher education in growing numbers, and colleges and universities are developing admissions policies for applicants who lack some of the usual criteria, such as transcripts. To determine whether these applicants are prepared for college, between 1998 and 2000, researchers from Georgia College and State University and Colorado State University compared first-year, degree-seeking home-schooled students at four-year public colleges and universities in Colorado with a random sample of freshmen graduated from traditional high schools. After matching the students by gender, race, ethnicity, and entrance-examination scores, the investigators found that the home schooled had higher grade-point averages and earned more credits in their first year, although the differences were too small to be statistically significant. "The academic performance analyses indicate that home school graduates are as ready for college as traditional high school graduates," the researchers concluded.[8]

Progress toward Inclusion

In 1997, Congress extended the life of the special-education law, whose new name, the Individuals with Disabilities Education Act (IDEA), reflected current preferences in terminology. The number of children determined to have disabilities was increasing, for several reasons. Methods of assessment had become more accurate;

disabilities were being diagnosed earlier; the number of children with autism was rising sharply, because of improved diagnosis or undetermined environmental factors; and definitions of learning disabilities had been broadened. By 2003, approximately half of children receiving special education services had learning disabilities. They were among the 6.2 million students, or 13 percent of schoolchildren, considered to have disabilities. This total represented an increase of 68 percent since the mid-1970s.

In many cases, a team of specialists works with disabled children in the classroom to ensure that their varied learning needs are met. The cost of special education depends on the nature of a child's disability and the services provided, but generally special education is twice as expensive as schooling for the nondisabled. Whether children with disabilities learn better in regular classrooms remains to be determined, but those who are included in regular classes are more likely than the graduates of special education to live on their own and hold jobs in adult life. Inclusion also alleviates some of the perceived negative aspects of special education, namely the possibility that teachers and principals might seek to have disruptive or failing students declared disabled in order to remove them from the classroom, and the stigma attached to children labeled abnormal or less able.

By 2004, more than 95 percent of children with physical, emotional, cognitive, or learning disabilities or impaired hearing or sight spent part or all of the school day in a regular classroom. The one group that generally has preferred separate, rather than inclusive, education is the deaf. Many deaf Americans consider themselves not disabled but rather members of a unique culture that employs its own means of communication, American Sign Language. Activists have worked toward having deaf students educated within this culture by deaf teachers employing their own language.

A Gap in Measured Achievement

At the start of the 21st century, the "achievement gap," the discrepancy in measured academic accomplishment between minority and economically disadvantaged students and their white counterparts, appeared to be decreasing. Nevertheless, according to information gathered with the National Assessment of Educational Progress, an instrument used by the U.S. Department of Education to measure subject-matter achievement in groups of students, in 2004, African-American and Hispanic 17-year-olds were performing at the level of white 13-year-olds in reading and mathematics, on average. In the same year, the dropout rate among urban African-American and Hispanic high school students was higher than 50 percent.

Keeping at-risk students in school through graduation remains a challenge to educators. In 2008, researchers at Rice University and the University of Texas at Austin released the results of a study demonstrating that the emphasis on accountability at the foundation of NCLB contributes to lower graduation rates. Tracking 271,000 students in Texas's public high schools, the researchers measured decreases in numbers of graduating students as school officials became accountable for academic performance. The dropouts included disproportionate numbers of African Americans, Latinos, and students speaking English as a second language. The researchers speculated that low-performing students became a liability to school administrators trying to raise average scores on standardized tests.

Corporate leaders and others are addressing the high school dropout crisis. In 2008, the AT&T Foundation (the philanthropic branch of the AT&T Corporation) pledged $100 million in grants to schools and nonprofit organizations working to keep students in school. The foundation also instituted a shadow program, permitting 100,000 students to visit the workplace and see for themselves the skills they will need for employment.

By 2007, Head Start, the school-readiness program for preschool children from economically disadvantaged families that was launched during Lyndon B. Johnson's presidency, had been educating children for more than 40 years—long enough for its effects to be measured. Most studies of Head Start children showed an initial rise in test scores as a result of the program, but any advantage gained disappeared after the children had spent several years in school. The cause of this discouraging finding is unknown, but under the administration of George W. Bush, Head Start was restructured to emphasize early reading and mathematical skills. The president and his advisors believed that with the availability of Medicaid, food stamps, and child nutrition programs, it was less important for Head Start to focus on health and nourishment than it had been in 1964, when the program was created.

Head Start enrolls children ages three to five, with most three and four years of age. Early Head Start, a program begun in 1995, works with children from birth through age three, in the belief that earlier intervention might yield better results. In 2006, Head Start programs educated 909,201 children in 18,875 locations nationwide, at a cost of $7,209 per child.

Schools Become More Segregated

It was becoming evident, as the new century began, that some of the progress made toward school integration had eroded. On January 21, 2003, the Civil Rights Project at Harvard University reported that the majority of African-American and Hispanic students attended schools at which most of the students belonged to minority groups, and the majority of white students attended schools that were predominantly white. In one state, New York, only 13.3 percent of Hispanic students and 13.6 percent of African-American students attended schools in which more than half the students were white.

In 1992, the U.S. Supreme Court ruled in the case *Freeman v. Pitts* that the purpose of court-supervised desegregation was to correct violations of the law. Once a district had done everything practicable to erase the effects of *de jure* segregation, then it could be released from judicial oversight. This ruling had the effect of returning to state and local authorities control of schools in districts that were in compliance with the Constitution; it affected the schools of Miami, Mobile, Denver, Buffalo, Cleveland, Minneapolis, Boston, and other large cities. Many of these districts subsequently chose to assign students to neighborhood schools, which resulted in greater segregation.

Of course, the flight of white city residents to suburbs in response to court-ordered desegregation had made integrated schooling less achievable than in earlier decades. In 2003, with more than one-third of African-American children living in large cities, the majority of students enrolled in the public schools of Chicago,

Philadelphia, Baltimore, Atlanta, Washington, D.C., and other cities were African American, and many of the rest were Hispanic. In contrast, most towns and cities with fewer than 100,000 people were more than 90 percent white.

At the same time, minority groups accounted for an increasing segment of the student population. Forty-three percent of public school students belonged to ethnic or racial minorities in 2004. The percentage had nearly doubled since 1972, when 23 percent of students fell into this category. The concentration differed according to region and was highest in the West, where minority enrollment was 57 percent of the total. The growth of the Hispanic population led to much of this increase and to the enormous rise in the number of children ages five to 17 who speak a language other than English at home. This figure nearly tripled between 1979 and 2004, rising from 3.8 million to 9.9 million.

During the 1990s, many Americans reconsidered the need for affirmative action in higher education and the fairness of using different criteria to evaluate white and minority students. In 1995, the regents of the University of California voted to end affirmative action on all campuses within the system. California's electorate endorsed the new policy in 1996 by narrowly passing Proposition 209, which prohibited any agency of the state government, including the university system, from considering race in employment, education, or contracting. The college-admission ban became effective in 1997 and had a significant impact on the racial and ethnic makeup of the student population. For example, the number of students who were African American, Latino, or Native American declined 61 percent on the Berkeley campus and 36 percent on the Los Angeles campus.

In 1998, voters in Washington State, thinking along the same lines as the California regents, passed Initiative 200, banning the state and local governments from using affirmative action in higher education, hiring, and contracting. The effect on education was immediate: The freshman class at the University of Washington included 40 percent fewer African Americans and 30 percent fewer Hispanics in 1999 than in the previous year.

In 2001, California pioneered a method for increasing minority enrollment while adhering to academic criteria. The board of regents voted to guarantee admission to the state university system to students in the top 4 percent of the graduating class of each high school in the state, based on grades in university-required courses. Students falling between the top 4 percent and 12.5 percent would be deemed eligible to attend a state university once they completed two years at a community college. Said University of California president Richard C. Atkinson, the new system "sends a signal to top-performing students, particularly those in disadvantaged high schools, that they have a clear path to a UC degree."[9]

The U.S. Supreme Court weighed in again on affirmative action in 2003, in its opinions in two cases concerning admission practices at the University of Michigan. In *Grutter v. Bollinger,* the court decided that the University of Michigan Law School could consider race in admissions to diversify its student body, because doing so enriched the learning experience for all students and brought differing perspectives to the legal profession. In *Gratz v. Bollinger,* however, the court ruled that the university's undergraduate College of Literature, Science, and Arts could not systematically add points to the applications of minority candidates to give them an advantage.

Over time, affirmative action improved the racial balance at U.S. colleges and universities, despite the controversy. In 1965, 4.8 percent of undergraduates were

African American. In 1998, 11 percent were African American, and 9 percent were Hispanic.

American Indian Students Face Challenges

Native Americans remain one of the most disadvantaged population groups in terms of educational achievement. In 1988, the dropout rate among American Indian high school students was 29 percent overall and slightly higher for girls. More than half of Indian students in elementary and secondary schools—65 percent—had poor attendance records.

In that year, the Bureau of Indian Affairs (BIA) created a profile of Indian students that helped explain the challenges these youngsters faced. Indian students frequently came from families with one parent or none living in the home, the bureau reported. Because English was a second language on many reservations, a significant number of Indian students lived in homes in which no English was spoken. Indian children had the highest incidence of disability in the United States. Their families were disproportionately poor, and their parents generally had little education themselves and offered the children minimal encouragement to do well in school. In addition, many Indian students lived with the home and community stressors that commonly affected impoverished young people of all racial and ethnic backgrounds, including alcohol and drug abuse, crime, and gang activity.

Too Many Illiterate Adults

Functional illiteracy remained a significant problem in the United States at the start of the 21st century. In 2003, an estimated 30 million Americans, or 14 percent of adults, were operating at the lowest level of literacy in English, as measured by the National Assessment of Adult Literacy, a survey administered to people age 16 and older by the National Center for Education Statistics.

The total included 61 percent of foreign-born residents between the ages of 16 and 65, which meant that immigration contributed significantly to the high level of adult illiteracy in English. It must be kept in mind, however, that many of these adults were literate in other languages. The 2000 U.S. Census counted 31.1 million immigrants in the United States, and one-third of these had arrived after 1990. Immigrants in the 16-to-65 age group typically had less formal education than U.S.-born adults. Yet many demonstrated a strong desire to improve their employability, prepare for citizenship, and help their children succeed in school by participating in adult literacy programs or preparing for and taking the General Educational Development (GED) test series, which was developed by the American Council on Education. A GED credential can be considered the equivalent of a high school diploma for employment or acceptance into some postsecondary educational programs.

Student mobility was also associated with adult illiteracy. More than half the students enrolled in U.S. schools at the start of the 21st century would make at least one unscheduled change of schools between grades one and 12, but those who changed schools frequently tended to be from poor, inner-city families. These mobile students demonstrated low levels of achievement and were at increased risk of dropping out of school before graduation or being pushed out by schools attempting to reduce their failure rates.

Author Eloise Greenfield speaks to children and parents at Kenilworth Elementary School in the District of Columbia, on February 28, 2007, as part of a Community Night sponsored by Turning the Page. *(Turning the Page)*

A low level of literacy also was associated with incarceration. In 2003, seven out of 10 people in U.S. prisons were functionally illiterate or able to read only at a fourth-grade level. Of men and women entering correctional facilities, only 30 percent had a high school diploma, and 14 percent had never been to high school. Among those who left prison, recidivism was lower for individuals who had improved their reading skills while behind bars.

Education and Employment

Poor academic preparedness has coincided with a shortage of qualified workers in recent years. In 2001, the American Management Association reported that in 1,627 companies surveyed, 43.1 percent of applicants fell short of the level of literacy needed for the jobs they sought. Eighty-five percent of the firms declined to employ these unqualified applicants, but the rest either allowed them to reapply and demonstrate improved skills at a later date or hired them and gave remedial training. In 2003, half of all Fortune 500 companies paid to educate employees in basic skills at a collective cost of $300 million for the year.

In 2005, Alan Greenspan, then chairman of the Federal Reserve, attributed the "income gap," the growing disparity in income between the nation's highest earners and workers at the middle and bottom of the pay scale, to differing levels of education and skill development. Total reported income in the United States increased nearly 9 percent in 2005, but the top 1 percent of earners—those with incomes of $348,000 or more—realized a gain of 14 percent. For the bottom 90 percent of workers, incomes dropped 0.6 percent, on average. This happened in part because people entering the job market without needed skills were competing for a shrinking number of jobs requiring minimal levels of ability and driving down wages in these occupations. At the same time, shortages of qualified workers drove up salaries in such specialized fields as information technology, health care, research, and corporate management, which increasingly require a strong educational background in science and mathematics. "I think it's a very disturbing trend," Greenspan said. "It is a reflection, as best I can judge, of a faulty educational system in the United States."[10]

The greater demand for workers with postsecondary degrees, coupled with a rise in the college-age population, led to a record enrollment in U.S. colleges and universities of 17.5 million in fall 2005. The U.S. Department of Education forecast that the number of postsecondary students would continue to grow, at least through 2015. According to the U.S. Census Bureau, the proportion of adults with bachelor's degrees rose from 24 percent in 1995 to 28 percent in 2005. The proportion of Americans age 25 and older who had earned a high school diploma or its equivalent rose from 82 percent to 85 percent over the same period. With more than half of two- and four-year institutions offering courses of study online and thus enabling people to learn at home, continuing education became possible for many adults.

Ever Learning

Americans continue to learn, as individuals and as a nation. Throughout their history, they have shared knowledge with the aims of forging a cohesive cultural group and equipping one another with the necessary skills to participate fully in society. Some efforts have been clumsy, some have been deplorable, and some have met with success.

The Learning Society that the National Commission on Excellence in Education defined in 1983—the society that strives to help every person realize his or her potential—has existed for more than 200 years. The educational system through which Americans have pursued this aim has evolved through trial and error, in response to research, or as a reflection of the prevailing social climate.

It is impossible to predict educational trends, to know whether the conservatism and back-to-basics approach of the early 21st century will yield one day to openness and experimentation reminiscent of the late 1960s and early 1970s; similarly, it cannot be known whether a major war or other emergency will require new approaches to teaching and learning and possibly lead to innovation. What is certain is that the American people will remain committed to meeting the educational needs of all.

Chronicle of Events

1980
- *May 7:* The U.S. Department of Education begins operations.
- *November:* Ronald Reagan defeats the incumbent, Jimmy Carter, in the presidential election.

1981
- There is one computer in U.S. schools for every 125 students.

1983
- The National Commission on Excellence in Education issues *A Nation at Risk,* a report documenting a decline in educational performance in the United States.

- *January:* California launches an ambitious initiative to raise educational standards and outcomes within the state.

1988
- Twenty-nine percent of American Indian students drop out of high school.
- According to the Bureau of Indian Affairs, many Indian students face challenges that include living apart from one or both parents, speaking English as a second language, having an increased likelihood of disability, and enduring poverty and its accompanying stressors.

1991
- There is one computer in U.S. schools for every 18 students.

Public school chorus members from Maryland and the District of Columbia rehearse for the 1989 Kennedy Center Honors program. *(John Reef)*

1992

- Minnesota is the first state to permit state support of charter schools.
- Edison Schools, a for-profit company that manages charter schools, is founded.
- The U.S. Supreme Court ruling in *Freeman v. Pitts* releases school districts in a number of large cities from judicial supervision of desegregation efforts.

1993

- Twenty percent of the 5.2 million students in California's public schools have limited knowledge of English.
- One hundred thousand students are entering the California public schools annually.
- In California, 96 percent more high school students take physics than in 1983, 87 percent more take chemistry, and 60 percent more take advanced mathematics.
- The number of seniors taking the SATs in California has increased by 14,500 since 1983.
- California's high school dropout rate has dropped by more than 27 percent since 1983.
- Nationwide, 11 percent of students in grades one through 12 attend public schools selected by their parents.

1994

- Congress reauthorizes the Elementary and Secondary Education Act, calling it the Improving America's Schools Act.
- *March 31:* President Bill Clinton signs the Goals 2000: Educate America Act.

1995

- Early Head Start is established to work with children from birth through age three.
- The regents of the University of California system vote to end affirmative action on all campuses.
- Twenty-four percent of adults in the United States have bachelor's degrees.

1996

- The federal government makes available $2 billion for computer technology in schools.
- California voters pass Proposition 209, prohibiting any state agency from considering race in employment, education, or contracting.

1997

- Three-fifths of charter school students surveyed report satisfaction with their teachers and schoolwork.

- The federal special-education law is reauthorized as the Individuals with Disabilities Act.
- The numbers of African-American, Latino, and Native American students entering the University of California at Berkeley and at Los Angeles decline 61 percent and 36 percent, respectively.

1998

- Washington State voters pass Initiative 200, barring the state and local governments from using affirmative action in higher education, hiring, and contracting.
- Eleven percent of undergraduates at U.S. colleges and universities are African American, and 9 percent are Hispanic.

1998–2000

- Home-schooled freshmen entering four-year public colleges and universities in Colorado perform as well academically as graduates of traditional high schools.

1999

- Approximately 850,000 students are home schooled in the United States.
- The freshman class at the University of Washington includes 40 percent fewer African Americans and 30 percent fewer Hispanics than in 1998.

2000

- There is one computer in U.S. schools for every five students.
- U.S. schools spend more than $5.5 billion, or $119 per student, on computer equipment, hardwiring of buildings, and technical support.
- Of the 31.1 million immigrants in the United States, one-third arrived after 1990.

2001

- California's board of regents guarantees admission to the state university system to the top 4 percent of all high school graduating classes in the state and eligibility to attend a state university after completing two years at a community college to the top 4 percent to 12.5 percent.
- In 1,627 companies surveyed by the American Management Association, 43.1 percent of applicants lack the level of literacy needed to perform their desired job.

2002

- In Illinois and Ohio, nearly 70 percent of charter school students and 30 percent of traditional public school students are from families with incomes falling below the poverty line.

- *January 8:* President George W. Bush signs the No Child Left Behind Act (NCLB), legislation intended to improve the performance of students and schools and to give alternatives to students in failing schools. NCLB increases federal funding for reading instruction from $300 million in 2001 to $900 million in 2002.

2002–2003
- The Milwaukee Parental Choice program provides for 15,000 children to receive school vouchers; fewer than 11,000 participate.

2003
- In this year, 8,600 schools are deemed in need of improvement, according to NCLB guidelines.
- Fifteen percent of students in grades one through 12 attend public schools selected by their parents.
- Approximately 1.1 million students are home schooled in the United States. Half their families employ prepared curriculums.
- About 6.2 million students, or 13 percent of schoolchildren, are determined to have disabilities; half of these have learning disabilities.
- More than one-third of African-American children live in large cities.
- Most towns and cities with fewer that 100,000 people are more than 90 percent white.
- In New York State, 13.3 percent of Hispanic students and 13.6 percent of African-American students attend schools whose enrollments are more than half white.
- In the case *Grutter v. Bollinger,* the U.S. Supreme Court rules that the University of Michigan Law School may consider race in admissions in order to ensure a diverse student body.
- In the case *Gratz v. Bollinger,* the U.S. Supreme Court decides that the College of Literature, Science, and Arts at the University of Michigan may not weight applications from minority students.
- Approximately 30 million U.S. adults operate at the lowest level of literacy in English.
- Seven out of 10 U.S. prisoners are functionally illiterate or able to read at a fourth-grade level.
- Thirty percent of people entering U.S. correctional facilities have a high school diploma; 14 percent have never been to high school.
- Half of Fortune 500 companies pay to educate employees in basic skills.

- *January 21:* The Civil Rights project at Harvard University reports that most African-American and Hispanic students attend schools whose enrollments are largely minority; most white students attend predominantly white schools.

2004
- More than 95 percent of children with disabilities spend all or part of the school day in a regular classroom.
- According to the results of the National Assessment of Educational Progress, African-American and Hispanic 17-year-olds are performing academically at the level of white 13-year-olds.
- Forty-three percent of public school students nationwide, and 57 percent in the West, belong to racial or ethnic minority groups.
- Some 9.9 million children ages five through 17 speak a language other than English at home.
- *January:* Bush creates the first federally funded school voucher program, for children in Washington, D.C.
- *fall:* About 1,700 low-income children in the District of Columbia receive up to $7,500 per year to attend a private or parochial school.

2005
- More than 3,400 charter schools are operating throughout the United States.
- Alan Greenspan, chairman of the Federal Reserve, attributes the growing income gap to disparities in education.
- Total reported income in the United States increases 9 percent; it increases 14 percent for the top 1 percent of earners and decreases 0.6 percent for the bottom 90 percent.
- Twenty-eight percent of adults in the United States have bachelor's degrees.
- *fall:* A record 17.5 million people are enrolled in U.S. colleges and universities.

2006
- Head Start programs educate 909,201 children in 18,875 locations, at a cost of $7,209 per child.

2006–07
- Eleven of 23 charter schools in Maryland fail to meet federal standards; three in Baltimore fall short for the second year in a row.

Uniforms may change, but the game remains the same: Two St. Albans School pitchers throw for their team, the Bulldogs. Pictured here are Jimmie Trimble (class of 1943) and Danny Hultzen (class of 2008). *(St. Albans School)*

2007

- Nine new charter schools, including six in Baltimore, open in Maryland.
- One-fourth of the 75,000 public school students in the District of Columbia attend the city's 55 charter schools.
- Fifty-five charter schools are scheduled to open in New Orleans.
- Nearly one-third of new teachers quit the profession within three years, and half leave within five years.
- New York City offers $5,000 toward a housing down payment to newly employed teachers certified in mathematics, science, or special education; Los Angeles offers a $5,000 bonus to teachers hired for low-performing schools.

- U.S. schools spend $7 billion to recruit and hire teachers.
- *June 12:* Mayor Adrian M. Fenty takes over the Washington, D.C., school system.

2008

- Researchers from two Texas universities find a link between holding schools responsible for students' academic performance and decreased graduation rates.
- The AT&T Foundation commits $100 million to efforts aimed at keeping students in school.
- *February 28:* California's Second District Court of Appeals decides that parents wanting to home school their children must possess a teaching credential.

Eyewitness Testimony

There is no blackboard jungle in Alex Costea's school-house. No one-way staircase to readily explain the stress. The daily tensions, which hunch the shoulders of this high school English teacher, are not so dramatic. But they sometimes churn his stomach nonetheless.

"Right now I need a hammer and a wedge to start pounding on something," jokes Costea to the first of his five classes at Arlington [Virginia]'s Washington-Lee High School after a 12th grader has asked a 4th grade question. "You'd think some of this stuff would have rubbed off."

Behold the conscientious teacher. After 28 years in the "education game," after 40 zillion incomplete sentences, misplaced commas and mangled verbs, Alex Costea, Doctor of Education, still teaches with enthusiasm. Successes, however small, are celebrated. But failures are also mourned. And the sum of those, he acknowledges, coupled with the sad economic reality of his profession, have taken their toll on the doctor.

"Sometimes the chore really becomes a chore," says the 53-year-old Costea. . . . "I'd like to retire as soon as I possibly can."

Denis Collins, Washington Post *staff writer, April 20, 1980, "The Beleaguered Teacher: Flare-Ups and Burnouts," p. 15.*

[P]ublic education in a democratic society must proceed from a common core of educational experiences for all children that will satisfy the requirements for a democratic education. Among the goals of the common core ought to be the provision of equal and appropriate educational opportunities for all children; exposure to ideas, values, political views, and individuals from backgrounds and cultures other than their own; fulfillment of basic requirements in a common language; familiarity with major technological issues; capability in numerical calculations and in reasoning; understanding of our system of government and the rights and responsibilities of individuals; and access to training opportunities for careers. . . . Given that schools are organized to produce these outcomes and the social benefits that should ensue from the common core, there is surely a substantial domain for educational choice within such a framework. It is only when individual and family choice in education undermines this common core and leads to social balkanization and privilege that it becomes injurious to the public interest.

If the basic goal of public education in a democratic society is to reproduce the common core so essential to the effective functioning of democracy, then any system of choice ought to be evaluated with respect to whether it contributes or supports such an objective or undermines it. Schemes that argue for private choice alone tend to ignore the external benefits of schooling in a democratic society by assuming that the sum of individual choices will always lead to a desirable social result. In particular, voucher approaches tend to understate the contradiction between the attainment of a common core of educational benefits and the fostering of a system of unfettered educational choice.

Henry M. Levin, 1983, "Educational Choice and the Pains of Democracy," p. 29.

Books and periodicals will continue to be vital resources in your learning activities at the library. But increasingly you will find the most modern informational and educational tools there. The computer, microfilm, and even the videocassette recorder and videodisc are being harnessed by librarians. Individuals can and do learn directly through these devices, which also handle administrative tasks, operate efficient links with other libraries both near and far, and store information.

So, the library is a place where you will be able to learn by yourself at your own time and pace. Others benefit there from one-on-one instruction in reading, computation, basic study skills, or research.

The reality is that learning services are already available to people of any age at libraries from Alaska, to Maine, to Texas, north and south, east and west, and to the outlying U.S. territories. The preschooler can be readied for school at the public library; boys and girls pursue classroom assignments in their school library media center; the college student rounds out an independent paper at the college/university library on campus; professionals verify facts and challenge assumptions in medical, law, business, or other special libraries; the adult voter, consumer, parent-to-be, taxpayer, or curious citizen can learn at the public library.

Center for Libraries and Education Improvement, U.S. Department of Education, July 1984, Alliance for Excellence: Librarians Respond to A Nation at Risk, *pp. 2–3.*

[T]he past few years have not been encouraging for the [school] library media center; budget cuts and other claims on resources have hit *all* areas, but school library media programs have been deeply hurt. As it stands, 15 percent of our public schools have no library media center; almost three million public school students attend schools with no library media center. Not far from the District of Columbia, 55 elementary school library media specialists in one county were released in 1982 due to budget shrinkage. In a major New England city, no elementary school library media center has a professional in charge; aides, technicians, or volunteers handle the work.

Center for Libraries and Education Improvement, U.S. Department of Education, July 1984, Alliance for Excellence: Librarians Respond to *A Nation at Risk, pp. 8–9.*

Once upon a time families would gather after dinner to play a round of Parchesi or Scrabble or Monopoly or Clue. Some families still do. But it is becoming evident that the computer is playing an increasingly strong role in family entertainment and learning. The major factor in bringing the computer into the mainstream of family life is the development of quality software.

Families are discovering how diverse a home computer can be. For example, during the course of a day a family might use its computer to compose music, to learn some Spanish, to practice landings and takeoffs at O'Hare Airport, to play a game, to draw a picture, to write a book report, to analyze home-heating costs, to communicate with a friend in a distant state, and to print out labels for invitations to a dinner party. Though these activities all take place at the computer, they are as different as weeding the garden, cooking a bouillabaisse, washing the car, and brushing one's teeth. And most computer programs for the home can be used by almost any member of the family over the age of 7. Naturally, no two people will approach a program in the same way or use it for the same purposes. But many adults are finding, much to their surprise, that children may start out using a program the way their parents do, but then go on to discover new possibilities that the adults were unaware of.

Henry Olds, member of the Governor's Advisory Committee on Computers in Education, Massachusetts, mid-October 1984, "Sometimes Children Are the Best Teachers," p. 47.

There won't be schools in the future. There'll be new kinds of social inventions that we can hardly even imagine, but they won't be anything like schools. And they won't be anything like children staying at home. I think the computer will blow up the school. That is, the school defined as something where there are classes, teachers running exams, people structured into groups by age, following a curriculum—all of that. The whole system is based on a set of structural concepts that are incompatible with the presence of the computer. These structural concepts are based on knowledge being handed out by a medieval process—exposition—rather than by a process of discovery. But this will happen only in communities of children who have access to computers on a sufficient scale. There's been a lot of ballyhoo about computers revolutionizing the schools, but in fact the relative number of computers in schools is so small that it's negligible. They aren't really having *any* effect. They *can't* have any effect.

Seymour Papert, professor of mathematics and education, Massachusetts Institute of Technology, mid-October 1984, in "Trying to Predict the Future," p. 38.

Few informed observers casting a careful, century-long look at schools could be blind to the changes that have occurred in public schools. Governance, curricula, and school organization, for example, have changed substantially since the closing decades on the nineteenth century. When observing changes in the classroom itself, however, there seem to have been only some modest alterations in classroom organization (more diversity in forms), teacher-student relationships (less formal), and instructional methods (a broader repertoire). What can hardly escape notice is the persistent core of practices that teachers have found to be efficient and resilient, engineered to fit the physics of the classroom. Thus, while governance, curricula, and organization have altered the district and school terrain sufficiently to be readily observed, shifts over the last century in classroom topography barely can be detected.

Larry Cuban, professor emeritus of education, Stanford University, 1986, Teachers and Machines: The Classroom Use of Technology Since 1920, *p. 104.*

In 1987, when Holly was 6, she wanted to know what school was like, so her parents arranged for her to spend a day as a student in a local public school's 1st grade classroom. It was a cheery room, not too crowded with students. Holly had her own desk, and the amiable and talented teacher was an acquaintance of her family. That evening, when her parents asked Holly what she thought of school, she replied that she liked recess. When asked whether she would like to go to school, Holly replied, "No, they're always sitting around doing nothing." She noticed the waiting—waiting in lines, waiting for the teacher's help with a math problem, and waiting for a classmate standing at the front of the room struggling through saying the names of the week in Spanish while others giggled and lost attention. Holly noticed that she could not move on to another engaging learning task or adventure when she was ready for it. There was a group for whom to wait. There was a structure to follow. At home, Holly knew that she could move on to new challenges when she was ready.

Brian D. Ray, president of the National Home Education Research Institute, describing the experience of a home-schooled child in 1987, "Customization through Homeschooling," pp. 51–52.

The only contact we had with the "normal" children was visual. We stared at each other. On those occasions, I can report my own feelings: embarrassment. . . . I can also report their feelings: Yech! We, the children in the "handicapped" class, were internalizing the "yech" message—plus a couple of others. We were in school because children go to school, but we were outcasts, with no future and no expectation of one.

A student from a special education class, 1987, in Massachusetts Advocacy Center, Out of the Mainstream, pp. 4–5.

As educators, we have a special responsibility because, in the United States, our schools have always played the key role in helping to integrate our society and this is the role we must play now. But how? By doing what we have always done.

First, we have to teach our students history. We have to teach them that the challenges that come from trying to integrate society are not new. Here are some statistics from a survey of 37 major cities: 58 percent of all students surveyed were children of immigrants; the vast majority of these children were in the primary grades; and 40 percent of these very young children were already behind grade level. These statistics would not surprise anyone who works in California schools today. What may be surprising is that they are from 1909.

Patrick Hayashi, associate vice chancellor for admissions and enrollment, University of California at Berkeley, winter 1991–92, "Affirmative Action: A Personal View," p. 33.

[I]t was easy to ridicule something that emphasized the importance of subject matter and standards as an old-fashioned piece of nonsense. States that tried to implement *A Nation at Risk* picked a few parts that were relatively easy to carry out and ignored the rest. For example, course requirements were increased in some places without looking at course content or changing the tests to bring them in line with the courses or making grades count for stu-

dents. This approach to reform is like trying to build a four-legged stool with only one leg, and it's no surprise that student achievement hardly improved. . . .

Until we agree on standards for what students should know and be able to do, assess them on their achievement of those standards, and give them a reason to work hard in school by linking their achievement with what they want—access to college or to jobs—we will not raise student achievement. *A Nation at Risk* told us this 10 years ago, but we missed it. If we don't listen now, we'll have 10 more years without progress in student achievement.

Albert Shanker, president of the American Federation of Teachers, May 9, 1993, "A Landmark Revisited," pp. 1–2.

So the country is going to hell in a handbasket, and the handbasket was made in America by public schools, and our kids can't write, won't read, and calculate only so long as the batteries in the pocket calculator hold out. They don't know a binomial from a bivalve; they are pretty sure that Robert E. Lee had something to do with Viet Nam and that Woodrow Wilson played outfield for Kansas City. Their favorite book is anything from *Cliff Notes*, and the idea of writing anything longer than a shopping list gives them the vapors. *And* they won't work, or honor their elders, let alone their fathers and mothers, or show any respect whatsoever for anything that doesn't give them something called instant gratification.

If all this is true, how can it be that, day after day, I walk away from my English 101 class at Essex Community College inspired and challenged by some of the most dedicated, honorable people I have ever known? Where did my students learn to write prose of force, style, and clarity? How can I account for the fact that they soak up each scrap of knowledge and insight I can give them, and leave me feeling that I owe them more energy than I can summon? How can I be having so much fun?

A. J. Downs, adjunct associate professor, Essex Community College, Baltimore, spring 1993, "Night School, English 101," p. 8.

Systems designed specifically to increase standardized test scores on basic skills and do record keeping as well have grabbed the largest share of the educational technology market. Schools' and policymakers' focus on raising test scores and a corresponding lack of investment in educating teachers and administrators about technology and about effective ways of learning have made school districts easy targets for hardware and software vendors' marketing claims. Vendors who can demonstrate that their technology is aligned with existing curricula and tests are more likely to make large sales than are those who push technology as a tool to transform teaching and learning. The bewilderment of educators and policymakers in the face of varied claims for technology simply adds to the appeal of individualized, self-paced student learning systems that require little, if any, teacher involvement. Moreover, such systems are typically placed in a computer laboratory with its own teacher or aide, further isolating classroom teachers from the technology.

Imagine how different U.S. schools might look today if the main goal for purchasing and using software during the 1980s had been to transform teaching and learning instead of to increase the efficiency of current practices.

Jane L. David, director of the Bay Area Research Group, Palo Alto, California, 1994, "Realizing the Promise of Technology: A Policy Perspective," p. 170.

The role that new technology should play in schools or anywhere else is something that needs to be discussed without the hyperactive fantasies of cheerleaders. In particular, the computer and its associated technologies are awesome additions to a culture, and they are quite capable of altering the psychic, let alone the sleeping, habits of our young. But like all important technologies of the past, they are Faustian bargains, giving and taking away, sometimes in equal measure, sometimes more in one way than the other. It is strange—indeed, shocking—that with the twenty-first century so close on our heels, we can still talk of new technologies as if they were unmixed blessings, gifts, as it were, from the gods. Don't we all know what the combustion engine has done for us and against us? What television is doing for us and against us?

Neil Postman, professor and chair, Department of Culture and Communications, New York University, 1995, The End of Education: Redefining the Value of School, p. 41.

I suppose it is possible that there are children who, waking at night, want to study algebra or who are so interested in their world that they yearn to know about Japan. If there be such children, and one hopes there are, they do not require expensive computers to satisfy their hunger for learning. They are on their way, with or without computers—unless, of course, they do not care about others, or have no friends, or little respect for democracy, or are filled with suspicion about those who are not like them. When we have machines that know how to do something about these problems, that is the time to rid ourselves of

the expensive burden of schools or to reduce the function of teachers to "coaches" in the use of machines.

Neil Postman, professor and chair, Department of Culture and Communications, New York University, 1995, The End of Education: Redefining the Value of School, pp. 48–49.

I think that even if you hate school, you've got to go. I just hate dealing with all this pressure, but I want to graduate. This one teacher hated [Indians] and said, "I'm going to tell you something." He didn't make it like a challenge or anything. He just told us like flat out, "Half of you kids aren't going to graduate from high school, and about half of you girls are going to get pregnant. The boys, you'll be fathers." And he was saying this stuff, and I was like, "No way, man. I'm going to graduate." I love challenges, but he was like not optimistic at all. If you hear something so many times, you are going to start to believe it and give up. I feel kind of down, but I try to ignore it. I try to calm myself down, but if I really, really get mad at something, it just like upsets me for the rest of the day. I can't think about school.

Maria, an Ojibway who lives on a reservation in the Midwest and attends a public high school, interviewed between 1997 and 2000, in Amy Bergstrom, Linda Miller Cleary, and Thomas D. Peacock, The Seventh Generation: Native Students Speak about Finding the Good Path, p. 7.

I went to [a Catholic school] and the only other Indian kid there was Beau. . . . I had some problems, especially when I was little. I was told animals had spirits in them, and my first theological argument was over that with my first-grade teacher. We were having a discussion one day, and Sister was telling us how they used to sacrifice lambs because lambs don't have spirits. . . . It's like, "But animals do have spirits. I know they have spirits because they are living, right?" "Everything has a spirit inside it, some kind of will for life." She goes, "Oh, no, they don't go to heaven. They don't have a spirit." I got really mad, and they had to take me down to the office. It blackballed me pretty well.

Quoetone, high school student of Kiowa and Ojibway heritage, interviewed between 1997 and 2000, in Amy Bergstrom, Linda Miller Cleary, and Thomas D. Peacock, The Seventh Generation: Native Students Speak about Finding the Good Path, p. 17.

[Ross Hensley's] parents started homeschooling tentatively, as an experiment, when Hensley was in sixth grade. He had attended a local public school and two private schools, where he remembers feeling bored with the workbook assignments. "They just piled on pointless, easy work."

He took advantage of the freedom of homeschooling to push himself beyond anything regular schools might allow. At age 13, for example, Hensley got a textbook and dove into the physics of special relativity, even though he hadn't been taught the calculus that most teachers would consider a prerequisite. Leaving school at an early age, he says, "gave me a tremendous amount of time to pursue my interests in depth."

Later, he sought more formal instruction. The Houston native—who passed seven advanced-placement exams, including the tough calculus test when he was just a high school sophomore—spent most of his senior year at nearby Rice University doing college-sophomore-level coursework in math and electrical engineering. He attended a Stanford-run summer program for gifted high schoolers and took distance-learning courses over the Internet through Stanford's Educational Program for Gifted Youth. Add all that together and you get enough credits to enter the University with junior standing. . . .

Christine Foster, freelance writer, November/December 2000, "In a Class by Themselves," p. 79.

The Indian view of the world tends to see unities both in the structure of physical things and in the behavior of things, and we have recently been describing it as "holistic" in that it tries to present a comprehensive picture in which the parts and their value are less significant than the larger picture and its meaning. . . .

Look at the curriculum Indian children are asked to use. Knowledge of the world is divided up into separate categories that seem to be completely isolated from each other. So profound is this separation that most children, Indian and non-Indian, rebel when they are asked to write complete sentences in classes other than English, or to show any comprehension of mathematics in any course except mathematics and physics/engineering. We are asking children to divide the world into predetermined categories of explanation and training them to avoid seeing the complete picture of what is before their eyes. Efforts of the last three decades have been somewhat bizarre when this question is faced directly. Quite often the images familiar to Indians are used instead of traditional white, middle-class images, and this change in pictorial representation is supposed to cure the defect in the child's perspective. If the child wants to understand the whole,

we simply dress up the parts in buckskin and pretend that we have answered the problem.

Vine Deloria, Jr., Standing Rock Sioux, writer, and educator, and Daniel Wildcat, Yuchi member of the Muscogee Nation of Oklahoma and professor of American Indian studies, Haskell Indian Nations University, 2001, Power and Place: Indian Education in America, *p. 155.*

It is seldom noted publicly, but many promoters of new technologies seem to have forgotten the historic civic idealism and broad social purposes public schools serve in a democracy. Well-intentioned reformers eager to make schools efficient instruments of American global economic competitiveness speak mostly about standards-based curriculum, test scores, and accountability as portals through which students move to become workers and consumers who help expand markets and contribute to soaring profits. They concentrate upon how schools serve the economy and how much individuals can gain, rather than on the public good. Recapturing the broad democratic purposes that Americans have sought through schooling and the critical importance of the schools in building and sustaining social capital challenges the assumptions passionately held by promoters of technology in schools.

Larry Cuban, professor emeritus of education, Stanford University, 2001, Oversold and Underused: Computers in the Classrooms.

The students in my class were gracious and compassionate as they struggled to make the environment conducive to Bobby's learning, even when it required some sacrifice on their part. The year was their success as much as it was Bobby's or mine. I was delighted by the students' sensitivity to Bobby and their willingness to put his needs before their own, such as waiting patiently (and sometimes for long periods of time) for Bobby to respond. Because Bobby felt secure in the classroom and was not bombarded with such distractions as excessive noise or commotion, he was able to challenge himself and perform many of the same tasks as the other students. Eventually, Bobby spoke in complete sentences. Granted, he never spoke as much as the other students, nor did he initiate conversations as often as they did. Nevertheless, his conversations revealed an increased awareness of the world around him.

Elizabeth Zylstra, doctoral candidate in curriculum and instruction at Boise State University and former second grade teacher, recalling the inclusion of a boy with autism in her class, November 2001, "A Year with Bobby," pp. 74–75.

Every school has a job to do. And that's to teach the basics and teach them well. If we want to make sure no child is left behind, every child must learn to read. And every child must learn to add and subtract. So in return for federal dollars, we are asking states to design accountability systems to show parents and teachers whether or not children can read and write and add and subtract in grades three through eight.

The fundamental principle of this bill is that every child can learn, we expect every child to learn, and you must show us whether or not every child is learning. I read a quote one time from a young lady in New York. She said, "I don't ever remember taking an exam. They just kept passing me along. I ended up dropping out in the 7th grade. I basically felt nobody cared."

The story of children being just shuffled through the system is one of the saddest stories in America. Let's just move them through. It's so much easier to move a child through than trying to figure out how to solve a child's problems. The first step to making sure that a child is not shuffled through is to test that child as to whether or not he or she can read and write, or add and subtract.

President George W. Bush, upon signing the No Child Left Behind Act, January 8, 2002, in "President Signs Landmark No Child Left Behind Education Bill," pp. 2–3.

[Laura] Brion was the first homeschooler in her small town, but over time her parents found others nearby, so the families joined forces. There were play dates, field trips to nature centers, and group classes in French and geology. One thing led to another. The piano lessons Brion began when she was nine led to a job as a church organist at sixteen. An interest in the Revolutionary War evolved into playing in a fife-and-drum corps. As a teenager Brion worked at

Mothers and fathers attend a parent-leadership program sponsored by Turning the Page in Washington, D.C., in March 2007. The parents gain information on such topics as No Child Left Behind, planned school improvements, and their rights and responsibilities under the law. *(Turning the Page)*

two small farms, one owned and run by a former physicist, the other by an ethnobotanist, both of whom welcomed her nonstop questions. "I realized learning was something I just couldn't get away from," she says. "Everything became a learning experience." It is, in fact, this aspect of homeschooling—learning as something that occurs at any time, in any place, throughout one's life—that explains so much of its appeal.

Jennifer Sutton, contributing editor, Brown Alumni Magazine, *January/February 2002, "Homeschooling Comes of Age," p. 47.*

For the past 20 years, the focus has been on preparing students for the workplace and developing a common academic curriculum so that everyone could be prepared for a globally competitive workplace. That emphasis has been so strong that it has actually shoved aside another purpose for U.S. tax-supported public schools, which is civic engagement. I hear a lot of talk about preparing students for citizenship, but I see very little action.

Larry Cuban, professor emeritus of education, Stanford University, April 2002, in Scott Willis, "Customization and the Common Good: A Conversation with Larry Cuban," p. 11.

Nearly every member of the political establishment in New York opposes private school vouchers for poor children while refusing to send their own children to public schools. As in other cities, the political and economic elite of New York views public schools as places for other people's children. The establishment provides the public school system with just enough support to keep it going but does not provide the commitment or determination to make it succeed.

Parents whose children get stuck in failing schools are told to be patient. Patience is an easy virtue when you do not need to live with the consequences of an inadequate education. But why is the public school system good enough for some kids and not for others? That position is no longer morally defensible. Indeed, it never was. That is why I have come around on school choice.

Joseph P. Viteritti, professor of public policy, New York University, April 2002, "Coming Around on School Choice," p. 47.

The future of U.S. society depends on people from different racial and ethnic backgrounds developing strong, positive, and lasting relationships with one another. I believe parents should do everything they can to expose their children to people who look different and behave, think, worship, and learn differently from the way they do.

But the first purpose of our public and private K-12 schools is to educate students. We have spent far too many years engaged in social engineering practices by seating diverse students next to one another in a classroom and calling that integration. Instead, we should focus on making sure that each student sitting in our classrooms has access to the best education opportunities and the best teachers we can provide.

Kaleem M. S. Caire, president and CEO of the Black Alliance for Educational Options, April 2002, "The Truth about Vouchers," p. 41.

The book of Exodus tells the story of the Israelites who, losing hope as they waited for Moses to return from the mountaintop, began to worship the golden calf. For African Americans, this story provides an important context for one of our greatest challenges—the education of our children.

Too many African Americans live in communities where public schools have been struggling for a long time. Like the Israelites waiting for Moses's return, they fear that they have been abandoned. Now they are being asked to turn their backs on public schools and replace them with a golden calf called vouchers.

Timothy McDonald, chair of the African American Ministers Leadership Council, April 2002, "The False Promise of Vouchers," p. 33.

What is happening? Are more kids in this country doing more poorly in school than ever before? New research on student mobility rates and their impacts certainly points in that direction. Whether mobility is a symptom or a cause, though, there are strong indications that growing numbers of students—most of them struggling academically—are leaving school in record numbers. Dropping out or getting pushed out, many of these young people want and need the assistance of the adult education and literacy system to get their lives and their educations back on track. Along with immigrants and their children, young adults leaving the school system are fueling the growth of the adult literacy challenge nationwide.

Robert Wedgeworth, president and CEO, ProLiteracy Worldwide, 2003, "The Number of Functionally Illiterate Adults in U.S. Is Growing," pp. 7–8.

In sharp contrast to a computer, a child possesses a *self,* which imbues her with the desire to give her life meaning, purpose, and a moral compass. A child is motivated to learn by the desire to be grounded in her family, in her community, and the natural order, and yet at the same time to express herself and place her own personal stamp on the world. Her thinking is infused with emotion, sensory and bodily kinesthetic experience, artistry, imagination, and soulfulness. It is through this uniquely *human* prism, in the service of uniquely *human* needs, that she processes information. Thus, it is a tragic irony that we idealize the disembodied, emotionless computer and try to teach our children to think according to its operating principles. Unfortunately, however, when mere information is what we seek to instill or elicit from our students, the content and context of the information at issue becomes completely secondary to one's ability to access and manipulate it.

Sharna Olfman, associate professor of psychology, Point Park College, Pittsburgh, 2003, "All Work and No Play: How Educational Reforms Are Harming Our Preschoolers," p. 8.

In the absence of sound guidelines to inform curriculum development, we have no qualms about taking a curriculum designed for students in grade one and forcing it on preschoolers to boost their achievement. At the same time, we demote play, artistic expression, and experiential learning to the status of mere diversions (in between the "real" work contained in worksheets) and substitute face time with computers for human mentoring. Then, when students struggle with the content or format of the curriculum, we bristle with an impressive array of psychiatric labels and a powerful pharmacopoeia of psychiatric drugs, when often what is needed is the patience and sensitivity to allow their development to unfold, and humane teaching methods that do not compartmentalize thought, feeling, and social development, as we typically insist on doing.

Sharna Olfman, associate professor of psychology, Point Park College, Pittsburgh, 2003, "All Work and No Play: How Educational Reforms Are Harming Our Preschoolers," p. 9.

Years ago, a person without good reading skills could get a job as a law firm receptionist. With training, this person could develop some typing skills and make a decent living. With the technology explosion of the past decade, it's virtually impossible for an uneducated person to get a job even as a receptionist.

What is even more ironic about the reality of the abilities of the average urban student is that the business community is sometimes forced to compensate for this lack of skills in order to have a pool of workers to pick from. One example is fast food restaurants where, because the young people who form their natural employee pool do not have even the most basic skills, the employers have taken to placing pictures of their offerings on the cash registers. Trainees who cannot read are taught to take orders by pushing the button with the appropriate picture on it, and the "smart" cash registers do all the work!

Kevin P. Chavous, chair of the Committee on Education, Libraries and Recreation, District of Columbia, 2004, Serving Our Children: Charter Schools and the Reform of American Public Education, pp. 12–13.

At one particularly poignant education committee hearing, a star female basketball player from a local high school delivered heart-wrenching testimony about her personal academic challenges with the D.C. school system. In front of several television cameras and a packed city council chamber, she recounted her learning experience starting in first grade when she was diagnosed as having a learning disability. She described her frustration when year after year, teachers and counselors who were supposed to help her advance academically failed to do so. As she entered high school and her basketball prowess emerged, she was still unable to read. But that didn't seem to matter. She was continuously promoted from grade to grade despite her clear lack of literacy. This young woman's story is not an anomaly.

Kevin P. Chavous, chair of the Committee on Education, Libraries and Recreation, District of Columbia, 2004, Serving Our Children: Charter Schools and the Reform of American Public Education, p. 56.

Daniel walks into his kindergarten classroom and drops his outerwear, backpack, and bus harness in a tangled heap in the middle of the floor. Daniel has a singular focus this morning: building a bridge and a house out of Lincoln Logs.

He does not notice as classmates step around or over him as he plays on the hard floor. If other children move into his space, he pushes them away. One or two children greet him, but he does not answer. Daniel keeps up a running dialogue as he plays, in jargon rarely understandable to anyone but himself.

Daniel's educational aide approaches him and, using a handmade schedule book with symbolic pictures, shows Daniel that this is not the time for playing. The first picture on the schedule is a locker, indicating that Daniel is to hang up his coat and backpack. Transitions to new activities are very difficult for Daniel, and he begins to scream and kick. Other children watch quietly or walk away.

Daniel is autistic. He is charming, intelligent, creative, and full of energy, just like his 18 classmates. However, he is unable to use language to interact with others. . . . Like other children with autism, Daniel would not understand the activities of the day without his schedule book. When events change and the day does not correspond to his schedule, Daniel may lose control and throw a tantrum. He requires the support of an educational assistant every minute of the school day.

Ann Christy Dybvik, winter 2004,
"Autism and the Inclusion Mandate," p. 43.

[W]hile the open classroom has clearly disappeared from the vocabulary of educators, another variation of open education is likely to reappear in the years ahead. Deep-seated progressive and traditional beliefs about rearing children, classroom teaching and learning, and the values and knowledge that should be instilled in the next generation will continue to reappear because schools historically have been battlegrounds for solving national problems and working out differences in values.

Since children differ in their motivations, interests, and backgrounds, and learn at different speeds in different subjects, there will never be a victory for either traditional or progressive teaching and learning. The fact is that no single best way for teachers to teach and for children to learn can fit all situations. Both traditional and progressive ways of teaching and learning need to be part of a school's approach to children. Smart teachers and principals have carefully constructed hybrid classrooms and schools that reflect the diversities of children. Alas, that lesson remains to be learned by the policymakers, educators, and parents of each generation.

Larry Cuban, professor emeritus of education, Stanford
University, spring 2004, "The Open Classroom," p. 71.

To the rational thinker, handing off children to paid agents of government makes as much sense as hiring the hangman as your babysitter. Yet today otherwise sane people consider it normal to frog-march a terrified 4-year-old child to the bus stop, and send him off into a penal system peopled with monsters and manipulators. "After all," the gulled parent says, "public school did me no harm!" Other than damaging your critical faculties to the point where you are unable to perceive the harm done to yourself.

Tom Smedley, writer and home-schooling parent, 2005,
"Homeschooling for Liberty," p. 70.

Unregulated home schooling opens up the possibility that children will never learn about or be exposed to competing or alternative ways of life. Home-schooled children can be sheltered and isolated in a way that students in schools, even sectarian private schools, cannot be. Parents can limit opportunities for social interaction, control the curriculum, and create a learning environment in which the values of the parents are replicated and reinforced in every possible way. With little or no exposure to competing ideas or interaction with people whose convictions differ from their parents', children who are home schooled can be raised in an all-encompassing or total environment that fails to develop their capacity to think for themselves. Parents can control the socialization of their children so completely as to instill inerrant beliefs in their own worldview or unquestioning obedience to their own or others' authority. . . . In short, children become unfree, unable to imagine other ways of living.

Rob Reich, assistant professor of political science and ethics
in society, Stanford University, 2005, "Why Home Schooling
Should Be Regulated," p. 114.

I lived and worked in New Orleans for the better part of the last six months, performing needs assessments for charter schools, and attempting to formulate responses. What I saw was simultaneously inspiring and depressing, with dark clouds teetering on the horizon. Schools like Singleton Charter, deep in the 'hood, opened as quickly after the storm as was humanly possible, volunteers and unpaid staff preparing the facility, adding a grade temporarily so that they could get older kids off the street, and providing the only stability that its deeply damaged students and families had. In January, when I first visited Franklin High, in the affluent Lakeview, there was a boat washed into the median of the road, unpaid staff were literally scooping mud out of the lower floor and surveying what weeks of ceiling-high, standing water could do to a library, not to mention servers. Within a week it was open.

Dirk Tillotson, attorney and school-improvement specialist,
December 2006/January 2007, "What's Next for New
Orleans?" pp. 70–71.

I packed up my classroom after three years of teaching to go back to school. I couldn't face a career of redecorating bulletin boards each month, unclasping tricky Bratz belts while little girls squirmed to hold in their pee, and screaming at little boys to stop throwing crayons across the room. The decision was made one sticky May day after a failed addition lesson, when Cory spat in Ladesha's face and my patience evaporated into the hot air.

But since I left I've realized a few things. For one, patience is a renewable resource. No matter what happened

On June 1, 2007, Secretary of Education Margaret Spellings visits the Cary Academy, a private school in Cary, North Carolina, where technology is integrated into the curriculum. These students are evaluating the effectiveness of Styrofoam for keeping liquids warm. *(U.S. Department of Education Archives)*

the day before, I revived loyally each dawn. Each morning I greeted my students with replenished serenity. When in command of 22 five-year-olds, part of me thinks exercising patience is giving them more than "enough."

I've also realized that altruism is somewhat selfish and addicting. I missed those small palms pressed adoringly into mine. And after a brief hiatus, I'm back—teaching children part-time. Am I doing it just to feel good about myself? Does it matter?

Katherine Newman, former New York City Teaching Fellow and instructor of writing at Emerson College, Boston, summer 2007, "Confessions from the Classroom," p. 1.

Enacted in 2001, the No Child Left Behind Act (NCLB) began with the resounding promise that every U.S. school-child will attain "proficiency" in reading and math by 2014. Noble, yes, but also naive, misleading, and in some respect dysfunctional. While nobody doubts that the number of "proficient" students in America can and should increase dramatically from today's woeful level, no edu-

cator believes that universal proficiency in 2014 is attainable. Only politicians promise such things. The inevitable result is weary cynicism among school practitioners and a "compliance" mentality among state and local officials.

In hindsight, NCLB's passage was less about improving schools or fostering results-based public sector accountability than about declaring fealty to a gallant but utopian ambition, one that the statute welded to a clumsy, heavy-handed set of procedural mandates.

NCLB is, in fact, a civil rights manifesto masquerading as an education accountability system. Its grand ambition provided a shaky basis for policymaking, rather as if Congress asserted in the name of energy reform that America will no longer need to import oil after 2014 or fought crime by declaring that by that date all U.S. cities would be peaceable kingdoms.

Frederick M. Hess, director of education policy studies at the American Enterprise Institute, and Chester E. Finn, Jr., president of the Thomas B. Fordham Foundation, fall 2007, "Crash Course," p. 1.

Appendix A
Documents

1. The Massachusetts School Law of 1647
2. Instructions for Schoolmasters, Society for the Propagation of the Gospel in Foreign Parts, 1706
3. Extracts from "A Bill for the More General Diffusion of Knowledge," presented by Thomas Jefferson to the Committee of Revisors of the Virginia Assembly, June 18, 1779
4. Extracts from Noah Webster's Introduction to *A Grammatical Institute, of the English Language,* 1783
5. Extract from "A Plan for Establishing Public Schools in Pennsylvania, and for Conducting Education Agreeably to a Republican Form of Government," presented by Benjamin Rush to the legislature and citizens of Pennsylvania, 1786
6. Extracts from the Massachusetts School Law of 1789
7. Announcement of the opening of the Warrenton [North Carolina] Female Academy, August 18, 1808
8. Extracts from Original Papers in Relation to a Course of Liberal Education [the Yale Report], September 11, 1827
9. An Act to amend the Laws in relation to Slaves and Free Persons of Color, South Carolina, 1840
10. The Massachusetts Compulsory School Law of 1850
11. Extracts from An Act Donating Public Lands to the Several States and Territories Which May Provide Colleges for the Benefit of Agriculture and the Mechanic Arts (Morrill Act), 1862
12. Extracts from the First Semi-Annual Report on Schools and Finances of Freedmen, Bureau of Refugees, Freedmen and Abandoned Lands, January 1, 1866
13. An Act to Compel Children to Attend School, Enacted and Amended by the Michigan Legislature at Its Session in 1871
14. Extracts from *Charles E. Stuart and Others v. School District No. 1 of the Village of Kalamazoo and Others* [the Kalamazoo Case], 1874
15. Extracts from "The Indian School at Carlisle Barracks," a Report to the U.S. Commissioner of Education, 1880
16. Extracts from Report of the Committee on Secondary School Studies [Committee of Ten], 1893
17. Regulations covering the use of school buildings adopted by the Rochester, New York, Board of Education, 1907
18. Extracts from Students' Army Training Corps Regulations, 1918

1. The Massachusetts School Law of 1647

It being one chiefe project of that ould deluder, Satan, to keepe men from the knowledge of the Scriptures, as in former times by keeping them in an unknowne tongue, so in these latter times by perswading from the used of tongues, that so at least the true sence and meaning of the originall might be clouded by false glosses of saint seeming deceivers, that learning may not be buried in the grave of our fathers in the church and commonwealth, the Lord assisting our endeavors,—

It is therefore ordered, that every towneship in this jurisdiction after the Lord hath increased them to the number of 50 housholders, shall then forthwith appoint one within their towne to teach all such children as shall resort to him to write and reade, whose wages shall be paid either by the parents or masters of such children, or by the inhabitants in generall, by way of supply, as the major part of those that order the prudentials of the towne shall appoint; provided, those that send their children be not oppressed by paying much more than they can have them taught for in other townes; and it is further ordered, that where any towne shall increase to the number of 100 families or househoulders, they shall set up a grammer schoole, the master thereof being able to instruct youth so farr as they may be fited for the university, provided, that if any towne neglect the performance hereof above one yeare, that every such towne shall pay £5 to the next schoole till they shall performe this order.

2. Instructions for Schoolmasters, Society for the Propagation of the Gospel in Foreign Parts, 1706

I. That they well consider the End for which they are employed by the Society, viz. The instructing and disposing Children to believe and live as Christians.

II. In order to this End, that they teach them to read truly and distinctly, that they may be capable of reading the Holy Scriptures, and other pious and useful Books, for informing their Understandings, and regulating their Manners.

III. That they instruct them thoroughly in the Church-Catechism; teach them first to read it distinctly and exactly, then to learn it perfectly by Heart; endeavouring to make them understand the Sense and Meaning of it, by the help of such Expositions as the Society shall send over.

IV. That they teach them to write a plain and legible Hand, in order to the fitting them for useful Employments; With as much Arithmetick as shall be necessary for the same Purpose.

V. That they be industrious, and give constant Attendance at proper School-Hours.

VI. That they daily use, Morning and Evening, the Prayers composed for their Use in this Collection, with their Scholars in the School, and teach them the Prayers and Graces composed for their use at home.

VII. That they oblige their Scholars to be constant at Church on the Lord's Day, Morning and Afternoon, and at all other times of Publick Worship; that they cause them to carry their Bibles and Prayer Books with them, instructing them how to use them there, and how to demean themselves in the Several Parts of Worship; that they be there present with them, taking care of their reverent and decent Behavious, and examine them afterwards as to what they have heard and learned.

VIII. That when any of their Scholars are fit for it, they recommend them to the Minister of the Parish, to be publickly Catechized in the Church.

IX. That they take special care of their Manners, both in their Schools and out of them; warning them seriously of those Vices to which Children are most liable; teaching them to abhor Lying and Falshood, and to avoid all sorts of Evil-speaking; to love Truth and Honesty; to be modest, gentle, well-behaved, just and affable; and courteous to all their Companions; respectful to their Superiors, particularly towards all that minister in the holy Things, and especially to the Minister of their Parish; and all this from a Sense and Fear of Almighty God; endeavouring to bring them in their tender Years to that Sense of Religion, which may render it the constant Principle of their Lives and Actions.

X. That they use all kind and gentle Methods in the government of their Scholars, that they may be loved as well as feared by them; and that when Correction is necessary, they make the Children to understand, that it is given them out of kindness, for their Good, bringing them to a Sense of their fault, as well as of their Punishment.

XI. That they frequently consult with the Minister of the Parish, in which they dwell, about the Methods of managing their Schools, and be ready to be advised by him.

XII. That they do in their whole Conversation shew themselves Examples of Piety and Virtue to their Scholars, and to all whom they shall converse.

XIII. That they be ready, as they have Opportunity, to teach and instruct the *Indians* and *Negroes* and their Children.

XIV. That they send to the Secretary of the Society, once in every six Months, an Account of the State of their respective Schools, the Number of their Scholars, with the Methods and Success of their Teaching.

3. Extracts from "A Bill for the More General Diffusion of Knowledge," presented by Thomas Jefferson to the Committee of Revisors of the Virginia Assembly, June 18, 1779

Whereas it appeareth that however certain forms of government are better calculated than others to protect individuals in the free exercise of their natural rights, and are at the same time themselves better guarded against degeneracy, yet experience hath shewn, that even under the best forms, those entrusted with power have, in time, and by slow operations, perverted it into tyranny; and it is believed that the most effectual means of preventing this would be, to illuminate, as far as practicable, the minds of the people at large, and more especially to give them knowledge of those facts, which history exhibiteth, that possessed thereby of the experience of other ages and countries, they may be enabled to know ambition under all its shapes, and prompt to exert their natural powers to defeat its purposes; And whereas it is generally true that that people will be happiest whose laws are best, and are best administered, and that laws will be wisely formed, and honestly administered, in proportion as those who form and administer them are wise and honest; whence it becomes expedient for promoting the publick happiness that those persons, whom nature hath endowed with genius and virtue, should be rendered by liberal education worthy to receive, and able to guard the sacred deposit of the rights and liberties of their fellow citizens, that they should be called to that charge without regard to wealth, birth or other accidental condition or circumstance; but the indigence of the greater number disabling them from so educating, at their own expence, those of their children

whom nature hath fitly formed and disposed to become useful instruments for the public, it is better that such should be sought for and educated at the common expence of all, than that the happiness of all should be confided for the weak or wicked:

Be it therefore enacted by the General Assembly, that in every county within this commonwealth, there shall be chosen annually, by the electors qualified to vote for Delegates, three of the most honest and able men of their county, to be called the Aldermen of the county; and that the election of the said Aldermen shall be held at the same time and place, before the same persons, and notified and conducted in the same manner as by law is directed for the annual election of Delegates for the county. . . .

The said Aldermen on the first Monday in October, if it be fair, and if not, then on the next fair day, excluding Sunday, shall meet at the court-house of their county, and proceed to divide their said county into hundreds, bounding the same by water courses, mountains, or limits, to be run and marked, if they think necessary, by the county surveyor, and at the county expence, regulating the size of the said hundreds, according to the best of their discretion, so as that they may contain a convenient number of children to make up a school, and be of such convenient size that all the children within each hundred may daily attend the school to be established therein, distinguishing each hundred by a particular name; which division, with the names of the several hundreds, shall be returned to the court of the county and be entered of record, and shall remain unaltered until the increase or decrease of inhabitants shall render an alteration necessary, in the opinion of any succeeding Aldermen, and also in the opinion of the court of the county. . . .

At every of these schools shall be taught reading, writing, and the common arithmetick, and the books that shall be used therein for instructing the children to read shall be such as will at the same time make them acquainted with Graecian, Roman, English, and American history. At these schools all the free children, male and female, resident within the respected hundred, shall be intitled to receive tuition gratis, for the term of three years, and as much longer, at their private expence, as their parents, guardians or friends, shall think proper. . . .

Every teacher shall receive a salary of —— by the year, which, with the expences of building and repairing the schoolhouses, shall be provided in such manner as other county expences are by law directed to be provided and shall also have his diet, lodging, and washing found him, to be levied in like manner, save only that such levy shall be on the inhabitants of each hundred for the board of their own teacher only.

And in order that grammar schools may be rendered convenient to the youth in every part of the commonwealth, Be it farther enacted, that on the first Monday in November, after the first appointment of overseers for the hundred schools, if fair, and if not, then on the next fair day, excluding Sunday, after the hour of one in the afternoon, the said overseers appointed for the schools . . . shall meet . . . and shall fix on such place in some one of the counties in their district as shall be most proper for situating a grammar school-house, endeavouring that the situation be as central as may be to the inhabitants of the said counties, that it be furnished with good water, convenient to plentiful supplies of provision and fuel, and more than all things that it be healthy. . . .

In these grammar schools shall be taught the Latin and Greek languages, English grammar, geography, and the higher part of numerical arithmetick, to wit, vulgar and decimal fractions, and the extraction of the square and cube roots. . . .

Every overseer of the hundred schools shall, in the month of September annually, after the most diligent and impartial examination and enquiry, appoint from among the boys who shall have been two years at the least at some of the schools under his superintendance, and whose parents are too poor to give them farther education, some one of the best and most promising genius and disposition, to proceed to the grammar school of his district; which appointment shall be made in the court-house of the county, on the court day for the month if fair, and if not, then on the next fair day, excluding Sunday, in the presence of the Aldermen, or two of them at the least, assembled on the bench for that purpose, the said overseer being previously sworn by them to make such appointment, without favor or affection, according to the best of his skill and judgment, and being interrogated by the said Aldermen, either on their own motion, or on suggestions from the parents, guardians, friends, or teachers of the children, competitors for such appointment; which teachers shall attend for the information of the Aldermen. On which interrogatories the said Aldermen, if they be not satisfied with the appointment proposed, shall have the right to negate it; whereupon the said visiter may proceed to make a new appointment, and the said Aldermen again to interrogate and negative, and so toties quoties until an appointment be approved.

Every boy so appointed shall be authorised to proceed to the grammar school of his district, there to be educated and boarded during such time as is hereafter limited; and his quota of the expences of the house together with a compensation to the master or usher for his tuition, at the rate of twenty dollars by the year, shall be paid by the Treasurer quarterly on warrant from the Auditors.

A visitation shall be held, for the purpose of probation, annually at the said grammar school on the last Monday in September, if fair, and if not, then on the next fair day, excluding Sunday, at which one third of the boys sent thither by appointment of the said overseers, and who shall have been there one year only, shall be discontinued as public foundationers, being those who, on the most diligent examination and enquiry, shall be thought to be of the least promising genius and disposition; and of those who shall have been there two years, all shall be discontinued, save one only the best in genius and disposition, who shall be at liberty to continue there four years or longer on the public foundation, and shall thence forward be deemed a senior.

The visiters for the districts which, or any part of which, be southward and westward of the James river, as known by that name, or by the names of Fluvanna and Jackson's river, in every other year, to wit, at the probation meetings held in the years, distinguished in the Christian computation by odd numbers, and the visiters for all the other districts at their said meetings to be held in those years, distinguished by even numbers, after diligent examination and enquiry as before directed, shall chuse one among the said seniors, of the best learning and most hopeful genius and disposition, who shall be authorised by them to proceed to William and Mary College, there to be educated, boarded, and clothed, three years; the expence of which annually shall be paid by the Treasurer on warrant from the Auditors. . . .

4. Extracts from Noah Webster's Introduction to *A Grammatical Institute, of the English Language,* 1783

To attack deep rooted prejudices and oppose the current of opinion, is a task of great difficulty and hazard. It commonly requires length of time and favourable circumstances to diffuse and establish a sentiment among the body of the people; but when a sentiment has acquired the stamp of time and the authority of general custom, it is too firm to be shaken by the efforts of an individual: Even errour becomes too sacred to be violated by the assaults of innovation.

But the present period is an era of wonders: Greater changes have been wrought, in the minds of men, in the short compass of eight years past, than are commonly effected in a century.

Previously to the late war, America preserved the most unshaken attachment to Great-Britain: The king, the constitution, the laws, the commerce, the fashions, the books, and even the sentiments of Englishmen were implicitly supposed to be the *best* on earth: not only their virtues and improvements, but their prejudices, their errours, their vices and their follies were adopted by us with avidity. But by a concurrence of those powerful causes that effect almost instantaneous revolutions in states, the political views of America have suffered a total change. She now sees a mixture of profound wisdom and consummate folly in the British constitution; a ridiculous compound of freedom and tyranny in their laws; and a few struggles of patriotism, overpowered by the corruptions of a wicked administration. She views the vices of that nation with abhorrence, their errours with pity, and their follies with contempt.

While the Americans stand astonished at their former delusion and enjoy the pleasure of a final separation from their insolent sovereigns, it becomes their duty to attend to the *arts of peace*, and particularly to the interests of *literature;* to see if there be not some errours to be corrected; some defects to be supplied, and some improvements to be introduced into our systems of education, as well as into those of civil policy. We find Englishmen practicing upon very erroneous maxims in politics and religion; and possibly we shall find, upon careful examination, that their methods of education are equally erroneous and defective.

The British writers remark it as one of the follies of their nation, that they have attended more to the study of ancient and foreign languages, than to the improvement of their own. The ancient Greek and Roman languages, and the modern French and Italian, have generally been made a necessary part of polite or learned education; while a grammatical study of their own language, has, till very lately been totally neglected. This ridiculous practice has found its way to America; and so violent have been the prejudices in support of it, that the whispers of common sense, in favour of our native tongue, have been silenced amidst the clamour of pedantry in favour of Greek and Latin.

The consequence is, that few attempts have been made to reduce our language to rules, and expunge the corruptions that ignorance and caprice, unguided by any standard, must necessarily introduce. It is but a short time since we have had a grammar of our own tongue, formed upon the true principals of its Saxon original: And those who have given us the most perfect systems, have confined themselves chiefly to the two last branches of grammar, Analogy and Syntax. In the two first, Orthography and Prosody, that is, in the spelling and pronunciation of words, we have no guide, or none but such as lead into innumerable errours. The want of some standard in schools has occasioned a great variety of dialects in Great-Britain and of course, in America. Every county in England, every State in America and almost every town in each State, has some peculiarities in pronunciation which are equally erroneous and disagreeable to its neighbors. And how can these distinctions be avoided? The sounds of our letters are more capricious and irregular than those of any alphabet with which we are acquainted. Several of our sounds are often expressed by five, six or seven different characters. The case is much the same with our consonants: And these different sounds have no mark of distinction. How would a child or a foreigner learn the different sounds of *o* in these words, *rove, move, dove* or of *oo* in *poor, door*? Or that *a, ai, ei,* and *e* have precisely the same sounds in *bare, laid, vein, there*? Yet these and fifty other irregularities have passed unnoticed by authors of Spelling Books and Dictionaries. They study the language enough to find the difficulties of it—they tell us that it is impossible to reduce it to order—that it is to be learnt only by the ear—they lament the disorder and dismiss it without a remedy.

Thus the pronunciation of our language, tho' the most important and difficult part of grammar, is *left* to parents and nurses—to ignorance and caprice—to custom, accident or nothing—Nay to something worse, to coxcombs, who have a large share in directing the *polite taste* of pronunciation, which of course is as vicious as that of any other class of people. And while this is the case, every person will claim a right to pronounce most agreably to his own fancy, and the language will be exposed to perpetual fluctuation.

This consideration gave rise to the following little system, which is designed to introduce uniformity and accuracy of pronunciation into common schools. It cost me much labour to form a plan that should be both *simple* and *accurate*. The one here adopted seems to unite these two articles; at least so far as to prevent any material errours. A more accurate method might have been invented; but it must have been too complicated to be useful. The rules for ascertaining a just pronunciation are so simple and concise, that I flatter myself they fall within the comprehension of the most indifferent capacity. Some may possibly be too indolent to study them; and others, from a principle of self-sufficiency, may affect to despise them. The former will be modest enough neither to approve nor condemn what they deem beneath their attention; and I would inform the latter that after I had devoted nine years to the acquisition of knowledge, three or four of which were spent in studying languages, and about the same period in teaching the English, I was astonished to find myself a stranger to its principle beauties and most obvious faults. Those therefore who disdain this attempt to improve our language and assist the instructors of youth, must be either much more or much less acquainted with the language than I am. The criticisms of those who know more, will be received with gratitude; the censure or ridicule of those who know less will be inexcusable.

The principal part of instructors are illiterate people, and require some easy guide to the *standard* of pronunciation, which is nothing else but the customary pronunciation of the most accurate scholars and literary Gentlemen. Such a standard, universally used in schools, would in time, demolish those odious distinctions of provincial dialects, which are the objects of reciprocal ridicule in the United States. . . .

The author wishes to promote the honour and prosperity of the confederated republics of America; and cheerfully throws his mite into the common treasure of patriotic exertions. This country must in some future time, be as distinguished by the superiority of her literary improvements, as she is already by the liberality of her civil and ecclesiastical constitutions. Europe is grown old in folly, corruption and tyranny—in that country laws are perverted, manners are licentious, literature is declining and human nature debased. For America in her infancy to adopt the present maxims of the old world, would be to stamp the wrinkles of decrepid age upon the bloom of youth and to plant the seeds of decay in a vigorous constitution. American glory begins to dawn at a favourable period, and under flattering circumstances. We have the experience of the whole world before our eyes; but to receive indiscriminately the maxims of government, the manners and the literary taste of Europe and make them the ground on which to build our systems in America, must soon convince us that a durable and stately edifice can never be erected upon the mouldering pillars of antiquity. It is the business of *Americans* to select the wisdom of all nations, as the basis of her constitutions,—to avoid their errours,   to prevent the introduction of foreign vices and corruptions and check the career of her own,—to promote virtue and patriotism,—to embellish

and improve the sciences,—to diffuse an uniformity and purity of *language*,—to add superiour dignity to this infant Empire and to human nature.

5. Extract from "A Plan for Establishing Public Schools in Pennsylvania, and for Conducting Education Agreeably to a Republican Form of Government," Presented by Benjamin Rush to the Legislature and Citizens of Pennsylvania, 1786

Before I proceed to the subject of this essay, I shall point out, in a few words, the influence and advantages of learning upon mankind.

I.   It is friendly to religion, inasmuch as it assists in removing prejudice, superstition and enthusiasm, in promoting just notions of the Deity, and in enlarging, our knowledge of his works.

II. It is favourable to liberty. Freedom can exist only in the society of knowledge. Without learning, men are incapable of knowing their rights, and where learning is confined to a few people, liberty can be neither equal nor universal.

III. It promotes just ideas of laws and government. "When the clouds of ignorance are dispelled (says the Marquis of Beccaria) by the radiance of knowledge, power trembles, but the authority of laws remains immoveable."

IV. It is friendly to manners. Learning in all countries, promotes civilization, and the pleasures of society and conversation.

V.   It promotes agriculture, the great basis of national wealth and happiness. Agriculture is as much a science as hydraulics, or optics, and has been equally indebted to the experiments and researches of learned men. The highly cultivated state, and the immense profits of the farms in England, are derived wholly from the patronage which agriculture has received in that country, from learned men and learned societies.

VI. Manufactures of all kinds owe their perfection chiefly to learning—hence the nations of Europe advance in manufactures, knowledge, and commerce, only in proportion as they cultivate the arts and sciences.

For the purpose of diffusing knowledge through every part of the state, I beg leave to propose the following simple plan.

I. Let there be one University in the state, and let this be established at the capital. Let law, physic, divinity, the law of nature and nations, œconomy, &c. be taught in it by public lectures in the winter season, after the manner of the European Universities, and let the professors receive such salaries from the State as will enable them to deliver their lectures at a moderate price.

II. Let there be four Colleges. One in Philadelphia; one at Carlisle; a third, for the benefit of our German fellow citizens, at Lancaster; and a fourth, some years hence at Pittsburg. In these Colleges, let young men be instructed in Mathematics and in the higher branches of science, in the same manner that they are now taught in our American Colleges. After they have received a testimonial from one of these Colleges, let them, if they can afford it, complete their studies by spending a season or two in attending the lectures in the University. . . .

III. Let there be free schools established in every township, or in districts consisting of one hundred families. In these schools let children be taught to read and write the English and German languages, and the use of figures. Such parents as can afford to send their children from home, and are disposed to extend their education, may remove them from the free school to one of the Colleges.

By this plan the whole State will be tied together by one system of education. The University will in time furnish masters for the Colleges, and the Colleges will furnish masters for the free schools, while the free schools, in their turns, will supply the Colleges and the University with scholars, students and pupils. The same systems of grammar, oratory and philosophy, will be taught in every part of the State, and the literary features of Pennsylvania will thus designate one great, and equally enlightened family. . . .

6. Extracts from the Massachusetts School Law of 1789

Every town or district within this Commonwealth, containing *fifty* families, or householders, shall be provided with a School-Master or School-Masters, of good morals, to teach children to read and write, and to instruct them in the English language, as well as in arithmetic, orthography, and decent behaviour, for such term of time as shall be equivalent to *six months* for one school in each year. And every town or district containing *one hundred* families, or householders, shall be provided with such School-Master or School-Masters, for such term of time as shall be equivalent to *twelve* months for one school in each year. And every town or district containing *one hundred and fifty* families, or householders, shall be provided with such School-Master or School-Masters, for such term of time as shall be equivalent to *six months* in each year; and shall, in addition thereto, be provided with a School-Master or School-Masters, as above described, to instruct children in the English language, for such term of time as shall be equivalent to *twelve months* for one school in each year. And every town or district containing *two hundred* families, or householders, shall be provided with a grammar School-Master, of good morals, well instructed in the Latin, Greek and English languages; and shall, in addition thereto, be provided with a School-Master or School-Masters, as above described, to instruct children in the English language, for such term of time as shall be equivalent to *twelve months* for each of said schools in each year. . . .

[N]o youth shall be sent to such grammar schools unless they shall have learned, in some other school or in some other way, to read the English language, by spelling the same; or the Selectmen of the town where such grammar school is, shall direct the grammar School-Master to receive and instruct such youth. . . .

[N]o person shall be allowed to be a Master or Mistress of such school, or to keep the same, unless he or she shall obtain a certificate from the Selectmen of such town or district where the same may be kept, or the Committee appointed by such town, district or plantation, to visit their schools, as well as from a learned Minister settled therein, if such there be, that he or she is a person of sober life and conversation, and well qualified to keep such a school. And it shall be the duty of such Master or Mistress, carefully to instruct the children, attending his or her school, in reading (and writing, if contracted for) and to instil into their minds a sense of piety and virtue, and to teach them decent behaviour. And if any person shall presume to keep such a school without a certificate as aforesaid, he or she shall forfeit and pay the sum of *Twenty Shillings*, one moiety thereof to the informer, and the other moiety to the use of the poor of the town, district or plantation where such school may be kept. . . .

No person shall be permitted to keep, within the Commonwealth, any school described in this Act, unless, in consequence of an Act of naturalization, or otherwise, he shall be a citizen of this or some other of the United States. And if any person who is not a citizen of this or some one of the United States, shall presume to keep any such school within this State for the space of one month, he shall be subjected to pay a fine of *Twenty Pounds,* and a proportionable sum for a longer or shorter time; the one half of which fine shall be to the use of the person who shall sue for the same, and the other half thereof to the use of this Commonwealth.

7. Announcement of the opening of the Warrenton (North Carolina) Female Academy, August 18, 1808

In conformity to the wishes of some respectable Patrons in this place and its vicinity, I propose to open an Institution for Female Improvement, on the first day of January next. The course of Instruction intended to be pursued, is the result of observation and some experience, and will be adopted to the varied dispositions of genius of my Pupils, not losing sight of systematic Arrangement and Progression. My object not merely to impart words and exhibit things, but chiefly to form the mind to the labour of thinking upon and understanding what is taught.— Whether my plan is judicious, a short experience will decide; and by the event I am content to be judged. The domestic arrangement for an efficient accommodation of my Scholars, will be an object of primary concern, and placed under the immediate inspection of Mrs. Mordecai—believing it to be no small part of Education bestowed on Females, to cultivate a *Taste* for neatness in their Persons and propriety of Manners: they will be placed under a superintendence calculated as much as possible to alleviate the solicitude of Parents.—In my Seminary will be taught the English Language, grammatically, *Spelling,* Reading, Writing, Arithmetic, Composition, History, Geography and use of the Globes. The plain and ornamental branches of Needle Work—Drawing, Vocal and Instrumental Music, by an approved Master of distinguished talents and correct deportment.

Terms:—For Board, Washing, Lodging and Tuition (Drawing and Music excepted) $105 per annum. An additional charge will be made for necessary Books, paper, Quills and Ink.

Warrenton, Aug, 18, 1808.
Jacob Mordecai.

8. Extracts from Original Papers in Relation to a Course of Liberal Education (the Yale Report), September 11, 1827

Report of the Faculty

PART I.

Containing a summary view of the plan of education in the college.

. . . We are decidedly of the opinion, that our present plan of education admits of improvement. We are aware that the system is imperfect: and we cherish the hope, that some of its defects may ere long be remedied. We believe that changes may, from time to time be made with advantage, to meet the varying demands of the community, to accommodate the course of instruction to the rapid advance of the country, in population, refinement, and opulence. We have no doubt that important improvements may be suggested, by attentive observation of the literary institutions in Europe; and by the earnest spirit of inquiry which is now so prevalent, on the subject of education.

The guardians of the college appear to have ever acted upon the principle, that it ought not to be stationary, but continually advancing. Some alteration has accordingly been proposed, almost every year, from its first establishment. It is with no small surprise, therefore, we occasionally hear the suggestion, that our system is unalterable; that colleges were originally planned, in the days of monkish ignorance; and that, "by being immovably moored to the same station, they serve only to measure the rapid current of improvement which is passing by them."

How opposite to all this, is the real state of facts, in this and the other seminaries in the United States. Nothing is more common, than to hear those who revisit the college, after a few years absence, express their surprise at the changes which have been made since they were graduated. Not only the course of studies, and the modes of instruction, have been greatly varied; but whole sciences have, for the first time, been introduced; chemistry, mineralogy, geology, political economy, &c. By raising the qualifications for admission, the standard of attainment has been elevated. Alterations so extensive and frequent, satisfactorily prove, that if those who are intrusted with the superintendence of the institution, still firmly adhere to some of its original features, it is from a higher principle, than a blind opposition to salutary reform. Improvements, we trust, will continue to be made, as rapidly as they can be, without hazarding the loss of what has been already attained.

But perhaps the time has come, when we ought to pause, and inquire, whether it will be sufficient to make *gradual* changes, as heretofore; and whether the whole system is not rather to be broken up, and a better one substituted in its stead. From different quarters, we have heard the suggestion, that our colleges must be *new-modelled*; that they are not adapted to the spirit and wants of the age; that they will soon be deserted, unless they are better accommodated to the business character of the nation. . . .

We shall in vain attempt to decide on the expediency of retaining or altering our present course of instruction, unless we have a distinct apprehension of the *object* of a collegiate education. A plan of study may well be adapted to a particular purpose, though it may be very unsuitable for a different one. Universities, colleges, academical, and professional seminaries, ought not to be all constituted upon the same model; but should be so varied as to attain the ends which they have severally in view.

What then is the appropriate object of a college? It is not necessary here to determine what it is which, in every case, entitles an institution to the *name* of a college. But if we have not greatly misapprehended the design of the patrons and guardians of this college, its object is to LAY THE FOUNDATION of a SUPERIOR EDUCATION. . . .

The two great points to be gained in intellectual culture, are the *discipline* and the *furniture* of the mind; expanding its powers, and storing it with knowledge. The former of these is, perhaps, the more important of the two. A commanding object, therefore, in a collegiate course, should be, to call into daily and vigorous exercise the faculties of the student. Those branches of study should be prescribed, and those modes of instruction adopted, which are best calculated to teach the art of fixing the attention, directing the train of thought, analyzing a subject proposed for investigation; following, with accurate discrimination, the course of argument; balancing nicely the evidence presented to the judgment; awakening, elevating, and controlling the imagination; arranging, with skill, the treasures which memory gathers; rousing and guiding the powers of genius. All this is not to be effected by a light and hasty course of study; by reading a few books, hearing a few lectures, and spending some months at a literary institution. The habits of thinking are to be formed, by long continued and close application. The mines of science must be penetrated far below the surface, before they will disclose their treasures. If a dex-

terous performance of the manual operations, in many of the mechanical arts, requires an apprenticeship, with diligent attention for years; much more does the training of the powers of the mind demand vigorous, and steady, and systematic effort.

In laying the foundation of a thorough education, it is necessary that *all* the important mental faculties be brought into exercise. It is not sufficient that one or two be cultivated, while others are neglected. . . . If a student exercises his reasoning powers only, he will be deficient in imagination and taste, in fervid and impressive eloquence. If he confines his attention to demonstrative evidence, he will be unfitted to decide correctly, in cases of probability. If he relies principally on his memory, his powers of invention will be impaired by disuse. In the course of instruction in this college, it has been an object to maintain, such a proportion between the different branches of literature and science, as to form in the student a *balance* of character. From the pure mathematics, he learns the art of demonstrative reasoning. In attending to the physical sciences, he becomes familiar with facts, with the process of induction, and the varieties of probable evidence. In ancient literature, he finds some of the most finished models of taste. By English reading, he learns the powers of the language in which he is to speak and write. By logic and mental philosophy, he is taught the art of thinking; by rhetoric and oratory, the art of speaking. By frequent exercise on written composition, he acquires copiousness and accuracy of expression. By extemporaneous discussion, he becomes prompt, and fluent, and animated. . . .

The course of instruction which is given to the undergraduates in the college, is not designed to include *professional* studies. Our object is not to teach that which is peculiar to any one of the professions; but to lay the foundation which is common to them all. There are separate schools for medicine, law, and theology, connected with the college, as well as in various parts of the country; which are open for the reception of all who are prepared to enter upon the appropriate studies of their several professions. With these, the academical course is not intended to interfere.

But why, it may be asked, should a student waste his time upon studies which have no immediate connection with his future profession? Will chemistry enable him to plead at the bar, or conic sections qualify him for preaching, or astronomy aid him in the practice of physic? Why should not his attention be confined to the subject which is to occupy the labors of his life? In answer to this, it may be observed, that there is no science which does not contribute its aid to professional skill. . . . The great object of a college education, preparatory to the study of a profession, is to give that expansion and balance of the mental powers, those liberal and comprehensive views, and those fine proportions of character, which are not to be found in him whose ideas are always confined to one particular channel. When a man has entered upon the practice of his profession, the energies of his mind must be given, principally, to its appropriate duties. But if his thoughts never range on other subjects, if he never looks abroad on the ample domains of literature and science, there will be a narrowness in his habits of thinking, a peculiarity of character, which will be sure to mark him as a man of limited views and attainments. Should he be distinguished in his profession, his ignorance on other subjects, and the defects of his education, will be the more exposed to public observation. On the other hand, he who is not only eminent in professional life, but also has a mind richly stored with general knowledge, has an elevation and dignity of character, which gives him a commanding influence in society, and a widely extended sphere of usefulness. . . .

Professional studies are designedly excluded from the course of instruction at college, to leave room for those literary and scientific acquisitions which, if not commenced there will, in most cases, never be made. They will not grow up spontaneously, amid the bustle of business. We are not here speaking of those giant minds which, by their native energy, break through the obstructions of a defective education, and cut their own path to distinction. These are honorable exceptions to the general law; not examples for common imitation. Franklins and Marshalls are not found in sufficient numbers to fill a college. And even Franklin would not have been what he was, if there had been no college in the country. . . .

9. An Act to amend the Laws in relation to Slaves and Free Persons of Color, South Carolina, 1840

If any person shall hereafter teach any slave to read or write, or shall aid or assist in teaching any slave to read or write, or cause or procure any slave to be taught to read or write, such person, if a free white person, upon conviction thereof, shall, for each and every offence against this Act, be fined not exceeding one hundred dollars, and imprisoned not more than six months; or if a free person of color, shall be whipped, not exceeding fifty lashes, and

fined not exceeding fifty dollars, at the discretion of the court of magistrates and freeholders before which such free person of color is tried; and if a slave, to be whipped at the discretion of the court, not exceeding fifty lashes; the informer to be entitled to one half of the fine, and to be a competent witness. And if any free person of color or slave shall keep any school, or other place of instruction, for teaching any slave or free person of color to read or write, such free person of color or slave shall be liable to the same fine, imprisonment, and corporal punishment, as are by this Act imposed and inflicted on free persons of color and slaves for teaching slaves to read or write.

10. The Massachusetts Compulsory School Law of 1850

Section 1.
Each of the several cities and towns in this Commonwealth is hereby authorized and empowered to make all needful provisions and arrangements concerning habitual truants, and children not attending school, without any regular and lawful occupation, growing up in ignorance, between the ages of six and fifteen years; and also all such ordinances and by-laws, respecting such children, as shall be deemed most conducive to their welfare, and the good order of such city or town; and there shall be annexed to such ordinances, suitable penalties, not exceeding, for any one breach, a fine of twenty dollars: *provided*, that said ordinances and by-laws shall be approved by the court of common pleas for the county, and shall not be repugnant to laws of the commonwealth.

Sec. 2.
The several cities and towns, availing themselves of the provisions of this act, shall appoint, at the annual meetings of said towns, or annually by the mayor and aldermen of said cities, three or more persons, who alone shall be authorized to make the complaints, in every case of violation of said ordinances or by-laws, to the justice of the peace, or other judicial officer, who, by said ordinances, shall have jurisdiction in the matter, which persons, thus appointed, shall alone have authority to carry into execution the judgments of said justices of the peace or other judicial officer.

Sec. 3.
The said justices of the peace, or other judicial officers, shall in all cases, at their discretion, in place of the fine aforesaid, be authorized to order children, proved before them to be growing up in truancy, and without the

benefit of education provided for them by law, to be placed, for such periods of time as they may judge expedient, in such institution of instruction or house of reformation, or other suitable situation, as may be assigned or provided for the purpose, under the authority conveyed by the first section of this act, in each city or town availing itself of the powers herein granted.

11. Extracts from An Act Donating Public Lands to the Several States and Territories Which May Provide Colleges for the Benefit of Agriculture and the Mechanic Arts (Morrill Act), 1862

Sec. 1.

Be it enacted by the Senate and House of Representatives of the United States of America in Congress assembled, That there be granted to the several States, for the purpose hereinafter mentioned, an amount of public land, to be apportioned to each State a quantity equal to thirty thousand acres for each senator and representative in Congress to which the States are respectively entitled by the apportionment under the census of eighteen hundred and sixty: Provided, That no mineral lands shall be selected or purchased under the provisions of this act.

Sec. 2.

And be it further enacted, That the land aforesaid, after being surveyed, shall be apportioned to the several States in sections or subdivisions of sections, not less than one quarter of a section; and whenever there are public lands in a State subject to sale at private entry at one dollar and twenty-five cents per acre, the quantity to which said State shall be entitled shall be selected from such lands within the limits of such State, and the Secretary of the Interior is hereby directed to issue to each of the States in which there is not the quantity of public lands subject to sale at private entry at one dollar and twenty-five cents per acre, to which said State may be entitled under the provisions of this act, land scrip to the amount in acres for the deficiency of its distributive share: said scrip to be sold by said States and the proceeds thereof applied to the uses and purposes prescribed in this act, and for no other use or purpose whatsoever. . . .

Sec. 4.

And be it further enacted, That all moneys derived from the sale of the lands aforesaid by the States to which the lands are apportioned, and from the sale of land scrip hereinbefore provided for, shall be invested in stocks of the United States, or of the States, or some other safe stocks; and that the moneys so invested shall constitute a perpetual find, the capital of which shall remain forever undiminished . . . and the interest of which shall by inviolably appropriated, by each State which may take and claim the benefits of this act, to the endowment, support, and maintenance of at least one college where the leading object shall be, without excluding other scientific and classical studies, and including military tactics, to teach such branches of learning as are related to agriculture and mechanic arts, in such manner as the legislatures of the State may respectively prescribe, in order to promote the liberal and practical education of the industrial classes in the several pursuits and professions in life. . . .

Sec. 6.

No State while in a condition of rebellion or insurrection against the government of the United States shall be entitled to the benefit of this Act. . . .

12. Extracts from the First Semi-Annual Report on Schools and Finances of Freedmen, Bureau of Refugees, Freedmen and Abandoned Lands, January 1, 1866

GENERAL: In obedience to your Special Order No. 84, appointing me inspector of schools and finances for freedmen, I have the honor to report that I left Washington on the 6th day of October last, and traveled through all the States south, below Tennessee, and this side of the Mississippi river. The cities and large towns visited were Baltimore, Maryland; Hampton, Norfolk, Petersburg, and Richmond, Virginia; Newbern, Goldsboro', and Wilmington, North Carolina; Florence, Charleston, and Beaufort, South Carolina; Savannah, Augusta, and Atlanta, Georgia; Fernandina, Jacksonville, and Tallahassee, Florida; Mobile and Montgomery, Alabama; Jackson, Vicksburg, and Natchez, Mississippi; and New Orleans, Louisiana; most of these places both on my outward and returning journey. My whole tour extended over 4,000 miles. Going by land I was enabled to see along the line, and by excursions into the interior and to the islands, much of the freedmen's condition upon the plantations. I also went among the colored troops, as I could find them in their various regimental encampments, or as detailed in companies on special duty.

SCHOOLS.

The desire of the freedmen for knowledge has not been overstated. This comes from several causes:

1. The natural thirst for knowledge common to all men.
2. They have seen power and influence among white people always coupled with *learning*; it is the sign of that elevation to which they now aspire.
3. Its mysteries, hitherto hidden from them in written literature, excites to the special study of *books*.
4. Their freedom has given wonderful stimulus to *all effort*, indicating a vitality which augurs well for their whole future condition and character.
5. But especially the practical business of life, now upon their hands, shows their immediate need of education. This they all feel and acknowledge; hence their unusual welcome and attendance upon schools is confined to no one class or age. Those advanced in life throw up their hands at first in despair, but a little encouragement places *even these* as pupils at the alphabet.

Such as are in middle life—the laboring classes—gladly avail themselves of the evening and Sabbath schools. They may often be seen during the intervals of toil, when off duty as servants, on steamboats, along the railroads, and when unemployed in the streets of the city, or on plantations, with some fragment of a spelling-book in their hands, earnestly at study. Regiments of colored soldiers have nearly all made improvement in learning. In some of them, where but few knew their letters at first, nearly every man can now read and many of them write. In other regiments one-half or two-thirds can do this. The officers of such regiments deserve great credit for their efforts in this respect. The 128th United States colored troops, at Beaufort, I found with regularly detailed teachers from the line officers; a neat camp school-house, erected by the regiment; and the colonel, with great interest, superintending the whole arrangement. Chaplains have also been the schoolmasters of their respective regiments with much success, and greatly increasing their usefulness.

Even in hospitals I discovered very commendable efforts at such elementary instruction.

But the great movement is among *children* of the *usual school age*. Their parents, if at all intelligent, encourage them to study. Your officers in all ways add their influence; and it is a fact, not always true of children, that among those recently from bondage, the school-house, however rough and uncomfortable, is of all other places the most attractive; the average attendance being nearly equal to that usually found at the north. . . . In the *comparison*, therefore, schools of colored children do not suffer (especially when we consider absence of home influence and opportunity for truancy) with the most vigorous system found among our own children. Love of their books is universally apparent. . . .

Evening and Sabbath schools . . . Evening schools for adults, of great utility, are becoming very numerous; often conducted by volunteer friends of the colored man, and with a modesty which forbids making public mention of their work. Sabbath schools among freedmen have been opened throughout the entire south; all of them giving elementary instruction, and reaching thousands who cannot attend the week-day teaching. These are not usually included in the regular returns, but are often spoken of with special interest by the superintendents. . . .

Self-teaching . . . Throughout the entire south an effort is being made by the colored people to educate themselves. In the absence of other teaching they are determined to be self-taught; and everywhere some elementary text-book, or the fragment of one, may be seen in the hands of negroes. They quickly communicate to each other what they already know, so that with very little learning many take to teaching. A willingness, even *an ambition*, to bear expenses is also noticed. They often say, "we want how much we can do *ourselves*, if you will only give us a chance."

Native schools.—The above may seem to those who doubt the character of the negro to be an over-statement; not that he is unwilling to be helped, but so universal is the feeling I am describing, that it seems as if some unseen influence was inspiring them to that intelligence which they now so immediately need. Not only are individuals seen at study, and under the most untoward circumstances, but in very many places I have found what I will call "native schools," often rude and very imperfect, but *there they are*, a group, perhaps, of all ages, *trying to learn*. Some young man, some woman, or old preacher, in cellar, or shed, or corner of a negro meeting-house, with the alphabet in hand, or a torn spelling-book, is their teacher. All are full of enthusiasm with the new knowledge THE BOOK is imparting to them.

Again, I saw schools (shall I call them) of somewhat higher order. A deserted house has been obtained. There is some organization and awkward classifying; larger numbers, better books, with tolerable exhibition of easy reading. A sample of such I met at Goldsboro', N.C. Two colored young men, who but a little time before commenced to learn themselves, had gathered 150 pupils, all quite orderly and hard at study. A small tuition fee was charged, and they needed books. These teachers told me that "no white man, before me, had ever come near them." At Halifax was a similar school, the first of *any kind* which had been opened in that county since the war.

The cities.—A still higher order of this native teaching is seen in the colored schools at Charleston, Savannah, and New Orleans. With many disadvantages they bear a very good examination. One I visited in the latter city, of 300 pupils, and wholly taught by educated colored men, would bear comparison with any ordinary school at the north. Not only good reading and spelling were heard, but lessons at the black-board in arithmetic, recitations in geography and English grammar. Very creditable specimens of writing were shown, and all the older classes could read or recite as fluently in French as in English. This was a free school, wholly supported by the colored people of the city, and the children were from the common class of families. They have six select schools where a better class attend. All the above cases illustrate the remark that this educational movement among the freedmen has in it a self-sustaining element. I took special pains to ascertain the facts on this particular point, and have to report that there are schools of this kind in some stage of advancement (taught and supported wholly by the people themselves) in all the large places I visited—often *numbers* of them, and they are also making their appearance through the *interior* of the entire country. The superintendent of South Carolina assured me that there was not a place of any size in the whole of that State where such a school was not attempted. I have much testimony, both oral and written, from others well informed, that the same is true of other States. There can scarcely be a doubt, and I venture the estimate, that at least 500 schools of this description are already in operation throughout the south. If, therefore, all these be added, and including soldiers and individuals at study, we shall have at least 125,000 as the *entire educational census of this lately emancipated people.*

This is a wonderful state of things. We have just emerged from a terrific war; peace is not yet declared. There is scarcely the beginning of reorganized society at the south; and yet here is a people long imbruted by slav-ery, and the most despised of any on earth, whose chains are no sooner broken than they spring to their feet and start up an exceeding great army, clothing themselves with intelligence. What other people on earth have ever shown, while in their ignorance, such a passion for education?

It is also seen that the children of the poor whites of the south are very ready to receive instruction, and that already considerable has been done for them.

The conclusions forced upon us from the above facts are:

1. *The experiment of educating the freedmen proves to be successful,* and the ignorant whites may be greatly benefited.

    It only remains to carry on with confidence the work so well begun.

    That colored children can at once compete with white children, who from the first have had high advantages, need not be said. It is enough that with early bad habits, bad example, and wholly unpracticed in study, they seize upon books gladly and learn rapidly. As well endowed naturally or not, we certainly see in the majority the same brightness, the same quick ambition, as with children of the more favored color; and, stimulated as they are by the novelty of study, there is at present an actual progress scarcely to be paralleled anywhere. In advanced studies, or at a mature age, pupils give no signs of having reached the limit of their capacity. I have discovered hesitation in their plans for using education. Their ardor is dampened by the well-known aversion to their occupying high position; but always, when assured that, as character and intelligence increase, ways and means of usefulness will be opened, they are ready to push on to new and higher tasks. When I have told the higher classes in the schools that they will be wanted as teachers, at least of their own color, a new stimulus is seen at once to excite them, and their instructors have always assured me that such promise has inspired an intense ambition. . . .

2. *The good influence of the schools upon all the habits of the freedmen is apparent.*—As the children repeat their lessons at home, parents become interested and thoughtful, acquire many new ideas, and are led to prize their families, who are thus increasing in knowledge. They at once make new exertion for self-support, especially for the schools, insuring both industry and economy. . . .

3. *The white population of the south feels the power of these schools.*—Assent, if not the favor, of the better men is

being gradually obtained. Popular education cannot well be opposed; free labor is found to be far more contented with its privileges. The major part may be indignant that negroes should have learning. All sorts of evil is predicted as the consequence; and yet a portion of this enmity is excited by the rivalry which their own children must now struggle with. The "poor whites" are provoked by hearing negroes read, while they are ignorant; and it is my belief that they will now receive schools, if furnished them, as never before. The educated class are not slow to perceive that their schools must be reopened, or fall behind humiliated, and that new schools must now be organized on a more popular plan than heretofore. Poverty, and perhaps pride, with the want of teachers, are the present difficulties in carrying out these convictions. . . .

4. *A class of schools is called for in which colored teachers can be taught.*—If dignified by the name "normal schools," they should commence with training in the simplest elements of art. Education for the freedmen, as a whole, must be at the very first rudimental, in which the text will be found mainly in the spelling book, but which can become, as soon as possible, universal. This people all want learning at once. . . .

4. [*sic*] *The people of the north are strongly seconding the educating efforts of this bureau.*—Educational associations were in the field almost as soon as our conquering armies gave them a foothold. They have increased in numbers and in arduous, well-directed effort. Their several corps of teachers deserve all praise for self-sacrifice and fidelity. Your appointment of State superintendents of schools has given organic unity to these efforts, and greatly enhanced their efficiency. Popular donations are rapidly increasing, and you may rely upon the continuance of sympathy and the increase of this important aid. . . .

5. In conclusion permit me distinctly to call attention to the fact that this whole educational movement among the freedmen must, for the present, be protected by the general government. I need not repeat, what appears all through this report, viz: that military force alone can save many of our schools from being broken up, or enable us to organize new schools. Such is the improper spirit in many parts of the south, that where as yet there have been no atrocities attempted against the schools, protecting power is called for to give that sense of quiet and consciousness of security

which the calm duties of both teacher and pupil always require. . . .

J. W. ALVORD,
Inspector of Schools and Finances.

Major General O. O. HOWARD,
Commissioner of Bureau of Refugees, Freedmen, &c.

13. An Act to Compel Children to Attend School, Enacted and Amended by the Michigan Legislature at Its Session in 1871

SECTION 1.

The People of the State of Michigan enact, That every parent, guardian, or other person in the State of Michigan having control and charge of a child or children between the ages of eight and fourteen years, shall be required to send any such child or children to a public school for a period of at least twelve weeks in each school year, commencing on the first Monday of September, in the year of our Lord eighteen hundred and seventy-one, at least six weeks of which shall be consecutive, unless such child or children are excused from such attendance by the board of the school district in which such parents or guardians reside, upon its being shown to their satisfaction that his bodily or mental condition has been such as to prevent his attendance at school or application to study for the period required, or that such a child or children are taught in a private school, or at home, in such branches as are usually taught in primary schools, or have already acquired the ordinary branches of learning taught in the public school: *Provided,* In case a public school shall not be taught for three months during the year, within two miles by the nearest traveled road, of the residence of any person within the school district, he shall not be liable to the provisions of this act.

SEC. 2.

It shall be the duty of the director of every school district, and president of every school board within this State, to cause to be posted three notices of this law in the most public places in such district, or published in one newspaper in the township for three weeks, during the month of August in each year, the expense of such publication to be paid out of the funds of said district.

SEC. 3.

In case any parent, guardian, or other person shall fail to comply with the provisions of this act, said parent, guardian or other person shall be liable to a fine of not less than five dollars or more than ten dollars for the first offense, nor less than ten or more than twenty dollars for the second and every subsequent offense; said fine shall be collected by the director of said district in the name of the district in an action of debt or on the case, and when collected shall be paid to the assessor of the district in which the defendant resided when the offense was committed, and by him accounted for the same as money raised for school purposes.

SEC. 4.

It shall be the duty of the director or president to prosecute any offense occurring under this act, and any director or president neglecting to prosecute for such fine within ten days after a written notice has been served on him by any tax-payer in said district, unless the person so complained of shall be excused by the district board, shall be liable to a fine of not less than twenty or more than fifty dollars, which fine shall be prosecuted for and in the name of the assessor of said district, and the fine when collected shall be paid to the assessor, to be accounted for as in section three of this act.

14. Extracts from *Charles E. Stuart and Others v. School District No. 1 of the Village of Kalamazoo and Others* (the Kalamazoo Case), 1874

Heard July 10 and 15. Decided July 21.
Appeal in Chancery from Kalamazoo Circuit. . . .

COOLEY, J.

The bill in this case is filed to restrain the collection of such portion of the school taxes assessed against complainants for the year 1872, as have been voted for the support of the high school in that village, and for the payment of the salary of the superintendent. While, nominally, this is the end sought to be attained by the bill, the real purpose of the suit is wider and vastly more comprehensive than this brief statement would indicate, inasmuch as it seeks a judicial determination of the right of school authorities, in what are called union school districts of the state to levy taxes upon the general public for the support of what in this state are known as high schools, and to make free by such taxation the instruction of children in other languages than the English. The bill is, consequently, of no small interest to all the people of the state; and to a large number of very flourishing schools, it is of the very

highest interest, as their prosperity and usefulness, in a large degree, depend upon the method in which they are supported, so that a blow at this method seems a blow at the schools themselves. The suit, however, is not to be regarded as a blow purposely aimed at the schools. It can never be unimportant to know that taxation, even for the most useful or indispensable purposes, is warranted by the strict letter of the law; and whoever doubts its being so in any particular case, may well be justified by his doubts in asking a legal investigation, that, if errors or defects in the law are found to exist, there may be a review of the subject in legislation, and the whole matter be settled on legal grounds, in such manner and on such principles as the public will may indicate, and as the legislature may prescribe.

The complainants rely on two objections to the taxes in question, one of which is general, and the other applies only to the authority or action of this particular district. The general objection has already been indicated; the particular objection is that, even conceding that the other districts in the state may have authority under special charters or laws, or by the adoption of general statutes, to levy taxes for the support of high schools in which foreign and dead languages shall be taught, yet this district has no such power, because the special legislation for its benefit, which was had in 1859, was invalid for want of compliance with the constitution in the forms of enactment, and it has never adopted the general law (*Comp. L., § 3742*), by taking a vote of the district to establish a union school in accordance with its provisions, though ever since that law was enacted the district has sustained such a school, and proceeded in its action apparently on the assumption that the statutes in all respects were constitutional enactments, and had been complied with.

Whether this particular objection would have been worthy of serious consideration had it been made sooner, we must, after this lapse of time, wholly decline to consider. The district existed *de facto*, and we suppose *de jure*, also, for we are not informed to the contrary, when the legislation of 1859 was had, and from that time to the present it has assumed to possess and exercise all the franchises which are now brought in question, and there has since been a steady concurrence of action on the part of its people in the election of officers, in the levy of large taxes, and in the employment of teachers for the support of a high school. The state has acquiesced in this assumption of authority, and it has never, so far as we are advised, been questioned by any one until, after thirteen years use, three individual tax payers, out of some thousands, in a suit instituted on their own behalf, and to which the public authorities give no countenance, come forward in this collateral manner and ask us to annul the franchises. To require a municipal corporation, after so long an acquiescence, to defend, in a merely private suit, the irregularity, not only of its own action, but even the legislation that permitted such action to be had, could not be justified by the principles of law, much less by those of public policy. We may justly take cognizance in these cases, of the notorious fact that municipal action is often exceedingly informal and irregular, when, after all, no wrong or illegality has been intended, and the real purpose of the law has been had in view and been accomplished; so that it may be said the spirit of the law has been kept while the letter has been disregarded. We may also find in the statutes many instances of careless legislation, under which municipalities have acted for many years, until important interests have sprung up, which might be crippled or destroyed, if then for the first time matters of form in legislative action were suffered to be questioned. If every municipality must be subject to be called into court at any time to defend its original organization and its franchises at the will of any dissatisfied citizen who may feel disposed to question them, and subject to dissolution, perhaps, or to be crippled in authority and powers if defects appear, however complete and formal may have been the recognition of its rights and privileges, on the part alike of the state and of its citizens, it may very justly be said that few of our municipalities can be entirely certain of the ground they stand upon, and that any single person, however honestly inclined, if disposed to be litigious, or over technical and precise, may have it in his power in many cases to cause infinite trouble, embarrassment and mischief.

It was remarked by Mr. Justice Campbell in *People v. Maynard*, 15 Mich., 470, that "in public affairs where the people have organized themselves under color of law into the ordinary municipal bodies, and have gone on year after year raising taxes, making improvements, and exercising their usual franchises, their rights are properly regarded as depending quite as much on the acquiescence as on the regularity of their origin, and no *ex post facto* inquiry can be permitted to undo their corporate existence. Whatever may be the rights of individuals before such general acquiescence, the corporate standing of the community can no longer be open to question.". . .

It may be said that this doctrine is not applicable to this case because here the corporate organization is not questioned, but only the authority which the district as-

serts to establish a high school and level taxes therefor. But we think that, though the statute may not in terms apply, in principle it is strictly applicable. The district claims and has long exercised powers which take it out of the class of ordinary school districts, and place it in another class altogether, whose organization is greatly different and whose authority is much greater. So far as the externals of corporate action are concerned, the two classes are quite distinct, and the one subserves purposes of a higher order than the other, and is permitted to levy much greater burdens. It is not very clear that the case is not strictly within the law; for the organization here claimed is that of a union school district, and nothing else, and it seems little less than an absurdity to say it may be presumed from its user of corporate power to be a school district, but not such a district as the user indicates, and as it has for so long a period claimed to be. But however that may be, we are clear that even if we might be allowed by law to listen to the objection after the two years, we cannot in reason consent to do so after thirteen. It cannot be permitted that communities can be suffered to be annoyed, embarrassed and unsettled by having agitated in the courts after such a lapse of time questions which every consideration of fairness to the people concerned and of public policy require should be raised and disposed of immediately or never raised at all.

The more general question which the record presents we shall endeavor to state in our own language, but so as to make it stand out distinctly as a naked question of law, disconnected from all considerations of policy or expediency; in which light alone are we at liberty to consider it. It is, as we understand it, that there is no authority in this state to make the high schools free by taxation levied on the people at large. The argument is that while there may be no constitutional provision expressly prohibiting such taxation, the general course of legislation in the state and the general understanding of the people have been such as to require us to regard the instruction in the classics and in living modern languages in these schools as in the nature of not of practical and therefore necessary instruction for the benefit of the people at large, but rather as accomplishments for the few, to be sought after in the main by those best able to pay for them, and to be paid for by those who seek them, and not by general tax. And not only has this been the general state policy, but this higher learning of itself, when supplied by the state, is so far a matter of private concern to those who receive it that the courts ought to declare it incompetent to supply it wholly at the public expense. This is in substance, as we understand it, the position of the complainants in this suit. . . .

It is not disputed that the dissemination of knowledge by means of schools has been a prominent object from the first, and we allude to the provision of the ordinance of 1787 on that subject, and to the donation of lands by congress for the purpose, only as preliminary to what we may have to say regarding the action of the territorial authorities in the premises. Those authorities accepted in the most liberal spirit the requirement of the ordinance that "schools and the means of education shall forever be encouraged," and endeavored to make early provision therefor on a scale which shows they were fully up to the most advanced ideas that then prevailed on the subject. The earliest territorial legislation regarding education, though somewhat eccentric in form, was framed in this spirit. It was "an act to establish the Catholepistemiad, or University of Michigania," adopted August 26, 1817, which not only incorporated the institution named in the title, with its president and thirteen professors, appointed by the governor, but it provided that its board of instruction should have power "to regulate all the concerns of the institution, to enact laws for that purpose," "to establish colleges, academies, schools, libraries, museums, atheneums, botanic gardens, laboratories and other useful literary and scientific institutions, consonant to the laws of the United States of America, and of Michigan, and to appoint officers and instructors and instructrices, in, among, and throughout the various counties, cities, towns, townships, and other geographical divisions of Michigan." To provide for the expense thereof the existing public taxes were increased fifteen per cent., and from the proceeds of all future taxes fifteen per cent. was appropriated for the benefit of this corporation. . . .

This act continued in force until 1821, when it was repealed to make way for one "for the establishment of an university," with more limited powers, and authorized only "to establish colleges, academies and schools depending upon the said university," and which, according to the general understanding at the time and afterwards, were to be schools intermediate the university and such common schools as might exist or be provided for. . . . In 1827 the education system was supplemented by "an act for the establishment of common schools," which is also worthy of special attention and reflection, as indicating what was understood at that day by the common schools which were proposed to be established.

The first section of that act provided "that every township within this territory, containing families or householders, shall be provided with a good schoolmaster or schoolmasters, of good morals, to teach children to read and write, and to instruct them in the English or French language, as well as in arithmetic, orthography. and decent behavior, for such term of time as shall be equivalent to six months for one school in each year. And every township containing one hundred families or householders, shall be provided with such schoolmaster or teacher for such term of time as shall be equivalent to twelve months for one school in each year. And every township containing one hundred and fifty families or householders shall be provided with such schoolmaster or teacher for such term of time as shall be equivalent to six months in each year, and shall, in addition thereto, be provided with a schoolmaster or teacher, as above described, to instruct children in the English language for such term of time as shall be equivalent to twelve months for one school in each year. And every township containing two hundred families or householders shall be provided with a grammar schoolmaster, of good morals, *well instructed in Latin, French and English languages,* and shall, in addition thereto, be provided with a schoolmaster or teacher, as above described, to instruct children in the English language, for such term of time as shall be equivalent to twelve months for each of said schools in each year." And the townships respectively were required under a heavy penalty, to be levied in case of default on the inhabitants generally, to keep and maintain the schools so provided for. . . .

Here, then, was a general law, which, under the name of common schools, required not only schools for elementary instruction, but also grammar schools to be maintained. The qualifications required in teachers of grammar schools were such as to leave it open to no doubt that grammar schools understood in the sense in England and the Eastern States were intended, in which instruction in the classics should be given, as well as in such higher branches of learning as would not usually be taught in the schools of lowest grade. How is it possible, then, to say, as the exigencies of complainants' case require them to do, that the term common or primary schools, as made use of in our legislation, has a known and definite meaning which limits it to the ordinary district schools, and that consequently the legislative authority to levy taxes for the primary schools cannot be held to embrace taxation for the schools supported by village and city districts in which a higher grade of learning is imparted. . . .

Thus stood the law when the constitution of 1835 was adopted. The article on education in that instrument contained the following provisions:

"2. The legislature shall encourage by all suitable means the promotion of intellectual, scientific and agricultural improvement. The proceeds of all lands that have been, or hereafter may be, granted by the United States to this date for the support of schools, which shall hereafter be sold or disposed of, shall be and remain a perpetual fund, the interest of which, together with the rents of all such unsold lands, shall be inviolably appropriated to the support of schools throughout the state.

"3. The legislature shall provide for a system of common schools, by which a school shall be kept up and supported in each school district at least three months in every year; and any school district neglecting to keep up and support such a school may be deprived of its equal proportion of the interest of the public fund."

The fifth section provided for the support of the university, "with such branches as the public convenience may hereafter demand for the promotion of literature, the arts and sciences," etc. Two things are specially noticeable in these provisions: *first*, that they contemplated provision by the state for a complete system of instruction, beginning with that of the primary school and ending with that of the university; *second*, that while the legislature was required to make provision for district schools for at least three months in each year, no restriction was imposed upon its power to establish schools intermediate to the common district and the university, and we find nothing to indicate an intent to limit their discretion as to the class or grade of schools to which the proceeds of school lands might be devoted, or as to the range of studies or grade of instruction which might be provided for in the district schools. . . .

The system adopted by the legislature, and which embraced a university and branches, and a common or primary school in every school district of the state, was put into successful operation, and so continued, with one important exception, until the adoption of the constitution in 1850. The exception relates to the branches of the university, which the funds of the university did not warrant keeping up. And which were consequently abandoned. Private schools to some extent took their place; but when the convention met to frame a constitution in 1850, there were already in existence, in a number of the leading towns, schools belonging to the general public system, which were furnishing instruction which fitted young men for the university. These schools for the most part had been organized under special laws, which, while leaving the primary school laws in general applicable, gave the districts a larger board of officers and larger powers of taxation for buildings and the payment of teachers. As the establishment and support of such schools were optional with the people, they encountered in some localities considerable opposition, which, however, is believed to have been always overcome, and the authority of the districts to provide instruction in the languages in these union schools was not, so far as we are aware, seriously contested. The superintendent of public instruction devotes a considerable portion of his annual report for 1848 to these schools, and in that of 1849 he says, "This class of institutions, which may be made to constitute a connecting link between the ordinary common school and the state university, is fast gaining upon the confidence of the public. Those already established have generally surpassed the expectations of their founders. . . ." This *common* free school was a union school equivalent in its instruction to the ordinary high school in most matters, and the report furnishes very clear evidence that the superintendent believed schools of that grade to be entirely competent under the primary school law.

It now becomes important to see whether the constitutional convention and the people, in 1850, did anything to undo what previously had been accomplished towards furnishing high schools as a part of the primary school system. The convention certainly did nothing to that end. On the contrary, they demonstrated in the most unmistakable manner that they cherished no such desire or purpose. The article on education as originally reported, while providing for free schools to be kept in each district at least three months in every year, added that "the English language and no other shall be taught in such schools." Attention was called to this provision, and it was amended so as to read that instruction should be "conducted in the English language." The reason for the change was fully given, that as it was reported it might be understood to prohibit the teaching of other languages than the English in the primary schools; a result that was not desired. . . .

The instrument submitted by the convention to the people and adopted by them provided for the establishment of free schools in every school district for at least three months in each year, and for the university. By the aid of these we have every reason to believe the people expected a complete collegiate education might be obtained. The branches of the university had ceased to exist; the university had no preparatory department, and it must either have been understood that young men were to be prepared for the university in the common schools, or else that they should go abroad for the purpose, or be prepared in private schools. Private schools adapted to the purpose were almost unknown in the state, and comparatively a very few persons were at that time of sufficient pecuniary ability to educate their children abroad. The inference seems irresistible that the people expected the tendency toward the establishment of high schools in the primary school districts would continue until every locality capable of supporting one was supplied. And this inference is strengthened by the fact that a considerable number of our union schools date their establishment from the year 1850 and the two or three years following. . . .

We content ourselves with the statement that neither in our state policy, in our constitution, or in our laws, do we find the primary school districts restricted in the branches of knowledge which their officers may cause to be taught, or the grade of instruction that may be given, if their voters consent in regular form to bear the expense and raise the taxes for the purpose. . . .

It follows that the decree dismissing the bill was right, and should be affirmed.

The other justices concurred.

15. Extracts from "The Indian School at Carlisle Barracks," a Report to the U.S. Commissioner of Education, 1880

. . . The barracks stand west of the town, on a well drained piece of land belonging to the Government. . . .

The buildings occupy the sides of a grassy square used for parade ground, &c. One row is occupied by the superintendent and his staff, another by the teachers' and female pupils' dormitories, a third by the boys' dormitories. Other buildings conveniently placed are used as chapel, school-house, refectory, infirmary, gymnasium, stable and coach-house, trade schools, &c. There is ample accommodation for double the actual number of pupils.

Lieutenant Pratt has at present under his charge about 110 boys and 44 girls, from several tribes. It was found impossible to obtain as many girls as boys, because the labor of the girls is so useful under the present ideas and social arrangements of the Indians.

A few of the older pupils had received some instruction and training before coming to this school. . . . More than a hundred of them, however, were last October without any civilized knowledge or training whatever. "They had never been inside of a school or a house," said one of the employes. They were brought to the barracks filthy, vermin covered, and dressed in their native garb. When they were assigned to their sleeping quarters "they lay down on the veranda, on their bellies, and glared out between the palings of the railings like wild beasts between the bars of their cages." The first thing to do was to clean them thoroughly and to dress them in their new attire. Baths are compulsory thrice a week. The vermin have been suppressed, all the more easily because the boys have allowed their hair to be cut in the fashion of the white people. Everything except swallowing, walking, and sleeping had to be taught; the care of person, clothing, furniture, the usages of the table, the carriage of the body, civility, all those things which white children usually learn from their childhood by mere imitation, had to be painfully inculcated and strenuously insisted on. In addition to this, there were to be taught the rudiments of an English school course and the practical use of tools. . . .

Three and a half months have passed, and the change is astonishing. . . .

The Schools

We entered one room after another. The first was one in which a number of the younger children were being exercised in the use of a vocabulary and in the formation of English sentences. On the teacher's desk was a large number of small familiar objects, drinking glasses, balls, cups, &c. The children successively were asked to name an object; the teacher phonetized the name into its sound elements and the children repeated it in the same way. Then the teacher placed one object on the top of another and the child made a sentence on the following model: "The cup is on the book."

In another room a class of boys was reciting a lesson in geography. One boy pointed out and named the continents, another the countries in North America, a third the oceans, a fourth the seas of Europe, and so on.

In another room a lesson in arithmetic was going on; a model of a fence afforded opportunities for questions in multiplication, division, &c. This seemed to me somewhat less satisfactory. A class of larger boys, however, wrote down . . . a long sum in addition, which was solved with satisfactory speed and correctness.

A number of children in another class were employed in making sentences, which they wrote at once on the blackboard. A child would be told to do something; then another would tell what had been done and write what he said. The writing was very fair.

A class in calisthenics was also seen. The scholars went through a variety of motions intended to develop the chest and arms, following the example set by one of the young ladies of the teaching corps. . . .

The Shops

We found some of the girls learning how to sew, others cooking, others mending clothes. Some of the boys were cobbling shoes, some were in the carpenter's shop, where a pinewood table was being finished by one pupil, while another was making tongues and grooves on the edges of boards, apparently for the top of another table; a third was working on table and chair legs. Two other boys were at a blacksmith's forge working away industriously. Three of the older boys had been apprenticed to a wagonmaker in Carlisle; one of these is painting wagons, another is making or putting together the parts of wheels and other woodwork; the third devotes his attention to the iron parts. I understood that these young men propose when they return home to pursue wagonmaking in partnership. The pupils are said to learn the use of tools as readily as white children do. There is a master blacksmith, master carpenter, and a shoemaker in the corps of instruction. . . .

CHARLES WARREN,
Chief Clerk

Hon. JOHN EATON,
Commissioner of Education.

16. Extracts from Report of the Committee on Secondary School Studies (Committee of Ten), 1893

The Committee of Ten, after a preliminary discussion on November 9th [1892], decided on November 10th to organize conferences on the following subjects:— 1. Latin; 2. Greek; 3. English; 4. Other Modern Languages; 5. Mathematics; 6. Physics, Astronomy, and Chemistry; 7. Natural History (Biology, including Botany, Zoölogy, and Physiology); 8. History, Civil Government, and Political Economy; 9. Geography (Physical Geography, Geology, and Meteorology). They also decided that each Conference should consist of ten members. They then proceeded to select the members of each of these Conferences, having regard in the selection to the scholarship and experience of the gentlemen named, to the fair division of the members between colleges on the one hand and schools on the other, and to the proper geographical distribution of the total membership. After selecting ninety members for the nine Conferences, the Committee decided on an additional number of names

to be used as substitutes for persons originally chosen who should decline to serve. . . .

The Committee next adopted the following list of questions as a guide for the discussions of all the Conferences, and directed that the Conferences be called together on the 28th of December:—

1. In the school course of study extending approximately from the age of six years to eighteen years—a course including the periods of both elementary and secondary instruction—at what age should the study which is the subject of the Conference first be introduced?
2. After it is introduced, how many hours a week for how many years should be devoted to it?
3. How many hours a week for how many years should be devoted to it during the last four years of the complete course; that is, during the ordinary high school period?
4. What topics, or parts, of the subject may reasonably be covered during the whole course?
5. What topics, or parts, of the subject may best be reserved for the last four years?
6. In what form and to what extent should the subject enter into college requirements for admission? Such questions as the sufficiency of translation at sight as a test of knowledge of a language, or the superiority of a laboratory examination in a scientific subject to a written examination on a text-book, are intended to be suggested under this head by the phrase "in what form."
7. Should the subject be treated differently for pupils who are going to college, for those who are going to a scientific school, and for those who, presumably, are going to neither?
8. At what stage should this differentiation begin, if any be recommended?
9. Can any description be given of the best method of teaching this subject throughout the school course?
10. Can any description be given of the best mode of testing attainments in this subject at college admission examinations?
11. For those cases in which colleges and universities permit a division of the admission examination into a preliminary and a final examination, separated by at least a year, can the limit between the preliminary and final examinations be approximately defined? . . .

All the Conferences sat for three days; their discussions were frank, earnest, and thorough; but in every

Conference an extraordinary unity was arrived at. . . . In the great majority of matters brought before each Conference, the decision of the Conference was unanimous. When one considers the different localities, institutions, professional experiences, and personalities represented in each of the Conferences, the unanimity developed is very striking, and should carry great weight. . . .

The experts who met to confer together concerning the teaching of the last four subjects in the list of Conferences all felt the need of setting forth in an ample way what ought to be taught, in what order, and by what method. They ardently desired to have their respective subjects made equal to Latin, Greek, and Mathematics in weight and influence in the schools; but they knew that educational tradition was adverse to this desire, and that many teachers and directors of education felt no confidence in these subjects as disciplinary material. . . . In less degree, the Conferences on English and Other Modern Languages felt the same difficulties, these subjects being relatively new as substantial elements in school programs. . . .

It might have been expected that every Conference would have demanded for its subject a larger proportion of time than is now commonly assigned to it in primary and secondary schools; but, as a matter of fact; the reports are noteworthy for their moderation in this respect,—especially the reports on the old and well-established subjects. The Latin Conference declares that,—"In view of the just demand for more and better work in several other subjects of the preparatory course, it seemed clear to the Conference that no increase in the quantity of the preparation in Latin should be asked for." Among the votes passed by the Greek Conference will be noted the following:—"That in making the following recommendations, this Conference desires that the average age at which pupils now enter college should be lowered rather than raised; and the Conference urges that no addition be made in the advanced requirements in Greek for admission to college." The Mathematical Conference recommends that the course in arithmetic in elementary schools should be abridged, and recommends only a moderate assignment of time to algebra and geometry. The Conference on geography says of the present assignment of time to geography in primary and secondary schools that "it is the judgment of the Conference that too much time is given to the subject in proportion to the results secured. It is not their judgment that more time is given to the subject than it merits, but that either more should be accomplished, or less time taken to attain it.". . .

[A]ll these bodies of experts desire to have the elements of their several subjects taught earlier than they now are; . . . the Conferences on all the subjects except the languages desire to have given in the elementary schools what may be called perspective views, or broad surveys, of their respective subjects—expecting that in later years of the school course parts of these same subjects will be taken up with more amplitude and detail. The Conferences on Latin, Greek, and the Modern Languages agree in desiring to have the study of foreign languages begin at a much earlier age than now,—the Latin Conference suggesting by a reference to European usage that Latin be begun from three to five years earlier than it commonly is now. The Conference on Mathematics wish to have given in elementary schools not only a general survey of arithmetic, but also the elements of algebra, and concrete geometry in connection with drawing. The Conference on Physics, Chemistry, and Astronomy urge that nature studies should constitute an important part of the elementary school course from the very beginning. The Conference on Natural History wish the elements of botany and zoölogy to be taught in the primary schools. The Conference on History wish the systematic study of history to begin as early as the tenth year of age, and the first two years of study to be devoted to mythology and to biography for the illustration of general history as well as of American history. Finally, the Conference on Geography recommend that the earlier course treat broadly of the earth, its environment and inhabitants, extending freely into fields which in later years of study are recognized as belonging to separate sciences.

In thus claiming entrance for their subjects into the earlier years of school attendance, the Conferences on the newer subjects are only seeking an advantage which the oldest subjects have long possessed. The elements of language, number, and geography have long been imparted young children. As things now are, the high school teacher finds in the pupils fresh from the grammar schools no foundation of elementary mathematical conceptions outside of arithmetic; no acquaintance with algebraic language; and no accurate knowledge of geometric forms. As to botany, zoölogy, chemistry, and physics, the minds of pupils entering the high school are ordinarily blank on these subjects. When college professors endeavor to teach chemistry, physics, botany, zoölogy, meteorology, or geology to persons of eighteen or twenty years of age, they discover that in most instances new habits of observing, reflecting, and recording have to be painfully acquired by the students,—habits which they should have acquired early in childhood. The college teacher of history finds in like manner that his subject has never taken any serious hold on the minds of pupils fresh from the secondary schools. He finds that they have devoted astonishingly little time to the subject; and that they have acquired no habit of historical investigation, or of the comparative examination of different historical narratives concerning the same periods or events. It is inevitable, therefore, that specialists in any one of the subjects which are pursued in the high schools or colleges should earnestly desire that the minds of young children be stored with some of the elementary facts and principles of their subject; and that all the mental habits, which the adult student will surely need, begin to be formed in the child's mind before the age of fourteen. . . .

If anyone feels dismayed at the number and variety of the subjects to be opened to children of tender age, let him observe that while these nine Conferences desire each their own subject to be brought into the courses of elementary schools, they all agree that these different subjects should be correlated and associated one with another by the programme and by the actual teaching. If the nine Conferences had sat all together as a single body, instead of sitting as detached and even isolated bodies, they could not have more forcibly expressed their conviction that every subject recommended for introduction into elementary and secondary schools should help every other; and that the teacher of each single subject should feel responsible for the advancement of the pupils in all subjects, and should distinctly contribute to this advancement. . . .

The 7th question is answered unanimously in the negative by the Conferences, and the 8th therefore needs no answer. . . . Ninety-eight teachers, intimately concerned either with the actual work of American secondary schools, or with the results of that work as they appear in students who come to college, unanimously declare that every subject which is taught at all in a secondary school should be taught in the same way and to the same extent to every pupil so long as he pursues it, no matter what the probable destination of the pupil may be, or at what point his education is to cease. Thus, for all pupils who study Latin, or history, or algebra, for example, the allotment of time and the method of instruction in a given school should be the same year by year. Not that all the pupils should pursue every subject for the same number of years; but so long as they do pursue it, they should all be treated alike. It has been a very general custom in American high schools and academies to make up

separate courses of study for pupils of supposed different destinations, the proportions of the several studies in the different courses being various. The principle laid down by the Conferences will, if logically carried out, make a great simplification in secondary school programmes. It will lead to each subject's being treated by the school in the same way by the year for all pupils, and this, whether the individual pupil be required to choose between courses which run through several years, or be allowed some choice among subjects year by year. . . .

[T]here is a general principle concerning the relation of the secondary schools to colleges which the Committee of Ten, inspired and guided by the Conferences, feel it their duty to set forth with all possible directness.

The secondary schools of the United States, taken as a whole, do not exist for the purpose of preparing boys and girls for colleges. Only an insignificant percentage of the graduates of these schools go to colleges or scientific schools. Their main function is to prepare for the duties of life that small proportion of all the children in the country—a proportion small in number, but very important to the welfare of the nation—who show themselves able to profit by an education prolonged to the eighteenth year, and whose parents are able to support them while they remain so long at school. There are, to be sure, a few private or endowed secondary schools in the country, which make it their principal object to prepare students for the colleges and universities; but the number of these schools is relatively small. A secondary school programme intended for national use must therefore be made for those children whose education is not to be pursued beyond the secondary school. The preparation of a few pupils for college or scientific school should in the ordinary secondary school be the incidental, and not the principal object. At the same time, it is obviously desirable that the colleges and scientific schools should be accessible to all boys or girls who have completed creditably the secondary course. Their parents often do not decide for them, four years before the college age, that they shall go to college, and they themselves may not, perhaps, feel the desire to continue their education until near the end of their school course. In order that any successful graduate of a good secondary school should be free to present himself at the gates of the college or scientific school of his choice, it is necessary that the colleges and scientific schools of the country should accept for admission to appropriate courses of their instruction the attainments of any youth who has passed creditably through a good secondary school course, no matter to what group of subjects he may have mainly devoted himself in the scondary school. . . .

17. Regulations Covering the Use of School Buildings Adopted by the Rochester, New York, Board of Education, 1907

Adult Civic Clubs: Upon application to the Board of Education any public school building may be used as a meeting place for non-exclusive adult organizations whose object is approved by the Board of Education.

Boys' and Girls' Clubs: Upon the written application to the Board of Education of fifty adult citizens of any school district, any public school building may be used at such times as the public day or evening schools are not in session, as a meeting place for organizations of young men or young women, boys or girls above the age of fourteen years, who are not in attendance upon any day school; and with the use of the school buildings the services of a responsible director shall be provided.

The use of the school buildings for this purpose and the services of the club director shall be withdrawn if during any two consecutive months the average attendance falls below twenty-five.

Gymnasiums: The use of a gymnasium where practicable and the services of a physical instructor may be provided upon the request of any club whenever the average club attendance during the preceding month shall be at least thirty-five.

The use of the gymnasium and the services of the physical instructor shall be withdrawn whenever the average gymnasium attendance during two consecutive months falls below twenty-five.

Library: The use of a library or reading room and the services of a librarian may be provided upon request of the clubs whenever the average weekly attendance in the club's meeting in the school building during any two months shall aggregate at least fifty.

The use of the library or reading room and the services of a librarian shall be withdrawn whenever the average attendance in the library or reading room during any two consecutive months falls below twenty-five or whenever the average number of books drawn falls below fifteen.

General neighborhood meetings for lectures or entertainments may be permitted upon the request of the clubs meeting in any public school building whenever, during any two consecutive months, the average weekly attendance aggregates at least 100.

The "general neighborhood-evenings" shall be discontinued when their average attendance during any two consecutive months falls below 100.

18. Extracts from Students' Army Training Corps Regulations, 1918

SECTION I.
GENERAL PRINCIPLES . . .

1. AUTHORIZATION FOR ESTABLISHMENT.—The Students' Army Training Corps is raised under authority of the act of Congress approved May 18, 1917, commonly known as the Selective Service Act, authorizing the President to increase temporarily the Military Establishment of the United States, as amended by the act of August 31, 1918, and under Section II, General Orders, No. 79, of the War Department, dated August 24, 1918. . . .

3. OBJECT.—The object of establishing units of the Students' Army Training Corps is to utilize effectively the plant, equipment, and organization of the colleges for selecting and training officer candidates and technical experts for service in the existing emergency.

SECTION II.
CONSTITUTION. . . .

4. ESTABLISHMENT OF UNITS.—The Students' Army Training Corps consists of units established by the President in qualified educational institutions which fulfill the requirements laid down in these regulations.

5. SECTIONS OF UNITS.—The members of the Students' Army Training Corps at an educational institution will form a single unit for purposes of military organization, but for purposes of instruction such unit may consist of one or more sections, according to the type of educational training given.

6. REQUIREMENTS FOR THE ESTABLISHMENT OF SECTIONS.—The sections of a unit of the Students' Army training Corps and the educational requirements for the establishment of the same are as follows:

   a. *Collegiate section.*—The establishment of a collegiate section (to be known as Section A) may be authorized at any civil educational institution which—

   (1) Requires for admission to its regular curricula graduation from a standard, four-year, secondary school, or an equivalent, and

(2) Ordinarily provides a general professional curriculum covering at least 2 years of not less than 32 weeks each, and

(3) Has a student attendance sufficient to maintain a collegiate section of a Students' Army Training Corps unit with a strength of at least 100 men.

So far as practicable an effort will be made to establish collegiate sections at institutions which have a smaller student attendance than that prescribed in the preceding paragraph. Applications from such institutions will be considered and granted so far as officers and equipment permit, and so far as arrangements for the establishment of joint units may be found practicable.

Provided the conditions of this paragraph are met, educational institutions qualified to maintain collegiate sections of Students' Army Training Corps units will include:

(1) Colleges and schools of—
  (a) Arts and sciences.
  (b) Technology.
  (c) Engineering.
  (d) Mines.
  (e) Agriculture and forestry.
  (f) Business administration, industry, and commerce.
  (g) Pharmacy.
  (h) Veterinary medicine.
  (i) Education.
  (j) Law.
  (k) Medicine.
  (l) Dentistry.
(2) Graduate schools.
(3) Normal schools.
(4) Junior colleges.
(5) Technical institutes.

b. *Vocational section.*—The establishment of a vocational section (to be known as Section B) may be authorized at any institution having an adequate shop or laboratory equipment and a staff of instructors capable of giving approved vocational training of military value. . . .

SECTION V.
SCOPE OF TRAINING. . . .

24. INSTRUCTION IN SECTION A.—For Section A the instruction will be partly military and partly in allied subjects that have value as a means of training officers and experts to meet the needs of the service.

The average number of hours to be devoted each week to those subjects will be as follows:

a. *Military subjects,* including practical instruction (drill, etc.), theoretical military instruction, and physical training—11 hours.

b. *Allied subjects,* including lectures, recitations, laboratory instruction and the necessary preparation therefor—42 hours. (Each hour of lecture or recitation will ordinarily require two hours of supervised study.)

The hours above set forth have reference to the normal course. In the case of students who have pursued for at least one year at an approved institution such studies as form part of the program of preparation for the Chemical Warfare Service, the Medical Corps, the Engineer Corps, the Ordnance Corps, or other technical branches of the service, the Committee on Education and Special Training may authorize a reduction in the hours of military instruction (including practical military instruction, theoretical military instruction, and physical training) to not less than six hours per week, provided that the reduction is made good by the substitution of a corresponding number of additional hours of instruction in approved technical subjects.

Provision will be made for approving general programs, as well as technical and special programs, in medicine, engineering, chemistry, and other technical courses.

25. APPROVAL OF COURSES IN ALLIED SUBJECTS.—The Committee on Education and Special Training will furnish from time to time suggestions regarding the treatment of allied subjects that are chosen as parts of the curriculum. . . .

26. LIST OF ALLIED SUBJECTS.—The allied subjects will ordinarily be selected from the following list: English, French, Italian, German, mathematics, physics, chemistry, biology, geology, psychology, topography and map making, meteorology, astronomy, hygiene, sanitation, descriptive geometry, mechanical and freehand drawing, surveying, economics, accounting, history, international law, military law, and government.

Permission may be granted for the recognition, as an allied subject, of not more than one subject outside the above list, provided that it occupies not more than three hours per week in lectures and recitations with corresponding time for study.

In the case of technical and professional schools provision will be made for approving general programs of study containing subjects other than those included in the above list of allied subjects.

The war-issues course.—The program of study in allied subjects must include a course on the underlying issues of the war. This may be planned as a special war-issues course with a minimum for Section A of three classroom hours per week, with corresponding time for study, covering three terms, or the requirement may be met by a course or courses in history, government, economics, philosophy, or modern literature where these courses are so planned as . . . to accomplish substantially the same purpose.

27. INSTRUCTION IN SECTION B.—For Section B the average number of hours to be devoted each week to military and vocational training will be as follows:
   a. *Military subjects*, including practical instruction (drill, etc.), and physical training—15½ hours.
   b. *Vocational subjects*—33 hours.
   c. *War-issues course* (see fourth subparagraph of paragraph 26 above)—1 hour. . . .

19. Extracts from Cardinal Principles of Education: A Report of the Commission on the Reorganization of Secondary Education, Appointed by the National Education Association, 1918

I. The Need for Reorganization.

Secondary education should be determined by the needs of the society to be served, the character of the individuals to be educated, and the knowledge of educational theory and practice available. These factors are by no means static. Society is always in process of development; the character of the secondary-school population undergoes modification; and the sciences on which educational theory and practice depend constantly furnish new information. Secondary education, however, like any other established agency of society, is conservative and tends to resist modification. Failure to make adjustments when the need arises leads to the necessity for extensive reorganization at irregular intervals. The evidence is strong that such a comprehensive reorganization of secondary education is imperative at the present time.

1. *Changes in society.*—Within the past few decades changes have taken place in American life profoundly affecting the activities of the individual. As a citizen,

he must to a greater extent and in a more direct way cope with problems of community life, State and National Governments, and international relationships. As a worker, he must adjust himself to a more complex economic order. As a relatively independent personality, he has more leisure. The problems arising from these three dominant phases of life are closely interrelated and call for a degree of intelligence and efficiency on the part of every citizen that can not be secured through elementary education alone, or even through secondary education unless the scope of that education is broadened.

The responsibility of the secondary school is still further increased because many social agencies other than the school afford less stimulus for education than heretofore. In many vocations there have come such significant changes as the substitution of the factory system for the domestic system of industry; the use of machinery in place of manual labor; the high specialization of processes with a corresponding subdivision of labor; and the breakdown of the apprentice system. In connection with home and family life have frequently come lessened responsibility on the part of the children; the withdrawal of the father and sometimes the mother from home occupations to the factory or store; and increased urbanization resulting in less unified family life. Similarly, many important changes have taken place in community life, in the church, in the State, and in other institutions. These changes in American life call for extensive modifications in secondary education.

2. *Changes in the secondary-school population.*—In the past 25 years there have been marked changes in the secondary-school population of the United States. The number of pupils has increased, according to Federal returns, from one for every 210 of the total population in 1889–90, to one for every 121 in 1899–1900, to one for every 89 in 1909–10, to one for every 73 of the estimated total population in 1914–15. The character of the secondary-school population has been modified by the entrance of large numbers of pupils of widely varying capacities, aptitudes, social heredity, and destinies in life. . . .

3. *Changes in educational theory.*—The sciences on which educational theory depends have within recent years made significant contributions. In particular, educational psychology emphasizes the following factors:
   (a) *Individual differences in capacities and aptitudes among secondary-school pupils.* . . .

(b) *The reexamination and reinterpretation of subject values and the teaching methods with reference to "general discipline."* . . .

(c) *Importance of applying knowledge.*—Subject values and teaching methods must be tested in terms of the laws of learning and the application of knowledge to the activities of life, rather than primarily in terms of the demands of any subject as a logically organized science.

(d) *Continuity in the development of children.*—It has long been held that psychological changes at certain stages are so pronounced as to overshadow the continuity of development. On this basis secondary education has been sharply separated from elementary education. Modern psychology, however, goes to show that the development of the individual is in most respects a continuous process and that, therefore, any sudden or abrupt break between the elementary and the secondary school or between any two successive stages of education is undesirable. . . .

III. The Main Objectives of Education.

In order to determine the main objectives that should guide education in a democracy it is necessary to analyze the activities of the individual. Normally he is a member of a family, of a vocational group, and of various civic groups, and by virtue of these relationships he is called upon to engage in activities that enrich the family life, to render important vocational services to his fellows, and to promote the common welfare. It follows, therefore, that worthy home-membership, vocation, and citizenship, demand attention as three of the leading objectives.

Aside from the immediate discharge of these specific duties, every individual should have a margin of time for the cultivation of personal and social interests. This leisure, if worthily used, will recreate his powers and enlarge and enrich life, thereby making him better able to meet his responsibilities. The unworthy use of leisure impairs health, disrupts home life, lessens vocational efficiency, and destroys civic-mindedness. The tendency in industrial life, aided by legislation, is to decrease the working hours of large groups of people. While shortened hours tend to lessen the harmful reactions that arise from prolonged strain, they increase, if possible, the importance of preparedness for leisure. . . .

To discharge the duties of life and to benefit from leisure, one must have good health. The health of the individual is essential also to the vitality of the race and to the defense of the Nation. Health education is, therefore, fundamental.

There are various processes, such as reading, writing, arithmetical computations, and oral and written expression, that are needed as tools in the affairs of life. Consequently, command of these fundamental processes, while not an end in itself, is nevertheless an indispensable objective.

And, finally, the realization of the objectives already named is dependent upon ethical character, that is, upon conduct founded upon right principles, clearly perceived and loyally adhered to. Good citizenship, vocational excellence, and the worthy use of leisure go hand in hand with ethical character; they are at once the fruits of sterling character and the channels through which such character is developed and made manifest. . . .

This commission, therefore, regards the following as the main objectives of education: 1. Health. 2. Command of fundamental processes. 3. Worthy home-membership. 4. Vocation. 5. Citizenship. 6. Worthy use of leisure. 7. Ethical character. . . .

20. Extracts from Program of Educational Activities for Emergency Camps and Shelters in California, State of California Department of Education Bulletin No. 5, March 1, 1934

Camp Program

Plans and schedules of instruction suitable for the needs of the particular camp or shelter should be prepared by the Educational Adviser aided by the local authorities. . . . It is recognized, however, that in every camp or shelter conditions vary so widely as to age, intelligence, aptitude, educational level, capacity, interest, availability of equipment, and many other factors, that it is essential to modify and adapt the program to the conditions found.

Voluntary Acceptance

The opportunity for instruction is offered to camp registrants, but it is not mandatory. Camp Directors and Advisers should, however, point out the advantage presented by this opportunity and should encourage camp registrants to avail themselves of it.

Hours

The hours available for instruction should not conflict with working hours. Periods after normal working hours and periods of inclement weather may be utilized. Also, the educational program should be scheduled in relation to other phases of camp routine.

Methods

Informal methods of instruction rather than formal classes should characterize the program. Also, the teaching methods and procedures used in the adult education program will be more effective.

GENERAL SUGGESTIONS

COORDINATION WITH OTHER CAMP ACTIVITIES

Educational Advisers and Local School Officials who participate in the program should, first of all, familiarize themselves thoroughly with the camp, the camp routine, the camp personnel, both officers and registrants, and all camp activities. The educational program is but one phase of camp life; to be successful it must be made to fit in with the work program and all other camp activities.

Informal Instruction

A new type of educational program is being developed in those camps and shelters. Preconceived ideas based upon formal school procedures should be discarded. Any program planned on the outside and imposed upon a camp has little chance of success. The educational activities must grow out of the needs, interests, and wishes of the camp registrants. While available adult classes may be used to excellent advantage in many cases, the camp program will be characterized by individual counseling, informal study, reading, and discussion. An exception to this general statement may be found in boys' camps and projects for girls, where formal schooling may be found advisable.

Locating Facilities

Resourcefulness in obtaining all possible aid from nearby schools, libraries, organizations, and community leaders will aid the program. Resourcefulness is also needed in securing necessary equipment, texts, and instructional materials, since there is seldom any provision for supplying these other than such as are available when adult classes are utilized. How to utilize camp activities and camp equipment in the educational program presents another challenge to the ingenuity of the educational adviser. This applies to enlisting camp officers, qualified camp registrants, and others as instructors and discussion leaders.

Motivation of Program

The program must be clearly motivated. Only as genuine motives impel the men and women to engage in edu-cational activities will the program succeed, and effort should be made to discover all such motives. The most compelling motive is interest in a job, and this may be utilized to stimulate the study of occupations, vocational studies, and other fields which may aid in future placement. The unemployment situation itself, and the social and economic crisis which has resulted in such widespread unemployment indicate motives which will stimulate such studies as civics, current events, economics, and the like. Many such motives may be found to exist and others may be aroused; the educational program should be built around these motives.

Morale Building

Cheerfulness and optimism should characterize all educational activities. The building of morale and restoration of self-confidence in these victims of the depression are as important as imparting knowledge. Group singing, choral clubs, harmonica clubs, games, are but a few of many activities which have in addition to educational values a high value for creating a happier atmosphere in any camp, with resultant beneficial effects to individuals and to society.

In the selection of instructional personnel, due consideration should be given to the important qualifications of enthusiasm, cheerfulness, and ability to inspire confidence.

PLANNING THE PROGRAM

The educational activities to be organized in a given camp or shelter must be based upon the interests and problems of the camp registrants. The first step, therefore, in planning the program will be to find out what these interests and problems are. Usually they will be found to be related to:

1. Readjustment to normal life after leaving camp
    a. Vocational interests.
    b. Connections and opportunities for employment.
    c. Reestablishment of family and home relationships.
    d. Preparation to meet changed economic conditions.
2. Present activities
    a. Camp problems involving cooperative responsibility with other camp registrants and with officers.
    b. Individual and personal problems, the solution of which are important to the individual's future.
    c. Individual educational needs and interests.

To discover these motivating interests and problems, the following methods may be helpful:

1. Consult freely with camp officers, welfare workers, and others who have been in touch with registrants, in order to have the benefit of their experience.

2. Talk with camp registrants informally, in order to gain their confidence and interest. Request the aid of responsive individuals with some leadership ability to assist in getting together small groups with like interest as a basis for further discussion, as well as a basis for possible educational activity.

3. Systematically interview all camp registrants as time may permit, recording the data on suitable forms, if the desired data are not already available on camp registration cards.

Eventually every person in the camp should be given a private interview, but this takes time and the establishment of various phases of the educational program need not await completion of all personal interviews.

With the information thus obtained, the educational program can be built up to meet the conditions found. Canvass should be made of all existing opportunities for adult education, and plans should be made to supplement existing facilities by the establishment of classes, discussion groups, lectures, interest-clubs, individual study procedures, reading courses, etc., as needed. . . . Assignment to educational activities should be made strictly on an individual basis and according to the needs of the individual.

It will probably be found advisable to start with small groups. As the work progresses more and more will be learned as to the interests and problems of the registrants and ways and means for meeting them will be discovered, thus gradually building up the program.

21. Extract from Unemployed Youth of New York City, a Report Published by the U.S. Bureau of Labor Statistics, February 1937

A heavy incidence of unemployment among young people 16 to 24 years of age, in New York City, was disclosed by a recent study made by the Welfare Council of that city, with the assistance of the Works Progress Administration. The study, made in 1935, though based upon a sample of the city's youth population and therefore not furnishing a complete census of the unemployed youth of the city, gives a basis for estimating the total numbers of young persons of each sex and of different ages who were unemployed. It also supplies information regarding education and previous work experience which is essential for the guidance of public and private agencies planning for unemployed youth. Any program, at least for New York City, set up with a view to providing training and work for this segment of the unemployed population should take account of the following findings:

1. Unemployed youth—that is, young persons 16 to 24 years of age who were out of school, able to work and desirous of employment but unable to obtain it—constituted one-third of the total sample of the youth population of that city.

2. The unemployed group contained almost as many girls (47 percent) as boys (53 percent).

3. A larger proportion of Negro than of the white youth was unemployed and seeking employment (43 percent as compared with 33 percent), so that the unemployed group contained a disproportionate number of Negroes.

4. Unemployed youth exhibited wide variations in degree of maturity, in educational achievement and vocational training, and in work experience. Almost one-fifth were found to be under 18, about two-fifths 18 to 20, and about two fifths 21 to 24 years of age. One-fourth had left school on finishing the eighth grade, and one-fifth on graduating from high school; one-tenth had not completed even the eighth grade, while, on the other hand, almost as many had from 1 to 7 years of college or university training. The unemployed young men and women who had never had work had a better education, measured in terms of school-grade attainment, than the others who were without jobs. As to work experience, half of the group under 21 years of age, compared with one-seventh of those 21 years of age or older, comprising altogether over one-third of the total, had never had a job of any kind. The other two-thirds had had work experience of varying lengths covering many types of employment, with about half in semiskilled and unskilled occupations and about two-fifths in clerical and kindred occupations.

These variations point to the necessity of a varied program in education, work projects, and other organized outlets for youthful energy, and also to the need of individualized treatment for many through the provision of counseling and other types of adjustment service.

5. The unemployed youth had been out of school for from a few weeks' time to 10 years or more. The average for those who had never had employment was between 1 and 2 years, and for those with work experience about 5. Almost all who had never had work, and a

large proportion of the others, had left school at a time when they must have been faced with the fact of scant likelihood of their getting a job. Even so, three-fourths had left without completing high school. It seems likely therefore that programs emphasizing a return to school for regular high school or college courses would be acceptable in comparatively few cases.

6. Of the unemployed youth with some work experience half had had no work for at least 1 year, and half had had at least 2 years' unemployment since leaving school. More than half had been idle at least half the time since they left school. This takes no account of the boys and girls who had been unable to obtain any employment, though out of school, on an average, between 1 and 2 years. What such facts as these may mean in the dissipation of youthful enthusiasm cannot be measured, but they must be considered in the formulation of programs for unemployed youth, both from the point of view of rehabilitating those whose morale has suffered from protracted idleness, and also on the preventive side through the provision of abundant facilities for the use of the enforced leisure.

7. Unemployed young persons who were themselves in receipt of relief or who were members of relief households (the group specially served by the National Youth Administration), who constituted one-fourth of the total unemployed, are seen, when compared with unemployed youth not on relief, to have had a more limited education and training, to have left school earlier, to have been out of work longer, and to have spent a larger proportion of their working lives without employment. The problem presented by this group is therefore more serious than that of the unemployed youth as a whole and as such will require especially careful and thorough attention in all its aspects, if the singling out of this group for special observation and treatment is to be continued. . . .

22. Extracts from the Servicemen's Readjustment Act (G.I. Bill of Rights), 1944

Title II
Chapter IV. Education of Veterans
Part VIII

1. Any person who served in the active military or naval service on or after September 16, 1940, and prior to the termination of the present war, and who shall have been discharged or released therefrom under conditions other than dishonorable, and who either shall have served ninety days or more, exclusive of any period he was assigned for a course of education or training under the Army specialized training program or the Navy college training program, which course was a continuation of his civilian course and was pursued to completion, or as a cadet or midshipman at one of the service academies, or shall have been discharged or released from active service by reason of an actual service-incurred injury or disability, shall be eligible for and entitled to receive education or training under this part: *Provided,* That such course shall be initiated not later than four years after either the date of his discharge or the termination of the present war, whichever is the later. *Provided further,* That no such education or training shall be afforded beyond nine years after the termination of the present war.

2. Any such eligible person shall be entitled to education or training at an approved educational or training institution for a period of one year plus the time such person was in the active service on or after September 16, 1940, and before the termination of the war, exclusive of any period he was assigned for a course of education or training under the Army specialized training program or the Navy college training program, which course was a continuation of his civilian course and was pursued to completion, or as a cadet or midshipman at one of the service academies, but in no event shall the total period of education or training exceed four years: *Provided,* That his work continues to be satisfactory throughout the period, according to the regularly prescribed standards and practices of the institution: *Provided further,* That wherever the period of eligibility ends during a quarter or semester and after a major part of such quarter or semester has expired, such period shall be extended to the termination of such unexpired quarter or semester.

3. (a) Such person shall be eligible for and entitled to such course of education or training, full time or the equivalent thereof in part-time training, as he may elect, and at any approved educational or training institution at which he chooses to enroll, whether or not located in the State in which he resides, which will accept or retain him as a student or trainee in any field or branch of knowledge which such insti-

tution finds him qualified to undertake or pursue: *Provided,* That for reasons satisfactory to the Administrator, he may change a course of instruction: *And provided further,* That any such course of education or training may be discontinued at any time, if it is found by the Administrator that, according to the regularly prescribed standards and practices of the institution, the conduct or progress of such person is unsatisfactory.

(*b*) Any such eligible person may apply for a short, intensive, post-graduate, or training course of less than thirty weeks: *Provided,* That the Administrator shall have the authority to contract with approved institutions for such courses if he finds that the agreed cost of such courses is reasonable and fair. . . .

(*c*) Any such eligible person may apply for a course of instruction by correspondence without any subsistence allowance: *Provided,* That the Administrator shall have authority to contract with approved institutions for such courses if he finds that the agreed cost of such courses is reasonable and fair. . . .

4. From time to time the Administrator shall secure from the appropriate agency of each State a list of the educational and training institutions (including industrial establishments), within such jurisdiction, which are qualified and equipped to furnish education or training (including apprenticeship, refresher or retraining and institutional on-farm training), which institutions, together with such additional ones as may be recognized by the Administrator, shall be deemed qualified and approved to furnish education or training to such persons as shall enroll under this part. . . .

5. The Administrator shall pay to the educational or training institution (including the institution offering institutional on-farm training), for each person enrolled in full time or part time course of education or training, the customary cost of tuition, and such laboratory, library, health, infirmary, and other similar fees as are customarily charged, and may pay for books, supplies, equipment and other necessary expenses, exclusive of board, lodging, other living expenses, and travel, as are generally required for the successful pursuit and completion of the course by other students in the institution: *Provided,* That in no event shall such payments, with respect to any person, exceed $500 for an ordinary school year unless the veteran elects to have such customary charges paid in excess of such limitation, in which event there shall be charged against his period of eligibility the

proportion of an ordinary school year which such excess bears to $500. . . .

6. While enrolled in and pursuing a course under this part, (including an institutional on-farm training course) such person, upon application to the Administrator, shall be paid a subsistence allowance of $65 per month, if without a dependent or dependents, or $90 per month, if he has a dependent or dependents, including regular holidays and leave not exceeding thirty days in a calendar year: Except, That (1) while so enrolled and pursuing a course of full-time institutional training, such person, shall be paid a subsistence allowance of $75 per month, if without a dependent or dependents, or $105 per month if he has one dependent or $120 per month if he has more than one dependent, and (2) while so enrolled and pursuing a course of part-time institutional training, including a course of institutional on-farm training, or other combination course, such person shall be paid, subject to the limitations of this paragraph, additional subsistence allowance in an amount bearing the same relation to the difference between the basic rates and the increased rates provided in (1) hereof as the institutional training part of such course bears to a course of full-time institutional training. . . .

23. Extracts from the Opinion of the U.S. Supreme Court in *Brown et al. v. Board of Education of Topeka et al.,* 1954

These cases come to us from the States of Kansas, South Carolina, Virginia, and Delaware. They are premised on different facts and different local conditions, but a common legal question justifies their consideration together in this consolidated opinion.

In each of these cases, minors of the Negro race, through their legal representatives, seek the aid of the courts in obtaining admission to the public schools of their community on a nonsegregated basis. In each instance, they had been denied admission to schools attended by white children under laws requiring or permitting segregation according to race. This segregation was alleged to deprive the plaintiffs of the equal protection of the laws under the Fourteenth Amendment. In each of the cases other than the Delaware case, a three-judge federal district court denied relief to the plaintiffs on the so-called "separate-but-equal" doctrine announced by this Court in

Plessy v. Ferguson, 163 U.S. 537. Under that doctrine, equality of treatment is accorded when the races are provided substantially equal facilities, even though these facilities be separate. In the Delaware case, the Supreme Court of Delaware adhered to that doctrine, but ordered that the plaintiffs be admitted to the white schools because of their superiority to the Negro schools.

The plaintiffs contend that segregated public schools are not "equal" and cannot be made "equal," and that hence they are deprived of the equal protection of the laws. Because of the obvious importance of the question presented, the Court took jurisdiction. Argument was heard in the 1952 Term and reargument was heard this Term on certain questions propounded by the Court.

Reargument was largely devoted to the circumstances surrounding the adoption of the Fourteenth Amendment in 1868. It covered exhaustively consideration of the Amendment in Congress, ratification by the states, then-existing practices in racial segregation, and the views of proponents and opponents of the amendment. This discussion and our own investigation convince us that, although these sources cast some light, it is not enough to resolve the problem with which we are faced. At best, they are inconclusive. The most avid proponents of the post-War Amendments undoubtedly intended them to remove all legal distinctions among "all persons born or naturalized in the United States." Their opponents, just as certainly, were antagonistic to both the letter and the spirit of the Amendments and wished them to have the most limited effect. What others in Congress and the state legislatures had in mind cannot be determined with any degree of certainty.

An additional reason for the inconclusive nature of the Amendment's history, with respect to segregated schools, is the status of public education at that time. In the South, the movement toward free common schools, supported by general taxation, had not yet taken hold. Education of white children was largely in the hands of private groups. Education of Negroes was almost non-existent, and practically all of the race were illiterate. In fact, any education of Negroes was forbidden by law in some states. Today, in contrast, many Negroes have achieved outstanding success in the arts and sciences as well as in the business and professional world. It is true that public school education at the time of the Amendment had advanced further in the North, but the effect of the Amendment on Northern States was generally ignored in the congressional debates. Even in the North, the conditions of public education did not approximate those existing today. The curriculum was usually rudimentary;

ungraded schools were common in rural areas; the school term was but three months a year in many states; and compulsory school attendance was virtually unknown. As a consequence, it is not surprising that there should be so little in the history of the Fourteenth Amendment relating to its intended effect on public education. . . .

In approaching this problem, we cannot turn the clock back to 1868 when the Amendment was adopted, or even to 1896 when *Plessy v. Ferguson* was written. We must consider public education in the light of its full development and its present place in American life throughout the Nation. Only in this way can it be determined if segregation in public schools deprives these plaintiffs of the equal protection of the laws.

Today, education is perhaps the most important function of state and local governments. Compulsory school attendance laws and the great expenditures for education both demonstrate our recognition of the importance of education to our democratic society. It is required in the performance of our most basic public responsibilities, even service in the armed forces. It is the very foundation of good citizenship. Today it is a principal instrument in awakening the child to cultural values, in preparing him for later professional training, and in helping him to adjust normally to his environment. In these days, it is doubtful that any child may reasonably be expected to succeed in life if he is denied the opportunity of an education. Such an opportunity, where the state has undertaken to provide it, is a right which must be made available to all on equal terms.

We come then to the question presented: Does segregation of children in public schools solely on the basis of race, even though physical facilities and other "tangible" factors my be equal, deprive children of the minority group of equal educational opportunities? We believe that it does. . . .

We conclude that in the field of public education the doctrine of "separate but equal" has no place. Separate educational facilities are inherently unequal. Therefore, we hold that the plaintiffs and others similarly situated for whom the actions have been brought are, by reason of the segregation complained of, deprived of the equal protection of the laws guaranteed by the Fourteenth Amendment. . . .

24. Code of Ethics of the Education Profession, National Education Association, 1975

Preamble

The educator believes in the worth and dignity of man. He recognizes the supreme importance of the pursuit of truth, devotion to excellence, and the nurture of democratic citizenship. He regards as essential to these goals the protection of freedom to learn and to teach and the guarantee of equal educational opportunity for all. The educator accepts his responsibility to practice his profession according to the highest ethical standards.

The educator recognizes the magnitude of the responsibility he has accepted in choosing a career in education, and engages himself, individually and collectively with other educators, to judge his colleagues, and to be judged by them, in accordance with the provisions of this code.

Principle I
Commitment to the Student

The educator measures his success by the progress of each student toward realization of his potential as a worthy and effective citizen. The educator therefore works to stimulate the spirit of inquiry, the acquisition of knowledge and understanding, and the thoughtful formulation of worthy goals.

In fulfilling his obligation to the student, the educator—

1. Shall not without just cause restrain the student from independent action in his pursuit of learning, and shall not without just cause deny the student access to varying points of view.
2. Shall not deliberately suppress or distort subject matter for which he bears responsibility.
3. Shall make reasonable effort to protect the student from conditions harmful to learning or to health and safety.
4. Shall conduct professional business in such a way that he does not expose the student to unnecessary embarrassment or disparagement.
5. Shall not on the ground of race, color, creed, or national origin exclude any student from participation in or deny him benefits under any program, nor grant any discriminatory consideration or advantage.
6. Shall not use professional relationships with students for private advantage.
7. Shall keep in confidence information that has been obtained in the course of professional service, unless disclosure serves professional purposes or is required by law.
8. Shall not tutor for remuneration students assigned to his class, unless no other qualified teacher is reasonably available.

Principle II
Commitment to the Public

The educator believes that patriotism in its highest form requires dedication to the principles of our democratic heritage. He shares with all other citizens the responsibility for the development of sound public policy and assumes full political and citizenship responsibilities.

The educator bears particular responsibility for the development of policy relating to the extension of educational opportunities for all and for interpreting educational programs and policies to the public.

In fulfilling his obligation to the public, the educator—

1. Shall not misrepresent an institution or organization with which he is affiliated, and shall take adequate precautions to distinguish between his personal and institutional or organizational views.
2. Shall not knowingly distort or misrepresent the facts concerning educational matters in direct and indirect public expressions.
3. Shall not interfere with a colleague's exercise of political and citizenship rights and responsibilities.
4. Shall not use institutional privileges for private gain or to promote political candidates or partisan political activities.
5. Shall accept no gratuities, gifts, or favors that might impair or appear to impair professional judgment, nor offer any favor, service, or thing of value to obtain special advantage.

Principle III
Commitment to the Profession

The educator believes that the quality of the services of the education profession directly influences the nation and its citizens. He therefore exerts every effort to raise professional standards, to improve his service, to promote a climate in which the exercise of professional judgment is encouraged, and to achieve conditions which attract persons worthy of the trust to careers in education. Aware of the value of united effort, he contributes actively to the support, planning and programs of professional organizations.

In fulfilling his obligation to the profession, the educator—

1. Shall not discriminate on grounds of race, color, creed, or national origin for membership in professional organizations, nor interfere with the free

participation of colleagues in the affairs of their association.

2. Shall accord just and equitable treatment to all members of the profession in the exercise of their professional rights and responsibilities.

3. Shall not use coercive means or promise special treatment in order to influence professional decisions of colleagues.

4. Shall withhold and safeguard information acquired about colleagues in the course of employment, unless disclosure serves professional purposes.

5. Shall not refuse to participate in a professional inquiry when requested by an appropriate professional association.

6. Shall provide upon the request of the aggrieved party a written statement of specific reason for recommendations that lead to the denial of increments, significant changes in employment, or termination of employment.

7. Shall not misrepresent his professional qualifications.

8. Shall not knowingly distort evaluations of colleagues.

Principle IV
Commitment to Professional Employment Practices

The educator regards the employment agreement as a pledge to be executed both in spirit and in fact in a manner consistent with the highest ideals of professional service. He believes that sound professional personnel relationships with governing boards are built upon personal integrity, dignity, and mutual respect. The educator discourages the practice of his profession by unqualified persons.

In fulfilling his obligation to professional employment practices, the educator—

1. Shall apply for, accept, offer, or assign a position of responsibility on the basis of professional preparation and legal qualifications.

2. Shall apply for a specific position only when it is known to be vacant, and shall refrain from underbidding or commenting adversely about other candidates.

3. Shall not knowingly withhold information regarding a position from an applicant, or misrepresent an assignment or conditions of employment.

4. Shall give prompt notice to the employing agency of any change in availability of service, and the employing agent shall give prompt notice of change in availability or nature of a position.

5. Shall adhere to the terms of a contract or appointment, unless these terms have been legally terminated, falsely represented, or substantially altered by unilateral action of the employing agency.

7. Shall not delegate assigned tasks to unqualified personnel.

8. Shall permit no commercial exploitation of his professional position.

9. Shall use time granted for the purpose for which it is intended.

25. Extracts from *A Nation at Risk*, National Commission on Excellence in Education, April 1983

Our Nation is at risk. Our once unchallenged preeminence in commerce, industry, science, and technological innovation is being overtaken by competitors throughout the world. This report is concerned with only one of the many causes and dimensions of the problem, but it is the one that undergirds American prosperity, security, and civility. We report to the American people that while we can take justifiable pride in what our schools and colleges have historically accomplished and contributed to the United States and the well-being of its people, the educational foundations of our society are presently being eroded by a rising tide of mediocrity that threatens our very future as a Nation and a people. What was unimaginable a generation ago has begun to occur—others are matching and surpassing our educational attainments.

If an unfriendly foreign power had attempted to impose on America the mediocre educational performance that exists today, we might well have viewed it as an act of war. As it stands, we have allowed this to happen to ourselves. We have even squandered the gains in student achievement made in the wake of the Sputnik challenge. Moreover, we have dismantled essential support systems which helped make those gains possible. We have, in effect, been committing an act of unthinking, unilateral educational disarmament.

Our society and its educational institutions seem to have lost sight of the basic purpose of schooling, and of the high expectations and disciplined effort needed to obtain them. This report, the result of 18 months of study, seeks to generate reform of our educational system in fundamental ways and to renew the Nation's commitment to schools and colleges of high quality throughout the length and breadth of our land.

That we have compromised this commitment is, upon reflection, hardly surprising, given the multitude of often conflicting demands we have placed on our nation's schools and colleges. They are routinely called on to provide solutions to personal, social, and political problems that the home and other institutions either will not or cannot resolve. We must understand that these demands on our schools and colleges often exact an educational cost as well as a financial one. . . .

The Risk

History is not kind to idlers. The time is long past when America's destiny was assured simply by an abundance of natural resources and inexhaustible human enthusiasm, and by our relative isolation from the malignant problems of older civilizations. The world is indeed one global village. We live among determined, well-educated, and strongly motivated competitors. We compete with them for international standing and markets, not only with products but also with the ideas of our laboratories and neighborhood workshops. America's position in the world may once have been reasonably secure with only a few exceptionally well-trained men and women. It is no longer. . . .

Our concern, however, goes well beyond such matters as industry and commerce. It also includes the intellectual, moral, and spiritual strengths of our people which knit together the very fabric of our society. The people of the United States need to know that individuals in our society who do not possess the levels of skill, literacy, and training essential to this new era will be effectively disenfranchised, not simply from the material rewards that accompany competent performance, but also from the chance to participate fully in our national life. A high level of shared education is essential to a free, democratic society and to the fostering of a common culture, especially in a country that prides itself on pluralism and individual freedom. . . .

Indicators of the Risk

The educational dimensions of the risk before us have been amply documented in testimony received by the Commission. For example:

- International comparisons of student achievement, completed a decade ago, reveal that on 19 academic tests American students were never first or second and, in comparison with other industrialized nations, were last seven times.

- Some 23 million American adults are functionally illiterate by the simplest tests of everyday reading, writing, and comprehension.

- About 13 percent of all 17-year-olds in the United States can be considered functionally illiterate. Functional illiteracy among minority youth may run as high as 40 percent.

- Average achievement of high school students on most standardized tests is now lower than 26 years ago when Sputnik was launched.

- Over half the population of gifted students do not match their tested ability with comparable achievement in school.

- The College Board's Scholastic Aptitude Tests (SAT) demonstrate a virtually unbroken decline from 1963 to 1980. Average verbal scores fell over 50 points and average mathematics scores dropped nearly 40 points.

- College Board achievement tests also reveal consistent declines in recent years in such subjects as physics and English.

- Both the number and proportion of students demonstrating superior achievement on the SATs (i.e., those with scores of 650 or higher) have also dramatically declined.

- Many 17-year-olds do not possess the "higher order" intellectual skills we should expect of them. Nearly 40 percent cannot draw inferences from written material; only one-fifth can write a persuasive essay; and only one-third can solve a mathematics problem requiring several steps.

- There was a steady decline in science achievement scores of U.S. 17-year-olds as measured by national assessments of science in 1969, 1973, and 1977.

- Between 1975 and 1980, remedial mathematics courses in public 4-year colleges increased by 72 percent and now constitute one-quarter of all mathematics courses taught in those institutions.

- Average tested achievement of students graduating from college is also lower.

- Business and military leaders complain that they are required to spend millions of dollars on costly remedial education and training programs in such basic skills as reading, writing, spelling, and computation. The Department of the Navy, for example, reported to the Commission that one-quarter of its recent recruits cannot read at the ninth grade level, the minimum needed simply to understand written safety instructions. Without remedial work they cannot even begin, much less complete, the sophisticated training essential in much of the modern military.

These deficiencies come at a time when the demand for highly skilled workers in new fields is accelerating rapidly. For example:

- Computers and computer-controlled equipment are penetrating every aspect of our lives—homes, factories, and offices.
- One estimate indicates that by the turn of the century millions of jobs will involve laser technology and robotics.
- Technology is rapidly transforming a host of other occupations. They include health care, medical science, energy production, food processing, construction, and the building, repair and maintenance of sophisticated scientific, educational, military, and industrial equipment. . . .

Hope and Frustration

Statistics and their interpretation by experts show only the surface dimension of the difficulties we face. Beneath them lies a tension between hope and frustration that characterizes current attitudes about education at every level.

We have heard the voices of high school and college students, school board members, and teachers; of leaders of industry, minority groups, and higher education; of parents and State officials. We could hear the hope evident in their commitment to quality education and in their descriptions of outstanding programs and schools. We could also hear the intensity of their frustration, a growing impatience with shoddiness in many walks of American life, and the complaint that this shoddiness is too often reflected in our schools and colleges. Their frustration threatens to overwhelm their hope.

What lies behind this emerging national sense of frustration can be described as both a dimming of personal expectations and the fear of losing a shared vision for America.

On the personal level the student, the parent, and the caring teacher all perceive that a basic promise is not being kept. More and more young people emerge from high school ready neither for college nor for work. This predicament becomes more acute as the knowledge base continues its rapid expansion, the number of traditional jobs shrinks, and new jobs demand greater sophistication and preparation. . . .

Excellence in Education. . . .

Our goal must be to develop the talents of all to their fullest. Attaining that goal requires that we expect and assist all students to work to the limits of their capabilities. We should expect schools to have genuinely high standards rather than minimum ones, and parents to support and encourage their children to make the most of their talents and abilities.

The search for solutions to our educational problems must also include a commitment to life-long learning. The task of rebuilding our system of learning is enormous and must be properly understood and taken seriously. Although a million and a half new workers enter the economy each year from our schools and colleges, the adults working today will still make up about 75 percent of the workforce in the year 2000. These workers, and new entrants into the workforce, will need further education and retraining if they—and we as a Nation—are to thrive and prosper.

The Learning Society

In a world of ever-accelerating competition and change in the conditions of the workplace, of ever-greater danger, and of ever-larger opportunities for those prepared to meet them, educational reform should focus on the goal of creating a Learning Society. At the heart of such a society is the commitment to a set of values and to a system of education that affords all members the opportunity to stretch their minds to full capacity, from early childhood through adulthood, learning more as the world itself changes. Such a society has as a basic foundation the idea that education is important not only because of what it contributes to one's career goals but also because of the value it adds to the general quality of one's life. Also at the heart of the Learning Society are educational opportunities extending far beyond the traditional institutions of learning, our schools and colleges. They extend into homes and workplaces; into libraries, art galleries, museums, and science centers; indeed, into every place where the individual can develop and mature in work and life. In our view, formal schooling in youth is the essential foundation for learning throughout one's life. But without life-long learning, one's skills will become rapidly dated. . . .

Thus, we issue this call to all who care about America and its future: to parents and students; to teachers, administrators, and school board members; to colleges and industry; to union members and military leaders; to governors and State legislators; to the President; to members of Congress and other public officials; to members of learned and scientific societies; to the print and electronic media; to concerned citizens everywhere. America is at risk.

We are confident that America can address this risk. If the tasks we set forth are initiated now and our recommendations are fully realized over the next several years, we can expect reform of our Nation's schools, colleges, and universities. This would also reverse the current declining trend—a trend that stems more from weakness of purpose, confusion of vision, underuse of talent, and lack of leadership, than from conditions beyond our control.

26. Extract from the Elementary and Secondary Education Act (No Child Left Behind Act), 2002

Title I—Improving the Academic Achievement of the Disadvantaged
SEC. 1001. STATEMENT OF PURPOSE

The purpose of this title is to ensure that all children have a fair, equal, and significant opportunity to obtain a high-quality education and reach, at a minimum, proficiency on challenging State academic achievement standards and State academic assessments. This purpose can be accomplished by—

(1) ensuring that high-quality academic assessments, accountability systems, teacher preparation and training, curriculum, and instructional materials are aligned with challenging State academic standards so that students, teachers, parents, and administrators can measure progress against common expectations for student academic achievement;

(2) meeting the educational needs of low-achieving children in our Nation's highest-poverty schools, limited English proficient children, migratory children, children with disabilities, Indian children, neglected or delinquent children, and young children in need of reading assistance;

(3) closing the achievement gap between high- and low-performing children, especially the achievement gaps between minority and nonminority students, and between disadvantaged children and their more advantaged peers;

(4) holding schools, local educational agencies, and States accountable for improving the academic achievement of all students, and identifying and turning around low-performing schools that have failed to provide a high-quality education to their students, while providing alternatives to students in such schools to enable the students to receive a high-quality education;

(5) distributing and targeting resources sufficiently to make a difference to local educational agencies and schools where needs are greatest;

(6) improving and strengthening accountability, teaching, and learning by using State assessment systems designed to ensure that students are meeting challenging State academic achievement and content standards and increasing achievement overall, but especially for the disadvantaged;

(7) providing greater decisionmaking authority and flexibility to schools and teachers in exchange for greater responsibility for student performance;

(8) providing children an enriched and accelerated educational program, including the use of schoolwide programs or additional services that increase the amount and quality of instructional time;

(9) promoting schoolwide reform and ensuring the access of children to effective, scientifically based instructional strategies and challenging academic content;

(10) significantly elevating the quality of instruction by providing staff in participating schools with substantial opportunities for professional development;

(11) coordinating services under all parts of this title with each other, with other educational services, and, to the extent feasible, with other agencies providing services to youth, children, and families; and

(12) affording parents substantial and meaningful opportunities to participate in the education of their children.

Appendix B
Biographies of Major Personalities

Abbott, Grace (1878–1939) *social worker, activist*
Grace Abbott was born in Grand Island, Nebraska. In 1898 she graduated from Grand Island College, and in 1902, while teaching high school in Grand Island, she pursued graduate study at the University of Nebraska at Lincoln. She moved to Chicago in 1907 to begin a career in social work. As a resident of Hull-House, the Chicago settlement house founded by Jane Addams and Ellen Gates Starr, she headed the Immigrants' Protection League. In 1909 Abbott earned a master's degree in political science from the University of Chicago. A member of the Women's Trade Union League, she supported striking garment workers in Chicago in 1910 and 1911. In 1917 she joined the U.S. Children's Bureau, and in 1919 she became its director. In that position she distributed funding for approximately 3,000 child and maternal health centers that were established nationwide in the 1920s. She helped draft the Social Security Act of 1935 and contributed suggestions for the Fair Labor Standards Act of 1938. Abbott's writings include *The Immigrant and the Community* (1917) and *The Child and the State* (1938). In 1976 she was inducted into the Nebraska Hall of Fame.

Addams, Jane (1860–1935) *social reformer, pacifist, Nobel laureate*
Jane Addams was born in Illinois and educated at the Rockford Female Seminary (now Rockford College), graduating in 1881. While in Europe in 1887 and 1888, she was inspired by the social reform movement. In 1889 she and college classmate Ellen Starr founded Hull-House, a social welfare center, or settlement house, in a poor immigrant neighborhood of Chicago. The Hull-House staff was active in child labor reform and education. The settlement provided the community with a day nursery and a gymnasium, among other services. Addams became chairperson of the Woman's Peace Party in 1915. That same year she also chaired the International Congress of Women at The Hague, Netherlands. She traveled in Europe at the start of World War I, urging peace through mediation. Her pacifism following U.S. entry into the war, however, earned her criticism at home. In 1931, she shared the Nobel Peace Prize with American educator Nicholas Murray Butler. Her 10 books include *Democracy and Social Ethics* (1902), *The Spirit of Youth and the City Streets* (1909), and *Twenty Years at Hull-House* (1910).

Armstrong, Samuel Chapman (1839–1893) *founder of Hampton University*
Samuel Armstrong was born on the island of Maui, Hawaii, to missionary parents. Soon after his birth, the family moved to Honolulu. In 1860 Armstrong's father died suddenly. The 21-year-old Armstrong, who had completed two years of study at the Royal School at Punahou (later Oahu College), left Hawaii to attend Williams College in Massachusetts. He graduated in 1862, during the Civil War, and enlisted in the Union army. He fought at Gettysburg and in late 1863, having attained the rank of lieutenant colonel, was placed in command of the 9th Regiment, U.S. Colored Troops. He was promoted to colonel, and in 1864 he led his regiment in the siege of Petersburg, Virginia. He was subsequently stationed with his unit at Ringgold Barracks, Texas, having been awarded the brevet rank of brigadier general, before being discharged from the army in December 1865. Armstrong joined the Freedmen's Bureau after the war and, with the aid of the American Missionary Association, founded the Hampton Normal and Industrial Institute (now Hampton University), at Hampton, Virginia. This school for

African Americans and American Indians trained some of its students as teachers and prepared others for employment as manual laborers. Armstrong was an instructor and fund-raiser for the school, and he was a mentor to Booker T. Washington, who entered the Hampton Institute in 1872. He recommended Washington to be the first principal of the Tuskegee Institute (now Tuskegee University) in Alabama, which began as a vocational school for African Americans. In 1892, Armstrong suffered a major stroke while in New York. He returned to Hampton in a private railroad car provided by a wealthy friend. He died at the Hampton Institute on May 11, 1893, and was buried with full military honors.

Banks, Nathaniel Prentice (Bobbin Boy Banks) (1816–1894) *Civil War general, politician*

Nathaniel Banks was born in Waltham, Massachusetts. He attended the local common school before going to work in a cotton mill and acquiring the lifelong nickname Bobbin Boy Banks. He subsequently apprenticed as a machinist, edited a Waltham newspaper, clerked in the customhouse in Boston, and studied law. He was admitted to the bar at age 23 and practiced law in Boston. He served in the Massachusetts legislature beginning in 1849 and for two years was Speaker of the House. He was elected to the U.S. House of Representatives in 1852 and served there until December 24, 1857, when he resigned to fill the post of governor of Massachusetts. In January 1861, Banks moved to Chicago to become vice president of the Illinois Central Railroad. Four months later, when the nation was divided by war, he entered the Union army as a major general of volunteers. President Abraham Lincoln had appointed him to one of the highest positions in the army despite his lack of military experience. After being defeated in battle in the Shenandoah Valley by Confederate general Thomas "Stonewall" Jackson, Banks was given command of the Military District of Washington. In October 1862 he took charge of the Gulf Department, where he established schools for African Americans. His military incompetence resulted in a failed attempt to open the Mississippi River from the south; heavy Union casualties at Port Hudson, Louisiana, in July 1863; and further defeats along the Red River in Louisiana in spring 1864. He was honorably discharged from the army on August 25, 1865, and returned to Massachusetts, where he was elected to Congress as a Republican to fill the seat of Daniel W. Gooch, who had resigned. He chaired the House Committee on Foreign Affairs and served until March 3, 1873, having lost the 1872 election. Banks was a

Massachusetts state senator in 1874 and was again elected to Congress, this time as an Independent, and served from March 4, 1875, to March 3, 1879. From March 11, 1879, through April 23, 1888, he held the appointed position of U.S. marshal for Massachusetts. In 1888 he was elected as a Republican to Congress. He served until March 3, 1891, and chaired the Committee on Expenditures in the Department of the Interior. Banks died in Waltham, where he had been born, on September 1, 1894.

Beecher, Catharine Esther (1800–1878) *advocate of education for women*

Catharine Beecher was born in East Hampton, New York. She was a daughter of the prominent clergyman Lyman Beecher and a sister of the abolitionist writer Harriet Beecher Stowe and the Congregationalist minister Henry Ward Beecher. Catharine Beecher was educated at home until age 10, when she began attending a private girls' school. At school, she studied the limited curriculum taught to girls, and at home she pursued wider knowledge. She became a teacher in 1821, and in 1823, with her sister Mary, she opened the Hartford Female Seminary in Connecticut. This school offered a broader education than was generally available to women, and it prepared them for the two roles for which Beecher believed they were suited: motherhood and teaching. Beecher encouraged instruction in domestic economy, or housekeeping, as a branch of study. She moved with her father to Cincinnati in 1832 and founded the Western Female Institute. She also established schools for women in Burlington, Iowa; Quincy, Illinois; and Milwaukee. In 1841, she published *A Treatise on Domestic Economy*, and in 1852, she founded the American Woman's Educational Association.

Bestor, Arthur (1908–1994) *historian, critic of public education*

Arthur Eugene Bestor, Jr., was born in Chautauqua, New York, where his father directed the Chautauqua Institution, an adult-learning center founded in 1874. As a child and youth he attended the Horace Mann School, a private elementary school in Riverdale, New York, and the Lincoln School, the laboratory school of Teachers College, Columbia University. He received baccalaureate and doctoral degrees in history from Yale University in 1930 and 1938, and he taught at Teachers College, beginning in 1936, and Stanford University, beginning in 1942. Upon the death of his father in 1944, he dropped his middle name and no longer used the suffix junior to distinguish himself from his elder. Bestor's early historical research concerned 18th- and 19th-century utopian communities in the United States, especially New Harmony, Indiana. His most notable work on this subject, *Backwoods Utopias*, was published in 1950, three years after he joined the faculty of the University of Illinois. In the 1950s, Bestor emerged as a leading critic of public education, especially the life-adjustment movement. He argued for more rigorous academic instruction in *Educational Wastelands* (1953) and *The Restoration of Learning* (1956). For the 1956–57 academic year he was Harmsworth professor of American history at Oxford University. From 1962 until his retirement in 1976, Bestor taught at the University of Washington. During this period he became a recognized authority on constitutional history and several times testified before Congress on constitutional matters.

Bethune, Mary McLeod (1875–1955) *educator, African-American leader*

Mary Jane McLeod was the 15th of 17 children born to Samuel and Patsy McLeod, former slaves living near Maysville, South Carolina. She attended a one-room school before studying on a scholarship at Scotia Seminary near Concord, North Carolina. After graduating in 1894, she was a scholarship student at the Bible Institute for Home and Foreign Missions in Chicago and hoped to become a missionary in Africa. She subsequently dedicated herself to education and political and social activism in the United States. She held several teaching jobs in the South and in 1898 married Albertus Bethune, a haberdasher. In 1904, Mary McLeod Bethune opened the Daytona Normal and Industrial Institute for Negro Girls in Daytona Beach, Florida. In 1924, this school merged with the Cookman Institute, a school for boys, to form Bethune-Cookman College, with Bethune as its president. Throughout her teaching career, Bethune pursued social goals, visiting prisoners and working for black voting rights. She became president of the Florida Federation of Colored Women in 1917 and the National Association of Colored Women in 1923. Bethune became the first African-American woman to head a federal agency in 1936, when President Franklin D. Roosevelt appointed her director of the National Youth Administration's Division of Negro Affairs. In 1940, she became vice president of the National Association for the Advancement of Colored People, and during World War II she was national commander of the Women's Army for National Defense, an organization of African-American women supporting the nation's war effort of the home front. She represented the United States at the inauguration of President William V. S. Tubman of Liberia in 1949, and President Harry Tru-

man named her to the Committee of Twelve for National Defense in 1951. Her awards included the Medal of Honor and Merit from Haiti and the title of commander of the Order of the Star of Africa from Liberia. Her own nation honored her with a postage stamp in 1985.

Binet, Alfred (1857–1911) *French psychologist, pioneer of intelligence testing*

Alfred Binet was born in Nice, in southeastern France. His parents divorced when he was young, and at age 15 he went with his mother to live in Paris. After being licensed to practice law in 1878, he began to work toward a medical degree. He discontinued formal learning when he developed a strong interest in psychology, preferring to read and study on his own. In 1883, he took a position at the Salpêtrière, a leading neurological research center in Paris that was under the direction of Jean-Martin Charcot, a physician researching the psychological basis of illness. In 1899, Binet joined the Free Society for the Psychological Study of the Child, and in 1890, he left the Salpêtrière to study the cognitive abilities of his two young daughters. He soon began working in a psychology laboratory at the Sorbonne, and in 1894, he became the laboratory's director. He also edited *l'Annee psychologique*, a French psychological journal. In 1903, he published *Experimental Studies of Intelligence*, a book describing his research in this area, and in 1904, he began work on the first intelligence test, which was intended to identify children needing specialized instruction because of low mental ability. With his colleague Theodore Simon he published this test, known as the Binet-Simon Scale, in 1905. Binet and Simon published their first revision in 1908 and their second in 1911, the year of Binet's death.

Braille, Louis (1809–1852) *inventor of the Braille alphabet for the blind*

Louis Braille was born in Coupvray, near Paris, France. An accident with an awl occurring in the workshop of his father, Simon-René Braille, a harness and saddle maker, caused him to lose the ability to see at age three. In 1818, he entered the National Institute for the Young Blind in Paris. He excelled in science and music, and he became known in Paris as an organist and cellist. At age 15, he modified a system employed for nighttime military communication, consisting of raised dashes and dots, to create an alphabet that the blind could use for reading and writing. He later developed the system further, adding mathematical and musical symbols. In 1828, Braille began teaching at the school where he had studied, and in 1829, he published his raised-dot alphabet, which continues to be used throughout the world. He died of tuberculosis at age 43.

Bridgman, Laura Dewey (1829–1889) *first blind and deaf American to learn language*

Laura Bridgman lost her sight and hearing and most of her ability to smell and taste to scarlet fever at age two, in an epidemic that killed her two sisters and brother. Her parents devised a simple system of signs that they used with Laura for basic communication, and they taught her to sew, knit, and do some simple chores on their Hanover, New Hampshire, farm. In October 1837, when she was almost eight years old, Bridgman enrolled in the Perkins School for the Blind in Boston, at the invitation of its founder, Samuel Gridley Howe, becoming the school's first blind and deaf student. At Perkins she learned to read using the raised-letter system and to communicate with others through signs. The press reported on her progress, and she became an attraction for visitors, including Charles Dickens, who toured the school in 1842. The Perkins School remained Bridgman's home after her formal education ended. She worked at the school, doing housekeeping and needle crafts. She also taught students, including Anne Sullivan, who would become Helen Keller's teacher.

Bush, George Walker (1946–) *43rd president of the United States*

George W. Bush was born in New Haven, Connecticut, and grew up in Midland and Houston, Texas, where his father, future president George H. W. Bush, was in the oil business. In 1968, he graduated from Yale University with a degree in history. He then served in the Texas Air National Guard, piloting an F-120 fighter jet. After receiving a master's degree in business administration from Harvard Business School in 1975, Bush returned to Texas and started his own oil business. In 1977, he ran unsuccessfully for the U.S. Congress as a Republican. In 1985, after his business was acquired by a Dallas firm, Bush became a paid advisor to his father's 1988 presidential campaign. The following year he assembled the investors who purchased the Texas Rangers baseball franchise. Bush became the first Texas governor elected to two consecutive four-year terms, in 1994 and 1998. In November 2000, he ran for president of the United States against Democrat Al Gore. The election, one of the closest in the nation's history, was the first to be decided in the U.S. Supreme Court. It was ultimately determined that Bush won, and he was sworn in to office on January 20, 2001. He achieved an easy victory in his bid for reelection in 2004. Bush has presided over military operations in Afghanistan and, more significantly, Iraq. His educational policy shaped the No Child Left Behind Act, which he signed into law on January 8, 2002. The act links federal support to measured academic achievement.

Child, Lydia Maria Francis (1802–1880) *writer, abolitionist*

Lydia Francis, born in Medford, Massachusetts, was 22 when she published her first novel, *Hobomok* (1824), concerning the marriage of a white woman and a Pequot Indian man. She followed this book with a short-story collection and a second novel. In 1825 she began publishing *Juvenile Miscellany,* a magazine for children. In 1828 she married David Lee Child, a lawyer and founder of the New England Anti-Slavery Society. Over the next several years, she wrote a series of books on home and family management, including *The Frugal Housewife* (1829) and *The Mother's Book* (1830). She next published *An Appeal in Favor of that Class of Americans Called Africans* (1833), in which she demanded an immediate end to slavery. Lydia Child continued working to further abolitionist goals and became editor of the *National Anti-Slavery Standard,* the journal of the American Anti-Slavery Society, in 1840. She withdrew from the society in 1843 to protest the call by its president, William Lloyd Garrison, for "no union with slaveholders." In 1865, she published *The Freedmen's Book,* an eclectic reader intended for use in schools educating former slaves. She distributed this book at her own expense.

Clinton, Bill (William Jefferson Clinton) (1946–) *42nd president of the United States*

Bill Clinton was born William Jefferson Blythe IV in Hope, Arkansas, three months after his father, a traveling salesman, died in an automobile accident. When he was four, his mother, Virginia, who was a nurse, married Roger Clinton of Hot Springs, Arkansas. Bill grew up in Hot Springs and as a teenager adopted his stepfather's surname. As a high school junior he participated in Boys Nation, a citizenship program conducted by the American Legion in Washington, D.C., and shook hands with President John F. Kennedy in the White House Rose Garden. The experience inspired Clinton to pursue a career in public service. In 1968, he received a bachelor's degree in international affairs from Georgetown University in Washington, D.C. The same year, he won a Rhodes scholarship to study at Oxford University in England. Then, after earning a law degree from Yale University in 1973, he returned to Arkansas to practice law. In 1976, he was elected state attorney general, and in 1978, he was elected governor of Arkansas. Clinton, a Democrat, lost the 1980 gubernatorial election, but he won the governorship again in 1982. He served in that post until 1992, when he defeated the incumbent president, Republican George H. W. Bush, and a third-party candidate, Ross Perot, in the presidential election. As president, Clinton signed the Goals 2000: Educate America Act, which set eight educational goals for the nation. He and his vice president, Al Gore, encouraged the use of computer technology in schools. Clinton was reelected in 1996, and in 1998, he was the second president in U.S. history to be impeached. He was tried in the Senate on grounds of perjury and obstruction of justice relating to his romantic involvement with a White House intern and was found not guilty of the charges against him.

Clinton, DeWitt (1769–1828) *political leader, proponent of public education*

DeWitt Clinton was born in Little Britain, New York. His father, James Clinton, held the rank of general in the American Revolution. DeWitt Clinton graduated from Columbia College (later Columbia University) in 1786. He then studied law and was admitted to the bar in 1789. In 1790, he became secretary to his uncle, George Clinton, who was governor of New York from 1777 to 1795, and in 1795, he was elected to the New York State assembly. DeWitt Clinton was a state senator from 1798 until 1802, when he was appointed to the U.S. Senate to serve out an unexpired term. Clinton was first appointed mayor of New York City in 1802; he held this position, with two interruptions, until 1815. From 1811 to 1813 he was New York State lieutenant governor. As mayor he expanded the city's public-education system and established a hospital and orphanage. Clinton also was a founder of the New-York Historical Society, the American Academy of the Arts, and the Literary and Philosophical Society. He was the Federalist Party's candidate for president in 1812, running on a platform of opposition to the impending war with Great Britain, but he lost this close race to the incumbent, James Madison. From 1817 to 1822, and again from 1825 to 1828, he was governor of New York. As governor he promoted and supervised the building of the Erie Canal, and in 1825 he presided over its opening.

Collier, John (1884–1968) *social worker, commissioner of Indian affairs*

John Collier was born in Atlanta, Georgia. His father, Charles A. Collier, was a banker and, from 1897 to 1899, mayor of Atlanta. John Collier was valedictorian of his high school class. In 1897, his mother died, and in 1900, his father committed suicide. In 1902, Collier enrolled in Columbia University, where he took a variety of courses with an emphasis on social concerns. His first attempt at social work was with New York City's immigrant population. In 1905, he became executive director of the newly formed Associated Charities of Atlanta. In 1906, he stud-

ied in Paris under the renowned psychologist Pierre M. F. Janet. In 1908, upon returning to New York, he joined the staff of the People's Institute, an organization that worked among immigrants on the Lower East Side of Manhattan. He directed the institute's National Training School for Community Workers beginning in 1915. Collier moved to California in 1919 to work for the state government. He resigned within a year, however, and went to Taos, New Mexico, where he studied the history and culture of the Pueblo Indians. In 1922, he mobilized opposition to the Bursum Bill, which would have opened 60,000 acres of Pueblo land to non-Indian settlement. After the bill was defeated he helped establish the American Indian Defense Association, an organization of whites dedicated to protecting Indians' rights, and served as its executive secretary. He also edited the association's magazine, *American Indian Life.* In 1933, Secretary of the Interior Harold Ickes appointed Collier commissioner of Indian affairs. In that post, Collier secured passage of the Indian Reorganization Act of 1934, which reversed government efforts to assimilate the Indians and encouraged Indian self-government and cultural and economic independence. Under Collier's leadership, Native culture assumed a more prominent place in the curriculum of federal Indian schools, and the government built 40 day schools with Indian labor. In 1945, Collier resigned as commissioner and became president of the Institute of Ethnic Affairs in Washington, D.C. Also in 1945, he attended the first session of the United Nations General Assembly in London. In 1947, he began teaching sociology and anthropology at the City College of New York. He retired in 1954 but fulfilled teaching commitments at Columbia University; the Merrill-Palmer Institute, a school of child and family development in Detroit; and Knox College in Galesburg, Illinois, before settling in Taos. His books include *Indians of the Americas* (1947) and *From Every Zenith* (1963).

Conant, James Bryant (1893–1978) *president of Harvard University, educational researcher, government official*

James Conant, who traced his ancestry to the early settlers of New England, was born in Dorchester, Massachusetts. His father, James Scott Conant, did engraving and etching. After graduating from the Roxbury Latin School in Boston, in 1910, James Bryant Conant earned baccalaureate and doctoral degrees in chemistry from Harvard University in 1914 and 1917. During World War I, he served with the Chemical Warfare Service, developing poisonous gases and achieved the rank of major. He returned to Harvard after the war to teach organic chemistry and was appointed assistant professor in 1919, associate professor in 1925, and professor in 1927. He also chaired the Division of Chemistry at Harvard and was a consultant to the Du Pont Company, a scientific adviser to the Rockefeller Institute for Medical Research, and a member of the Board of Trustees of the Carnegie Foundation for the Advancement of Teaching. In 1933, Conant became president of Harvard. Between 1941 and 1946, he chaired the National Defense Research Committee, which oversaw the military's scientific research during World War II, including the Manhattan Project, the successful effort to develop the first nuclear bomb. In 1944, the American Chemical Society awarded him its highest honor, the Priestley Medal. From 1947 to 1952, Conant was an adviser to the National Science Foundation and Atomic Energy Commission. In 1953, he retired as president of Harvard and entered government service, first as U.S. high commissioner and then as U.S. ambassador to Germany. He came back to the United States in 1957 to conduct a study of U.S. high schools that was financed by the Carnegie Foundation. This work resulted in the book *The American High School Today* (1959), which influenced the academic curriculum in high schools throughout the United States. In 1963, President John F. Kennedy presented Conant with the Medal of Freedom, the nation's highest civilian honor. The next year, Conant began an 18-month stint as an educational adviser in Berlin, supported by the Ford Foundation. Conant retired to New York City; in spring 1977, he fell ill while vacationing in Hanover, New Hampshire. He remained in Hanover until his death.

Crandall, Prudence (1803–1890) *educator of African-American girls*

Prudence Crandall was born into a white Quaker family in Hopkinton, Rhode Island. She was educated at the New England Friends' Boarding School in Providence and briefly taught school in her home state. In 1831, she moved to Canterbury, Connecticut, and opened a girls' boarding school. In 1833, she admitted an African-American student who wished to train as a teacher. Following strong community protest, Crandall closed her school, reopened it as a school for African-American girls, and recruited students throughout New England. The town of Canterbury responded by outlawing the education of any African American from outside Connecticut. Crandall was arrested, tried, and convicted of violating this law, but the conviction was reversed on appeal in July 1834. Local opposition to the school continued, and in September 1834, mob violence forced Crandall to close her school permanently. She moved with her husband, the Reverend Calvin Philleo, to Illinois. Following Philleo's death, she lived with her brother in Elk Falls, Kansas.

Dewey, John (1859–1952) *philosopher, educator*

John Dewey earned a bachelor's degree from the University of Vermont in 1879 and a doctorate from Johns Hopkins University in 1884. From 1884 until his retirement, he taught at the University of Michigan (1884–88; 1889–94), the University of Minnesota (1888–89), the University of Chicago (1894–1904), and Columbia University (1904–31). Dewey gained national recognition as a philosopher while at Chicago. He viewed human beings as creatures of the natural world who must seek life's meaning in their present surroundings. He recognized as truth any idea that works in practical experience. He contributed to *Studies in Logical Theory* (1903), an essay collection that marked the appearance of the Chicago school in philosophy. In 1896, Dewey established the laboratory school at the University of Chicago to experiment with teaching methods, especially those that actively involved students. His work led to a shift in teaching practices in the early 20th century, as educators focused on students' needs and interests. Dewey was politically active and favored progressive, even radical, approaches to international and economic issues. His many books include *The School and Society* (1899), *Democracy and Education* (1916), *Human Nature and Conduct* (1922), and *Problems of Men* (1946).

DuBois, William Edward Burghardt (1868–1963) *scholar, writer, a founder of the National Association for the Advancement of Colored People (NAACP)*

In 1895, W. E. B. DuBois became the first African American to earn a Ph.D. from Harvard University. From 1897 to 1910, he taught history and economics at Atlanta University. He emerged as a spokesman for African Americans in the early 20th century when he objected in print to Booker T. Washington's advocacy of manual training for young blacks. DuBois called instead for education of the "Talented Tenth" of his race to serve as leaders and role models in the African-American community. DuBois led the Niagara Movement, a group that first met in Niagara Falls, Canada, in 1905 to demand an end to racial inequality. After the NAACP was formed in 1910, he served as director of publications. He also edited *The Crisis*, the journal of the NAACP. DuBois became an advocate of pan-Africanism after World War I and organized several international pan-African conferences. He worked again with the NAACP from 1944 to 1948. In 1959, the Soviet Union awarded DuBois the Lenin Peace Prize. In 1961, he joined the Communist Party and moved to Ghana. His 20 books include *The Philadelphia Negro* (1899), *The Souls of Black Folk* (1903), *Black Reconstruction* (1935), and *Worlds of Color* (1961). He died before completing his final project, *Encyclopedia Africana*.

Eisenhower, Dwight David (1890–1969) *Allied supreme commander during World War II, 34th president of the United States*
Born in Texas, Dwight Eisenhower grew up in Abilene, Kansas. He attended the U.S. Military Academy at West Point and was commissioned an infantry officer upon graduation in 1915. He commanded a tank corps training center during World War I. His service in World War II began with an assignment in Washington, D.C. He subsequently commanded the Allied force that landed in North Africa in 1942 and was supreme commander of the Allied invasion of France on June 6, 1944. In December 1944, Eisenhower was promoted to general of the army and given overall responsibility for the Allied forces. He became president of Columbia University in 1948 but left in 1951 to be supreme commander of the North Atlantic Treaty Organization. He was elected president of the United States in 1952. As president, he worked to reduce cold war tensions and maintain world peace. In September 1955, he sent troops to Little Rock, Arkansas, to ensure compliance with court-ordered school desegregation. Eisenhower was elected to a second term as president in 1956. In 1960, he accepted responsibility for a U-2 spy-plane flight over the Soviet Union, an event that strained relations between the United States and USSR.

Eliot, Charles William (1834–1926) *president of Harvard University*
Charles Eliot was born in Boston to a prominent New England family. He graduated from Harvard University in 1853 and taught mathematics and chemistry there from 1854 until 1863. Between 1863 and 1865, he traveled in Europe, continuing his study of chemistry and observing methods of instruction. Upon returning to the United States he became a professor of mathematics at the Massachusetts Institute of Technology and wrote articles on educational reform. His writings impressed Harvard's leaders, and in 1869, they elected him president of the university. Eliot's 40-year presidency is remembered as a period of innovation, when Harvard developed into one of the world's leading centers of advanced study and research. Eliot gradually implemented the elective system for undergraduates. He also reorganized and modernized the law school, having students discuss actual court cases rather than abstract principles. He introduced laboratory work to the medical school, made clinical instruction available at Boston hospitals, and required medical students to pass written examinations in all subjects. Under Eliot's leadership, the university added graduate schools of arts and sciences, applied science, and business administration.

Eliot was a member of the Committee of Ten, appointed in 1892 by the National Education Association (NEA) to make recommendations on the high school curriculum. In 1903, he was president of the NEA, and in 1909, he retired from active professional life. In 1910, he edited the Harvard Classics, inexpensive editions of great books that he believed readers could use to educate themselves.

Faubus, Orval Eugene (1910–1994) *governor of Arkansas who resisted school desegregation*
Orval Faubus grew up in northwest Arkansas, where his father was active in socialist politics. Although he was a bookish child, Orval Faubus left school after completing the eighth grade. He nevertheless acquired a teaching certificate in 1928 and taught school in rural Pinnacle, Arkansas. He eventually earned a high school diploma and spent a year at Commonwealth College, a left-leaning school in northwest Arkansas that has since closed. He ran unsuccessfully for the Arkansas House of Representatives in 1936 and subsequently served two terms as a circuit clerk and recorder. He saw combat in World War II as an intelligence officer with General George S. Patton's Third Army and after the war was state highway commissioner. Faubus ran for governor as a Democrat in 1954, winning the election, and was reelected in 1956. As governor he oversaw the desegregation of public transportation in Arkansas and allowed school integration to proceed at the local level—except in Little Rock. Feeling pressure from segregationists and fearing it would hurt his chances in the 1958 election, Faubus in September 1957 ordered the Arkansas National Guard to block African-American students from entering all-white Central High School. President Dwight D. Eisenhower responded by federalizing the national guard and sending the 101st Airborne Division to Little Rock to enforce the Supreme Court's mandate to integrate. Faubus won election to four more terms as governor; in 1966, he retired from elected office. He subsequently held various jobs, managing Dogpatch USA, a theme park in the Ozark Mountains, and working as a bank teller in Huntsville, Arkansas. He sought the Democratic nomination for governor in 1970, 1974, and 1986 but was defeated in the primaries. In 1981, Governor Frank D. White appointed him to head the Arkansas Department of Veterans Affairs, but in 1983, Governor Bill Clinton named someone to replace him.

Franklin, Benjamin (1706–1790) *statesman, scientist, writer, printer*
Benjamin Franklin was the 15th of 17 children born to a Boston chandler and soap maker. He attended school for two years before going to work for his father at age 10. Two

years later, he was apprenticed to his older half-brother, James, a printer. For the next five years, he educated himself by reading, and he submitted anonymous essays to James Franklin's newspaper, the *New England Courant*. In 1723, following a quarrel with his half-brother, Franklin moved to Philadelphia, where he planned to establish his own print shop. He traveled to London to buy equipment but was unable to transact business because he lacked the necessary letters of credit. He worked for two years as a printer in London to earn enough to return to Philadelphia, and by 1730, he was publishing the *Pennsylvania Gazette*, which he had purchased. From 1732 to 1757, Franklin published *Poor Richard's Almanac*, which contained many of his aphorisms. In 1748, he gave up printing to devote himself to scientific experiments. He is credited with inventing a stove that reduced chimney smoke, bifocals, and the lightning rod. In 1749, he proposed for Philadelphia an English-language grammar school that emphasized scientific and practical knowledge. He also participated in government, serving in the Pennsylvania Assembly for 14 years, beginning in 1750. As postmaster general of the colonies, from 1753 to 1774, he reduced inefficiency in the colonial postal system. In 1754, at an intercolonial conference held in Albany, New York, he suggested that the colonies unite against the French and Native Americans. His farsighted plan was accepted by the delegates but rejected by the colonial assemblies and British government. Three years later, Franklin went to England on behalf of the Pennsylvania Assembly to petition for the right to levy taxes on proprietary lands. He spent five years in Britain as a representative of the American colonies. He went again to England as an agent of Pennsylvania in 1764, to negotiate a new charter. During this stay he persuaded Parliament to repeal the Stamp Act. After returning to America in 1775, he was a member of the Second Continental Congress and helped to draft the Declaration of Independence. Throughout most of the American Revolution Franklin was in France, where he negotiated a commercial and defensive alliance. In 1778, he became the first U.S. minister to France, and in 1783 he helped to conclude the Treaty of Paris, the agreement ending the war between the United States and Great Britain. Franklin sailed home to Philadelphia in 1785 and was a member of the Constitutional Convention in 1787. His autobiography, published in 1791, continues to be widely read.

Froebel, Friedrich Wilhelm August (1782–1852)
German educator, founder of the first kindergarten
Friedrich Froebel, son of a Lutheran minister, was born in Oberweissbach, Saxony (now part of Germany). In his youth, Froebel acquired an extensive knowledge of plant life. As a young man, he drifted from one occupation to another, working as a forester, surveyor, and architect before becoming a teacher. He also studied briefly in Jena, Gottingen, and Berlin. From 1806 to 1810, he worked at a school run by the Swiss educator Johann Pestalozzi. Between 1813 and 1815, he served in the Prussian army and supervised the mineralogical museum at the University of Berlin. In 1816, Froebel founded the Universal German Educational Institute, where he developed his program for educating preschool children. In 1827, he opened a school for young children at Blankenburg, Thuringia, which he called a *Kindergarten*, or children's garden. The Prussian government banned kindergartens in 1851, suspecting that Froebel held radical political ideas; the ban was lifted in 1860. Froebel's writings include *The Education of Man* (1826) and *Mother Play and Nursery Songs* (1843).

Gallaudet, Edward Miner (1837–1917) *educator of the deaf*
Edward Gallaudet was born in Hartford, Connecticut. He was the son of Thomas Hopkins Gallaudet, founder of the American School for the Deaf, and Sophia Fowler Gallaudet, a deaf graduate of the school. Gallaudet taught at the school part-time while attending nearby Trinity College, where he considered becoming a minister, and he continued teaching there after leaving college. In 1857, he accepted an invitation from the philanthropist Amos Kendall to head a new school in Washington, D.C., the Columbia Institution for the Instruction of the Deaf and Dumb and Blind. In 1864, he successfully lobbied Congress to permit the school to grant degrees, and in 1867, following visits to European schools for the deaf, he instituted a combined oral and manual communication system for instruction at the school, which was renamed Gallaudet College, after Thomas Hopkins Gallaudet, in 1894 (and Gallaudet University in 1986). Gallaudet married twice and had eight children. He wrote numerous articles on deaf education as well as a book, *Life of Thomas Hopkins Gallaudet*, published in 1888. In 1895, he became the first president of the Convention of American Instructors of the Deaf. In 1910, he retired and moved back to Hartford, and in 1912, he was named a chevalier of the French Legion.

Gallaudet, Thomas Hopkins (1787–1851) *educator of the deaf*
Thomas Gallaudet was born in Philadelphia but grew up in Hartford, Connecticut, where his family moved soon after he was born. He earned a bachelor's degree in 1805 and a master's degree in 1810, both from Yale University. In 1811, he entered the Andover Theological

Seminary in Massachusetts, and in 1814, he was licensed to preach. Gallaudet became concerned about the lack of educational opportunities for the deaf in the United States after befriending Alice Cogswell, the nine-year-old deaf daughter of a neighbor. In 1815, he traveled to London, Edinburgh, and Paris to study methods used there for teaching the deaf and to learn sign language. Upon returning to the United States, he raised the funds needed to open a school for the deaf and in 1817 began educating seven pupils, including Alice Cogswell, in his home. This effort grew into the American School for the Deaf, the first such institution in the United States. Gallaudet served as president of the school until 1830, when ill health forced him to resign. He remained one of its directors, however. In 1838, he became chaplain of the Hartford Retreat for the Insane, and he held this position for the rest of his life. He wrote a number of books on educational and religious subjects for children and adults.

Hall, Granville Stanley (1844–1924) *psychologist, educator*

G. Stanley Hall was a native of Ashfield, Massachusetts. Over an 11-year period, from 1868 to 1878, his interest shifted from theology to philosophy and then to psychology. He spent a year at Union Theological Seminary in New York City, pursued further study in Germany, and taught at Antioch College. In 1878, at Harvard University, he earned the first Ph.D. in psychology granted in the United States. In 1883, he joined the faculty of Johns Hopkins University and founded one of the nation's earliest psychology laboratories. He began publishing the *American Journal of Psychology* in 1887, and in 1888 he was a founder of Clark University in Worcester, Massachusetts. He also served as the school's first president. Hall promoted the study of child development, and he defined the term *adolescence*. He established the *Pedagogical Seminary* (later the *Journal of Genetic Psychology*) in 1893 and was one of the first Americans to recognize the importance of psychoanalysis. In 1909, he arranged for Sigmund Freud and Carl Jung to visit Clark University. Hall's 489 written works include *Adolescence* (1904), *Youth* (1906), *Senescence* (1922), and *Life Confessions of a Psychologist* (1923).

Harris, William Torrey (1835–1909) *educator, student of philosophy, government official*

William Harris, who was born in North Killingly, Connecticut, attended Phillips Andover Academy in Andover, Massachusetts. He completed two years of study at Yale before moving west. He began teaching in St. Louis in 1857 and became superintendent of the city's public schools in 1868.

In 1873, Harris established public kindergartens in St. Louis, and in 1875, he served as president of the National Educational Association. In 1880, he represented the U.S. Bureau of Education at an international congress of educators in Brussels. During this period he also pursued his interest in the German philosopher Georg Wilhelm Friedrich Hegel, founding, in 1866, the St. Louis Philosophical Society and, in 1867, the *Journal of Speculative Philosophy*. Until 1893, Harris edited this publication, which was one of the most influential American philosophical journals of the late 19th century. In summer 1879, Harris was on the faculty of the first Concord School of Philosophy and Literature, which was founded by the Transcendentalist teacher and writer A. Bronson Alcott. He moved to Concord, Massachusetts, in 1880, and purchased Orchard House, Alcott's former home, in 1888. He took part in every session of Alcott's summer school until it closed in 1888, after Alcott's death. From 1889 until 1906, Harris was U.S. commissioner of education. With Benjamin Franklin Sanborn he authored the two-volume biography and memoir *A. Bronson Alcott: His Life and Philosophy* (1893). He also was editor in chief of *Webster's New International Dictionary* (1909).

Harvard, John (1607–1638) *Puritan minister, benefactor of Harvard College*

John Harvard was born in Southwark, Surrey, England. He was the fourth of nine children born to Robert Harvard, a butcher who served as vestryman for St. Saviour's Church, Southwark, and trustee of the parish grammar school, and Katherine Harvard, who was from Stratford-on-Avon. Robert Harvard and two of his sons died of plague in summer 1625, and Katherine Harvard married twice again. Details of John Harvard's education before December 1627 are nonexistent. In that month he entered Emmanuel College, Cambridge. The date of his ordination as a Puritan minister is unknown as well. Harvard's mother died in 1635, and his brother Thomas died in spring 1637. With each death, Harvard's share of the family wealth increased. In summer 1637, Harvard immigrated to Massachusetts with his wife, Ann. The Harvards settled in Charlestown, where John served as one of the church's two clergymen. He died of consumption on September 14, 1638, and left half his estate of 1,500 pounds and his library of 320 books to the college at Cambridge, Massachusetts, that was named for him.

Hoover, Herbert Clark (1874–1964) *31st president of the United States*

Herbert Hoover was born into a Quaker family in rural Ohio. He studied geology and mining at Stanford University and began his career managing mining properties in Western Australia and China. He performed relief work during World War I, arranging transportation home for 120,000 American tourists stranded in Europe and securing food for war-torn Belgium. Following the war, he headed the American Relief Administration, which distributed food, clothing, and medical supplies in eastern Europe. Between 1921 and 1928, he was secretary of commerce under presidents Warren G. Harding and Calvin Coolidge. Hoover, a Republican, was elected president in 1928. Although he took unprecedented steps to combat the Great Depression, sanctioning government spending for public works and federal loans to businesses through the Reconstruction Finance Corporation, the public perceived him as insensitive to their distress, and he lost the 1932 election to Franklin D. Roosevelt. Hoover headed commissions under Presidents Harry S. Truman and Dwight D. Eisenhower to streamline the executive branch of the federal government. He was the author of *American Individualism* (1922), *Challenge to Liberty* (1934), and the three-volume *Memoirs* (1951–52).

Howe, Samuel Gridley (1801–1876) *educator of the blind*

Samuel Howe was born in Boston to Joseph N. Howe, a rope merchant, and Patty Gridley Howe. He graduated from Brown University in 1821 and Harvard Medical School in 1824. His studies complete, he sailed to Europe and served as a surgeon in the Greek army during Greece's war for independence from Turkish rule. In 1827, he returned to the United States and raised $60,000 for provisions and clothing for Greeks enduring hardship in the aftermath of war. He worked in Greece to improve living conditions for war refugees, and he wrote *Historical Sketch of the Greek Revolution* (1828). Once again in Boston, Howe in 1831 agreed to oversee the establishment of the first residential school for the blind in the United States. First, though, he went to Europe to observe institutions for the blind there and involved himself in the Polish revolt of 1831. He was arrested while carrying American contributions across the Prussian frontier and imprisoned in Berlin. Released through the efforts of the U.S. minister to Paris, he was back in Boston by July 1832 and receiving his first blind students at home. In 1833, the Massachusetts legislature appropriated funds for the New England School for the Blind, and in 1839, the philanthropy of trader Thomas H. Perkins allowed the school to purchase and convert a hotel for its use. The school was subsequently renamed the Perkins School for the Blind. Howe added workshops to the school as well as the first printing shop for the blind in the United States. He was an abolitionist, and from

1851 to 1853, with his wife, Julia Ward Howe, he edited the *Commonwealth*, an antislavery newspaper. Beginning in 1856, he also served, without pay, as superintendent of the Massachusetts School for Idiotic and Feeble-Minded Youth (later the Walter E. Fernald State School). Although he was director of the Perkins School for the Blind for the rest of his life, by 1866, Howe had begun to question the effectiveness of large institutions and asylums for the disabled. In 1867, he once more aided Greece in its struggles with Turkey, and in 1868 he earned a law degree from Brown University. In 1871, he served on a commission that investigated for the U.S. government the possible annexation of Santo Domingo.

Jefferson, Thomas (1743–1826) *third president of the United States, principal author of the Declaration of Independence, founder of the University of Virginia*

Thomas Jefferson grew up on a Virginia plantation and attended the College of William and Mary. He was admitted to the bar in 1857 and elected to the Virginia House of Burgesses in 1859. Throughout his life, Jefferson was a voracious reader and a prolific writer. He wrote the *Summary View of the Rights of British America* for the Virginia delegates to the First Continental Congress in 1774. In June 1776, he drafted the Declaration of Independence for the Second Continental Congress. He was governor of Virginia from 1779 until 1781. Jefferson had many interests, including architecture and agriculture. He devoted much time and energy to designing and building his Virginia estate, Monticello. His interest in the people, politics, and commerce of his home state inspired him to write *Notes on the State of Virginia*. Jefferson was minister to France from 1786 to 1789 and the first U.S. secretary of state from 1789 to 1794. He was a candidate for president in the election of 1796; because he received the second largest number of votes, he became vice president under John Adams, the victor, in accordance with the electoral system in use at the time. The presidential election of 1800 resulted in a tie between Jefferson and Aaron Burr, which the House of Representatives decided in Jefferson's favor. As president, Jefferson was responsible for the Louisiana Purchase, which significantly increased the territory of the United States. He founded the University of Virginia in 1819.

Johnson, Lyndon Baines (1908–1973) *36th president of the United States*

Lyndon Johnson was born on a farm in Gillespie County, Texas. In 1913, he moved with his parents to Johnson City, a community that his forebears had helped to found. He graduated from Southwest Texas State Teachers College in 1930 and taught high school briefly before moving to Washington, D.C., in 1931, as secretary to Congressman Richard M. Kleberg. He also attended Georgetown University Law School in 1934. On November 17, 1934, Johnson married Claudia "Lady Bird" Taylor. The couple would have two daughters, Lynda Byrd (born 1944) and Luci Baines (born 1947). In 1937, President Franklin D. Roosevelt appointed Johnson to direct the National Youth Administration (NYA) in Texas. In 1937, Johnson was elected to Congress as a Democrat to fill the seat left vacant by the death of Representative James P. Buchanan. He was elected to five succeeding Congresses. In 1941, Johnson was the first member of Congress to enlist in World War II. He served in the navy as a lieutenant commander and earned a Silver Star in the South Pacific. He returned to government in 1942, when Roosevelt recalled members of Congress from active duty. Johnson was first elected to the U.S. Senate in 1948. He distinguished himself during 12 years in the Senate, serving as Democratic whip (1951–53), minority leader (1953–55), and majority leader (1955–61). In November 1960, he was elected vice president on the ticket with John F. Kennedy. He assumed the presidency on November 22, 1963, after Kennedy's assassination. President Johnson envisioned a "Great Society" and pursued educational, economic, and cultural initiatives toward that end. Declaring "War on Poverty," he signed into law the 1964 Economic Opportunity Act. Also, during his administration such social programs as Head Start, food stamps, Medicare, and Medicaid had their beginnings. Johnson was elected president in 1964, but faced with racial violence at home and deepening military involvement in Vietnam, he did not seek reelection in 1968. He retired to his ranch near Johnson City and died on January 22, 1973.

Kennedy, John Fitzgerald (1917–1963) *35th president of the United States*
John Kennedy graduated from Harvard University in 1940; his expanded senior thesis, *Why England Slept*, was published the same year. He served in the navy during World War II. In August 1943, he was commanding a PT boat that was rammed and sunk by a Japanese destroyer off the Solomon Islands. Kennedy, severely injured, led the surviving crew members to safety. After the war he entered politics. Massachusetts voters elected him to the U.S. House of Representatives as a Democrat in 1946 and to the U.S. Senate in 1952. Kennedy wrote *Profiles in Courage* (1956) while recovering from back surgery. In 1960 he was elected president. As president, he took decisive steps internationally, sending the first U.S. military personnel to South Vietnam in December

1961 and responding to the installation of Soviet missiles in Cuba with a naval blockade of the island. He also attended to domestic issues, including education. He signed the Higher Education Act of 1963 and at the time of his death was preparing legislation to address poverty. Kennedy was assassinated in Dallas on November 22, 1963.

Lancaster, Joseph (1778–1838) *British educator who perfected the monitorial system of education*
Joseph Lancaster attended school only briefly before leaving his London home at age 14 and joining the navy. Friends secured his discharge, and in 1798, he began teaching children in the home of his father, a sieve maker. He soon moved his school to roomier quarters and, to cut expenses, enlisted older students to teach the younger ones. From this beginning he developed a complex monitorial system of instruction, order, and discipline. Lancaster traveled throughout Great Britain to promote his method and won converts in North and South America. Lancasterian schools were first established in Canada in 1814. In 1818, financial difficulties and scandal forced Lancaster to leave England and settle in the United States. His health declined, and in 1820, he moved to Venezuela. In 1828, he lived in New York; he moved in 1829 to Montreal, where he opened a school. He endeavored to publish a periodical, the *Gazette of Education and Friend of Man*, in 1830, but produced only one issue. Soon afterward he closed his school due to a lack of funds. Lancaster returned to New York, where he died in 1838 after being run over by a breakaway horse.

Locke, John (1632–1704) *English philosopher*
John Locke was born to Anglican parents in Wrington, Somerset, and educated at Oxford. From 1661 to 1664, he lectured to undergraduates on Greek, rhetoric, and moral philosophy. He went on to hold a series of government appointments. In 1669, as one of his official duties, he wrote a constitution for the Carolina Colony, but it was never adopted. From 1675 until 1678, Locke lived in France. He spent the years 1683 through 1688 in Holland because he opposed Roman Catholicism, the faith of the British monarchy in those years. He returned to England after the Glorious Revolution of 1688 brought William of Orange to the throne and restored Protestantism to favor. In 1689, Locke published *An Essay Concerning Human Understanding*, in which he compared a newborn's mind to a *tabula rasa*, or blank slate, on which knowledge is recorded as a result of experience. In the same year, he also published *Two Treatises of Government*, which included an attack on the theory of the divine right of kings and the assertion that power resides in a nation's people. Many of the ideas

Locke put forth, such as the duty of government to protect people's rights and the right of the majority to rule, influenced the authors of the U.S. Constitution. King William III appointed Locke to the Board of Trade in 1696, but ill health forced him to resign in 1700. Locke's writings also include *Some Thoughts Concerning Education* (1693) and *The Reasonableness of Christianity* (1695).

Mann, Horace (1796–1859) *first secretary of the Massachusetts Board of Education, U.S. senator*
Horace Mann was born into poverty in Franklin, Massachusetts. He attended school irregularly during childhood but studied independently at the Franklin library. He graduated first in his class from Brown University and continued his education at Litchfield Law School, Litchfield, Connecticut. Mann was admitted to the bar in 1823 and served in the Massachusetts House of Representatives from 1827 to 1833. As a representative, he worked to open the nation's first hospital for the insane at Worcester, Massachusetts. In 1835, he was elected to the Massachusetts Senate. Mann left the Senate in 1837 to become the first secretary of the Massachusetts Board of Education. In this position he lobbied for improved schools and teaching methods and the establishment of normal, or teacher-training, schools. His speeches and writings influenced trends in education throughout the United States. Mann resigned from the Board of Education in 1848 to take the seat in the U.S. Senate left empty by the death of former president John Quincy Adams. He became president of Antioch College, a new institution in Yellow Springs, Ohio, in 1853, and held this position until his death.

Martin, Luther (1748–1826) *politician, lawyer*
Luther Martin was born in Metuchen, New Jersey, and graduated first in his class from the College of New Jersey (later Princeton University) in 1766. He taught school in Maryland for three years before studying law. He was admitted to the bar in Virginia in 1771. Martin was a proponent of American independence from Great Britain, and after being appointed attorney general of Maryland in 1778, he tirelessly prosecuted loyalists residing in the state. He joined a militia company, the Baltimore Light Dragoons, while continuing to serve as attorney general. In 1787, he attended the Constitutional Convention at Philadelphia, but he opposed ratification of the Constitution on several grounds, especially his objection to a strong central government. He resigned as Maryland attorney general in 1805. Martin argued two high-profile legal cases. In 1805, he won an acquittal at the impeachment trial of Supreme Court Justice Samuel Chase, who

was his friend. In 1807, he was a defense lawyer at Aaron Burr's trial for treason. From 1813 to 1816, he was chief judge of the Court of Oyer and Terminer for the City of Baltimore, and in 1818, he again assumed the duties of attorney general of Maryland. Martin retired in 1822 due to illness. He died at Burr's home in New York City in 1826 and was buried in an unmarked grave.

Mather, Cotton (1663–1728) *Congregational minister, author*
Cotton Mather was born in Boston, the son of Increase Mather, pastor of Boston's North Church. Cotton Mather was educated at Harvard College (now Harvard University) and in 1685 he was formally ordained and joined his father in ministering to the North Church. Increase Mather continued his ecclesiastical duties while serving as president of Harvard from 1685 until 1701, and until his death in 1723. Cotton Mather became the sole pastor of the North Church and served there for the rest of his life. He was an influential author who wrote on theology, science, witchcraft, history, and biography. *Wonders of the Invisible World* (1693) recounted some of the cases leading to the Salem witch trials; *Magnalia Christi Americana* (1702) traced the history of Protestantism in New England and is considered one of the most significant scholarly works produced in colonial America; *Essays to Do Good* (1710) offered advice on charitable living; and *Ratio Disciplinae* (1726) dealt with governance of the Congregational Church. Between 1712 and 1724, Mather published his *Curiosa Americana*, dealing with natural phenomena in the New World. In 1713, he became the first American-born member of the Royal Society of London, Britain's national academy of science. In 1721, he advocated smallpox inoculation, which was new and controversial.

McGuffey, William Holmes (1800–1873) *educator, textbook author*
William McGuffey was born near Claysville, Pennsylvania. Two years later, his family moved to Youngstown, Ohio. McGuffey began teaching on the Ohio frontier at age 13. He attended Washington College (now Washington and Jefferson College) in Pennsylvania and in 1826, he joined the faculty of Miami University in Oxford, Ohio, where he taught languages. In 1836, he was appointed president of Cincinnati College (now Cincinnati University), and in 1839, he became president of Ohio University. In 1845, he accepted a professorship in mental and moral philosophy at the University of Virginia, and he held that position for the rest of his life. McGuffey is best remembered for compiling a series of readers for

American schoolchildren. Published between 1835 and 1857, the McGuffey readers progressed in difficulty from basic exercises to excerpts from English and American classics. They were widely used in classrooms throughout the United States for half a century.

Meredith, James Howard (1933–) *first African American to attend the University of Mississippi*

James Meredith, who was born in Kosciusko, Mississippi, joined the U.S. Air Force in 1951, after graduating from high school. He completed a tour of duty in Japan and was discharged in 1960. He then spent two years at Jackson State College, a school for African Americans in his home state, and in 1962 gained acceptance to the University of Mississippi in Oxford, which previously had admitted only whites. On September 20, 1962, when the fall semester began, protesters barred Meredith from registering. President John F. Kennedy sent federal troops to Oxford to enforce Meredith's right to attend the university, and on October 1, he enrolled. This event triggered riots on campus that left two people dead and 48 soldiers and 30 U.S. marshals wounded. On August 18, 1963, Meredith graduated from the University of Mississippi with a degree in history. He continued his studies for a year at the University of Ibadan in Nigeria and in 1966 published a book, *Three Years in Mississippi*, based on his university experience. Shortly afterward, he conceived of and led the Walk against Fear, which was to be an equal-rights march from Memphis to Jackson. This demonstration ended prematurely when a sniper wounded Meredith. He completed the march after his recovery and was joined by the Reverend Martin Luther King, Jr., and other civil rights leaders. Meredith earned a law degree from Columbia University in 1968 and worked for a time as a stockbroker. He made several unsuccessful attempts to be elected to Congress as a Republican and in 1989 began 18 months as a domestic adviser to Senator Jesse Helms of North Carolina. On March 21, 1997, he presented his papers to the University of Mississippi. In 2002, when the university commemorated the 40th anniversary of its desegregation, Meredith was operating a used-car business in Jackson.

Morrill, Justin Smith (1810–1898) *U.S. representative and senator from Vermont*

Justin Morrill was born in Strafford, Vermont, where his father was a blacksmith. He left school at 14, disappointed that his family could not afford to send him to college, and worked as a store clerk in Strafford and a bookkeeper in Portland, Maine. In 1834, he formed a partnership with one of Strafford's most prosperous merchants, and together they maintained four stores. Acknowledged as one of Strafford's leading citizens, Morrill became active in Whig politics. He was a delegate to the Whig National Convention in 1852 and was elected to the U.S. House of Representatives from the Second Vermont District in 1854. Following the collapse of the Whig Party in 1855, Morrill was a founder of the Republican Party. He served on the House Committees on the Territories, Agriculture, and Ways and Means, and was responsible for significant pieces of legislation, including the Internal Revenue Act of 1862, which initiated the federal income tax, and the Morrill Land Grant Act of 1862, which funded colleges through the transfer of federal land to the states for the purpose of generating revenue. In 1866, Morrill was elected to the U.S. Senate, and he served there until his death in 1898. As a senator he chaired the Finance and Buildings and Grounds Committees. He took a strong interest in the beautification of public areas in Washington and spurred completion of the Capitol and Washington Monument and the landscaping of the Capitol grounds by Frederick Law Olmsted. He also secured the land for the Supreme Court Building. Morrill's record for continuous service in Congress stood until December 1956, when it was broken by Carl T. Hayden of Arizona.

Neef, Joseph (1770–1854) *innovative educator*

Joseph Neef was born Joseph Näef in Alsace, France. At age 21, he joined the French army and served under Napoleon Bonaparte. He was shot in the head in 1796; while recovering he read the early writings of the Swiss educator Johann Heinrich Pestalozzi. In 1800, he joined the faculty of Pestalozzi's school at Burgdorf, Switzerland, teaching foreign languages and gymnastics. In 1802, he opened his own school for orphans in Paris. In 1803, he married Luise Buss, whom he had met in Switzerland, and in 1804, the couple's son was born. One visitor to Neef's school was William Maclure, a Scottish-born U.S. immigrant who had come to France to study geology. Maclure invited Neef to open a similar school in Philadelphia, and in 1806, he paid the Neefs' passage to the United States. Neef then spent two years studying English. Three daughters were born to Joseph and Luise Neef between 1807 and 1812. In 1808, Joseph Neef published *Sketches of a Plan of Education*, and in 1809, he opened a school for boys at the Falls of Schuylkill, near Philadelphia. Rather than directing his efforts toward the poor, as Pestalozzi did, Neef considered all potential pupils to be equally deserving. He encouraged his students to think rationally, analyze data, and ask questions. Neef became a member of the Philadelphia Academy of Natural Sciences in 1812. In 1813, he opened a boarding school for boys at Village Green, Pennsylvania, and published *Method of Instructing Children Rationally*. In 1815, he moved with his family to Louisville, Kentucky, where two more daughters were born. Neef opened a school in Louisville with assistance from a former student, Josiah Warren. In 1821, after this school failed, he and his family moved to a farm in Shelby County, Kentucky. They moved again in 1826, at Maclure's request, to the utopian community of New Harmony, Indiana. Neef was to teach Pestalozzi's method there, but disagreements caused the family to move once more, to Cincinnati. Neef briefly ran a school before taking up farming in Clarke County, Indiana. The Neefs returned to New Harmony in 1835, and Joseph Neef directed the community's printing department. After Luise Neef died, in 1845, he lived with a daughter and her husband. Following his death, doctors removed the metal ball that had been lodged in his head since 1796, in accordance with his wishes.

Nixon, Richard Milhous (1913–1994) *37th president of the United States*
Richard Nixon was born to poor parents in Yorba Linda, California. He attended public schools and Whittier College in Whittier, California, from which he graduated second in his class in 1934. In 1937, he graduated third in his class from Duke University Law School in Durham, North Carolina. The same year he was admitted to the bar and began practicing law in Whittier. Nixon was an attorney in the Office of Emergency Management in Washington, D.C., for several months before enlisting in the U.S. Navy in August 1942. He served as a supply officer in the South Pacific and was discharged in January 1946 as a lieutenant commander. In November 1946, he was elected to the U.S. House of Representatives as a Republican. Nixon gained a national reputation as a member of the House Committee on Un-American Activities in 1949. In 1950, he was elected to the U.S. Senate, and in 1952, he was elected vice president of the United States on the ticket with Dwight D. Eisenhower. In 1960, he was the Republican nominee for president but lost the election to John F. Kennedy. He returned to the practice of law in California and New York and in 1962 ran unsuccessfully for governor of California. Nixon was elected president of the United States in 1968 and reelected in 1972. In 1970, he authorized military operations in Cambodia, which led to nationwide demonstrations that left four students dead at Kent State University in Ohio. Nixon also ordered the gradual withdrawal of 500,000 Americans from Vietnam, and he established diplomatic relations with China. He resigned the presidency on August 9, 1974, after the House Judiciary Committee began impeachment proceedings against him for allegedly covering up the burglary and wiretapping of the Democratic National Committee Headquarters at the Watergate Hotel in Washington. He accepted a pardon from his successor, President Gerald R. Ford, on September 8, 1974. After resigning, Nixon lived in New York City and then Park Ridge, New Jersey.

Peabody, Elizabeth Palmer (1804–1894) *New England educator who promoted kindergartens in the United States*
Elizabeth Peabody was born in Billerica, Massachusetts, and educated in Salem, at a school conducted by her mother. Peabody herself taught at the Salem school before establishing a school in Brookline, Massachusetts, with her sister Mary. She was a founding member of the Transcendentalist Club in 1837. Soon afterward, she operated a bookstore in Boston from which she published *The Dial*, a transcendentalist journal, from 1842 until 1843. In 1860, Peabody opened a kindergarten in Boston, the first in the United States. She traveled to Europe in 1867 to learn more about the kindergarten movement and returned to the United States to write and lecture on the subject. Her writings include *Kindergarten Culture* (1870) and *Letters to Kindergartners* (1886). She published the *Kindergarten Messenger* from 1873 to 1875, and in 1877, she became founder and first president of the American Froebel Union, an educational organization.

Penn, William (1644–1718) *founder of Pennsylvania*
William Penn was born in London, the eldest son of Admiral Sir William Penn, a British naval hero. He was educated at Chigwell School, Essex, and at Christ Church, Oxford. While at Oxford, he joined the Religious Society of Friends, or Quakers, in a move that distressed his father and caused him to be expelled. English authorities viewed Quakers with suspicion because they refused to swear loyalty to the king. In 1666, Penn went to Ireland to oversee his father's estates in County Cork. There, his beliefs landed him in prison. Upon his return to England, he wrote *The Sandy Foundation Shaken*, an attack on the doctrine of the Trinity, which was published in 1668 without a license and caused him to be imprisoned again, this time in the Tower of London. In prison, he wrote *No Cross, No Crown* (1669), on following Christ's teachings, and *Innocency with Open Face* (1669), a modification of his anti-Trinity position. Penn continued to write and speak on matters of faith and was repeatedly imprisoned. In 1681, King Charles II granted him territory in North America in payment for a debt to his late father. Penn sailed to the New World in 1682 and established a colony called Sylvania, from the Latin word for woods;

King Charles changed the name to Pennsylvania, in honor of Penn's father. As governor of the colony, Penn founded Philadelphia and established relations with the Indians that were based on fairness. He returned to England in 1684 to aid persecuted Quakers there. In 1699, he made a second visit to Pennsylvania during which he issued the Charter of Privileges, guaranteeing religious freedom to all believers residing in the colony. Mismanagement of his affairs forced him to go back to England in 1701, and he spent the next decade involved in legal action against his financial adviser. A severe stroke in 1712 left Penn permanently disabled, and he died six years later in Buckinghamshire.

Pestalozzi, Johann Heinrich (1746–1827) *Swiss educational theorist*

Johann Pestalozzi was born in Zurich. Following the death of his father, a barber-surgeon, he was raised in poverty by his mother and a loyal maidservant. He attended his city's free schools and studied theology and law at the University of Zurich. In 1767, Pestalozzi married Anna Schulthess, who was eight years his senior, against the wishes of her parents. The couple lived on a farm and estate in the village of Birr. In 1775, inspired by the French philosopher Jean-Jacques Rousseau, Pestalozzi opened an experimental school for the poor peasant children living on his estate, which was called Neuhof. In 1780, financial difficulties forced him to close the school and sell some of his land. He spent the next 15 years developing his ideas on educational reform and putting them into writing. He published *The Evening Hours of a Hermit* (1781), a book of aphorisms, and *Leonard and Gertrude* (1781–85), a four-volume didactic novel. Pestalozzi founded a school for orphans at Stans in 1798, but it closed within months of opening. A school established at Burgdorf in 1799 proved more successful, and Pestalozzi moved it to Yverdon in 1805. By this time he was a famous educator, and his school attracted pupils from all over Europe. The school at Yverdon was a laboratory for testing Pestalozzian methods, especially teacher training and a focus on the individuality of each child and learning through practice and observation. The school closed in 1825, and Pestalozzi returned to Neuhof with the goal of starting an institute to counteract poverty, but he died before he could act on his plans.

Piaget, Jean (1896–1980) *Swiss psychologist*

Growing up in Neuchâtel, Switzerland, where he was born, Jean Piaget displayed a strong interest in zoology. His father, a professor of medieval literature, and his mother, a woman with socialist leanings, encouraged his intellectual curiosity, and he published his first scientific papers in adolescence. As a student at the University of Neuchâtel during World War I, Piaget was active in student socialist and Christian organizations. He earned a doctorate in natural science in 1918 and subsequently studied psychology in Zurich. He next taught at a boys' school in France, where he noticed a pattern in children's responses to intelligence tests. Study of his own three children and child subjects at the Rousseau Institute in Geneva, which he joined in 1921, led Piaget to formulate a theory of learning that he called genetic epistemology. Piaget stated that children mentally build and rebuild a model of the world, based on their observations and experiences. He further stated that children pass through four stages of cognitive development: the sensorimotor state, in which they experience the world through movement and their senses, the preoperational stage, in which they acquire finer motor skills; the concrete operational stage, in which they begin to think logically; and the formal operational stage, in which they become capable of abstract reasoning. Piaget first gained international recognition in the 1920s. In 1929, he became a professor of psychology at the University of Geneva; he taught as well at the University of Lausanne and the Sorbonne. From 1929 through 1968, he was director of the International Bureau of Education, a private organization founded in Geneva to collect and disseminate the findings of scientific research in education. In 1955, he founded the International Center for Genetic Epistemology. In the United States, Piaget's thinking influenced the open education movement of the 1960s and 1970s. A prolific writer, Piaget produced hundreds of articles and more than 50 books, among them *Play, Dreams, and Imitation* (1951), *The Origins of Intelligence* (1952), and *The Construction of Reality* (1954).

Pratt, Richard Henry (1840–1924) *army officer, educator of Native Americans*

Richard Pratt was born in Rushford, New York, but grew up in Logansport, Indiana, where he was apprenticed to a tinsmith. He enlisted in the Union army in 1861 to serve in the Civil War and rose to the rank of lieutenant. He reenlisted in 1867 and was assigned to the 10th Cavalry, an African-American unit stationed on the western frontier. In 1875, Pratt was assigned to escort Native American prisoners of war to Fort Marion in St. Augustine, Florida. At Fort Marion, he developed a program of education for the Indian prisoners that emphasized vocational training. Some of the prisoners were sent to the Hampton Institute in Virginia in 1878, and Pratt went there to teach. He was at Hampton until 1879, when the War Department authorized him to establish and supervise the first federally funded boarding school for Indian youth, located in abandoned barracks at Carlisle, Pennsylvania. The school served as a model for other Indian boarding schools. Pratt resigned from the army in 1903; in 1904 he was removed as supervisor of the Carlisle school for speaking out against the reservation system and the U.S. Indian Bureau. He continued to work on behalf of Indian education and to promote assimilation of Native peoples into mainstream American life.

Reid, Whitelaw (1837–1912) *journalist, politician, diplomat*
Whitelaw Reid was born into a devout Presbyterian farming family living near Xenia, Ohio. He attended Xenia Academy, where his uncle was principal, and at age 15 enrolled as a sophomore in Miami University in Oxford, Ohio. He graduated with scientific honors in 1856 and spent a year as a schoolmaster in South Charleston, Ohio. In 1857, Reid and his brother purchased the *Xenia News*, and he served as editor for nearly two years. A zealous member of the new Republican Party, Reid supported Abraham Lincoln in the 1860 presidential campaign. Beginning in 1861, he was a war correspondent for the *Cincinnati Gazette*. He covered the Battles of Shiloh and Gettysburg; the capture of Richmond, Virginia; and the funeral of Abraham Lincoln, all to widespread acclaim. He was also one of the first eastern correspondents for the Western Associated Press, a news-gathering agency founded in Detroit during the Civil War. In 1863, as a result of his Republican connections, Reid became librarian of the House of Representatives. He also was named clerk of the House Committee on Military Affairs during the third session of the 37th Congress. In May 1865, he accompanied Chief Justice Salmon P. Chase on an inspection tour of the war-ravaged South. In 1866, he published his observations in a book, *After the War*. In 1867, he tried raising cotton in the South but quickly gave it up. He returned to writing and in 1868 published *Ohio and the War*. In 1868, at age 31, Reid joined the staff of Horace Greeley's *New York Tribune*, and within a short time he became its editor. He was campaign manager when Greeley ran unsuccessfully for president against the incumbent, Ulysses S. Grant. Greeley died a month after the 1872 election, and with a loan from financier Jay Gould, Reid took control of the *Tribune*. As editor-in-chief he built the paper into a forum of national importance. In 1889, President Benjamin Harrison appointed Reid minister to France. Reid returned to the United States in 1892 to be Harrison's running mate in his bid for reelection. Harrison and Reid lost the race to Grover Cleveland, and Reid retired from public life until 1897, when President William McKinley sent him to Great Britain as special ambassador to the Queen's Jubilee. In 1898, Reid served

on the U.S. commission that negotiated peace following the Spanish-American War, and in 1900 he published a book on colonialism, *Problems of Expansion*. President Theodore Roosevelt named Reid special ambassador to the coronation of King Edward VII in 1902 and ambassador to Great Britain in 1905. Reid died in London.

Rickover, Hyman George (1900–1986) *naval officer, engineer who developed the nuclear-powered submarine*
Hyman Rickover came to the United States from Russia as a child. He grew up in Chicago and moved east to attend the U.S. Naval Academy, from which he graduated in 1922. He earned a master's degree in engineering from Columbia University in 1929. Rickover served aboard submarines and a battleship, the USS *New Mexico*, before assuming command of a minesweeper, the USS *Finch*, in 1937. During World War II, he was assigned to the Electrical Station of the navy's Bureau of Ships in Washington, D.C. In 1946 and 1947, Rickover was in Oak Ridge, Tennessee, for training in nuclear science through the Manhattan Project, the operational unit that developed the atomic bomb. Subsequently, he supervised the planning and construction of the USS *Nautilus*, the first nuclear-powered submarine, which was launched in 1954. Rickover attained the rank of rear admiral in 1953 and was promoted to vice admiral in 1959. In the late 1950s, he was an outspoken critic of U.S. schools. He discussed perceived flaws in the educational system and their remedies in such books as *Education and Freedom* (1959). He was promoted to admiral in 1973 and retired in 1986, having spent a record 63 years on active duty, because Congress had exempted him from mandatory retirement at the standard age for senior admirals. In 1980, President Jimmy Carter presented Rickover with the Medal of Freedom.

Roosevelt, Anna Eleanor (1884–1962) *first lady, social activist, U.S. representative to the United Nations*
Eleanor Roosevelt became active in Democratic politics in 1920, assisting her husband, Franklin Delano Roosevelt, in his career in New York State. She was influential in his administration after he was elected president in 1932, although she held no official position. She was particularly active in helping the poor during the depression, furthering civil rights for African Americans, and providing educational opportunities for unemployed and discouraged youth. In the 1930s, she established an experimental manufacturing program in the impoverished coal-mining community of Arthurdale, West Virginia, and she was a supporter of the National Youth Administration. In 1939,

when the Daughters of the American Revolution denied African-American singer Marian Anderson permission to perform in Constitution Hall in Washington, D.C., which the organization owned, Roosevelt arranged for her to sing at the Lincoln Memorial. Roosevelt visited American service personnel overseas during World War II, and she called for desegregation of the armed forces. As U.S. delegate to the United Nations from 1945 to 1953, she was instrumental in drafting the Universal Declaration of Human Rights. President John F. Kennedy appointed her to the UN again in 1961. Her books include *This Is My Story* (1937), *This I Remember* (1949), and *On My Own* (1958).

Roosevelt, Franklin Delano (1882–1945) *32nd president of the United States*

The only child of wealthy parents, Franklin Roosevelt spent his early childhood in New York City and Hyde Park, New York. He graduated from Harvard University in 1904, and after studying law at Columbia University, he was admitted to the New York State bar in 1907. In 1905 he married a distant cousin, Eleanor Roosevelt. His political career began with his election to the New York State Senate in 1910. President Woodrow Wilson appointed him secretary of the navy during World War I. In 1920, Roosevelt was the Democratic candidate for vice president, sharing the ticket with James M. Cox, but Cox lost the election to Warren G, Harding. Although an attack of poliomyelitis in 1921 left Roosevelt unable to walk, he was elected governor of New York in 1928. In 1932, he defeated the incumbent, Herbert Hoover, in the presidential election. He would be elected to an unprecedented four terms. During his first three months in office, Roosevelt prevailed on Congress to pass legislation to combat the economic instability and unemployment of the Great Depression. Some of the programs established by New Deal legislation had educational components. Many of the boys and young men employed on conservation and public works projects through the Civilian Conservation Corps (1933) attended classes in the evening; jobs obtained through the National Youth Administration (1935) enabled many high school and college students to remain in school. The second crisis of Roosevelt's presidency was World War II. He asked Congress to declare war following the December 7, 1941, Japanese attack on Pearl Harbor, Hawaii. Roosevelt died in 1945, before the United States and its allies achieved victory.

Rush, Benjamin (1746–1813) *physician, statesman*

After graduating from the College of New Jersey (now Princeton University) in 1760, Benjamin Rush spent six years as a physician's apprentice. He continued his studies in Europe, earning a medical degree from the University of Edinburgh in 1768. He returned to America in 1769 and was appointed professor of chemistry at the College of Philadelphia. In 1770, he published *Syllabus of a Course of Lectures on Chemistry,* the first American chemistry text and the first of many scientific and medical books that he would write. Rush gained a reputation as a leading American physician. He taught a great many apprentices and students, and his lectures attracted crowds. He is remembered as the father of American psychiatry because he pushed for humane treatment of the mentally ill. He also advocated bloodletting and purging as remedies for a wide range of ailments, however, and was largely responsible for the continued use of those treatments in the United States after European doctors had cast doubt on their value. He was a member of the Continental Congress in 1776–77 and a signer of the Declaration of Independence. During the American Revolution, he was surgeon general of the Continental army, and after 1783, he was on the staff of the Pennsylvania Hospital, where he founded the first free dispensary in the United States. In 1786, he published a plan for a national system of education to promote American cultural unity. He became treasurer of the U.S. Mint in 1799 and held this position for the rest of his life. His 1812 book *Medical Inquiries and Observations upon Diseases of the Mind* was the first work on psychiatry published in the United States.

Savio, Mario (1942–1996) *leader in the Free Speech Movement*

The son of a Sicilian sheet-metal worker, Mario Savio was born and raised in Queens, New York. While a student at Martin Van Buren High School in Queens, he was a finalist in the Westinghouse Science Talent Search, having completed a project on the transmission of sound through water. He graduated first in his class and attended Manhattan College on a scholarship and Queens College before enrolling in 1963 at the University of California at Berkeley as a philosophy major. Savio spent the summer of 1964 with the Student Nonviolent Coordinating Committee in Mississippi, helping African Americans register to vote. During the fall 1964 semester, he emerged as a leader in the Free Speech Movement that arose at Berkeley to assert students' right to freedom of political expression. He left Berkeley without graduating and worked as a salesclerk in a bookstore, bartender, and mathematics tutor. He returned to college and in 1984 graduated *summa cum laude* from San Francisco State University with a degree in physics. In 1989, he received a master's degree in physics from the same university and was named outstanding graduate student by the School of Science. In 1990, he joined the faculty of Sonoma State University and was still teaching there when he died of a heart ailment at age 53.

Terman, Lewis Madison (1877–1956) *psychologist, developer of the Stanford-Binet Intelligence Scale*
The child of farmers, Lewis Terman was born in Johnson County, Indiana. From 1892 through 1898, he attended Central Normal College in Danville, Indiana, earning baccalaureate degrees in pedagogy, science, and the classics. He supported himself while in college by teaching school. He next worked as a high school principal, but in 1901, his desire to teach pedagogy or psychology at the college level brought him to Indiana University, from which he received baccalaureate and master's degrees in psychology. In 1905, he earned a doctorate in psychology from Clark University in Worcester, Massachusetts, studying under G. Stanley Hall. Terman spent a year as a high school principal in San Bernardino, California, and between 1906 and 1910 taught child study and pedagogy at Los Angeles State Normal School. In 1910, he joined the education faculty at Stanford University. In 1916, Terman published the Stanford-Binet Scale, which represented a significant revision of Alfred Binet's 1905 intelligence test. Terman's test—the first to yield a result calculated as an intelligence quotient, or IQ—became the most widely used tool for measuring human intelligence. During World War I, Terman led the development of intelligence tests for the army that made possible the examination of many people at one time. After the war, his efforts to adapt group testing for schools led to the National Intelligence Tests, designed for use in grades three through eight, which became available in 1920. In 1922, Terman was named head of the Psychology Department at Stanford. He undertook a long-term study of so-called gifted children and published the first results in 1925. He continued to develop psychological-assessment instruments, including the Stanford Achievement Test (1923) and a gender-identity assessment (1936). In 1937, with Stanford colleague Maud A. Merrill, he revised the Stanford-Binet test. Terman's books include *The Measurement of Intelligence* (1916), the five-volume *Genetic Studies of Genius* (1925–59), *Sex and Personality* (1936), and *Psychological Factors in Marital Happiness* (1938).

Truman, Harry S. (1884–1972) *33rd president of the United States*
Harry Truman was born in Lamar, Missouri, where his father was a livestock trader and farmer. After attending high school in the town of Independence, Missouri, he spent 12 years farming and working at various jobs. During World War I, he served in France as an artillery captain. He settled in Kansas City after the war, married Elizabeth "Bess" Wallace, and opened a men's clothing store. The nation was experiencing an economic downturn, however, and this business failed. In 1922, Truman entered politics as a Democrat and was elected to an administrative position as judge of the Jackson County Court. In 1934, he won a seat in the U.S. Senate, where he supported President Franklin D. Roosevelt's New Deal legislation. Truman gained national recognition during World War II when he chaired a Senate committee investigating waste and corruption in the war effort. The committee's work saved the government as much as $15 billion. In 1944, Roosevelt chose Truman to be his running mate. In April 1945, just weeks into his fourth term, Roosevelt died; Truman succeeded him as president and commander in chief. Thus, Truman was president when the Allies achieved victory in Europe and made the decision to explode atomic bombs over the Japanese cities of Hiroshima and Nagasaki, in August 1945, causing Japan to surrender. In the postwar years, Truman pursued a policy of containment toward the Soviet Union, China, and other communist nations. He sent U.S. troops to South Korea in 1950, without the consent of Congress, to help that nation repel an invasion by communist North Korea. Truman's ambitious domestic agenda, the six-point Fair Deal, met with little success. His plan for federal aid to education, for example, was defeated. Truman won a narrow victory against Republican Thomas E. Dewey in 1948 but decided not to seek reelection in 1952. He retired to Independence.

Washington, Booker Taliaferro (1856–1915) *educator, founder of the Tuskegee Institute, spokesperson for African Americans*
Booker T. Washington, who was born a slave in Franklin County, Virginia, moved with his family to Malden, West Virginia, following the Civil War. There, from the age of nine, Washington worked in a salt furnace and in coal mines. In 1872, he enrolled in the Hampton Normal and Agricultural Institute in Virginia. He taught for two years in Malden after graduating in 1875, and then entered the Wayland Seminary in Washington, D.C. He returned to the Hampton Institute to teach in 1879. In 1881, the institute's director, Samuel Chapman Armstrong, chose Washington to head the recently established Tuskegee Institute, a trade school for African Americans in Alabama. Washington's advocacy of vocational training and temporary social inferiority for African Americans persuaded

whites to recognize him as a spokesperson for his race. Although many black Americans accepted Washington's line of thinking, his opinions brought criticism from other African-American leaders, most notably the scholar W. E. B. DuBois. Washington's books include *The Future of the Negro* (1899); his autobiography, *Up from Slavery* (1901); *Life of Frederick Douglass* (1907); *The Story of the Negro* (1909); and *My Larger Education* (1911).

Webster, Noah (1758–1843) *lexicographer, writer, educator*
Noah Webster, who served in the American Revolution, graduated from Yale College in 1778. He was admitted to the bar in 1781 but soon was hired as a teacher in Goshen, New York. In 1782, he embarked on his life's work: standardizing and cataloguing American English. Between 1783 and 1785, he published *A Grammatical Institute of the English Language*, a series consisting of *The American Spelling Book*, a grammar book, and a reader. An estimated 60 million copies of the *Grammatical Institute* were sold over the next 100 years. In 1793, Webster moved to New York City and founded two newspapers: a daily, the *Minerva*; and a semiweekly, the *Herald*. Both supported the Federalist Party. He was living in New Haven, Connecticut, in 1806, when he published the *Compendious Dictionary of the English Language*. Between 1802 and 1812, he published the four-volume *Elements of Useful Knowledge*, a series on U.S. history and scientific progress written for students. From 1812 until 1822, Webster lived in Amherst, Massachusetts. He was a founder of Amherst College, which opened in 1821. In 1828 he published *An American Dictionary of the English Language*, containing 70,000 definitions, approximately half of which were appearing in a dictionary for the first time. To prepare this work, Webster had gained familiarity with 20 languages and traveled to France and England to use research materials unavailable in the United States. An enlarged edition was published in 1840.

Willard, Emma Hart (1787–1870) *pioneer of female education*
Emma Hart was born in Berlin, Connecticut, the 16th of 17 children. Her father encouraged her to learn, and she attended the district school in Worthington Point, Connecticut, before enrolling in the Berlin Academy in 1802. At age 17, she began teaching at the academy, and in 1806, at age 19, she ran the school for a year. In 1807, Emma Hart took a teaching job in Middlebury, Vermont, and in 1809, she married John Willard, a physician. In 1814, she opened the Middlebury Female Seminary in her home, offering a rigorous curriculum similar to that studied by

males. In 1819, after the Willards moved to Waterford, New York, Emma Willard opened the Waterford Academy. The academy closed in 1821 because of a lack of funding, but later that year Willard founded the Troy Female Seminary in Troy, New York, which was later named the Emma Willard School. This private secondary school for girls was prosperous and successful. John Willard died in 1825, and Emma Willard toured Europe in 1830. In 1833, she published *Journals and Letters from Great Britain* and gave the proceeds to a school for women that she had helped establish in Athens, Greece. Willard also authored several textbooks. In 1838, she married Dr. Christopher C. Yates and moved to Boston, and her son took over the Troy Female Seminary. Willard and her second husband lived together less than a year and later divorced. She died in Troy.

Yerkes, Robert Mearns (1876–1956) *psychologist*
Intent on pursuing a career in medicine rather than a life of farming, like his parents, Robert Yerkes attended Ursinus College, in his home state, Pennsylvania, with financial help from an uncle. After graduating in 1897, he entered Harvard University, intending to study biology, but his interest soon shifted to psychology, and he earned a doctorate in comparative psychology in 1902. He then joined the Harvard faculty, first as an instructor and later as an assistant professor of comparative psychology. In the decade leading up to U.S. participation in World War I he published *The Dancing Mouse: A Study in Animal Behavior* (1907), served as director of psychological research at the Boston State Psychopathic Hospital (1913–17), and studied at the Hunterian Laboratory for Experimental Medicine at Johns Hopkins University and the Marine Biological Laboratory at Woods Hole, Massachusetts. In 1915, he was a developer of the Yerkes-Bridges Point Scale, an early intelligence test, and in 1917, he became president of the American Psychological Association. Yerkes chaired the committee on the psychological examination of recruits, which developed the Alpha and Beta intelligence tests and administered them to more than a million soldiers during World War I. After the war, he headed the National Research Council's Committee for Research in Problems of Sex. In the 1920s, Yerkes began to study chimpanzees. This work led to his 1924 book *Almost Human*. In 1924, he became a professor of psychobiology at Yale University. In 1930, he founded the Yale University Laboratories of Primate Biology, located at Orange Park, Florida. When he retired, in 1941, Yale renamed the facility the Yerkes Laboratory of Primate Biology. Emory University assumed ownership of the lab in 1956.

Appendix C
Maps

1. Federal Emergency Relief Administration Resident Schools for Unemployed Women, 1934
2. National Youth Administration Educational Camps for Unemployed Women, 1935
3. Expenditure per Pupil in Average Daily Attendance in the United States, 1935–1936
4. School Segregation-Desegregation in the Southern and Border States, 1964–1965
5. Percentage Change in Public Elementary and Secondary Enrollment, by State, 1996–2001
6. Location of Bureau of Indian Affairs Schools, 2007–2008
7. Land-grant Colleges and Universities, 2008

FEDERAL EMERGENCY RELIEF ADMINISTRATION RESIDENT SCHOOLS
FOR UNEMPLOYED WOMEN, 1934

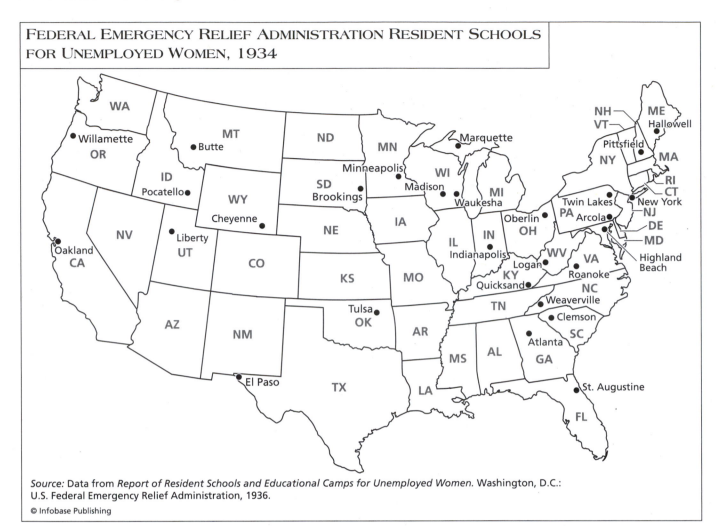

Source: Data from *Report of Resident Schools and Educational Camps for Unemployed Women.* Washington, D.C.:
U.S. Federal Emergency Relief Administration, 1936.
© Infobase Publishing

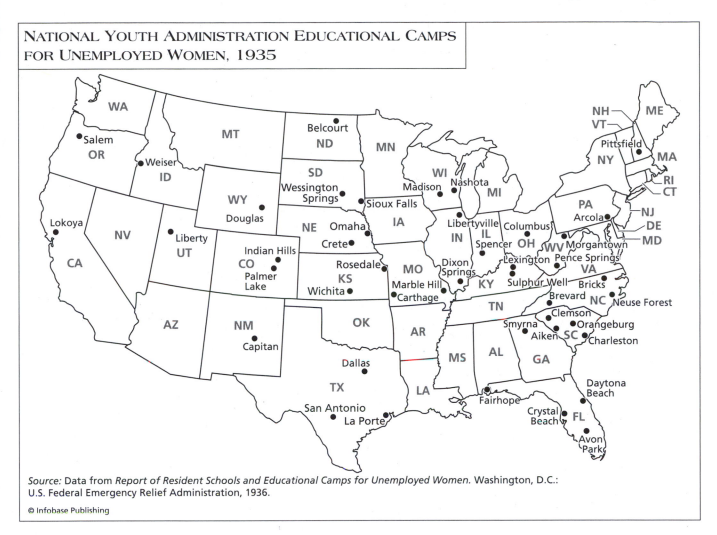

NATIONAL YOUTH ADMINISTRATION EDUCATIONAL CAMPS
FOR UNEMPLOYED WOMEN, 1935

Source: Data from *Report of Resident Schools and Educational Camps for Unemployed Women.* Washington, D.C.:
U.S. Federal Emergency Relief Administration, 1936.

© Infobase Publishing

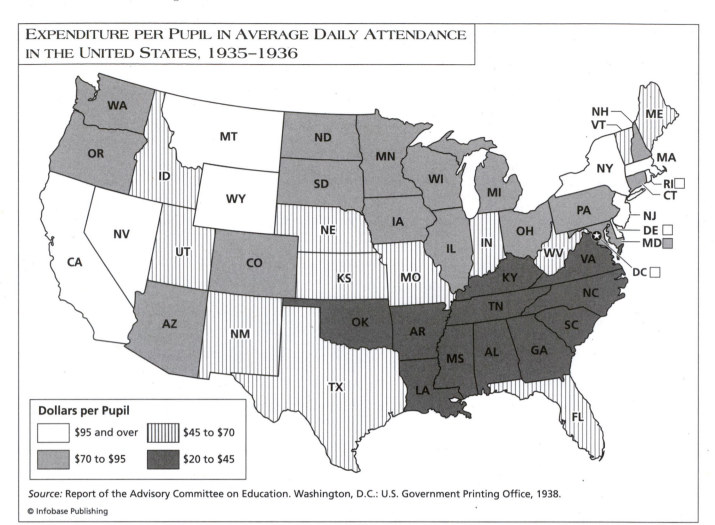

EXPENDITURE PER PUPIL IN AVERAGE DAILY ATTENDANCE IN THE UNITED STATES, 1935–1936

Dollars per Pupil

$95 and over	$45 to $70
$70 to $95	$20 to $45

Source: Report of the Advisory Committee on Education. Washington, D.C.: U.S. Government Printing Office, 1938.

© Infobase Publishing

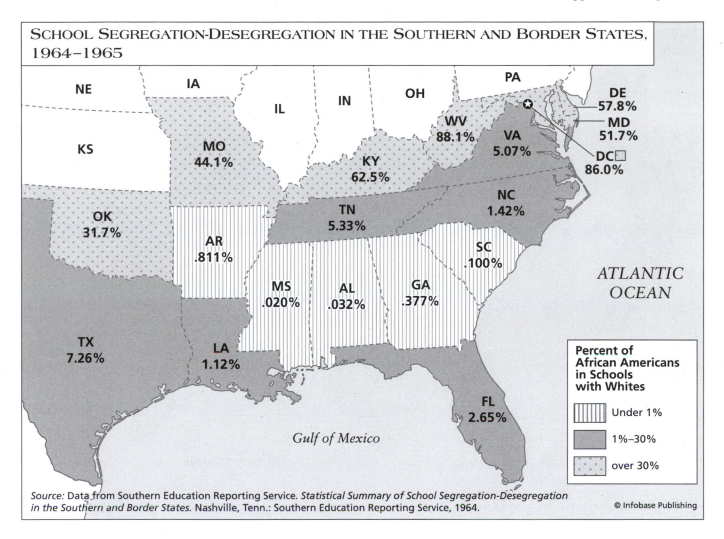

SCHOOL SEGREGATION-DESEGREGATION IN THE SOUTHERN AND BORDER STATES, 1964–1965

NE

IA

IL

IN

OH

PA

MO 44.1%

KS

KY 62.5%

WV 88.1%

VA 5.07%

DE 57.8%

MD 51.7%

DC☐ 86.0%

OK 31.7%

AR .811%

TN 5.33%

NC 1.42%

SC .100%

MS .020%

AL .032%

GA .377%

TX 7.26%

LA 1.12%

FL 2.65%

ATLANTIC OCEAN

Gulf of Mexico

Percent of African Americans in Schools with Whites

Under 1%

1%–30%

over 30%

Source: Data from Southern Education Reporting Service. *Statistical Summary of School Segregation-Desegregation in the Southern and Border States.* Nashville, Tenn.: Southern Education Reporting Service, 1964.

© Infobase Publishing

PERCENTAGE CHANGE IN PUBLIC ELEMENTARY AND SECONDARY ENROLLMENT, BY STATE, 1996–2001

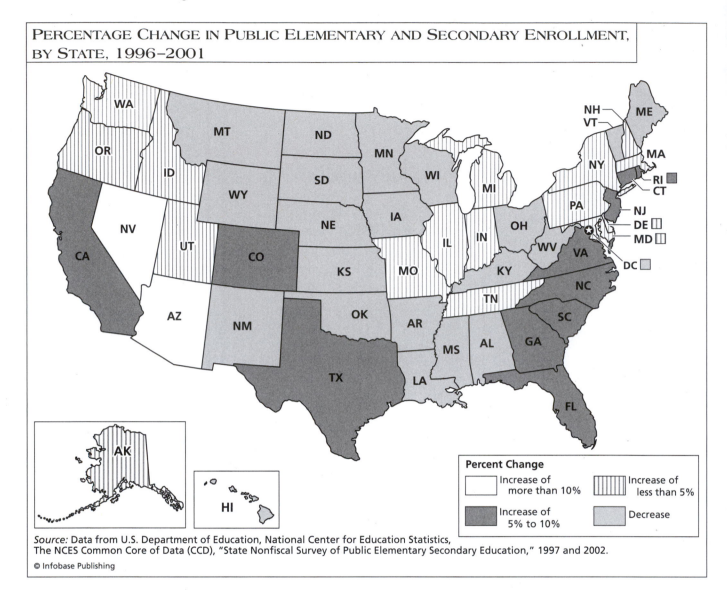

Percent Change

Increase of more than 10%	Increase of less than 5%
Increase of 5% to 10%	Decrease

Source: Data from U.S. Department of Education, National Center for Education Statistics, The NCES Common Core of Data (CCD), "State Nonfiscal Survey of Public Elementary Secondary Education," 1997 and 2002.

© Infobase Publishing

LOCATION OF BUREAU OF INDIAN AFFAIRS SCHOOLS, 2007–2008

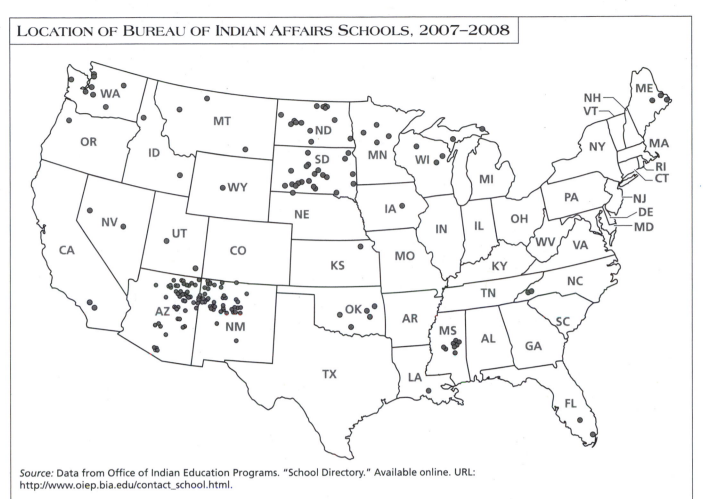

Source: Data from Office of Indian Education Programs. "School Directory." Available online. URL:
http://www.oiep.bia.edu/contact_school.html.

LAND-GRANT COLLEGES AND UNIVERSITIES, 2008

1	Alabama A&M University	24	University of Kentucky	46	North Carolina State University
2	Auburn University	25	Louisiana State University	47	North Dakota State University
3	University of Alaska	26	Southern University	48	Ohio State University
4	University of Arizona	27	University of Maine	49	Langston University
5	University of Arkansas, Fayetteville	28	University of Maryland, College Park	50	Oklahoma State University
6	University of Arkansas, Pine Bluff	29	University of Maryland, Eastern Shore	51	Oregon State University
7	University of California	30	Massachusetts Institute of Technology	52	Pennsylvania State University
8	Colorado State University	31	University of Massachusetts, Amherst	53	University of Rhode Island
9	University of Connecticut	32	Michigan State University	54	Clemson University
10	Delaware State University	33	University of Minnesota	56	South Dakota State University
11	University of Delaware	34	Alcorn State University	57	Tennessee State University
12	University of the District of Columbia	35	Mississippi State University	58	University of Tennessee, Knoxville
13	Florida A&M University	36	Lincoln University	59	Prairie View A&M
14	University of Florida	37	University of Missouri	60	Texas A&M University
15	Fort Valley State University	38	Montana State University	61	Utah State University
16	University of Georgia	39	University of Nebraska	62	University of Vermont
17	University of Hawaii	40	University of Nevada, Reno	63	Virginia Polytechnic Institute
18	University of Idaho	41	University of New Hampshire		& State University
19	University of Illinois	42	Rutgers, the State University	64	Washington State University
20	Purdue University		of New Jersey	65	West Virginia State University
21	Iowa State University	43	New Mexico State University	66	University of Wisconsin-Madison
22	Kansas State University	44	Cornell University	67	University of Wyoming
23	Kentucky State University	45	North Carolina A&T State University		

Source: Data from Robert O'Neil. *Factbook*. Washington, D.C.: National Association of Land Grant Colleges, 1989, 39–41.

© Infobase Publishing

Appendix D
Graphs and Tables

1. Earliest Harvard College Schedule, ca. 1638
2. Primary School Books and Supplies in Boston, Colonial Days and 1907
3. School-Age Attendance and Adult Literacy, 1860
4. Location and Opening Date for Off-Reservation American Indian Boarding Schools, 1879–1902
5. Total Population, Urban and Rural, and School-Age Population, Urban and Rural (Six to Twenty Years of Age, Inclusive), 1910
6. Illiteracy of the Population Ten Years of Age and Over, Total Urban and Rural, 1910
7. Minimal Laboratory Equipment Recommended for Teaching General Science, Missouri Department of Education, 1915
8. Basic Legal Provisions for State-Aided Programs of Special Education in Local School Districts, 1948
9. Status of School Segregation-Desegregation, 1964
10. Enrollment in Educational Institutions, by Level and Control of Institution, Selected Years, 1869–1870 to Fall 2013 (in thousands)
11. Percentage Distribution of Students by Sex and Race or Ethnicity, 2003–2004
12. Number of Students, Teachers, Schools, Principals, School Libraries, and Districts, by School Type and Selected School Characteristics, 2003–2004
13. Percentage of Years of School Completed by Persons Age 25 and Older, by Race/Ethnicity, and Sex, Selected Years, 1910–2002
14. Number and Percentage of Home-Schooled Students, Ages Five through Seventeen with a Grade Equivalent of Kindergarten through Twelfth Grade, by Various Characteristics, 1999 and 2003
15. Percentage of 25- to 29-Year-Olds Who Completed at Least Some College, by Race/Ethnicity and Sex, March 1971–2006
16. Ratios of One-Teacher Schools to All Schools and Teachers in These Schools to All Teachers, 1917–1947

Earliest Harvard College Schedule, ca. 1638

Classes	Monday	Tuesday	Wednesday	Thursday	Friday	Saturday
First Year	Logic Physics Disputes	Logic Physics Disputes	Greek etymology, Syntax, "Precepts of Grammar in such authors as have variety of words"	Hebrew grammar, Bible practice, "Eastern tongues"	Rhetoric, declamations (once monthly), "vacat rhetoricis studiis"[1]	Divinity, catecheticall, Commonplaces, History, Nature of plants
Second Year	Ethics Politics Disputes	Ethics Politics Disputes	Greek prosodia & dialects, Poesy; Nonnus, Duport "or the like"	Chaldee, Ezra & Daniel	Rhetoric, declamations (once monthly), "vacat rhetoricis studiis"	Divinity, catecheticall, Commonplaces, History, Nature of plants
Third Year	Arithmetic Geometry Astronomy Disputes	Arithmetic Geometry Astronomy Disputes	"perfect their theory and exercise style, Composition, Imitation, Epitome, both in prose and verse"	Syraic, Trostius, New Testament	Rhetoric, declamations (once monthly), "vacat rhetoricis studiis"	Divinity, catecheticall, Commonplaces, History, Nature of plants[2]

[1]"Vacat is here used in the sense of *is reserved* for rhetorical studies." *The Study of History in American Colleges and Universities,* by H. B. Adams, Circular No. 2, U.S. Bureau of Education.

[2]*First Fruits of New England;* 1643, pp. 244–245, vol. I, Massachusetts Historical Society Collections.

Source: Meriwether, Colyer. *Our Colonial Curriculum: 1607–1776.* Washington, D.C.: Capital Publishing Co., 1907.

Primary School Books and Supplies in Boston, Colonial Days and 1907

Colonial Days	Primary Schools 1907

Hornbook	The Finch Primer
	Stepping Stones to Literature $1
	   ” ” ” ” $2
	   ” ” ” ” $3
	Cyr's The Children's Primer
	The Werner Primer
	Progressive Course in Reading, First Book
	   ” ” ” ” Second ”
	   ” ” ” ” Third ”
	Franklin Primer and First Reader
	   ” Second Reader.
	   ” Advanced Second Reader.
	   ” Third Reader
	   ” Primary Arithmetic
	American System of Music, Reader $1
	McLaughlin & Veazie's Introductory Music Reader
	National Music Course, New First Reader
	Normal ” ” First Reader
	Natural ” ” Primer
	McLaughlin & Veazie's Introductory Music Reader
	Educational Music Reader, $1
	First Lesson in Natural History and Language
	Two number work blocks
	Drawing Pencils
	Common lead pencils
	Rubber
	Paper
	Clay

Source: Meriwether, Colyer. *Our Colonial Curriculum: 1607–1776.* Washington, D.C.: Capital Publishing Co., 1907.

School-Age Attendance and Adult Literacy, 1860

States	School Age: 5–20 Years						Total Attending School	Total Not Attending School	Total of School Age
	White			Black					
	Attending School	Not Attending School	Total	Attending School	Not Attending School	Total			
Alabama	98,090	115,916	214,006	114	172,976	173,090	98,204	288,892	387,096
Arkansas	42,721	91,015	133,736	5	44,313	44,318	42,726	135,328	178,054
California	25,763	34,469	60,232	153	433	586	25,916	34,902	60,818
Connecticut	88,558	45,196	133,754	1,378	1,466	2,844	89,936	46,662	136,598
Delaware	18,442	14,167	32,609	250	8,476	8,726	18,672	22,663	41,335
Florida	8,494	21,967	30,461	9	24,520	24,529	8,503	46,487	54,990
Georgia	94,680	141,774	236,454	7	187,495	187,502	94,687	329,269	423,956
Illinois	404,510	206,902	611,412	611	2,074	2,685	405,121	208,976	614,097
Indiana	336,969	179,350	516,319	1,122	3,407	4,529	338,091	182,757	520,848
Iowa	167,470	79,574	247,044	138	244	382	167,608	79,818	247,426
Kansas	13,318	23,105	36,423	14	210	224	13,332	23,315	36,647
Kentucky	182,450	171,500	353,950	209	98,344	98,553	182,659	269,844	452,503
Louisiana	47,748	74,393	122,141	275	115,586	115,861	48,023	189,979	238,002
Maine	188,918	25,792	214,710	292	161	453	189,210	25,953	215,163
Maryland	78,320	103,885	182,205	1,355	64,659	66,014	79,675	168,544	248,219
Massachusetts	217,678	113,030	360,708	1,615	1,344	2,959	249,293	114,364	363,667
Michigan	187,499	70,787	258,286	1,105	1,282	2,387	188,604	72,069	260,673
Minnesota	24,132	27,513	51,645	18	68	86	24,150	27,581	51,731
Mississippi	66,522	74,757	141,279	2	163,740	163,742	66,524	238,497	305,021
Missouri	203,333	192,740	396,673	155	50,756	50,911	203,488	243,496	446,984
New Hampshire	82,854	16,166	99,020	80	67	147	82,934	16,233	99,167
New Jersey	116,475	98,620	215,095	2,741	6,220	8,961	119,216	104,840	224,056
New York	799,856	440,270	1,240,126	5,694	9,879	15,573	805,550	450,149	1,255,699
North Carolina	116,434	121,946	238,380	133	150,636	150,769	116,567	272,582	389,149
Ohio	599,985	250,386	850,371	5,671	8,528	14,199	605,656	258,914	1,031,719
Oregon	10,814	6,076	16,890	2	35	37	10,816	6,111	16,927
Pennsylvania	662,388	351,362	1,013,750	1,573	12,202	19,775	669,961	363,564	1,033,525
Rhode Island	31,036	21,108	52,144	532	673	1,205	31,568	1,781	53,349
South Carolina	46,225	64,788	111,013	365	162,431	162,796	46,590	227,219	273,809
Tennessee	162,970	162,107	325,077	52	117,958	118,010	163,042	280,155	443,087
Texas	63,614	94,989	158,603	11	74,690	74,701	63,625	169,679	233,304
Vermont	79,450	23,184	102,634	115	127	242	79,565	23,311	102,876
Virginia	154,922	238,184	393,106	41	217,878	217,919	154,963	456,062	611,025
Wisconsin	184,597	86,556	271,153	112	281	393	184,709	86,837	271,546
Dist. of Columbia	9,048	10,540	19,588	678	4,612	5,290	9,726	15,152	24,878
New Mexico	1,466	27,858	29,324	—	29	29	1,466	27,887	29,353
Total	5,647,729	3,821,972	9,469,701	32,627	1,707,800	1,740,427	5,680,356	5,529,772	11,210,128

States	Adults: Over 20 Years						Total Adults	Total Population
	Able to Read and Write			Not Able to Read and Write				
	White	Black	Total	White	Black	Total Illiterate Adults		
Alabama	188,764	803	189,567	37,605	190,547	228,152	417,719	964,201
Arkansas	110,143	49	110,192	23,642	48,248	71,890	182,082	435,450
California	238,328	2,416	240,744	18,989	704	19,693	260,4 37	379,994
Connecticut	255,085	4,503	259,588	8,488	345	8,833	268,421	460,147
Delaware	37,841	2,522	40,363	6,661	7,156	13,817	54, 180	112,216
Florida	29,331	306	29,627	5,341	27,454	32,795	62,422	140,424
Georgia	214,877	1,104	215,981	43,684	196,509	24 0,193	456,174	1,057,286
Illinois	742,826	2,344	746,170	58,037	1,327	59,36 4	804,534	1,711,951
Indiana	536,269	3,438	539,707	60,943	1,773	62, 716	602,423	1,350,428
Iowa	282,215	363	282,578	19,782	169	19,951	302,52 9	674,913
Kansas	48,811	258	49,069	3,004	63	3,067	52,136	107,206
Kentucky	345,964	3,156	349,120	67,577	93,793	161,370	510,490	1,155,684
Louisiana	163,330	8,653	171,983	17,808	178,183	195,991	367,974	708,002
Maine	284,433	691	285,124	8,552	46	8,598	293,722	628,279
Maryland	242,760	20,703	263,463	15,819	58,928	74,747	338,210	687,049
Massachusetts	664,191	4,974	669,165	46,262	659	46,921	716,086	1,231,066
Michigan	348,098	2,322	354,420	17,441	1,044	18, 485	369,905	749,113
Minnesota	79,116	114	79,230	4,751	12	4,763	83,993	172,123
Mississippi	140,920	282	141,202	15,526	203,961	2 19,487	360,689	791,305
Missouri	424,663	1,276	425,939	59,660	45,251	104,911	530,850	1,182,012
New Hampshire	186,922	253	187,175	4,683	34	4,717	191,892	326,073
New Jersey	317,942	9,350	327,275	19,276	3,805	23,099	350,373	672,035
New York	1,950,732	22,241	1,972,973	115,965	5,913	121,878	2,094,851	3,880,735
North Carolina	227,434	6,494	233,928	68,128	142,269	210,397	444,325	992,622
Ohio	10,943	1,045,662	58,642	6,186	64,8 28	1,110,490	2,339,514	
Oregon	23,961	62	24,023	1,499	12	1,511	25,534	52,465
Pennsylvania	1,328,258	20,671	1,348,927	72,156	9,359	81,515	1,430,444	2,906,215
Rhode Island	92,428	2,079	94,507	5,852	260	6,112	100,619	174,620
South Carolina	122,328	3,089	125,417	14,792	178,769	193,561	3 18,978	703,708
Tennessee	297,119	1,613	298,732	70,359	113,446	183,805	482,537	1,109,801
Texas	169,661	101	169,762	18,414	76,000	94,414	264,176	604,215
Vermont	165,598	337	165,935	8,869	47	8,916	174,851	315,098
Virginia	415,800	4,706	420,506	74,055	228,959	303,014	723,520	1,596,318
Wisconsin	348,520	490	349,059	16,488	98	16,546	3 65,605	775,881
Dist. of Columbia	27,859	2,474	30,331	3,506	4,869	8,375	28,400	75,080
New Mexico	8,157	15	8,172	32,758	27	32,785	42,009	93,516
Total	12,086,156	145,185	12,231,34 1	1,124,974	1,827,265	2,952,239	15,183,580	31,316,642

Note: The changes in population and boundaries of the Territories during the last decade have been so great that they are omitted, excepting New Mexico, from this and the two succeeding tables.

* In 1860, seventy out of every one hundred children of school age in the free States were attending school, while in the slave States but thirty-three out of every one hundred were at school.

Source: Circular of Information of the Bureau of Education, for August, 1870. Washington, D.C.: Government Printing Office, 1870.

Location and Opening Date for Off-Reservation American Indian Boarding Schools, 1879–1902

Location of School	Date of Opening
Carlisle, Pennsylvania	1879
Chemawa, Oregon (Salem)	1880
Chilocco, Oklahoma	1884
Genoa, Nebraska	1884
Albuquerque, New Mexico	1884
Lawrence, Kansas	1884
Grand Junction, Colorado	1886
Santa Fe, New Mexico	1890
Fort Mojave, Arizona	1890
Carson, Nevada	1890
Pierre, South Dakota	1891
Phoenix, Arizona	1891
Fort Lewis, Colorado	1892
Fort Shaw, Montana	1892
Flandreau, South Dakota	1893
Pipestone, Minnesota	1893
Mount Pleasant, Michigan	1893
Tomah, Wisconsin	1893
Wittenberg, Wisconsin	1895
Greenville, California	1895
Morris, Minnesota	1897
Chamberlain, South Dakota	1898
Fort Bidwell, California	1898
Rapid City, South Dakota	1898
Riverside, California	1902

Note: The school at Riverside, California, was a replacement for a boarding school at Perris, California, which was opened in 1893.
Source: Annual Report of the Commissioner of Indian Affairs, 1905, 41.

Total Population, Urban and Rural, and School-Age Population, Urban and Rural (Six to Twenty Years of Age, Inclusive), 1910

States	Total Population	Urban Population	Rural Population	Ratio of Rural to Total	Total Population, 6–20 inclusive	Urban Population, 6–20 inclusive	Rural Population, 6–20 inclusive	Ratio of Rural to Total, 6–20 inclusive
United States	91,972,266	42,623,383	49,348,883	*Per ct.* 53.7	27,750,599	11,520,193	16,230,406	*Per ct.* 58.5
North Atlantic Division	25,868,573	19,178,718	6,689,855	25.9	7,086,368	5,219,818	1,866,550	26.3
South Atlantic Division	12,194,895	3,092,153	9,102,742	74.6	4,139,759	877,545	3, 262,214	78.8
South Central Division	17,194,435	3,531,685	13,662,750	79.4	5,946,923	1,017,114	4,929,809	82.9
North Central Division	29,888,542	13,490,987	16,397,555	54.9	8,811,377	3,624,762	5,186,615	58.9
Western Division	6,825,821	3,329,840	3,495,981	51.2	1,766,172	780,954	98 5,218	55.7
North Atlantic Division								
Maine	742,371	381,443	360,928	48.6	195,197	100,246	94,951	48.6
New Hampshire	430,572	255,099	175,473	40.8	111,634	69,490	42,144	37.8
Vermont	355,956	168,943	187,013	52.5	94,701	44,661	50,040	52.8
Massachusetts	3,366,416	3,125,367	241,049	7.1	881,024	820,776	60,248	6.8
Rhode Island	542,610	524,654	17,956	3.3	148,102	143,747	4,355	2.9
Connecticut	1,114,756	999,839	114,917	10.3	298,454	269 ,119	29,335	9.8
New York	9,113,614	7,185,494	1,928,120	21.2	2,454,428	1,959,243	495, 185	20.2
New Jersey	2,537,167	1,907,210	629,957	24.8	708,525	535,853	172,672	24.4
Pennsylvania	7,665,111	4,630,669	3,034,442	39.6	2,194,303	1,276,683	917,620	41.8
South Atlantic Division								
Delaware	202,322	97,085	105,237	52.0	57,932	25,674	32,258	55.7
Maryland	1,295,346	658,192	637,154	49.2	388,486	182,2 69	206,217	53.0
District of Columbia	331,069	331,069	0	.0	79,249	79,249	0	.0
Virginia	2,061,612	476,529	1,585,083	76.9	697,649	136,3 10	561,339	80.5
West Virginia	1,221,119	228,242	992,877	81.3	396,818	63,697	333,121	83.9
North Carolina	2,206,287	318,474	1,887,813	85.6	785,583	100,262	685,32 1	87.2
South Carolina	1,515,400	224,832	1,290,568	85.2	564,260	70,007	494,253	87.6
Georgia	2,669,121	538,650	2,070,471	79.4	925,865	157,8 01	768,064	83.0
Florida	752,619	219,080	533,539	70.9	243,917	62,276	181,641	74.4
South Central Division								
Kentucky	2,280,905	555,442	1,734,463	75.7	755,709	153, 661	602,048	79.7
Tennessee	2,184,789	441,045	1,743,744	79.8	738,478	12 3,371	615.107	83.3
Alabama	2,138,093	370,431	1,767,662	82.7	750,357	107, 524	642,833	85.7
Mississippi	1,797,114	207,311	1,589,803	88.5	644,805	61 ,151	583,654	90.5
Louisiana	1,656,388	496,516	1,159,872	70.0	575,866	148 ,296	427,570	74.3
Texas	3,896,542	938,104	2,958,438	75.9	1,363,713	275,9 94	1,087,719	79.7
Arkansas	1,574,449	202,681	1,371,768	87.1	551,672	57,9 89	493,683	89.5
Oklahoma	1,657,155	320,155	1,337,000	80.7	566,323	89, 128	477,195	84.3
North Central Division								
Ohio	4,767,121	2,665,143	2,101,978	44.1	1,313,809	695, 794	618,015	47.0
Indiana	2,700,876	1,143,835	1,557,041	57.6	777,889	299, 012	478,877	61.1

(continues)

Total Population, Urban and Rural, and School-Age Population, Urban and Rural (Six to Twenty Years of Age, Inclusive), 1910 *(continued)*

States	Total Population	Urban Population	Rural Population	Ratio of Rural to Total	Total Population, 6–20 inclusive	Urban Population, 6–20 inclusive	Rural Population, 6–20 inclusive	Ratio of Rural to Total, 6–20 inclusive
Illinois	5,638,591	3,476,929	2,161,662	38.3	1,615,914	94 3,719	672,195	41.6
Michigan	2,810,173	1,327,044	1,483,129	52.8	796,887	357,122	439,765	55.2
Wisconsin	2,333,860	1,004,326	1,329,540	57.0	732,544	294,468	438,076	59.8
Minnesota	2,075,708	850,294	1,225,414	59.0	648,775	228,293	420,482	64.8
Iowa	2,224,771	689,054	1,544,717	69.4	675,222	182,100	493,122	73.0
Missouri	3,293,335	1,398,817	1,894,518	57.5	993,998	369,451	624,547	62.8
North Dakota	577,056	63,236	513,820	89.0	183,336	17,267	166,069	90.6
South Dakota	583,888	76,673	507,215	86.9	183,979	20,267	163,712	89.0
Nebraska	1,192,214	310,852	881,362	73.9	373,868	83,182	290,686	77.7
Kansas	1,690,949	493,790	1,197,159	70.8	515,156	134,087	381,069	74.0
Western Division								
Montana	376,053	133,420	242,633	64.5	93,771	31,943	61,828	65.9
Wyoming	145,965	43,221	102,744	70.4	35,776	10,326	25,450	71.1
Colorado	799,024	404,840	394,184	49.3	215,940	101,727	114,213	52.9
New Mexico	327,301	46,571	280,730	85.7	105,403	13,648	91,755	87.0
Arizona	204,354	63,260	141,094	69.0	56,897	16,169	40,728	71.6
Utah	373,351	172,934	200,417	53.7	121,016	51,982	69,034	57.0
Nevada	81,875	13,367	68,508	83.7	16,132	2,730	13,402	83.1
Idaho	325,594	69,898	255,696	78.5	96,819	17,812	79,007	81.6
Washington	1,141,990	605,530	536,460	47.0	293,478	140,271	153,207	52.2
Oregon	672,765	307,060	365,705	54.4	175,386	68,465	106,921	61.0
California	2,377,549	1,469,739	907,810	38.2	555,554	325,881	229,673	41.3

Source: Monahan, A. C. *The Status of Rural Education in the United States.* Washington, D.C.: U.S. Government Printing Office, 1913.

Illiteracy of the Population Ten Years of Age and Over, Total and Urban and Rural, 1910[1]

States	Urban and Rural			Urban			Rural		
		Illiterate			Illiterate			Illiterate	
	Total	Number	Percent	Total	Number	Percent	Total	Number	Percent
United States	71,580,270	5,516,693	7.7	34,649,175	1,766,135	5.1	36,931,095	3,750,028	10.2
North Atlantic Division	20,777,429	1,154,818	5.6	15,467,962	801,706	5.8	5,309,467	262,912	5.0
South Atlantic Division	9,012,826	1,444,294	16.0	2,493,359	211,146	8.5	6,519,467	1,233,148	18.9
South Central Division	12,572,621	1,917,706	15.3	2,842,222	134,803	4.7	9,730,399	1,682,901	17.2
North Central Division	23,666,260	755,426	3.2	11,035,304	364,029	3.3	12,630,956	390,959	3.3
Western Division	5,551,134	244,449	4.4	2,810,328	64,451	2.3	2,740,806	180,108	6.6
North Atlantic Division									
Maine	603,893,	24,554	4.1	312,251	14,982	4.8	291,642	9,572	3.3
New Hampshire	354,118	16,386	4.6	208,549	11,740	5.6	145,569	4,646	3.2
Vermont	289,128	10,806	3.7	138,047	5,425	3.8	151,081	5,381	3.5
Massachusetts	2,742,684	141,541	5.2	2,543,364	133,259	5.2	199,320	8,282	4.1
Rhode Island	440,065	33,854	7.7	425,215	32,923	7.7	14,850	931	6.1
Connecticut	901,026	53,665	6.0	806,986	48,814	6.0	94,040	4,851	5.1
New York	7,410,819	406,220	5.5	5,821,825	343,712	5.9	1,588,994	62,308	3.9
New Jersey	2,027,946	113,502	5.6	1,519,977	87,980	5.8	507,969	25,522	5.0
Pennsylvania	6,007,750	354,290	5.9	3,691,748	212,871	5.8	2,316,002	141,419	6.1
South Atlantic Division									
Delaware	163,080	13,240	8.1	79,374	5,185	6.5	83,706	8,055	9.6
Maryland	1,023,950	73,397	7.2	536,900	25,366	4.7	487,050	48,031	9.9
District of Columbia	279,088	13,812	4.9	279,088	13,812	4.9			
Virginia	1,536,297	232,911	15.2	385,258	35,277	9.2	1,151,039	197,634	17.2
West Virginia	903,822	74,866	8.3	182,597	7,229	3.8	721,225	67,637	9.4
North Carolina	1,578,595	291,497	18.5	240,920	30,508	12.3	1,331,675	269,989	19.7
South Carolina	1,078,161	276,980	25.7	177,169	27,326	15.4	900,992	249,654	27.7
Georgia	1,885,111	389,775	20.7	430,544	51,757	12.0	1,454,567	338,018	23.2
Florida	564,722	77,816	13.8	175,509	14,686	8.4	389,213	63,130	16.2
South Central Division									
Kentucky	1,722,644	208,084	12.1	459,544	30,619	6.7	1,263,100	177,465	14.1
Tennessee	1,621,179	221,071	13.6	361,536	32,212	8.8	1,259,643	188,859	15.0
Alabama	1,544,575	352,710	22.9	293,843	38,151	13.0	1,247,732	314,559	25.2
Mississippi	1,293,180	290,235	22.4	164,754	21,049	12.8	1,128,426	269,186	23.9
Louisiana	1,213,576	352,179	29.0	397,718	42,430	10.7	815,858	309,749	38.0
Texas	2,848,904	282,904	9.9	747,547	53,209	7.1	2,101,357	229,695	10.9
Arkansas	1,131,087	142,954	12.6	162,523	10,461	6.5	971,564	132,493	13.6
Oklahoma	1,197,476	67,569	5.6	254,757	6,672	2.6	942,719	60,895	6.5
North Central Division									
Ohio	3,848,747	124,774	3.2	2,186,020	71,811	3.3	1,662,727	52,963	3.2
Indiana	2,160,405	66,213	3.1	940,419	28,485	3.0	1,219,986	37,728	3.1
Illinois	4,493,734	168,241	3.7	2,820,830	115,243	4.1	1,672,904	53,051	3.2
Michigan	2,236,252	74,800	3.3	1,075,314	37,572	3.5	1,160,938	37,228	3.1

(continues)

Illiteracy of the Population Ten Years of Age and Over, Total and Urban and Rural, 1910[1] *(continued)*

States	Urban and Rural			Urban			Rural		
	Total	Illiterate		Total	Illiterate		Total	Illiterate	
		Number	Percent		Number	Percent		Number	Percent
Wisconsin	1,829,811	57,770	3.2	809,007	24,289	3.0	1,020,804	33,480	3.3
Minnesota	1,628,635	49,337	3.0	702,070	19,799	2.8	926,565	29,537	3.2
Iowa	1,760,286	29,889	1.7	564,111	10,303	1.8	1,196,175	19,586	1.6
Missouri	2,594,600	111,604	4.3	1,162,899	38,047	3.3	1,431,701	73,069	5.1
North Dakota	424,730	13,070	3.1	51,226	1,114	2.2	373,504	11,956	3.2
South Dakota	443,466	12,751	2.9	63,172	1,038	1.6	380,294	11,712	3.1
Nebraska	924,032	18,000	1.9	255,568	6,581	2.6	668,464	11,428	1.7
Kansas	1,321,562	28,968	2.2	404,668	9,747	2.4	916,894	19,221	2.1
Western Division									
Montana	303,551	14,348	4.7	110,008	3,648	3.3	193,543	10,809	5.6
Wyoming	117,585	3,874	3.3	36,077	1,003	2.8	81,508	2,871	3.5
Colorado	640,846	23,780	3.7	337,179	8,011	2.4	303,667	15,769	5.2
New Mexico	240,990	48,697	20.2	36,451	2,842	7.8	204,539	45,855	22.4
Arizona	157,659	32,953	20.9	50,667	5,036	9.9	106,992	27,917	26.1
Utah	274,778	6,821	2.5	132,961	2,153	1.6	141,817	4,668	3.3
Nevada	69,822	4,702	6.7	11,467	302	2.6	58,355	4,400	7.5
Idaho	249,018	5,453	2.2	57,762	967	1.7	191,256	4,486	3.8
Washington	933,556	18,416	2.0	511,822	6,697	1.3	421,734	11,719	2.8
Oregon	555,631	10,504	1.9	264,881	3,371	1.3	290,750	7,133	2.5
California	2,007,698	74,901	3.7	1,261,053	30,421	2.4	746,645	44,481	5.9

[1] The figures here given were furnished by the Bureau of the Census, as a preliminary report. The final figures differ slightly from those here given.

Source: Monahan, A. C. *The Status of Rural Education in the United States.* Washington D.C.: U.S. Government Printing Office, 1913.

Minimal Laboratory Equipment Recommended for Teaching General Science, Missouri Department of Education, 1915

Quantity	Item	Cost
1	Balance, horn pan	$1.90
1	Set of weights, 50 g. to 1 mg.	2.00
1	Brass globe for weighing air	2.25
1	Set beakers, 150 cc. to 1000 cc.	1.69
4	Wide mouth bottles, 2, 8, 16 and 32 oz.	.24
2	Blast lamps provided the laboratory is not supplied with gas (or 2 Bunsen burners and 21 ft. each rubber tubing if laboratory is supplied with gas, .80)	5.50
1	Burette clamp for iron stand	.30
1	Hoffman clamp, medium	.18
1	Rattail file, 5"	.09
1	Triangular file, 5"	.09
3	Florence flasks, 100, 300, 500 cc.	.50
1	Round bottom flask, 1000 cc.	.35
1	Iron forceps, 4"	.10
3	Funnels, 2, 4 and 8"	.85
4	Glass plates, 2" square	.12
2 lb.	Glass tubing, 7 mm. diam. outside	1.00
1	Measure cylinder, 50 cc.	.50
1	Measure cylinder, 250 cc.	.90
8	One-hole rubber stoppers, Nos. 0–6	.45
8	Two-hole rubber stoppers, Nos. 0–6	.43
1	Ring stand, No. 3, three rings	.55
6	Test tubes, 1×6"	.14
2	Thermometers centigrade	2.20
2	Thermometers Fahrenheit	2.20
4	Thistle tubes, straight stem	.40
1	Wing top (burner attachment)	.08
6	Squares iron wire gauze 10 cm. sq.	.24
1	Exhaust and compression pump	4.00
6	Tin pans	.30
4	Lamp chimneys	.24
2	Sq. ft. dental rubber	.60
6	Candles	.15
6	Drinking tumblers	.30
1	Spool copper wire, No. 18	.25
1	Spool linen thread	.12
1	Hard glass test tube, 1×8"	.10
1	Funnel separatory bell shape with glass stop cock (2 in.) 4 oz.	1.25
1	Barometer tube	.25
6	Magnifiers	1.92
100	Filter papers, 13"	.55
1	Meter stick	.25
1	Yardstick, plain	.10

(continues)

Minimal Laboratory Equipment Recommended for Teaching General Science, Missouri Department of Education, 1915 *(continued)*

Quantity	Item	Cost
1 lb.	Marble chips	.10
2 lb.	Mercury	5.50
2	Glass prisms	.60
1	Set of lenses	1.00
1	Reading glass	.50
1	Horseshoe magnet	.12
2	Bar magnets	.40
1	Electrolysis apparatus	3.25
1	Dry cell battery	.35
1	Electric bell	.40
2	Pinchcocks	.24
1	Pinchcock, screw compression	.15
2	Battery jars, 5×7	.40
	Total	$48.64

Source: Missouri Department of Education. *Sixty-Sixth Report of the Public Schools of the State of Missouri.* Jefferson City, Mo.: Hugh Stephens Co., (for school year ending June 30, 1915), n.d.

Basic Legal Provisions for State-Aided Programs of Special Education in Local School Districts, 1948

State	Children Specified by Law	Permissive (P) or Mandatory (M)	Basis of Annual State Aid
Arizona	Crippled in Pima County and Maricopa County	M	Special appropriation for administrative use.
Arkansas	Physically handicapped (except those enrolled at State schools for deaf and blind).	P	Excess cost up to $200 per pupil in residence; up to $350 per nonresident.
California	Physically handicapped	P[1]	Excess cost up to $400 per unit of average daily attendance.
	Mentally retarded	M for 15 or more pupils	75 percent of excess cost, but not to exceed $75 per unit of average daily attendance.
Colorado	Physically handicapped	P	Special appropriation for administrative allotment; up to $300 for nonresident pupil; total cost of home and hospital instruction.
Connecticut	Educationally exceptional children	P; M for 7 or more children upon petition of parents and approval of State Board of Education.	Physically handicapped: 2/3 of disbursements of town for their education, but not to exceed $200 per resident pupil, and $300 per nonresident. Children with two defects may be counted twice. (Mentally handicapped: no State aid.)
Florida	Exceptional children: physical, mental, or emotional deviates.	M, insofar as practicable	10 or more exceptional children considered one instruction unit in apportionment of State funds.
Illinois	Physically handicapped	P	Excess cost up to $300 per pupil.
	Maladjusted	P	Excess cost up to $190 per pupil.
	Mentally handicapped	P	Excess cost up to $250 per pupil.
Indiana	Handicapped children, with physical or mental disability (except totally blind or deaf, eligible for residential schools).	P	Excess cost.
Iowa	Physically handicapped, emotionally maladjusted, or intellectually incapable (excluding those for whom special institutions are provided).	P	Special appropriation for equitable reimbursement for excess cost per pupil, to be made by administrative allotment. For deaf children: $20 per month per child.
Kentucky	Physically handicapped	P	Excess cost up to $275 per pupil.
	Mentally handicapped	P	Excess cost up to $125 per pupil.
Louisiana	Crippled or physically disabled	P	Special appropriation for administrative allotment.
Maine	Physically handicapped	P; M for local school board to request State services upon petition of parents of 5 or more children.	Excess cost up to $200 per pupil in residence and $350 per nonresident pupil.
Maryland	Physically handicapped	P	Approved cost up to $200 per pupil.
	Mentally handicapped	P	Each special class considered a separate unit in determining equalization fund for county. (Baltimore not included.)
Massachusetts	Physically handicapped	M	Total cost of classes for deaf in 6 towns. Special appropriation for other groups for administrative allotment.
Michigan	Physically handicapped	P	For reimbursable expenditures, up to $200 per pupil in residence and $300 per non-resident pupil. Total reimbursement for speech-defective, home-bound, and hospitalized.

(continues)

Basic Legal Provisions for State-Aided Programs of Special Education in Local School Districts, 1948 *(continued)*

State	Children Specified by Law	Permissive (P) or Mandatory (M)	Basis of Annual State Aid
Minnesota	Deaf	P; M upon petition of parents of 8 children and with approval of State Commissioner of Education.	Excess cost not to exceed $250 per resident pupil, $400 per nonresident.
	Blind	"	Excess cost not to exceed $300 per resident pupil, $450 per nonresident.
	Crippled	"	Excess cost not to exceed $250 per pupil for home or class instruction.
Minnesota	Speech-defective	"	Excess cost not to exceed $1500 for each teacher.
	Subnormal	"	Excess cost not to exceed $100 per pupil.
Missouri	Physically handicapped	P	Excess cost not to exceed per pupil allowance of: $300 for orthopedically handicapped.$250 for deaf and hard-of-hearing.$225 for blind and partially seeing.$20 for speech-defectives.
	Mentally deficient or mentally retarded	P; M for 10 or more children.	$100 for mentally deficient and mentally retarded.
Nebraska	Deaf	P	$150 to $300 per pupil, depending upon the size of the class.
New Jersey	Physically handicapped	P; M for 10 or more children.	One-half of excess cost as approved by Commissioner of Education.
	Subnormal	"	Each special class considered a special unit in apportionment of State funds.
New Mexico	Crippled	P	An additional teacher allowed in apportionment of State funds for each 5 to 15 crippled children; and an additional teacher for each additional 15 crippled children or major fraction thereof.
New York	Physically handicapped	P; M for 10 or more children.	$800 for each approved special class;[2] one-half of cost incurred for individual cases.
	Mentally retarded	"	$800 for each approved special class.
	Delinquents	"	do
North Carolina	Physically handicapped	P	Equitable reimbursement for excess cost of instruction.
	Mentally handicapped	P	do
Ohio	Physically handicapped	P; M for crippled upon direction of State Superintendent of Public Instruction.	Excess cost up to $300 per pupil; plus transportation costs and $250 per pupil for maintenance of nonresident pupils.$1,000 per teaching unit of 24 or more pupils served by a teacher on circuit.
	Slow-learning	P	$750 per teaching unit of 12 pupils, plus cost of transportation of nonresident pupils.(Children with multiple defects may be counted for each defect.)
Oklahoma	Physically handicapped	P	Excess cost up to $200 per pupil; plus transportation and boarding (up to $250) for non-resident pupils.
	Mentally handicapped	P	$750 per teaching unit of not less than 6 children; plus transportation and boarding (up to $250) for nonresident pupils.
Oregon	Physically handicapped	M (with approval of State Superintendent of Public Instruction).	Excess cost up to 1 1/2 times the per capita cost of educating nonhandicapped children.
	Maladjusted (exclusive of mental retardation)	P	do

State	Children Specified by Law	Permissive (P) or Mandatory (M)	Basis of Annual State Aid
Pennsylvania	Physically handicapped	M for 10 or more children.	$30 per pupil in average daily membership of class; for home instruction, an amount determined by applying State financial formula.
	Mentally handicapped	"	$20 per pupil in average daily membership of class.
South Dakota	Crippled in hospitals	P	Special appropriation for administrative allotment.
Tennessee	Physically handicapped (excluding those eligible for State schools for blind and deaf).	P	Special appropriation for administrative allotment.
Texas	Physically handicapped (except those eligible for State schools).	P	Excess cost up to $200 per pupil.
Virginia	Not specified by law.[3]	P	Special appropriation for administrative allotment.
Washington	Physically handicapped	P	Administrative allocations made from special funds.
West Virginia	Home-bound crippled children	P	Special appropriation for administrative allotment.
Wisconsin	Physically handicapped	P	Reimbursement for amount expended, as approved by the State Superintendent; full cost of transportation and maintenance for nonresident pupils.
	Mentally handicapped	P	do
Wyoming	Physically handicapped	M (upon State Board of Education's approval).	All necessary expenses allowed by State Board of Education; full cost of home instruction.
	Mentally handicapped	"	Special appropriation for administrative allotment.

[1] But "any school district which does not maintain facilities for the education of physically handicapped minors shall enter into a contract with a school district in the same county maintaining such facilities" or any other county. Deering's California Codes, §9601.2.

[2] Quota for classes of fewer than 10 is $80 per pupil.

[3] Classes for "blind and partially blind" children are operated jointly by local school boards and the Virginia Commission for the Blind.

Source: Data from Martens, Elise H. *State Legislation for Education of Exceptional Children.* Washington, D.C.: Federal Security Agency and U.S. Office of Education, 1949.

Status of School Segregation-Desegregation, 1964

State	School Districts			Enrollment		In Desegregated Districts		Blacks in Schools with Whites	
	Total	With Blacks & Whites	Deseg.	White	Black	White	Black	No.	+%
Alabama	118	118	8	549,543**	293,476**	152,486**	88,952**	94	.032
Arkansas	412	228	24	333,630**	114,651**	93,072	28, 943	930	.811
Florida	67	67	21	1,001,611*	.246,215*	812,268*	174,52 2*	6,524	2.65
Georgia	196	180	11	752,620	354,850	195,598	133,888	1,337	.377
Louisiana	67	67	3	489,000*	321,000*	61,885	86,248	3,581	1.12
Mississippi	150	150	4	308,409**	295,962**	34,620**	21,929**	58	.020
North Carolina	171	171	84	828,638	349,282	548,705	201,394	4,949	1.42
South Carolina	108	108	16	371,921	260,667	156,346	83,608	260	.100
Tennessee	152	141	61	724,327*	173,673*	459,162*	135,001*	9,265*	5.33
Texas	1,380	862	291	2,086,752*	344,312*	1,500,000*	225,000*	25,000*	7.26
Virginia	130	128	81	733,524**	234,176**	585,491	189 ,046	11,883	5.07
SOUTH									
	2,951	2,220	604	8,179,975	2,988,264	4,599,633	1,368,531	63,881	2.14
Delaware	78	43	43	83,325	19,497	78,346	14,484	11 ,267	57.8
Dist. of Columbia	1	1	1	17,487	123,906	17,487	123,906	106,578	86.0
Kentucky	204	165	164	620,000*	56,000*	540,000*	55, 900*	35,000*	62.5
Maryland	24	23	23	565,434	166,861	560,359	166,861	86,203	51.7
Missouri	1,542	212*	203*	818,000*	102,000*	NA	94,000*	44,000*	43.1
Oklahoma	1,118	242	200	542,103*	43,954*	324,981*	37,026*	13,923*	31.7
West Virginia	55	44	44	425,821*	21,000*	389,921*	21,000*	18,500*	88.1
Border									
	3,022	730	678	3,073,170	533,218	1,911,094††	513,177	315,471	59.2
Region									
	5,973	2,950	1,282	11,253,145	3,521,482	6,510,727††	1,881,708	379,352	10.8

*Estimated

**1963–64

†Number of Negroes in schools with whites, compared to total Negro enrollment

††Mo. not included

Source: Data from the Southern Education Reporting Service. *Statistical Summary of School Segregation-Desegregation in the Southern and Border States.* Fourteenth Revision. Nashville, 1964.

Enrollment in Educational Institutions, by Level and Control of Institution, Selected Years, 1869–1870 to Fall 2013 (in thousands)

Year	Total Enrollment, all Levels	Elementary and Secondary, Total	Public Elementary and Secondary Schools			Private Elementary and Secondary Schools[a]			Degree-Granting Institutions[b]		
			Total	Prekindergarten through Grade 8	Grades 9 through 12	Total	Prekindergarten through Grade 8	Grades 9 through 12	Total	Public	Private
1869–70	—	—	6,872	6,792	80				52	—	—
1879–80	—	—	9,868	9,757	110			—	116		
1889–90	14,491	14,334	12,723	12,520	203	1,611	1,516	95	157	—	—
1899–1900	17,092	16,855	15,503	14,984	519	1,352	1,241	111	238	—	—
1909–10	19,728	19,372	17,814	16,899	915	1,558	1,441	117	355	—	—
1919–20	23,876	23,278	21,578	19,378	2,200	1,699	1,486	214	598	—	—
1929–30	29,430	28,329	25,678	21,279	4,399	2,651	2,310	341	1,101	—	—
1939–40	29,539	28,045	25,434	18,832	6,601	2,611	2,153	458	1,494	797	698
1949–50	31,151	28,492	25,111	19,387	5,725	3,380	2,708	672	2,659	1,355	1,304
Fall 1959	44,497	40,857	35,182	26,911	8,271	5,675	4,640	1,035	3,640	2,181	1,459
Fall 1969	59,055	51,050	45,550	32,513	13,037	5,500[c]	4,200[c]	1,300[c]	8,005	5,897	2,108
Fall 1970	59,838	51,257	45,894	32,558	13,336	5,363	4,052	1,311	8,581	6,428	2,153
Fall 1971	60,220	51,271	46,071	32,318	13,753	5,200[c]	3,900[c]	1,300[c]	8,949	6,804	2,144
Fall 1972	59,941	50,726	45,726	31,879	13,848	5,000[c]	3,700[c]	1,300[c]	9,215	7,071	2,144
Fall 1973	60,047	50,445	45,445	31,401	14,044	5,000[c]	3,700[c]	1,300[c]	9,602	7,420	2,183
Fall 1974	60,297	50,073	45,073	30,971	14,103	5,000[c]	3,700[c]	1,300[c]	10,224	7,989	2,235
Fall 1975	61,004	49,819	44,819	30,515	14,304	5,000[c]	3,700[c]	1,300[c]	11,185	8,835	2,350
Fall 1976	60,490	49,478	44,311	29,997	14,314	5,167	3,825	1,342	11,012	8,653	2,359
Fall 1977	60,003	48,717	43,577	29,375	14,203	5,140	3,797	1,343	11,286	8,847	2,439
Fall 1978	58,897	47,637	42,551	28,463	14,088	5,086	3,732	1,353	11,260	8,786	2,474
Fall 1979	58,221	46,651	41,651	28,034	13,616	5,000[c]	3,700[c]	1,300[c]	11,570	9,037	2,533
Fall 1980	58,305	46,208	40,877	27,647	13,231	5,331	3,992	1,339	12,097	9,457	2,640
Fall 1981	57,916	45,544	40,044	27,280	12,764	5,500[c]	4,100[c]	1,400[c]	12,372	9,647	2,725
Fall 1982	57,591	45,166	39,566	27,161	12,405	5,600[c]	4,200[c]	1,400[c]	12,426	9,696	2,730
Fall 1983	57,432	44,967	39,252	26,981	12,271	5,715	4,315	1,400	12,465	9,683	2,782
Fall 1984	57,150	44,908	39,208	26,905	12,304	5,700[c]	4,300[c]	1,400[c]	12,242	9,477	2,765
Fall 1985	57,226	44,979	39,422	27,034	12,388	5,557	4,195	1,362	12,247	9,479	2,768
Fall 1986	57,709	45,205	39,753	27,420	12,333	5,452[c]	4,116[c]	1,336[c]	12,504	9,714	2,790
Fall 1987	58,253	45,487	40,008	27,933	12,076	5,479	4,232	1,247	12,767	9,973	2,793
Fall 1988	58,485	45,430	40,189	28,501	11,687	5,242[c]	4,036[c]	1,206[c]	13,055	10,161	2,894
Fall 1989	59,279	45,741	40,543	29,152	11,390	5.198[c]	4,035[c]	1,163[c]	13,539	10,578	2,961
Fall 1990	60,269	46,451	41,217	29,878	11,338	5,234	4,084	1,150	13,819	10,845	2,974
Fall 1991	61.681	47,322	42,047	30,506	11,541	5,275[c]	4,113[c]	1,162[c]	14,359	11,310	3,049
Fall 1992	62,633	48,145	42,823	31,088	11,735	5,322[c]	4,175[c]	1,147[c]	14,487	11,385	3,103
Fall 1993	63,118	48,813	43,465	31,504	11,961	5,348[c]	4,215[c]	1,132[c]	14,305	11,189	3,116

(continues)

Enrollment in Educational Institutions, by Level and Control of Institution, Selected Years, 1869–1870 to Fall 2013 (in thousands)

Year	Total Enrollment, all Levels	Elementary and Secondary, Total	Public Elementary and Secondary Schools			Private Elementary and Secondary Schools[a]			Degree-Granting Institutions[b]		
			Total	Prekindergarten through Grade 8	Grades 9 through 12	Total	Prekindergarten through Grade 8	Grades 9 through 12	Total	Public	Private
Fall 1994	63,888	49,609	44,111	31,898	12,213	5,498[c]	4,335[c]	1,163[c]	14,279	11,134	3,145
Fall 1995	64,764	50,502	44,840	32,341	12,500	5,662	4,465	1,197	14,262	11,092	3,169
Fall 1996	65,743	51,375	45,611	32,764	12,847	5,764[c]	4,551[c]	1,213[c]	14,368	11,120	3,247
Fall 1997	66,470	51,968	46,127	33,073	13,054	5,841	4,623	1,218	14,502	11,196	3,306
Fall 1998	66,982	52,475	46,539	33,346	13,193	5,937[c]	4,702[c]	1,235[c]	14,507	11,138	3,369
Fall 1999	67,667	52,876	46,857	33,488	13,369	6,018	4,765	1,254	14,791	11,309	3,482
Fall 2000	68,678	53,366	47,204	33,688	13,515	6,162[d]	4,875[d]	1,287[d]	15,312	11,753	3,560
Fall 2001	69,818	53,890	47,688	33,952	13,736	6,202[d]	4,880[d]	1,322[d]	15,928	12,233	3,695
Fall 2002[d]	70,260	54,158	47,918	33,942	13,976	6,241	4,885	1,356	16,102	12,354	3,749
Fall 2003[d]	70,657	54,296	48,040	33,843	14,198	6,256	4,876	1,379	16,361	12,546	3,814
Fall 2004[d]	70,923	54.455	48,175	33,669	14,506	6,279	4,871	1,408	16,468	12,627	3,841
Fall 2005[d]	71,294	54,615	48,304	33,534	14,770	6,311	4,878	1,433	16,679	12,786	3,893
Fall 2006[d]	71,794	54,907	48,524	33,589	14,936	6,383	4,933	1,449	16,887	12,942	3,945
Fall 2007[d]	72,069	55,049	48,640	33,654	14,986	6,409	4,950	1,458	17,020	13,042	3,978
Fall 2008[d]	72,292	55,124	48,690	33,791	14,899	6,434	4,975	1,459	17,168	13,153	4,015
Fall 2009[d]	72,597	55,223	48,761	33,994	14,767	6,461	5,001	1,461	17,374	13,308	4,066
Fall 2010[d]	72,927	55,386	48,890	34,243	14,648	6,495	5,040	1,455	17,541	13,431	4,110
Fall 2011[d]	73,342	55,618	49,084	34,597	14,487	6,534	5,091	1,443	17,724	13,566	4,158
Fall 2012[d]	73,873	55,946	49,367	35,006	14,361	6,579	5,148	1,430	17,927	13,716	4,211
Fall 2013[d]	74,515	56,364	49,737	35,430	14,307	6,627	5,208	1,419	18,151	13,883	4,268

— Not available.

[a] Beginning in fall 1980, data include estimates for an expanded universe of private schools. Therefore, direct comparisons with earlier years should be avoided.

[b] Data for 1869–70 through 1949–50 include resident degree-credit students enrolled at any time during the academic year. Beginning in 1959, data include all resident and extension students enrolled at the beginning of the fall term.

[c] Estimated.

[d] Projected.

Note: Elementary and secondary enrollment includes pupils in local public school systems and in most private schools (religiously affiliated and nonsectarian), but generally excludes pupils in subcollegiate departments of colleges, federal schools, and home-schooled children. Based on the National Household Education Survey, the home-schooled children numbered approximately 850,000 in the spring of 1999. Public elementary enrollment includes most preprimary school pupils. Private elementary enrollment includes some preprimary students. Beginning in 1996–97, data are for degree-granting institutions. Degree-granting institutions are 2-year and 4-year institutions that were eligible to participate in Title IV federal financial aid programs. Data for degree-granting institutions for 1999 were imputed using alternative procedures. Some data have been revised from previously published figures. Detail may not sum to totals due to rounding.

Source: Thomas D. Snyder, Alexandra G. Tan, and Charlene M. Hoffman, "Table 3. Enrollment in Educational Institutions, by Level and Control of Institution: Selected Years, 1869–70 to Fall 2013." *Digest of Education Statistics, 2003,* NCES 2005-025, U.S. Department of Education, National Center for Education Statistics. Washington, D.C. Available online. URL: http://nces.ed.gov/programs/digest/d03/tables/dt003.asp. Accessed on July 26, 2005.

Percentage Distribution of Students by Sex and Race or Ethnicity, 2003–2004

School Type and Selected School Characteristic	Sex		Race/Ethnicity				
	Male	Female	White, Non-Hispanic	Black, Non-Hispanic	Hispanic, Regardless of Race	American Indian/ Alaska Native	Asian/ Pacific Islander
All schools	50.0	50.0	61.8	16.0	16.7	1.7	3.6
All public schools	**50.1**	**49.9**	**60.3**	**16.8**	**17.7**	**1.3**	**3.9**
School Classification							
Traditional public	50.1	49.9	60.6	16.6	17.6	1.3	3.9
Charter school	48.6	51.4	43.4	29.7	21.7	1.4	3.8
Community Type							
Central city	49.5	50.5	36.0	28.4	28.9	0.8	5.9
Urban fringe/large town	50.3	49.7	68.2	12.3	14.6	1.0	3.8
Rural/small town	50.5	49.5	77.5	10.6	7.8	3.0	1.1
School Level							
Elementary	49.9	50.1	57.8	17.7	19.6	1.2	3.8
Secondary	50.0	50.0	63.4	15.7	15.0	1.2	4.6
Combined	52.7	47.3	74.2	11.6	9.0	3.6	1.6
Student Enrollment							
Less than 100	57.8	42.2	59.3	13.8	22.2	4.0	0.8
100–199	52.0	48.0	71.3	12.9	10.5	4.0	1.2
200–499	50.7	49.3	67.3	16.8	11.0	1.9	3.0
500–749	50.1	49.9	60.3	16.9	18.5	1.1	3.3
750–999	49.3	50.7	55.4	18.2	21.5	0.8	4.1
1,000 or more	49.5	50.5	55.8	16.2	21.5	0.9	5.6
All Bureau of Indian Affairs (BIA)schools	**48.0**[1]	**52.0**[1]	**1.4**	**0.6**	**0.8**	**97.1**	**0.1**
All private schools	**49.8**	**50.2**	**76.5**	**9.3**	**8.3**	**5.0**	**0.8**
School Classification							
Catholic	48.5	51.5	74.1	8.5	11.3	5.1	0.9
Other religious	49.7	50.3	80.0	10.3	5.5	3.5	0.7
Nonsectarian	53.0	47.0	75.9	9.4	6.1	7.7	0.9
Community Type							
Central city	48.6	51.4	68.6	13.0	10.9	7.0	0.5
Urban fringe/large town	50.4	49.6	80.9	7.4	7.0	4.0	0.7
Rural/small town	51.8	48.2	88.8	3.1	3.2	1.9	3.1
School Level							
Elementary	50.4	49.6	74.3	10.3	9.1	5.2	1.1
Secondary	48.5	51.5	76.4	7.9	9.7	5.4	0.6
Combined	49.5	50.5	80.4	8.4	6.1	4.5	0.6
Student Enrollment							
Less than 100	54.0	46.0	73.5	13.4	8.3	3.9	0.9
100–199	51.4	48.6	71.8	13.3	7.9	4.6	2.4
200–499	48.8	51.2	76.9	8.8	9.0	4.8	0.5
500–749	47.1	52.9	81.5	6.1	6.4	5.7	0.3
750 or more	50.0	50.0	78.5	6.1	8.6	6.5	0.3

(continues)

Percentage Distribution of Students by Sex and Race or Ethnicity, 2003–04
(continued)

[1] For the item that measured male student enrollment in grades K-12 and comparable ungraded levels, the response rate was below 70 percent on the BIA School Data File. This item was also used to calculate female student enrollment.

Note: BIA school refers to schools funded by the Bureau of Indian Affairs (BIA) that are operated by the BIA, a tribe, or a private contractor and not by a regular school district.

Source: U.S. Department of Education, National Center for Education Statistics, Schools and Staffing Survey, 2003–04, Public School, BIA School, and Private School Data Files.

Number of Students, Teachers, Schools, Principals, School Libraries, and Districts, by School Type and Selected School Characteristics, 2003–2004

School Type and Selected School Characteristic	Students	Teachers[1]	Schools	Principals[1]	Libraries	Districts
Total	52,419,400	3,722,000	116,665	115,478	78,411	15,500
All public schools	**47,315,700**	**3,250,600**	**88,113**	**87,621**	**78,257**	†
School Classification						
Traditional public	46,689,000	3,208,500	85,934	85,451	77,319	†
Charter school	626,700	42,100	2,179	2,170	938	†
Community Type						
Central city	13,972,000	929,400	21,985	21,849	18,490	1,400
Urban fringe/large tow	24,915,800	1,704,200	42,326	42,110	38,411	6,800
Rural/small town	8,427,900	617,000	23,802	23,662	21,356	7,300
School Level						
Elementary	29,953,900	2,107,900	61,572	61,477	57,404	†
Secondary	15,301,300	975,200	19,886	19,697	16,268	†
Combined	2,060,400	167,500	6,655	6,447	4,586	†
Student Enrollment						
Less than 100	320,900	48,700	6,895	6,476	2,905	†
100–199	1,182,300	118,800	7,922	7,911	5,995	†
200–499	12,543,200	978,900	35,685	35,893	33,104	†
500–749	12,290,800	850,300	20,156	19,818	19,253	†
750–999	7,229,600	466,300	8,396	8,428	7,868	†
1,000 or more	13,748,800	787,700	9,059	9,096	9,132	†
All Bureau of Indian Affairs (BIA) schools	**44,300**	**4,000**	**168**	**167**	**154**	†
All private schools	**5,059,400**	**467,400**	**28,384**	**27,690**	†	†
School Classification						
Catholic	2,320,000	164,000	7,919	7,900	†	†
Other religious	1,746,500	178,300	13,659	13,092	†	†
Nonsectarian	992,900	125,100	6,806	6,698	†	†
Community Type						
Central city	2,087,100	182,300	9,757	9,666	†	†
Urban fringe/large town	2,533,500	235,700	14,129	13,749	†	†
Rural/small town	438,800	49,400	4,499	4,275	†	†
School Level						
Elementary	2,676,000	222,900	17,331	16,748	†	†
Secondary	832,300	76,700	2,657	2,514	†	†
Combined	1,551,200	167,800	8,397	8,427	†	†
Student Enrollment						
Less than 100	577,700	82,400	13,492	12,712	†	†
100–199	913,600	95,900	6,263	6,216	†	†
200–499	2,063,300	170,400	6,646	6,717	†	†
500–749	735,900	55,500	1,228	1,237	†	†
750 or more	769,000	63,200	754	808	†	†

(continues)

Number of Students, Teachers, Schools, Principals, School Libraries, and Districts, by School Type and Selected School Characteristics, 2003–2004 *(continued)*

† Not applicable.

[1] Includes full- and part-time head counts.

Note: BIA school refers to schools funded by the Bureau of Indian Affairs (BIA) that are operated by the BIA, a tribe, or a private contractor and not by a regular school district. Detail may not sum to totals because of rounding. Community type for students, teachers, schools, principals, and libraries is based on the locale of the related school. Community type for district is based upon the locale of the majority of the schools located in the district and may differ from the community type of a school sampled from the district.

Source: U.S. Department of Education, National Center for Education Statistics, Schools and Staffing Survey, 2003–04, Public School, BIA School, Private School, Public School Teacher, BIA School Teacher, Private School Teacher, Public School Principal, BIA School Principal, Private School Principal, Public School Library Media Center, BIA School Library Media Center, and District Data Files.

Percentage of Years of School Completed Persons Age 25 and Older, by Race/Ethnicity, and Sex, Selected Years, 1910–2002

Age and Year	Total			White, Non-Hispanic[a]			Black, Non-Hispanic[a]			Hispanic		
	Less than 5 Years of Elementary School	High School Completion or Higher[b]	4 or More Years of College[c]	Less than 5 Years of Elementary School	High School Completion or Higher[b]	4 or More Years of College[c]	Less than 5 Years of Elementary School	High School Completion or Higher[b]	4 or More Years of College[c]	Less than 5 Years of Elementary School	High School Completion or Higher[b]	4 or More Years of College[c]
Males and Females												
25 and older												
1910[d]	23.8	13.5	2.7	—	—	—	—	—	—	—	—	—
1920[d]	22.0	16.4	3.3	—	—	—	—	—	—	—	—	—
1930[d]	17.5	19.1	3.9	—	—	—	—	—	—	—	—	—
April 1940	13.7	24.5	4.6	10.9	26.1	4.9	41.8	7.7	1.3	—	—	—
April 1950	11.1	34.3	6.2	8.9	36.4	6.6	32.6	13.7	2.2	—	—	—
April 1960	8.3	41.1	7.7	6.7	43.2	8.1	23.5	21.7	3.5	—	—	—
March 1970	5.3	55.2	11.0	4.2	57.4	11.6	14.7	36.1	6.1	—	—	—
March 1975	4.2	62.5	13.9	2.6	65.8	14.9	12.3	42.6	6.4	18.2	38.5	6.6
March 1980	3.4	68.6	17.0	1.9	71.9	18.4	9.1	51.4	7.9	15.8	44.5	7.6
March 1985	2.7	73.9	19.4	1.4	77.5	20.8	6.1	59.9	11.1	13.5	47.9	8.5
March 1986	2.7	74.7	19.4	1.4	78.2	20.9	5.3	62.5	10.9	12.9	48.5	8.4
March 1987	2.4	75.6	19.9	1.3	79.0	21.4	4.9	63.6	10.8	11.9	50.9	8.6
March 1988	2.4	76.2	20.3	1.2	79.8	21.8	4.8	63.5	11.2	12.2	51.0	10.0
March 1989	2.5	76.9	21.1	1.2	80.7	22.8	5.2	64.7	11.7	12.2	50.9	9.9
March 1990	2.4	77.6	21.3	1.1	81.4	23.1	5.1	66.2	11.3	12.3	50.8	9.2
March 1991	2.4	78.4	21.4	1.1	82.4	23.3	4.7	66.8	11.5	12.5	51.3	9.7
March 1992	2.1	79.4	21.4	0.9	83.4	23.2	3.9	67.7	11.9	11.8	52.6	9.3
March 1993	2.1	80.2	21.9	0.8	84.1	23.8	3.7	70.5	12.2	11.8	53.1	9.0
March 1994	1.9	80.9	22.2	0.8	84.9	24.3	2.7	73.0	12.9	10.8	53.3	9.1
March 1995	1.8	81.7	23.0	0.7	85.9	25.4	2.5	73.8	13.3	10.6	53.4	9.3
March 1996	1.8	81.7	23.6	0.6	86.0	25.9	2.2	74.6	13.8	10.3	53.1	9.3
March 1997	1.7	82.1	23.9	0.6	86.3	26.2	2.0	75.3	13.3	9.4	54.7	10.3
March 1998	1.6	82.8	24.4	0.6	87.1	26.6	1.7	76.4	14.8	9.3	55.5	11.0
March 1999	1.6	83.4	25.2	0.6	87.7	27.7	1.7	77.4	15.5	9.0	56.1	10.9
March 2000	1.6	84.1	25.6	0.5	88.4	28.1	1.6	78.9	16.6	8.7	57.0	10.6
March 2001	1.6	84.3	26.1	0.5	88.7	28.6	1.3	79.5	16.1	9.3	56.5	11.2
March 2002	1.6	84.1	26.7	0.5	88.7	29.4	1.6	79.2	17.2	8.7	57.0	11.1
25 to 29												
1920[d]	—	—	—	12.9	22.0	4.5	44.6	6.3	1.2	—	—	—
April 1940	5.9	38.1	5.9	3.4	41.2	6.4	27.0	12.3	1.6	—	—	—
April 1950	4.6	52.8	7.7	3.3	56.3	8.2	16.1	23.6	2.8	—	—	—
April 1960	2.8	60.7	11.0	2.2	63.7	11.8	7.2	38.6	5.4	—	—	—
March 1970	1.1	75.4	16.4	0.9	77.8	17.3	2.2	58.4	10.0	—	—	—

(continues)

Percentage of Years of School Completed Persons Age 25 and Older, by Race/Ethnicity, and Sex, Selected Years, 1910–2002 *(continued)*

Age and Year	Total			White, Non-Hispanic[a]			Black, Non-Hispanic[a]			Hispanic		
	Less than 5 Years of Elementary School	High School Completion or Higher[b]	4 or More Years of College[c]	Less than 5 Years of Elementary School	High School Completion or Higher[b]	4 or More Years of College[c]	Less than 5 Years of Elementary School	High School Completion or Higher[b]	4 or More Years of College[c]	Less than 5 Years of Elementary School	High School Completion or Higher[b]	4 or More Years of College[c]
March 1975	1.0	83.1	21.9	0.6	86.6	23.8	0.5	71.1	10.5	8.0	53.1	8.8
March 1980	0.8	85.4	22.5	0.3	89.2	25.0	0.6	76.7	11.6	6.7	58.0	7.7
March 1985	0.7	86.1	22.2	0.2	89.5	24.4	0.4	80.5	11.6	6.0	60.9	11.1
March 1986	0.9	86.1	22.4	0.4	89.6	25.2	0.5	83.5	11.8	5.6	59.1	9.0
March 1987	0.9	86.0	22.0	0.4	89.4	24.6	0.4	83.4	11.5	4.8	59.8	8.7
March 1988	1.0	85.9	22.7	0.3	89.7	25.1	0.3	80.9	12.0	6.0	62.3	11.3
March 1989	1.0	85.5	23.4	0.3	89.3	26.3	0.5	82.3	12.6	5.4	61.0	10.1
March 1990	1.2	85.7	23.2	0.3	90.1	26.4	1.0	81.7	13.4	7.3	58.2	8.1
March 1991	1.0	85.4	23.2	0.4	89.8	26.7	0.5	81.8	11.0	5.8	56.7	9.2
March 1992	0.9	86.3	23.6	0.3	90.7	27.2	0.8	80.9	11.0	5.2	60.9	9.5
March 1993	0.7	86.7	23.7	0.3	91.2	27.2	0.2	82.6	13.3	4.0	60.9	8.3
March 1994	0.8	86.1	23.3	0.2	91.1	27.1	0.6	84.1	13.6	3.6	60.3	8.0
March 1997	0.8	87.4	27.8	0.1	92.9	32.6	0.6	86.9	14.2	4.2	61.8	11.0
March 1998	0.7	88.1	27.3	0.1	93.6	32.3	0.4	88.2	15.8	3.7	62.8	10.4
March 1999	0.6	87.8	28.2	0.1	93.0	33.6	0.2	88.7	15.0	3.2	61.6	8.9
March 2000	0.7	88.1	29.1	0.1	94.0	34.0	*	86.8	17.8	3.8	62.8	9.7
March 2001	0.8	87.7	28.6	0.2	93.3	33.0	0.1	87.0	17.8	4.7	63.2	11.1
March 2002	1.1	86.4	29.3	0.1	93.0	35.9	0.6	87.6	18.0	4.7	62.4	8.9
Males												
25 and older												
April 1940	15.1	22.7	5.5	12.0	24.2	5.9	46.2	6.9	1.4	—	—	—
April 1950	12.2	32.6	7.3	9.8	34.6	7.9	36.9	12.6	2.1	—	—	—
April 1960	9.4	39.5	9.7	7.4	41.6	10.3	27.7	20.0	3.5	—	—	—
March 1970	5.9	55.0	14.1	4.5	57.2	15.0	17.9	35.4	6.8	—	—	—
March 1980	3.6	69.2	20.9	2.0	72.4	22.8	11.3	51.2	7.7	16.5	44.9	9.2
March 1990	2.7	77.7	24.4	1.3	81.6	26.7	6.4	65.8	11.9	12.9	50.3	9.8
March 1995	2.0	81.7	26.0	0.8	86.0	28.9	3.4	73.5	13.7	10.8	52.9	10.1
March 1996	1.9	81.9	26.0	0.7	86.1	28.8	2.9	74.6	12.5	10.1	53.0	10.3
March 1997	1.8	82.0	26.2	0.6	86.3	29.0	2.9	73.8	12.5	9.2	54.9	10.6
March 1998	1.7	82.8	26.5	0.7	87.1	29.3	2.3	75.4	14.0	9.3	55.7	11.1
March 1999	1.6	83.4	27.5	0.6	87.7	30.6	2.0	77.2	14.3	9.0	56.0	10.7
March 2000	1.6	84.2	27.8	0.6	88.5	30.8	2.1	79.1	16.4	8.2	56.6	10.7
March 2001	1.6	84.4	28.0	0.6	88.6	30.9	1.7	80.6	15.9	9.4	55.6	11.1
March 2002	1.7	83.8	28.5	0.5	88.5	31.7	1.9	79.0	16.5	9.0	56.1	11.0

Percentage of Years of School Completed Persons Age 25 and Older, by Race/Ethnicity, and Sex, Selected Years, 1910–2002 *(continued)*

Age and Year	Total			White, Non-Hispanic[a]			Black, Non-Hispanic[a]			Hispanic		
	Less than 5 Years of Elementary School	High School Completion or Higher[b]	4 or More Years of College[c]	Less than 5 Years of Elementary School	High School Completion or Higher[b]	4 or More Years of College[c]	Less than 5 Years of Elementary School	High School Completion or Higher[b]	4 or More Years of College[c]	Less than 5 Years of Elementary School	High School Completion or Higher[b]	4 or More Years of College[c]
Females												
25 and older												
April 1940	12.4	26.3	3.8	9.8	28.1	4.0	37.5	8.4	1.2	—	—	—
April 1950	10.0	36.0	5.2	8.1	38.2	5.4	28.6	14.7	2.4	—	—	—
April 1960	7.4	42.5	5.8	6.0	44.7	6.0	19.7	23.1	3.6	—	—	—
March 1970	4.7	55.4	8.2	3.9	57.7	8.6	11.9	36.6	5.6	—	—	—
March 1980	3.2	68.1	13.6	1.8	71.5	14.4	7.4	51.5	8.1	15.3	44.2	6.2
March 1990	2.2	77.5	18.4	1.0	81.3	19.8	4.0	66.5	10.8	11.7	51.3	8.7
March 1995	1.7	81.6	20.2	0.6	85.8	22.1	1.7	74.1	13.0	10.4	53.8	8.4
March 1996	1.7	81.6	21.4	0.5	85.9	23.2	1.6	74.6	14.8	10.5	53.3	8.3
March 1997	1.6	82.2	21.7	0.5	86.3	23.7	1.3	76.5	14.0	9.5	54.6	10.1
March 1998	1.6	82.9	22.4	0.6	87.1	24.1	1.2	77.1	15.4	9.2	55.3	10.9
March 1999	1.5	83.3	23.1	0.5	87.6	25.0	1.5	77.5	16.5	9.0	56.3	11.0
March 2000	1.5	84.0	23.6	0.4	88.4	25.5	1.1	78.7	16.8	9.3	57.5	10.6
March 2001	1.5	84.2	24.3	0.4	88.8	26.5	1.0	78.6	16.3	9.1	57.4	11.3
March 2002	1.5	84.4	25.1	0.5	88.9	27.3	1.4	79.4	17.7	8.3	57.9	11.2

Note: Total includes other racial/ethnic groups not shown separately.

* Rounds to zero.

— Not available.

[a] Includes persons of Hispanic origin for years prior to 1980.

[b] Data for years prior to 1993 include all persons with at least 4 years of high school.

[c] Data for 1993 and later years are for persons with a bachelor's or higher degree.

[d] Estimates based on Bureau of the Census retrojection of 1940 Census data on education by age.

Source: Data from Snyder, Thomas D., Alexandra G. Tan, and Charlene M. Hoffman, "Table 8. Percent of Persons Age 25 and Over and 25 to 29, by Years of School Completed, Race/Ethnicity, and Sex: Selected Years, 1910–2002," in *Digest of Education Statistics, 2003*, NCES 2005-025, U.S. Department of Education, National Center for Education Statistics, Washington, DC, December 2004. Available online. URL: http://nces.ed.gov/programs/digest/d03/tables/dt008.asp. Accessed on July 26, 2005.

Number and Percentage of Home-Schooled Students, Ages Five through Seventeen with a Grade Equivalent of Kindergarten through Twelfth Grade, by Various Characteristics, 1999 and 2003

Characteristic	1999			2003		
	Number of Students[1]	Number Home Schooled	Percent Home Schooled	Number of Students[1]	Number Home Schooled	Percent Home Schooled
Total	50,188,000	850,000	1.7	50,707,000	1,096,000	2.2
Grade equivalent[2]						
K–5	24,428,000	428,000	1.8	24,269,000	472,000	1.9
Kindergarten	3,790,000	92,000	2.4	3,643,000	98,000	2.7
Grades 1–3	12,692,000	199,000	1.6	12,098,000	214,000	1.8
Grades 4–5	7,946,000	136,000	1.7	8,528,000	1 60,000	1.9
Grades 6–8	11,788,000	186,000	1.6	12,472,000	302,000	2.4
Grades 9–12	13,954,000	235,000	1.7	13,958,000	315,000	2.3
Race/ethnicity						
White, non-Hispanic	32,474,000	640,000	2.0	31,584,000	843,000	2.7
Black, non-Hispanic	8,047,000	84,000	1.0	7,985,000	103,000	1.3
Hispanic	7,043,000	77,000	1.1	8,075,000	59,000	0.7
Other	2,623,000	49,000	1.9	3,063,000	91,000	3.0
Sex						
Female	24,673,000	434,000	1.8	24,888,000	527,000	2.1
Male	25,515,000	417,000	1.6	25,819,000	569,000	2.2
Number of children in the household						
One child	8,226,000	120,000	1.5	8,033,000	11 0,000	1.4
Two children	19,883,000	207,000	1.0	20,530,000	306,000	1.5
Three or more children	22,078,000	523,000	2.4	22,144,000	679,000	3.1
Number of parents in the household						
Two parents	33,007,000	683,000	2.1	35,936,000	886,000	2.5
One parent	15,454,000	142,000	0.9	13,260,000	196,000	1.5
Nonparental guardians	1,727,000	25,000	1.4	1,511,000	14,000	0.9
Parents' participation in the labor force						
Two parents–both in labor force	22,880,000	237,000	1.0	25,108,000	274,000	1.1
Two parents–one in labor force	9,628,000	444,000	4.6	10,545,000	594,000	5.6
One parent in labor force	13,907,000	98,000	0.7	12,045,000	174,000	1.4
No parent in labor force	3,773,000	71,000	1.9	3,008,000	54,000	1.8
Household Income						
$25,000 or less	16,776,000	262,000	1.6	12,375,000	283,000	2.3
25,001–50,000	15,220,000	278,000	1.8	13,220,000	311,000	2.4
50,001–75,000	8,576,000	162,000	1.9	10,961,000	2 64,000	2.4
75,001 or more	9,615,000	148,000	1.5	14,150,000	238,000	1.7
Parents' highest educational attainment						
High school diploma or less	18,334,000	160,000	0.9	16,106,000	269,000	1.7
Voc/tech degree or some college	15,177,000	287,000	1.9	16,068,000	338,000	2.1
Bachelor's degree	8,269,000	213,000	2.6	9,798,000	274,000	2.8
Graduate/professional school	8,407,000	190,000	2.3	8,734,000	215,000	2.5

Characteristic	1999			2003		
	Number of Students[1]	Number Home Schooled	Percent Home Schooled	Number of Students[1]	Number Home Schooled	Percent Home Schooled
Urbanicity[3]						
Urban	37,415,000	575,000	1.5	40,180,000	794,000	2.0
Rural	12,773,000	275,000	2.2	10,527,000	302,000	2.9
Region						
Northeast	10,220,000	114,000	1.1	9,220,000	168,000	1.8
South	17,366,000	355,000	2.0	17,232,000	445,000	2.6
Midwest	12,040,000	166,000	1.4	11,949,000	238,000	2.0
West	10,560,000	215,000	2.0	12,305,000	245,000	2.0

Number of students refers to all students in public and private schools and home-schooled students.

[2] Students whose grade equivalent was "ungraded" were excluded from the grade analysis. The percent of students with an "ungraded" grade equivalent was 0.02 percent in 2003 and 0.03 percent in 1999.

[3] Urbanicity is based on a U.S. Census classification of places. Urban is a place with at least 50,000 people. Rural is a place not classified as urban.

Note: Detail may not sum to totals because of rounding. Number and percent of home schoolers excludes students who were enrolled in school for more than 25 hours a week and students who were home schooled due to a temporary illness.

Source: Data from the U.S. Department of Education, National Center for Education Statistics, Parent Survey of the 1999 National Household Education Surveys Program (NHES); Parent and Family Involvement in Education Survey of the 2003 NHES.

Percentage of 25- to 29-Year-Olds Who Completed at Least Some College, by Race/Ethnicity and Sex, March 1971–2006

Year	Total[1]			White			Black			Hispanic		
	Total	Male	Female	Total	Male	Female	Total	Male	Female	Total	Male	Female
1971	33.9	38.5	29.4	36.7	41.7	31.8	18.1	16.5	19. 5	14.7	19.7	10.5!
1972	36.0	40.9	31.3	38.6	44.0	33.3	21.4	19.6	22. 8	15.3	17.4	13.5
1973	36.3	41.4	31.4	39.2	44.6	33.7	21.5	21.2	21.8	16.6	21.4	12.4
1974	40.1	44.7	35.6	43.1	47.8	38.4	24.2	26.4	22. 4	21.3	24.7	18.2
1975	41.6	47.4	36.0	44.3	50.4	38.3	27.5	29.7	25. 8	21.8	26.3	17.6
1976	44.1	50.1	38.4	47.2	53.5	41.0	27.5	29.5	25. 9	21.1	24.4	18.3
1977	45.5	50.3	40.8	48.6	53.4	43.7	31.1	34.3	28. 5	23.8	26.5	21.5
1978	46.4	51.0	41.9	49.5	54.6	44.4	34.7	35.7	33. 9	24.7	27.6	22.0
1979	46.3	49.8	42.9	49.6	53.3	45.9	31.2	30.2	32. 0	25.1	28.2	22.3
1980	44.7	47.6	41.9	48.0	51.1	44.9	32.4	32.6	32. 3	23.2	25.9	20.5
1981	43.2	45.6	40.9	46.0	48.5	43.5	33.0	33.9	32. 3	23.6	24.6	22.7
1982	43.0	44.5	41.6	45.1	46.6	43.7	37.1	38.1	36. 3	24.1	24.6	23.7
1983	43.5	44.8	42.2	46.1	47.7	44.4	33.0	33.2	32. 9	25.0	23.8	26.3
1984	43.0	43.6	42.5	45.6	46.2	45.0	32.9	31.5	34. 1	26.7	27.0	26.4
1985	43.7	44.2	43.3	46.4	46.8	46.0	34.4	34.2	34. 5	26.9	26.9	27.0
1986	44.0	44.1	43.8	46.8	46.9	46.8	36.3	35.9	36. 6	25.3	24.9	25.8
1987	43.6	43.1	44.0	46.0	45.7	46.2	35.9	32.4	38. 8	26.7	27.1	26.2
1988	43.6	43.7	43.6	46.4	46.4	46.5	33.3	34.7	32. 1	28.0	26.5	29.6
1989	43.8	43.9	43.7	47.2	47.1	47.2	34.6	34.0	35. 1	27.0	27.3	26.7
1990	44.5	43.7	45.3	48.3	47.3	49.3	36.1	35.0	36. 9	23.4	22.9	23.9
1991	45.3	44.4	46.2	49.3	48.8	49.9	35.3	32.0	38. 2	23.9	23.1	24.8
1992	48.9	48.2	49.6	53.3	52.6	53.9	36.2	34.9	37. 2	28.5	27.2	30.1
1993	51.0	49.5	52.5	55.6	54.7	56.6	40.0	37.0	42. 5	29.7	26.9	33.1
1994	52.1	49.8	54.3	57.1	54.9	59.3	41.8	40.3	43. 0	31.0	28.0	34.6
1995	54.1	52.3	55.8	59.8	57.5	62.1	45.1	45.3	44. 8	28.7	26.7	30.9
1996	56.5	54.5	58.5	62.0	60.3	63.7	48.1	47.9	48. 3	31.1	28.1	35.0
1997	57.1	54.9	59.4	63.3	61.3	65.3	46.6	43.0	49. 6	33.3	30.7	36.4
1998	57.8	54.6	61.0	64.1	61.3	66.9	49.9	46.8	52. 6	32.5	29.3	36.3
1999	58.0	54.7	61.3	63.9	60.7	67.0	51.3	45.9	55. 5	31.2	27.4	35.0
2000	58.3	55.1	61.5	64.1	60.5	67.7	52.7	50.4	54. 6	32.8	29.0	36.6
2001	58.4	54.4	62.5	64.8	60.5	69.1	50.5	46.7	53. 6	32.2	28.2	36.4
2002	58.0	54.5	61.6	65.8	62.0	69.5	53.4	51.8	54. 6	30.9	28.3	34.1
2003	57.4	53.8	61.1	65.5	61.9	69.2	51.2	49.6	52. 5	31.1	27.9	34.9
2004	57.3	53.4	61.3	64.7	60.8	68.6	51.9	49.3	54. 0	32.3	27.9	37.7
2005	56.7	52.1	61.4	64.3	59.7	68.9	49.0	41.9	55. 1	32.8	31.8	34.0
2006	57.8	53.3	62.4	66.3	62.1	70.4	49.9	44.8	54. 3	31.7	28.3	35.9

! Interpret data with caution (estimates are unstable).

[1] Included in the totals but not shown separately are estimates for those from other racial/ethnic categories.

Note: *Some college* also includes those with a bachelor's degree or higher. Prior to 1992, *some college* referred to those who completed 1 or more years of college; beginning in 1992, the term referred to those who completed any college at all. In 1994, the survey instrument for the Current Population Survey (CPS) was changed and weights were adjusted. Some estimates are revised from previous publications. Race categories exclude persons of Hispanic ethnicity.

Source: U.S. Department of Commerce, Census Bureau, Current Population Survey (CPS), March and Annual Social and Economic Supplement, 1971–2006.

RATIOS OF ONE-TEACHER SCHOOLS TO ALL SCHOOLS AND TEACHERS IN
THESE SCHOOLS TO ALL TEACHERS, 1917–1947

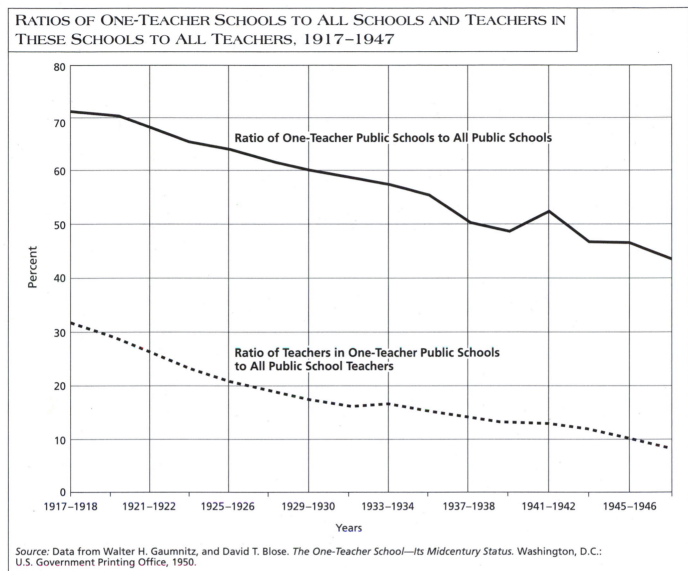

Source: Data from Walter H. Gaumnitz, and David T. Blose. *The One-Teacher School—Its Midcentury Status.* Washington, D.C.:
U.S. Government Printing Office, 1950.

© Infobase Publishing

Glossary

academy A private secondary school. Academies first gained popularity in the 1700s. Most offered a classical education to boys, but some instructed girls in basic academic skills and social refinement. Some academies were boarding schools.

achievement gap A disparity in academic performance between two population groups. Achievement gaps have been measured, for example, between whites and blacks and between whites and Hispanics.

affirmative action Policies and initiatives to increase the participation of minorities and women in education and employment, especially in fields in which they have been underrepresented.

American Missionary Association (AMA) An evangelical organization founded in 1846 to help African Americans acquire the full rights of citizenship. The AMA established primary schools for African Americans in the South during and after the Civil War, and it founded several historically black colleges and universities, including Atlanta University, Fisk University, and Howard University.

apprentice A youth bound by contract to an artisan for a period of years during which he or she will learn the master's trade. The apprentice system flourished in the colonial and early national periods.

Army Specialized Training Program (ASTP) A program to prepare army officers trained in scientific and technological fields during World War II. ASTP was active on college campuses from late 1942 until early 1944. The army also sponsored the Army Air Forces College Training Program on college campuses during the war to prepare pilots, meteorologists, and ground-crew personnel.

assimilation Replacing the customs, language, and beliefs of an ethnic minority with those of the predomi-nant culture. Assimilation, or amalgamation, was the goal of schools for American Indians in the 19th and early 20th centuries.

baby boom Any period of great elevation in the birth rate within geographical bounds. In the United States, the term usually refers to the post–World War II baby boom of 1946–64, when 76 million babies were born.

Brown v. Board of Education A group of court cases challenging the constitutionality of segregated public schooling considered collectively by the U.S. Supreme Court. In their unanimous decision, read on May 17, 1954, the justices declared that segregation was incompatible with equal educational opportunity.

busing (for school integration) The mandatory transport of children by bus among city neighborhoods to achieve a racial balance in the schools. Court-ordered busing began in 1971.

Carnegie unit A unit for measuring high school coursework developed by the Carnegie Foundation for the Advancement of Teaching, an organization established in 1905. One Carnegie unit was a course taught for 120 one-hour sessions or the equivalent in an academic year.

catechism Subject matter, nearly always religious, to be learned through memorization. Catechisms most often are written in a question-and-answer format.

charity schools Schools operated in the 19th century by Protestant and Catholic groups to educate poor urban children. Sunday schools were charity schools that offered instruction twice a day on Sunday and were popular from about 1800 to 1830. The curriculums at charity schools emphasized religion.

charter school A public school founded by parents or others in the community as an alternative to the existing public schools. Charter schools employ various approaches to education, but their students must meet the same standards of academic progress as those in traditional public schools.

Civilian Pilot Training Program   A flight-training program sponsored by the U.S. government and established in 1939 to increase the number of civilian pilots and improve military preparedness prior to U.S. entry into World War II.

cold war   The hostile, nonviolent ideological conflict involving the United States, the Soviet Union, and their respective allies that lasted roughly from 1946 until 1989, when the Soviet Union collapsed.

College Entrance Examination Board (CEEB)   An organization founded in 1900 to standardize college admission testing.

Committee on Public Information   An independent agency of the federal government established in April 1917, upon U.S. entry into World War I, by executive order under President Woodrow Wilson, to influence public opinion in favor of the war effort. In addition to other activities, the committee cooperated with the U.S. Bureau of Education and National Board for Historical Service to draft a wartime curriculum for the public schools. The committee ceased operation on August 21, 1919.

Committee on Secondary School Studies (Committee of Ten)   A committee formed in 1892 by the National Education Association to formulate national goals in secondary education and encourage consistency in high school curriculums nationwide.

common school   A name used in the 18th and 19th centuries for a public or district elementary school.

community college   A two-year institution of higher learning that addresses the needs of adults within commuting distance. Community colleges, which gained popularity after World War II, offer academic classes for college credit, two-year professional and technical courses, and cultural enrichment.

consolidation   The replacement of several small rural schools with a larger, centralized facility. School consolidation began in the Midwest in the early 20th century as a way to modernize rural education and make it more efficient and cost-effective.

constructivism   Jean Piaget's theory of learning. Piaget taught that children build knowledge from within and that their method of processing information progresses from sensory exploration to abstract thought, according to their interests and level of development.

contraband   An African American who fled slavery during the Civil War and sought protection with the Union army.

cooperative extension   A partnership among the federal, state, and county governments for delivering research-based education to the public, usually through the land-grant colleges and universities. Offerings typically relate to agriculture, food preparation and storage, home economy, family well-being, and community development.

de facto, de jure   Legal terms borrowed from Latin that mean "by custom" (*de facto*) and "by law" (*de jure*) and have been used to describe school segregation. *De facto* segregation results from patterns of residence, whereas *de jure* segregation is legislated.

domestic science   A vocational course of study developed in the late 19th century and applying science to household management. Girls studying domestic science learned, for example, to prevent disease by sanitizing surfaces, prepare economical and nutritious meals, and balance a family budget.

dust bowl   A large section of the southwestern United States that suffered from drought and wind erosion in the 1930s. Because economic conditions forced many families fleeing the dust bowl to adopt a nomadic lifestyle, the drought interrupted the education of thousands of children.

Elementary and Secondary Education Act (ESEA)   Federal legislation enacted April 11, 1965, and marking the start of increased government involvement in public education. ESEA funded building and instructional programs in schools with large percentages of low-income students.

Enlightenment   An 18th-century philosophical movement occurring in Europe and the American colonies that emphasized reason, science, and human goodness. Enlightenment thinking influenced a shift toward secularism in American education at the time of the Revolution.

Extended School Services   A program directed by the U.S. Office of Education during the 1942–43 school year that provided supervised recreation for the school-age children of working parents in the hours when school was closed.

Fair Deal   A legislative package proposed by President Harry S. Truman in 1949 that was intended to redistribute income and address social problems and included federal aid to education. Congress rejected most of the Fair Deal, including aid to education.

Freedmen's Bureau (Bureau of Refugees, Freedmen and Abandoned Lands)   A federal agency formed on March 3, 1865, to help African Americans make the transition from slavery to freedom. The Freedmen's Bureau distributed food and supplies, established schools, resettled people, and protected them in their efforts to find paying employment. The bureau was discontinued in 1869 and its programs were terminated by 1872.

Free Speech Movement   An organization formed at the University of California at Berkeley during the fall 1964 semester to coordinate student demonstrations to secure the right to free political expression.

functional illiteracy   Minimal ability to read and write. A person who is functionally illiterate lacks the ability to perform many simple tasks that are common to everyday life.

graded school   A school in which the student body has been divided into separate classes according to the level of instruction completed. Graded education began in U.S. schools in response to increasing numbers of students in the mid-19th century.

grammar school   In the colonial and early national periods, a grammar school was a publicly supported secondary school that prepared boys for college. Instruction often was in Latin and focused on classical languages and literature.

Great Depression   A catastrophic worldwide economic decline beginning in 1929 and lasting a decade

or more that led to widespread unemployment and poverty. The depression reversed important advancements in education in the United States.

high school   A secondary school that offers academic and vocational training to prepare students for college or employment. High schools became popular in the United States after 1860. Today they include grades nine or 10 through 12.

High School Victory Corps   A learning and service organization established by U.S. Commissioner of Education John W. Studebaker and active during World War II. Participants completed fitness and war-training classes in their schools and did volunteer patriotic and community-service work.

home schooling   Educating children at home. Home schooling gained popularity in the 1990s as an alternative to public and private schools. Home-schooling families follow varied educational approaches, but they must meet state curriculum requirements.

hornbook   A primer used in colonial schools that consisted of a sheet of basic reading exercises affixed to a board and protected by a transparent sheet of cow's horn.

inclusion (also called mainstreaming)   Placing a child with disabilities in a class with children without disabilities. Inclusion increased with passage of the Education for All Handicapped Children Act of 1975, which mandated that children with disabilities be educated with their non-disabled peers as much as possible.

instrumentalism   John Dewey's philosophy of learning by doing. Dewey taught that learning resulted from interaction between the individual and the environment, and knowledge served as an instrument for controlling this interaction.

intelligence quotient (IQ)   A measurement of intelligence based on the results of a standardized test. IQ is determined by dividing a person's mental age by his or her chronological age and multiplying the result by 100.

junior high school   A transitional school between elementary and high school. Junior high schools were developed to make the passage from childhood to adulthood more gradual and to introduce vocational and college-preparatory course work to students younger than high school age. The first junior high schools in the United States opened in 1909.

kindergarten A school or class in which young children develop manual dexterity and learn through games, songs, handwork, and other guided play. Kindergartens originated in Europe in the first half of the 19th century and gained acceptance in the United States in the 1870s.

Lancasterian school A school operating on the monitorial system developed by Joseph Lancaster, in which student monitors instructed less advanced pupils and maintained order, allowing one teacher to oversee the education of hundreds of children. Lancasterian schools gained popularity in U.S. cities in the first half of the 19th century.

land grant Federal public land transferred to a state for the purpose of supporting a college or university offering agricultural and mechanical instruction and military training. The land-grant system began in 1862 with passage of the first Morrill Act.

learning disability A condition that appears to affect the brain's ability to receive, process, or retain information and interferes with learning. Learning disabilities may be related to brain development; heredity and the environment may also play contributing roles.

life-adjustment education Instruction tailored to the needs of the majority of high school students in the late 1940s and early 1950s who planned neither to go to college nor to enter a skilled trade. Course offerings varied greatly, and as a result life-adjustment education never was clearly defined.

mental age A score on a standardized intelligence test that reflects the chronological age at which this level of performance is average.

National Japanese American Student Relocation Council A private organization founded on May 29, 1942, that helped Japanese-American students of college age whose education had been interrupted by federal exclusion orders to be placed in institutions of higher learning away from the West Coast.

natural philosophy The study of matter, energy, and physical forces that in the 19th century became the field of physics.

New Deal A series of laws enacted under President Franklin Delano Roosevelt that were intended to revive the economy and boost morale. Some New Deal initiatives, especially the Works Progress Administration, employed teachers, and others, including the Civilian Conservation Corps and National Youth Administration, offered academic and vocational instruction to young adults.

New England Primer A reader that was first printed in 1690 or earlier and used in schools in colonial New England. The text combined reading exercises with instruction in faith.

No Child Left Behind (NCLB) The 2002 reauthorization of the Elementary and Secondary Education Act. NCLB differs from the earlier law in its requirement that schools demonstrate measured student progress in reading and mathematics.

normal school A school for training teachers. The first normal school in the United States opened in Lexington, Massachusetts, in 1839. American teachers are now educated at colleges and universities.

open classroom A space that encourages children to learn independently at their own pace and according to their own interests. In the open classroom, desks, letter grades, and rigid schedules give way to learning stations, flexibility, and freedom of movement. Open education began in Great Britain and reached its height of popularity in the United States in the early 1970s.

Operation Head Start A program established under Title II of the Economic Opportunity Act of August 20, 1964, to prepare preschoolers from economically disadvantaged families for kindergarten. Participating children engage with one another socially and receive educational enrichment, health checkups, and nutritious meals and snacks.

Reconstruction Finance Corporation (RFC) An agency established in 1932 by President Herbert Hoover to make emergency loans to banks, railroads and other businesses at risk of collapsing during the Great Depression. The RFC disbursed $1.5 million in its first year.

retrench   To economize or cut back. In times of declining budgets, schools have coped by retrenching, or cutting staff and services.

schoolmaster, schoolmistress   A schoolmaster was a man, and a schoolmistress was a woman, hired to teach school. These terms were widely used in the 18th and 19th centuries but fell into disuse.

Serviceman's Readjustment Act (GI Bill of Rights; GI Bill)   Federal legislation enacted in 1944 that provided several financial benefits to the veterans of World War II, including tuition and living expenses for those wishing to attend institutions of higher learning. Approximately 2,323,000 veterans attended college on the GI Bill between 1944 and 1956, when the program was terminated.

settlement house   A community center, usually in a poor, urban, immigrant neighborhood, staffed by resident social workers. The first U.S. settlement houses were founded in 1886 and offered instruction in English, child care for working mothers, health services, classes, and cultural and recreational activities. Several hundred settlement houses continue to operate in the United States, although they no longer serve as residences for their personnel.

Students' Army Training Corps   A cooperative effort of the U.S. War Department and institutions of higher learning to train qualified officer candidates in skills needed by the military during World War I.

Students for a Democratic Society (SDS)   A national student political organization formed in 1962. SDS was active in the antiwar movement of the late 1960s and early 1970s; by 1972, it was defunct.

U.S. Bureau of Education   A federal bureau created in 1867 to track and report on educational thought and developments. In 1939, it was renamed the Office of Education; in 1980, its programs became the responsibility of the newly created Department of Education.

U.S. Cadet Nurse Corps   A program directed by the U.S. Public Health Service that subsidized the education of nurses to meet military and civilian needs during World War II. In return for tuition, books, uniforms, and a stipend, nurse cadets agreed to serve, after graduation, wherever the need was greatest for the duration of the war.

U.S. School Garden Army (USSGA)   A federal agency that enlisted 1.5 million schoolchildren to contribute to the nation's food supply during World War I by raising vegetables on home and community plots. The USSGA was dismantled soon after the November 11, 1918, armistice.

V-12 Navy College Training Program   A program that employed the resources and faculties of U.S. colleges and universities to prepare naval officers trained in scientific and technical fields during World War II. The V-12 program was active from December 1942 through June 1946.

voucher   A grant of public funds that enables a low-income student from a poorly performing public school to attend a private or parochial school.

work-study   Any program that allows students to combine academic study with paid employment, in order to earn money toward tuition or gain workplace experience.

Notes

Introduction

1. Sterling M. McMurrin, "A Crisis of Conscience," in *American Education Today,* eds. Paul Woodring and John Scanlon (New York: McGraw-Hill Book Co., 1963), p. 19.
2. William T. O'Hara, ed., *John F. Kennedy on Education* (New York: Teachers College Press, Columbia University, 1966), p. 133.
3. Walter Herbert Small, *Early New England Schools* (Boston: Ginn and Co., 1914), p. 109.
4. John McWilliams, *Recollections of John McWilliams* (Princeton, N.J.: Princeton University Press, 1921), p. 36.
5. O. L. Davis, Jr. "The Educational Association of the C.S.A.," *Civil War History* (March 1964): 68.
6. W. E. B. DuBois, *The Souls of Black Folk* (New York: Gramercy Books, 1994), p. 34.
7. David M. Kennedy, *Over Here: The First World War and American Society* (Oxford, U.K.: Oxford University Press, 2004), p. 55.
8. C. S. March, "The Education Program of the Civilian Conservation Corps," *School and Society* (March 31, 1934): 402.
9. Fred Kingsley Elder, "Chaos in Education—The Liberal Arts," *School and Society* (October 2, 1943): 241.
10. David Burner, *Making Peace with the Sixties.* (Princeton, N.J.: Princeton University Press, 1996), p. 177.
11. Diane Ravitch, *The Troubled Crusade: American Education, 1945–1980* (New York: Basic Books, 1983), p. 152.
12. "A Nation at Risk," *U.S. Department of Education* (URL: http://www.ed.gov/pubs/NatAtRisk/risk.html), p. 5.

1. "That Our Schools May Flourish" : Education in Colonial America: 1636–1792

1. Alexander S. Rippa, ed., *Educational Ideas in America: A Documentary History* (New York: David McKay Co., 1969), p. 49.
2. Alexander S. Rippa, *Education in a Free Society* (New York: Longman, 1997), p. 36.
3. Ibid.
4. Willard Elsbree, *The American Teacher: Evolution of a Profession in a Democracy* (New York: American Book Co., 1939), p. 33.
5. Ibid., p. 42.
6. Ibid., pp. 26–27.
7. Walter Herbert Small, *Early New England Schools* (Boston: Ginn and Co., 1914), p. 109.
8. Ibid., p. 110.
9. Tony W. Johnson and Ronald F. Reed, eds., *Historical Documents in American Education* (Boston: Allyn and Bacon, 2002), p. 11.
10. Edwin H. Brown, Jr. "First Free School in Queen Anne's County," *Maryland Historical Magazine* (March 1911): 2–3.
11. Ibid., p. 4.
12. Ibid.
13. David Humphreys, *An Historical Account of the Incorporated Society for the Propagation of the Gospel in Foreign Parts* (New York: Arno Press and the New York Times, 1969), pp. 232–233.
14. William Webb Kemp, *The Support of Schools in Colonial New York by the Society for the Propagation of the Gospel in Foreign Parts* (New York: Teachers College, Columbia University, 1913), p. 239.
15. Gerald L. Gutek, *Education in the United States: An Historical Perspective* (Englewood Cliffs, N.J., 1986), p. 132.

16. Colyer Meriwether, *Our Colonial Curriculum: 1607–1776* (Washington, D.C.: Capital Publishing Co., 1907), pp. 249–250.

17. "Dartmouth—A Brief History," *Dartmouth College* (URL: http://www.dartmouth.edu/home/about/history.html), p. 1.

2. Schooling a New Nation: 1783–1859

1. David Barton, *Benjamin Rush: Signer of the Declaration of Independence* (Aledo, Tex.: WallBuilder Press, 1999), p. 37.

2. Ibid.

3. Alexander S. Rippa, *Education in a Free Society* (New York: Longman, 1997), p. 54.

4. Allen Oscar Hansen, *Liberalism and American Education in the Eighteenth Century* (New York: Macmillan Co., 1926), p. 115.

5. E. Jennifer Monaghan, *A Common Heritage: Noah Webster's Blue-Back Speller* (Hamden, Conn.: Archon Books, 1983), p. 42.

6. Hansen, p. 239.

7. Noah Webster, *An American Dictionary of the English Language*, 3rd ed. (New York: S. Converse, 1830), p. iv.

8. Ibid., p. v.

9. Gerald L. Gutek, *Education in the United States: An Historical Perspective* (Englewood Cliffs, N.J., 1986), p. 44.

10. "A Brief History of the United States Naval Academy," *United States Naval Academy* (URL: http://www.usna.edu/VirtualTour/150years/), p. 1.

11. Carl F. Kaestle, *Pillars of the Republic: Common Schools and American Society, 1780–1860* (New York: Hill and Wang, 1983), p. 44.

12. Ibid., p. 38.

13. "A Canterbury Tale: A Document Package for Connecticut's Prudence Crandall Affair," *The Gilder Lehrman Center for the Study of Slavery, Resistance, and Abolition at the MacMillan Center* (URL: http://www.yale.edu/glc/crandall/05.htm), p. 2.

14. Stanley K. Schultz, *The Culture Factory: Boston Public Schools, 1789–1860* (New York: Oxford University Press, 1973), p. 192.

15. Ibid.

16. Lawrence A. Cremin, *American Education: The National Experience, 1783–1876* (New York: Harper & Row, 1980), p. 234.

17. "The Missionary Impulse," *Digital History* (URL: http://www.digitalhistory.uh.edu/native_voices/voices_display.cfm?id=45), p. 1.

18. John D. Pulliam and James J. Van Patten, *History of Education in America*, 7th ed. (Upper Saddle River, N.J.: Merrill, 1999), p. 93.

19. Sabrina Holcomb, "Answering the Call: The History of the National Education Association," *National Education Association* (URL: http://www.nea.org/neatoday/0601/neahistory.html), p. 3.

3. Adversity and Increase: The Civil War and Its Aftermath: 1860–1880

1. David W. Galenson, "Determinants of the School Attendance of Boys in Early Chicago," *History of Education Quarterly* (winter 1995): 397.

2. James Marten, *The Children's Civil War* (Chapel Hill: University of North Carolina Press, 1998), p. 54.

3. Christopher Clausen, "Some Confederate Ideas about Education," *Mississippi Quarterly* (spring 1977): 241.

4. James Marten, *The Children's Civil War* (Chapel Hill: University of North Carolina Press, 1998), p. 55.

5. L. Branson, *First Book in Composition, Applying the Principles of Grammar to the Act of Composing: Also, Giving Full Directions for Punctuation; Especially Designed for the Use of Southern Schools* (Raleigh, N.C.: Branson, Farrar and Co., 1863), p. 14.

6. O. L. Davis, Jr., "The Educational Association of the C.S.A.," *Civil War History* (March 1964): 72.

7. Ibid., p. 75.

8. Christopher Clausen, "Some Confederate Ideas about Education," *Mississippi Quarterly* (spring 1977): 245.

9. "Militia Act of July 17, 1862 [Extracts]," *University of Massachusetts* (URL: http://www.umass.edu/afroam/aa133c.html), p. 1.

10. Joe M. Richardson, *Christian Reconstruction: The American Missionary Association and Southern Blacks, 1861–1890* (Athens: University of Georgia Press, 1986), p. 48.

11. Ibid., p. 28.

12. Robert F. Engs, *Freedom's First Generation: Black Hampton, Virginia, 1861–1890* (New York: Fordham University Press, 2004), p. 39.

13. William F. Messner, "Black Education in Louisiana, 1863–1865," *Civil War History*, March 1976, p. 45.

14. Robert C. Morris, "Introduction," *Freedmen's Schools and Textbooks*, vol. 1: *Semi-Annual Report on Schools for Freedmen, by John W. Alvord, Numbers 1–10, January,*

1866–July, 1870, edited by Robert C. Morris (New York: AMS Press, 1980), N.p.

15. Carolyn L. Karcher, *The First Woman in the Republic: A Cultural Biography of Lydia Maria Child* (Durham, N.C.: Duke University Press, 1994), p. 496.

16. Jurgen Herbst, *The Once and Future School: Three Hundred and Fifty Years of American Secondary Education* (New York: Routledge, 1996), p. 63.

17. Michael Steven Shapiro, *Child's Garden: The Kindergarten Movement from Froebel to Dewey* (University Park: Pennsylvania State University Press, 1983), p. 77.

18. Frederick Rudolph, *The American College and University: A History* (Athens: University of Georgia Press, 1990), p. 252.

19. David Wallace Adams, *Education for Extinction: American Indians and the Boarding School Experience, 1875–1928* (Lawrence: University Press of Kansas, 1995), p. 29.

20. Ibid., p. 49.

4. Meeting Diverse Needs: 1881–1916

1. Robert A. Trennert, "Educating Indian Girls at Nonreservation Boarding Schools, 1878–1920," *Western Historical Quarterly* (July 1982): 277.

2. David Wallace Adams, *Education for Extinction: American Indians and the Boarding School Experience, 1875–1928* (Lawrence: University Press of Kansas, 1995), pp. 57–58.

3. Owen R. Lovejoy, "Will Trade Training Solve the Child-Labor Problem?" in Edna D. Bullock, comp., *Selected Articles on Child Labor* (White Plains, N.Y.: H. W. Wilson Co., January 1915), p. 91.

4. Selma Cantor Berrol, *Immigrants at Schools in New York City, 1898–1914* (New York: Arno Press, 1978), p. 55.

5. "Selections on Education from the Pronouncements of the Third Plenary Council of Baltimore," in *Education in the United States: A Documentary History,* ed. Sol Cohen, vol. 2. (New York: Random House, 1974), p. 1167.

6. William W. Cutler, III, "Cathedral of Culture: The Schoolhouse in American Educational Thought and Practice since 1820," *History of Education Quarterly* (spring 1989): 30.

7. Edwin L. Miller, "The Lunch-Room at the Englewood High School," *School Review* (March 1905): 205.

8. Neil R. Fenske, *A History of American Public High Schools, 1890–1990: Through the Eyes of Principals* (Lewiston, N.Y.: Edwin Mellen Press, 1997), pp. 10–11.

9. *Report of the Committee on Secondary School Studies Appointed at the Meeting of the National Educational Association, July 9, 1892, with the reports of the Conferences Arranged by This Committee and Held December 28–30, 1892* (Washington, D.C.: Government Printing Office, 1893), p. 52.

10. David B. Tyack, ed., *Turning Points in American Educational History* (Waltham, Mass.: Blaisdell Publishing Co., 1967), p. 355.

11. "Booker T. Washington's Atlanta Exposition Address," in Sol Cohen, *Education in the United States: A Documentary History,* vol. 3 (New York: Random House, 1974), p. 1673.

12. Ibid., p. 1674.

13. John Hope Franklin and Alfred A. Moss, Jr., *From Slavery to Freedom,* 6th ed. (New York: McGraw-Hill, 1988), p. 249.

14. Ibid.

5. Scientific Management: 1917–1929

1. Steven Jantzen, *Hooray for Peace, Hurrah for War: The United States During World War I* (New York: Facts On File, 1991), p. 3.

2. "Columbia's Dismissed Professors," *Literary Digest* (October 20, 1917): 24.

3. Thomas H. Briggs, *Secondary Education* (Washington, D.C.: Government Printing Office, 1919), p. 35.

4. David M. Kennedy, *Over Here: The First World War and American Society* (Oxford, U.K.: Oxford University Press, 2004), p. 54.

5. Ibid., p. 55.

6. Lewis Paul Todd, *Wartime Relations of the Federal Government and the Public Schools, 1917–1918* (New York: Teachers College, Columbia University, 1945), p. 60.

7. J. H. Francis, *The United States School Garden Army* (Washington, D.C.: Government Printing Office, 1919), p. 6.

8. William T. Bawden, *Vocational Education* (Washington, D.C.: Government Printing Office, 1919), p. 15.

9. *Cardinal Principles of Secondary Education: A Report of the Commission on the Reorganization of Secondary Education, Appointed by the National Education Association* (Washington, D.C.: Government Printing Office, 1918), pp. 10–11.

10. George D. Strayer, N. L. Engelhardt, and F. W. Hart, *Possible Consolidations of Rural Schools in Delaware* (Wilmington, Del.: Service Citizens of Delaware, 1919), p. 4.

11. Jon Reyhner and Jeanne Eder, *American Indian Education: A History* (Norman: University of Oklahoma Press, 2004), p. 148.

12. Raymond E. Fancher, *The Intelligence Men: Makers of the IQ Controversy* (New York: W. W. Norton and Co., 1985), p. 124.

13. Robert M. Thorndike with David F. Lohman, *A Century of Ability Testing* (Chicago: Riverside Publishing Co., 1990), p. 49.

14. Stephen Jay Gould, *The Mismeasure of Man* (New York: W. W. Norton and Co., 1981), p. 174.

15. Theodore A. Zornow and l. A. Pechstein, "An Experiment in the Classification of First-Grade Children through the Use of Mental Tests," *Elementary School Journal* (October 1922): 137.

16. Jean N. Nazzaro, *Exceptional Timetables: Historic Events Affecting the Handicapped and Gifted* (Reston, Va.: Council for Exceptional Children, 1977), p. 21.

6. The Hardest of Times: Schools Withstand the Great Depression: 1930–1940

1. David Tyack, Robert Lowe, and Elisabeth Hansot, *Public Schools in Hard Times: The Great Depression and Recent Years* (Cambridge: Harvard University Press, 1984), p. 39.

2. F. Raymond Daniell, "Crisis Threatens Alabama Schools, *New York Times*, 23 April 1933, sec. 2, p. 1.

3. Betty Lindley and Ernest K. Lindley, *A New Deal for Youth* (New York: Viking Press, 1938), p. 195.

4. Julia Wright Merrill, "What the Depression Has Done to Public Libraries," *Public Management* (May 1934): 137.

5. Dominic W. Moreo, *Schools in the Great Depression* (New York: Garland Publishing, 1996) p. 57.

6. Russell Freedman, *Franklin Delano Roosevelt* (New York: Clarion Books, 1990), p. 80.

7. "National Youth Administration," *Eleanor Roosevelt Historic Site* (URL: http://www.nps.gov/archive/elro/glossary/nya.htm), p. 2.

8. Benjamin Fine, "70,000 Adults Here Go to School Daily," *New York Times*, 9 May 1937, sec. 2, p. 7.

9. "'Glaring Inequalities,'" *Time* (URL: http://www.time.com/time/printout/0,8816,795224,00.html), p. 2.

10. Leonard Ephraim Meece, *Negro Education in Kentucky* (Lexington: University of Kentucky, March 1938), p. 172.

11. A. C. Monahan, "The Indian Education Program," *Indians at Work* (August 15, 1935): 12.

12. Ibid., p. 11.

7. "Every Life Is Affected" : Education for Victory in World War II: 1941–1946

1. *Educational Adjustments to War and Post-War Conditions* (Baltimore: City of Baltimore Department of Education, November 1943), p. 185.

2. Ibid., p. 103.

3. N. L. Engelhardt, Jr., *Education for the Air Age* (New York: Macmillan Co., 1942), p. 2.

4. Gerard Giordano, *Wartime Schools: How World War II Changed American Education* (New York: Peter Land, 2004), p. 27.

5. Ethel L. Cornell, *High School Adjustments to War Needs* (Albany: University of the State of New York Press, 1944), p. 5.

6. A. H. Bryan, "The Highschool in Wartime," *Journal of the National Education Association* (February 1942): 60.

7. William H. Johnson, "Chicago Public Schools Contribute to the War Effort," *Chicago Schools Journal* (January–June 1943): 52.

8. R. R. Palm, *War Policies for American Schools* (Los Angeles County, Calif.: Office of the County Superintendent of Schools, March 1942), p. 9.

9. *From Camp to College: The Story of Japanese American Student Relocation* (Philadelphia: National Japanese American Student Relocation Council, n.d.), *unnumbered page.*

10. Headquarters Western Defense Command, Office of the Commanding General, Presidio of San Francisco, California, "Public Proclamation No. 21," December 19, 1944, p. 1.

11. Sallie B. Marks, "Educational News and Editorial Comment," *Elementary School Journal* (April 1943): 442.

12. Carolyn Alison, "V-12: The Navy College Training Program," *V-12 Program* (URL: http://homepages.rootsweb.com/~uscnrotc/V-12/v12-his.htm), p. 2.

13. Raymond Walters, "Facts and Figures of Colleges at War," *Annals of the American Academy of Political and Social Science* (January 1944): 13.

14. Alison p. 2.

8. Toward Equal Educational Opportunity for All: 1946–1963

1. U.S. Department of Health, Education and Welfare. *Vitalizing Secondary Education* (Washington, D.C.: U.S. Government Printing Office, 1951), p. 32.
2. Ibid., pp. 32–33.
3. Arthur Bestor, *The Restoration of Learning: A Program for Redeeming the Unfulfilled Promise of American Education* (New York: Alfred A. Knopf, 1955), p. 4.
4. H. G. Rickover, *Education and Freedom* (New York: E. P. Dutton and Co., 1959), p. 146.
5. James Bryant Conant, *The American High School Today* (New York: McGraw-Hill, 1959), p. 19.
6. James Bryant Conant, *Slums and Suburbs: A Commentary on Schools in Metropolitan Areas* (New York: McGraw-Hill, 1961), p. 2.
7. Elise H. Martens, *State Legislation for Education of Exceptional Children* (Washington, D.C.: Federal Security Agency and U.S. Office of Education, 1949), p. 3.
8. Paul A. Witty, "Who Are the Gifted?" in *Education for the Gifted*, edited by Nelson B. Henry (Chicago: University of Chicago Press, 1958), p. 62.
9. Samuel A. Kirk, *Educating Exceptional Children* (Boston: Houghton Mifflin Co., 1962), p. 263.
10. *Brown v. Board of Education*, 347 U.S. 483 (1954).
11. *Brown v. Board of Education*, 349 U.S. 294 (1955).
12. Juan Williams, *Eyes on the Prize: America's Civil Rights Years, 1954–1965* (New York: Viking, 1987), p. 215.
13. Benjamin Muse, *Ten Years of Prelude: The Story of Integration Since the Supreme Court's 1954 Decision* (New York: Viking Press, 1964), p. 267.
14. Williams, p. 195.

9. Turbulent Years: 1963–1980

1. Diane Ravitch, *The Troubled Crusade: American Education, 1945–1980* (New York: Basic Books, 1983), p. 143.
2. Lyndon B. Johnson, "State of the Union Address, January 8, 1964," *State of the Union* (URL: http://stateoftheunion.onetwothree.net/texts/19640108.html), p. 2.
3. Sol Cohen, *Education in the United States: A Documentary History*, vol. 5 (New York: Random House, 1974), p. 3373.
4. "The *Green* Decision of 1968," *Virginia Historical Society* (URL: http://www.vahistorical.org/civilrights/green.htm), p. 1.
5. Ravitch, p. 176.

6. Gerald L. Gutek, *Education in the United States: An Historical Perspective* (Englewood Cliffs, N.J.: Prentice-Hall, 1986), p. 298.
7. Roger I. Abrams, "Not One Judge's Opinion: Morgan v. Hennigan and the Boston Schools," *Harvard Educational Review* (November 1975): 9.
8. "Education: Morgan vs. Hennigan," *Massachusetts Historical Society* (URL: http://www.masshist.org/longroad/02education/morgan.htm), p. 1.
9. David Burner, *Making Peace with the Sixties* (Princeton, N.J.: Princeton University Press, 1996), p. 141.
10. *The Report of the President's Commission on Campus Unrest* (Washington, D.C.: U.S. Government Printing Office, 1970), p. 459.
11. Ravitch, p. 274.
12. Estelle Fuchs and Robert J. Havighurst, *To Live on This Earth: American Indian Education* (Garden City, N.Y.: Doubleday, 1972), p. 299.
13. Francis Paul Prucha, *The Great Father: The United States Government and the American Indian*, vol. 2 (Lincoln: University of Nebraska Press, 1984), p. 1144.
14. Arlene Silberman, "Excitement in North Dakota," in Charles E. Silberman, *The Open Classroom Reader* (New York: Random House, 1973), p. 45.
15. Ravitch, p. 308.

10. The Learning Society: 1980–2008

1. Catherine O'Neill, "A Syllabus for Education," *Washington Post Book World*, 20 April 1980, p. 15.
2. "Findings," *U.S. Department of Education* (URL: http://www.ed.gov/pubs/NatAtRisk/findings.html), p. 1.
3. Ibid.
4. "Recommendations," *U.S. Department of Education* (URL: http://www.ed.gov/pubs/NatAtRisk/recomm.html), p. 1.
5. "A Nation at Risk," *U.S. Department of Education* (URL: http://www.ed.gov/pubs/NatAtRisk/risk.html); p. 6.
6. Jennifer Hochschild and Nathan Scovronick, *The American Dream and the Public Schools* (New York: Oxford University Press, 2003), p. 117.
7. "Mission Statement," *Nueva Esperanza Academy Charter High School* (URL: http://www.neacademy.org/home.aspx), p. 1.
8. Paul Jones and Gene Gloeckner, "First-Year College Performance: A Study of Home School Graduates

and Traditional School Graduates," *The Journal of College Admissions* (spring 2004): 20.

9. "Regents Approve 'Dual Admissions' Plan, Expanding UC Access for High-Achieving Students," *University of California Office of the President Newsroom* (URL: http://www.ucop.edu/news/archives/2001/july-19art2.htm), p. 1.

10. Patrice Hill, "Income Gap Grows in U.S.," *Washington Times* (URL: http://washingtontimes.com/functions/print.php?StoryID=20050730-114005-1449r), p. 1.

Bibliography

Abbott, Allan. "'In These Bad Days.'" *Teachers College Record* 42, no. 4 (January 1941): 334–339.

Abbott, Grace. *The Immigrant and the Community.* New York: Century Co., 1917.

Abrams, Roger I. "Not One Judge's Opinion: *Morgan v. Hennigan* and the Boston Schools." *Harvard Educational Review* 45, no. 4 (November 1975): 5–16.

Adams, David Wallace. *Education for Extinction: American Indians and the Boarding School Experience, 1875–1928.* Lawrence: University Press of Kansas, 1995.

Adams, Olga. "Educational News and Editorial Comment." *Elementary School Journal* 43, no. 10 (June 1943): 563–575.

Alison, Carolyn. "V-12: The Navy College Training Program." *V-12 Program.* Available online. URL: http://homepages.rootsweb.com/~uscnrotc/V-12/v12-hit.htm. Downloaded on May 1, 2007.

Alliance for Excellence: Librarians Respond to A Nation at Risk. Washington, D.C.: U.S. Government Printing Office, July 1984.

Americanization as a War Measure: Report of a Conference Called by the Secretary of the Interior, and Held in Washington, April 13, 1918. Washington, D.C.: Government Printing Office, 1918.

Andrews, Charles C. *The History of the New-York African Free Schools.* New York: Negro Universities Press, 1969.

Antin, Mary. *At School in the Promised Land.* Boston: Houghton Mifflin, 1912.

Armstrong, Samuel Chapman. *Armstrong's Ideas on Education for Life.* Hampton, Va.: Hampton Institute Press, 1940.

———. *The Indian Question.* Hampton, Va.: Normal School Steam Press, 1883.

Ashcroft, Samuel C. "Exceptionality and Adjustment," in *Exceptional Children in the Schools,* edited by Lloyd M. Dunn. New York: Holt, Rinehart and Winston, 1963, 521–556.

Baltimore Department of Education. *Educational Adjustments to War and Post-War Conditions.* Baltimore: City of Baltimore Department of Education, November 1943.

Barth, Roland S. *Open Education and the American School.* New York: Agathon Press, 1972.

Barton, David. *Benjamin Rush: Signer of the Declaration of Independence.* Aledo, Tex.: WallBuilder Press, 1999.

Bawden, William T. *Vocational Education.* Washington, D.C.: Government Printing Office, 1919.

Beals, Melba Pattillo. *Warriors Don't Cry: A Searing Memoir of the Battle to Integrate Little Rock's Central High.* New York: Washington Square Press, 1994.

Beard, Charles A., and William G. Carr. "The Schools Weathering a Storm." *Journal of the National Education Association,* 24, no. 5 (May 1935): 149–152.

Bergstrom, Amy, Linda Miller Cleary, and Thomas D. Peacock. *The Seventh Generation: Native Students Speak about Finding the Good Path.* Charleston, W.Va.: Clearinghouse on Rural Education and Small Schools, 2003.

Berrol, Selma Cantor. *Immigrants at School in New York City, 1898–1914.* New York: Arno Press, 1978.

Bestor, Arthur. *Educational Wastelands: The Retreat from Learning in Our Public Schools.* Urbana: University of Illinois Press, 1985.

———. *The Restoration of Learning: A Program for Redeeming the Unfulfilled Promise of American Education.* New York: Alfred A. Knopf, 1955.

Biggs, Fannie B. "The Teacher's Side of It." *New York Times,* February 2, 1934, 16.

Boler, John F. "Behind the Protests at Berkeley," in *Revolution at Berkeley,* edited by Michael V. Miller and Susan Gilmore. New York: Dial Press, 1965, 107–115.

"Booker T. Washington's Atlanta Exposition Address," in *Education in the United States: A Documentary History,* vol. 3, edited by Sol Cohen. New York: Random House, 1974, 1,672–1,675.

Branson, L. *First Book in Composition, Applying the Principles of Grammar to the Act of Composing; Also, Giving Full Direction for Punctuation; Especially Designed for the Use of Southern Schools.* Raleigh, N.C.: Branson, Farrar and Co., 1863.

Brickman, William W. "Anarchy vs. Freedom in Academia." *School and Society* 96, no. 2310 (October 26, 1968): 356.

———. "Student Power and Academic Anarchy." *School and Society* 96, no. 2300 (January 6, 1968): 6–7.

"A Brief History of the United States Naval Academy." *United States Naval Academy.* Available online. URL: http://www.usna.edu/VirtualTour/150years/. Downloaded on August 16, 2006.

Briggs, Thomas H. *Secondary Education.* Washington, D.C.: Government Printing Office, 1919.

Brim, Orville G. "The Curriculum Problem in Rural Elementary Schools." *Elementary School Journal* 23, no. 8 (April 1923): 586–599.

Brown, Edwin H., Jr. "First Free School in Queen Anne's County." *Maryland Historical Magazine* 6, no. 1 (March 1911): 1–15.

Bryan, A. H. "The Highschool in Wartime." *Journal of the National Education Association* 31, no. 2 (February 1942): 60–61.

Buisson, Ferdinand E. "The Free School System." *Circulars of Information of the Bureau of Education: No. 5, 1879.* Washington, D.C.: Government Printing Office, 1879.

Burner, David. *Making Peace with the Sixties.* Princeton, N.J.: Princeton University Press, 1996.

Burton, Warren. *The District School as It Was.* New York: T. Y. Crowell Co., 1928.

Butler, Vera M. *Education as Revealed by New England Newspapers Prior to 1850.* n.p., 1935.

Caire, Kaleem M. S. "The Truth about Vouchers." *Educational Leadership* 59, no. 7 (April 2002): 38–42.

Calhoun, Daniel, ed. *The Educating of Americans: A Documentary History.* New York: Houghton Mifflin, 1969.

Cardinal Principles of Secondary Education: A Report of the Commission on the Reorganization of Secondary Education, Appointed by the National Education Association. Washington, D.C.: Government Printing Office, 1918.

Carlson, Avis D. "Deflating the Schools." *Harper's Monthly Magazine* 167, no. 5 (November 1933): 705–714.

Carmichael, O. C. "Some Educational Frontiers." *School and Society* 68, no. 1761 (September 25, 1948): 193–96.

Carter, Hodding. "Desegregation Does Not Mean Integration," in *Integration vs. Segregation,* edited by Hubert H. Humphrey. New York: Thomas Y. Crowell, 1964.

Cassell, George F. "English and Its Value to Our Schools." *Texas Outlook* 14, no. 8 (August 1930): 42–43.

Castor, G. M. "Punishments." *North-Western Journal of Education* 1, no. 9 (April 1891): 250–251.

Chaudron, A. de V. *Chaudron's Spelling Book, Carefully Prepared for Family and School Use.* Mobile, Ala.: S. H. Goetzel, 1865.

Chavous, Kevin P. *Saving Our Children: Charter Schools and the Reform of American Public Education.* Sterling, Va.: Capital Books, 2004.

Clausen, Christopher. "Some Confederate Ideas about Education." *Mississippi Quarterly* 30, no. 2 (spring 1977): 235–247.

Cohen, Ronald D. *Children of the Mill: Schooling and Society in Gary, Indiana, 1906–1960.* Bloomington: Indiana University Press, 1990.

Cohen, Sol., ed. *Education in the United States: A Documentary History.* 5 vols. New York: Random House, 1974.

Coleman, James S. "Equal Schools or Equal Students?" *Public Interest,* no. 4 (summer 1966): 70–75.

College Entrance Examination Board. *The Work of the College Entrance Examination Board, 1901–1925.* Boston: Ginn and Co., 1926.

Collier, John. Introduction. *Indians at Work* 3, no. 1 (August 15, 1935): 1–7.

Collins, Denis. "The Beleaguered Teacher: Flare-Ups and Burnouts." *Washington Post Book World* 15 (April 20, 1980): 22–23.

"Columbia's Dismissed Professors." *Literary Digest* 55, no. 16 (October 20, 1917): 24.

Commission on Life Adjustment Education for Youth. *Vitalizing Secondary Education.* Washington, D.C.: U.S. Government Printing Office, 1951.

Conant, James Bryant. *The American High School Today.* New York: McGraw-Hill, 1959.

———. *Slums and Suburbs: A Commentary on Schools in Metropolitan Areas.* New York: McGraw-Hill, 1961.

Cooke, W. Henry. "The Segregation of Mexican-American School Children in Southern California." *School and Society* 67, no. 1745 (June 5, 1948): 417–421.

Cornell, Ethel L. *High School Adjustments to War Needs.* Albany: University of the State of New York Press, 1944.

Countryman, Gratia A. "Value of Library Must Be Sold to City Officials." *Public Management* 16, no. 5 (May 1934): 140–141.

Counts, George S. *Dare the School Build a New Social Order?* New York: John Day Co., 1932.

———. *Secondary Education and Industrialism.* Cambridge: Harvard University Press, 1929.

Craig, Gerald S. "Childhood Education and the World Crisis." *Teachers College Record* 43, no. 2 (November 1941): 108–119.

Cremin, Lawrence A. *American Education: The National Experience, 1783–1876.* New York: Harper and Row, 1980.

Cuban, Larry. "The Open Classroom." *Education Next* 4, no. 2 (spring 2004): 69–71.

———. *Oversold and Underused: Computers in the Classroom.* Cambridge: Harvard University Press, 2001.

———. *Teachers and Machines: The Classroom Use of Technology.* New York: Teachers College Press, 1986.

Cutler, William W., III. "Cathedral of Culture: The Schoolhouse in American Educational Thought and Practice Since 1820." *History of Education Quarterly* 29, no. 1 (spring 1989): 1–40.

Cyr, Frank W. "Looking Ahead in Rural Education." *Teachers College Record* 42, no. 8 (May 1941): 700–708.

Daniell, F. Raymond. "Crisis Threatens Alabama Schools." *New York Times,* April 23, 1933, 1, 3.

"Dartmouth—A Brief History." *Dartmouth College.* Available online. URL: http://www.dartmouth.edu/home/about/history.html. Downloaded on May 20, 2006.

David, Jane L. "Realizing the Promise of Technology: A Policy Perspective," in *Technology and Education Reform: The Reality behind the Promise,* edited by Barbara Means. San Francisco: Jossey-Bass, 1994.

Davis, O. L., Jr. "The Educational Association of the C.S.A." *Civil War History* 10, no. 1 (March 1964): 67–79.

Davis, William R. *The Development and Present Status of Negro Education in East Texas.* New York: Teachers College, Columbia University, 1934.

Deloria, Vine, Jr., and Daniel Wildcat. *Power and Place: Indian Education in America.* Golden, Colo.: Fulcrum Resources, 2001.

Dewey, John. *The School and Society.* Chicago: University of Chicago Press, 1899.

Downs, A. J. "Night School, English 101." *College Board Review,* no. 167 (spring 1993): 8–11, 26.

DuBois, W. E. B. *The Souls of Black Folk.* New York: Gramercy Books, 1994.

Duffus, Robert L. *Our Starving Libraries: Studies in Ten American Communities during the Depression.* Boston: Houghton Mifflin, 1933.

Duncan, Clyde. "Salaries of Public School Teachers." *Texas Outlook* 14, no. 6 (June 1930): 10.

Duncan, Richard R. "The Impact of the Civil War on Education in Maryland." *Maryland Historical Magazine* 61, no. 1 (March 1966): 37–52.

Dunlap, Knight. "Mental Tests," in *Readings from Progressive Education: A Movement and Its Journal,* vol. 1, edited by Stephen I. Brown and Mary E. Finn. Lanham, Md.: University Press of America, 1988, 123–133.

Dybvik, Ann Christy. "Autism and the Inclusion Mandate." *Education Next* 4, no. 1 (winter 2004): 43–49.

Eaton, John, Jr. *The Relation of the National Government to Public Education: An Address Delivered before the National Teachers' Association at Cleveland, Ohio, Aug. 17. 1870.* N.p., n.d.

Edelman, Marian Wright. "Winson and Dovie Hudson's Dream." *Harvard Education Review* 45, no. 4 (November 1975): 417–450.

The Editors. "Busing for Racial Balance." *Harvard Educational Review* 45, no. 1 (February 1975): 1–4.

Education in Colorado: A Brief History of the Early Educational Interests of Colorado, Together with the History of the State Teachers' Association, and Short Sketches of Private and Denominational Institutions. Denver: News Printing Co., 1885.

"Education: Morgan vs. Hennigan." *Massachusetts Historical Society.* Available online. URL: http://www.masshist.org/longroad/02education/morgan.htm. Downloaded on July 18, 2007.

Educational Adjustments to War and Post-War Conditions. Baltimore: City of Baltimore Department of Education, November 1943.

Educational Policies Commission. *American Education and the War in Europe.* Washington, D.C.: The National Education Association of the United States and the American Association of School Administrators, October 1939.

———. *A War Policy for American Schools.* Washington, D.C.: The National Education Association of the United States and the American Association of School Administrators, February 1942.

The Eighteenth Annual Report of the American Missionary Association. New York: American Missionary Association, 1864.

Elder, Fred Kingsley. "Chaos in Education—The Liberal Arts." *School and Society* 58, no. 1501 (October 2, 1943): 241–244.

Eliot, Charles W. "The New Education." *Atlantic Monthly* 23, no. 136 (February 1869): 203–220.

Elsbree, Willard S. *The American Teacher: Evolution of a Profession in a Democracy.* New York: American Book Co., 1939.

Engs, Robert F. *Freedom's First Generation: Black Hampton, Virginia, 1861–1890.* New York: Fordham University Press, 2004.

"Equal Schools in Virginia." *Crisis* 43, no. 11 (November 1936): 333.

Fancher, Raymond E. *The Intelligence Men: Makers of the IQ Controversy.* New York: W. W. Norton and Co., 1985.

Farish, Hunter Dickinson, ed. *Journal and Letters of Philip Vickers Fithian, 1773–1774: A Plantation Tutor of the Old Dominion.* Williamsburg, Va.: Colonial Williamsburg, 1943.

Fenske, Neil R. *A History of American Public High Schools, 1890–1990: Through the Eyes of Principals.* Lewiston, N.Y.: Edwin Mellen Press, 1997.

Filler, Louis, ed. *Horace Mann on the Crisis in Education.* Lanham, Md.: University Press of America, 1983.

"Findings." *U.S. Department of Education.* Available online. URL: http://www.ed.gov/pubs/NatAtRisk/findings.html. Downloaded on July 22, 2007.

Fine, Benjamin. "70,000 Adults Here Go to School Daily." *New York Times,* May 9, 1937, sec. 2, 7.

———. *Our Children Are Cheated: The Crisis in American Education.* New York: Henry Holt and Co., 1947.

First Ten Annual Reports of the American Board of Commissioners for Foreign Missions, with Other Documents of the Board. Boston: Crocker and Brewster, 1834.

Fleming, Robert. *The Elementary Spelling Book, Revised and Adapted to the Youth of the Southern Confederacy, Interspersed with the Bible Readings on Domestic Slavery.* Atlanta, Ga.: Franklin Steam Printing House, 1863.

Flexner, Abraham. *Universities: American English German.* New York: Oxford University Press, 1930.

Formisano, Ronald P. *Boston against Busing: Race, Class, and Ethnicity in the 1960s and 1970s.* Chapel Hill: University of North Carolina Press, 1991.

Forten, Charlotte L. *The Journals of Charlotte Forten Grimke.* New York: Oxford University Press, 1988.

Foster, C. R. "The Latimer Junior High School." *Elementary School Journal* 24, no. 4 (December 1923): 279–289.

Foster, Christine. "In a Class by Themselves." *Stanford* (November/December 2000): 76–81.

Fowlkes, John Guy. *Planning Schools for Tomorrow: The Issues Involved.* Washington, D.C.: U.S. Government Printing Office, 1942.

Fox, Lorene K. *The Rural Community and Its School.* Morningside Heights, N.Y.: King's Crown Press, 1948.

Francis, J. H. *The United States School Garden Army.* Washington, D.C.: Government Printing Office, 1919.

Franklin, Benjamin. "Proposals Relating to the Education of Youth in Pensilvania," in *The Papers of Benjamin Franklin.* Vol. 3: *January 1, 1745, through June 30, 1750,* edited by Leonard W. Larabee. New Haven, Conn.: Yale University Press, 1961.

Freedman, Russell. *Franklin Delano Roosevelt.* New York: Clarion Books, 1990.

Freeman, Frank N. "Sorting the Students." *Educational Review* 68, no. 4 (November 1924): 169–174.

From Camp to College: The Story of Japanese American Student Relocation. Philadelphia: National Japanese American Student Relocation Council, n.d.

Fryatt, F. E. "A Free Kindergarten." *Harper's New Monthly Magazine.* 57, no. 342 (November 1878): 801–806.

Fuchs, Estelle, and Robert J. Havighurst. *To Live on This Earth: American Indian Education.* Garden City, N.Y.: Doubleday, 1972.

Fuller, Wayne E. *One-Room Schools of the Middle West: An Illustrated History.* Lawrence: University Press of Kansas, 1994.

Galenson, David W. "Determinants of the School Attendance of Boys in Early Chicago." *History of Education Quarterly* 35, no. 4 (winter 1995): 371–400.

Gardner, W. H. "High Schools—Suggestions for Their Improvement." *North-Western Journal of Education* 1, no. 9 (April 1891): 253.

"Glaring Inequalities." *Time.* Available online. URL: http://www.time.com/time/printout/0,8816,759224,00.html. Downloaded on March 20, 2007.

Giordano, Gerard. *Wartime Schools: How World War II Changed American Education.* New York: Peter Lang, 2004.

Goodlad, John L. "The Schools vs. Education." *Saturday Review* (April 19, 1969): 59–61, 80–82.

Godson, Susan H., Ludwell H. Johnson, Richard B. Sherman, Thad W. Tate, and Helen C. Walker. *The College of William and Mary: A History.* Vol. 1: *1693–1888.* Williamsburg, Va.: King and Queen Press, 1993.

Goldberg, Miriam L. "Factors Affecting Educational Attainment in Depressed Urban Areas," in *Education in Depressed Areas,* edited by A. Harry Passow. New York: Bureau of Publications, Teachers College, Columbia University, 1963.

Goodwin, Edward J. "The Curriculum of a Small High School." *School Review* 3, no. 5 (May 1895): 268–281.

Gordon, Kate. "Wherein Should the Education of a Woman Differ from That of a Man." *School Review* 13, no 10 (December 1905): 789–794.

Gould, Stephen Jay. *The Mismeasure of Man.* New York: W. W. Norton and Co., 1981.

"The *Green* Decision of 1968." *Virginia Historical Society.* Available online. URL: http://www.vahistorical.org/civilrights/green.htm. Downloaded on June 25, 2007.

Greenberg, Cheryl Lynn. *"Or Does It Explode?" Black Harlem in the Great Depression.* New York: Oxford University Press, 1991.

Gutek, Gerald L. *Education in the United States: An Historical Perspective.* Englewood Cliffs, N.J.: Prentice-Hall, 1986.

Hall, G. Stanley, and Theodate L. Smith. "Curiosity and Interest," in Hall, G. Stanley, *Aspects of Child Life and Education.* Boston: Ginn and Co., 1907, 84–141.

Hall, Theodore. *Gifted Children: The Cleveland Story.* Cleveland: World Publishing Co., 1956.

Halleck, Reuben Post. "Why Do So Many Pupils Leave the Public High School during the First Year?" *School Review* 13, no. 7 (September 1905): 551–559.

Hampton Institute, Hampton, Va. *Ten Years' Work for Indians at the Hampton Normal and Agricultural Institute at Hampton, Virginia.* Hampton, Va.: Printed by Colored and Indian Students Trained in the Office of the Hampton Institute, 1888.

Handbook on Education and the War. Washington, D.C.: U.S. Government Printing Office, 1943.

Hansen, Allen Oscar. *Liberalism and American Education in the Eighteenth Century.* New York: Macmillan Co., 1926.

Harlan, Louis R., ed. *The Booker T. Washington Papers.* Vol. 2: *1860–89.* Urbana: University of Illinois Press, 1972.

Harris, William Torrey. *The Early Withdrawal of Pupils from School: Its Causes and Its Remedies.* St. Louis: Western Publishing and School Furnishing Co., 1872.

Hayashi, Patrick. "Affirmative Action: A Personal View." *College Board Review,* no. 162 (winter 1991–92): 19, 30–33.

Henry, David D. *What Priority for Education? The American People Must Soon Decide.* Urbana: University of Illinois Press, 1961.

Henry, Nelson B. "Educational News and Editorial Comment." *Elementary School Journal* 43, no. 6 (February 1943): 317–328.

Herbst, Jurgen. *The Once and Future School: Three Hundred and Fifty Years of American Secondary Education.* New York: Routledge, 1996.

Herrick, Cheesman A. "Commercial Education in Secondary Schools." *Education Review* 52, no. 3 (October 1916): 247–264.

Herrick, Virgil E. "Educational News and Editorial Comment." *Elementary School Journal* 43, no. 3 (November 1942): 129–741.

Hess, Frederick M., and Chester E. Finn, Jr. "Crash Course." *Education Next* (fall 2007). Available online. URL: http://www.hoover.org/publications/ed-next/9223491.html. Downloaded on August 31, 2007.

"Highlights from Denver Speeches." *Journal of the National Education Association* 31, no. 6 (September 1942): 17.

Hill, Patrice. "Income Gap Grows in U.S." *Washington Times.* Available online. URL: http:washingtontimes.com/functions/print.php?StoryID=20050730-114005-1449r. Downloaded on July 4, 2006.

Hochschild, Jennifer, and Nathan Scovronick. *The American Dream and the Public Schools.* New York: Oxford University Press, 2003.

Hofstadter, Richard, and Wilson Smith, eds. *American Higher Education: A Documentary History.* Vol. 2. Chicago: University of Chicago Press, 1961.

Hogan, David. "The Market Revolution and Disciplinary Power: Joseph Lancaster and the Psychology of the Early Classroom System." *History of Education Quarterly* 29, no. 3 (fall 1989): 381–417.

Holcomb, Sabrina. "Answering the Call: The History of the National Education Association." *National Education Association.* URL: http://www.nea.org/neatoday/0601/neahistory.html. Downloaded on October 7, 2006.

Horn, John Louis. *The Education of Exceptional Children: A Consideration of Public School Problems and Policies in the Field of Differentiated Education.* New York: Century Co., 1924.

———. *Principles of Elementary Education.* New York: Century Co., 1929.

Horst, Samuel L., ed. *The Fire of Liberty in Their Hearts: The Diary of Jacob E. Yoder of the Freedmen's Bureau School, Lynchburg, Virginia, 1866–1870.* Richmond, Va.: Library of Virginia, 1996.

Huckaby, Elizabeth. *Crisis at Central High: Little Rock, 1957–58.* Baton Rouge: Louisiana State University Press, 1980.

Humphreys, David. *An Historical Account of the Incorporated Society for the Propagation of the Gospel in Foreign Parts.* New York: Arno Press and the New York Times, 1969.

Hutchinson, Woods. "Overworked Children on the Farm and in School," in Edna D. Bullock, comp., *Selected Articles on Child Labor.* White Plains, N.Y.: H. W. Wilson Co., January 1915, 112–115.

Indiana Department of Public Instruction. *The Gifted Child.* Indianapolis, 1958.

Institute for Government Research. *The Problem of Indian Administration.* Baltimore: Johns Hopkins University Press, 1928.

Jacoway, Elizabeth. *Turn Away Thy Son: Little Rock, the Crisis that Shocked the Nation.* New York: Free Press, 2007.

Jantzen, Steven. *Hooray for Peace, Hurrah for War: The United States during World War I.* New York: Facts On File, 1991.

"Japanese Who Get Clearance May Attend the University of Minnesota." *School and Society* 59, no. 1521 (February 1944): 135–36.

Johnson, Lyndon B. "State of the Union Address, January 8, 1964." *State of the Union.* Available online. URL: http://stateoftheunion.onetwothree.net/texts/19640108.html. Downloaded on July 18, 2007.

Johnson, Mauritz, Jr. "The Rise and Fall of Life Adjustment," in *American Education Today,* edited by Paul Woodring and John Scanlon. New York: McGraw-Hill Book Co., 1963.

Johnson, Palmer O., and Oswald L. Harvey. *The National Youth Administration.* Washington, D.C.: Government Printing Office, 1938.

Johnson, Tony W., and Ronald F. Reed, eds. *Historical Documents in American Education.* Boston: Allyn and Bacon, 2002.

Johnson, William H. "Chicago Public Schools Contribute to the War Effort." *Chicago Schools Journal* 44, nos. 5–10 (January–June 1943), 49–56.

Jones, Charles C. *The Religious Instruction of the Negroes in the United States.* New York: Negro Universities Press, 1969.

Jones, Hugh. *Present State of Virginia: Giving a Particular and Short Account of the Indiana, English, and Negroe Inhabitants of That Colony.* London: J. Clarke, 1724.

Jones, Jacqueline. *Soldiers of Light and Love: Northern Teachers and Georgia Blacks, 1865–1878.* Chapel Hill: University of North Carolina Press, 1980.

Jones, Paul, and Gene Gloeckner. "First-Year College Performance: A Study of Home School Graduates and Traditional School Graduates." *Journal of College Admission* no. 183 (spring 2004): 17–20.

Jordan, June B., ed. *Teacher, Please Don't Close the Door: The Exceptional Child in the Mainstream.* Reston, Va.: Council for Exceptional Children, 1976.

Kaestle, Carl F. *Pillars of the Republic: Common Schools and American Society, 1780–1860.* New York: Hill and Wang, 1983.

———, ed. *Joseph Lancaster and the Monitorial School Movement.* New York: Teachers College Press, 1973.

Karcher, Carolyn L. *The First Woman in the Republic: A Cultural Biography of Lydia Maria Child.* Durham, N.C.: Duke University Press, 1994.

Keithahn, Edward L. "Eskimo School." *Progressive Education* 9, no. 2 (February 1932): 136–37.

Keller, George C. "The Search for 'Brainpower.'" *Public Interest,* no. 4 (summer 1966): 59–69.

Kemp, William Webb. *The Support of Schools in Colonial New York by the Society for the Propagation of the Gospel in Foreign Parts.* New York: Teachers College, Columbia University, 1913.

Kennedy, David M. *Over Here: The First World War and American Society.* Oxford, U.K.: Oxford University Press, 2004.

Kennedy, John F. *Message from the President of the United States Relative to a Proposed Program for Education.* Washington, D.C.: U.S. Government Printing Office, 1963.

Kephart, Newell C. *The Slow Learner in the Regular Classroom.* Columbus, Ohio: Charles E. Merrill Books, 1960.

Kerfoot, John B. *An Address Delivered at the Commencement of the College of St. James, Washington County, Maryland, in 1862.* Baltimore: Joseph Robinson, 1862.

Kirk, Samuel A. *Educating Exceptional Children.* Boston: Houghton Mifflin Co., 1962.

Kirkpatrick, Marion G. *The Rural School from Within.* Philadelphia: J. B. Lippincott Co., 1917.

Knight, Edgar W., ed. *A Documentary History of Education in the South before 1860.* Vol. 5. *Educational Theories and Practices.* Chapel Hill: University of North Carolina Press, 1953.

Kohl, Herbert R. *The Open Classroom: A Practical Guide to a New Way of Teaching.* New York: New York Review, 1969.

Kozol, Jonathan. *Death at an Early Age: The Destruction of the Hearts and Minds of Negro Children in the Boston Public Schools.* Boston: Houghton Mifflin, 1967.

Kuschman, William E. "Education and Society in Disadvantaged Suburbia." *School and Society* 94, no. 2281 (November 12, 1966): 386–387.

Langstaff, John Brett, ed. *Harvard of Today from the Undergraduate Point of View.* Cambridge: Harvard Federation of Territorial Clubs at the Harvard Union, 1913.

Lawhead, Helen E. "Teaching Navajo Children to Read." *Progressive Education* 9, no. 2 (February 1932): 131–35.

Lenz, Frank B. "The Education of the Immigrant." *Educational Review* 51, no. 5 (May 1916): 469–477.

Leonard, George B. "How School Stunts Your Child." *Look* 32, no. 19 (September 17, 1968): 31–42.

Lessinger, Leon M. *Every Kid a Winner: Accountability in Education.* New York: Simon and Schuster, 1970.

Levin, Henry M. "Educational Choice and the Pains of Democracy," in Thomas James and Henry M. Levin, eds., *Public Dollars for Private Schools: The Case of Tuition Credits.* Philadelphia: Temple University Press, 1983.

Lindley, Betty, and Ernest K. Lindley. *A New Deal for Youth.* New York: Viking Press, 1938.

Locke, John. *An Essay Concerning Human Understanding.* New York: Prometheus Books, 1995.

Lovejoy, Owen R. "Will Trade Training Solve the Child-Labor Problem?" in Edna D, Bullock, comp., *Selected Articles on Child Labor.* White Plains, N.Y.: H. W. Wilson Co., January 1915, 89–96.

Mackie, Romaine P. *Education of Crippled Children in the United States.* Washington, D.C.: U.S. Government Printing Office, 1949.

Magill, Edward Hicks. *Sixty-Five Years in the Life of a Teacher.* Boston: Houghton Mifflin, 1907.

Malott, Deane W. "Will Liberal Education Survive?" *School and Society* 59, no. 1538 (June 17, 1944): 417–419.

Marcelli, Nino. "An Unfortunate Trend in School Music." *School and Society* 59, no. 1538 (June 17, 1944): 428–429.

Marks, Sallie B. "Educational News and Editorial Comment." *Elementary School Journal* 43, no. 8 (April 1943): 439–449.

Marsh, C. S. "The Educational Program of the Civilian Conservation Corps." *School and Society* 39, 1005 (March 31, 1934): 400–405.

Marten, James. *The Children's Civil War.* Chapel Hill: University of North Carolina Press, 1998.

Martens, Elise H. *State Legislation for Education of Exceptional Children.* Washington, D.C.: Federal Security Agency and U.S. Office of Education, 1949.

Martin, Edwin. "Integration of the Handicapped Child into Regular Schools," in *Mainstreaming: Origins and Implications,* edited by Maynard Reynolds. Reston, Va.: Council for Exceptional Children, 1977.

Massachusetts Advocacy Center. *Out of the Mainstream.* Boston: Massachusetts Advocacy Center, 1987.

McDonald, Timothy. "The False Promise of Vouchers." *Educational Leadership* 59, no. 7 (April 2002): 33–37.

McFarland, John W. *The Development of Life Adjustment Education in the United States with Special Reference to Texas.* Austin: Texas Study of Secondary Education, April 1952.

McMurrin, Sterling M. "A Crisis of Conscience," in *American Education Today,* edited by Paul Woodring and John Scanlon. New York: McGraw Hill Book Co., 1963, 17–25.

McWilliams, John. *Recollections of John McWilliams.* Princeton, N.J.: Princeton University Press, 1921.

Meece, Leonard Ephraim. *Negro Education in Kentucky.* Lexington: University of Kentucky, March 1938.

Melby, Ernest O., ed. *Mobilizing Educational Resources for Winning the War and the Peace.* New York: Harper and Brothers, 1943.

Meredith, James. *Three Years in Mississippi.* Bloomington: Indiana University Press, 1966.

Meriwether, Colyer. *Our Colonial Curriculum: 1607–1776.* Washington, D.C.: Capital Publishing Co., 1907.

Merrill, Julia Wright. "What the Depression Has Done to Public Libraries." *Public Management* 16, no. 5 (May 1934): 135–39.

Messner, William F. "Black Education in Louisiana, 1863–1865." *Civil War History* 22, no. 1 (March 1976): 41–59.

Meyer, Agnes E. *Journey through Chaos.* New York: Harcourt, Brace and Co., 1944.

"Military Act of July 17, 1862 [Extracts]." *University of Massachusetts.* Available online. URL: http://www.umass.edu/afroam/aa133c.html. Downloaded on November 15, 2006.

Miller, Edwin L. "The Lunch-Room at the Englewood High School." *School Review* 13, no. 3 (March 1905): 201–12.

Milson, Andrew J., Chara Haeussler Bohan, Perry L. Glanzer, and J. Wesley Null, eds. *Readings in American Educational Thought: From Puritanism to Progressivism.* Greenwich, Conn.: Information Age Publishing, 2004.

"Mission Statement." *Nueva Esperanza Academy Charter High School.* Available online. URL: http://www.neacademy.org/home.aspx. Downloaded on August 11, 2007.

"The Missionary Impulse." *Digital History.* Available online. URL: http://www. digitalhistory.uh.edu/native_voices/voices_display.cfm?id=45. Downloaded on August 20, 2006.

Missouri Department of Education. *Sixty-Fifth Report of the Public Schools of the State of Missouri.* Jefferson City, Mo.: Hugh Stephens Printing Co., n.d.

———. *Sixty-Sixth Report of the Public Schools of the State of Missouri.* Jefferson City, Mo.: Hugh Stephens Co., n.d.

Monaghan, E. Jennifer. *A Common Heritage: Noah Webster's Blue-Back Speller.* Hamden, Conn.: Archon Books, 1983.

Monahan, A. C. "The Indian Education Program." *Indians at Work* 3, no. 1 (August 15, 1935): 9–12.

———. *The Status of Rural Education in the United States.* Washington, D.C.: U.S. Government Printing Office, 1913.

Moreo, Dominic W. *Schools in the Great Depression.* New York: Garland Publishing, 1996.

Morris, Willie. *North toward Home.* Boston: Houghton Mifflin, 1967.

Morris, Robert C. *Reading, 'Riting, and Reconstruction: The Education of Freedmen in the South, 1861–1870.* Chicago: University of Chicago Press, 1981.

Morris, Robert C., ed. *Freedmen's Schools and Textbooks.* Vol. 1. *Semi-Annual Report on Schools for Freedmen.* New York: AMS Press, 1980.

Morrison, J. Cayce. "Some Issues for Postwar Elementary Education." *Elementary School Journal* 45, no. 1 (September 1944): 15–22.

Muse, Benjamin. *Ten Years of Prelude: The Story of Integration Since the Supreme Court's 1954 Decision.* New York: Viking Press, 1964.

"A Nation at Risk." *U.S. Department of Education.* Available online. URL: http://www.ed.gov/pubs/NatAtRisk/risk.html. Downloaded on July 23, 2007.

National Board for Historical Service. *Opportunities for History Teachers.* Washington, D.C.: Government Printing Office, 1917.

National Education Association of the United States. *Wartime Handbook for Education.* Washington, D.C.: National Education Association of the United States, January 1943.

"National Youth Administration." *Eleanor Roosevelt National Historic Site.* Available online. URL: http://www.nps.gov/archive/elro/glossary/nya.htm. Downloaded on March 12, 2007.

Nazzaro, Jean N. *Exceptional Timetables: Historic Events Affecting the Handicapped and Gifted.* Reston, Va.: Council for Exceptional Children, 1977.

Newman, Katherine. "Confessions from the Classroom." *Education Next* (summer 2007). Available online. URL: http://www.hoover.org/publications/ednext/7561652.html. Downloaded on August 31, 2007.

The Nineteenth Annual Report of the American Missionary Association. New York: American Missionary Association, 1865.

Nixon, Richard M. "Academic Freedom Today." *School and Society* 94, no. 2283 (December 10, 1966): 451–454.

O'Hara, William T., ed. *John F. Kennedy on Education.* New York: Teachers College Press, Columbia University, 1966.

Ohles, John F. "The University and the Unstudent." *School and Society* 96, no. 2310 (October 26, 1968): 360–361.

Olds, Henry. "Sometimes Children Are the Best Teachers." *Popular Computing* (mid-October 1984): 47–52.

Olfman, Sharna, ed. *All Work and No Play: How Educational Reforms Are Harming Our Preschoolers.* Westport, Conn.: Praeger, 2003.

O'Neill, Catherine. "A Syllabus for Education." *Washington Post,* April 20, 1980, 15–18.

Orcutt, Hiram. *The Parents' Manual; or, Home and School Training.* Boston: Thompson, Brown, and Co., 1874.

———. *Reminiscences of School Life.* Cambridge, Mass.: University Press, 1898.

———. *The Teacher's Manual; Containing a Treatise upon the Discipline of the School, and Other Papers Upon the Teacher's Qualification and Work.* Boston: Thompson, Bigelow, and Brown, 1871.

Orfield, Gary. *Must We Bus? Segregated Schools and National Policy.* Washington, D.C.: Brookings Institution, 1978.

Orr, Gustavus J. "The Needs of Education in the South." *Circulars of Information of the Bureau of Education: No. 2—1879.* Washington, D.C.: Government Printing Office, 1879.

Orton, Dwayne. "The Community College: Fad or Fundamental?" *School and Society* 68, no. 1772 (December 11, 1948): 401–405.

Osborne, Ernest G. "Education's Task in a World at War." *Teachers College Record* 43, no. 7 (April 1942): 538–547.

Palm, R. R. *War Policies for American Schools.* Los Angeles County, Calif.: Office of the County Superintendent of Schools, March 1942.

Paolucci, Beatrice. "A Look at Today's Homemaking Programs." *Bulletin of the National Association of Secondary-School Principals* 37, no. 196 (October 1953): 1–14.

Parsons, Edward S. "The Social Life of the Coeducational College." *School Review* 13, no. 5 (May 1905): 382–389.

Paschal, Billy J. "Goals for Space Age Education." *School and Society* 95, no. 2295 (October 28, 1967): 390–391.

Peabody, Elizabeth Palmer. "Kindergarten—What Is It?" *Atlantic Monthly* 10, no. 61 (November 1862): 586–593.

Perry, Clarence Arthur. *Wider Use of the School Plant.* New York: Charities Publication Committee, 1910.

Personal Justice Denied: Report of the Commission on Wartime Relocation and Internment Camps. Washington, D.C.: U.S. Government Printing Office, 1982.

Phillips, John Aristotle, and David Michaelis. *Mushroom: The Story of the A-Bomb Kid.* New York: William Morrow and Co., 1978.

Postman, Neil. *The End of Education: Redefining the Value of School.* New York: Alfred A. Knopf, 1995.

Powell, Lyman P. *History of Education in Delaware.* Washington, D.C.: Government Printing Office, 1893.

Pratt, Richard Henry. *Battlefield and Classroom: Four Decades with the American Indian, 1867–1904.* Lincoln: University of Nebraska Press, 1987.

"President Signs Landmark No Child Left Behind Education Bill." *The White House.* Available online. URL: http://www.whitehouse.gov/news/releases/2002/01/print/20020108-1.html. Downloaded on August 20, 2007.

Preston, Carleton E. "Are Our Schools Hitting the Mark?" *Educational Review* 51, no. 3 (March 1916): 275–285.

Price, J. St. Clair, "General Summary and Conclusions." *Journal of Negro Education* 1, no. 2 (July 1932): 325–335.

"The Problem of Student Nurses of Japanese Ancestry." *American Journal of Nursing* 43, no. 10 (October 1943): 895–896.

"Proceedings of the Department of Superintendence of the National Education Association for 1877." *Circulars of Information of the Bureau of Education: No. 2—1879.* Washington, D.C.: Government Printing Office, 1879.

Prucha, Francis Paul. *The Great Father: The United States Government and the American Indian.* Vol. 2. Lincoln, Neb.: University of Nebraska Press, 1984.

Public Proclamation No. 21. San Francisco: Headquarters of Western Defense Command, Office of the Commanding General, Presidio of San Francisco, California, December 17, 1944.

Pulliam, John D., and James J. Van Patten. *History of Education in America.* 7th ed. Upper Saddle River, N.J.: Merrill, 1999.

Rafferty, Max. *Suffer, Little Children.* New York: Devin-Adair Co., 1962.

Ravitch, Diane. *Troubled Crusade: American Education, 1945–1980.* New York: Basic Books, 1983.

Ray, Brian D. "Customization through Homeschooling." *Educational Leadership* 59, no. 7 (November 2002): 50–54.

Raywid, Mary Anne. *The Ax-Grinders: Critics of Our Public Schools.* New York: Macmillan, 1962.

"Recommendations." *U.S. Department of Education.* Available online. URL: http://www.ed.gov/pubs/NatAtRisk/recomm.html. Downloaded on July 22, 2007.

"Regents Approve 'Dual Admissions' Plan, Expanding UC Access for High-Achieving Students." *University of California Office of the President News Room.* Available online. URL: http://ucop.edu/news/archives/2001/july19art2.htm. Downloaded on August 14, 2007.

Reich, Rob. "Why Home Schooling Should Be Regulated," in *Home Schooling in Full View: A Reader,* edited by Bruce S. Cooper. Greenwich, Conn.: Information Age, 2005, 109–120.

Reid, Whitelaw. *After the War: A Southern Tour.* New York: Moore, Wilstach and Baldwin, 1866.

Report of the Advisory Committee on Education. Washington, D.C.: U.S. Government Printing Office, 1938.

Report of the Committee on Secondary School Studies Appointed at the Meeting of the National Educational Association, July 9, 1892, with the Reports of the Conferences Arranged by This Committee and Held December 28–30, 1892. Washington, D.C.: Government Printing Office, 1893.

Report of Resident Schools and Educational Camps for Unemployed Women. Washington, D.C.: U.S. Federal Emergency Relief Administration, May 1936.

The Report of the President's Commission on Campus Unrest. Washington, D.C.: U.S. Government Printing Office, 1970.

Reyhner, Jon, and Jeanne Eder. *American Indian Education: A History.* Norman: University of Oklahoma Press, 2004.

Rice, J. M. *Scientific Management in Education.* New York: Hinds, Noble and Eldredge, 1914.

Richardson, Joe M. *Christian Reconstruction: The American Missionary Association and Southern Blacks, 1861–1890.* Athens: University of Georgia Press, 1986.

Richardson, Martin D., and Le Roy M. Washington. "A Picture of Florida's Schools." *Crisis* 44, no. 9 (September 1937): 270–271.

Richmond, W. Kenneth. *Education in the U.S.A.: A Comparative Study.* London: Alvin Redman, 1956.

Rickover, H. G. *Education and Freedom.* New York: E. P. Dutton and Co., 1959.

Riessman, Frank. *The Culturally Deprived Child.* New York: Harper and Brothers, 1962.

———. *The Inner-City Child.* New York: Harper and Row, 1976.

Rippa, S. Alexander. *Education in a Free Society.* New York: Longman, 1997.

———, ed. *Educational Ideas in America: A Documentary History.* New York: David McKay Co., 1969.

Roberts, Isaac Phillips. *Autobiography of a Farm Boy.* Albany, N.Y.: J. B. Lyon Co., 1916.

Roby, Maud Frothingham. "Implications of the Present World Situation for the Elementary School." *Elementary School Journal* 43, no. 5 (January 1943): 267–272.

Rudd, Mark. "Columbia: Notes on the Spring Rebellion," in *The New Left Reader*, edited by Carl Oglesby. New York: Grove Press, 1969, 290–312.

Rudolph, Frederick. *The American College and University: A History*. Athens: University Press of Georgia, 1990.

———, ed. *Essays on Education in the Early Republic*. Cambridge, Mass.: Belknap Press of Harvard University, 1965.

Russell, David H. "The Elementary School Child and the War." *California Journal of Education* 11, nos. 3 and 4 (February and May 1943): 144–153.

Russell, John Dale, ed. *Higher Education under War Conditions*. Chicago: University of Chicago, 1943.

Ryan, W. Carson, Jr., and Rose K. Brandt. "Indian Education Today." *Progressive Education* 9, no. 2 (February 1931): 81–86.

Savio, Mario. "An End to History," in *The Berkeley Student Revolt: Facts and Interpretations*, edited by Seymour Martin Lipset and Sheldon S. Wolin. Garden City, N.Y.: Doubleday and Co., 1965.

Scantlin, Roy. *War Problems and Responsibilities of Missouri Schools*. Jefferson City, Mo.: Mid-State Printing Co., 1943.

Scheifele, Marian. *The Gifted Child in the Regular Classroom*. New York: Teachers College, Columbia University, 1953.

Schneir, Walter, and Miriam Schneir. "The Joy of Learning—in the Open Corridor." *New York Times Magazine* (April 4, 1971): 30–31, 72–80, 92–97.

"Selections on Education from the Pronouncements of the Third Plenary Council of Baltimore," in *Education in the United States: A Documentary History*, vol. 2, edited by Sol Cohen. New York: Random House, 1974, 1,166–1,171.

Shanker, Albert. "A Landmark Revisited." *Hoover Institution*. Available online. URL: http://www.hoover.org/publications/ednext/3352881.html. Downloaded on July 29, 2007.

Shapiro, Michael Steven. *Children's Garden: The Kindergarten Movement from Froebel to Dewey*. University Park: Pennsylvania State University Press, 1983.

Silber, Kate. *Pestalozzi: The Man and His Work*. London: Routledge and Kegan Paul, 1973.

Silberman, Arlene. "Excitement in North Dakota," in *The Open Classroom Reader*, edited by Charles E. Silberman. New York: Random House, 1973, 42–52.

Silberman, Charles E. *Crisis in the Classroom: The Remaking of American Education*. New York: Random House, 1970.

———. "Technology Is Knocking at the Schoolhouse Door." *Fortune* 74, no. 3 (August 1966): 120–25, 198, 203–205.

Siljestrom, P. A. *Educational Institutions of the United States*. New York: Arno Press and the New York Times, 1969.

Simmons, Warren. "A Stranger in Two Worlds." *Education Next* 4, no. 4 (fall 2004): 21–25.

Small, Walter Herbert. *Early New England Schools*. Boston: Ginn and Co., 1914.

Smedley, Tom. "Homeschooling for Liberty," in *Home Schooling in Full View: A Reader*, edited by Bruce S. Cooper. Greenwich, Conn.: Information Age, 2005, 69–74.

Stanley, Jerry. *Children of the Dust Bowl: The True Story of the School at Weedpatch Camp*. New York: Crown, 1992.

Stern, Edith M. "Jim Crow Goes to School in New York." *Crisis* 44, no. 7 (July 1937): 201–202.

Stetar, Joseph M. "In Search of Direction: Southern Higher Education after the Civil War," in *ASHE Reader on the History of Higher Education,* edited by Lester F. Goodchild and Harold S. Wechsler. Needham Heights, Mass.: Ginn Press, 1989, 237–261.

Stockwell, Thomas B., ed. *A History of Public Education in Rhode Island, from 1636 to 1876.* Providence, R.I.: Providence Press Co., 1876.

Strainchamps, Ethel. "The Plight of the Intellectual Girl," in *American Education Today,* edited by Paul Woodring and John Scanlon. New York: McGraw-Hill Book Co., 1963.

Strayer, George D., N. L. Engelhardt, and F. W. Hart. *Possible Consolidation of Rural Schools in Delaware.* Wilmington, Del.: Service Citizens of Delaware, 1919.

"Students Answer the Professor." *Crisis* 37, no. 10 (October 1930): 336–37, 356.

"The Students' Army Training Corps: Entire University Reorganized as Army Post—Soldiers in Khaki March to Class." *Vanderbilt Alumnus* 4, no. 1 (November 1918): 5–7.

Sutton, Jennifer. "Homeschooling Comes of Age." *Brown Alumni Magazine* 102, no. 3 (January/February 2002): 47–53.

Terman, Lewis M. *The Intelligence of School Children.* Boston: Houghton Mifflin Co., 1919.

"Think Straight." *Texas Outlook* 14, no. 6 (June 1930): 5.

Thorndike, Robert M., with David F. Lohman. *A Century of Ability Testing.* Chicago: Riverside Publishing Co., 1990.

Thurber, S. "Rigid Courses *versus* Optional Studies." *School Review* 3, no. 4 (April 1895): 206–211.

Tillotson, Dirk. "What's Next for New Orleans?" *High School Journal* 90, no. 2 (December 2006/January 2007): 69–74.

Tocqueville, Alexis de. *Democracy in America.* Vol. 1. New York: Vintage Books, 1954.

Todd, Helen M. "Why Children Work: The Children's Answer," in Edna D. Bullock, comp., *Selected Articles on Child Labor.* White Plains, N.Y.: H. W. Wilson Co., January 1915, 208–222.

Todd, Lewis Paul. *Wartime Relations of the Federal Government and the Public Schools, 1917–1918.* New York: Teachers College, Columbia University, 1945.

Trennert, Robert A. "Educating Indian Girls at Nonreservation Boarding Schools, 1878–1920." *Western Historical Quarterly* 13, no. 3 (July 1982): 271–290.

"Trying to Predict the Future." *Popular Computing* (mid-October 1984): 30–32, 35–36, 38, 43–44.

Tyack, David, Robert Lowe, and Elisabeth Hansot. *Public Schools in Hard Times: The Great Depression and Recent Years.* Cambridge: Harvard University Press, 1984.

Tyack, David B., ed. *Turning Points in American Educational History.* Waltham, Mass.: Blaisdell Publishing Co., 1967.

U.S. Bureau of Education. *Secondary Schools and the War.* Washington, D.C. U.S. Government Printing Office, January 1918.

U.S. Commission on Civil Rights. *The Navajo Nation: An American Colony.* Washington, D.C.: U.S. Commission on Civil Rights, 1975.

U.S. Department of Health, Education and Welfare. *Vitalizing Secondary Education.* Washington, D.C.: U.S. Government Printing Office, 1951.

U.S. President's Commission on Higher Education. *Higher Education for American Democracy.* New York: Harper and Brothers, 1948.

U.S. President's Committee on Civil Rights. *To Secure These Rights*. Washington, D.C.: U.S. Government Printing Office, 1947.

"The Value of Common School Education to Common Labor." *Circulars of Information of the Bureau of Education: No. 3—1879*. Washington, D.C.: Government Printing Office, 1879.

Van Sickle, J. H., John Whyte, and W. S. Deffenbaugh. *Public Education in the Cities of the United States*. Washington, D.C.: Government Printing Office, 1919.

Viteritti, Joseph P. "Coming Around on School Choice." *Educational Leadership* 59, no. 7 (April 2002): 44–48.

Walters, Raymond. "Facts and Figures of Colleges at War." *Annals of the American Academy of Political and Social Science* 231 (January 1944): 8–13.

Ward, John William. "The Trouble with Higher Education." *Public Interest*, no. 4 (summer 1966): 76–88.

Webster, Noah. *An American Dictionary of the English Language*. 3rd ed. New York: S. Converse, 1830.

Wedgeworth, Robert. "The Number of Functionally Illiterate Adults in U.S. Is Growing." *ProLiteracy*. Available online. URL: http://www.proliteracy.org/downloads/ProLiteracyStateOfLiteracy%2010-25-04.pdf. Downloaded on July 22, 2007.

Wesley, Edgar B. *NEA: The First Hundred Years*. New York: Harper and Brothers, 1957.

Wickersham, J. P., ed. *A History of Education in Pennsylvania*. Lancaster, Pa.: Inquirer Publishing Co., 1886.

Willey, Malcolm M. "The College Training Programs of the Armed Services." *Annals of the American Academy of Political and Social Science* 231 (January 1944): 14–28.

Williams, Clement C. "Higher Education Without Students." *School and Society* 59, 1536 (June 3, 1944): 385–387.

Williams, Juan. *Eyes on the Prize: America's Civil Rights Years, 1954–1965*. New York: Viking, 1987.

Willis, Scott. "Customization and the Common Good: A Conversation with Larry Cuban." *Educational Leadership* 59, no. 7 (April 2002): 6–11.

Winthrop, John. *The History of New England from 1630 to 1649*. Vol. 2. Edited by James Savage. Boston: Phelps and Farnham, 1826.

Witty Paul A. "Who Are the Gifted?" in *Education for the Gifted*, edited by Nelson A. Henry. Chicago: University of Chicago Press, 1958, 42–63.

Woodson, Carter G. "The Miseducation of the Negro." *Crisis* 38, no. 8 (August 1931): 266–267.

Young, Raymond Y. "Life Adjustment Education after Five Years." *Bulletin of the National Association of Secondary-School Principals* 37, no. 197 (November 1953): 64–60.

Zorbaugh, Harvey, Rhea Kay Boardman, and Paul Sheldon. "Some Observations of Highly Gifted Children." In *The Gifted Child*, edited by Paul Witty. Boston: D. C. Heath and Co., 1951, 86–105.

Zornow, Theodore A., and L. A. Pechstein. "An Experiment in the Classification of First-Grade Children through the Use of Mental Tests." *Elementary School Journal* 23, no. 2 (October 1922): 136–146.

Zylstra, Elizabeth. "A Year with Bobby." *Educational Leadership* 59, no. 3 (November 2001): 74–75.

Index

Locators in *italic* indicate illustrations. Locators in **boldface** indicate main entries/topics and biographies. Locators followed by *m* indicate maps. Locators followed by *t* indicate graphs and tables. Locators followed by *g* indicate glossary entries. Locators followed by *c* indicate chronology entries.

A

AAA. *See* Agricultural Adjustment Act
Abbott, Allan 195
Abbott, Grace 134, **326**
ABCFM. *See* American Board of Commissioners for Foreign Missions
abolitionism 31
"Academic Freedom Today" (Nixon) 250
academy 382*g*
accelerated programs 181
ACE. *See* American Council on Education
achievement gap 269–270, 277*c*, 382*g*
An Act Donating Public Lands to the Several States and Territories Which May Provide Colleges for the Benefit of Agriculture and the Mechanic Arts. *See* Morrill Act (1862)
activism. *See* student activism
An Act to amend the Laws in relation to Slaves and Free Persons of Color, South Carolina (1840) **299**
An Act to Compel Children to Attend School (Michigan, 1871) **303–304**
Acworth, New Hampshire 46–47
Addams, Jane 92, 100*c*, 111, **326**
adolescence (as developmental stage) 98–99, 101*c*
Adolescence (Hall) 99, 101*c*
adult education 154, 222, 229–230. *See also* community college
Advisory Committee on Education 158–159, 165*c*, 177–178
aeronautics xx
affirmative action 382*g*
　　Bakke case 238–239, 247*c*
　　Gratz v. Bollinger 271, 277*c*
　　Grutter v. Bollinger 271, 277*c*
　　and higher education 238–239
　　and immigration 281
　　Initiative 200 (Washington State) 271, 276*c*
　　overall effect of 271–272
　　Proposition 209 (California) 271, 276*c*
　　referenda against (1990s) 271, 276*c*
"Affirmative Action: A Personal View" (Hayashi) 281
African-American history 241–242
African Americans. *See also* integration; segregation
　　achievement gap xxiv, 269, 277*c*
　　Cadet Nurse Corps 190

Civil Rights Act (1964) 235–236
during Civil War xiv, 69*c*
college enrollment (1998) 276*c*
college enrollment after anti–affirmative action initiatives 271, 276*c*
colleges (late 1800s) xv, 66
colleges (mid-1800s) 27
colonial America 15–17
Columbia University antiwar protests 240–241
Prudence Crandall's school xiii, 30–31, 37*c*, 38*c*, **331**
education debate (1880s–early 1900s) 97–98
federal aid to education 207
Fifteenth Amendment *70*
Fourteenth Amendment 61, 71*c*
during Great Depression 159–161, *160*, 164*c*, 168, 170, 174, 176–178
industrial training (late 1800s) xv
Keyes v. School District No. 1 237
land-grant colleges for 96
as majority in urban areas 270–271
Manumission Society school 30, 36*c*
Morgan v. Hennigan 237–238
in North (1800s) xiii, 30, 36*c*, 37*c*
in North (early 1900s) 128
Oberlin College 27, 37*c*
poverty (1960s) xxii
in South (early 1800s) xi, xiii, 31–32
in South (early 1900s) 128, *128*, 132*c*, 140
Sunday schools 30
as teachers (1800s) 52
as teachers during Great Depression 178
as teachers in Alabama (1917) 128, 132*c*
as teachers in Virginia (1917) 135
Tuskegee Institute 103–104
in urban ghettos 210
urban migration (World War I era) 128
in V-12 Program 188, 193*c*
in Washington, D.C. 72
during World War I 123, 127–128
African Methodist Episcopal Church 27
after-school programs 193*c*
After the War: A Southern Tour (Reid) 77–78
Agricultural Adjustment Act (AAA) 151
agricultural experiment stations 96
agricultural instruction 65, 69*c*
agricultural research 96–97
agriculture 121–123, 132*c*, 203
AIM. *See* American Indian Movement
air-raid drills 197
Alabama 127–128, 132*c*, 149, 163*c*, 170. *See also* University of Alabama
Alabama National Guard 216

Alaska 169
Alcatraz Island occupation 242, 246*c*
Alderman, L. R. 140
Alexander, Margaret Walker 255
Alford, Thomas Wildcat 104
Alliance for Excellence: Librarians Respond to A Nation at Risk 279–280
"All Work and No Play" (Olfman) 285–286
alphabet method 24
Alpha test 130
AMA. *See* American Missionary Association
amalgamation xiii, 32
American Board of Commissioners for Foreign Missions (ABCFM) xiii, 32, 37*c*
American Council on Education (ACE) 186, 190–191, 194*c*
American Dictionary of the English Language (Webster) xii, 24, 37*c*
American Education and the War in Europe (Educational Policies Commission) 178
American Friends Service Committee 183, 193*c*
American Higher Education: A Documentary History, vol. 2 (Hofstadter and Smith, eds.) 79
The American High School Today (Conant) 210, 219*c*, 228–229
American Indian boarding schools
　　during 1870s xv, 67–68
　　during 1880s–early 1900s 85, 87–88
　　during 1920s 128–130, 133*c*
　　Carlisle Indian Industrial School xv, 67–68, 71*c*, 87, 103, 161
　　during Great Depression 161, 163*c*
American Indian day schools 161–162, 174–175
American Indian Movement (AIM) 242, 246*c*
American Indians
　　ABCFM schools 37*c*
　　achievement gap xxiv, 272
　　activism (late 1960s) 242
　　amalgamation xiii, 32
　　assimilation 66–68
　　bilingual education 242
　　boarding schools. *See* American Indian boarding schools
　　Cadet Nurse Corps 190
　　Civilization Fund 37*c*
　　college enrollment after anti–affirmative action referenda 276*c*
　　College of William and Mary 9
　　colonial America 10–11
　　Dartmouth College 9, 13*c*, 19–20
　　dropout rate (1969) 242
　　dropout rate (1988) 272, 275*c*
　　educational challenges (1990s) 282, 283
　　employment problems (1880s) 104
　　enrollment in Indian schools (1965) 245*c*

B

E